T0215695

Lecture Notes in Computer Science 12193

More information about this series at http://www.springer.com/series/7409

Pei-Luen Patrick Rau (Ed.)

Cross-Cultural Design

Applications in Health, Learning, Communication, and Creativity

12th International Conference, CCD 2020
Held as Part of the 22nd HCI International Conference, HCII 2020
Copenhagen, Denmark, July 19–24, 2020
Proceedings, Part II

 Springer

Editor
Pei-Luen Patrick Rau
Tsinghua University
Beijing, China

ISSN 0302-9743   ISSN 1611-3349   (electronic)
Lecture Notes in Computer Science
ISBN 978-3-030-49912-9   ISBN 978-3-030-49913-6   (eBook)
https://doi.org/10.1007/978-3-030-49913-6

LNCS Sublibrary: SL3 – Information Systems and Applications, incl. Internet/Web, and HCI

This Springer imprint is published by the registered company Springer Nature Switzerland AG
The registered company address is: Gewerbestrasse 11, 6330 Cham, Switzerland

Foreword

The 22nd International Conference on Human-Computer Interaction, HCI International 2020 (HCII 2020), was planned to be held at the AC Bella Sky Hotel and Bella Center, Copenhagen, Denmark, during July 19–24, 2020. Due to the COVID-19 coronavirus pandemic and the resolution of the Danish government not to allow events larger than 500 people to be hosted until September 1, 2020, HCII 2020 had to be held virtually. It incorporated the 21 thematic areas and affiliated conferences listed on the following page.

A total of 6,326 individuals from academia, research institutes, industry, and governmental agencies from 97 countries submitted contributions, and 1,439 papers and 238 posters were included in the conference proceedings. These contributions address the latest research and development efforts and highlight the human aspects of design and use of computing systems. The contributions thoroughly cover the entire field of human-computer interaction, addressing major advances in knowledge and effective use of computers in a variety of application areas. The volumes constituting the full set of the conference proceedings are listed in the following pages.

The HCI International (HCII) conference also offers the option of "late-breaking work" which applies both for papers and posters and the corresponding volume(s) of the proceedings will be published just after the conference. Full papers will be included in the "HCII 2020 - Late Breaking Papers" volume of the proceedings to be published in the Springer LNCS series, while poster extended abstracts will be included as short papers in the "HCII 2020 - Late Breaking Posters" volume to be published in the Springer CCIS series.

I would like to thank the program board chairs and the members of the program boards of all thematic areas and affiliated conferences for their contribution to the highest scientific quality and the overall success of the HCI International 2020 conference.

This conference would not have been possible without the continuous and unwavering support and advice of the founder, Conference General Chair Emeritus and Conference Scientific Advisor Prof. Gavriel Salvendy. For his outstanding efforts, I would like to express my appreciation to the communications chair and editor of HCI International News, Dr. Abbas Moallem.

July 2020

Constantine Stephanidis

HCI International 2020 Thematic Areas and Affiliated Conferences

Thematic areas:

- HCI 2020: Human-Computer Interaction
- HIMI 2020: Human Interface and the Management of Information

Affiliated conferences:

- EPCE: 17th International Conference on Engineering Psychology and Cognitive Ergonomics
- UAHCI: 14th International Conference on Universal Access in Human-Computer Interaction
- VAMR: 12th International Conference on Virtual, Augmented and Mixed Reality
- CCD: 12th International Conference on Cross-Cultural Design
- SCSM: 12th International Conference on Social Computing and Social Media
- AC: 14th International Conference on Augmented Cognition
- DHM: 11th International Conference on Digital Human Modeling and Applications in Health, Safety, Ergonomics and Risk Management
- DUXU: 9th International Conference on Design, User Experience and Usability
- DAPI: 8th International Conference on Distributed, Ambient and Pervasive Interactions
- HCIBGO: 7th International Conference on HCI in Business, Government and Organizations
- LCT: 7th International Conference on Learning and Collaboration Technologies
- ITAP: 6th International Conference on Human Aspects of IT for the Aged Population
- HCI-CPT: Second International Conference on HCI for Cybersecurity, Privacy and Trust
- HCI-Games: Second International Conference on HCI in Games
- MobiTAS: Second International Conference on HCI in Mobility, Transport and Automotive Systems
- AIS: Second International Conference on Adaptive Instructional Systems
- C&C: 8th International Conference on Culture and Computing
- MOBILE: First International Conference on Design, Operation and Evaluation of Mobile Communications
- AI-HCI: First International Conference on Artificial Intelligence in HCI

Conference Proceedings Volumes Full List

1. LNCS 12181, Human-Computer Interaction: Design and User Experience (Part I), edited by Masaaki Kurosu
2. LNCS 12182, Human-Computer Interaction: Multimodal and Natural Interaction (Part II), edited by Masaaki Kurosu
3. LNCS 12183, Human-Computer Interaction: Human Values and Quality of Life (Part III), edited by Masaaki Kurosu
4. LNCS 12184, Human Interface and the Management of Information: Designing Information (Part I), edited by Sakae Yamamoto and Hirohiko Mori
5. LNCS 12185, Human Interface and the Management of Information: Interacting with Information (Part II), edited by Sakae Yamamoto and Hirohiko Mori
6. LNAI 12186, Engineering Psychology and Cognitive Ergonomics: Mental Workload, Human Physiology, and Human Energy (Part I), edited by Don Harris and Wen-Chin Li
7. LNAI 12187, Engineering Psychology and Cognitive Ergonomics: Cognition and Design (Part II), edited by Don Harris and Wen-Chin Li
8. LNCS 12188, Universal Access in Human-Computer Interaction: Design Approaches and Supporting Technologies (Part I), edited by Margherita Antona and Constantine Stephanidis
9. LNCS 12189, Universal Access in Human-Computer Interaction: Applications and Practice (Part II), edited by Margherita Antona and Constantine Stephanidis
10. LNCS 12190, Virtual, Augmented and Mixed Reality: Design and Interaction (Part I), edited by Jessie Y. C. Chen and Gino Fragomeni
11. LNCS 12191, Virtual, Augmented and Mixed Reality: Industrial and Everyday Life Applications (Part II), edited by Jessie Y. C. Chen and Gino Fragomeni
12. LNCS 12192, Cross-Cultural Design: User Experience of Products, Services, and Intelligent Environments (Part I), edited by P. L. Patrick Rau
13. LNCS 12193, Cross-Cultural Design: Applications in Health, Learning, Communication, and Creativity (Part II), edited by P. L. Patrick Rau
14. LNCS 12194, Social Computing and Social Media: Design, Ethics, User Behavior, and Social Network Analysis (Part I), edited by Gabriele Meiselwitz
15. LNCS 12195, Social Computing and Social Media: Participation, User Experience, Consumer Experience, and Applications of Social Computing (Part II), edited by Gabriele Meiselwitz
16. LNAI 12196, Augmented Cognition: Theoretical and Technological Approaches (Part I), edited by Dylan D. Schmorrow and Cali M. Fidopiastis
17. LNAI 12197, Augmented Cognition: Human Cognition and Behaviour (Part II), edited by Dylan D. Schmorrow and Cali M. Fidopiastis

38. CCIS 1224, HCI International 2020 Posters - Part I, edited by Constantine Stephanidis and Margherita Antona
39. CCIS 1225, HCI International 2020 Posters - Part II, edited by Constantine Stephanidis and Margherita Antona
40. CCIS 1226, HCI International 2020 Posters - Part III, edited by Constantine Stephanidis and Margherita Antona

http://2020.hci.international/proceedings

12th International Conference on Cross-Cultural Design (CCD 2020)

Program Board Chair: **Pei-Luen Patrick Rau, Tsinghua University, China**

The full list with the Program Board Chairs and the members of the Program Boards of all thematic areas and affiliated conferences is available online at:

http://www.hci.international/board-members-2020.php

HCI International 2021

The 23rd International Conference on Human-Computer Interaction, HCI International 2021 (HCII 2021), will be held jointly with the affiliated conferences in Washington DC, USA, at the Washington Hilton Hotel, July 24–29, 2021. It will cover a broad spectrum of themes related to Human-Computer Interaction (HCI), including theoretical issues, methods, tools, processes, and case studies in HCI design, as well as novel interaction techniques, interfaces, and applications. The proceedings will be published by Springer. More information will be available on the conference website: http://2021.hci.international/.

General Chair
Prof. Constantine Stephanidis
University of Crete and ICS-FORTH
Heraklion, Crete, Greece
Email: general_chair@hcii2021.org

http://2021.hci.international/

Contents – Part II

Culture, Learning and Communication

Culture and Creativity

Contents – Part I

Culture-Based Design

Cross-Cultural Behavior and Attitude

Cultural Facets of Interactions with Autonomous Agents and Intelligent Environments

Health, Well-Being and Social Design Across Cultures

Usability Evaluation on Intuitive Interaction Between Product Interfaces and Older Adults with Dementia

Li-Hao Chen[1]([⊠]), Yi-Chien Liu[2], and Pei-Jung Cheng[3]

[1] Fu Jen Catholic University, Xinzhuang District,
New Taipei City 24205, Taiwan
ahao55@gmail.com
[2] Cardinal Tien Hospital, Xindian District, New Taipei City 23148, Taiwan
milkgen@gmail.com
[3] National Chengchi University, Wenshan District, Taipei 11605, Taiwan
admufy@gmail.com

Abstract. The objective of this study was to explore interface features for intuitive interactions for older people with dementia. Research experiments were conducted by examining cooking power configuration settings in the user interfaces of microwave ovens, and the participants involved 25 older people with mild dementia. The initial reaction times and task completion times of the participants were recorded. During the experiments, we also observed the participants to note any difficulties experienced by them while executing the tasks. The results showed that user interfaces that presented information clearly resulted in better perception of affordance for operability and were more likely to elicit intuitive reactions among older people with dementia. However, the elicitation of intuitive reactions does not equate to intuitive usability, as the prior experiences of users facilitate their perceived intended functions and plays an important role in intuitive use. Therefore, user interfaces should be designed in accordance with user prior experiences. These results can serve as a reference for designing product interfaces that are intuitively interactive for older people with dementia.

Keywords: Old age · Interface design · Intuitive interaction · Dementia

1 Introduction

Because Taiwan is gradually entering an aging society, product development and designs that conform to changes in aging lifestyles are imperative. Moreover, how older people use and interact with products has been investigated more frequently. Of previous studies regarding various facets of user interface usability, few have examined the interaction between older users and product interfaces, and numerous relevant issues merit further exploration. In recent years, the concept of intuitive interactions has received increasing attention in the fields of human-machine interaction and product design. The ultimate goal of intuitive interactions is to enable novice or inexperienced users to easily operate a product without the needs to reference a user's manual. Design

© Springer Nature Switzerland AG 2020
P.-L. P. Rau (Ed.): HCII 2020, LNCS 12193, pp. 3–11, 2020.
https://doi.org/10.1007/978-3-030-49913-6_1

psychologist Norman [1] asserted that a good product enables users to operate it adequately on their first attempt. If a product requires users to read a manual, the product design has failed. Therefore, applying the concept of intuitive interactions to user interface designs enables providing older users with user-friendly product interfaces that help resolve the usability issues.

Cognitive functions gradually decline with age, and older people are often faced with difficulties operating products in their daily lives. Lee [2] examined product designs for older users and found that their ability to operate products was affected by their declining motor and cognitive functions. In the aging society, the number of patients with dementia has increased. Dementia is a neurodegenerative condition among the elderly and begins with the atrophy of the hippocampus. Assessing cognitive functions is essential to diagnosing dementia [3], and memory decline is considered an important indicator of cognitive deterioration. The clinical assessment of dementia includes evaluating cognitive skills such as long-term memory, short-term memory, attention, focus, temporal and spatial orientation, general abstractions and judgments, language and other basic cognitive skills, hand-eye coordination in composing pictures, and fluency of thought. In particular, short-term memory decline prevents patients from recalling events experienced or knowledge acquired in the recent past. The progression of this condition leads to long-term memory loss, which in turn affects cognitive functions. Because of the gradual decline in cognitive functions, patients with dementia are often faced with difficulties operating products in their daily lives. For example, such patients may suddenly forget how to operate a once-familiar product. In addition, executive dysfunction is a core symptom of dementia. Executive functions pertain to higher cortical functions that are crucial to an individual's ability to survive in society, but such functions are very difficult for physicians to explain clearly. Simply put, a specific goal might necessitate multiple steps to achieve, and intact executive functioning is required to arrange and execute these steps in a fluent order. For example, withdrawing money from a bank account requires a number of steps, which may include walking to a convenience store, finding an automated teller machine, retrieving a debit card, and entering a personal identification number. Similarly, in user-product interactions, the completion of a task requires a sequence of steps. Numerous factors affect how older people with dementia interact with product interfaces. Therefore, understanding how they perceive the affordances of user interface features facilitates demonstrating affordances for promoting product intuitive usability.

The concept of intuitive interactions has received increasing attention in the field of design in recent years. It primarily addresses topics on designing interfaces that enable users to understand how to interact with a product on the first attempt. In addition, many relevant topics require further examination. Hurtienne and Blessing [4] stated that intuitive interfaces allow users to operate a device without assistance. In his book *The Design of Everyday Things*, Norman [1] discussed how the concept of affordances is applied to intuitive interactions. For example, a round doorknob naturally leads users to believe that it can be grasped and turned, but a flat plate naturally guides users to push on it. However, intuitive interactions cannot be explained thoroughly by purely physical user actions. As mentioned above, Silver [5] stated that even in purely physical user actions, such as pressing a button, the user has learned certain functional conventions: buttons are for pressing, knobs are for turning, electronic keys are for tapping, and ropes are for pulling. With affordance in design, it involves two dimensions, namely the observer's motor skills [6–8] and experiences and culture [9–11]. The perceived affordances of users are affected by their physical motor skills and by prior experiences and knowledge. Perception of affordances involves the process through which people receive perceptual information from the environment. As shown in Fig. 1, users must pick up perceptual information from the external environment to perceive the affordances of the environment. Decoding such perceptual information requires user's motor skills and prior experiences and knowledge. Previous relevant studies have primarily employed these two dimensions (i.e., users' motor skills and prior knowledge) to address applying the concept of affordances to product, interaction, and interior designs. These two dimensions are of equal importance and interact mutually.

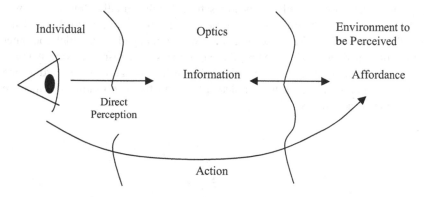

Fig. 1. Model of the perception of affordances [10].

A user's past experiences deeply influence the occurrence of intuitive interactions. Scholars in the field of intuitive interactions [12, 13] found that prior experiences and knowledge are key factors in intuitive interactions between users and product interfaces because their familiar experiences and knowledge allow them to operate products non-consciously and rapidly. These scholars also asserted that examining intuitive interactions among older users must account for their familiarity with technology. User characteristics are indeed crucial to intuitive interactions. Designers must understand the characteristics of the target user group to design interfaces that are genuinely intuitive for older people with dementia. This study explored the intuitive usability regarding the affordances established between products and older people with dementia.

2 Method

The objective of this study was to examine the intuitive usability of user interface elements and shapes for older people with dementia. Experimental testing was performed through the user interfaces of microwave ovens. The participants were older people with mild dementia. Compared to other user groups, older users may be faced with more difficulties operating products. The experimental tasks set in this study is adjusting cooking power. Patients with mild dementia and acceptable communicative and cognitive functions were nominated by their physicians to participate in this study.

2.1   Test Interfaces and Experimental Procedures

With cooking power adjustment task, we examined current microwave models and compiled six different types of interface for adjusting cooking power. Graphics software was used to draw the basic contours of the interfaces (Fig. 2). Interfaces A, B, and F were operated by pressing buttons at the bottom of the interface to cycle through the available power settings. Interface C was operated by directly pressing the buttons labeled with the different power settings. Interface D was operated by pressing the round buttons directly underneath the power setting labels. Finally, Interface E was operated by sliding a bar underneath the power setting labels. Similar to those of the first stage, the test interfaces in the second stage were displayed on a tablet computer with a 10-in. touch screen. During the test, these interfaces were displayed one at a time on the tablet. The test interfaces also involved the custom program for recording the amount of time a participant took to complete a task and for determining whether the task was completed accurately.

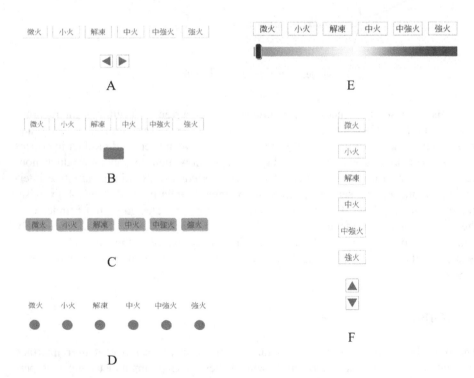

Fig. 2.   Test interfaces for adjusting cooking power.

In this test, the participants were asked to adjust the cooking power to medium-high. The custom program recorded two different times: the time elapsed before a participant touched the screen on the first attempt (i.e., the initial reaction time) and the time elapsed before a participant completed the cooking power adjustment task (i.e., the task completion time). During the test, the participants each sat in front of a 10-inch touch-screen tablet and read the task instructions displayed on the screen. If the participants did not understand the written instructions, verbal explanations of the task were provided. After the participants confirmed that they understood the task, they manipulated the test interface on the tablet computer. No time limit was set for completing the task. Video recording equipment was used to capture the entire test process. Some participants forgot the goal of the task or did not understand the test objective. When this happened, researchers verbally guided the participants to complete the task.

2.2 Experimental Task and Participants

The experimental task is cooking power adjustment, with no time limits imposed on the participants. The cooking power task was aimed to examine the participants' direct observation and operation of a particular function and setting. Therefore, the participants were asked to complete an identical task (i.e., adjusting the cooking power to medium-high) with each test interface. The primary goal of the test was to compare the intuitive usability and effectiveness of each test interface. After completing each task, the participants pressed a "confirm" button to signal that he or she was finished. The custom program then recorded the time elapsed.

The tests were performed in a hospital clinic. Hospital neurologists nominated 25 participants who had mild dementia, demonstrated acceptable communicative and cognitive functions, and were experienced in using home appliances. The participants averaged 81.8 years (SD = 7.2 years) of age. The definition of mild dementia was based on a score of 0.5 or 1 in the clinical dementia rating scale. Regarding cognitive skill assessments, patients who scored moderately low in short-term memory function, long-term memory function, and hand-eye coordination were chosen as the participants.

3 Results

By comparing the initial reaction times, task completion times and observations of the participants, we learned which elements of the user interfaces could elicit more favorable intuitive interactions and demonstrate more desirable usability. Summarizing the analyses results enabled determining the correspondence of intuitive interactions and affordances between older people with dementia and user interface features. These results can serve as a reference for designing user interfaces that are intuitively interactive for older people.

3.1 Initial Reaction Times

For each of the six test interfaces in the cooking power task, the mean initial encounter reaction time of the 25 participants was calculated and compared. As shown in Table 1, the mean reaction times for Interfaces A, D, and F were relatively slow, with Interface E attaining the shortest mean reaction time. The post-hoc ANOVA results showed statistically significant differences between the mean reaction times of Interfaces E and F, indicating that the slider interface was more likely to entice the participants in their initial encounters with the interface.

Table 1. ANOVA results for the initial reaction times of the cooking power task.

Initial Reaction Times in the Cooking Power Task					
Test Sample	Average Time	Standard Deviation	Number of Samples	Significance	p
A	14.2	10.5	25		0.186
B	13.4	8.8	25		
C	13.9	8.8	25		
D	14.9	10.8	25		
E	10.5	4.6	25	*F	
F	15.2	8.9	25	*E	

3.2   Task Completion Times

Between the six test interfaces, the ANOVA results showed that the mean times required by the 25 participants to complete the cooking power task were significantly different (Table 2). The post-hoc analysis results further revealed that Interfaces C and D attained relatively short mean times, which were statistically different from the times attained through Interfaces A, B, E, and F. This is attributable to how Interfaces C and D are "directly" manipulated by pressing the buttons that correspond to the different cooking power settings. By contrast, Interfaces A, B, E, and F are "indirectly" manipulated by pressing the buttons or sliders that cycle through the available settings. The results confirmed that the interfaces which allow users to directly selecting a setting resulted in more favorable task performance.

Table 2. ANOVA results for the completion times of the cooking power task.

Completion Times in the Cooking Power Task					
Test Sample	Average Time	Standard Deviation	Number of Samples	Significance	p
A	34.7	22.1	25	*C, D	0.000
B	32.2	18.2	25	*C, D	
C	18.8	9.6	25	*A, B, E, F	
D	22.3	12.9	25	*A, B, E, F	
E	32.7	13.1	25	*C, D	
F	34.5	14.7	25	*C, D	

3.3 Observational Analysis

Table 3 displays the number of failed participants in the cooking power task and the reasons for their mistakes. The primary reason for failing the task was that the participants forgot the goal of the task and pressed the incorrect buttons. For Interface B or E, some participants did not realize that the buttons at the bottom of the interface could be manipulated to adjust the cooking power settings, thereby configuring the wrong settings.

Table 3. Observation records of the cooking power task.

Test Interface	Observation		
	Number of participants who failed to complete the task accurately	Percentage	Reasons
A	1	4%	Did not understand the task and chose the wrong cooking power
B	2	8%	Did not understand the task and chose the wrong cooking power. Did not understand that the buttons underneath the labels could be pressed to adjust cooking power and chose the wrong cooking power
C	0	0%	
D	0	0%	
E	3	12%	Did not understand that the slider could be moved. Inadvertently chose the wrong cooking power
F	0	0%	

4 Discussions

For the cooking power task, the results showed that the indirect user interfaces (i.e., those that require the user to cycle through the settings) required more time to complete. This finding accords with those of Drewitz and Brandenburg [14] and maybe attributable to how the manipulation action for cycling through the available settings required additional time. Notably, Interface E was more enticing to the participants in their initial encounters with the interface, but the mean time required to complete the tasks using this interface was undesirable. In the cooking power task, Interface F was the only interface with buttons that were arranged vertically. The mean initial reaction time and task completion time attained through this interface were relative long compared with those achieved through the other interfaces. Whether intuitive interactions are affected by vertical or horizontal arrangements of buttons merits further investigation. With completion times, interfaces C and D attained relatively short mean times. From the observation, some participants did not realize that the buttons at the bottom of the interface could be manipulated. Except the reason of the way to manipulate interfaces C and D, "directly pressing" the buttons to complete the tasks set in this study, the participants' prior or familiar experiences in manipulating product interfaces might influence user-product intuitive interaction. As the scholars [12, 13] mentioned above noted that prior experiences and knowledge are key factors in intuitive interactions between users and product interfaces because their familiar experiences and knowledge allow them to operate products non-consciously and rapidly.

This study examined intuitive interactions between older people with dementia and user interfaces. We endeavored to formulate design principles for intuitively interactive product interfaces that are easy to use and less prone to mistakes by older people with dementia. The results showed that simple user interfaces are more likely to elicit intuitive reactions among older people with dementia, but this does not necessarily equate to facilitating the intuitive use of such interfaces. The prior experiences of users are crucial to intuitive use; hence, user interfaces should be designed to comply with users' prior experiences. Understanding user characteristics is the key to designing elements that promote intuitive interactions. However, older people with dementia may experience temporary short-term or long-term memory loss because of their disease condition, causing them to forget how to operate once-familiar products. Therefore, designers may experience difficulty accounting for the prior experiences of this user group, and they may need to instead examine the direct relationship between users and product external features noted in the theory of affordances. Alternatively, the designers may employ voiced instructions to remind the users of how to operate a product. Thus, designing user interfaces that are intuitively usable for older people with dementia require additional efforts.

5 Conclusions

In the present study, we tested and analyzed the effective data of 25 older patients with mild dementia. The findings enabled proposing a model describing the perceived affordances between in the intuitive interactions of product interfaces and older people with dementia, despite participant selection being a notable limitation of this study. In addition, the physicians advised us to avoid subjecting the participants to complex interface operating procedures and a high amount of test interfaces. Therefore, we could not adopt comprehensive operating procedures, such as asking the participants to place food in the microwave, turn on the microwave, input cooking time, adjust cooking power, wait for the food to finish cooking, and then remove the food from the microwave. The experimental tasks were designed to involve abbreviated instructions. Subsequent studies are suggested to increase the number of participants and examine additional tasks and user interfaces, thereby providing research implications for designers to create user interfaces that are intuitively interactive for older people with dementia.

Acknowledgements. This research was supported by the grant from the Ministry of Science and Technology, Taiwan, Grant MOST 107-2410-H-030-059-MY2.

References

1. Norman, D.A.: The Design of Everyday Things. Basic Books Inc., New York (1990)
2. Lee, C.F.: Approaches to product design for the elderly. J. Des. **11**(3), 65–79 (2006)
3. Hsu, R.L., Chen, W.H., Chiu, H.C., Shen, H.M.: Cognitive function in different stages of dementia. Formosan J. Med. **4**(4), 371–378 (2000)
4. Hurtienne, J., Blessing, L.: Design for intuitive use – testing image schema theory for user interface design. In: Proceedings of the 16th International Conference on Engineering Design, No. DS42_P_386, Paris, France (2007)
5. Silver, M.: Exploring Interface Design. Thomson, New York (2005)
6. Landwehr, K.: Ecological Perception Research, Visual Communication, and Aesthetics. Springer, New York (1990). https://doi.org/10.1007/978-3-642-84106-4
7. You, H., Chen, K.: Application of affordance and semantics in product design. Des. Stud. **28** (3), 22–38 (2007)
8. Gero, J.S., Kannengiesser, U.: Representational affordances in design, with examples from analogy making and optimization. Res. Eng. Design **23**(3), 35–249 (2012)
9. Cooper, A.: About Face The Essentials of User Interface Design. IDG Books Worldwide, CA (1995)
10. McGrenere, J., Ho, W.: Affordance: clarifying and evolving a concept. In: Proceedings of Graphics Interface 2000, pp. 179–186. Lawrence Erlbaum Associates Press, Montreal (2000)
11. Krippendorff, K.: The Semantic Turn: A New Foundation for Design. Taylor & Francis, Boca Raton (2006)
12. Blacker, A., Hurtienne, J.: Towards a unified view of intuitive interaction: definitions, models and tools across the World. MMI-Interaktiv **13**, 36–54 (2007)
13. Blacker, A., Popovic, V., Lawry, S., Reddy, R., Mahar, D., Kraal, B., Chamorro-Koc, M.: Researching Intuitive Interaction. In: Diversity and unity: Proceedings of IASDR2011), Delft, The Netherlands (2011)
14. Drewitz, U., Brandenburg, S.: From design to experience: towards a process model of user experience. In: Proceedings of the 9th Pan-Pacific Conference on Ergonomics, pp. 117–122, Kaohsiung, Taiwan (2010)

Reliability and Validity Assessment of the Chinese Version of MBI-PPD Self-efficacy Scale

Hao Chen[1(✉)], Chao Liu[1(✉)], Chia-Yi Liu[2], Liang-Ming Lo[3],
Rungtai Lin[4(✉)], Ding-Hau Huang[5], and Wen-Ko Chiou[6(✉)]

[1] Graduate Institute of Business and Management,
Chang Gung University, Taoyuan City, Taiwan
174673015@qq.com, victory666666@126.com
[2] Department of Psychiatry, Chang Gung Memorial Hospital,
Taipei City, Taiwan
liucy752@cgmh.org.tw
[3] Department of Obstetrics and Gynecology, Chang Gung Memorial Hospital,
Taipei City, Taiwan
lmlo@cgmh.org.tw
[4] Graduate School of Creative Industry Design,
National Taiwan University of Arts, New Taipei City, Taiwan
rtlin@mail.ntua.edu.tw
[5] Institute of Creative Design and Management,
National Taipei University of Business, Taoyuan City, Taiwan
hau1012@gmail.com
[6] Department of Industrial Design, Chang Gung University,
Taoyuan City, Taiwan
wkchiu@mail.cgu.edu.tw

Abstract. MBI - PPD refers to Mindfulness-Based Intervention in Postpartum Depression. This study aimed to develop a Chinese version of the Mindfulness-Based Intervention in Postpartum Depression Parenting Self-Efficacy (MBI-PPD S-E) tool and then test its reliability and validity using Taiwanese mothers of hospitalized neonates. For this, the Perceived Maternal Parenting Self-Efficacy (PMP S-E) questionnaire was first translated into Chinese and then back-translated into English (to ensure translation accuracy). After translation, the MBI-PPD S-E was implemented using an app to help pregnant women relieve symptoms of postpartum depression. Participants: We recruited 300 pregnant and lying-in women in Taiwan. Ethical considerations: This study was approved by the Institutional Review Boards, and the anonymity of participants was respected. For construct validity, confirmatory factor analysis (CFA) was used to assess the fit of the PMP S-E measurement model. Specifically, we employed the following fit indices: chi^2 test, root mean square error of approximation (RMSEA), normed fit index (NFI), comparative fit index (CFI), and non-normed fit indices (NNFI). For concurrent validity, the Chinese version of the MBI-PPD S-E for research and treatment of pregnant and lying-in woman 20-item core quality of Self-Efficacy (S-E) questionnaire was used as a criterion measure for S-E. Reliability was evaluated according to internal consistency and test-retest reliability measures. Results: The Chinese version of the MBI-PPD S-E

© Springer Nature Switzerland AG 2020
P.-L. P. Rau (Ed.): HCII 2020, LNCS 12193, pp. 12–24, 2020.
https://doi.org/10.1007/978-3-030-49913-6_2

comprised four factors and 20 items and showed good reliability and validity. Conclusions: The MBI-PPD S-E was successfully translated into Chinese. Psychometric results indicated good internal consistency and validity for this newly constructed instrument. To further validate the Chinese MBI-PPD S-E, future studies should conduct additional testing and investigate its application in a number of contexts.

Keywords: Mindfulness-Based Intervention in Postpartum Depression · PMP S-E · Chinese version · Reliability and validity

1 Introduction

1.1 Mindfulness-Based Intervention in Postpartum Depression (MBI – PPD)

MBI - PPD refers to Mindfulness-Based Intervention in Postpartum Depression. Pregnant and postpartum women have a high probability of suffering from depression due to the drastic hormone changes they experience during and after pregnancy, and this affect emotional responses. Indeed, pregnant and postpartum women frequently suffer from postpartum depression (PPD), leaving them emotionally handicapped. Women who develop PPD are often unable to handle a normal mother-infant relationship, and some of these women may even have suicidal ideations or consider harming their newborn. Therefore, to relieve their depression, these women need professional medical assistance and other supports, such as mindfulness practices.

Mindfulness involves maintaining attention and awareness of the present moment and accepting what's going on in the present moment without judgment (Bodhi 2011; Kabat-Zinn 2003, 2006); to achieve a peaceful state of mind. Bishop et al. (2004) similarly described mindfulness as the self-regulation of attention in order to achieve non-elaborative awareness of present experiences. Many previous studies have demonstrated that mindfulness can reduce anxiety (Anderson et al., 2007) and depression (Shapiro et al. 2005).

With the rapid development of technology, Electronic Mental Health (EMH) services have recently been embraced as a non-pharmacological treatment trend. These services provide professional functions and relevant information through online social media to help users alleviate mental health problems. With the increasing popularity of smartphones and tablets, the mobile health (mHealth) service model is becoming most popular EMH model. Improving and reducing the risk of postpartum depression in women as well as effectively combining EMH with mindfulness are two of the most important goals of EMH services.

This study was performed using the EMH APP, a mindfulness-based intervention system named We'll. This system (1) promotes social support and mindfulness exercises for mothers and (2) provides effective opportunities for self-examination using the Motherhood Self-Efficacy Scale (PMP S-E) (Barnes and Adamson-Macedo 2007a) in order to relieve and prevent postpartum depression and associated emotional problems.

1.2   Parenting Self-efficacy

Self-efficacy is defined as how an individual perceives their ability to perform a specific task or behavior (Bandura 1997a). Self-efficacy has also been defined as (1) the judgement of one's own ability to perform a task and (2) the ability to successfully develop and implement a plan of action (Bandura 1986). Whether a person believes that they have the requisite abilities to successfully complete a specific task (Coleman and Karraker 1997) is the core of self-efficacy theory (Bandura 1977). Self-efficacy affects peoples' thoughts, feelings, and behaviors (Schwarzer 1992) and is therefore a major determinant of human motivations.

Parental self-efficacy refers to parents' perception of their abilities to care for and cultivate their children's growth and development (Coleman and Karraker 1997; (Kuhn and Carter 2006; Teti and Gelfand 1991a). Parental self-efficacy, defined as a belief in one's ability to successfully address parenting challenges (Hess et al. 2004), is an important mechanism which guides mothers' interactions with hospitalized babies. Parents must possess qualities related to a strong sense of self-efficacy in order to be successful at parenting. Parental self-efficacy is influenced by a number of factors, including characteristics of parents and children as well as external factors related to the social environment (Hess et al. 2004). Determining whether a woman feels competent in various aspects of parenting should enable healthcare professionals to better manage and support pregnant and postpartum mothers (Barnes and Adamson-Macedo 2007b).

One of the biggest sources of postpartum psychological stress is a mother's (accurate or inaccurate) belief that she lacks child rearing skills (Miles et al. 1993; Miles and Holditch 1997). Mothers are effective at performing and managing various tasks in parenting roles. Sexual beliefs also play a key role in the theory of self-efficacy (Bandura 1997b). Self-efficacy in parenting can help predict long-term outcomes and potential risk factors for dysfunctional mother-child relationships (Aarnoudse et al., 2009; Jones and Prinz 2005; Melnyk et al. 2001a). Parents' self-efficacy and parenting abilities are regulated by how well they understand their baby's condition and emotional state (Pedrini et al., 2018). For these reasons, parental self-efficacy has been classified as a target for direct postnatal intervention (Benzies, Magill-Evans, Hayden, and Ballantyne 2013). Beliefs about parenting self-efficacy mediate the effects of depression, social support, and infant temperament on parenting behaviors (Teti and Gelfand 1991b) In fact, interventions aimed at encouraging mother-child interactions have positively impacted mothers, particularly when it comes to reducing maternal stress (Melnyk et al. 2006; Kaaresen, Rønning Ulvund and Da 2006) and improving their confidence in dealing with children (Ohgi et al. 2004). These improvements can in turn help alleviate postpartum depression.

To better support pregnant and postpartum mothers, a tool which can effectively measure their understanding of and ability to care for their baby is needed. Perceptions of their ability and sensitivity to various levels and tasks in parenting. In addition, knowing whether mothers consider themselves to be competent childcare providers will enable health care professionals to determine which mothers require further intervention and support (Hsiao et al. 2016).

1.3 PMP S-E

The Perceived Maternal Parenting Self-Efficacy (PMP S-E) tool, developed by Barnes and Adamson-Macedo (2007a), is a self-report questionnaire which assesses maternal self-efficacy and focuses on mothers of at-risk infants. Initial validation studies on the PMP S-E tool showed high internal consistency and sufficient retest reliability, indicating that the psychometric characteristics of the questionnaire are adequate (Barnes and Adamson-Macedo 2007b). The PMP S-E was also shown to be reliable and effective in assessing general self-efficacy levels of UK-born, neonatal mothers (Hsiao et al. 2016). The PMP S-E is consistent with the recognized Bandurian theory of self-efficancy. That is to say, the PMP S-E is a domain-specific tool because it explicitly refers to specific parenting tasks and activities. Thus, it is a highly predictive of actual behavior (Bandura 1977). In addition, as the PMP S-E was developed to assess parental self-efficacy during the early stages of neonatal development, it is consistent with a family-centered approach to care (Westrup 2015; Als et al. (2012; Bracht et al. 2013; Montirosso, Del Prete et al. 2012). The PMP S-E is critical to the ethical behavior of clinical research; however, the PMP S-E scale has not yet been translated into Chinese.

1.4 Research Objective

The primary objective of this study was to translate the PMP S-E tool into Chinese and then evaluate the effectiveness and reliability of the Chinese version of the tool. There are no similar Chinese instruments specifically formulated for mothers of neonates; therefore, the results of this study may benefit clinical and research applications.

2 Methods

2.1 Procedures

The study was conducted in the Department of Obstetrics and Gynecology of Chang Gung Memorial Hospital, Taipei, and included 300 mothers. To be included in our study, mothers had to meet the following selection criteria: (1) had given birth to a healthy baby within the past month and (2) were fluent in Mandarin (listening, speaking, reading and writing). All mothers provided written, informed consent prior to being included in this study. Mothers who had given birth to a baby with genetic or congenital abnormalities were not included. All mothers included in this study were asked to complete the PMP S-E questionnaire and other questionnaires. All questionnaires were completed anonymously.

2.2 The Chinese Adaptation of the PMP S-E

The PMP S-E questionnaire was translated into Chinese and then back-translated into English. Briefly, in translating the English version of PMP S-E, two bilingual, native-Chinese speakers completed two independent translations. Both translators were medical doctoral students with academic and clinical backgrounds. After translation, the translators consulted with each other and with a translation expert and then further revised Chinese version of the PMP S-E tool based on discussion and feedback. Subsequently, two new translators who were unfamiliar with the original PMP S-E translated the Chinese version back into English to ensure that the content of both versions of the PMP S-E was consistent. The Chinese text was then reviewed by two additional expert translators and two other translators who specialized in the neonatal field before an updated translation was prepared.

To evaluate the surface validity of the Chinese PMP S-E tool, questionnaire items were administered to 30 relatively healthy mothers of hospitalized newborns. These mothers were asked to assess the significance of each item and to consider whether each item was relevant in a neonatal context. We also had these mothers complete the PMP S-E to ensure that questionnaire items were clear and easy to understand. Finally, the 30 mothers were asked if they had questions about the format, layout, description, or answer scale of the questionnaire. The interviewer then wrote a detailed report, which noted any difficulties these 30 mothers had in completing the questionnaire and included suggestions for additional revisions to the Chinese version of the PMP S-E. Following this, the final version of the Chinese PMP S-E was completed and submitted to the expert committee.

2.3   Measures

The Perceived Maternal Parenting Self-Efficacy (PMP S-E) scale is a 20-item self-report questionnaire which measures the parental self-efficacy of new mothers (Barnes and Adamson-Macedo 2007a). The questionnaire requires mothers to answer questions using a four-point Likert scale which includes responses that range from "strongly disagree" to "strongly agree". (In other words, the questionnaire asks mothers to rate how strongly they agree with given parenting skills statements.) The range of total scores for all items is between 20 and 80, whereby higher scores indicate a stronger sense of parental self-efficacy. The initial confirmatory study included four subscales: (1) care-taking procedures (4 items), which refers to the ability of mothers to perform specific activities and tasks (e.g. feeding); (2) evoking behaviour (7 items), which refers to how mothers perceive their ability to change their infant's behavior; (3) reading behaviour or signalling (6 items), which refers to how mothers perceive their ability to understand and recognize their infant's behavioural changes; (4) situational beliefs (3 items), which refers to how mothers perceive their ability to judge overall interactions with their baby. The PMP S-E was analysed using a sample of 165 mothers who had given birth to relatively healthy neonates at NICU. Our results showed that the Chinese PMP S-E had high internal consistency for both the overall scale (Cronbach's alpha = 0.91) and for each subscale (Cronbach's alpha ranged from 0.72 to 0.89). Furthermore, over a 10-day interval, test–retest reliability was also high for both the overall score ($r = .96$; $p < .001$) and subscale scores (care-taking procedures: $r = .92$, $p = .01$; evoking behaviour: $r = .92$, $p = .01$; reading behaviour or signaling: $r = .93$, $p = .01$; situational beliefs: $r = .88$, $p = .01$).

2.4   Statistical Analysis

To test the validity of the factor structure included in the original English verification study (Barnes and Adamson-Macedo 2007b), Exploratory Factor Analysis (EFA) and Confirmatory Factor Analysis (CFA) were conducted. In accordance with recommendations on scale development and validation studies (Cabrera-Nguyen 2010; Worthington and Whittaker, 2006), we randomly split our study population in order to conduct EFA and CFA on different samples. Specifically, we first performed EFA on half of the study population (i.e. the calibration sample), and we then performed CFA on the other half of the study population (i.e. the validation sample) to test the factor structure derived from EFA. The following indices and thresholds were used to determine the goodness of fit of the model: a Root Mean Square Error of Approximation (RMSEA) smaller than 0.08, Comparative Fit Index (CFI) and Non-Normed Fit Index (NNFI) values greater than 0.90, and a ratio of Chi-square value to degrees of freedom (chi2/df) less than 3.0. Exploratory Factor Analysis (EFA) with varimax rotation was used to determine the factor structure of the PMP S-E. The Kaiser–Meyer–Olkin (KMO) test was performed to verify sampling adequacy for this analysis, and Barlett's Test of Sphericity was performed to assess the degree of intercorrelation between variables. Factor extraction was determined using Kaiser's criterion (eigen values $\geq$ 1). For this, a factor loading greater than 0.5 was considered to indicate that the item contributed sufficiently to its factor. Cronbach's alpha coefficients were calculated to determine the internal consistency for both the overall scale and its factors, whereby values $\geq$ 0.70 were considered adequate. All statistical analyses were performed using SPSS 21.0 and LISREL 8.80 software. Statistical significance was set at p = .05.

3   Results

Overall, we observed large variability in perceptions of maternal self-efficacy, with PMP S-E scores ranging from 20–80. Figure 1 shows the distribution of scores. For the overall study, the mean self-efficacy score of the sample was 59.24 (SD = 8.957); the median was 59; and the mode was 59. The large spread of scores suggests that the PMP S-E tool had a reasonable degree of discrimination. Skewness was not significant at the 2% level, indicating that PSP S-E scores were normally distributed.

3.1   Construct Validity of the Chinses PMP S-E

After splitting the study population into two samples, EFA was conducted on one sample (validation sample) to determine the optimal factor structure of the Chinese version of the PMP S-E (Table 1). The eigen values of the four factors in this analysis were all greater than 1 and explained 71.5% of the total variability. The factors were easily interpretable and were labelled according to item content, as follows: evoking behaviours (which explained 52.6% of variance); reading behavior or signalling (which explained 6.6% of variance), situational beliefs (which explained 6.5% of variance), and care-taking procedures (which explained 5.8% of variance). None of the items showed loadings below the cut-off value (0.5), and none of the items loaded onto more than one factor. This indicates that (1) all items were relevant to the measurement of the parenting self-efficacy construct and (2) all factors were distinct. The fit of the EFA-derived model was then tested by performing CFA on the second sample (calibration sample). As shown in Fig. 2, the fit of the model to the data was excellent (RMSEA = 0.053; CFI = 0.99; NNFI = 0.99; chi^2/df = 1.833, p < .001).

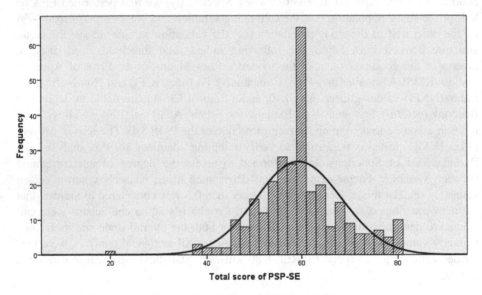

Fig. 1. Distribution of PSP-SE scores

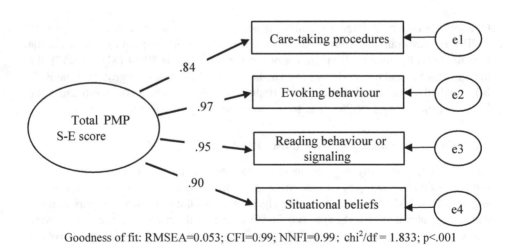

Goodness of fit: RMSEA=0.053; CFI=0.99; NNFI=0.99; chi^2/df = 1.833; p<.001

Fig. 2. CFA validation of EFA-derived factor structure. Model was developed using a Chinese sample

3.2 Internal Consistency of the Chinses PMP S-E

The Chronbach's alpha value ($\alpha = 0.953$) we obtained confirmed that the overall scale had high internal consistency. As reported in Table 1, alpha values were low when any item was removed from the scale. Cronbach's alpha values for the subscales were as follows: reading behaviour or signalling ($\alpha = 0.888$); evoking behaviour ($\alpha = 0.919$); situational beliefs ($\alpha = 0.767$); care-taking procedures ($\alpha = 0.816$).

Table 1. Factor structure and internal consistency of the Chinese PMP S-E

	Factor loading	α if item is removed	Item-total correlation
Factor 1. Care-taking procedures			
I am good at keeping my baby occupied	0.630	0.950	0.642***
I am good at feeding my bab	0.748	0.951	0.570***
I am good at changing my baby	0.771	0.949	0.703***
I am good at bathing my baby	0.771	0.949	0.700***
Factor 2. Evoking behaviour(s)			
I can make my baby happy	0.787	0.949	0.689***
I can make my baby calm when he/she has been crying	0.730	0.948	0.740***
I am good at soothing my baby when he/she becomes upset	0.780	0.948	0.769***
I am good at soothing my baby when he/she becomes fussy	0.800	0.948	0.764***
I am good at soothing my baby when he/she continually cries	0.778	0.948	0.734***
I am good at soothing my baby when he/she becomes more restless	0.660	0.948	0.784***
I am good at getting my baby's attention	0.512	0.949	0.699***
Factor 3. Reading behaviour(s) or signalling			
I believe that I can tell when my baby is tired and needs to sleep	0.731	0.950	0.655***
I believe that I have control over my baby	0.542	0.950	0.643***
I can tell when my baby is sick	0.800	0.949	0.694***
I can read my baby's cues	0.730	0.949	0.719***
I am good at understanding what my baby wants	0.555	0.949	0.731***
I am good at knowing what activities my baby does not enjoy	0.574	0.949	0.671***
Factor 4. Situational beliefs			
I believe that my baby responds well to me	0.793	0.950	0.639***
I believe that my baby and I have good interactions with each other	0.729	0.949	0.680***
I can show affection to my baby	0.580	0.952	0.526***

*** P < .001

Table 2. Reliability and validity of PSP S-E across multiple studies

	Studies		
	Barnes and Adamson, 2007	Pedrini et al., 2018	Current study
Reliability			
Cronbach's α of total score	0.91	0.93	0.95
Cronbach's α of Factor 1	0.74	0.88	0.82
Cronbach's α of Factor 2	0.89	0.87	0.92
Cronbach's α of Factor 3	0.74	0.77	0.89
Cronbach's α of Factor 4	0.72	0.88	0.77
Validity			
Goodness of fit:	No data	RMSEA = 0.000 CFI = 1.000 NNFI = 1.000 chi2/df = 0.068	RMSEA = 0.053 CFI = 0.990 NNFI = 0.990 chi2/df = 1.833
Total variability explained	61.6%	68%	71.5%
Variance explained by Factor 1	41.%	46%	52.6%
Variance explained by Factor 2	7.5%	12%	6.6%
Variance explained by Factor 3	6.8%	5%	6.5%
Variance explained by Factor 4	6.3%	5%	5.8%

Factor 1. Care-taking procedures; Factor 2. Evoking behaviour(s); Factor 3. Reading behaviour (s) or signalling; Factor 4. Situational beliefs.

4   Discussion

The purpose of this study was to translate the PMP S-E tool into Chinese and evaluate its reliability and validity. Our results provide support for Chinese version of this tool, which can be used by Taiwanese mothers of hospitalized neonates during the neonatal period. We developed a Chinese version of this tool for the following reasons. Firstly, understanding the parental self-efficacy construct can benefit both healthcare providers and recipients in multiple ways. Specifically, it provides information that can be used to empower new parents to make choices that should enhance their ability to care for their babies (10). The PMP S-E also features a unique methodology to help medical professionals screen mothers' parenting abilities. We recommend using the overall PMP S-E score to gain general insight into self-efficacy level and using the subscales to determine specific types of support that individual mothers may benefit from. The PMP S-E questionnaire only takes 10 min to complete, making it easy to administer in clinical settings. Furthermore, the PMP S-E is unique among measures used to assess parenting self-efficacy in that it was specifically designed for postpartum mothers. The neonatal period is a stressful time, and this stress may affect mothers' perceptions of their abilities to be successful parents. Thus, the PMP S-E could be useful during this stressful period.

This study addresses the lack of tools to assess self-efficacy among mothers of neonates in Taiwan. An assessment of maternal self-efficacy should allow more effective, family-centered interventions to be implemented in treating mothers with postpartum depression (Westrup 2015). This study also confirmed the multidimensional structure of the PMP S-E. Specifically, EFA clearly identified four factors which pertain to different parenting skills. In addition, the Chinese version of the MBI-PPD S-E includes 20 items. None of the items loaded on more than one factor, and alpha coefficients revealed high internal consistency for each of the four factors. The factor "care-taking procedures" refers to a mother's perception of her ability to perform tasks related to her baby's basic needs (e.g. feeding). The factor "evoking behaviours" refers to a mother's perception of her ability to elicit certain changes in her baby's behaviour (e.g. soothing). The factor "reading behaviour or signaling" refers to the mother's perception of her ability to identify and understand the body cues of her baby (e.g. tiredness). The factor "situational beliefs" refers to the mother's perception of her ability to identify and manage changes in her baby's behaviour based on emotional cues (e.g. when the baby is upset). The PMP S-E had high internal consistency, and the removal of any item resulted in a larger overall alpha coefficient, indicating that all items are significant components of the parental self-efficacy construct.

Table 2 compares reliability and validity scores for the PMP S-E that were obtained by the current study and by previous studies. For the current study, alpha values were high regardless of whether overall reliability or the reliability of subscales was being assessed. With regard to validity, all of the indicators we employed confirmed that our CFA model had adequate goodness of fit. Furthermore, the amount of variability explained by our EFA model was relatively high. Overall, our findings confirm the nature of the PMP S-E as a "domain-specific" measure of self-efficacy (Barnes and Adamson-Macedo 2007a). According to the well-accepted Bandurian theory of self-efficacy (Bandura 1997c), "domain-specific" measures refer to specific activities, and this makes them more predictive of parenting competence than general measures of self-efficacy (Bandura 1997d). In this sense, the PMP S-E fits well with current approaches to neonatal care that combine technological and pharmacological interventions with interventions that address "relationship-based needs" (Westrup 2015; Als et al. 2012; McAnulty et al. 2010). Effectively assessing mother-baby interactions requires that specific observation and coding procedures be employed (Jones and Prinz 2005; Morsbach and Prinz 2006). Indeed, attachment representations are the factors with the greatest influence over mother-baby interactions (Fonseca, Nazaré, Canavarro et al., 2013). However, assessments of perceived parental self-efficacy can still be informative. Cognitive processes (i.e. obtaining knowledge, acquiring beliefs, developing values and attitudes) influence the acquisition of new behavioural patterns and the ability to change existing behavioural patterns (Bandura 1977). This may explain why parental self-efficacy has been associated with parenting competence (Jones and Prinz2005; Teti and Gelfand 1991b; Teti et al. 2005).

5 Conclusions

This is the first study to develop a Chinese translation of a tool that is capable of measuring maternal self-efficacy among mothers of hospitalized neonates. This study was completed using a large sample of Taiwanese mothers of neonates, and our results indicated that the Chinese version of the PMP S-E had good validity, reliability, and consistency. Therefore, this tool is worthy of further testing and application. Given that parental self-efficacy is likely associated with the quality of parent-baby interactions, the PMP S-E questionnaire should greatly benefit clinical and research applications. Improving parent–baby interactions has long-term benefits for the neurodevelopment process of neonates. This study also deepened existing knowledge about parental self-efficacy and provided evidence of its manifestation in Taiwan. Future studies should employ the Chinese version of the MBI-PPD S-E scale developed in this study to further investigate the relationship between parental self-efficacy and postpartum depression, and further investigate the role of mindfulness interventions in improving maternal self-efficacy and alleviating postpartum depression.

References

Bandura, Albert, Adams, Nancy E.: Analysis of self-efficacy theory of behavior change. Cognitive Therapy Res. **1**(4), 287–310 (1977)

Als, H., et al.: NIDCAP improves brain function and structure in preterm infants with severe intrauterine growth restriction. J. Perinatol. **32**, 797–803 (2012)

Bandura, A.: The anatomy of stages of change. Am. J. Health Promot. **12**(1), 8–10 (1997a)

Bodhi, B.: What does mindfulness really mean? a canonical perspective. Contemporary Buddhism **12**(1), 19–39 (2011)

Bandura, A.: Self-efficacy: toward a unifying theory of behavioural change. Psychol. Rev. **84**, 191–215 (1977)

Bandura, A.: Self-efficacy: The Exercise of Control. W. H. Freeman, New York (1997b)

Bandura, A.: Self-efficacy mechanism in human agency. Am. Psychol. **37**(2), 122 (1982)

Coleman, P.K., Karraker, K.H.: Self-efficacy and parenting quality: findings and future application. Dev. Rev. **18**, 47–85 (1997a)

Bandura, A., Cervone, D.: Differential engagement of self-reactive influences in cognitive motivation. Organ. Behav. Hum. Decision Process. **38**(1), 92–113 (1986)

Bandura, A.: Self-Efficacy: The Exercise of Control. Freeman and Co, New York (1997c)

Bandura, A.: The explanatory and predictive scope of self-efficacy theory. J. Soc. Clin. Psychol. **4**(3), 359–373 (1997d)

Barnes, C.R., Adamson-Macedo, E.N.: Perceived Maternal Parenting Self-Efficacy (PMP S-E) tool: Development and validation with mothers of hospitalized preterm neonates. J. Adv. Nurs. **60**, 550–560 (2007a)

Melnyk, B.M., Alpert-Gillis, L., Feinstein, N.F., Fairbanks, E., Sinkin, R.A.: Improving cognitive development of low-birth-weight premature infants with the cope program: a pilot study of the benefit of early nicu intervention with mothers. Res. Nurs. Health **24**(5), 373–389 (2001a)

Bishop, S.R.: Mindfulness: a proposed operational definition. Clinical Psychol. Sci. Practice **11** (3), 230–241 (2004)

Bracht, M., O'Leary, L., Lee, S.K., O'Brien, K.: Implementing family-integrated care in the NICU: a parent education and support program. Adv. Neonatal Care, **13**, 115–126 (2013)

Cabrera-Nguyen, P.: Author Guidelines for reporting scale development and validation results. J. Soc. Soc. Work Res. **1**, 99–103 (2010)

Barnes, C.R., Adamson-Macedo, E.N.: Perceived maternal parenting self-efficacy (pmp s-e) tool: development and validation with mothers of hospitalized preterm neonates. J. Adv. Nurs. **60** (5), 550–560 (2007b)

Teti, Douglas M., Gelfand, Donna M.: Behavioral competence among mothers of infants in the first year: the mediational role of maternal self-efficacy. Child Dev. **62**(5), 918–929 (1991a)

Fonseca, A., Nazaré, B., Canavarro, M.C.: Parental psychological distress and confidence after an infant's birth: The role of attachment representations in parents of infants with congenital anomalies and parents of healthy infants. J. Clin. Psychol. Med. Settings **20**, 143–155 (2013)

Hess, C.R., Teti, D.M., Hussey-Gardner, B.: Self-efficacy and parenting of high-risk infants: the moderating role of parent knowledge of infant development. Appl. Dev. Psychol. **25**, 423–437 (2004)

Jones, T.L., Prinz, R.J.: Potential roles of parental selfefficacy in parent and child adjustment: a review. Clin. Psychol. Rev. **25**(3), 341–363 (2005)

Kabat-Zinn, J.: Mindfulness-based interventions in context: past, present, and future. Clin. Psychol. Sci. Practice **10**(2), 144–156 (2003)

Kaaresen, P.I., Ronning, J.A., Ulvund, S.E., Dahl, L.B.: A randomized, controlled trial of the effectiveness of an early-intervention program in reducing parenting stress after preterm birth. Pediatrics **118**(1), e9–e19 (2006)

Benzies, K.M., MagillEvans, J.E., Hayden, K.A., Ballantyne, M.: Key components of early intervention programs for preterm infants and their parents: a systematic review and meta-analysis. BMC Pregnancy & Childbirth, **13** (2013)

Kuhn, J.C., Carter, A.S.: Maternal self-efficacy and associated parenting cognitions among mothers of children with autism. Am. J. Orthopsychiatry **76**, 564–575 (2006)

Miles, M.S., Holditch-Davis, D.: Parenting the prematurely born child. Annual Rev. Nurs. Res. **15**(1) (1997)

McAnulty, G.B., Duffy, F.H., Butler, S.C., Bernstein, J.H., Zurakowski, D., Als, H.: Effects of the newborn individualized developmental care and assessment program (NIDCAP) at age 8 years: preliminary data. Clin. Pediatr. **49**, 258–270 (2010)

Melnyk, B.M., Alpert-Gillis, L., Feinstein, N.F., Fairbanks, E., Schultz-Czarniak, J., et al.: Improving cognitive development of low-birth-weight premature infants with the COPE program: a pilot study of the benefit of early NICU intervention with mothers. Res. Nurs. Health **24**, 373–389 (2001b)

Miles, M.S., Funk, S.G., Carlson, J.: Parental Stressor Scale: neonatal intensive care unit. Nurs. Res. **42**, 148–152 (1993)

Miles, M.S., Holditch-Davis, D.: Parenting the prematurely born child: pathways of influence. Semin. Perinatol. **21**, 254–266 (1997)

Montirosso, R., Del Prete, A., Bellù, R., Tronick, E., Borgatti, R.: Neonatal Adequate Care for Quality of Life (NEO-ACQUA) Study Group: Level of NICU quality of developmental care and neurobehavioral performance in very preterm infants. Pediatrics **129**, e1129–e1137 (2012)

Montirosso, R., Provenzi, L., Calciolari, G., Borgatti, R.: NEOACQUA Study Group: measuring maternal stress and perceived support in 25 Italian NICUs. Acta Paediatr. **101**, 136–142 (2012)

Morsbach, S.K., Prinz, R.J.: Understanding and improving the validity of self-report of parenting. Clin. Child Family Psychol. Rev. **9**, 1–21 (2006)

Coleman, P.K., Karraker, K.H.: Self-efficacy and parenting quality: findings and future applications. Dev. Rev. **18**(1), 47–85 (1997b)

Schwarzer, R., Bandura, A., Schwarzer, R.: Self-efficacy: thought control of action (1992)

Shapiro, S.L., Astin, J.A., Bishop, S.R., Cordova, M.: Mindfulness-based stress reduction for health care professionals: results from a randomized trial. Int. J. Stress Manage. **12**(2), 164–176 (2005)

Ohgi, S., Gima, H., Akiyama, T.: Neonatal behavioural profile and crying in premature infants at term age. Acta Paediatr. **95**(11), 1375–1380 (2006)

Teti, D.M., et al.: Intervention with African American premature infants: four-month results of an early intervention program. Journal of Early Intervention **31**, 146–166 (2009)

Teti, D.M., Gelfand, D.M.: Behavioral competence among mothers of infants in the first year: the mediational role of maternal self-efficacy. Child Dev. **62**, 918–929 (1991b)

Teti, D.M., Hess, C.R., O'Connell, M.: Parental perceptions of infant vulnerability in a preterm sample: pre diction from maternal adaptation to parenthood during the neonatal period. J. Dev. Behav. Pediatrics **26**, 283–292 (2005)

Westrup, B.: Family-centered developmentally supportive care: the Swedish example. Archives of Pediatrics **22**, 1086–1091 (2015)

We'll App and Corporate Mandala Improves Mental Health and Creativity

Wen-Ko Chiou[1]([✉]), Mei-Ling Lin[1]([✉]), Kuo-Jung Hsieh[1]([✉]),
Ying-Chieh Liu[1]([✉]), Ding-Hau Huang[2], Chia-Yi Liu[3],
and Rungtai Lin[4]

[1] Department of Industrial Design, Chang Gung University,
Taoyuan City, Taiwan
{wkchiu,khsieh,ycl30}@mail.cgu.edu.tw,
march19670324@gmail.com
[2] Institute of Creative Design and Management,
National Taipei University of Business, Taoyuan City, Taiwan
hau1012@gmail.com
[3] Department of Psychiatry, Chang Gung Memorial Hospital,
Taipei City, Taiwan
liucy752@cgmh.org.tw
[4] Graduate School of Creative Industry Design,
National Taiwan University of Arts, New Taipei City, Taiwan
rtlin@mail.ntua.edu.tw

Abstract. People in this modern era now live in a stressful environment and in a civilization full of competition to such an extent that their bodies, minds, and souls have contracted to incompleteness. The aims of this study are to improve and identify ways to cope with this condition, by following the process of "question—main factor—coping strategy—case study—research challenge." The main factors listed are (1) prioritizing mind-body dualism, especially the material body, (2) active sympathetic nerves as a norm, and (3) dominant left brain activity inhibiting the right brain. The coping strategies are (1) transformation through meditation, (2) surrender and self-inquiry on the consciousness of oneness, and (3) spiritual covenant. The case studies analyzed are (1) We'll app and (2) Corporate Mandala. Following a literature review and reviewing case studies, this study proposes 6 preliminary dimensions and 12 hypotheses aimed to improve the increasing problems in creativity limitation and depression.

Keywords: Depression · Mandala · Mental health · Creativity · App · Meditation · Mindfulness

© Springer Nature Switzerland AG 2020
P.-L. P. Rau (Ed.): HCII 2020, LNCS 12193, pp. 25–40, 2020.
https://doi.org/10.1007/978-3-030-49913-6_3

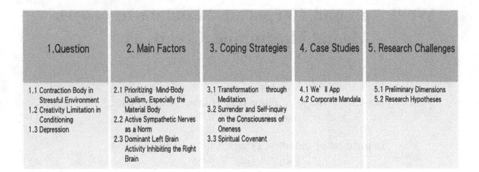

Fig. 1. The process of "question—main factor—coping strategy—case study—research challenge".

1 Questions

1.1 Contraction Body in Stressful Environment

As people nowadays deal with large amounts of information, they pursue efficiency and convenience. In an era that is also filled with distractions and multitasking, our fast-paced lives force our ideas to change quickly because in this world, we tend to receive never-ending information through our senses [1] (Fig. 1).

And through constantly living hectic lives, our brains cannot help but create a virtual reality. In fact, our brains are not apt to deal with these constant motions in time; thus, pressure is imposed [2]. When our mind is under stress or crises, it naturally has effects on our body, manifesting as anxiety or contractions, for example [3]. Our grievances and emotions, coming from losses, breakups, or being wronged in life, accumulate on an emotional level and can directly affect our body in many ways, from our behavior and life values to even physical health. These are consequences from our past that have ultimately conditioned us in the present [4].

Whether it is pain, insecurity, unhappiness, trouble, or loss, in the end, what remains is fear—the fear of pain, insecurity, and loss. All kinds of fear bring forth a sense of powerlessness and discomfort that we are all too familiar with. As fear arises, it stimulates our sympathetic nervous system and dominates over all of our bodily reactions [5]. Our contracted body turns pain into grief. Coupled with incredibly immense fear that is concentrated and condensed, this conditioning is difficult to be unconditioned. In the light of Qi or energy, a contracted body allows neither Qi nor energy to flow. All that remains are knots of Qi and energy scars. It not only affects this life but also leaves a collective wound on mankind, as if these contractions are stored in the DNA of our civilization that are passed onto future generations [6].

1.2 Creativity Limitation in Conditioning

Since childhood, our mind has been conditioned by constant brainwashing. Our mind transforms itself into a limitation/condition and constructs everything in life through ideas and phenomenon. All of these are the products of conditioning [7]. Throughout one's life, one thought after another, one cannot escape the constraints brought by thoughts. Each idea and phenomenon limits a life, convincing one that a life potential is limited and that it can only be lived in this way. It is a pity that even the next generation will grow up under conditioned education, enter a conditioned society, and establish conditioned relationships [8]. It turns a life into a large scope conditioning throughout the course of adulthood and aging, thereby establishing a conditioned culture and life. Human history is inseparable from conditioning, and the evolution of civilization is even more inseparable from materiality, from "motion", from pursuit, from comparison and differentiation, and from "I" [9].

As the message of insecurity promotes the growth of negative emotion in an emotional circle, it directly stimulates various self-defense systems in our body and keeps the body and mind in a constant state of stress. At this time, all physiological indexes become disordered, and signals and feedback mechanisms come in full swing. However, in a positive state, the amygdala of the brain remains calm and enters a stable and harmonious state of mind and body [10]. At this time, the hippocampus is operating normally, maximizing memory, concentration, and creativity. In a happy and safe environment, the highest learning efficiency can be achieved in a relaxed state of mind and body in which the potential of the left and right brains is simultaneously in full development [11]. As human hand motions relating to the establishment of a neural network in the brain, each muscle cell responds to many nerve cells. The muscle cells then send signals back to the nerve cells to form a continuous feedback loop, accelerating the potential of neural pathways. A happy manual activity not only stimulates the brain's potential but also can cultivates aesthetic, artistic, and creative abilities in all aspects, creating a complete and positive mind and personality [12].

1.3 Depression

Rapid economic development, advancement in technology, and the rapid progress of society have created prosperous human achievements and a large amount of material wealth. At the same time, these have also accelerated the pace of society that have led to many problems. People are now too often tense and stressed. The atmosphere of tension and anxiety has been spreading rapidly in our society. The psychological problems of people in our modern world have become more and more severe [13]. Sensing stress is a part of our instinct and is a dynamic mechanism that is always in adjustments and balances. The stress response is an inherent adaptive response to a stressor. Its role is to restore the body to a state of non-stress. Like an immune response, a stress response is essential for survival, but it can cause disorders if imbalanced. Gradual accumulation of psychological problems and long-term unease of emotions lead to the development of psychological and mental illness [14].

The World Health Organization (WHO) has indicated that depression is one of the three major diseases in the world that demand attention in 2020. With more than 300 million patients worldwide, depression is prominent in modern society and has been suggested to be a disease of modern civilization caused by western culture [15]. Long-term moderate or severe depression can turn into a serious illness. Patients can be greatly affected to the point where their performance at work, school, or home is poor.

Furthermore, depression can lead to suicide. In fact, suicide accounts for nearly 800,000 deaths each year and is the second leading cause of death among people aged 15–29. Women are also twice as likely to suffer from depression than men. Depression and chronic disorders caused by depression have become the most common health problems in women. It is similarly a major problem for men, in addition to cardio-vascular diseases [16]. More than a quarter of Americans experience severe depression at least once in their lives, and more than 16% of college students in Mainland China have moderate or more severe emotional problems [17].

2 Main Factors

2.1 Prioritizing Mind-Body Dualism, Especially the Material Body

The concept of mind-body dualism proclaims that the world has consciousness and matter from two independent origins, emphasizing that matter and consciousness exist equally. Dualism essentially insists that consciousness exists independently, separate from matter. The core idea of contemporary science is to verify based on evidence using the senses. Both the natural and social sciences test hypotheses through observations and experiments. However, semi-empirical evidence is often used to describe axioms, established scientific theories, or theoretical methods based on the experimental studies. It is used to conduct rational model constructions and theoretical exploration [18]. The brain can only operate through binary oppositions, such as distinction and comparison. The logic of the mind is somewhat comparative and linear that relies on a causal relationship. However, the body is different. It is not affected by nerves at every turn. A large part of our good health is not directly controlled by nerve cells but is rather governed by the consciousness of oneness, a kind of consciousness of non-thought [19].

No knowledge can be deduced, unless it is summarized from a person's sensory experience, which is generally considered to be in opposition to rationalism. Rationalism is the idea that knowledge can be derived from reason, not just from the senses. One of the greatest discoveries of modern physics is the "mass–energy equivalence." [20] There is nothing in matter; the essence of matter is not matter but energy [21]. A body appears to be constituted by solid matter, which can be decomposed into molecules and atoms. But according to quantum physics, the interior of each atom is almost empty. Its subatomic particles orbiting at lightning speed in space are in fact bundles of vibrational energy [22, 23]. They are not random vibrations but actually "information carriers." The entire information field will transmit the information to the quantum field in the universe, creating the reality that we see in the material world [24]. Arthur Eddington once said that "We used to think that matter is a thing; now, it is no more so. Matter is more like a thought than like a thing." Indeed, matter comes from ideas, from our thoughts [25].

2.2 Active Sympathetic Nerves as a Norm

In the nervous system, the cerebellum in the brain controls breathing, blood circulation, and digestion. This system is divided into the sympathetic and parasympathetic nervous systems. The sympathetic nervous system can accelerate metabolism and heartbeat, expand the bronchi in the lungs, and promote the release of stress hormones, which can negatively affect muscles. All of these are changes that occur during the fight-or-flight response [26]. The sympathetic nervous system, also known as the stress response system, allows us to suppress other physiological functions to fully deal with stress in an emergency. People nowadays are constantly stressed almost every day. When one wakes up, one cannot help but worry, for example, about work, study, or relationships [27]. Long hours of work leave little spare time to eat and rest. Furthermore, constant troubles cloud our minds even during sleep. This puts one in a state of long-term sympathetic nervous overload. The activation of the fight-or-flight response, which biologically and evolutionarily was a life-saving mechanism in times of danger, has now become mainstream and something that we are unfortunately accustomed to in modern life [28].

Stress in life is inevitable. Secretion of adrenaline and adrenal cortisol reduces insulin secretion in order to prepare one for what is coming next. At the same time, the liver increases glucose secretion and reduces its absorption, leading to an increase in levels of blood sugar. In the long run, however, persistent stress leaves one susceptible to diabetes or other chronic diseases. Cortisol is another hormone secreted in times of stress. When its levels remain high over a long period of time, an excess of free radicals is generated that inhibits immunity; affects sleep, digestion, and cardiovascular health; and causes inflammatory reactions [29]. In addition, jealousy is a combination of the three perceptions of fear, worry, and anger. According to one study, when jealousy emerges, sympathetic nervous activity increases, blood pressure rises, and adrenaline secretion increases whereas serotonin activity and immune function decrease, which can cause anxiety and insomnia [30].

2.3 Dominant Left Brain Activity Inhibiting the Right Brain

Roger Wolcott Sperry discovered brain asymmetry—the division of left and right brain functions—through the well-known "Split Brain Experiments." The normal human brain has two hemispheres, connected by the corpus callosum to form a complete unity [31]. The left hemisphere is responsible for logical comprehension, memory, time, language, judgement, arrangement, classification, logics, analysis, writing, deduction, suppression, and the five senses. Its way of thinking is continuity, sustainability, and analysis. However, under the collective imbalance among modern people and the extreme evolution of Earth, the division of left and right brain functions is severely imbalanced [32]. Too much emphasis has been put on the left brain, that is, too much on reason and thinking, and as such, thoughts have repeatedly brought us back to fear and survival. People have not dared to guard against the threats that may be caused by the moment and thus constantly confront everything occurring in the moment. This is the beginning of our worries [33].

The left brain is rational whereas the right brain is artistic and energetic. The balance of both hemispheres and of the autonomic nervous system is closely related to our physical and mental health [34]. A loss of function in the left brain, such as in the event of a stroke that causes extensive damage, can result in one's loss of function in speech, logic, temporal and spatial positioning, and junctional thinking [35]. When one looks at the world all as interactive energy, then everything becomes an energy spectrum, where there is no stress nor worry; the concept of "ego" is absent. The cerebrum, midbrain, and cerebellum inherently form a complete nerve network, enabling us to appreciate another level of life that is beyond the left brain, beyond the sympathetic system, beyond limitations, and beyond nerves, all of which are tied to the realm of time and space [36]. Our most basic nervous system can rest itself in a state of love, joy, and peace in the most relaxed situations. It experiences the moment itself, and even transcends.

3 Coping Strategies

3.1 Transformation Through Meditation

Meditation stimulates parasympathetic nerves, relaxes the mind, and returns the body to a state of harmony and completeness. During meditation, brain waves change from awaking and fast beta waves to relaxing and focusing alpha waves, which activate unconscious areas in the brain, enhancing intelligence, cognition, creativity, emotional stability; creating positive emotions and relaxation; and strengthening moral reasoning and self-confidence [37]. Meditation helps us integrate the ability to coordinate space, vision, feeling, perception, and motions, adjusting the physical and mental burden in response to messages of stress. It can improve cardiovascular health and restore the unity of the heart. It can also stimulate digestive glands to secrete saliva and enzymes to help digestion and bowel movements [38]. Additionally, meditation can correct posture in complete relaxation and adjustment of body and mind. It has been reported that serotonin values increase by up to two-fold following transcendental meditation. Furthermore, after twenty minutes of transcendental meditation, 5-HIAA, a metabolite of serotonin, significantly increases by 50%. This suggests that there are long-term increases in serotonin levels in those who practice transcendental meditations [39]. When practicing transcendental meditation, the body almost immediately goes into a deep state of rest that is more effective than several hours of sleep [40].

Post-traumatic stress disorder (PTSD) an urgent problem tormenting war-torn veterans and is generally considered incurable. As a result, an increasing number of American soldiers have committed suicide after returning from war over the past 15 years [41]. The figure is actually more than the total death toll on the battlefields of Iraq and Afghanistan. In a similar study of veterans of the Vietnam War, those who practiced transcendental meditation exhibited significant improvements after only three months [42]. Their PTSD, anxiety, depression, insomnia, alcoholism, and other symptoms were reduced, and their stress resistance also improved. As a result, 70% of the veterans participating in the experiment no longer needed further treatment [43]. Moreover, the control group, who received standard psychotherapy, showed no improvement. In a study of veterans of the Iraq War, their PTSD and depression symptoms were reduced by 50% after just eight weeks of practicing transcendental meditation [44]. Because these results were so surprising and exciting, CNN reported these findings on US Veteran's Day [45, 46]. In addition, the US military is now actively supporting and promoting the techniques of transcendental meditation for its soldiers [47].

3.2   Surrender and *Self-inquiry* on the Consciousness of Oneness

More and more biased is slipping into contemporary research, and there is a trend that research is falling to reductionism. Science can simplify very complicated matters into smaller and smaller units until they cannot be even smaller anymore. This is sometimes the case in modern science. The oneness and the origin have been forgotten and cornered by our limited brain. An animal, a flower, and a stone all have one body. One wants to be liberated, to jump out of the human condition, and surpass human quality [48]. There is no second timing in human development that is more mature than now. Everyone can find the unity of life through the strongest and even extreme "binary opposition." One or all is actually a concept of "presence." It is not something that the mind can imagine, nor is it something that the mind can pursue [49]. It at most, through our developed mind, does a reversal, letting it stop by itself and naturally falling to the "heart."

Compassion motivates action, coexistence, coevolution among people. The pulsation of the Earth is my pulsation, and the frequency of the Earth my frequency. Coexistence can also extend to animals, plants, the Earth, and even the universe. When we embrace it completely, people and things in life are neither good nor bad. We will not be envious with a comparative heart. Even negative thoughts will not be criticized but accepted. Surrender is the easiest and the most elegant gesture in life [50]. Only it can free the mind. It is not weakness but a very powerful spiritual force. Only by changing what can be changed in life, accepting what cannot be changed in life, and surrendering and joyfully trusting all arrangements of life can one understand that all causes and deaths are in perfect progress [51]. Only by acceptance can one truly move towards healing and live in the present and become a master of life [52].

3.3   Spiritual Covenant

By means of daily purification rituals—gratitude, repentance, hope, and giving back—the healing of heart can be facilitated. Verbal expression of feelings is not only the most powerful tool but also a positive tool. Positive language naturally brings people physically and mentally together. People expecting to be healthy will soon see the effects if they say "thank you" more. Practicing it in good faith can change the energy of the body and further the chemical structure of the body [53]. Living with the energy of the heart also means that one will fulfill the covenant that one has made with the soul. By following this agreement with oneself, one's health is significantly better in all aspects [54]. Living in harmony with nature, one may start from diet, exercise, breathing, thoughts, and emotional management. Moreover, remind oneself that the covenant of mind should always be present. Compassion is the greatest healing power in the universe! One needs to completely change one's thoughts to restore health [55]!

The first assignment one may start from is to be grateful, doing so unconditionally. One may begin even if obstacles are ahead. If this is the case, soon one's views will be different. One will be sincere and will practice repentance. This results from one's realization in human limits. Then through faith, religion, or meditative practice, one gains strength and hope [56]. As for giving back, it is about the heart. One's actions and behaviors must be consistent with the heart [57]. The method of giving back may be different for everyone, but the most important thing is to forsake oneself and think about the people around you, that is, to return to the heart, where it is the starting point of everything [58]. A person can be reborn once he practices these assignments every day. The value of life changes from the negative to the positive and to the light. Not only does one affect oneself personally, but everyone around can feel the encouragement and energy that are brought [59].

4 Case Studies

4.1 We'll App

This case combines "surrendering" and "self-inquiry" with spiritual covenant of mindfulness intervention therapy (MBI). The state of mindfulness demands that the mind is always noticing what is happening in front of us while also experiencing its own feelings. As long as one is sincere, the power of the rebound effect weakens each time that it is accepted. If accepted again and again, the emotional rebound gradually subsides, and one gets a gap to escape from the "ego" storm [60]. By "surrendering" and "self-inquiry" in every part of life, our consciousness will no longer be limited by momentary thoughts, moments of encounters, nor moments of joy and sorrow. We will move towards a broad or deep understanding. As "surrender" and "self-inquiry" influence the operation of the mind bit by bit, "ego" is moved aside. The tranquility, joy, happiness, satisfaction, and love of life naturally emerge like the sun [61, 62]. "We'll app" can put the minds of pregnant women in a state of mindfulness, withdrawing them from painfulness and emotions and reducing the pain caused by the symptoms. Through establishing mindfulness, they are able to reset the baseline of the current context. This mechanism frees them from the rigid framework. This is a thorough psychological treatment [63].

The use of We'll app not only transforms and reduces depression in pregnant women, but it also develops their self-efficacy. Self-efficacy is the belief that an individual has ownership to one's success on an action that leads to a desired result. Being confident plays an important role in the regulation of the stage of intention, of specific behavior change, and of preventing relapses when developing a healthy lifestyle. Many external factors and internal factors, such as personal experiences, can affect behavior through self-efficacy [64, 65]. Through the use of We'll app, pregnant women can share their different experiences, which then generate self-efficacy through observing the behaviors, practices, and experiences of others. The more similar the role models are, the more practical persuasion in the community there is, which can improve their self-efficacy and encourage them to work hard towards success, and thus lastingly encourage them through their parenting process [66, 67].

4.2 Corporate Mandala

According to Jung's discovery, each of us had a prototype so divided that we need a mandala to integrate it. The mandala can connect our inner perfection through precise totems. Mandala energy, a structural mystery of body in geometry and the power of color, creates a powerful circle of energy [68]. The magic of mandala is that in the beginning, you do not know what you are going to draw, but in the end, what you draw is beyond not only your own expectations but of the expectations of others as well [69]. Similarly, we do not really know what things can really satisfy us, but when we explore, we will discover our true dream and make it come true. Through Corporate Mandala, you can meditate; you can channel bad emotions; you can treat depression; you can learn to live in the present; you can activate your inner energy; you can use the law of attraction by using energy, will, time, and space; and you can achieve what you want! More importantly, it can teach us to release our inner child, to create and play innocently and happily [70, 71]!

The operation of the human mind is divided into two levels—consciousness and sub-consciousness. The consciousness is usually at work when we think. In the time test, most use the conscious mind. If you want to explain and understand what happens in your life, or why you are afraid of something, you need to understand your heart and solve the problem of life, which can be achieved through Corporate Mandala [72]. In addition, some people who are more introverted, or not good at expressing or not willing to speak, are also suitable to express their emotions and feelings through this. It is purely "drawing my mind." It is only for personal use, or for leisure and stress release [73]. In this case, by creating Corporate Mandala, the reification of subjects' adventure is in the dark. Researchers of educational aesthetics connect their unconsciousness and nonverbal artistic expressions in consciousness through the viewpoint of a "mythical hero." Moreover, they allow their subjects to create a complete world by the Corporate Mandala. By connecting the collective unconsciousness that is deep in the soul, the unconsciousness in the sober state can be embodied and the imagination can be used to rescue an endangering split-self to reconnect with "the conscious" self [74, 75] (Fig. 2).

5 Research Challenges

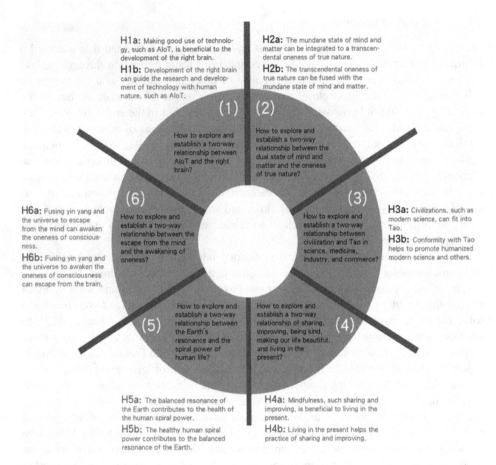

H1a: Making good use of technology, such as AIoT, is beneficial to the development of the right brain.

H1b: Development of the right brain can guide the research and development of technology with human nature, such as AIoT.

H2a: The mundane state of mind and matter can be integrated to a transcendental oneness of true nature.

H2b: The transcendental oneness of true nature can be fused with the mundane state of mind and matter.

(1) How to explore and establish a two-way relationship between AIoT and the right brain?

(2) How to explore and establish a two-way relationship between the dual state of mind and matter and the oneness of true nature?

H6a: Fusing yin yang and the universe to escape from the mind can awaken the oneness of consciousness.

H6b: Fusing yin yang and the universe to awaken the oneness of consciousness can escape from the brain.

(6) How to explore and establish a two-way relationship between the escape from the mind and the awakening of oneness?

(3) How to explore and establish a two-way relationship between civilization and Tao in science, medicine, industry, and commerce?

H3a: Civilizations, such as modern science, can fit into Tao.

H3b: Conformity with Tao helps to promote humanized modern science and others.

(5) How to explore and establish a two-way relationship between the Earth's resonance and the spiral power of human life?

(4) How to explore and establish a two-way relationship of sharing, improving, being kind, making our life beautiful, and living in the present?

H5a: The balanced resonance of the Earth contributes to the health of the human spiral power.

H5b: The healthy human spiral power contributes to the balanced resonance of the Earth.

H4a: Mindfulness, such sharing and improving, is beneficial to living in the present.

H4b: Living in the present helps the practice of sharing and improving.

Fig. 2. Research challenges of improving the increasing problems in creativity limitation and depression.

5.1 Preliminary Dimensions

(1) Making the best use of technology, such as a combination of artificial intelligence (AI) and the Internet of Things (IoT) (AIoT), by taking advantage of its speed and convenience [77–79].

(2) Cultivating the inner self of the eastern spirit along the duality of the western mind and body [80–82].

(3) Making science, medicine, industry, commerce, and other civilizations compatible with Tao [83, 84].

(4) Sharing, improving, being kind, making our life beautiful together, and living in and enjoying the present [85, 86].

(5) Helping the spiral power of the Earth and human life return to balance and harmony [87, 88].

(6) Thinking outside the box, designing the merge of yin yang and the universe, and awakening the oneness of consciousness [88, 89].

5.2 Research Hypotheses

(1) **How to explore and establish a two-way relationship between AIoT and the right brain?**

   H1a: Making good use of technology, such as AIoT, is beneficial to the development of the right brain.

   H1b: Development of the right brain can guide the research and development of technology with human nature, such as AIoT.

(2) **How to explore and establish a two-way relationship between the dual state of mind and matter and the oneness of true nature?**

   H2a: The mundane state of mind and matter can be integrated to a transcendental oneness of true nature.

   H2b: The transcendental oneness of true nature can be fused with the mundane state of mind and matter.

(3) **How to explore and establish a two-way relationship between civilization and Tao in science, medicine, industry, and commerce?**

   H3a: Civilizations, such as modern science, can fit into Tao.

   H3b: Conformity with Tao helps to promote humanized modern science and others.

(4) **How to explore and establish a two-way relationship of sharing, improving, being kind, making our life beautiful, and living in the present?**

   H4a: Mindfulness, such sharing and improving, is beneficial to living in the present.

   H4b: Living in the present helps the practice of sharing and improving.

(5) **How to explore and establish a two-way relationship between the Earth's resonance and the spiral power of human life?**

   H5a: The balanced resonance of the Earth contributes to the health of the human spiral power.

   H5b: The healthy human spiral power contributes to the balanced resonance of the Earth.

(6) **How to explore and establish a two-way relationship between the escape from the mind and the awakening of oneness?**

   H6a: Fusing yin yang and the universe to escape from the mind can awaken the oneness of consciousness.

   H6b: Fusing yin yang and the universe to awaken the oneness of consciousness can escape from the brain.

References

1. Chen, L., Nath, R., Tang, Z.: Understanding the determinants of digital distraction: an automatic thinking behavior perspective. Comput. Hum. Behav. **104**, 106195 (2020)
2. O'Connor, D.B., Walker, S., Hendrickx, H., Talbot, D., Schaefer, A.: Stress-related thinking predicts the cortisol awakening response and somatic symptoms in healthy adults. Psychoneuroendocrinology **38**(3), 438–446 (2013)
3. Huang, L., Whitson, J.: Organizational costs of compensating for mind-body dissonance through conspiracies and superstitions. Organ. Behav. Hum. Decis. Process. **156**, 1–12 (2020)
4. Hussain, M.B., Püntmann, V.O., Mayr, M., Khong, T., Singer, D.R.: The role of oxidant stress in angiotensin II-mediated contraction of human resistance arteries in the state of health and the presence of cardiovascular disease. Vascul. Pharmacol. **45**(6), 395–399 (2006)
5. Haaker, J., et al.: Making translation work: Harmonizing cross-species methodology in the behavioural neuroscience of Pavlovian fear conditioning. Neurosci. Biobehav. Rev. **107**, 329–345 (2019)
6. Williams, L.M., Gatt, J.M., Schofield, P.R., Olivieri, G., Peduto, A., Gordon, E.: 'Negativity bias' in risk for depression and anxiety: brain–body fear circuitry correlates, 5-HTT-LPR and early life stress. NeuroImage **47**, 804–814 (2009)
7. Xie, Q.W., Chan, C., Lau, B., Tam, M., Fung, Y., Chan, C.: Effectiveness of an integrative body-mind-spirit group intervention in improving the skin symptoms and psychosocial well-being in children living with atopic dermatitis: a randomized-waitlisted controlled trial. Child Youth Serv. Rev. **110**, 104739 (2020)
8. Stuhlmüller, A., Goodman, N.D.: Reasoning about reasoning by nested conditioning: modeling theory of mind with probabilistic programs. Cogn. Syst. Res. **28**(1), 80–99 (2013)
9. Diamantopoulos, A., Arslanagic-Kalajdzic, M., Moschik, N.: Are consumers' minds or hearts guiding country of origin effects? conditioning roles of need for cognition and need for affect. J. Bus. Res. **108**, 487–495 (2020)
10. Walsh, E.C., et al.: Pretreatment brain connectivity during positive emotion upregulation predicts decreased anhedonia following behavioral activation therapy for depression. J. Affect. Disord. **243**, 188–192 (2018)
11. Koush, Y., Pichon, S., Eickhoff, S., Van De Ville, D., Vuilleumier, P., Scharnowski, F.: Brain networks for engaging oneself in positive-social emotion regulation. Neuroimage **189**, 106–115 (2019)
12. Zhang, Q., Lee, M.: A hierarchical positive and negative emotion understanding system based on integrated analysis of visual and brain signals. Neurocomputing **73**, 3264–3272 (2010)
13. Chan, R.C.H., Operario, D., Mak, W.W.S.: Bisexual individuals are at greater risk of poor mental health than lesbians and gay men: the mediating role of sexual identity stress at multiple levels. J. Affect. Disord. **260**, 292–301 (2019)
14. Valikhani, A., Ahmadnia, F., Karimi, A., Mills, P.: The relationship between dispositional gratitude and quality of life: the mediating role of perceived stress and mental health. Personality Individ. Differ. **141**, 40–46 (2019)
15. https://www.who.int/news-room/fact-sheets/detail/depression
16. Collaborators, G.B.D., Nomura, S.: Global, regional, and national incidence, prevalence, and years lived with disability for 354 diseases and injuries for 195 countries and territories, 1990–2017: a systematic analysis for the Global Burden of Disease Study 2017. The Lancet **392**, 1789–1858 (2018)

17. Gold, P.W.: The organization of the stress system and its dysregulation in depressive illness. Mol. Psychiatry **20**(1), 32–47 (2015)
18. Tayeb, H.O.: Epilepsy stigma in Saudi Arabia: the roles of mind–body dualism, supernatural beliefs, and religiosity. Epilepsy Behavior **95**, 175–180 (2019)
19. Ross, A.M., Fotheringham, D., Crusoe, K.: Re-valuing nursing's currency: shifting away from hierarchical binary opposition. Nurse Educ. Today **34**(5), 687–690 (2014)
20. Perkovic, D., Stefancic, H.: Dark sector unifications: dark matter-phantom energy, dark matter - constant w dark energy dark matter-dark energy-dark matter. Phys. Lett. B **797**, 134806 (2019)
21. Lennon, M.: Decolonizing energy: black lives matter and technoscientific expertise amid solar transitions. Energy Res. Soc. Sci. **30**, 18–27 (2017)
22. Liu, T.: The scientific hypothesis of an "energy system" in the human body. J. Trad. Chinese Med. Sci. **5**, 29–34 (2018)
23. Mark, G., Lyons, A.: Conceptualizing mind body spirit interconnections through and beyond spiritual healing practices. Explore: The J. Sci. Heal. **10**, 294–299 (2014)
24. Atmanspacher, H.: Mind and matter as asymptotically disjoint inequivalent representations with broken time-reversal symmetry. Bio Syst. **68**, 19–30 (2003)
25. Gherab-Martín, K.J.: From structuralism to neutral monism in Arthur S. Eddington's philosophy of physics. Stud. History and Philosophy Sci. Part B: Stud. History Philosophy Modern Phys. **44**, 500–512 (2013)
26. Thompson, K.L., Hannan, S., Miron, L.: Fight, flight, and freeze: threat sensitivity and emotion dysregulation in survivors of chronic childhood maltreatment. Personality Individ. Differ. **69**, 28–32 (2014)
27. Ma, I.C., Chang, W.H., Wu, C.L., Lin, C.H.: Risks of post-traumatic stress disorder among emergency medical technicians who responded to the 2016 Taiwan earthquake. J. Formos. Med. Assoc. (2019). https://doi.org/10.1016/j.jfma.2019.11.021
28. Roos, L.E., Knight, E.L., Beauchamp, K.G., Berkman, E.T., Fisher, P.A.: Acute stress impairs inhibitory control based on individual differences in parasympathetic nervous system activity. Biol. Psychol. **125**, 58–63 (2017)
29. Stetler, C.A., Guinn, V.: Cumulative cortisol exposure increases during the academic term: links to performance-related and social evaluative stressors. Psychoneuroendocrinology **114**, 104584 (2020)
30. Bethea, C.L., Pau, K.Y., Fox, S., Hess, D., Berga, S., Cameron, J.: Sensitivity to stress-induced reproductive dysfunction linked to activity of the serotonin system. Fertil. Steril. **83**, 148–155 (2005)
31. Pearce, J.M.S.: The "split brain" and Roger Wolcott Sperry (1913–1994). Revue Neurologique **175**, 217–220 (2019)
32. Bogen, J.E.: My developing understanding of Roger Wolcott Sperry's philosophy. Neuropsychologia **36**, 1089–1096 (1998)
33. Rangarajan, V., Parvizi, J.: Functional asymmetry between the left and right human fusiform gyrus explored through electrical brain stimulation. Neuropsychologia **83**, 29–36 (2016)
34. Passingham, R.E., Chung, A., Goparaju, B., Cowey, A., Vaina, L.M.: Using action understanding to understand the left inferior parietal cortex in the human brain. Brain Res. **1582**, 64–76 (2014)
35. Skrandies, W., Jedynak, A.: Associative learning in humans- conditioning of sensory-evoked brain activity. Behav. Brain Res. **107**, 1–8 (2000)
36. Pessiglione, M., Petrovic, P., Daunizeau, J., Palminteri, S., Dolan, R.J., Frith, C.D.: Subliminal instrumental conditioning demonstrated in the human brain. Neuron **59**(4), 561–567 (2008)

37. Travis, F., Parim, N., Shrivastava, A.: Higher theta and alpha1 coherence when listening to Vedic recitation compared to coherence during Transcendental Meditation practice. Conscious. Cogn. **49**, 157–162 (2017)
38. Avvenuti, G., et al.: Reductions in perceived stress following Transcendental Meditation practice are associated with increased brain regional connectivity at rest. Brain Cogn. **139**, 105517 (2020)
39. Travis, F., Parim, N.: Default mode network activation and Transcendental Meditation practice: focused attention or automatic self-transcending? Brain Cogn. **111**, 86–94 (2017)
40. Gathright, E.C., et al.: The Impact of transcendental meditation on depressive symptoms and blood pressure in adults with cardiovascular disease: a systematic review and meta-analysis. Complementary Therapies in Medicine **46**, 172–179 (2019)
41. Bujatti, M., Riederer, P.: Serotonin, noradrenaline, dopamine metabolites in Transcendental Meditation technique. J. Neural Trans. **39**, 257–267 (1976)
42. Wallace, R.K.: Physiological effects of transcendental meditation. Science **167**(3926), 1751–1754 (1970)
43. Dillbeck, M.C., Orme-Johnson, D.W.: Physiological differences between transcendental meditation and rest. Am. Psychol. **42**(9), 879–881 (1987)
44. Rosenthal, J.Z., Grosswald, S., Ross, R., Rosenthal, N.: Effects of transcendental meditation in veterans of operation enduring freedom and operation Iraqi freedom with posttraumatic stress disorder: a pilot study. Mil. Med. **176**(6), 626–630 (2011)
45. https://www.youtube.com/watch?v=SsIvJHrtAlw
46. https://www.army.mil/article/139778/
47. Brooks, J.S., Scarano, T.: Transcendental meditation in the treatment of post-Vietnam adjustment. J. Counsel. Dev. **64**(3), 212–215 (1985)
48. Fullanaa, M.A., Dunsmoorc, J.E., Schruersd, K.R., Savagef, H.S., Bachg, D., Harrisonf, B.J.: Human fear conditioning: from neuroscience to the clinic. Behav. Res. Ther. **124**, 103528 (2019)
49. Viegas, C.V., Bond, A., Rodrigues Vaz, C., João Bertolo, R.: Reverse flows within the pharmaceutical supply chain: a classificatory review from the perspective of end-of-use and end-of-life medicines. J. Clean. Prod. **238**, 117719 (2019)
50. Deb, A.: 'Surrender to nature': worldviews and rituals of the small-scale coastal fishers of Bangladesh. Marine Policy **92**, 1–12 (2018)
51. Schacter, D.L., Addis, D.R., Buckner, R.L.: Remembering the past to imagine the future: the prospective brain. Nat. Rev. Neurosci. **8**, 657–661 (2007)
52. Kim, A.E., Sikos, L.: Conflict and surrender during sentence processing: an ERP study of syntax-semantics interaction. Brain Lang. **118**, 15–22 (2011)
53. Ferry, G.: Paul Greengard, Ph.D. (1925–2019). Nature, **569**, 488 (2019). https://doi.org/10.1038/d41586-019-01532-9
54. Vintila, I.: Actual state and perspectives of Christian religious dietary laws and certification in Romania. Trends Food Sci. Technol. **45**, 147–152 (2015)
55. De Coteau, T., Anderson, J., Hope, D.A.: Adapting manualized treatments: treating anxiety disorders among native Americans. Cognit. Behav. Pract. **13**(4), 304–309 (2006)
56. Murdoch, K.C., et al.: The efficacy of the strength, hope and resourcefulness program for people with Parkinson's disease (SHARP-PWP): a mixed methods study. Parkinsonism Related Disorders **70**, 7–12 (2019)
57. Zhou, X., Tang, J., Zhao, Y., Wang, T.: Effects of feedback design and dispositional goal orientations on volunteer performance in citizen science projects. Comput. Hum. Behav. 106266 (2020)

58. Paterson, C., Paterson, N., Jackson, W., Work, F.: What are students' needs and preferences for academic feedback in higher education: a systematic review. Nurse Educ. Today **85**, 104236 (2020)
59. Center, E.G., Knight, R., Fabiani, M., Gratton, G., Beck, D.M.: Examining the role of feedback in TMS-induced visual suppression: a cautionary tale. Conscious. Cogn. **75**, 102805 (2019)
60. Reyes, A.T., Bhatta, T.R., Muthukumar, V., Gangozo, W.J.: Testing the acceptability and initial efficacy of a smartphone-app mindfulness intervention for college student veterans with PTSD. Archives of Psychiatric Nursing (2020). In Press Journal Pre-Proof
61. Linardon, J.: Can acceptance, mindfulness, and self-compassion be learnt by smartphone apps? a systematic and meta-analytic review of randomized controlled trials. Behavior Therapy, In Press, Corrected Proof (2019). https://doi.org/10.1016/j.beth.201
62. Clarke, J., Draper, S.: Intermittent mindfulness practice can be beneficial, and daily practice can be harmful. an in depth, mixed methods study of the "Calm" app's (mostly positive) effects. Internet Interventions, **19**, 100293 (2019)
63. Hunter, J.E., et al.: Feasibility of an app-based mindfulness intervention among women with an FMR1 premutation experiencing maternal stress. Res. Dev. Disabil. **89**, 76–82 (2019)
64. Chittaro, L., Vianello, A.: Evaluation of a mobile mindfulness app distributed through on-line stores: a 4-week study. Int. J. Hum-. Comput. Stud. **86**, 63–80 (2016)
65. Torous, J., Lipschitz, J., Ng, M., Firth, J.: Dropout rates in clinical trials of smartphone apps for depressive symptoms: a systematic review and meta-analysis. J. Affect. Disord. **263**, 413–419 (2019)
66. García-Magariño, I., Plaza, I.: ABS-MindHeart: an agent based simulator of the influence of mindfulness programs on heart rate variability. J. Comput. Sci. **19**, 11–20 (2017)
67. Wasil, A., Venturo-Conerly, K., Shingleton, R.M., Weisz, J.R.: A review of popular smartphone apps for depression and anxiety: assessing the inclusion of evidence-based content. Behav. Res. Ther. **123**, 103498 (2019)
68. Kim, H., Kim, S., Choe, K., Kim, J.: Effects of mandala art therapy on subjective well-being, resilience, and hope in psychiatric inpatients. Arch. Psychiatr. Nurs. **32**, 167–173 (2017)
69. Schrade, C., Tronsky, L., Kaiser, D.H.: Physiological effects of mandala making in adults with intellectual disability. Arts Psychotherapy **38**, 109–113 (2011)
70. Kim, S., Ghil, J., Choi, E., Kwon, O., Kong, M.: A computer system using a structured mandala to differentiate and identify psychological disorders. Arts Psychotherapy **41**, 181–186 (2014)
71. Elkis-Abuhoff, D., Gaydos, M., Goldblatt, R., Chen, M., Rose, S.: Mandala drawings as an assessment tool for women with breast cancer. Arts Psychotherapy **36**, 231–238 (2009)
72. Kim, S., Kim, Y.H., Kim, E.J.: An expert system for interpretation of structured mandala. Arts Psychotherapy **35**, 320–328 (2008)
73. South, B.: Combining mandala and the Johari Window: an exercise in self-awareness. Teach. Learn. Nurs. **2**, 8–11 (2007)
74. Kim, S., Betts, D.J., Kim, H.M., Kang, H.S.: Statistical models to estimate level of psychological disorder based on a computer rating system: an application to dementia using structured mandala drawings. Arts Psychotherapy **36**, 214–221 (2009)
75. Kim, S., Kang, H., Kim, Y.: A computer system for art therapy assessment of elements in structured mandala. Arts Psychotherapy **36**, 19–28 (2009)
76. Andreasen, N.C.: Linking mind and brain in the study of mental illnesses: a project for a scientific psychopathology. Science **275**(5306), 1586–1593 (1997)
77. Aziz-Zadeh, L., Liew, S.L., Dandekar, F.: Exploring the neural correlates of visual creativity. Soc. Cogn. Affect. Neurosci. **8**(4), 475–480 (2013)

78. Bratman, G.N., et al.: Nature and mental health: an ecosystem service perspective. Sci. Adv. **5**(7), 1 (2019). https://doi.org/10.1126/sciadv.aax0903
79. Demertzi, A., et al.: Human consciousness is supported by dynamic complex patterns of brain signal coordination. Sci. Adv. **5**(2) (2019). https://doi.org/10.1126/sciadv.aat7603
80. Engert, V., Kok, B.E., Papassotiriou, I., Chrousos, G.P., Singer, T.: Specific reduction in cortisol stress reactivity after social but not attention based mental training. Sci. Adv. **3**(10) (2017). https://doi.org/10.1126/sciadv.1700495
81. Garland, E.L., Atchley, R.M., Hanley, A.W., Zubieta, J.K., Froeliger, B.: Mindfulness-oriented recovery enhancement remediates hedonic dysregulation in opioid users: neural and affective evidence of target engagement. Sci. Adv. **5**(10) (2019). https://doi.org/10.1126/sciadv.aax1569
82. Ge, J., et al.: Cross-language differences in the brain network subserving intelligible speech. Proc. Natl. Acad. Sci. U.S.A. **112**, 2972–2977 (2015)
83. Labarthe, D.R., Kubzansky, L.D., Boehm, J.K., Lloyd-Jones, D., Berry, J.D., Seligman, M. E.: Positive cardiovascular health: a timely convergence. J. Am. Coll. Cardiol. **68**, 860–867 (2016)
84. Mashour, G.A.: The controversial correlates of consciousness. Science **360**(6388), 493–494 (2018)
85. Michaels, R., Huber, M., McCann, D.: Evaluation of transcendental meditation as a method of reducing stress. Science **192**(4245), 1242–1244 (1976)
86. Pinto, Y., et al.: Split brain: divided perception but undivided consciousness. Brain **140**(5), 1231–1237 (2017)
87. Stefaniak, J.D., Halai, A.D., Lambon Ralph, M.A.: The neural and neurocomputational bases of recovery from post-stroke aphasia. Nat. Rev. Neurol. **16**, 43–55 (2019)
88. Valk, S.L., et al.: Structural plasticity of the social brain: differential change after socio-affective and cognitive mental training. Sci. Adv. **3**(10) (2017). https://doi.org/10.1126/sciadv.1700489
89. Wolman, D.: The split brain: a tale of two halves. Nature **483**(7389), 260–263 (2012)

Design as Mediation for Social Connection Against Loneliness of Older People

Yumei Dong[1] , Haoxin Weng[2] , Hua Dong[3] ,
and Long Liu[1(✉)]

[1] Tongji University, Shanghai 20092, China
liulong@tongji.edu.cn
[2] Delft University of Technology, 2600 AA Delft, The Netherlands
[3] Loughborough University, Leicestershire LE11 3TU, UK

Abstract. In the social background of population ageing, this paper addressed the issue of social isolation and loneliness. Reflecting on the current design for social connectedness. We advocate a positive perspective to older people and consider design as mediation for social connection. Practice cases and research show the potential of design mediation connection, however, there is a lack of summarized knowledge of how to design for mediation. This paper aims to answer the research question-How does design as mediation facilitate social connection? This question was answered from two aspects. One focused on the form or features as regards to the design as a result, the other is reflecting design as an ideating process. This research follows a Research through Design (RtD) approach. A design project was launched in a design course for design students. Research materials, including the design process and design outcome, were documented and reflected. As a result, the design elements for enhancing social connection was clarified and conceptualized. It includes five categories from abstract to concrete level, namely role, partnership, encounter, facility and trigger. Design strategies were also concluded according to the five elements. The paper also proposed an ideation process of designing for social connection by linking the design elements with the ideation activities. This research criticized viewing socializing as a functional activity and advocated a new perspective of design as mediation for social connection among older people. The results provided practice guidance and reference for designers in designing intervention for social connection.

Keywords: Design mediation · Older people · Population ageing · Social connection · Loneliness · Research through Design (RtD)

1 Introduction

1.1 Population Ageing and Loneliness

Populations around the world are rapidly ageing [1]. Two billion, 22% of the total population in the world can expect to live into their 60s and beyond [2, 3]. And those who reach 60 years of age can expect to live longer than ever before [1]. Longevity presents a triumph of human development, however, it means many people will live

© Springer Nature Switzerland AG 2020
P.-L. P. Rau (Ed.): HCII 2020, LNCS 12193, pp. 41–52, 2020.
https://doi.org/10.1007/978-3-030-49913-6_4

more years than before after retirement, during which losing spouse and friends will happen and social networks tend to shrink. According to Age UK, more than 2 million people in England over the age of 75 live alone, and more than a million older people say they go for over a month without speaking to a friend, neighbour or family member [4].

Social isolation leads to loneliness and it consequently becomes a serious social phenomenon in the ageing society. The impact of loneliness on physical and mental health has been widely studied. Many empirical studies are supporting the social network's and social support's influence the physical health. A survey including 755 samples indicates the negative impact of the lack of social support in the physical health of older people and proposes using social variables to predict health outcome [5]. Studies prove that loneliness may lead to a cognitive decline [6, 7], heart disease, stroke [8] and accelerated risk of depression [9].

Due to the huge negative impact, loneliness has attacked much attention all around the world. Social facilitation [10], psychological therapies [11], animal interventions [12], leisure and skill development interventions [13] are taken to reduce loneliness in the discipline of social work, nursing and public health [14]. Policymaking departments and social sectors have also taken measures to address this problem from a top-down to a bottom-up approach. The UK attaches great importance to loneliness by appointing one minister specifically to tackle this problem. While in the Netherlands, the Dutch government has spent over 26 million euro on the plan to address the problem from a top-down approach. There are organizations such as The National Elderly Fund and De Zonnebloem approaching the problem by organizing volunteer activities for older people who are socially isolated.

1.2 Design Response to Loneliness

How can design approach the issue of social isolation and loneliness among older people? Age-friendly neighbourhoods are planned and designed in many cities to support older people going out. Communication technologies are designed following the inclusive design principles so that it is easy to use for older people. Games were designed to relieve loneliness through a nostalgic visual style and a plants-growing theme to improve the sense of purpose [15]. Many robots can accompany older people and provide emotional support. Alice is one of the examples. It is a social robot, developed to alleviate loneliness among vulnerable elderly people. With the sensors and connections with other objects and tools, Alice can chat with older people, send WhatsApp messages and ordering messages [16]. Tests proved that Alice performs functionally well in various conversations and situations. Despite the great potential for positive impact, there are some doubts if Alice creates a social connection or reduces social connection. Research indicates a negative impact of interactive technology, e.g. reduced quality of face-to-face interactions, decreased measures of mental health, e.g. higher stress levels, and lower psychological functioning e.g. increased loneliness [17].

Social loneliness cannot be prevented by tackling a single point. It is connected to both the individual and the society, such as the person's self-esteem, physical condition, his or her social network and environment, accessibility to a social resource and so on [18]. Design for reducing loneliness should open the opportunities for social participation of older people, but not only provide companionship at home and close the door for real social interaction. What is more, the passive way to consume social welfare requires a large number of resources. There is a concern that the demographic pressures of population ageing will lead to an unprecedented rise in healthcare expenditures and unsustainable financial arrangement [19]. Research also shows activities or interventions which support productive engagement seems to be more successful in reducing social isolation than those involving passive activities [20]. Therefore, Public welfare approach seeks for transformation from a passive to an active way, where older people themselves play an important role to tackle their problem and create social value. From this perspective, the design should not only support for psychological therapy to relieve the sense of loneliness but a channel to provide active social interaction.

1.3 Design as Mediation

Generally, there are two functions of design. One is the practical function, the other is the symbolic function. Focusing more on the practical function adds the risk of cutting off the meaningful relations between human and the world. Philosophers on technology distinguish artificial into two categories, one is the 'thing'; the other is the 'device' [21]. Device is what provides a close form of functionality and follows a consumption relation and restricts the interaction with the world of people. Borgmann advocates escaping from the consumption relation to participation through focused practice [22]. Verbeek follows this advocate and focuses on the mediating function of things. He considers this function as the third function of design [23]. Researchers introduced mediated empowerment [24] and transformative mediation [25] into urban design, which mean 'that does not necessarily lead to direct policy or action but is nonetheless empowering' and 'a process of a process of placing the decision-making power in the hands of participating parties and allowing participants to become more self-aware' respectively [26]. Buchanan supports to pay attention to the mediating influence of product to support interactions between people or people and their social and natural environments [27]. Design research in subjective well-being also advocates products' contribution to well-being is grounded in their potential to support well-being-enhancing activities rather than in their material value [28]. Following this advocacy, we argue that design against loneliness should be the mediation to bridge social connection, rather than a product with social function. From this perspective, Design itself can not relieve loneliness, but the social and contributing opportunities it brings do.

Even though the mediation function was not elaborated obvious in design literature related to design for reducing loneliness for older people, many cases present the potential to trigger social interaction. For example, a PhD project at the Eindhoven University of Technology explored the possibilities of Design for Connectedness for older people. As a result, Tangible products with embedded technologies such as a machine called Slot-Memento to transfer the memory of two generations were designed and provided to bridge the connection between older people and their family members [29]. Nevay et al. designed a responsive device which can be shared on a table or across participants. Sounds and music from the city were embedded into fabric patches depicting scenes from the city. By listening to the sounds and interact with the fabric together, participants were encouraged towards storytelling, sharing, conversation and relationship building towards connectedness [30]. The above cases in the literature show older people engaged in social activities with the mediation of design.

Even though the cases of designs were given, there was a lack of knowledge and methods for design as mediation for social connection. Therefore, this research aims at proving practical knowledge through answering the question of how design as mediation facilitates social connection. This question was answered from two aspects. One focused on the form or features regarding design as a result, the other is reflected the designing as an ideating process.

2 Method

To answer the research question, this research follows a Research through Design (RtD) approach, a research approach that employs methods and processes from design practice as a legitimate method of inquiry [31]. A connection was made between RtD and the Action Research approach used in the humanities and the social sciences [32]. Similar to Action Research, RtD emphasizes reflection in design practice and aims to generate knowledge. As one of the outcomes of RtD, the artefact is a type of implicit and theoretical contribution [33]. We generalize artefact into different stages of actualization, from concept to prototype to final commodity. Reflection on the design process also generates design knowledge.

In this study, Design project addressing social isolation and loneliness was conducted in design courses for design students. This project follows a process of design thinking which includes five phases (i.e. empathize, define, ideate, prototype and test). User interview was conducted in empathize phase, 19 retired older people in the Netherlands participated in the interview. The daily routine, social network, social activities, moments feeling loneliness and their own efforts to overcome loneliness were asked in the interview. Insights from user interview nurtured the design ideation. For example, one lady said 'feeling loneliness is a shame, so I do not like the social activities with an obvious purpose of making friends.' This point was taken into consideration into the ideate process. It also helped researchers understand mediation was necessary for social connection. Cases were collected and analyzed after problem definition to spark innovation. Table 1 presents the collected cases and shows how people overcome loneliness.

Table 1. Design cases to show how people overcome loneliness

Cases	Brief introduction	Methods to overcome loneliness
Experience Corps	A program made up of volunteers who are above 50 years old to helping children become great readers	-Cross-generation interaction -Productive activities
Abtswoude Bloeit	A nursing home where older people, students and marginalized people live under one roof and share times with cultural and art activities	-Cross-cultural interaction -cultural and art activities
Agewell	A care project: employing able older people as companions of less able older people through home visits and health screening	-peer-to-peer support -technology-enabled productive activities

The first author was one of the tutors of the course and the second author is the student participated in this course. Researchers sometimes participated in the project, and sometimes jump out of the process to gain new insights. Students generated different ideas range from product design to service design. Those results and ideating process, as well as materials generated during the process, was documented as raw materials for analysis. Analysis on design proposals and referred cases (material generated in the ideate and prototype phases) generates knowledge of design outcome. Reflection on the ideation process (material generated in ideate phase) generates knowledge of ideating activities. Analysis on user research data (material generated in emphasize phase) generates knowledge of users. This is how the design thinking as a design process interweaved with the RtD as a design research process. Due to the limited space, this paper does not present the knowledge of users.

Therefore, the analysis process will present in two parts. In the first part, the design elements in students proposals and cases were decomposed and clustered through the card sorting method. For example, we extracted the 'peer-to-peer' as an element from the case of Agewell [34] and 'older people, students and marginalized people living under one roof' from the case of Abtswoude Bloeit [35]. Those elements were then clustered into one category, partnership, by a similar function in each case. To make the phrase more precise, we conceptualized the categories of design elements by comparison with the theory from other fields. In the second part, research focused on the ideating process. Students' ideating activities were reflected, we tried to link the ideating activities with the design elements so that it can provide guidance for design practice.

3 Results

The results section will present the five design elements and related strategies, and the ideation process linked to the five design elements. A student's proposal will also be presented as a demonstration of how the five elements integrate.

3.1 Five Elements and the Strategies

Role - from Dissipative to Generative. The first element is the generative role. Regarding older people as a dissipative role in society requires a large amount of resource input and makes the design solutions unsustainable. Instead, to mediating social connection, a generative role is crucial to motivate older people for a sense of accomplishment. Older people who retired from work are still competent in many aspects and they seek opportunities for generative involvement for social value creation [36]. Erikson's research implies that harnessing the untapped desire for generativity in an ageing population could lead to benefits for both society and older adults [37, 38]. Empirical studies have also demonstrated significant correlations between generative involvement and late-life satisfaction and happiness [39]. The positive psychological feedback will encourage active social participation.

Partnership - Based on Homogeneity and Heterogeneity. The second element is the reciprocal partnership. To build and sustain a social connection for older people, a reciprocal partnership with a common language is significant to guarantee a sustainable relationship. Research finds that interest and friendship information is highly relevant and correlated [40]. The shared background such as interests, education and professional experience, and demographic information reinforce trust. while the difference is beneficial for benefit exchange. Granovetter has analyzed the social tie and identifies several factors that influence the strength [41]. His research indicates resource is more likely exchanged reciprocally between weak tie where people have different resources [42]. Studies in social capital also indicate heterogeneous between people more likely to open new avenues for resource exchange and create social capital [43]. To facilitate resource exchange, heterogeneous factors also have to be taken into consideration.

Agewell is an elder-to-elder peer care project in Cape Town [34]. The project recruits able older people to become companions, called 'AgeWells' to help less abled people. The partnership is based on a different health condition. However, the peers also matched with shared language based on several factors including demographics, geography, gender, language, personality, and interests [34]. The results of the test show a reduction in depression among people who receive visits. Agewells who do the visit also benefit from a sense of purpose and accomplishment. This model has been proved to be effective and replicated to different countries.

Facility - Supportive and Inviting. The third element is the facility. The facility is any physical or virtual products that support to achieve a specific goal. Facilities should be flexible so that it can adjust to a wide range of activities. Facilities themselves are not the aim of design but the mediating function to support social connection. Plain features can make them inviting for more participation.

Abtswoude Bloeit is a former nursing home where students, older people and marginalized people live together under one roof [35]. For older people who are frail and difficult to move out, this project provides a Living Room open for everyone. Students and people from the neighborhoods are welcomed to organize and participate in activities together. The Living Room combined multiple functions, café, library, art gallery and stage performance, with the support of many facilities. The facilities are very flexible. It can meet different needs of social activities. Besides the physical facilities, this project also provides a website where everyone can apply to organize the activities and call for participation.

Encounter - from Intentional to Natural. The third element is the encounter. The term 'Encounter' comes from the concept 'service encounter' [44], which refers to 'dyadic interaction between a customer and service provider' [45] and 'a period of time during which a consumer directly interacts with the service' [46]. In this paper, encounter means the physical or virtual social interaction between people. The forms of encounter range from a home visit, a coffee break to an email or a call. Studies in service design have found encounter perceptions are critical to the perceived level of service satisfaction [47, 48]. It seems apparent that the experience of a specific encounter will affect the quality of social connection. Much contextual information, such as location and timing can affect the quality of social encounter. Interview on older people shows they don't want to make friends intentionally since it tells that 'you are lonely'. They think 'feeling lonely is a shame'. Therefore, how to create a natural experience, for example, embedding social encounter in people's daily routine, is significant for creating an expected experience.

Chatty bus is the service in the UK, that creates a social space and a community hub in elderly daily transportation [49]. Volunteers could initiate talks with the older people in the bus in a natural way. Without extra effort, older people can have a conversation in their daily transportation. This service also helps the government to approach the lonely older people who are difficult to identify. This case presents a good timing and location which help create a special encounter for social connection.

Trigger - from Compulsory to Spontaneous. User research in this project shows many older people are eager to make friends with other people. However, it is very difficult to start a conversation. Therefore, in many neighbourhood centres, there are facilitators to organize activities and guide conversations. To make sure everyone can participate in a conversation, a roll-call strategy was usually employed but not welcomed, because people do not like the compulsory way. Therefore, a trigger is required to spark conversation spontaneously. Fogg's behaviour model conclude 3 elements of behaviour change, namely motivation, ability and trigger. Without an appropriate trigger, the behaviour will not occur even if both motivation and ability are as high as required [50]. Fogg states timing is a crucial factor for triggering a behaviour. The low motivation makes a trigger distracting, while a lack of ability makes a trigger frustrated. A well-timed trigger can stimulate a vivid conversation and social connection.

In the early phase of field research, students find older people like having breakfast at IKEA restaurant for meeting people. However, how to find a proper topic with strangers is not easy. To tackle this problem, the idea, a placard with interesting topics was proposed. Another idea is a distinguished plate indicating different interests with different colours. People with similar interests can chat with each other starting from the shared interest by selecting a plate that shows the interest. The conversation is not compulsory. When people do not want to chat with others, he or she can use a white plate which indicates no willingness for chatting.

3.2 Framing the Ideation Process

These five elements integrate to achieve social connection in the following ideation process (see Fig. 1). The first stage is the **envision**. As a start, designers change the mindset of regarding older people as passive social welfare consumers and endow them with a positive role based on their resources, such as life experience, professional knowledge and daily life skill. After that, a partnership can be ideated to bridge the resource and social need. For example, older people know the history of the city and are full of life stories related to the city, while visitors want to know about the historical memory of the city. Thus, a partnership can be built by matching the resource of stories and need to know the stories together. This stage is the **bridge**. To make the partnership built, it is crucial to create opportunities for an encounter. What to do, how and where to meet have to be considered. Once the activities are determined, the facilities are needed to **support** to achieve the goal. After that, designers should think about how to **stimulate** contact by triggers. This ideation process makes sure design can ground from planning at a strategic level to design details.

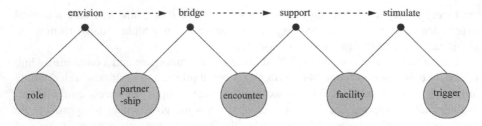

Fig. 1. An ideation process of design for social connection

3.3 A Design Proposal-Likebrary

Following the design strategies and process and combined with insights from user research, a design concept-Likebrary was proposed. This design proposal will be presented to demonstrate how to design for social connection.

User research shows older people who live alone tend to stay at home and read books by themselves. For this kind of person, they want to share their comments with people who have the same taste of reading. They do not want to make friends intentionally because they think feel loneliness is a shame. Therefore students found reading as a mediation activity can trigger social interaction. Likebrary is a decentralized book-circulating system. In this system, books are not stored at one certain place such as the traditional library. Instead, they are distributed and circulated among people. Users could borrow a book from the last person who is keeping it. It makes a connection between people who are willing to know people with similar reading taste. The book could be the filter to find those who share the same interest. In this proposal, People borrow books not only for reading but also meet friends. However, the social intention is behind the stage, so that people will not feel 'a shame' of loneliness. Books and reading purpose mediate social contact with people. Once the connection is bridged, they are free to talk about any other topics related or not related to reading. Likebrary encourages older people with shared reading interests and in a close distance but a different background to meet with each other. Thus, the system will match partners following this principle with a specific recommendation algorithm. To remove the barrier of technology use of older people, the website was designed with simple logic and characters in big-size.

Designers ideate different encounters. 'Likebrary Coffee' is one of the physical encounters of them. A website and App were designed as facilities to find expected books, make an appointment and so on. This service collaborates with café offline. Once readers choose to meet at a recommended cafe, they could get a special coupon for this appointment from the website. 'Likebrary Cup' is designed in this situation to trigger a conversation with a unique appearance that differs from the normal coffee cup. When users use the special coupon to buy a coffee, the cafe will serve them coffee with the 'Likebrary Cup'. Then the two users could identify each other by looking for who in the cafe also has the unique 'Likebrary Cup'. After they find each other, the unique appearance of the cup could trigger a conversation.

In comparison to the traditional library, this service is less efficient for reading purpose. However, in mediating a connection, efficiency is not the core criterion. The following activities mediated by reading determined the quality of design. What is more, this service also has the potential to improve physical activities to improve health condition of older people.

4 Discussion and Conclusion

With the process of population ageing, loneliness and social isolation have become a serious social problem. This research tries to address the problem from a design perspective. Following a Research through Design approach, this paper concludes five categories of design elements which can connect isolated older people with others, namely generative role, reciprocal partnership based on both homogeneity and heterogeneity, encounter embedded naturally in older people's daily routine, supportive and inviting facilities, and triggers that stimulates spontaneous action for connection.

The five elements provides not only the forms of design as a results, but also broadens the roles that design play for social connectedness. We tend to differentiate design by their disciplinary attributes. Normally, there are product design, interaction design, service design from a disciplinary attributes. This paper gets rid of this consideration and pay attention to their functionality. It provides designer new perspective for design especially design for social connection. Those five elements are integrated into a coherent ideation process, from envision to bridge to support to stimulate. This ideation process starts from a strategic level and ground on design details. It can be used to guide design ideation. Following this process, a design proposal can be innovative in both vision and practical details. A service design proposal was given as a case. Even though the social aim hides behind the reading purpose in this service, older people could develop new linkages and receive social support from it through this service. The reading service plays a role as mediation for social connection. The results of this research provided a new perspective of design for ageing as well as practice guidance and reference for designers in designing intervention for social connection.

From a theoretical perspective, as the third function of design, mediation is abstract for designers. This research makes it more concrete from both the design results aspect and the ideation process aspects. However, there are a couple of limitations of this research. Firstly, the framework generated only from a limited cases and design practice. Secondly, the proposed framework was not validated in the field. Future work should be done to implement the framework in design projects and evaluate the design proposals in the field.

References

1. Beard, J.R., Officer, A.M., Cassels, A.K.: The world report on ageing and health. The Gerontologist 56(2), S163–S166 (2016). https://doi.org/10.1093/geront/gnw002

2. UNDESA: World economic and social survey 2007: development in an ageing world, United Nations Department of Economic and Social Affairs, New York, (2007). https://doi.org/10.18356/5e23a8b3-en
3. Bloom, D.E., Chatterji, S., Kowal, P., Lloyd-Sherlock, P., McKee, M., Rechel, B., Smith, J. P.: Macroeconomic implications of population ageing and selected policy responses. The Lancet 385(9968), 649–657 (2015). https://doi.org/10.1016/s0140-6736(14)61464-1
4. Ageuk.org.uk, Combating loneliness. https://www.ageuk.org.uk/information-advice/health-wellbeing/loneliness
5. Tomaka, J., Thompson, S., Palacios, R.: The relation of social isolation, loneliness, and social support to disease outcomes among the elderly. J. Aging Health 18(3), 359–384 (2006). https://doi.org/10.1177/0898264305280993
6. Cacioppo, J.T., Hawkley, L.C.: Perceived social isolation and cognition. Trends Cognitive Sci. 13(10), 447–454 (2009). https://doi.org/10.1016/j.tics.2009.06.005
7. Litwin, H., Börsch-Supan, A., Brandt, M., Weber, G.: Active Ageing and Solidarity between Generations in Europe. De Gruyter, Berlin (2013). https://doi.org/10.1515/9783110295467.fm
8. Valtorta, N.K., Kanaan, M., Gilbody, S., Ronzi, S., Hanratty, B.: Loneliness and social isolation as risk factors for coronary heart disease and stroke: systematic review and meta-analysis of longitudinal observational studies. Heart 102(13), 1009–1016 (2016). https://doi.org/10.1136/heartjnl-2015-308790
9. Singh, A., Misra, N.: Loneliness, depression and sociability in old age. Ind. Psychiatry J. 18 (1), 51 (2009). https://doi.org/10.4103/0972-6748.57861
10. Alaviani, M., Khosravan, S., Alami, A., Moshki, M.: The effect of a multi-strategy program on developing social behaviors based on Pender's health promotion model to prevent loneliness of old women referred to Gonabad urban health centers. Int. J. Commun. Based Nurs. Midwifery 3(2), 132–140 (2015). https://doi.org/10.29252/hehp.6.4.129
11. Creswell, J.D., Irwin, M.R., Burklund, L.J., et al.: Mindfulness-Based Stress Reduction training reduces loneliness and proinflammatory gene expression in older adults: a small randomized controlled trial. Brain Behav. Immun. 26(7), 1095–1101 (2012). https://doi.org/10.1016/j.bbi.2012.07.006
12. Krause-Parello, C.A.: Pet ownership and older women: the relationships among loneliness, pet attachment support, human social support, and depressed mood. Geriatric Nurs. 33(3), 194–203 (2012). https://doi.org/10.1016/j.gerinurse.2011.12.005
13. Heo, J., Chun, S., Lee, S., Lee, K.H., Kim, J.: Internet use and well-being in older adults. Cyberpsychol. Behav. Soc. Network. 18(5), 268–272 (2015). https://doi.org/10.1089/cyber.2014.0549
14. Gardiner, C., Geldenhuys, G., Gott, M.: Interventions to reduce social isolation and loneliness among older people: an integrative review. Health Soc. Care Commun. 26(2), 147–157 (2018). https://doi.org/10.1111/hsc.12367
15. Li, Y.-J., Ren, W.-Q.: A study of game design based on sense of loneliness of the elderly. In: Stephanidis, C. (ed.) HCI 2018. CCIS, vol. 851, pp. 175–182. Springer, Cham (2018). https://doi.org/10.1007/978-3-319-92279-9_24
16. Deloitte, Hello my name is Alice. https://www2.deloitte.com/nl/nl/pages/over-deloitte/articles/zorgrobot-alice-zorgen-voor-morgen.html
17. Castellacci, F., Tveito, V.: Internet use and well-being: a survey and a theoretical framework. Res. Policy 47(1), 308–325 (2018). https://doi.org/10.1016/j.respol.2017.11.007
18. Shen, S.: Hospital to home: Design to prevent social loneliness among people with chronic heart failure. Delft University of technology (2015)

19. Howdon, D., Rice, N.: Health care expenditures, age, proximity to death and morbidity: implications for an ageing population. J. Health Econ. **57**, 60–74 (2018). https://doi.org/10.1016/j.jhealeco.2017.11.001
20. Toepoel, V.: Ageing, leisure, and social connectedness: how could leisure help reduce social isolation of older people? Soc. Indic. Res. **113**(1), 355–372 (2013). https://doi.org/10.1007/s11205-012-0097-6
21. Borgmann, A.: Technology and the character of contemporary life: A philosophical inquiry. University of Chicago Press, Chicago (1987). https://doi.org/10.7208/chicago/9780226163581.001.0001
22. Borgmann, A.: Crossing the Postmodern Divide. University of Chicago Press, Chicago (1993). https://doi.org/10.7208/chicago/9780226161488.001.0001
23. Verbeek, P.P.: What Things do: Philosophical Reflections on Technology, Agency, and Design. The Pennsylvania State University Press, Pennsylvania (2005)
24. Rocha, E.: A ladder of empowerment. J. Plann. Educ. Res. **17**(1), 31–44 (1997). https://doi.org/10.1177/0739456x9701700104
25. Bush, R.A., Folger, J.P.: The Promise of Mediation: Responding to Conflict through Empowerment and Recognition. Jossey-Bass, San Francisco (1994)
26. Senbel, M., Church, S.P.: Design Empowerment. J. Plann. Educ. Res. **31**(4), 423–437 (2011). https://doi.org/10.1177/0739456x11417830
27. Buchanan, R.: Design research and the new learning. Des. Issues **17**(4), 3–23 (2001). https://doi.org/10.1162/07479360152681056
28. Wiese, L., Pohlmeyer, A., Hekkert, P.: Activities as a gateway to sustained subjective well-being mediated by products. In: Proceedings of the 2019 on Designing Interactive Systems Conference, pp. 85–97. ACM (2019). https://doi.org/10.1145/3322276.3322297
29. Lin, X., Kang, K., Li, C., Hengeveld, B., Hummels, C., Raterberg, M.: Design for Connectedness: interaction design explorations for elderly people in care home context. Creation and Des. **3**, 5–18 (2019). https://doi.org/10.3969/J.ISSN.1674-4187.2019.03.001
30. Nevay, S., Lim, C.S., Gowans, G.: The Soft Touch: Design vs Disruption. Des. J. **22**(sup1), 601–613 (2019). https://doi.org/10.1080/14606925.2019.1595441
31. Zimmerman, J., Stolterman, E., Forlizzi, J.: An analysis and critique of Research through Design: towards a formalization of a research approach. In: Proceedings of the 8th ACM Conference on Designing Interactive Systems, pp 310–319. ACM (2010). https://doi.org/10.1145/1858171.1858228
32. Koskinen, I., Binder, T., Redström, J.: Lab, field, gallery, and beyond. Artifact **2**(1), 46–57 (2009). https://doi.org/10.1080/17493460802303333
33. Zimmerman, J., Forlizzi, J., Evenson, S.: Research through design as a method for interaction design research in HCI. In: Proceedings of the SIGCHI Conference on Human Factors in Computing Systems, pp 493–502. ACM (2007). https://doi.org/10.1145/1240624.1240704
34. Agewell Globle Homepage. https://www.agewellglobal.com/sa-pilot/
35. Abtswoude Bloeit Homepage. https://abtswoudebloeit.nl/
36. Mor-Barak, M.E.: The meaning of work for older adults seeking employment: the generativity factor. Int. J. Aging Hum. Dev. **41**(4), 325–344 (1995). https://doi.org/10.2190/vgtg-epk6-q4bh-q67q
37. Erikson, E.H., Erikson, J.M.: The Life Cycle Completed (Extended Version). W.W Norton, New York (1998)
38. Erikson, E.H.: Adulthood. W.W Norton, New York (1978)
39. McAdams, D.P., St Aubin, E.D., Logan, R.L.: Generativity among young, midlife, and older adults. Psychol. Aging **8**, 221–230 (1993). https://doi.org/10.1037/0882-7974.8.2.221

40. Yang, S.H., Long, B., Smola, A., Sadagopan, N., Zheng, Z., Zha, H.: Like like alike: joint friendship and interest propagation in social networks. In: Proceedings of the 20th International Conference on World Wide Web, pp 537–546. ACM (2011). https://doi.org/10.1145/1963405.1963481
41. Granovetter, M.S.: The strength of weak ties. In: Social networks. Academic Press, pp 347–367 (1977). https://doi.org/10.1016/b978-0-12-442450-0.50025-0
42. Sheldon, K.M., Kasser, T.: Getting older, getting better? personal strivings and psychological maturity across the life span. Dev. Psychol. **37**(4), 491–501 (2001). https://doi.org/10.1037/0012-1649.37.4.491
43. Glass, T.A., et al.: Experience Corps: design of an intergenerational program to boost social capital and promote the health of an aging society. J. Urban Health **81**(1), 94–105 (2004). https://doi.org/10.1093/jurban/jth096
44. Bitner, M.J., Wang, H.S.: Service encounters in service marketing research. In: Handbook of Service Marketing Research. Edward Elgar Publishing (2014). https://doi.org/10.4337/9780857938855.00019
45. Surprenant, C.F., Solomon, M.R.: Predictability and personalization in the service encounter. J. Market. **51**(2), 86–96 (1987). https://doi.org/10.2307/1251131
46. Wong, A.: The role of emotional satisfaction in service encounters. Manag. Serv. Qual. Int. J. **14**(5), 365–376 (2004). https://doi.org/10.1108/09604520410557976
47. Crosby, L.A., Stephens, N.: Effects of relationship marketing on satisfaction, retention, and prices in the life insurance industry. J. Mark. Res. **24**(4), 404–411 (1987). https://doi.org/10.2307/3151388
48. Brown, S.W., Swartz, T.A.: A gap analysis of professional service quality. J. Market. **53**(2), 92–98 (1989). https://doi.org/10.2307/1251416
49. Go-Ahead. https://www.go-ahead.com/sustainability/case-studies/chatty-bus-initiative
50. Fogg, B.J.: A behavior model for persuasive design. In: Proceedings of the 4th International Conference on Persuasive Technology, p. 40. ACM (2009). https://doi.org/10.1145/1541948.1541999

A Hybrid Conversational Agent with Semantic Association of Autobiographic Memories for the Elderly

Yu-Ting Hsiao[1] , Edwinn Gamborino[2]([⊠]) , and Li-Chen Fu[1,2]

[1] Department of Electrical Engineering, National Taiwan University,
Taipei, Taiwan
{r06921010, lichen}@ntu.edu.tw
[2] Center for Artificial Intelligence and Advanced Robotics,
National Taiwan University, Taipei, Taiwan
gamborino@ntu.edu.tw

Abstract. Socially Assistive Robots are becoming essential in the field of elderly care, as they can support caregivers in their tasks, for instance, by providing senior users with emotional and psychological support through verbal communication. In this paper, we present the results of a project where we developed an interactive dialogue system so that a robot could engage elderly users in conversations about their personal life stories. A task that seems almost mundane for the average person, is in fact extremely challenging for a machine to achieve. Through the development of a comprehensive platform with a variety of modules, the system is able to extract essential keywords from a user utterance and classify them according to sentence context and word meaning. These keywords are then indexed in a user-specific knowledge base, where semantic associations between items are made, relating them, for instance, by time or place. These items are used by the robot to generate responses to the user's speech by leveraging a hybrid template/data-driven mechanism. As the user interacts with the system, it learns more details which further enrich the generated sentences. The system was evaluated on a human-in-loop experiment, where the results showed the ability of the system to understand human speech, memorize personal information of each user and generate coherent responses in dialogic interactions. These results highlight the potential of a robot not only to provide companionship, but also to build a social relationship with its user.

Keywords: Dialogue system · Autobiographic memory · Natural Language Understanding

1 Introduction

Worldwide, with the improvement of general healthcare and living standards, the number of elderly people relative to the rest of the population is rising at an accelerating pace, more so in developed nations. This leads to a number of problems in the seniors' livelihood, including an increased demand for related care facilities, and a deterioration in the Quality-of-Life due to social isolation. To address these issues,

P.-L. P. Rau (Ed.): HCII 2020, LNCS 12193, pp. 53–66, 2020.
https://doi.org/10.1007/978-3-030-49913-6_5

experts from different areas have focused their efforts to fill the gap in the needs and requirements of senior citizens. Aside from solutions such as the establishment of nursing homes, long-term care policies and provision of daily care from social workers, which already have been implemented to some success, solutions that leverage AI are becoming popular in the research communities, where we have observed progress in technological propositions that are able to provide both physical and psychological assistance to their users [1].

One such example can be found in the field of social robotics. These robots are able to assist humans in several different situations. For instance, *Pepper* [2] is one of the most famous android robots, which can be found in banks, stores and hotels, standing at the front door or in behind the information desk, providing guidance for customers, guests and visitors. Another example is *Jibo* [3], a robot designed for the home environment, which can deliver a variety of information to its users such as the daily news and weather forecast, among other useful functions. Social robots have also been introduced to healthcare institutions to take care of senior citizens; for instance, *Miro* [4] not only keeps elders company but also watches over their health status.

One of the most essential capabilities for a social robot is to be able to communicate with humans. Furthermore, verbal communication is the most intuitive and natural way for people to communicate with others. Even though several powerful conversational agents have been made available to the public in the form of artificial personal assistants such as *Siri* [5], *Alexa* [6], or *Google Assistant* [7], a large gap still exists between human-human conversation and human-robot conversation. One of the main differences being that artificial agents lack the ability to remember previous conversations. On top of that, elderly users often have trouble interacting with electronic devices; for them, being able to interface with robots through speech is a highly desirable feature.

We connect with each other through communication. As we are able to remember mutual interests, passions, and past experiences, we can establish long-term relationships with each other. For artificial agents, with the currently available technology being limited to a command-response based paradigm, it is not possible to build such relationships. If robots cannot remember details about their conversational partner's shared experiences, it is unlikely that people will ever see robots as companions instead than merely as tools, which in turn limits the effectiveness of the social support that robots could provide to their users.

Therefore, enabling a conversational agent to understand, recall and smartly use facts previously mentioned by their users is paramount if we are to push the boundary of human-computer interaction. To this purpose, in this paper we propose a conversational agent embedded with a computational autobiographical memory model. The system leverages a Natural Language Understanding (NLU) module, which was designed in order to extract essential information from human utterances in Mandarin Chinese. These data are stored in a computational autobiographical memory model, which has the ability to maintain human information and do probabilistic inferences to make semantic relations between items. Finally, in order to utilize the parsed data in conversation, we implemented a hybrid sentence generation method, which combines template-based and machine-learning based methods, making conversations at the same time more robust and diverse.

The rest of this paper is organized as follows: In Sect. 2 we discuss related works and the State-of-the-Art in conversational agents and memory management systems. Section 3 describes in detail the software architecture and the technical details of how the conversational agent is able to extract and remember facts from the user's speech, make semantic inferences and use them later in speech. In Sect. 4 we go over the experiments designed to validate the proposed system and the results obtained from them. We close the paper in Sect. 5 with discussion on the limitation of the system and future works.

2 Background and Related Works

Our conversational agent consists of two main parts: the autobiographical memory model and the hybrid dialogue system. As there are few examples of previous attempts to combine these two into a single platform, we conducted a literature review to highlight the most relevant works in each field independently.

2.1 Autobiographical Memory Model

The concept of autobiographical memory was first formulated by Tulving. In [8], he describes the two main cognitive components of it being semantic knowledge and episodic knowledge. The autobiographical memory is fundamentally significant to human beings; given that it can be understood as a recollection of episodes from one's life experiences. Research on autobiographical memory has lasted over 40 years in various subareas of psychology, yet it had not been organized into a framework until Conway et al. [9] proposed the self-memory system in the year 2000.

A more comprehensive systematic review of the self-memory system can be found in [10]. In the context of autobiographical memory knowledge bases, memories are stored hierarchically and can be roughly divided into two layers: the conceptual self and episodic memories. The top layer, which is the conceptual self, aims to store semantic knowledge whereas the lower layer, which is the episodic memories, aims to store episodic knowledge. In this work, we realized an implementation of this theory into a system that is able to store and retrieve memories simulating this structure.

There have been a few other attempts in the literature to introduce autobiographical memory into artificial conversational agents. Pointeau et al. [11] proposed an autobiographical memory system implemented on the humanoid robot iCub [12], so that it could accumulate its experiences while interacting with humans and form composite knowledge in its memory. Elsewhere, Evans et al. [13] used deep learning methods to mimic the hippocampus architecture, which fulfilled the functional requirements of autobiographical memory, enabling robots to imitate the physiology of the human brain. In addition of improving the artificial agent's interaction ability, the integration of memory models has also been used for the consolidation of human-robot interactions. In [14] Ho et al. tried to integrate a computational autobiographical memory model with an intelligent virtual agent so as to create coherent life stories for them, with the goal of achieving long-term believability. In a follow-up paper [15], Ho et al.

proposed a memory model to enable robots to remember events which are significant or relevant to themselves or users, so as to make long-term companion achievable.

There are relatively few works that have attempted to integrate a dialogue system and a memory models under one platform. Campos *et al.* [16] developed a memory-gathering conversational virtual companion, MAY, to interact with users. Their experiment showed that even providing the smallest perception of understanding of the user's personal life resulted in a more positive attitude towards human-robot relationships. However, MAY's dialogue system was based on A.L.I.C.E. [17], which is a script-based *chatbot*, which depends on pre-scripted templates in a knowledge base to interact with its users. Therefore, its structure is rigid and it is unable to extend its own speech abilities through interaction.

2.2   Dialogue System

Researchers have worked on artificial dialogue systems for several decades, with the ultimate goal of endowing machines with the ability to talk with humans in a naturalistic fashion, as similar as possible to human-human conversation.

Several outstanding works are worth mentioning. Eliza [18] is known as the first *chatbot*. A simulation of a Rogerian psychotherapist, through hand-crafted scripts and methods of pattern matching, Eliza can accept textual inputs and then generate appropriate responses. Even though the conversation between users and Eliza can be quite successful, due to the limitation of its knowledge base, Eliza can only talk about a constrained domain. A.L.I.C.E. [17] is another world-famous script-based *chatbot*. It was one of the first agents to use the Artificial Intelligence Markup Language (AIML) to enable developers or even the end user to customize its knowledge base, potentially expanding the domain of the conversation to any topic, as long as someone would create the semantic rules to follow a conversation. The main advantage of AIML over previous attempts at rule-based conversational agents was that, being a type of markup language, it had a robust and well defined syntax and rules, which allowed other people to easily learn how to add new contents to the agent's knowledge base. An example of an A.L.I.C.E. based agent with an extensive knowledge base is Mitsuku [19], which has won the Loebner Prize [20] for four times. Given that the responses of the agent are hard-coded to match a template, as long as the user's query can be found in the knowledge base, the robot will be able to issue a coherent response, often giving its users the sensation of being smarter than it actually is.

All the previous references are instances of rule-based dialogue systems. While relatively robust, one of their main weaknesses is the limitation on the handcrafted knowledge base. On the other hand, data-driven dialogue systems learn to respond to humans by training with data from human-human conversations, human-machine conversations and even non-dialogic texts. Using machine learning algorithms to learn from massive datasets, data driven agents have the ability to learn the relationships between words and phrases. Therefore, due to their adaptability, they can generate naturalistic sentences without the need of pre-scripted templates. Data-driven agents [21, 22, 23] are typically constructed in an encoder-decoder framework, which is also known as Sequence-to-Sequence (Seq2Seq). Several modified versions of Seq2Seq have been proposed in order to achieve higher quality sentence generation. For example,

Li *et al.* [24] proposed using Maximum Mutual Information (MMI) instead of maximum log-likelihood as the objective function so that the agent could generate more diverse and interesting responses. Gu *et al.* [25] incorporated a copying mechanism into Seq2Seq so as to replicate certain segments of the input queries into the output responses. Xing *et al.* [26] tried to bring external knowledge into the generated sentences. They obtained topic words using a Latent Dirichlet Allocation (LDA) model; then, a joint attention mechanism is used to affect the decoding process. Extra probability was added to topic words in order to let bias the generator towards certain words.

In this paper, we adopt a hybrid method to generate robot utterances. We leverage a script-based method utilizing AIML in order to maintain the robustness of conversations whereas a data-driven method modified from the model framework proposed by Xing *et al.* [26] plays the role of generating robot's utterances based on the memory items in the user database.

3 System Design

The proposed dialogue system can be divided into five major parts, as shown in Fig. 1. In this chapter, each component of the system is described in detail.

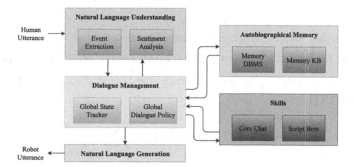

Fig. 1. The architecture of the proposed dialogue system. The NLU module extracts informative memory items and sentiment analysis from the users' utterances. This information is passed to the Dialogue Management (DM) module, which maintains data and commands other modules to start. New data items are stored and related concepts are retrieved from the memory knowledge base. The skills module contains data-driven and script-based methods for sentence generation. DM will decide which sentence to use depending on context. Finally, the Natural Language Generation (NLG) module helps output robot's responses.

3.1 Natural Language Understanding

The NLU module is one of the most essential components of a conversational agent. It provides the ability to parse the users' utterances, where the results may have a large influence on the performance of the overall dialogue system. In this paper, the main task of the NLU module is to extract memory events the user's utterances in order to fill the memory knowledge base. Furthermore, sentiment analysis is also performed to classify the emotion associated with each retrieved item. This is achieved in a process called event extraction.

Briefly, user utterances are first segmented into words. Words of interest include theme, people, locations, activities, objects, facts, thoughts and user age, which are required attributes for the memory knowledge base. In order to classify each word in a sentence into these categories, we propose the use of pattern-matching, which has been successfully applied previously in instances of Mandarin NLP systems [27, 28]. Instead of developing new tools for parsing, we leverage LTP [29] a well-known Chinese language analysis platform. Using the POS tagging tool from LTP, each word in a sentence is assigned a grammatical tag (e.g. noun, verb, pronoun, etc.).

We designed over 20 different patterns to identify word categories based on these tags. Each type of item is classified using uni-gram patterns, bi-gram patterns, tri-gram patterns and other special patterns if needed. A few instances are shown in Table 1.

Table 1. Pattern matching examples.

Category	Pattern	Example
Human	$w_1 \rightarrow nickname$, if $w_1 \in List$	"Classmate"
Location	$w_1 \rightarrow gen$, if "at" $+ w_1$ and w_1 is n	"Classmate"
Fact	$w_1 + w_2 \rightarrow fact$ if w_1 is a and w_2 is n	"Good people"
Time	$w_1 \rightarrow age$ if w_1 is nt	"1995"

After extracting various items, biased term frequency-inverse document frequency is used to rank the extracted items. Formally, given a set of sentences $S = \{s_j\}_{j=1}^{M}$ and sets of words $W_j = \{w_{ij}\}_{i=1}^{N_j}$ for each sentence, the biased tf-idf score of w_{ij} is computed using Eq. (1):

$$tfidf_{bias}(w_{ij}) = \beta_{ij} * tfidf(w_{ij}), \beta_{ij} = \sum_{\{j:w_{ij} \in s_j\}} \frac{N_j}{\sum_{k=1}^{M} N_k} \quad (1)$$

In a nutshell, this algorithm will rank the parsed items by the length of the sentence that contained them, words which belong to longer utterances should gain higher scores than words which belong to shorter utterances.

3.2 Autobiographical Memory Module

The autobiographical memory can be thought of as a representation of oneself. In this paper, the conceptual model of the autobiographical memory knowledge base was developed utilizing a SQL database. With this memory model, the proposed system was able to collect items from the user's speech as well as retrieve them later to generate sentences. An instance of a partially filled knowledge base is shown in Fig. 2. The knowledge base is composed of four layers, namely:

- Theme layer: It separates the users' life into several meaningful themes commonly present in peoples' lives. In this work, this layer contains nine predefined themes:

living, travel, family, friends, partner, study, work, hobby and others. In this layer, one node cannot be connected to other theme nodes, but only to nodes in the lifetime period layer.

- Lifetime period layer: Specifies the age of the user when a memory occurred, either as a specific age, or a period (e.g. my twenties). A node in this layer can have connection to only one theme node, but multiple connections to the general event layer.
- General event layer: Nodes in this layer are represented by three attributes:
  - Person: Contains name and, optionally, nickname.
  - Location: Contains general (e.g. park, zoo) or specific locations (e.g. Taiwan).
  - Verb-noun: Contains either verbs (e.g. eat), nouns (e.g. noodles) or both.
- Episodic memory layer: According to [8], an instance of episodic memory usually includes details such as actions, thoughts, feelings, locations and facts. To model this structure in our database, episodic memory nodes can be connected to one or more items in both the lifetime period layer and the general event layer. Furthermore, they can contain two additional parameters:
  - Thoughts: Subjective sentiments and emotions (e.g. like this place)
  - Facts: Objective and descriptive phrases (e.g. hot noodles)

It is worth noting that the nodes in the episodic memory layer (thoughts and facts) are unique to an event, whereas the nodes in the general event (person, location and verb-noun) and lifetime period layers can be shared by several events. Nodes in the lifetime period, general event and episodic memory layers have three more attributes:

- Sentiment polarity: Represents qualitatively the general feeling associated with a given item. In numerical terms, it is represented by −1 (negative) or 1 (positive).
- Count: Represent the number of times that a specific node has been mentioned by the user. It is used to calculate the edge weight between items and in the Bayesian retrieval model.
- Edge weight: It represents the strength of the relation between two nodes. It is calculated by the number of times that the tags of both nodes are mentioned together.

Instead of equally retrieving all items, Bayes' theorem is adopted here to compute the probability of each item being retrieved, so as to increase the accuracy of retrieval of Memory knowledge base. For instance, given a set of episodic memories, $EP = \{ep_j\}_{j=1}^{M}$ and a set of items of EP, $ITEM = \{item_i\}_{i=1}^{N}$, then the probability of observing a specific item $item_i$ is described by Eq. (2):

$$p(item_i) = \alpha_i \sum_{j=1}^{M} p(item_i|ep_j)p(ep_j) \tag{2}$$

$$p(ep_j) = \frac{n_j}{\sum_{k=1}^{M} n_k}, \quad p(item_i|ep_j) = \frac{n_{ij}}{n_j}$$

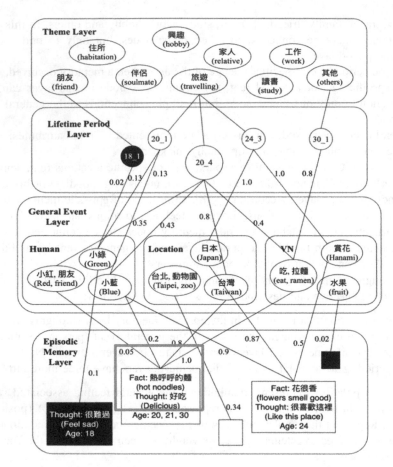

Fig. 2. An instance of a partially filled knowledge base. The nodes in the lifetime period layer are named with age and instance. For example, the node "20_4" denotes that there are four items in the general event layer connected to it. The episodic memory node highlighted in red memory stores "hot noodles" into fact and "Delicious" into thought. It links to "Red, friend" and "Blue" in human table, "Taiwan" in location table, and "eat, ramen" in the verb/noun table and to ages 20, 21 and 30 in the lifetime period layer. Each edge has a weight which indicates the importance of the linked items to an episodic memory node. Sentiment polarity is represented as white or black for positive and negative instances, respectively. (Color figure online)

where $p(ep_j)$ is the probability of observing ep_j from *EP*, computed using n_j, which is the count of ep_j. And p $(item_i|ep_j)$ is the probability of observing $item_i$ conditioned ep_j, computed through n_{ij} and n_j. n_{ij} indicates the count of $item_i$ of ep_j. α_i is a bias computed using scores of episodic memories in order to inherit scores of episodic memories into the probability of each node, which is given by Eq. (3):

$$\alpha_i = \frac{s(item_i)}{\sum_{l=1}^{N} s(item_l)}, \quad s(item_i) = \sum_{\{j:item_i \in ep_j\}} s(ep_j) \quad (3)$$

3.3   Skills Module

The skills module generates responses based on the information obtained from the current user utterance and the data extracted from the knowledge base. There are two sentence generators based on these data: a data-driven model and a script-based model.

The data-driven model was designed to generate both general responses as well as responses embedded with items retrieved from the memory knowledge base. In order to embed items from the memory knowledge base into these responses, the architecture of TA-Seq2Seq model [26] is adapted, as shown in Fig. 4. Formally, given an input sequence $X = \{x_i\}_{i=1}^{N}$, a series of hidden vectors $\{h_i\}_{i=1}^{N}$ are generated through a bidirectional GRU. At the same time, several memory words $M = \{m_j\}_{j=1}^{M}$ are transformed into hidden vectors $\{k_j\}_{j=1}^{M}$ through an embedding look-up table. At time step t, message attention generates a context vector c_t and a memory vector o_t is generated by memory attention (Fig. 3).

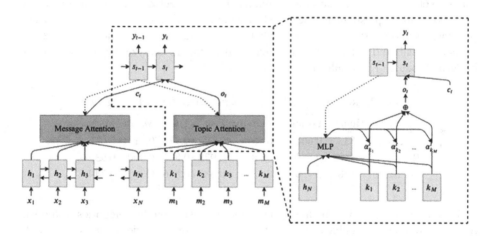

Fig. 3. The architecture of core chat module (adapted from [26])

The script-based model generates responses through rule-based methods written in AIML. This module is mostly used for pre-determined interactions, such as greetings and to say goodbye. It also contains a few patterns that can be applied to thought and fact nodes from the episodic memory layer, which did not show a good performance with the data-driven model.

3.4   Dialog Management and Language Generation

The dialog management module coordinates all the other modules. It controls the general behavior of the conversational agent, activating different modules depending on the system state. Furthermore, it controls the information flow between modules.

On the other hand, in the scenario where the skills module generated more than one response from either of its models, the purpose of the language generation module is to select which of the sentences will be played out. This decision is hard-coded based on heuristic rules derived from observation.

4   Experimental Validation

In this section, we introduce the validation methodology, results and discussion for the three main modules.

4.1   NLU Module

The evaluation of NLU module demonstrates its ability to understand user utterances and extract essential memory information. 50 posts collected from *Dcard*, a Taiwanese social network, were used as the testing data. The length of the collected items ranges from 6 to 60 sentences. Humans raters annotated each collected item. For each item, the rater had to fill a questionnaire designed to obtain the same data as the NLU module (persons, location, time, etc.). These labels are considered as ground truth. We use precision, recall and F-1 Score (both macro and micro) to analyze the performance of the NLU module. The results are shown in Table 2.

Table 2. Results of NLU module performance for each category

Category	Human	Location	Activity	Fact	Time	Macro	Micro
Precision	0.833	0.667	0.587	0.525	0.972	0.717	0.612
Recall	0.843	0.884	0.981	0.978	0.814	0.900	0.935
F-1 Score	0.838	0.760	0.734	0.683	0.886	0.790	0.740

Results show that NLU module gains higher precision on the categories of human, location and time. A possible reason is that items in these categories are more similar to each other and more concrete compared to items in the categories of activity and fact.

The recall is relatively high across the board. Furthermore, it can be observed that there is not much difference between macro and micro precision, recall and F-1 Score, where micro scores are more suitable for the case when postings are not equally distributed in chosen categories. In general, the proposed NLU module is capable of extracting meaningful information from human speech.

4.2   Autobiographical Memory Module

To validate the Autobiographical Memory module, we wanted to measure its performance when retrieving relevant memory items from memory KB given a sentence.

20 posts collected from *Dcard* were used as human memories and stored into the memory KB. Hand-written summaries for each post are used to test the retrieval of relevant memory items.

We tested the performance of the system under the condition of high memory density. That is, for any given user utterance, all the nodes in the memory knowledge base will be queried. We use a recall matrix to show the result of high memory density experiment, as shown in Fig. 4. The darker the block is, the higher the recall is. Ideally, if only the specific post is retrieved given its summary, elements in the main diagonal should be dark. However, in the practical implementation this is not always the case. This is given that, if the density of memory stored in Memory KB increases, items from similar postings may be retrieved, resulting in the decrease of precision and recall. Furthermore, with an increase of memory density, it becomes likely for the memory DBMS to treat similar items as the same item, especially if the attributes of each item are similar. In the authors' opinion, this is not necessarily a negative outcome, as it demonstrates that the system can retrieve related items, even when they do not belong to exactly the same story.

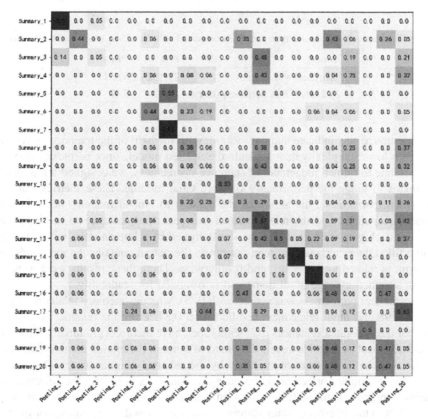

Fig. 4. Recall matrix under high memory density condition, threshold = 3.

4.3   Data-Driven Model for Sentence Generation

The performance of the data-driven model is validated and compared with a Seq2Seq with Attention model. Furthermore, human evaluations are also conducted.

To train and validate the model, we use *Douban Conversation Corpus* [30] which is a multi-turn conversation dataset collected for retrieval-based response generation, containing over 1 million training data points. A threshold of 30 words is set to build the both input and output sentences. The input memory words are extracted from both queries and responses through our proposed NLU module, belonging to the categories of people, location, activity and fact. The maximum number of input memory items is set to 10. The embedding dimension is set to 256, the encoder dimension and the decoder dimension are set to 512, and both attention dimensions are set to 128. The model is trained using the Adam optimizer [31].

Since most of the evaluation metrics are not able to represent human judgements on responses generated by a dialogue system [32], to prove that our model can learn better from the training data compared to Seq2Seq with Attention model, we compute the perplexity for validation and testing data, denoted as PPL_D and PPL_T respectively. The results are shown in Table 3.

Table 3. Perplexity of data driven module compared to a Seq2Seq model with attention.

Model	$PPPL_D$	$PPPL_T$
Seq2Seq with attention	27.132	26.851
Adapted T-A Seq2Seq (ours)	**5.82**	**5.47**

While this results indicate that our system, with the help of the memory knowledge base, has a lower perplexity than a standard Seq2Seq model, since perplexity does not fully correlate to human judgement of sentence correctness, we designed three metrics for humans to judge the performance of Core Chat module. These metrics stand for grammatical correctness, the ability of the system to embed memory items into the generated responses, and the relatedness of the generated sentence to the input sentence. For each generated item, a score was assigned by a human rater, with 1 being if the item filled the criteria (e.g. correct grammar, the output contains the memories, and the output is related to the input), and 0 otherwise. Then, these results were weighted with the summed average of all items and normalized for readability.

Grammatical correctness was scored with 0.70, whereas memory relatedness got a score of 0.98 and input relatedness resulted with 0.84. From the results, we can conclude that the generated sentences may sometimes have incorrect grammar which is not pleasant for most people. However, they tend to contain the related memory items and are related to the input sentence as shown by the relatively higher scores. One reasons for the low grammar correctness is because the dataset comes from the Internet, so it contains expressions not suitable to use in oral conversations. Moreover, utterances collected from the Internet contain various abbreviations and combinations of multiple sentences.

5 Discussion

A dialogue system integrated with a computational memory model was proposed. Its main purpose was to provide a conversational agent with the ability to store and retrieve memories while communicating with their users. Through the assistance offered by the computational memory model, results showed that the robot could extract meaningful information from the user's speech, perform some semantic inferences on the content and retrieve relevant content in subsequent utterances.

Although the responses generated by the system have shown to contain memory items relevant to the input sentence, the quality of the output is not always satisfactory, as it lacks coherency because of poor grammatical correctness. This is mainly caused by the dataset used to train the model. As larger and less "noisy" datasets are released in the future, a more accurate version of the sentence generation module may be devised.

References

1. Broekens, J., Heerink, M., Rosendal, H.: Assistive social robots in elderly care: a review. J. Gerontechnol. **8**(2), 94–103 (2009)
2. Pepper|Softbank Robotics. https://www.softbankrobotics.com/us/pepper. Accessed 17 Feb 2020
3. Robot, J.: He can't wait to meet you. https://www.jibo.com/. Accessed 17 Jan 2020
4. Consequential Robotics. http://consequentialrobotics.com/miro. Accessed 17 Jan 2020
5. Siri – Apple. https://www.apple.com/tw/siri/. Accessed 17 Jan 2020
6. Keyword Research, Competitive Analysis & Website Ranking|Alexa. https://www.alexa.com/. Accessed 17 Jan 2020
7. Google Assistant, your own personal Google. https://assistant.google.com/. Accessed 17 Jan 2020
8. Tulving, E.: Episodic and semantic memory. In: Tulving, E., Donaldson, W. (eds.) Organization of Memory. Academic Press, Oxford (1972)
9. Conway, M.A., Pleydell-Pearce, C.W.: The construction of autobiographical memories in the self-memory system. Psychol. Rev. **107**(2), 261–288 (2000)
10. Conway, M.A.: Memory and the self. J. Mem. Lang. **53**(4), 594–628 (2005)
11. Pointeau, G., Petit, M., Dominey, P.F.: Successive developmental levels of autobiographical memory for learning through social interaction. IEEE Trans. Auton. Ment. Dev. **6–3**, 200–212 (2014)
12. Metta, G., Sandini, G., Vernon, D., Natale, L., Nori, F.: The iCub humanoid robot: an open platform for research in embodied cognition. In: Proceedings of the 8th Workshop on Performance Metrics for Intelligent Systems, pp. 50–56 (2008)
13. Evans, M.H.W., Fox, C.W., Prescott, T.: Machines learning - towards a new synthetic autobiographical memory. In: Conference on Biomimetic and Biohybrid Systems, Living Machines, pp. 84–96 (2014)
14. Ho, W.C., Dautenhahn, K.: Towards a narrative mind: the creation of coherent life stories for believable virtual agents. In: Prendinger, H., Lester, J., Ishizuka, M. (eds.) IVA 2008. LNCS (LNAI), vol. 5208, pp. 59–72. Springer, Heidelberg (2008). https://doi.org/10.1007/978-3-540-85483-8_6

15. Ho, W.C., Dautenhahn, K., Lim, M.Y., Vargas, P.A., Aylett, R., Enz, S.: An initial memory model for virtual and robot companions supporting migration and long-term interaction, In: Proceedings of the 18th IEEE International Symposium on Robot and Human Interactive Communication, pp. 277–284 (2009)
16. Campos, J., Paiva, A.: MAY: my memories are yours. In: International Conference on Intelligent Virtual Agents (IVA), pp. 406–412 (2010)
17. Shawar, B.A., Atwell, E.S.: Using corpora in machine learning chatbot systems. Int. J. Corpus Linguist. **10–4**, 489–516 (2005)
18. Weizenbaum, J.: ELIZA - a computer program for the study of natural language communication between man and machine. Commun. ACM **9–1**, 36–45 (1966)
19. Mitsuku. https://www.pandorabots.com/mitsuku. Accessed 17 Jan 2020
20. Homepage - AISB - The Society for the Study of Artificial Intelligence and Simulation of Behaviour. http://www.aisb.org.uk. Accessed 17 Jan 2020
21. Shang, L., Lu, Z., Li, H.: Neural responding machine for short-text conversation. In: Proceedings of the ACL 2015 Annual Meeting of the Association for Computational Linguistics (2015)
22. Vinyals, O., Le, Q.: A neural conversational model. In: International Conference on Machine Learning (ICML), Deep Learning Workshop (2015)
23. Sordoni, A., et al.: A neural network approach to context-sensitive generation of conversational responses. In: Proceedings of the 2015 Conference of the North American Chapter of the Association for Computational Linguistics: Human Language Technologies, pp. 196–205 (2015)
24. Li, J., Galley, M., Brockett, C., Gao, J., Dolan, B.: A diversity-promoting objective function for neural conversation models. In: Proceedings of the 2016 Conference of the North American Chapter of the Association for Computational Linguistics: Human Language Technologies (2016)
25. Gu, J., Lu, Z., Li, H., Li, V.O.: Incorporating copying mechanism in sequence-to-sequence learning. In: Proceedings of the 54th Annual Meeting of the Association for Computational Linguistics, vol. 1 (2016)
26. Xing, C., et al.: Topic aware neural response generation. In: Proceedings of the Thirty-First AAAI Conference on Artificial Intelligence, pp. 3351–3357 (2017)
27. Xu, H., Huang, C.-R.: A rule system for chinese time entity recognition by comprehensive linguistic study. In: Proceedings of the Sixth International Joint Conference on Natural Language Processing. Asian Federation of Natural Language Processing, pp. 795–801 (2013)
28. Xia, J., Xie, F., Zhang, M., Su, Y., Luan, H.: CNME: a system for chinese news meta-data extraction. In: Proceedings of the 2015 Joint International Semantic Technology Conference (JIST), pp. 91–107 (2015)
29. LTP: Language Technology Platform. https://github.com/HIT-SCIR/ltp/. Accessed 17 Jan 2020
30. Wu, Y., Wu, W., Xing, C., Zhou, M., Li, Z.: Sequential matching network: a new architecture for multi-turn response selection in retrieval-based chatbots. In: Proceedings of the 55th Annual Meeting of the Association for Computational Linguistics, vol. 1, pp. 496–505 (2017)
31. Kingma, D., Ba, J.: Adam: a method for stochastic optimization. In: Proceedings of the 3rd International Conference on Learning Representations (2014)
32. Liu, C.-W., et al.: How NOT to evaluate your dialogue system: an empirical study of unsupervised evaluation metrics for dialogue response generation. In: Proceedings of the 2016 Conference on Empirical Methods in Natural Language Processing, pp. 2122–2132 (2016)

The Reliability and Validity of Multidimensional Scale Perceived Social Support of Chinese Version for MBI-PPD

Szu-Erh Hsu[1]([⊠]), Wen-Ko Chiou[1]([⊠]), Hao Chen[2], Tai-He Hong[3], Liang-Ming Lo[3], and Ding-Hau Huang[4]

[1] Department of Industrial Design, Chang Gung University,
Taoyuan City, Taiwan
h410@hotmail.com, wkchiu@mail.cgu.edu.tw
[2] Graduate Institute of Business and Management, Chang Gung University,
Taoyuan City, Taiwan
174673015@qq.com
[3] Department of Obstetrics and Gynecology, Chang Gung Memorial Hospital,
Taipei, College of Medicine, Chang Gung University, Taoyuan City, Taiwan
{thh20,lmlo}@cgmh.org.tw
[4] Institute of Creative Design and Management,
National Taipei University of Business, Taoyuan City, Taiwan
hau1012@gmail.com

Abstract. MBI - PPD refers to mindfulness-based intervention in postpartum depression. The research mainly used mindfulness-based intervention and integrated social support theory into an APP so that depression of maternal can be improved after using the APP. The research was conducted in Chang Gung Hospital, Taipei. Researchers translated and tested the reliability and validity of the MBI-PPD MSPSS Chinese version on 300 maternal. Questionnaire was translated back to English after translated from English to Chinese to confirm the consistency of the questionnaire in Chinese and the questionnaire in English. Subjects: We recruited 300 maternal to conduct the test. Moral consideration: The research was approved by the IRB review committee at Chang Gung Hospital to ensure the safety and confidentiality of each subject. To ensure the validity of questionnaire construction, confirmatory factor analysis (CFA) was used to evaluate MSPSS. Its index includes chi2 inspection results, root mean square error of approximation (RMSEA) and normed fit index (NFI) to compare fit index and non-normed fit index. To ensure its validity at the same time, MBI-PPD MSPSS in Chinese version was used to understand the social support level of maternal. Internal consistency and test-retest reliability were applied to confirm whether the questionnaire can have valid use in future experiment. Results: MBI-PPD MSPSS tool in Chinese version show good reliability and validity at relevant aspect. Conclusion: MBI-PPD MSPSS in Chinese version has good reliability and validity. It can provide a new research tool to the Chinese speaking countries for testing applications in the future.

Keywords: Mindfulness-based intervention in postpartum depression · Social support · MSPSS · Chinese version · Reliability and validity

© Springer Nature Switzerland AG 2020
P.-L. P. Rau (Ed.): HCII 2020, LNCS 12193, pp. 67–77, 2020.
https://doi.org/10.1007/978-3-030-49913-6_6

1 Introduction

1.1 MBI-PPD

MBI-PPD refers to mindfulness-based intervention in postpartum depression. PDD was one of the non-psychotic major depression with prevalence around 10%–15% (Cox et al. 1993; Darcy et al. 2011; Gavin et al. 2005; O'hara et al. 1991; Vesga-Lopez et al. 2008; Wisner et al. 2002) and had serious negative consequences on the puerpera (Da Costa et al. 2006), spouse (Goodman 2004), new-born baby and mother and baby interaction (Stanley et al. 2004). Most puerpera did not realize one has depression symptoms herself and seek for relevant assistance with PDD, causing delayed medical treatment. In the severe case, they can have suicidal intention and harm the newborn baby. There were around 20% pregnant women committed suicide.

Postpartum depression is one of the illnesses that could harm the physical and mental health of a perinatal woman. When postpartum depression occurs, it was often neglected if the symptom was mild. However, it could harm the safety of mothers and babies in severe cases. In the results of a retrospective study, Pearlstein et al. (2009) shows the probability of women having mild postpartum depression within 10 days after delivery is between 15–85%, with possible symptoms of crying easily, being tired and anxious. However, most of these symptoms were temporary and do not require medication. The probability of a more severe postpartum depression occurs at 2–6 months after delivery, which is in the range of 6.5–12.9%. A woman suffering depression could not only take actions harmful to herself, but also her babies. Hence, postpartum depression is a women health issue required to be valued.

Mindfulness is to maintain the current focus and awareness, as well as accept the current time without conducting any judgment and evaluation to obtain peace and happiness. Many research (Bodhi 2011; Kabat-Zinn 2003, 2006) stated that mindfulness can reduce anxiety and depression.

Research team in the past developed a set of postpartum emotion assistance system, We'll, through social support and self-efficacy theory. With the mindfulness practice by We'll, we hope to ease and prevent obstacles and depression problems in emotions postpartum.

1.2 Social Support

Social support was broadly defined as support and assistance given by members or specialists in the social network through materials, cognition and emotion (Gottlieb and Bergen 2010; Thoits 2011). It had been extensively discussed for over the past decades that social support provided multiple benefits to the physiological and mental health of puerpera and is one of the influencing factors helpful in prediction and reduction of PPD risks (Beck 2001; Robertson et al. 2004; WHO 2003b).

Specialists and members of the social network are included as subjects providing social support. Hogan et al. (2002) divided social supporter into two categories, formal support and informal support. Formal support comes from specialists, such as medical personnel and social groups, providing relevant professional information. General puerpera can learn the baby caring knowledge from nurses and midwifes, which is helpful for puerpera to accommodate themselves from being a woman to the role of "a mother" (Logsdon and Davis 2003; Wilkins 2006). Non-formal support comes from natural relationships, which are members of the social network and the major support source of puerpera (Leahy-Warren 2005), such as family members, close partner, friends and peers. The people whom puerpera contact most frequently are their spouses, mothers and sisters (Leahy-Warren et al. 2012). The actual assistance obtained from their partners and mothers of the puerpera is very important to puerpera (Häggman and Laitila 2003).

Many studies in the past pointed out that poor parturition, such as stillbirth, deadbirth, birth defects and infant sex, can induce conflicts in family relationship. The lack of social support and assistance (Brugha et al. 1998; Honey et al. 2003; Nielsen et al. 2000; Seguin et al. 1995; Xie et al. 2009) and low family cohesion affected the interaction level between puerpera and their family members. However, family support has huge impact on the puerpera. Thus, psychological social factor is a very important link in the cause of PDD (Da Costa et al. 2000). Moreover, this kind of non-traditional assistance method for clinical treatment have been valued more and more. Many literature also pointed out that social support was related to depression and also related to postpartum depression (Howell et al. 2009; Haslam et al. 2006). Some research even stated that social support was the largest factor affecting postpartum depression (Beck 1996, 2001; O'Hara and Swain 1996).

1.3 MSPSS

Multidimensional Perceived Social Support Scale (MSPSS) is a research tool developed by Zimet et al (1988), which is a scale consisting of 12 questions and measures social support awareness in three dimensions: family, friends and important others. There are four questions in each dimension. Likert 7-point scale was adopted to score the scale. Higher score represents higher awareness in social support (from "strongly disagree" to "strongly agree"). The lowest score in the scale is 12 and the highest score in the scale is 84. Currently, Iran has conducted verification and reliability test on this research. The research stated that Cronbach'α in each dimension ("family", "friends" and "important others") of the social support was 0.8, 0.9 and 0.8, respectively. According to Rajabi and Sheikhshabani (2012), validity test was also conducted on each dimension ("family", "friends" and "important others") and the result was 0.84, 0.7 and 0.82, respectively.

1.4 Research Purpose

Currently, there were only few studies applying social support on MBI-PPD and no one applied the social support scale of Zimet et al. (1988) in Chinese. Hence, the purpose of the research is to provide a new research tools for MBI-PPD through the reliability and validity confirmation on the social support scale in Chinese.

2 Method

2.1 Procedure

The research was conducted in Chang Gung Hospital. Maternal were recruited according to the following standards: (1) women who are around 36–40 weeks pregnant and puerpera who gave birth within 4 weeks; (2) capable of fluent language skills in Chinese; (3) stable status with the new-born baby; (4) signing the subject agreement by the maternal. Maternal with major illness or puerpera having newborn with birth defects were ruled out in this research. After oral explanations from the researchers, informed consent was obtained from maternal with their signature on the subject agreement. Then the researchers gave them MSPSS questionnaire and they started answering the 12 questions. The questionnaires were handed back after the questions were filled out. All the content was completed anonymously to ensure information safety of the subjects.

2.2 The Chinese Adaptation of MSPSS

First, we obtained consent from the original author of the MSPSS questionnaire and translated the questionnaire into Chinese. MSPSS was translated into two separate Chinese versions by two bilingual translators whose mother tongue language is Chinese. The two translators are local PhD candidates having medical and clinical background. After translation, the two translators discussed, made revisions and prepared the tool in confirmed version. Then, another two translators translated the scale in Chinese version back to English to understand whether the Chinese version and the English version have the same meaning. After that, another two translators with relevant background in Medicine and Obstetrics and Gynecology reviewed the Chinese version and confirmed the final Chinese version of MSPSS. To evaluate the validity of the MSPSS structure, these questions were first conducted on 30 maternal. Each subject was required to fill out the questionnaire accurately to evaluate whether they can understand the meaning in each item and ensure each item is related to family, friends and partners in the structure and the words and sentences are easy to understand. Meanwhile, the subjects were interviewed and asked whether problems exist on the format and content of the questionnaire and when filling out the scale. Detailed report was written from the opinions of the 30 maternal, including the validity test results on the structure and revisions were made to the final version. Then the final version was submitted to specialist committee.

2.3 Measures

Multidimensional Perceived Social Support Scale (MSPSS) tool developed by Zimet et al. (1988) is a 12-question self-report questionnaire used to measure the social support level on maternal. Questionnaires were filled out by maternal and Likert 7-point scale was adopted. Higher score represents higher social support. The questions consist of three dimensions: family support, friend support and partner support. Scores were given on the supporting level of each party to themselves from "strongly disagree" to "strongly agree". Verification was conducted on the scale with three factors: (1) supporting level to yourself by family; (2) supporting level to yourself by friends; (3) supporting level to yourself by important others.

2.4 Statistical Analysis

To test the validity of the factor structure included in the original English verification study Zimet at al. (1988), Exploratory Factor Analysis (EFA) and Confirmatory Factor Analysis (CFA) were conducted. In accordance with recommendations on scale development and validation studies (Cabrera-Nguyen 2010; Worthington and Whittaker 2006), we randomly split our study population in order to conduct EFA and CFA on different samples. Specifically, we first performed EFA on half of the study population (i.e. the calibration sample), and we then performed CFA on the other half of the study population (i.e. the validation sample) to test the factor structure derived from EFA. The following indices and thresholds were used to determine the goodness of fit of the model: a Root Mean Square Error of Approximation (RMSEA) smaller than 0.08, Comparative Fit Index (CFI) and Non-Normed Fit Index (NNFI) values greater than 0.90, and a ratio of Chi-square value to degrees of freedom (chi2/df) less than 3.0. Exploratory Factor Analysis (EFA) with varimax rotation was used to determine the factor structure of the MSPSS. The Kaiser–Meyer–Olkin (KMO) test was performed to verify sampling adequacy for this analysis, and Barlett's Test of Sphericity was performed to assess the degree of intercorrelation between variables. Factor extraction was determined using Kaiser's criterion (eigen values $\geq$ 1). For this, a factor loading greater than 0.5 was considered to indicate that the item contributed sufficiently to its factor. Cronbach's alpha coefficients were calculated to determine the internal consistency for both the overall scale and its factors, whereby values $\geq$ 0.70 were considered adequate. All statistical analyses were performed using SPSS 21.0 and LISREL 8.80 software. Statistical significance was set at p = .05.

3 Results

3.1 Sample Characteristics

The average social support score of all the research samples was 68.38 (SD = 9,183) with the median being 69 and mode being 68. The p-values in Kolmogorov-Smirnov test and Shapiro-Wilk test were greater than 0.05 and there were no extreme values in the scale, which explains that the scale presents normal distribution.

3.2 Construct Validity of the Chinses MSPSS

CFA analysis was conducted on all the samples to evaluate model fitting goodness-of-fit on the structural factors of the scale proposed in the research of Zimet et al. (1988) in the beginning. As shown in Fig. 1, the results show good model fitting: RMSEA = 0.02; CFI = 0.91; NNFI = 0.89; chi2/ df = 2.78; p < .001. EFA test was conducted on all the samples to ensure the factor structure in the Chinese version of MSPSS (Table 1) has similar factor structure in the original English scale. Quantitative value of 0.915 in Kaiser-Meyer-Olkin test shows that the characteristic values of the three factors in the analysis on the data samples were greater than 1, explaining the total variation of 76.3% sufficiently while Barlett "test of sphericity" with p < .001 explained such data sample was not unit matrix and EFA test can be conducted. These factors seemed easily explained and labels were marked according to the item content as follows: the factor, important others, explained 60.5% variance; the factor, family, explained 9.6% difference; the factor, friends, explained 6.2% difference. All the questions did not show factor load lower than the threshold (0.5) and did not show high factor load, either, which explained that all items were related to the measurement of parental self-efficacy and differences clearly existed between the factors.

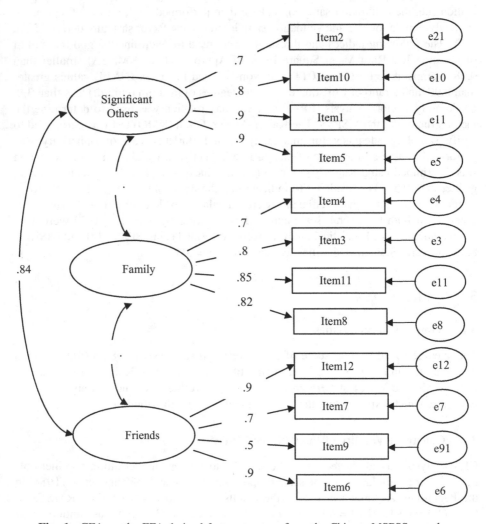

Fig. 1. CFA on the EFA-derived factor structure from the Chinese MSPSS sample

3.3   Internal Consistency of the Chinese MSPSS

The scale shows higher overall internal consistency, which created Cronbach's α = 0.937. As shown in Table 2, higher alpha value was not found if any item in the scale was omitted. Cronbach's α values of the subscale were as follows: family (α = 0.829); friends (α = 0.920); and important others (α = 0.882).

Table 1. Factor structure and internal consistency of the Chinese version of the MSPSS

	Factor loadings	α if item is removed	Item-total correlation
Factor 1. Significant Others			
There is a special person with whom I can share joys and sorrows	0.805	0.932	0.714***
There is a special person in my life who cares about my feelings	0.794	0.930	0.768***
There is a special person who is around when I am in need	0.759	0.936	0.622***
I have a special person who is the real source of comfort to me	0.808	0.931	0.744***
Factor 2. Family			
I get the emotional help and support I need from my family	0.696	0.929	0.801***
My family really tries to help me	0.652	0.930	0.772***
My family is willing to help me make decisions	0.907	0.941	0.512***
I can talk about my problems with my family	0.642	0.931	0.740***
Factor 3. Friends			
I can talk about my problems with my friends	0.849	0.931	0.750***
I can count on my friends when things go wrong	0.817	0.930	0.769***
I have friends with whom I can share my joys and sorrows	0.811	0.931	0.757***
My friends really try to help me	0.794	0.931	0.754***

*** P < .001

Table 2. Reliability and validity of MSPSS across multiple studies

Studies									
	Zimet (Zimet et al. 1988)	Başol (2008)	Ng et al. (2010)	Wongparan et al. (2011)	Guan et al. (2013)	Osman et al. (2013)	Canty-Mitchell and Zimet (2016)	Shumaker et al. (2017)	This study
Reliability									
Cronbach's α of total score	0.88	0.90	0.89	0.91	0.924	0.869	0.93	0.94	0.937
Cronbach's α of Factor 1	0.91	0.92	0.94	0.86	0.859	0.941	0.91	0.94	0.829
Cronbach's α of Factor 2	0.87	0.87	0.88	083	0.891	0.929	0.91	0.94	0.920
Cronbach's α of Factor 3	0.85	0.90	0.82	0.91	0.904	0.942	0.89	0.94	0.882
Validity									
Goodness of fit:	No data	No data	No data	No data	No data	No data	No data	No data	RMSEA = 0.02 CFI = 0.91 NNFI = 0.89 chi2/df = 2.78
Total variability explained	70.48%	77.24%	No data	No data	No data	No data	68%	83%	76.3%
Variance explained by Factor 1	No data	27.10%	No data	No data	No data	No data	No data	61.8%	60.5%
Variance explained by Factor 2	No data	24.87%	No data	No data	No data	No data	No data	11.5%	9.6%
Variance explained by Factor 3	No data	25.27%	No data	No data	No data	No data	No data	9.8%	6.2%

4 Discussion

The purpose of the research is to translate and evaluate the reliability and validity of the MSPSS scale. From statistical results, it can be seen that the Chinese MSPSS scale has reliability. Chinese version of MSPSS can be provided for maternal in Taiwan. The choice to use MSPSS tool is to allow the maternal to gain a better understanding of the level of social support they have received. Through the acquisition of such information, it is hoped that support from her family, friends and important others can be enhanced. In addition, there were only 12 questions in MSPSS, which can be easily completed within 10 min, which allowed for the convenience in effective management of clinical experiment. All these dimensions present perspectives on maternal from different parties. (1) the support level on maternal from family; (2) the support level on maternal from friends; (3) the support level on maternal from important others.

The research solves the problem of lacking tools to evaluate the awareness of social support level in maternal in Taiwan and confirms the multidimensional structure of MSPSS. High internal consistency was found in family, friends and important others.

Higher alpha value was not found if any item was omitted from the scale, presenting that all items made important contributions to awareness of social support in maternal.

Table 2 compares reliability and validity scores for the PMP S-E that were obtained by the current study and by previous studies. For the current study, alpha values were high regardless of whether overall reliability or the reliability of subscales was being assessed. With regard to validity, all of the indicators we employed confirmed that our CFA model had adequate goodness of fit. Furthermore, the amount of variability explained by our EFA model was relatively high.

5 Conclusion

The research result shows that the Chinese version of MSPSS is a reliable and valid tool in the test on 300 maternal in Chang Gung hospital, Taipei. The psychometric performances of such tool in terms of reliability and validity are both impressive. The scale and its subscale of the tool have high internal consistency, meaning that there is high homogeneity between each item, and the reliability is high as well.

Three factors were obtained from the factor analysis on the 12 items in MSPSS, which proved the three-dimensional structure proposed in the initial research of the original author (Zimet et al. 1988), supported by most subsequent research. Moreover, the subjects in the research can separate the three supporting sources in MSPSS, that is, family, friends and important others. In general, the Chinese version of MSPSS presents good psychometric performances in social support aspect in the measurement on 300 maternal in Chang Gung hospital, Taipei, representing good reliability and validity. It can measure the different dimension in social support, family, friends and important others. However, two limitations of the research were found in other similar studies (Kee 2000). First, the research sample used was maternal. The study has a certain reference value to the psychometric properties and factor structure of other groups. Secondly, the cause and effect relationship between social support and mental depression is not clear yet but can be further clarified in future studies.

References

Beck, C.T.: Predictors of postpartum depression: an update. Nurs. Res. **50**(5), 275–285 (2001)

Bodhi, B.: What does mindfulness really mean? A canonical perspective. Contemporary Buddhism **12**(1), 19–39 (2011)

Brugha, T.S., et al.: The Leicester 500 Project Social support and the development of postnatal depressive symptoms a prospective cohort survey. Psychol. Med. **28**(1), 63–79 (1998)

Cox, J.L., Holden, J.M., Sagovsky, R.: Detection of postnatal depression: development of the 10-item edinburgh postnatal depression scale. British J. Psychiatry **150**(6), 782–786 (1987)

Da Costa, D., Dritsa, M., Rippen, N., Lowensteyn, I., Khalife, S.: Health-related quality of life in postpartum depressed women. Archives Women's Mental Health **9**(2), 95–102 (2006)

Darcy, J.M., Grzywacz, J.G., Stephens, R.L., Leng, I., Clinch, C.R., Arcury, T.A.: Maternal depressive symptomatology: 16-month follow-up of infant and maternal health-related quality of life. J. Am. Board Family Med. **24**(3), 249–257 (2011)

Dennis, C.L.: Can we identify mothers at risk for postpartum depression in the immediate postpartum period using the Edinburgh postnatal depression scale? J. Affect. Disord. **78**(2), 163–169 (2004). https://doi.org/10.1016/S0165-0327(02)00299-9

Gavin, N.I., Gaynes, B.N., Lohr, K.N., Meltzer-Brody, S., Gartlehner, G., Swinson, T.: Perinatal depression: a systematic review of prevalence and incidence. Obstet. Gynecol. **106**(5), 1071–1083 (2005)

Goodman, J.H.: Paternal postpartum depression, its relationship to maternal postpartum depression, and implications for family health. J. Adv. Nurs. **45**(1), 26–35 (2004)

Gottlieb, B.H., Bergen, A.E.: Social support concepts and measures. J. Psychosom. Res. **69**(5), 511–520 (2010)

Häggman-Laitila, A.: Early support needs of Finnish families with small children. J. Adv. Nurs. **41**(6), 595–606 (2003)

Honey, K.L., Bennett, P., Morgan, M.: Predicting postnatal depression. J. Affect. Disord. **76**(1–3), 201–210 (2003)

Kabat-Zinn, J.: Gesund durch Meditation. Fischer-Taschenbuch, Frankfurt/M (2006)

Kabat-Zinn, J.: Mindfulness-based interventions in context: past, present, and future. Clin. Psychol. Sci. Pract. **10**(2), 144–156 (2003)

Leahy Warren, P.: First-time mothers: social support and confidence in infant care. J. Adv. Nurs. **50**(5), 479–488 (2005)

Logsdon, M.C., Davis, D.W.: Social and professional support for pregnant and parenting women. MCN: The American J. Maternal/Child Nurs. **28**(6), 371–376 (2003)

Nielsen, D., Videbech, P., Hedegaard, M., Dalby, J., Secher, N.J.: Postpartum depression: identification of women at risk. BJOG: Int. J. Obstetrics Gynaecol. 107(10), 1210–1217 (2000)

O'Hara, M.W., Schlechte, J.A., Lewis, D.A., Varner, M.W.: Controlled prospective study of postpartum mood disorders: psychological, environmental, and hormonal variables. J. Abnorm. Psychol. **100**(1), 63 (1991)

Orr, S.T.: Social support and pregnancy outcome: a review of the literature. Clin. Obstet. Gynecol. **47**(4), 842–855 (2004)

Orr, S.T., James, S.A., Blackmore Prince, C.: Maternal prenatal depressive symptoms and spontaneous preterm births among African-American women in Baltimore Maryland. Am. J. Epidemiol. **156**(9), 797–802 (2002)

Pearlstein, T., Howard, M., Salisbury, A., Zlotnick, C.: Postpartum depression. Am. J. Obstet. Gynecol. **200**(4), 357–364 (2009)

Robertson, E., Grace, S., Wallington, T., Stewart, D.E.: Antenatal risk factors for postpartum depression: a synthesis of recent literature. Gen. Hosp. Psychiatry **26**(4), 289–295 (2004)

Séguin, L., Potvin, L., Denis, M.S., Loiselle, J.: Chronic stressors, social support, and depression during pregnancy. Obstet. Gynecol. **85**(4), 583–589 (1995)

Thoits, P.A.: Mechanisms linking social ties and support to physical and mental health. J. Health Soc. Behav. **52**(2), 145–161 (2011)

Vesga-Lopez, O., Blanco, C., Keyes, K., Olfson, M., Grant, B.F., Hasin, D.S.: Psychiatric disorders in pregnant and postpartum women in the United States. Arch. Gen. Psychiatry **65** (7), 805–815 (2008)

WHO (2003). Risk factors for postpartum depression: WHO

Wahn, E.H., Nissen, E.: Sociodemographic background, lifestyle and psychosocial conditions of Swedish teenage mothers and their perception of health and social support during pregnancy and childbirth. Scandinavian J. Public Health **36**(4), 415–423 (2008)

Wilkins, C.: A qualitative study exploring the support needs of first-time mothers on their journey towards intuitive parenting. Midwifery **22**(2), 169–180 (2006)

Wisner, K.L., Parry, B.L., Piontek, C.M.: Postpartum depression. N. Engl. J. Med. **347**(3), 194–199 (2002)

Xie, R.H., He, G., Koszycki, D., Walker, M., Wen, S.W.: Prenatal social support, postnatal social support, and postpartum depression. Ann. Epidemiol. **19**(9), 637–643 (2009)

Zimet, G.D., Dahlem, N.W., Zimet, S.G., Farley, G.K.: The multidimensional scale of perceived social support. J. Pers. Assess. **52**(1), 30–41 (1988)

Development of Health Care System Based on Smart Clothes

Pin-Chieh Huang[1] , Chung-Chih Lin[1,2(✉)] , Hisang-Jen Hsieh[1] ,
Wei-Chia Chen[1] , and Ho-Huan Chiang[1]

[1] Department of Computer Science and Information Engineering,
Chang Gung University, Taoyuan, Taiwan (R.O.C.)
astyle1l07@gmail.com, cclin@mail.cgu.edu.tw,
garygh159357@yahoo.com.tw, viga3437@gmail.com,
chainglars@gmail.com

[2] Department of Rehabilitation, Chang Gung Memorial Hospital Linkou
Medical Center and College of Medicine, Taoyuan, Taiwan (R.O.C.)

Abstract. With the rapid growth of the world's aging population, health care for the elderly has become an important issue in all countries. In order to reduce the manpower burden, reduce medical costs and improve the quality of care services, wearable devices are viewed as a solution to improve the situation. This research developed a wearable device of smart clothing, which has been used to record user physiological parameters. After uploading the original physiological parameters to the cloud server, the data will convert into a personal health report. Once the abnormal situation happened, the system will remind the caregivers immediately. This health care system has been applied to long-term care institutions and smart wards to provide care. By using this system, users can monitor self-physiological parameters and abnormal events for a long time to achieve the effect of self-health management.

Keywords: Wearable devices · Smart clothes · Health care system · Long term care

1 Introduction

According to the statistic report of the United Nations Population Fund (UNFPA), the world's population aged 65 and over will reach 703 million in 2019. It is expected that until 2050, the number of elderly will reach 1.5 billion. The proportion of the elderly population will continue to increase from 6% in the 1990s to 9% in 2019 and up to 16% in 2050. One-sixth people worldwide will be over 65 [1]. In elderly society, chronic diseases are one of the biggest health threats. More than 75% of the elderly suffer from more than one type of chronic disease [2]. For such elders, issues such as elderly care, long-term care services, and medical institutions have become a major issue and test that the world needs to face.

P.-L. P. Rau (Ed.): HCII 2020, LNCS 12193, pp. 78–88, 2020.
https://doi.org/10.1007/978-3-030-49913-6_7

Faced with the challenge of manpower shortage, most countries around the world are supplemented by telecommunications technology and high-quality medical systems, and constructing a service model based on smart medical services. With the rapid development of wearable devices, assisted care with smart technology provides a solution to alleviate the shortage of care manpower. Through device miniaturization, 24-h physiological monitoring, indoor positioning to prevent the loss, real-time notification of abnormal events, and automatic promotion of health information, etc., can be used for early health monitoring and prevention of accidents through long-term health trend analysis [3], which can help to improve the overall care quality, not only enable caregivers to focus on key care items but can gradually extend the medical system-centric service model to home care to provide more diversified services. In recent years, wearable devices have flourished. The development and production of health smart textiles have had a huge impact on home care, institutional nursing care, personal health care, and even electronic communications and the textile industry. Due to the development of miniature sensors that can be attached to the human body without interference, it can also be sewn on clothes and become a part of clothes. Such as the sensor element embedded in the fabric of the clothes, becoming smart clothing. Smart clothes can collect patients' physiological parameters for a long time, which offers countless possibilities of long-term care [4] and enhances disease prevention capabilities [5, 6]. The smart clothes use physiological signal sensors to capture physiological signals and pass them to the back-end database for analysis and recording through the Bluetooth module. As smart clothes are used personally, electronic devices have tended to be miniaturized, highly flexible, low power, sweat-resistant, and high-humidity [7]. The development of physiological monitoring textiles includes breathing, electrocardiogram, posture, electromyography, heartbeat detection, etc. Among them, the application of the heartbeat is the most common item. Conductive fiber weaving is a key technology that makes smart clothing a carrier of telecommunication signals. By combining cloud servers with smart clothes, a personal physical health database can be established to assist the promotion of health management and solve the problem of manpower shortage. In this study, we designed smart clothing. By collecting physiological parameters through smart clothes, and upload data to the cloud server to build a health care system. We use smart clothing as a carrier, combined with ECG, posture sensors, and indoor positioning, Bluetooth, and wireless transmission, through cloud server collecting data, we can achieve real-time data processing and feedback, reducing the workload of medical staff by using automated systems.

2 Methodology

The smart clothes collect physiological signals through four electrode pads, transmits the signals to the sensing components through conductive fibers, and uploads the data to the back-end cloud database analysis platform for analysis. The system can set personal thresholds according to different conditions of patients. Once the patient's measured value exceeds the threshold, the system will proactively notify the caregivers. The system architecture diagram shows in Fig. 1.

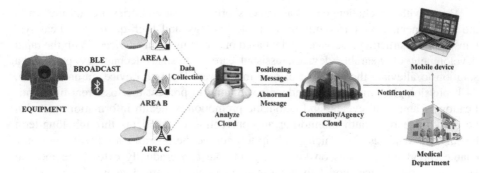

Fig. 1. System architecture diagram

2.1   Design of Smart Clothes

Smart clothes are wearable smart textiles. To meet the demand of wearable sensing device that can move with users and collect physiological signals anytime and anywhere, the smart clothes must meet six main features: (1) detect physiological signals accurately, (2) the device must be light and convenient to wear, (3) long standby time, (4) provide reliable information storage, and can record physiological data even when the network is disconnected, (5) physiological signals can be transmitted to the cloud server for data processing and analysis, and (6) conduct fabrics are able to be washed. The design and development of smart clothes integrate three industries of electronic information, health care, and textile weaving to conduct cross-field research. The smart clothes are made of highly elastic conductive fibers as the main material, which improves the wearing comfort by reducing the friction between the sensing fabric and the skin. Conductive fiber weaving is a key technology to make smart clothing a carrier of signal transmission. The smart clothes must meet the requirements of washability, flexibility, oxidation resistance, etc., the conductive fibers are made on the surface by wrapping a thin layer of metal or penetrating alloy, or using a metal material to convert the coating or directly extract the conductive fibers, and then directly or twisted into conductive yarn. Smart clothes can continuously measure personal vital signs. Users only need to put on their clothes in the usual way and can enjoy functions such as external entertainment links to life and entertainment, sports and leisure status detection, safety protection for people, personal health management and abnormal condition monitoring. Four pieces of fabric electrode made of stainless steel wire (see Fig. 2) are sewn on the smart clothes. The size of the stainless steel wire is about 10^{-3} mm. A smart sensing element is attached to the smart clothing to calculate ECG, heartbeat, and posture, and transmit data through Bluetooth.

Fig. 2. Smart clothes and fabric electrodes

The position of the electrodes for measuring ECG signals is shown in Fig. 3. Electrode yarns are sewed on both sides' shoulders and lower ribs. The ECG signals sensed by the electrode yarns are transmitted to the metal buttons on the clothes through physiological conductive fibers. Snap-on physiological signal wireless transmission device is used to collect and process the wireless signal to the computer or mobile device to display and analyze the ECG signal synchronously.

Fig. 3. The position of smart clothing electrode

The sensing element contains 4 parts: microprocessor (MCU), analog to digital converter (ADC), G-sensor, BLE to WIFI. The MCU is used to calculate the received information, the ADC is used to converting the ECG analog signal received by the electrode patch into a digital signal. The G-sensor receives the acceleration of the three axes. BLE to WIFI is used to transmit data. In order to meet the needs of the market, the design of smart clothes is streamlined the shape to provide a sense of fashion. In addition, when designing a commercially-available wearable device, there are two issues that need to be faced (1) power-saving problems (2) volume issues. It is expected that battery life should under continuous operation for more than 40 h and should not exceed 50 g. Figure 4 shows the architecture of smart clothing and physiological signal wireless transmission components.

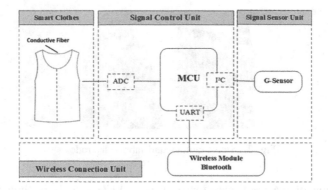

Fig. 4. Architecture diagram of smart clothing and physiological signal wireless transmission components

This study uses the results of previous clinical trials to improve the style and performance of smart clothing. According to different objects according to their needs and care situations, we design a variety of smart clothing styles, including sports vest smart clothing and home smart clothing (see Fig. 5). Product use objects and application scenarios are shown in Table 1. The sensed physiological data signals, such as ECG, heart rate, and body temperature, are calculated by algorithms. The results are will transmit to a cloud server for data analysis. The smart clothes have already run the ECG algorithm test and its accuracy performance is over 99.5% [8].

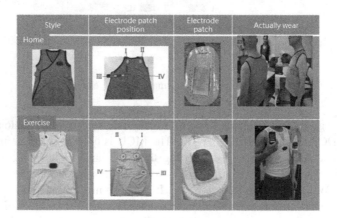

Fig. 5. Different type of smart clothes

Table 1. Product use objects and application scenarios

Smart clothes	Object	Application scenarios
Posture and movement monitoring smart vest	Normal people	People with poor sleep quality
	Mid-aged people	Walking posture characteristic value detection
	Postoperative patient	Move detection and fall detection
Heart function smart clothes	Patients with heart disease	Acute myocardial infarction detection
	Normal elderly	Detect abnormal ECG signal
	Patients with chest pain	Detect abnormal ECG signal
	Patients after cardiovascular surgery	Detect abnormal ECG signal
Body temperature smart clothes	Normal people	Body temperature detection
	Women	Basal body temperature
Sweat sensing smart clothes	Athlete	Sweat and ion measurement
	Soldier	Abnormal monitoring of heat stroke and heat exhaustion

2.2 System Integration

After collecting vital signs by the sensor recorder, the result will be transferred to the cloud server through Bluetooth. The cloud server algorithm will evaluate the emergency situation and notification the caregivers. The construction of the cloud server contains personal health files and the indicators of physiological health. The health file contains personal measurement data, health information and consultation records, etc., which is convenient for tracking the health status and personal health management. The establishment of health indicators has mainly established the correlation between various parameters and diseases, and define health indicators and risk levels. Through the establishment of health indicators, once the abnormal emergency situation occurs, the system will notify the caregivers immediately to handle the situation. The currently defined health indicators are shown in Table 2.

Table 2. Health care indicators

Health indicator	Application scenario
All day rest time statistic	Daily and monthly rest analysis based on the get-up and lie data
Sit for too long	The indoor positioning algorithm detects and records the activity tracking of the residents', and monitor whether they have abnormal activities or sitting for too long
Activity	Step detection is performed by the G-sensor on the device. Steps analysis can be performed
Guard zone detection	Detect if seniors approach the guarded area or not

(continued)

84   P.-C. Huang et al.

Table 2. (*continued*)

Health indicator	Application scenario
Leave the bed at night	Leave bed at night often falls due to poor eyesight, the system can remind the caregivers to assist
Inside of toilet for too long	Toilets usually occur falls. Detecting inside toilets for too long can remind caregivers to care and assist
Emergency service bell	The physiological signal wireless transmission element provides an emergency service bell button. Once residents feel abnormal or encounter an emergency, they can call for help through the physiological signal wireless transmission element

In addition to the item mentioned above, there is also a low battery warning and loss of signal warning. When the component power is less than 20%, the nursing staff will be informed to make an instant replacement. The overall system of the cloud server provides a personal information input page, which can quickly establish a patient's personal health file. The personal health records contain physiological data, exercise data, activity trajectory, care records and care indicators. In addition to querying personal health records, the cloud server also provides a nursing station management page. Nursing staff can instantly understand the patient's location, physiological parameters, abnormal status, device status, and abnormal event records. The system screenshot is shown in Fig. 6.

Fig. 6. Screenshot of the cloud server

3   Experiment Design and Result

The health care system has installed in a long-term care institution and smart ward.

3.1   Long-Term Care Institution

The system has been established in a long-term care institution in Taoyuan, Taiwan. Most patients in this field are elderly with chronic diseases and dementia patients. The elderly dress in smart clothes to collect physiological parameters, and the data will be uploaded through the network to the cloud database. The actual field pictures show in Fig. 7.

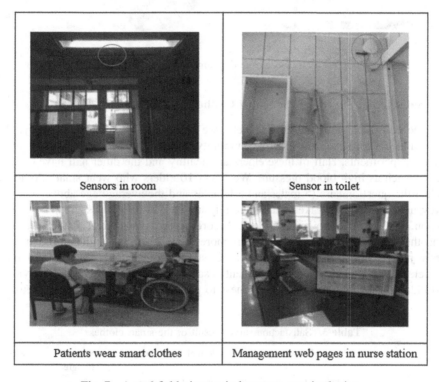

Fig. 7. Actual field pictures in long-term care institution

3.2   Smart Ward

The establishment of the smart ward mainly monitors the physiological parameters such as heart rate and posture of patients after operation. As patient safety has been an important item of hospital evaluation. It will reduce many accidents if monitoring of physiological parameters, posture activities of patients in time. The schematic diagram of the smart ward is shown in Fig. 8. The care indicators of the smart ward can be set by the hospital for monitoring physiological parameters.

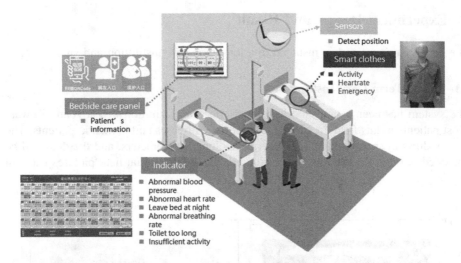

Fig. 8. Schematic diagram of smart ward

3.3   Satisfaction Survey of the Smart Clothes

After the construction of the clinical field, we conducted a satisfaction survey. We recruited elders who live in an elderly community in Taoyuan, Taiwan to conduct smart clothing experiments. Half of these elders are healthy and the other half have chronic diseases such as high blood pressure. We select 10 elders who wear smart clothes to conduct the questionnaire (5 males and 5 females and the average age above 70). The survey uses a five-point Likert scale (strongly agree: 5, strongly disagree: 1) for calculation. The result is shown in Table 3. According to the statistical results, it can be found that the average satisfaction rate is more than 3.3 points, indicating that most elderly people think that wearing the ECG smart clothes to collect physiological parameters for personal health management is satisfactory. Through verbal interviews, most elderly also indicated their willingness to pay to use this health care system.

Table 3. Satisfaction survey result of the smart clothes

Item	Strongly agree		Agree		Normal		Disagree		Strongly disagree		Average
	Times	%	Times	%	Times	%	Times	%	Times	%	
1. If I have a smart clothes with ECG record, I will be happy to use it	1	10%	7	70%	1	10%	1	10%	0	0%	3.8
I think the ECG record smart clothing is helpful for my health care	1	10%	8	80%	1	10%	0	0%	0	0%	4
3. The use of smart clothes is not difficult for me	0	0%	7	70%	3	30%	0	0%	0	0%	3.7

(continued)

Table 3. (*continued*)

Item	Strongly agree		Agree		Normal		Disagree		Strongly disagree		Average
	Times	%	Times	%	Times	%	Times	%	Times	%	
4. The experience of using the ECG to record the smart clothes was pleasant	0	0%	6	60%	4	40%	0	0%	0	0%	3.6
5. My doctor thinks I should use smart clothes	0	0%	5	50%	5	50%	0	0%	0	0%	3.5
6. I think using the ECG record smart clothes is an advanced health concept	2	20%	4	40%	4	40%	0	0%	0	0%	3.8
7. Smart clothes are closely related to my health care	0	0%	5	50%	5	50%	0	0%	0	0%	3.5
8. I feel satisfied with the quality of smart clothes	0	0%	7	70%	3	30%	0	0%	0	0%	3.7
9. I will communicate with other people about the experience of using smart clothes	1	10%	3	30%	4	40%	2	20%	0	0%	3.3
10. I am voluntary to use smart clothes	1	10%	5	50%	4	40%	0	0%	0	0%	3.3

4 Conclusions

With the advent of an aging society, health care issues have become more important and urgent. In this study, a health care system based on smart clothes was designed. The wearable devices were used to collect the user's physiological parameters for a long time under the premise of not disturbing the daily routine of the user. The data will upload to the cloud server to analysis and perform the personal health report. Once the emergency situation occurs, the system will notify the caregivers proactively to handle and assist. With the health care system, it will effectively record users' personal health management and analyze their health trends, it can also reduce the frequency of accidents and improve care efficiency. The system can flexibly adjust care indicators for different fields. At present, it has been installed in the long-term care institution and the postoperative smart ward to provide care services. We will also conduct a system use satisfaction survey for caregivers to improve the system operation process. In the future, it can be extended to home health care and other medical wards. With the system, it can not only reduce the manpower shortage of care but enhances the important concept of personal health management.

Acknowledgement. This work was supported in part by the Ministry of Science and Technology under Grant MOST 108-2221-E-182-032.

References

1. United Nations. World Ageing Population 2019
2. https://www.un.org/en/development/desa/population/publications/pdf/ageing/WorldPopulation Ageing2019-Highlights.pdf
3. Lin, C.-C., Chiu, M.-J., Hsiao, C.-C., Lee, R.-G., Tsai, Y.-S.: Wireless health care service system for elderly with dementia. IEEE Trans. Inf. Technol. Biomed. **10**(4), 696–704 (2006)
4. Yilmaz, T., Foster, R., Hao, Y.: Detecting vital signs with wearable wireless sensors. Sensors **10**(12), 10837–10862 (2010)
5. Bonato, P.: Advances in wearable technology and applications in physical medicine and rehabilitation. J. NeuroEng. Rehabilit. **2**, 2 (2005)
6. Caldeira, J.M.L.P., Rodrigues, J.J.P.C., Lorenz, P.: Toward ubiquitous mobility solutions for body sensor networks on healthcare. IEEE Communi. Magazine **50**(5), 108–115 (2012)
7. Pandian, P.S., et al.: Smart vest: wearable multi-parameter remote physiological monitoring system. Med. Eng. Phys. **30**(4), 466–477 (2008)
8. Taiwan Electrical and Electronic Manufacturers' Association, the first general rule of smart clothes standards. http://www.teema.org.tw/download/doc/001[20171207].pdf
9. Wang, J., Lin, C.-C., Yu, Y.-S., Yu, T.-C.: Wireless sensor-based smart-clothing platform for ECG monitoring. Comput. Math. Methods in Med. **15**, 1–8 (2015)

Effectiveness of the Immersive Virtual Reality in Upper Extremity Rehabilitation

Lan-Ling Huang[1] and Mei-Hsiang Chen[2(✉)]

[1] Fujian University of Technology, Fuzhou City, Fujian, China
[2] Chung Shan Medical University/Chung Shan Medical University Hospital,
Taichung City, Taiwan
cmh@csmu.edu.tw

Abstract. Stroke has been one of the leading causes of death worldwide for the past 15 years. Upper limb dysfunction is one of the main symptoms in stroke patients. The purpose of is to evaluate the treatment effectiveness of Immersive virtual reality system in upper limb rehabilitation. A single-blind clinical trial, and pretest–posttest control group design trial was conducted. The Fugl-Meyer Assessment of Physical Performance, Box and Block Test of Manual Dexterity, and FIM self-care score were used at baseline and post intervention. All subjects were asked to complete a total of twenty training sessions over eight weeks. The results of this project can be summarized as follows: (1) A total of eighteen stroke patients were involved in the trial, 15 males and 3 females, with an average age of 57.42 years (SD 12.75), and time from stroke (Mean 8.78 months, SD 5.51). (2) Results of the differences between the two groups pretest–posttest showed that the two groups were significantly differences in FMA (Conventional group, $p = 0.021$; Immersive virtual reality group, $p = 0.014$). It is known from the above results that the immersive virtual reality game device contributes to the improvement of the functions of the upper limbs. The results of this project are expected to provide a reference for innovative design in the medical industry and the entertainment industry.

Keywords: Virtual reality · Occupational therapy · Upper extremity rehabilitation · Effectiveness

1 Introduction

Stroke is one of the biggest killers in the world. It has been one of the leading causes of death globally for the past fifteen years [1, 2]. In 2018, cerebrovascular disease was the fourth leading cause of death in Taiwan [3]. Upper limb motor deficit is one of the main symptoms of stroke patients. Upper limb dysfunction occurs in 85% of patients at the beginning of a stroke, and 40% of patients suffer from upper limb dysfunction after the chronic phase [4]. In order to restore the patient's ability to live independently, all patients need to undergo rehabilitation activities.

With the development of digital technology, clinical therapists in Taiwan have used virtual reality game systems (for example: Nintendo Wii and Kinect for XBOX360 ™, XaviX, etc.) for upper limb rehabilitation treatment in stroke cases. The results of the

© Springer Nature Switzerland AG 2020
P.-L. P. Rau (Ed.): HCII 2020, LNCS 12193, pp. 89–98, 2020.
https://doi.org/10.1007/978-3-030-49913-6_8

study found that virtual reality game-assisted rehabilitation can indeed help improve the efficacy of upper limb rehabilitation and improve the motivation of patients to receive treatment [5]. Virtual reality (VR) shows promise in the application of healthcare and because it presents patients an immersive, often entertaining, approach to accomplish the goal of improvement in performance [6].

Immersive virtual reality system create an environment that surrounds the user. When the user enters the virtual environment, it will be fully integrated into the system and completely isolated from the outside world. In the system, the computer will send messages to stimulate the user's senses, including vision, hearing, and touch; and the user's limb movements will be transmitted back to the computer through peripheral devices to present appropriate images. Immersive virtual reality has become increasingly popular to improve the assessment and treatment of health problems. The availability of afordable headsets that deliver high quality immersive experiences [7]. Immersive virtual reality (IVR) offers new possibilities to perform treatments in an ecological and interactive environment with multimodal online feedbacks [8].

Literature review in immersive virtual reality device, the immersive virtual reality device used in rehabilitation were HTC Vive [9, 10], The GRAIL System [8], Oculus Rift DK2 and Intel® RealSense™ [5]. Jared et al. (2018) demonstrated the increasing availability of immersive VR technology offers the potential for engaging therapy in traumatic brain injury rehabilitation [11]. Lee et al. (2019) showed that a fully immersive VR rehabilitation program using an HMD for rehabilitation of the upper extremities following stroke is feasible. Immersive virtual reality improves movement patterns in patients after ACL reconstruction [10]. Gagliardi et al. (2018) researched on sixteen school-aged children with Bilateral CP—diplegia for a pilot study in a pre–post treatment experimental design. The effect could have been due to the possibility of IVR to foster integration of motor/perceptual competences beyond the training of the walking ability, giving a chance of improvement also to older and already treated children. Baldominos et al. (2015) developed a game using Oculus Rift DK2 and Intel® RealSense™ that required patients to perform a set of rehabilitation exercises for abduction and adduction arms. Preliminary assessment by physiotherapy experts had showed encouraging results.

Most of the digital gaming devices currently in clinical use (Nintendo Wii and Kinect for XBOX360 ™, XaviX, etc.) are mostly non-immersive interactions, lacking the presence and authenticity associated with daily life environments. For example, the action training for reaching out may be similar to the boxing game action of Kinect for XBOX360 ™. However, in immersive virtual reality devices (for example: HTC Vive, Oculus Rift DK2, etc.), it is actually simulating the real living environment for targeted action training (for example: simulating the real kitchen environment, removing the cup from the cabinet). This is highly correlated with the actual environment and living functions. Therefore, the authenticity provided by the immersive virtual reality system may be more in line with the purpose and expectations of functional therapy.

There are few studies on the effectiveness evaluation of immersive virtual reality system in the treatment of upper limb rehabilitation, and further trials are still needed to confirm the efficacy intensity. The purpose of this study was to evaluate the effectiveness of the application of the virtual reality system (for example: HTC Vive) in upper limb rehabilitation.

2   Methods

2.1   Subjects

Stroke patients were recruited from an outpatient occupational therapy department of Chung Shan Medical University Hospital in Taiwan.

Inclusion criteria were as follows: (a) hemiparesis with upper extremity dysfunction following a single unilateral stroke; (b) first-time stroke (3–24 months post-stroke); (c) upper extremity rehabilitation to convalescent levels of Brunnstrom stages III to V; (d) ability to communicate, and to understand and follow instructions; and e) ability to maintain sitting and standing balance unsupported for two minutes under supervision (score $\geq$ 3 on the Berg Balance Scale).

Exclusion criteria were as follows: (a) engagement in any other rehabilitation studies during the study; and (b) serious aphasia or cognitive impairment. Each patient gave informed consent. This study was approved by the Human Research Ethics Board of a local hospital.

2.2   Devices

VIVE is a virtual reality brand building hardware, software and creative platforms to unleash imaginations from the limits of our world. Sub-millimeter-precise tracking technology from Steam VR. High-fidelity hardware and an ecosystem of innovation from VIVE. Together, they make a superlative experience unlike any other [12]. HTC Vive includes a hardware, controllers, and base stations (see Fig. 1).

Fig. 1. The HTC Vive.

Fig. 2. The use scene.

Table 1. Devices were used in two groups.

Groups	Devices were used in trail
Conventional group	Conventional devices

Climbing bar   Ball bearing   Pulley

Immersive virtual reality group	Immersive virtual reality game

Shoot balloon   Electric current stick

Shooting game

The system requires a few meters of space to set up a complete system. Participants wore a head-mounted display to provide a 90-Hz virtual picture update frequency and scene sound effects, while each hand held an interactive controller to provide the subject to interact with the virtual script. Set up two sensors in the space to track the subject's position, and construct a corresponding virtual environment as the subject's visual experience. The virtual reality system must have sufficient computer hardware specifications to support the operation of the virtual script. The use scenes showed in Fig. 3.

2.3   Outcome Measures

Three assessments were used frequently in this study, as following: The Fugl-Meyer Assessment of Physical Performance (FMA) [13], Box and Block Test of Manual Dexterity (BBT) [14], and FIM self-care score (FIM) [15] were used at baseline and post intervention.

2.4   Procedure

This study was a single-blind clinical trial and used a pretest–posttest control group design. The functional ability of each subject's affected upper extremity was assessed by one of the assessors in two stages: (1) prior to the interventions, and (2) immediately after completing all the training sessions.

Stroke patients were randomly assigned to conventional rehabilitation equipment (conventional group) and immersive virtual reality system (IVR group).

All subjects were asked to complete a total of twenty training sessions over eight weeks, scheduled at three 30-mins sessions per week (excluding set-up time). In addition to the training sessions in this study, all subjects also received at least one hour of occupational therapy and physical therapy, respectively.

After one hour of conventional upper limb rehabilitation, these three devices (Climbing bar, Ball bearing, and Pulley) were performed for an additional 30 min in

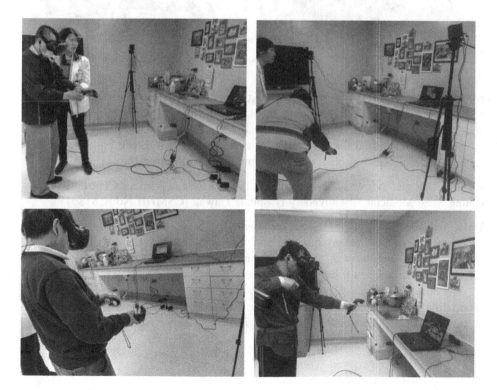

Fig. 3. Stroke patients used the HTC Vive in trial.

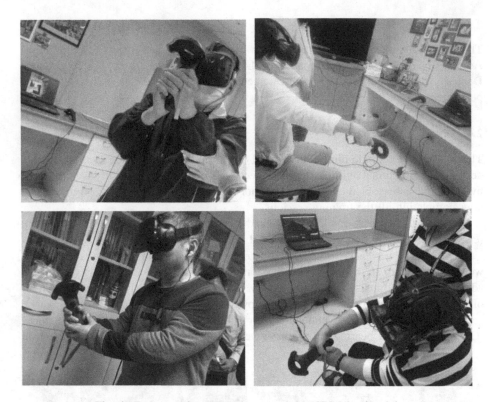

Fig. 4. Postures of stroke patients used the HTC Vive in trial.

conventional group. For the Immersive virtual reality group, After sixty minutes of conventional upper limb rehabilitation, these three devices (Climbing bar, Ball bearing, and Pulley) were performed for an additional 30 min.

Stroke patients used the HTC Vive in trial (see Fig. 3). Stroke patient Postures, such as: holding the controller, and performing in a sitting (see Fig. 4).

Ethics. This research was approved by the Human Research Ethics Committee of the Chung Shan Medicine of University Hospital, Taiwan (CSMUH No: CS18017).

Data Analysis. All data were analyzed with SPSS for Windows version 22. The characteristics of the three groups were analyzed with descriptive statistics. The paired samples T-test analysis was used for within-group analyses. Differences were considered significant when $p < 0.05$.

The effect size d was calculated for each measurement to indicate the magnitude of group differences in performance [16]. When $d \geqq 0.50$, it means a high effect; when $d \geqq 0.30$, it means a moderate effect; $d \geqq 0.10$, it means a low effect.

3   Results

3.1   Characteristics of Stroke Patients

A total of eighteen subjects participated in the trial, fifteen males and three females, with an average age of 57.42 years (standard deviation 12.75). Each group had nine stroke patients.

In conventional group, three patients with the affected side on the left side and five patients with the affected side on the right side. In immersive virtual reality group, four patients with the affected side on the left side and four patients with the affected side on the right side. The characteristics of the subjects was shown in Table 2.

From the results, there was no significant difference between the two groups in age, time from stroke, and the previous measurements of the three assessments (FMA, BBT and FIM).

Table 2. Characteristics of stroke patients.

Groups	Conventional group			IVR group			
	N	Mean	SD	N	Mean	SD	p-value[a]
Number of subjects	9			9			
Gender, male/female (n)	7/2			8/1			
Paretic side, left/right (n)	3/5			4/4			
Age in years		55.36	10.48		59.48	15.02	0.509
Time from stroke, months		7.87	7.07		9.69	3.57	0.500
FMA (pretest)		52.44	10.11		38.22	19.57	0.071
BBT (pretest)		29.67	19.26		17.44	17.11	0.174
FIM (pretest)		99.33	27.02		112.67	13.11	0.202

[a]p for differences between two groups.
FMA: Fugl-Meyer Assessment of motor function; BBT: Box and Block Test of Manual Dexterity; FIM: Functional Independence Measure.

3.2   Differences of Pretest and Posttest in Each Group

Regarding within-group changes, the groups showed significant improvements in upper extremity function (Table 3). The Conventional group and the IVR group had significant differences on FMA. Both were not significant differences on BBT and FIM.

Table 3. Effectiveness of pretest and posttest in each group.

Outcome measures	Conventional group			Immersive virtual reality group		
	Mean	SD	p-value[b]	Mean	SD	p-value[b]
FMA (pretest)	52.44	10.11	0.021*	38.22	19.57	0.014*
FMA (posttest)	55.56	8.06		46.78	18.55	
BBT (pretest)	29.67	19.26	0.102	17.44	17.11	0.122
BBT (posttest)	35.44	24.61		29.67	18.17	
FIM (pretest)	99.33	27.02	0.117	112.67	13.11	0.251
FIM (posttest)	104.11	28.19		108.56	17.54	

*Significant at ≤ 0.05 level.
[b]p for Within-group differences in change of scores for pre- and posttests.

3.3   Effectiveness Differences Between Groups

The results showed that there was no significant difference in the magnitude of group differences in performance between the two groups in the three assessments, FMA (p = 0.084), BBT (p = 0.417), and FIM (p = 0.055) (see in Table 4).

Comparing the average value of the FMA's progress index between the two groups, it was found that the IVR group had a larger improvement amount than the traditional group (mean 0.13, standard deviation 0.12); the BBT had a slightly larger improvement amount (mean 0.08, standard deviation 0.14).

The effect size was used to calculate the effect value intensity between the two groups. Analyzing the effect size of the IVR group compared with the conventional group, it was found that in the FMA, the effect size between the two groups was 0.61, which means that the IVR group had a higher effect amount than the conventional group.

The moderate effects were presented separately in the FIM scale of the conventional group compared with the IVR group (d = 0.69), which means that the conventional group has a higher effect amount than the IVR group.

Table 4. Effectiveness differences between groups.

Outcome measures	Conventional group		Immersive virtual reality group			Conventional group vs. Immersive virtual reality group
	Mean	SD	Mean	SD	p-value[c]	Effect size (d)
FMA	0.05	0.05	0.13	0.12	0.084	0.61
BBT	0.04	0.06	0.08	0.14	0.417	0.28
FIM	0.04	0.06	0.03	0.08	0.055	0.69

[c]p for Within-group differences in change of scores for pre- and posttests.

4 Discussion

The purpose of this project is to evaluate the effectiveness of the immersive virtual reality system in upper limb rehabilitation. These results are consistent with those of other studies[8] reported that HTC Vive games for the upper extremities rehabilitation is feasible.

The results of this project can be summarized as follows: (1) A total of eighteen stroke patients were involved in the trial, 15 males and 3 females, with an average age of 57.42 years (SD 12.75), and time from stroke (Mean 8.78 months, SD 5.51). (2) Results of the differences between the two groups pretest–posttest showed that the two groups were significantly differences in FMA (Conventional group, $p = 0.021$; Immersive virtual reality group, $p = 0.014$). It is known from the above results that the immersive virtual reality game device contributes to the improvement of the functions of the upper limbs.

Three limitations of this trial are noteworthy. First, because of the difficulty in finding eligible patients who met all the inclusion criteria of this study in just one hospital, we had a relatively small sample size. Second, the time since stroke onset (3–24 months) may have been too long, and this factor may have influenced the recovery potential. Third, considering the rules of research ethics and the interests of patients, their regular treatment was not discontinued; therefore, we had difficulty determining the intensity of the therapeutic effectiveness in the Conventional group or IVR group. Thus, further research is needed to examine the long-term effects and intensity of using video games in rehabilitation.

The research results of this project can be summarized as follows: 1) A total of 18 stroke cases participated in the trial, 15 males and 3 females, with an average age of 57.42 years (standard deviation 12.75), and an average of 8.78 months (standard deviation 5.51). 2) Analyze the difference between the two groups before and after the measurement, and find that both groups have significant differences in FMA ($p = 0.021$). From this, it can be seen that virtual reality game devices can help improve upper limb motor function.

From the above results, it is known that the immersive virtual reality game device helps to improve the effect of rehabilitation of upper limbs; in the operation of the device, it needs to be improved so that patients can use it easily. The results of this study are expected to provide a reference for innovative designs in the medical and entertainment industries.

Acknowledgment. This study was partly supported by the Ministry of Science and Technology (No. MOST 107-2221-E-040-006), the Fujian Provincial Social Science Planning Project (A study on the usage and design suggestions of upper limb rehabilitation products in Fujian and Taiwan hospitals with grant No. FJ2018B150), and Chung Shan Medical University (CSH-2020-A-039).

References

1. Hatem, S.M., et al.: Rehabilitation of motor function after stroke: a multiple systematic review focused on techniques to stimulate upper extremity recovery. Front. Hum. Neurosci. (2016). https://doi.org/10.3389/fnhum.2016.00442
2. Global Health Estimates 2016: Deaths by Cause, Age, Sex, by Country and by Region, 2000–2016. Geneva, World Health Organization (2018)
3. Ministry of Health and Welfare: Statistics on the cause of death of Taiwan in 2018. https://www.mohw.gov.tw/cp-16-48057-1.html. Accessed 20 Oct 2019
4. McCrea, P.H., Eng, J.J., Hodgson, A.J.: Biomechanics of reachin: clinical implications for individuals with acquired brain injury. Disabil. Rehabil. **24**, 534–541 (2002)
5. Baldominos, A., Saez, Y., Pozo, C.G.: An approach to physical rehabilitation using state-of-the-art virtual reality and motion tracking technologies. Procedia Comput. Sci. **64**, 10–16 (2015)
6. Rose, T., Nam, C.S., Chen, K.B.: Immersion of virtual reality for rehabilitation – review. Appl. Ergonom. **69**, 153–161 (2018)
7. Huygelier, H., Schraepen, B., Ee, R., Abeele, V.V., Gillebert, C.R.: Acceptance of immersive headmounted virtual reality in older adults. Sci. Rep. **9**, 4519 (2019)
8. Gagliardi, C., et al.: Immersive virtual reality to improve walking abilities in cerebral palsy: a pilot study. Ann. Biomed. Eng. **46**(9), 1376–1384 (2018)
9. Lee, S.H., Jung, H.Y., Yun, S.J., Oh, B.M., Seo, H.G.: Upper extremity rehabilitation using fully immersive virtual reality games with a head mount display: a feasibility study. The Journal of Injury, Function and Rehabilitation (2019). https://doi.org/10.1002/pmrj.12206
10. Marsha Bisschop, A.G., et al.: Immersive virtual reality improves movement patterns in patients after ACL reconstruction: implications for enhanced criteria-based return-to-sport rehabilitation. Knee Surg. Sports Traumatol. Arthroscopy **24**(7), 2280–2286 (2016)
11. Jareda, A., Brianb, C., Justinc, D.: Immersive virtual reality in traumatic brain injury rehabilitation: a literature review. Neuro Rehabilit. **42**(4), 441–448 (2018)
12. HTC Vive. https://www.vive.com/us/experiences/. Accessed 21 Nov 2019
13. Sanford, J., Moreland, J., Swanson, L.R., Stratford, P., Gowiand, C.: Reliability of the fugl-meyer assessment for testing motor performance in patients following stroke. Phys. Ther. **73**(7), 447–454 (1993)
14. Wilson, R.: Box and Block Test of Manual Dexterity (2002). http://healthsciences.qmuc.ac.uk/labweb/Equipment/Box%20and%20Block%20test.htm. Accessed 27 Dec 2010
15. Ravaud, J.F., Delcey, M., Yelnik, A.: Construct validity of the functional independent measure (FIM): questioning the unidimensionality of the scale and the "value" of FIM scores. Scand. J. Rehabil. Med. **31**(1), 31–41 (1999)
16. Cohen, J.: Statistical power analysis. Curr. Direct. Psychol. Sci. **1**, 98–101 (1992)
17. Baldominos, A., Saez, Y., Pozo, C.G.: An approach to physical rehabilitation using state-of-the-art virtual reality and motion tracking technologies. Procedia. Comput. Sci. **64**, 10–16 (2015)

mHealth Strategies to Promote Uptake and Adherence to PrEP: A Systematic Review

Morgan LaBelle[1], Carol Strong[2(✉)], and Yuan-Chi Tseng[3,4]

[1] School of Human Kinetics, University of Ottawa,
Ottawa, Canada
[2] Department of Public Health, National Cheng Kung University,
Tainan, Taiwan
carolcj@mail.ncku.edu.tw
[3] Institute of Service Science, National Tsing Hua University, Hsinchu, Taiwan
[4] Department of Industrial Engineering and Engineering Management,
National Tsing Hua University, Hsinchu, Taiwan

Abstract. Pre-exposure Prophylaxis (PrEP) is the use of antiretroviral medications by high-risk HIV-negative individuals to prevent HIV infection and when taken consistently, PrEP can effectively reduce HIV infection risk. The purpose of this literature review was to research existing studies that have used mHealth strategies to prevent HIV and promote uptake and adherence to PrEP. This review is meant to aid in the future development of an app for PrEP adherence and HIV prevention in Taiwan. A systematic journal review of published, peer-reviewed literature was conducted in May and June 2019 to identify and evaluate existing interventions for HIV prevention and PrEP adherence in humans. We identified 22 papers published during or after 2016. Social Cognitive Theory was used by most studies to formulate their intervention strategies. There were several common design features found in studies involving mHealth interventions, such as gamification, notifications, medication log, and education. While the diary feature, including both a sexual activity log and medication log, is critical for preventing HIV, a few more elements should be added to improve the diary feature, including a mood log to show correlations and trends in mental health, and a drug use log to track drug use with PrEP adherence. As more studies that are focusing on the formulation of apps for HIV prevention complete their clinical trial phases, more data will exist to aid researchers in developing the best possible app.

Keywords: mHealth · Behavioral intervention · HIV prevention

1 Introduction

Human immunodeficiency virus (HIV) impedes the immune system from activating and suppresses various innate immunity mechanisms [1]. In Taiwan, an average of 2082 new cases of HIV infection have occurred each year since 2007 [2]. Pre-exposure Prophylaxis (PrEP) is the use of antiretroviral medications by high-risk HIV-negative individuals to prevent HIV infection [3]. Clinical trials estimate that, when taken consistently, PrEP can reduce HIV infection risk by as much as 99% [4]. However,

© Springer Nature Switzerland AG 2020
P.-L. P. Rau (Ed.): HCII 2020, LNCS 12193, pp. 99–113, 2020.
https://doi.org/10.1007/978-3-030-49913-6_9

access to PrEP is often limited by certain barriers such as misinformation, fear of side effects, fear of judgment, stigma, and price [3].

Electronic Health (eHealth) refers to healthcare services provided electronically via the Internet [5]. One branch of eHealth is Mobile Health (mHealth) which is the use of mobile devices such as mobile phones or tablets to provide healthcare services. mHealth services can be very valuable as they provide instantaneous and direct access to health information and care [6]. Numerous mobile device applications (apps) have been formulated as health strategies for many different medical and health issues [7].

The purpose of this literature review was to research existing studies that have used mHealth strategies to prevent HIV and promote uptake and adherence to PrEP. This review is meant to aid in the future development of an app for PrEP adherence and HIV prevention in Taiwan.

2   Methods

A systematic journal review of published, peer-reviewed literature was conducted in May and June 2019 to identify and evaluate existing interventions for HIV prevention and Pre-exposure Prophylaxis (PrEP) adherence in humans. The review focused more directly on papers that evaluate mHealth strategies. Key search terms were used to identify potential articles (see Table 1). The following databases were searched: Web of Science- Core Collection, PubMed, SCOPUS. The search returned 140 articles. In addition, 12 papers were added manually from other sources. The titles of articles, abstracts, and papers were reviewed and duplicates were eliminated which reduced the

Table 1. Search terms for systematic review.

Database	Search algorithm	Filtered by
Web of science - core collection	(ALL = (PrEP OR antiretroviral prophylaxis OR pre-exposure prophylaxis) AND ALL = (HIV negative NOT TB NOT tuberculosis) AND ALL = (intervention OR behavior change OR RCT) AND ALL = (adherence OR self-management OR self-monitoring OR retention))	All fields
PubMed	((Adherence OR self-management OR self-monitoring OR retention) AND (PrEP OR antiretroviral prophylaxis OR pre-exposure prophylaxis) AND (HIV negative) AND (intervention OR RCT OR behaviour change) AND (Humans))	All fields
SCOPUS	((Adherence OR self-management OR self-monitoring OR retention) AND (prep OR antiretroviral AND prophylaxis OR pre-exposure AND prophylaxis) AND (HIV AND negative) AND (intervention OR RCT OR behaviour AND change) AND (humans)) AND (LIMIT-TO (ACCESSTYPE(OA)))	All fields
Web of science - core collection	(ALL = (PrEP OR antiretroviral prophylaxis OR pre-exposure prophylaxis) AND ALL = (HIV) AND ALL = (mobile app OR chatbot OR app OR mHealth) AND ALL = (adherence OR self-management OR self-monitoring OR retention) NOT ALL = (tuberculosis OR TB))	All fields
Pubmed	((PrEP OR antiretroviral prophylaxis OR pre-exposure prophylaxis) AND (HIV) AND (mobile app OR chatbot OR app OR mHealth) AND (adherence OR self-management OR self-monitoring OR retention) NOT (tuberculosis OR TB))	All fields
SCOPUS	((Prep OR antiretroviral AND prophylaxis OR pre-exposure AND prophylaxis) AND (HIV) AND (mobile AND app OR chatbot OR app OR mhealth) AND (adherence OR self-management OR self-monitoring OR retention) AND NOT (tuberculosis OR tb)) AND (LIMIT-TO (ACCESSTYPE(OA)))	All fields

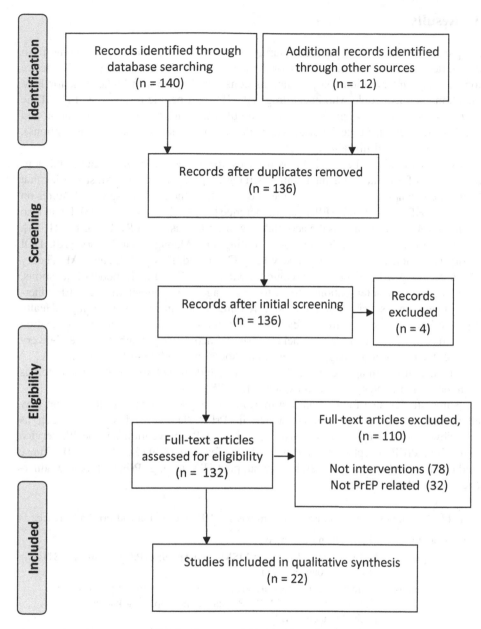

Fig. 1. Process of systematic review.

sample to 22 articles (see Fig. 1). Inclusion criteria included: using an mHealth strategy, Human Immunodeficiency Virus (HIV), an intervention of some type, human studies, and PrEP Exclusion criteria included: treatment of HIV, incomplete papers, and papers focusing on tuberculosis.

3 Results

All papers reviewed were published during or after 2016 and the majority come from the United States of America. Many of the papers from the United States of America focused their interventions on populations considered to be at a higher risk for HIV infection such as people who inject drugs (PWID) and people of color [8–14]. Of the 22 papers reviewed, 14 approached the issue of interventions for HIV prevention and PrEP adherence using technology (formulating apps, social media interventions). Features were listed in Table 2.

Social Cognitive Theory [15] was used by most studies (both mHealth and non-mHealth) to formulate their intervention strategies [10, 14, 16–20]. Most studies that formulated an app as an intervention method examined the effect of specific features on increasing HIV testing and PrEP uptake/adherence [11, 12, 14, 16–19, 21–23]. It was also common for groups to assess the acceptability of an app using an RCT [16, 17, 21, 23]. Other theories used in studies include: Contingency Management Theory [18], DOI theory [10], Self-Determination Theory [13], Grounded Theory [8], and KAP Theory [24] used along with the Fogg behavioural model [17, 18] and IMB model of questions.

Features of all interventions served to encourage HIV prevention and PrEP adherence. There were several common design features found in studies involving mHealth interventions. The most common features were: gamification, notifications, medication log, and education. Other features included: sexual activity log, chatbot service, delivery service, testing location map, interviews, and social network [8–12, 14, 16–26].

The use of health apps combined with wearable devices (Applewatch, fitbit etc.) as an intervention strategy was also explored [27, 28].

Some studies also focused on non-mHealth strategies to evaluate factors that may affect individuals' uptake and adherence in PrEP. These used strategies such as interviews and surveys to assess risk behaviors, HIV prevention and health service utilization, PrEP acceptability, and desired app features [8, 9, 24, 26, 29, 30]. These studies also used counselling sessions to support HIV testing, PrEP refills and adherence counselling [13, 25].

Table 2. Primary features of app interventions for HIV prevention and PrEP adherence.

Ref.	Feature[a]	Description of Feature
10	Sample	- 152 black and Latinx YMSM aged 18-29: E-PrEP group (n = 81), Control group (n = 71)
	Intervention	- Social media intervention with the aim of increasing self-reported intention to use PrEP, PrEP uptake, and impacting knowledge and attitudes about PrEP - Participants were added to a private Facebook or Instagram group with a group leader who posted the E-PrEP information - After completing recruitment, peer leaders launched the intervention by posting materials according to the timeline developed during the training and intervention refinement period
	Education	- Posts about: PrEP awareness, how to talk about sex and PrEP, talking to partners and friends, overcoming barriers to PrEP, how to get on PrEP, finding a doctor to prescribe you PrEP and affording PrEP

(continued)

Table 2. (*continued*)

Ref.	Feature[a]	Description of Feature
	Testing	- List of local doctors and link to PrEP providers in country provided
	Privacy	- Private social media groups and questions can be asked over direct messaging
	Adherence support	- Posts about: overcoming barriers to PrEP, how to get on PrEP, finding a doctor to prescribe you PrEP and affording PrEP
	Social	- Participants can participate and interact with the posts on the private social-media pages
11	Sample	- 25 HIV-uninfected YMSM of color aged 18–25 years
	Intervention	- PrEPTECH is an online program that provides: telemedicine appointments that can help one get medication, home delivered free prescriptions (Truvada), and STI testing kits
	Testing	- An STI kit from Quest Diagnostics was home-delivered by mail to participants at baseline and 90 days
	Privacy	- An infectious disease physician conducted telehealth visits through telephone at baseline, 30, 90, and 180 days through telephone rather than in a clinic to review laboratory results and gather information on medical history, sexual behaviors, and PrEP adherence - During telehealth appointments, counseling was provided for incident STIs, as well as treatment referral and verification
	Adherence support	- Participants informed of local, free, or low-cost PrEP source using pleaseprepme.org and community organization referrals - Telemedicine appointments, free supply of Truvada home-delivered, reminders for check-ups, and encouragements
12	Sample	- 16 YMSM of color ages 20–25 years
	Intervention	- Developed and refined mock-ups for a mHealth app (participants discussed the content and features of the mock-ups) - Identified barriers and facilitators to the use of mHealth technology for HIV prevention for high-risk MSM, developed 'use cases' and identified relevant functional content and features for inclusion in a design document to guide future app development
	Education	- Ask a doctor forum: chat with a provider or HIV testing counselor - Myths and facts, nutrition & fitness information
	Testing	- Resources for: HIV/AIDS medical care locations, general services (e.g. LGBTQ centers), substance use, law/advocacy, chat with HIV testing counselor, testing information
	Privacy	- Chosen profile picture, password, and alerts can be changed in settings
	Adherence support	- My medication information, lab reports, my providers contact information, health appointments
	Social	- Interactive blogs
	Diary	- Partner logs
14	Sample	- 20 MSM ages 18–35 years; 85% identified as African American
	Intervention	- A smart pill bottle cap (that measures adherence) integrated with an app gaming intervention (ViralCombat) to promote PrEP adherence

(*continued*)

Table 2. (*continued*)

Ref.	Feature[a]	Description of Feature
	Education	- The game follows HIV prevention and PrEP adherence themes and wrong answers are corrected and explained during gameplay
	Privacy	- The terms "HIV" & "PrEP" are never part of an audio feature, so stigmatizing information cannot be overhead by another person
	Gamification	- As players successfully battle HIV, engage with providers, and take medication, they move to new, distinct levels. Messages from the doctors, nurses and friends encourage and provide clues during difficult twists and turns in the battle - Answering quiz questions from clinician avatars allows each player to earn strength and points; wrong answers are corrected and explained. Players find medication, strength, and points by acting on positive suggestions. During each mission, the player's score (pill count and health) is shown
	Adherence support	- If players were less than 90% adherent during the week, phrases such as "Missing you in Combat" and "Get back in the game" are texted to their phones - Congratulatory short message service (SMS) text messages such as "Great job in battle" and "You are fighting off virus well" are sent for greater than 90% adherence
16	Sample	- Theater testing: 30 YMSM; Beta testing: 15 YMSM; Pilot RCT: 60 YMSM (ages 15–24)
	Intervention	- MyChoices app designed to increase HIV testing and PrEP uptake
	Education	- Quizzes, infographics, and GIFs that focus on the promotion of HIV prevention and regular HIV testing - Links to videos related to·PrEP, reasons for routine HIV testing, and the importance of engaging in care if one tests positive - Provides answers to questions about HIV transmission behaviors and testing history
	Testing	- Information on and links to testing sites and local PrEP clinics (e.g., contact number, address, and testing hours) as determined using GPS technology, allowing men to locate clinics that are nearby their current location (provides map) - Users can order home testing kits for HIV and STIs - Users can create an individually tailored HIV testing plan by having them compare and choose different options
	Privacy	- OraQuick HIV test can be ordered online and different types of condoms and lubricant that can be shipped to a location of choice
	Gamification	- Quizzes on information provided
	Adherence support	- "My Test Plan" (planning of when user will go for regular HIV testing) - "Help me Choose" (a quiz to help recommend a preferred setting/option for HIV testing)
17	Sample	- RCT testing: up to 240 HIV-uninfected MSM or MSTW (currently recruiting); ages 16–24; assigned male sex at birth; currently on or planning to take PrEP and have an active PrEP prescription

(*continued*)

Table 2. (*continued*)

Ref.	Feature[a]	Description of Feature
	Intervention	- P3 or P3 + app on a smartphone device (P3 + also includes two–way text messaging sessions with trained adherence counselors) - P3 is an interactive mobile phone app for HIV-uninfected YMSM to improve PrEP adherence and retention in preventive care
	Education	- Information provided about STIs and PrEP (symptoms, how to screen, how to treat, preventive measures, etc.) through articles and a multimedia library. Quizzes, daily quests (routine tasks) and interactive exercises help users build and check knowledge and skills - Knowledge Center Multimedia library: Includes PrEP -related information and information about safer sex, relationships, and general health and wellness. Users are prompted with a reflection question after each article to apply the material to their lives. A visual shows progress toward completing each section
	Privacy	- Avatars, pseudonyms, confidential personal identification number to open the app, and app time-out after 5 min of inactivity - Discreet reminders that can be personalized
	Gamification	- Train avatars through the completion of tasks, including whether to take daily or read articles, etc. Participants level up and earn in-game currency based on app use. Participants redeem currency to unlock narratives and other app features - Daily actionable routine tasks help users set goals and build knowledge and skills - "Choose-your own adventure" narratives feature young men who have sex with men or young transwomen who have sex with men navigating common situations that impact PrEP care and adherence (e.g., substance use, stigma). Playing through story paths allows users to face hard choices that impact health and practice problem solving
	Adherence support	- Personalized reminders (PrEP refill, medication adherence) and habit building solutions (ex: take when I brush my teeth) to promote PrEP adherence. The app uses information provided during the initial set up (ex: time of day PrEP is taken) to suggest adherence strategies. Tailored feedback on new strategies is provided when adherence falters - Automated "canned" and tailored messages can be delivered to provide support and encouragement - Next Step Counseling conducted in-app through text messaging. Key features include reviewing participant adherence experiences, exploring adherence facilitators and barriers, identifying adherence needs and strategies to meet needs, and developing an adherence action plan
	Social	- Ability to share medication experience and strategy with others and count how many people think this strategy is useful and how many people think this strategy is not useful - Can read and comment on articles.
18	Sample	- 10 YMSM, ages 18–30 - Mostly white (n = 7); mostly earning at least an undergraduate degree (n = 7)

(*continued*)

Table 2. (*continued*)

Ref.	Feature[a]	Description of Feature
	Intervention	- Adaptation of mSMART smartphone app where participants logged PrEP dosage and learned about PrEP adherence - Participants received feedback that they earned US \$2 every time they logged a dose within a 2-h window of their daily dosing. Feedback about money earned upon taking their daily dose was provided immediately by mSMART and could be seen on the app
	Education	- Behavioral skill instruction on how to improve adherence and how to cope with short-term side effects that may deter adherence - SMART Desk: An interactive space where mSMART prompted brief daily surveys (i.e., 1–4 questions per day pertaining to knowledge or concerns about PrEP, knowledge about HIV, and general medication use concerns or problems) - Education about different aspects of PrEP (ex: explaining why daily adherence is important, describing a typical medical visit schedule once on PrEP, and addressing concerns regarding possible long-term health effects of PrEP), financial aspects related to being on PrEP, information about communicating with health care workers about PrEP and sexual behavior, and eliciting support from family and friends to support PrEP adherence
	Adherence support	- Contingent reinforcement when doses were logged daily and daily medication reminders - Notifications informing participants of missing a PrEP dose provided through the SMART Desk - Daily self-assessments of general medication adherence difficulties and visual feedback about logging doses each day - Skill instruction on how to improve adherence (ex: how to remember to take a daily dose if forgetfulness is a barrier to adherence) and how to cope with short-term side effects that may deter daily adherence - Participants were able to set up their preferred time to receive medication reminders. Participants could change this setting at any time and therefore could modify it on days they anticipated taking PrEP at a different time
	Diary	- Feedback about overall PrEP adherence in the form of percentage of days they logged a dose
19	Sample	- 121 HIV-negative MSM with a median age of 28 who use Android smartphones; most (85.9%, 104/121) were gay-identified - Nearly half (48.8%, 59/121) were nonwhite
	Intervention	- A mobile phone app for HIV prevention (healthMindr) that included self-assessment tools; prevention recommendations; commodity (condoms, HIV self-tests, lubricant) ordering; reminders to MSM for basic HIV prevention services, HIV testing, condom use, screening for PrEP and nPEP eligibility; and prevention and treatment provider locators - Free at-home HIV test kits, a variety condom styles, and silicone and water-based personal lubricants were offered

(*continued*)

Table 2. (*continued*)

Ref.	Feature[a]	Description of Feature
	Education	- Tailored, HIV-related prevention suggestions for users to consider based on monthly risk assessment quiz responses - Frequently asked questions related to HIV were included for users to reference - Reminders to MSM for basic HIV prevention services, HIV testing, condom use, screening for PrEP and nPEP
	Testing	- "Find My Frequency": Suggests HIV testing frequency of every 3 or 6 months based on five questions, including number of partners, partners' HIV status, bacterial STI infections in the last 12 months, and injection drug, meth, or poppers use - Help Me Choose: Allows users to prioritize the most important aspects of an HIV testing experience based on location type, sample collection method, cost, HIV counseling available, wait time for results, and window period of test. Users can filter tests based on their preferences or complete a quiz for recommendations based on their stated preferences - My Test Plan: users can plan an HIV test by date, time, and location. Automated reminders can be set based on a chosen frequency - Free at-home HIV test kits (OraQuick and Home Access) - Provides a map and details about testing locations, including address, phone number, type of organization, web address, days/hours of operation, service eligibility requirements (if any), fee information, languages available, and clinical services offered (HIV testing, HIV treatment, PrEP, nPEP, vaccinations, and so on). GPS was enabled to show user's location relative to testing locations. Locations were able to be filtered by the above characteristics to display locations with select characteristics
	Privacy	- HIV test kits, a variety condom styles, and silicone and water-based personal lubricants can be delivered to home - Preferences can be set for how users receive testing and assessment reminders as pop-up notification, email, or neither; users can choose the text of the reminder from a list of preset phrases or write their own message
	Adherence support	- Screening for PrEP and nPEP eligibility
	Diary	- After being tested, users can record their HIV/STI test results within the app to keep a record of testing history
20	Sample	- 60 preadolescents aged 11–14 years; 30 used for intervention - 1 guardian for each child in the intervention group (n = 30), these were mostly female (n = 25)
	Intervention	- Participants were provided with smartphones on which the Tumaini game was loaded so that they could play it 1 h a day - Tumaini is a game designed to promote learning related to gender, consent, goal setting, planning delaying sex, condom use, puberty, sexual health and HIV stigma. Tumaini is also designed to build risk-avoidance and risk-reduction skills related self-efficacy; challenging and to promote dialogue with adult mentors

(*continued*)

Table 2. (*continued*)

Ref.	Feature[a]	Description of Feature
	Education	- In-game learning
	Gamification	- A choose-your-own-adventure game, where players role-play 6 diverse characters, making choices for them that determine the course of their lives with themes like peer pressure, puberty, violence, and decisions about smoking, alcohol, drugs, and sex - A set of mini games designed to reinforce knowledge and skills relating to puberty; HIV and other sexually transmitted infections (STIs); pregnancy and avoiding pregnancy; identifying, avoiding, and responding to risk situations; and resisting peer pressure - My Story, in which players create an avatar of themselves, set personal goals, and relate the game narrative knowledge and skills (ex: setting goals and how they will achieve them) to their own lives. The topics coordinate with the main role-playing narrative - The player is rewarded with prizes (furniture and other items for the player's virtual home) upon successful completion of game components - Once the player finishes the last chapter and observes the long-term outcomes for the characters, they can replay and collect the remaining prizes by making different choices and observing different outcomes. This rewards system thus encourages players to explore the game and experience the consequences of both health-protective and harmful choices
21	Sample	- 374 MSM and TSM; 18 + (mean age was 40.6)
	Intervention	- AMPrEP app for adherence support for daily PrEP users - Participants were requested to report daily PrEP intake and sexual behavior in the app during study by answering 2–8 daily questions: (1) "Did you take the pill today?", to be answered by "yes" or "no"; and: (2) "Did you have anal sex today?", to be answered by "yes" or "no"; and if "yes": (3) "With an unknown partner?"; (4) "With a known partner?"; and (5) "With a steady partner?", each to be answered by "yes" or "no." If "yes" to questions 3, 4 or 5, the number of partners and condom use was asked - Self-administered computer-assisted questionnaire about sexual risk behavior and adherence every 3 months containing questions on the same topics as the app but formulated differently
	Privacy	- Data were saved at a protected server using a unique study identifier
	Adherence support	- Visualization of self-reported pill use and sexual activity
	Diary	- Daily report PrEP intake and sexual behavior in the app during study participation

(*continued*)

Table 2. (*continued*)

Ref.	Feature[a]	Description of Feature
22	Sample	- Participants on PrEP at the San Francisco (n = 48) and Chicago (n = 8) iPrEx OLE sites - 25% (n = 14) were ≥ 30 y.o.a.; Median age was 49 years (range, 21–66) - Most San Francisco site participants were white (68%), while 100% of the Chicago site participants were men of color - Most (88%) had completed some college
	Intervention	- Weekly bidirectional text or e-mail support messages to encourage PrEP adherence - Participants were registered on the iText platform which allowed them to the messages during the days and times they requested - The platform offered three outgoing message options to choose from: How are you doing?, Are you okay?, or How is PrEP going? - Participants were given the option to choose the responses they could text or e-mail back (ex: Ok or not Ok, Fine or not fine)
	Privacy	- The iText platform stored all responses securely, which were accessible only to study staff
	Adherence support	- SMS and e-mail check-in messages sent weekly - For participants that responded "not Ok," or those that did not respond to the weekly message, even after a reminder message was sent within a 48-h period, study staff would contact them by phone
23	Sample	- 60 HIV-uninfected YMSM at risk for HIV acquisition
	Intervention	- Mobile app designed to increase HIV/STI testing and support PrEP uptake among YMSM
	Education	- PrEP resources: PrEP videos, bidirectional chat function with study staff, assistance with linkage to care - Sex Pro: a personalized risk score provided to promote accurate risk perception displayed on a *speedometer* (based on data from several large MSM cohort studies). Information will be provided on aspects of behaviors (ex: number of anal sex partners, condom use) that contributed to their score
	Testing	- Quarterly HIV/STI testing reminders with 2 options for testing: (1) Order a home HIV/STI testing kit to be mailed to a location of their choosing free of charge (2) A geo-located map of the closest HIV/STI testing sites - Information about next steps for linkage to care is included in the testing section of the app, including a phone number for an on-call clinician available 24 h a day - Any participant who enters a positive HIV test result into the app will be contacted by the study team and provided supportive counseling and referral to treatment services

(*continued*)

Table 2. (*continued*)

Ref.	Feature[a]	Description of Feature
	Privacy	- Reminder notifications are nonspecific, but inside the app, the participant is linked to a customizable reminder - Must create log-in credentials and set up a password to access the password-protected app - All data collected by the app are encrypted and stored on a secure web-based cloud environment
	Gamification	- Sex Pro speedometer and earn badges for completing in-app activities (ex: sexual diary entries and ordering a testing kit)
	Adherence support	- Reminders personalized by the user for day, time, and message content - Chat function in which participants can contact LYNX staff for support and assistance with linkage to care.
	Diary	- Electronic diary to track sexual behavior

MSM = Men who have sex with men; MSTW = Men who have sex with Transgender Women; YMSM = Young men who have sex with men; TSM = Transgender individuals who have sex with men; YTWSM = Young transgender individuals who have sex with men; HIV = Human Immunodeficiency Virus; AIDS = acquired immune deficiency syndrome; PrEP = preexposure prophylaxis; nPEP = nonoccupational postexposure prophylaxis; STI = Sexually Transmitted Infection

[a]Features in Table 2 include "Education", "Testing", "Privacy", "Gamification", "Adherence Support", "Social", and "Sex/Medication Log". If a feature was not a part of the app, it was not included in the table.

4   Discussion

An interesting feature found in this review was the incorporation of social network into PrEP interventions [10, 12, 17]. The interaction between those using a prevention service may aid in "humanizing" the experience of taking and adhering to PrEP. A correlate of PrEP adherence found was knowledge of male partner taking PrEP [13]; knowledge of others or a community taking PrEP may function in a similar way.

A key feature found in this review was the diary feature. This element includes both a sexual activity log and medication log. Right now, apps like LYNX allow users to create a log all sexual activity and partners [23]. Medication logging is also an important features that allows users to understand when medication must be taken and their level of risk for HIV [21, 23]. While these features are both critical elements of a diary for preventing HIV, it was suggested that a few more elements should be added to improve the diary feature. These include: a mood log to show correlations and trends in mental health, and a drug use log to track drug use with PrEP adherence.

Other features found in this review found to be key features include: education, gamification, notifications, privacy, and improving access to resources. The education feature would help users to understand HIV prevention and educate themselves on STIs and PrEP use. This information could potentially be provided using studies, games, quizzes, videos, and articles. A proposed addition to this feature would be information on how to get the price of PrEP covered (by organisations, government funding, etc.).

Another key element of education is a Chatbot service. Users could potentially use this feature to answer any questions they have about PrEP quickly and accurately and to help get access to health services.

The gamification feature would allow users to play games while learning about HIV, STIs, adhering to PrEP, and heath strategies. This feature could also allow users to win real-life incentives for playing games and using the app such as: gift cards, discount codes, condoms, VIP upgrades on HORNET, etc.

Notifications are also a key feature found in this review. This element promotes adherence to PrEP in users by reminding medication PrEP use and promotes health in users by reminding HIV testing, condom use, doctor appointments, etc. A key and related feature is that of privacy. Using encoded or encrypted notifications, users can retain privacy (in the case of their phone being seen or used by another person). Having a log in for the app would also be useful for promoting the privacy of users. In terms of the social interaction feature mentioned above, privacy could mean users going by pseudonyms or avatars in the app.

An important feature found was access to resources. A service to deliver HIV testing kits, condoms, and medicine to home promotes privacy and reduces fear of judgement by individuals using the service. Additionally, providing information about local health service providers can link users with the important resource of health care and testing as well as linking users to locations where they can meet with a health care professional to inquire about taking PrEP.

The findings of this review can be useful for the formulation of an app for HIV prevention in Taiwan. Currently, results on the practicality of app features in HIV prevention are very limited. As more studies that are focusing on the formulation of apps for HIV prevention complete their RCT phases, more data will exist to aid researchers in developing the best possible app for the Taiwanese people [16, 17].

5 Conclusion

The purpose of this literature review was to aid in the future development of an mHealth application for PrEP adherence and HIV prevention in Taiwan. Many potential features were identified from numerous studies testing HIV prevention apps in relation to PrEP. This information will be used alongside results from ongoing studies to help formulate features for an HIV prevention app in Taiwan by the team working on that project. Future researchers may also focus on the efficacy of these HIV prevention apps once their RCT trials have been completed.

References

1. Root-Bernstein, R.: Human immunodeficiency virus proteins mimic human T cell receptors inducing cross-reactive antibodies. Int. J. Mol. Sci. **18**, 2091 (2017)
2. https://www.cdc.gov.tw/En/Category/MPage/kt6yIoEGURtMQubQ3nQ7pA

3. Holloway, I.W., et al.: Facilitators and barriers to pre-exposure prophylaxis willingness among young men who have sex with men who use geosocial networking applications in California. AIDS Patient Care STDs **31**, 517–527 (2017)
4. Anderson, P.L., et al.: Emtricitabine-tenofovir concentrations and pre-exposure prophylaxis efficacy in men who have sex with men. Sci. Trans. Med. **4**, 151ra125 (2012)
5. Eysenbach, G.: What is e-health? J. Med. Internet Res. **3**(2), e20 (2001). https://doi.org/10.2196/jmir.3.2.e20. https://www.jmir.org/2001/2/e20. PMID: 11720962,PMCID: PMC1761894
6. Marcolino, M.S., Oliveira, J.A.Q., D'Agostino, M., Ribeiro, A.L., Alkmim, M.B.M., Novillo-Ortiz, D.: The impact of mHealth interventions: systematic review of systematic reviews. JMIR mHealth uHealth **6**(1), e23 (2018)
7. Payne, H.E., Lister, C., West, J.H., Bernhardt, J.M.: Behavioral functionality of mobile apps in health interventions: a systematic review of the literature. JMIR mHealth uHealth **3**(1), e20 (2015)
8. Arnold, T., et al.: Social, structural, behavioral and clinical factors influencing retention in Pre-Exposure Prophylaxis (PrEP) care in Mississippi. PloS one **12**(2), e0172354 (2017). https://doi.org/10.1371/journal.pone.0172354
9. Biello, K., et al.: Perspectives on HIV pre-exposure prophylaxis (PrEP) utilization and related intervention needs among people who inject drugs. Harm Reduct. J. **15**, 55 (2018)
10. Patel, V.V., et al.: Empowering with PrEP (E-PrEP), a peer-led social media–based intervention to facilitate HIV preexposure prophylaxis adoption among young Black and Latinx gay and bisexual men: protocol for a cluster randomized controlled trial. JMIR Res. Protoc. **7**(8), e11375 (2018)
11. Refugio, O.N., Kimble, M.M., Silva, C.L., Lykens, J.E., Bannister, C., Klausner, J.D.: Brief report: PrEPTECH a Telehealth-based initiation program for HIV pre-exposure prophylaxis in young men of color who have sex with men. A pilot study of feasibility. Jaids J. Acquir. Immune Defic. Syndr. **80**, 40–45 (2019)
12. Schnall, R., et al.: A user-centered model for designing consumer mobile health (mHealth) applications (apps). J. Biomed. Inf. **60**, 243–251 (2016)
13. Wheeler, D.P., et al.: Pre-exposure prophylaxis initiation and adherence among Black men who have sex with men (MSM) in three US cities: results from the HPTN 073 study. J. Int. AIDS Soc. **22**(2), e25223 (2019)
14. Whiteley, L., Mena, L., Craker, L.K., Healy, M.G., Brown, L.K.: Creating a theoretically grounded gaming app to increase adherence to pre-exposure prophylaxis: lessons from the development of the viral combat mobile phone game. JMIR Serious Games **7**(1), e11861 (2019)
15. Bandura, A.: Social cognitive theory: an agentic perspective. Annu. Rev. Psychol. **52**, 1–26 (2001)
16. Biello, K.B., Marrow, E., Mimiaga, M.J., Sullivan, P., Hightow-Weidman, L., Mayer, K.H:. A mobile-based app (MyChoices) to increase uptake of HIV testing and pre-exposure prophylaxis by young men who have sex with men: protocol for a pilot randomized controlled trial. JMIR Res. Protoc. **8**(1), e10694 (2019)
17. LeGrand, S., et al.: Testing the efficacy of a social networking gamification app to improve pre-exposure prophylaxis adherence (P3: prepared, protected, emPowered): protocol for a randomized controlled trial. JMIR Res. Protoc. **7**(12), e10448 (2018)
18. Mitchell, J.T., et al.: Smartphone-based contingency management intervention to improve pre-exposure prophylaxis adherence: pilot trial. JMIR mHealth uHealth **6**(9), e10456 (2018)
19. Sullivan, P.S., et al.: Usability and acceptability of a mobile comprehensive HIV prevention app for men who have sex with men: a pilot study. JMIR mHealth uHealth **5**(3), e26 (2017)

20. Winskell, K., et al.: A smartphone game-based intervention (Tumaini) to prevent HIV among young Africans: pilot randomized controlled trial. JMIR mHealth uHealth **6**(8), e10482 (2018)
21. Finkenflugel, R.N.N., et al.: A mobile application to collect daily data on preexposure prophylaxis adherence and sexual behavior among men who have sex with men: use over time and comparability with conventional data collection. Sex. Transm. Dis. **46**, 400–406 (2019)
22. Fuchs, J.D., et al.: A mobile health strategy to support adherence to antiretroviral preexposure prophylaxis. AIDS Patient Care and STDs **32**, 104–111 (2018)
23. Liu, A., et al.: Developing a mobile app (LYNX) to support linkage to HIV/sexually transmitted infection testing and pre-exposure prophylaxis for young men who have sex with men: protocol for a randomized controlled trial. JMIR Res. Protoc. **8**(1), e10659 (2019)
24. Qu, D., Zhong, X., Lai, M., Dai, J., Liang, H., Huang, A.: Influencing factors of pre-exposure prophylaxis self-efficacy among men who have sex with men. Am. J. Men's Health **13**(2), 1557988319847088 (2019)
25. Hightow-Weidman, Lisa B., Kathryn Muessig, Eli Rosenberg, Travis Sanchez, Sara LeGrand, Laura Gravens, and Patrick S. Sullivan. `University of North Carolina/Emory Center for Innovative Technology (iTech) for addressing the HIV epidemic among adolescents and young adults in the United States: protocol and rationale for center development.' JMIR research protocols 7, no. 8 (2018): e10365
26. McMahan, V.M., et al.: Development of a targeted educational intervention to increase pre-exposure prophylaxis uptake among cisgender men and transgender individuals who have sex with men and use methamphetamine in Seattle (WA, USA). Sex. Health **16**, 139–147 (2019)
27. Carreiro, S., Chai, P.R., Carey, J., Lai, J., Smelson, D., Boyer, E.W.: mHealth for the detection and intervention in adolescent and young adult substance use disorder. Curr. Addict. Rep. **5**, 110–119 (2018)
28. Ferreri, F., Bourla, A., Mouchabac, S., Karila, L.: e-Addictology: an overview of new technologies for assessing and intervening in addictive behaviors. Front. Psychiatry **9**, 51 (2018)
29. Hightow-Weidman, L.B., et al.: University of North Carolina/Emory Center for Innovative Technology (iTech) for addressing the HIV epidemic among adolescents and young adults in the United States: protocol and rationale for center development. JMIR Res. Protoc. **7**(8), e10365 (2018)
30. Zhang, A., Reynolds, N.R., Farley, J.E., Wang, X., Tan, S., Yan, J.: Preferences for an HIV prevention mobile phone app: a qualitative study among men who have sex with men in China. BMC Public Health **19**, 297 (2019)

Research on Social Service Education System from the Perspective of Chinese Welfare Culture

Jinze Li[1,2]($\boxtimes$), Mingming Zong[1]($\boxtimes$), and Yu Wang[1]($\boxtimes$)

[1] Zhuhai College, Beijing Institute of Technology,
Beijing, People's Republic of China
564960767@qq.com, zmm77800@126.com, 252656279@qq.com
[2] Studying School for Doctor's Degree, Bangkok Thonburi University,
Bangkok, Thailand

Abstract. At present, Internet technology is changing with each passing day, the globalization process is booming, and the rapid development of technology products is inseparable from the meaning given to society by design itself. Convenient life and high-quality service experience make people's lives happy, which have given new meaning to "well-being". Welfare services are about social stability and people's happiness. Social needs and industrial ecology determine the direction of design. From the perspective of social design itself, this is a systematic progress, which determines the new thinking paradigm of innovation, service, design, and education. It is a new direction of designing and educating people to cut into the "social service" from the culture of well-being. Taking the vision of Chinese well-being culture and people's livelihood service as the research purpose, we will deeply study the principles and methods of educating people about ecological design education. It is the focus of this article to cultivate design talents who are in line with society and take on the future.

Keywords: Welfare culture · Social services · Design education system

1 Chinese Well-Being Culture and Society

The continuous development of society is always closely linked with the history and culture of different periods. The high-quality culturally rich life experience and living standards are related to the happiness of the people. In this long river of time, the rich history and culture of different periods cannot be separated from culture The inheritance of education is inseparable from the social responsibility and historical significance given to "people" by education. Welfare refers to happiness, benefits, and well-being. It also refers to a happy and peaceful living environment, a stable and secure social environment, and a relaxed and open political environment. Social well-being is a collective name for a very complex social component element, which covers many fields, involving economic, political, cultural and other elements. Welfare culture emphasizes the construction of social well-being culture. It concerns the individuals in the social unit, and takes "people" as the starting point, cares for the physical and mental health of "people", and builds a harmonious society as the cornerstone to link

© Springer Nature Switzerland AG 2020
P.-L. P. Rau (Ed.): HCII 2020, LNCS 12193, pp. 114–125, 2020.
https://doi.org/10.1007/978-3-030-49913-6_10

social needs, social policies, and social welfare. Social education, social medical care, and related infrastructure construction, and other related directions, promote the harmonious and stable development of society as the fundamental purpose.

2 Establishment of Welfare Service System

2.1 Prospects for Welfare Culture Services

The country is stable, the people are happy, the elderly are dependent, elderly people can enjoy basic security, and social harmony is the ideal living environment and living conditions for the citizens of the country in the new period. Therefore, striving to create a stable living environment for the long-term happiness of the people requires the country and society. Joint efforts of all parties. In recent years, more and more related researches on the theme of "welfare culture" have marked that more and more researchers have begun to pay attention to people's livelihood, society and the basic needs of citizens. This requires a full understanding of the needs of citizens and groups. Organically integrate the well-being system with the needs of groups, formulate well-being service models, determine guarantee mechanisms, encourage active participation from all walks of life, and mobilize regional participation (see Table 1).

Table 1. Basic model of social welfare needs (drawed by the author)

Welfare \mode	Country	Society	Family/group	Personal
Types	People happiness	Social care	Group welfare	Obtain
Object	National citizen	Society as a whole	Group area	Individual
demand	Well-being system	Group	Organizational needs	Individual needs
Standard	mode	Guarantee	participate	Vitality

2.2 Social Service System

The service object of social services is the "people" involved in social construction. The society itself is a unified whole composed of multiple social individuals. Therefore, social services must first meet the needs of people. Human needs include multiple dimensions. In Maslow's hierarchy of needs theory, it was mentioned that "people's needs from low to high are divided into physiological needs, safety needs, social needs, respect needs, and self-realization needs." "People" in the process of social life During a period (age, stage), there will be multiple choices and choices when dealing with problems, and different service needs or education needs will also arise. At the same time, the root of these needs comes from various aspects, such as life, career, etc. Based on this, the needs of "people" at different ages are inherently diverse and dynamic. These needs are fulfilled after the service, which makes the work of the service itself rich and impressive.

2.3   Welfare Culture Service Design System

In the continuous development of the country, with the continuous emergence of social needs, we adjust and control domestic demand to stimulate the development of society, give play to its own initiative, and fully mobilize different social groups and social organizations, which covers Different social strata have achieved social stability and guaranteed the positive production and life of citizens (see Fig. 2). In this environment, social needs, social well-being, social policies, social environment and social behavior need to be organically unified. In the welfare culture system, the needs of social individuals form a certain scale, and can be met and realized in a unified cultural background. Demand itself represents the needs of society. These needs protect the interests of the people, are positive needs, and enable individual expectations to be realized (see Fig. 1).

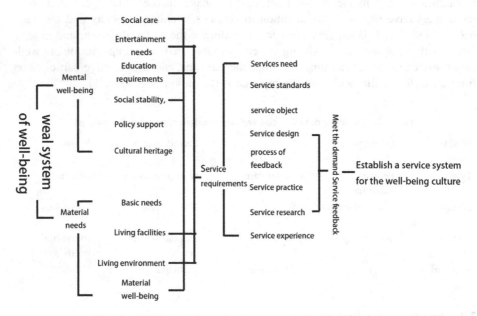

Fig. 1. Welfare service cultural system (author self-drawn)

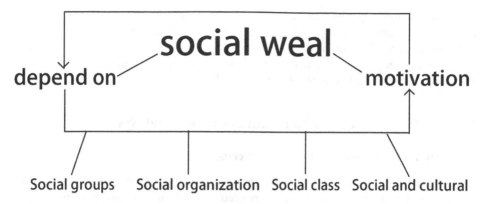

Fig. 2. The framework of welfare culture needs (drawn by the author)

3   Establishment of Social Service System

To improve the social service system, we need to formulate relevant systems and service systems for social services based on social needs (see Table 2). In particular, we need to pay attention to the implementation of services and needs of disadvantaged groups, including early childhood education and elderly education. They need a complete set of service demand models and a guarantee system. Take "education" as an example, all stages of a person's life are constantly learning, there are learning from different institutions and schools, there is learning from individual needs, and there is learning about new things, new technology, In these learning processes, there are both active and passive education, but it is undeniable that based on the educational content and educational needs of education itself, it runs through one's life.

Table 2. Social service system (self-drawn by the author)

Social services target	Mechanism	Organization	Community	Individual
Service Subject	Government agency	Social organization	Society's strength	Volunteer service
Service object	Vulnerable Groups	Elderly children	Empty nest seniors	left behind children
Service Content	Community care	Life medical	Legal service	Mental Health
Service method	Home services	Community service	Institutional Services	Volunteer service

A sound social service system requires a sound social system to maintain it. A sound social system requires a complete social security system, and a complete social security system needs to further stimulate internal demand to maintain positive initiative and ensure protection in stages Evaluation to ensure continued stability and further positive development. In the social education service system, education is the most important link. It itself gives society a step into civilization, a rule of law, and a step into harmony. In addition to compulsory education in the education service system, more attention needs to be paid to the education of people with mental retardation and vulnerable groups, and they also need social care.

4 Establishment of a Social Education Demand System

4.1 Multi-level Needs Based on Basic Needs

The basic education needs in social education refer to the basic education needs of individuals and groups that are socially oriented and oriented towards employment. It contains the needs and needs of individuals or groups in order to pursue self-worth and the realization of ambitious goals. Surviving in the social environment faces multi-dimensional and multi-dimensional needs, which cover spiritual, material and other levels. These needs come from the individual's hobbies and social needs, including active acceptance and passive acceptance. The ultimate goal is to complete the realization of personal value. These multi-level needs and needs serve as the internal motivation for the realization of personal value [7].

The social environment includes the birth, growth, life, work, and elderly environment of social individuals. When the basic needs of social individuals are met and realized, individuals will face a new period of stepping into society and engaging in related work. Individuals in society are restricted by relevant aspects of the social environment, social needs, and natural resources and the opinions of surrounding groups before choosing a direction or facing a decision.

4.2 Universal Compulsory Education and Professional Vocational Training

"Universal" is a paraphrase of the Latin oecumenicus. The word originally originated from the Greek. In addition to the meaning of "universal", it also contains the meaning of "root". Universal education refers to the general public, the most basic the most universal education. Compulsory education is a uniform education for all school-age children. Adolescents must receive it. China currently implements nine-year compulsory education, and some coastal cities implement 12-year compulsory education. After compulsory education, students pass the national unified examination and pass grades to choose themselves. In the direction of life, professional vocational training refers to professional vocational and technical training, which is mainly oriented to social needs, and further cultivates technical talents with social needs, focusing on practical and operational capabilities.

4.3 Social Education Extension Model for Urban and Rural Elderly

With the continuous acceleration of the global aging process, a series of problems such as the reduction of labor force and the reduction of urban area construction rate and infrastructure utilization rate have been seeking better ways to cope with it. The actual needs of people are presented to us. Advances in science and technology have changed our production and life. The application of artificial intelligence and AI technology has made our lives more convenient and increased production efficiency. However, elderly people often feel at a loss when facing new science and new technologies. Although some technologies are simple to operate, the lack of understanding of the technology and improper operation methods have led to many new technologies and technologies in most elderly users There is no way to better apply and run [2, 3]. Elderly people in most cities and towns in China still have high vitality, such as traveling outdoors or dancing in city squares. Some seniors choose to enter a senior university for continuous learning as a hobby. Another part of the elderly is gradually derailed from society, which is mainly reflected in the use and understanding of new technology. The application and operation of some technologies seem simple, but they need to understand the application direction and experience behind the technology. There is a certain degree of obstacles in understanding physiological conditions in this respect. Therefore, how to help the elderly adapt to new technology and new technology more quickly requires professional technical talents. Through further analysis and statistics, the elderly in social education are Education is an extension of the educational model [4].

4.4   Left-Behind and Migrant Children Adapt to Education Model

Left-behind and migrant children refer to school-age children who meet the educational requirements led by non-resident migrants between urban and rural areas. Some of these children usually follow their parents to another city. Another part of the children chose to stay home and be taken care of by grandparents. In the first part, children choose local schools for study. They need to adapt to the new education environment. Because the new location is relatively unfamiliar to the children, the children need to further strengthen their willpower, task awareness and personal management. In terms of education, this class of children can use class services and behaviors as carriers to carry out social development and service awareness-based communicative and experiential education while educating students, in order to cultivate students 'sense of gratitude to the school and avoid students' The resistance of the environment requires continuous attention to children's social communication ability, social emotions, and social learning, and refines these three major directions, so as to further perceive and experience in interpersonal communication in a collective environment. So that children can adapt to the new teaching environment and class collective as soon as possible. For the other children who choose to stay behind, although the educational environment has not changed, they have not seen parents need more spiritual care for a long time. Therefore, teachers need to plan to inspire the class, people, things, resources, and design with real "caring" as a link to inspire The multiple interactions of children, classmates, teachers, and schools form an organic life education system.

5 Social and Welfare Education

5.1 Infant Enlightenment

Toddler refers to a 1-year-old child who has gone through infancy, and generally refers to the period of 1–6 years. Parents of children during this period have gradually started to consciously train them in basic life skills and behaviors, such as: Wearing clothes and eating fruits such as melon peels know how to cut skins. Children in this period have just opened up their psychology and intelligence. Therefore, the education of young children is particularly important. First of all, children in this period are generally distinguished by being lively and active. In outdoor activities, they accept more natural factors such as sunlight, air, and water, and have strong adaptability. Therefore, children need to be trained in natural activities to accumulate in the natural activities. Knowledge and experience, promote the development of abilities, and enrich the spiritual world. At the same time, more intellectual sports games and hands-on activities need to be created and compiled to help children understand the world and understand the world. Imagine creating role-playing games that simulate real-life occupations, help young children to establish ideals, and embody humane care in simulated scenarios.

5.2 Youth Education

Youth education is an important stage in the construction of education. The youth stage refers to the age of 13–17, and the youth stage refers to the age of 18 to 45. Youth is the root of the country, and the youth stage is the easiest stage to absorb knowledge compared to other stages. As teachers of higher education institutions, they must strive to complete basic education while creating equal opportunities for education. Concept, carry out correct future career planning, when out of school, adapt to society as soon as possible, improve their overall quality and professional core competitiveness. Expand the third and fourth classrooms, enter the society, into the community, enrich after-school life, expand the field of youth volunteer services, advocate new social trends, strengthen mutual love between people, promote social harmony, focus on society, and focus on nature.

5.3 Older Age Well-Being

With the continuous acceleration of the global population aging, more and more countries are about to enter the elderly society. After entering the aging society, the increasing number of elderly people has led to an increase in the needs of the elderly society. Most of the urban elderly are retired. From a spiritual and cultural perspective, the frequency of most seniors participating in social activities has increased. Traveling and cultivating hobbies are one of the choices of most seniors. The continued stability of society requires a stable society Environment, continuous education for the elderly in cities and towns helps the elderly to adapt to the social changes brought about by new technology and new technology as soon as possible, and increases the social environment, such as related institutions and facilities such as senior colleges and welfare centers for the elderly, Establish a perfect follow-up education system, integrate forces, resources at all levels of society, guarantee social welfare and cultural construction, and promote social harmony.

5.4 Special Education

The main body of special education is people with disabilities and people with other special education needs who are demented. They are part of the education system, and they are the responsibility and obligation to achieve fair education and ensure that people with disabilities have the right to education. Based on the special education group, there are differences in the process of treating the special education population between the East and the West. This is determined by different national systems. Oriental philosophy and culture have been passed down for thousands of years. Emphasis is on etiquette, and more emphasis on the relationship between people and people. Harmony, social stability, and equality in education. Some western countries pay attention to logic and practice. There are special management methods and education standards for special groups. There is a complete education system and special talents for education management and program implementation.

Specially educated groups, as citizens of the country, should enjoy equal educational rights. Professionals responsible for the subject of education need to continuously improve their professional knowledge, and have the professional and psychological adjustment capabilities of general education and special education. Education, teaching, extra-curricular counseling, psychological intervention, treatment and rehabilitation are integrated, and the needy people are psychologically constructed and groomed in a timely manner. At the same time, they need to have "love" to understand the specific needs of this group of people, and pass the care through In life and classroom, further improve their professional skills and practical ability.

6 Welfare Professional Education and Thinking Formula

6.1 School Building

A good modern university should face the society, the country, and the world. It should have excellent discipline construction, a sound talent training mechanism, high standards of teachers and management teams, first-class disciplines and professional construction, a number of high-quality research results, and perfection. Logistics support mechanism and excellent students. The school needs long-term development and must have core competitiveness. This includes both the soft and hard environment. The hard environment refers to the construction of majors and teachers, and the soft environment refers to the construction of campus infrastructure. The ultimate goal of talents cultivated by schools and disciplines is to enter the society, realize the value of individuals' lives and become modernized construction talents useful for the development of the country. This requires the school to coordinate all aspects of the factors, invest a lot of people, materials, money, and make the school all departments go hand in hand. At the same time, managers have a higher education vision and a forward-looking view of construction. They constantly improve the construction of teachers, focus on break-throughs in scientific research difficulties, drive each department to find the right direction, and realize the cultivation of senior socially responsible seniors in a new environment. Application-oriented composite talents.

6.2 Professional Education

Welfare education refers to the cultivation of caring, professional, and professional technical talents with social responsibility, modern application, complex, and social welfare services. The main body of well-being education is for the general public and the wider population, and the groups and individuals who have needs and are committed to the education of well-being culture. The well-being and educating team requires the construction of a professional teacher team and a long-term teacher development plan. This requires a comprehensive logistical support mechanism and multi-party cooperation to achieve this. At the same time, teachers and managers also need to have a higher vision of welfare education management and a high sense of social responsibility. Facing the society, we focus on cultivating various professional and innovative service talents with social responsibility, a sense of national mission, an international perspective, and extensive practical capabilities.

In the teaching environment, the main body of education is students, and teachers are the organizers and implementers of professional and teaching activities. They are at the core of teaching. In the teaching process, the teaching content and teaching methods mainly rely on teachers to achieve. In the process of well-being cultural education and practice, students need to have a keen sense of social service, a high sense of responsibility, and complete professional skills and practical experience. The direction of cultivating people and practice covers social service design, related design for vulnerable groups, and caring design. Majors and directions in social care and social services.

6.3 Thinking Formula

The thinking formula refers to a stable thinking pattern formed through the accumulation of experience and lessons learned over a certain period of time and after repeated use and verification. In short, the thinking model of social welfare education services is based on social needs, combined with various majors, and on the premise of improving the professional skills, to cultivate students' social service capabilities and service awareness, and to improve themselves through continuous social experience To form an independent social thinking cognitive system, and become a modern talent with responsibility, ability and responsibility.

7 Smart Education Model and Industry Demand

7.1 Demand of Modern Industry

The advent of the Internet era has brought new development opportunities to various industries. The modern industry has shifted to network and integration. As a result, new demands have been created for talents. Highly professional and highly-complex application talents are the majority of industries. Urgently needed talents, so the professional training plan should be developed on the premise of combining the internal needs of society and enterprises. Only in this way can the professional talents with social needs be targeted. In the new era, we need responsible, responsible, capable, and caring Talent, of course, it also needs to excavate and cultivate talents in-depth professional ability. In the process of training, continuous feedback and improvement to adapt to the continuous development of society.

7.2 5G and Virtual Education

With the popularity of mobile data intelligent terminals and the continuous development of high-speed network technology, the era of 5G technology and virtual education has arrived. Virtual teaching and transmission of three-dimensional dynamic images through virtual robots will not be a dream. The full name of 5G technology is 5th generation mobile networks (5th generation mobile networks or 5th generation wireless systems). Compared with 4G technology, 5G technology will provide users with faster download and transmission speeds and more stable link capabilities. Traffic transmission and high link density and multi-scenario applications. In the future, 5G technology will have a stronger driving force for virtual education. Strong network transmission and stability guarantee will bring continuous and stable output of virtual education dynamic images and gesture dynamics. Recognition and capture, it is convenient for users to make timely feedback and analysis when conducting virtual education, and it will be more intuitive to watch and experience virtual image education.

7.3 Mobile Learning and Remote Interaction

With the rapid development of global science and technology, after human beings have fully entered the information society, the innovation of information technology has promoted the use of more information technology in various fields, and the development and innovation of electronic components have led to the application of more intelligent mobile terminal equipment to educate In terms of methods and education models, the application of the Internet and information technology has promoted the transformation of education to diversification, mobility, intelligence, and humanization. The original face-to-face classroom teaching method has become a way for people and interactive devices to learn through the Internet. The utilization rate of students' fragmented time is integrated, so that people who record courses and study courses can control their learning progress and learning time according to their own time, and can repeatedly watch instructional videos, which greatly improves the efficiency of student learning.

7.4   Smart Education Platform

Educational informationization and modernization are needed by the times. Before establishing a modern online education platform, it must be strategic, global, diverse and serviceable. This requires that we fundamentally change our consciousness and make the content of education connotative. To establish a service concept, improve the level and technology of platform operations, develop a comprehensive guarantee and evaluation, feedback mechanism, strengthen the construction of management and service systems, and build a public education service platform [6].

Wisdom education is a brand-new education method and education concept. It mainly uses information technology and methods to integrate high-speed development of network technology to integrate education resources. Through audit mechanism and system construction, it focuses on resource management and services, and uses mobile terminals. And interactive technology to realize the interaction between people and knowledge, promote the innovation of new technologies and technologies, and realize the sharing of online knowledge. At the same time, it has promoted the reform of educational communication channels, and promoted the development of education with technology and shared knowledge. Quality improvement.

8   Education and Continuous Promotion of Welfare

8.1   Focus on Service Demand

The formation of a student-service teaching model that is guided by social needs and professional needs will more closely meet the needs of individuals in the society for a desired career, thereby forming a targeted, targeted, and more structured education and teaching system to promote discipline development. Education first serves human beings, and is inspired by life experience and skills inheritance. Educational application itself should come from life. Service-oriented education aims to promote a better life for human beings and to become a human being's existence. Way to create the meaning of new life.

8.2   Education for Social Stability

Education promotes social civilization, and science and technology promote social progress. In view of the popularity of education, China has transitioned from nine-year compulsory education to twelve-year compulsory education, extending from the development of young children, preschool education, primary education, intermediate education, vocational and higher education to university education, greatly It has increased the popularity of education and promoted social harmony. At the same time, with the continuous improvement of the knowledge system, it will train more professionals in various aspects, increase the national cultural level, and promote social stability with education and knowledge.

8.3   Continue to Promote Educational Welfare

The construction of society is inseparable from the development of "people", and the development of individuals is inseparable from the reflection of the individual's personal value in society and the life plan formulated to achieve life goals. This includes the integration of three dimensions in the personal value system That is, values, goals, and plans. They are not isolated from each other. They are related to each other. Before the goal of life is achieved, the potential synergy and connection between these three dimensions need to be included in the scope of thinking to promote the achievement of goals.

Achieving life goals requires learning relevant skills and knowledge to improve one's own knowledge reserve so that it has core professional competitiveness, and education and learning need continuity. The overall goal of education-based social welfare and cultural construction is to provide all people with equal and quality education and free lifelong learning opportunities, so that everyone can enjoy universal and free learning opportunities And through the teachers to produce effective learning results, in the new era, new technologies continue to emerge, while reforming the old way of life while "education" as an important institution of national development and social stability, has given teachers new social and historical responsibilities In the training of various professional talents, we will continue to promote the construction of social welfare culture and the stable and harmonious development of society through "education and education services".

References

1. Yu, H.: Construction and Enlightenment of Korea's senior human resource development system. Vocat. Educ. Forum. **06**, 93–96 (2017)
2. Liu, T.: Construction of Chinese lifelong education system from the perspective of citizens' right to learn. High. Educ. Explor. **05**, 155–158 (2014)
3. Gu, Y., Zhang, X.: Evaluation and analysis of Japanese elderly well-being policy from the perspective of lifelong education. Mod. Educ. Manag. **11**, 115–117 (2010)
4. Jie, W.: Research on the classification of elderly education: reasons, goals and types. J. Guangzhou City Vocat. Coll. **04**, 48–52 (2017)
5. Wang, W.: The change of the family pension model in Japan. Japan J. **03**, 98–107 (2004)
6. Wang, X.: Research on the development of elderly education from the perspective of informationization. Times Agric. Mach. **10**, 97–98 (2018)
7. Cai, G., Tao, J.: The status quo and effective implementation of elderly education. China Natl. Expo. **11**, 72–73 (2018)
8. Chen, Y., Ning, K.: Development of elderly education under the background of population aging. Soc. Welf. (Theor. Edn.) **12**, 13–17 (2018)
9. Xue, H.: Research on the construction of community elderly education curriculum under the background of aging. Curric. Educ. Res. **48**, 42–43 (2018)

Interactive Assistive Technology with Corporate Sponsor and Crowdfunding for Children with Physical Disabilities

Chien-Yu Lin[(⊠)]

Department of Special Education, National University of Tainan, Tainan, Taiwan
linchienyu@mail.nutn.edu.tw

Abstract. The goal is to solve problems of promoting assistive technology with corporate sponsorship and crowdfunding for children with special needs. There are 7 cases application in special needs in Taiwan. The results show the game-base free support system could be allowed the special needs participants some clues, so they could have the motivation to do physical activities by themselves. This program design is based on Arduino and 3D printing interactive technology being applied on the activity for children with physical disabilities.

This research is based on Maker's development of Arduino, coin switch and 3D printing technology to make interactive assistive device switches. Due to the special needs device are expensive, this study share the 3D model files and arduino coding for free, it also provided low-cost interactive device for schools and families in need. This study uses interactive games enhance the body strength of children with disabilities. This research focus on the significant effect using multimedia feedback from interactive interface and real objects integrated in activity. Launched Jar-to-happiness in 2018, and has successfully reached a fundraising plan in FlyingV, then deliver 500 resource classes or children with special needs, reaching the university social responsibility.

Keywords: Children · Special needs · Assistive technology · Crowdfunding

1 Introduction

1.1 A Subsection Sample

Interactive game is more popular, special using pc mouse left click could find many resource in online games or App, thus, allowing for revise the function using of technology for physical activities. Arduino micro could using coding to do problem solving, just as operated automobile air conditioning system [1], Self-balancing robot design [2], control a gear pump [3], A photovoltaic blocks mutualization system [4], teaching tools for students [5]. Various technologies are used Arduino as an interactive switch, we used the concept and design the interactive device for children with disabilities.

Interactive games such as the Microsoft Xbox, Nintendo Wii or Sony PlayStation are not only for the play function, but have also been used in physical activities [6]. But Xbox, Nintendo Wii or Sony PlayStation are business product, there are not enough

P.-L. P. Rau (Ed.): HCII 2020, LNCS 12193, pp. 126–137, 2020.
https://doi.org/10.1007/978-3-030-49913-6_11

resource to arrange these interactive game tools in classroom. Recently, many open source could be applied, with their share their program, the users could design customers' interface, Recently, many open source or free platform have become available, which share their ideas and technology, so users can via this support to create their specific interfaces. Just as Arduino system, write code and share in share your sketches on the arduino web editor [7], Thingivers [8, 9]. This study via Arduino, which is an open-source hardware and software company, project and user community that designs and manufactures single-board microcontrollers and microcontroller kits for building digital devices. Arduino boards are available commercially in preassembled form or as do-it-yourself (DIY) kits. Arduino Web site (https://www.arduino.cc/) support a free online interactive community, with people sharing, discussing their programs, designers could be designing, creating, and remixing one another's projects [10].

The advantage of this study is that it could be used in laptop or mobile phone, the content easy to redesign or remix, thus we can focus on children preference to do physical training. There are limitations application on special switches due to the expensive facilities, stand on family economic status, it is a big burden who have children with special needs at home. Therefore, this research will emphasize facilities with a low-cost and maker design for investigation and researches, which will apply a real-time feedback system for children with physical disabilities, it could be practically applied for the promotion to classes with lower budgets on customized assistive device design.

2 Materials and Methods

2.1 Participants

There were 7 cases in different elementary, kindergarten, special school in Taiwan, all of the children from resource classes. In Sect. 3, this study will describe.

2.2 Apparatus, Material and Setting

The author and her team members are special education teachers from elementary schools, junior high school and senior high school and special schools, occupational therapist, physical therapists; we all work in the field of special education, assistive technology and industrial design. We design the interactive program for children with special needs via Arduino micro, 3d printing and McDonald support materials. Relative information just as URL: https://sites.google.com/site/nutnspeat/happiness.

We design the interactive teaching materials and share the coding and 3d model files on thingverse (https://www.thingiverse.com/thing:3422304). In this study, all the children know when they throw coin, ball or triangle object; he/she could get the feedback including audio and visual feedback from laptop or mobile phone. The concept of the study is shown in Fig. 1. In the study, we focus not only on the result, but also consider the applications and service in the future. The hardware used Jar-to-Happiness via laptop and mobile phone, it is easy to setup could attract teachers and parents want to learn and share their experiences. Figure 1 shows the concept.

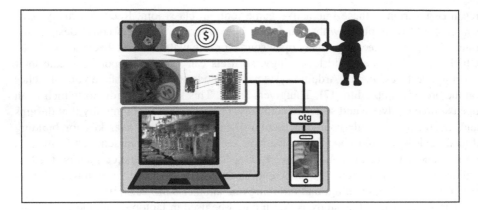

Fig. 1. The concept of this study

2.3   General Procedure

This study focused on how the interactive multimedia feedback can enhance the motivation of hand-eye coordination training for children with disabilities. The function of the Jar-to-Happiness is replace pc mouse left click, thus, the corresponding teaching materials could be easy to used, just as online games, YouTube, PowerPoint or scratch and so on. The laptop or the mobile phone was arranged in front of the participants, when the participants throw something in to the hole; the participants received the multimedia feedback. Figure 2 shows the experimental setup.

Fig. 2. The experimental process

The experimental process used Arduino micro, coin switch and 3d printing, the experimental process use laptop or mobile phone to detect throw something to start the mouse left click function and feedback effect. When the participant throw things in the hole; the coin switch as a sensor. Because our participants were children from resource class, their response maybe not as quick as normal, and consider their ability and disabilities, arrange different interactive teaching materials.

2.4 Preliminary Teaching Services

Promoting self-made assistive technology could be reduced costs and adjust for special needs. At the beginning, we arrange an event for special education teachers from elementary and preschool at Tainan University, make a two-way communication to identify potential problems, make adjustments and problems solving, In order to establish standard processes on teaching services in other counties and cities nationwide. Figure 3 shows the experimental setup.

Fig. 3. Teaching services in Tainan/Taiwan

2.5 Teaching Extensive Services

Our team used to develop self-made technology assistive devices, but only for children with special needs in Tainan area. Our team hopes via interactive assistive devices could improve hand-eye coordination for children with special needs, especially physical disabilities and cerebral palsy. Considering that the most familiar promotion method through workshops for special educational teachers. It was planned to hold 16 workshops, Table 1 shows all teaching extensive services in Taiwan. Figure 4 shows a part of workshop processes from these 16 workshops.

Table 1. All teaching extensive services

No.	yyyy-mm-dd	City or county/location	Amount
1	2018-10-20	Tainan/National University of Tainan	136
2	2018-10-27	Penghu/County Government Spe-edu Complex	22
3	2018-11-07	Tainan/Chi Mei Medical Center	5
4	2018-11-10	Chiayi/McDonalds	22
5	2018-11-10	Yunlin/McDonalds	11
6	2018-11-10	Changhua/McDonalds	13
7	2018-11-11	Nantou/McDonalds	4
8	2018-11-14	Pingtung/National Pingtung Spe-edu School	25
9	2018-12-01	Kaohsiung/Shih-Hu elementary School	65
10	2018-12-02	Kinmen/Kinmen Hospital, kindergarten	4
11	2018-12-08	Hsinchu/National Chiao Tung University	36
12	2018-12-15	Taipei/National Taiwan Normal University	105

(continued)

Table 1. (*continued*)

No.	yyyy-mm-dd	City or county/location	Amount
13	2019-01-05	Taichung/Li Sing elementary School	33
14	2019-01-11	Taitung/Binlang elementary School	11
15	2019-01-12	Hualien/National Hualien Special School/Yichang Junior high school	18
16	2019-01-13	Yilan/Ching Gou Elementary	5
	Total		515

Fig. 4. Teaching services in parts of counties and cities/Taiwan

3   Results

3.1   Case 1 (Hualien County)

This student is a cerebral palsy with good cognitive function, Fig. 5 left, he practices his hands for fine motor skills. Because the student like the effect of computer interaction, their special education teacher arranges for a full body rehabilitation after turning over, he could get the Jar-to-Happiness as a reinforce. In the special education school, special education teachers use this interactive assistive device, whether it's training fine motor skills or gross motor skills.

Fig. 5. Case 1 environment setup and instructions

3.2   Case 2 (Hualien County)

In normal course schedule, case 2 will use big yoga ball for rehabilitation, such as lying on the big yoga ball or sitting on the ball to practice stability. Big yoga ball is a tool often used in rehabilitation courses, special education teacher incorporates the Jar-to-Happiness into the course, students must lie on the big yoga ball steadily for a certain period of time, then they could throw balls in to the Jar-to-Happiness to receive the multimedia feedback from computer. Figure 6 right shows after the participant sat on the big yoga ball and maintain stability, he could use one hand to execute throw action, teachers use teaching techniques to add interactive feedback in the training process of students' physical exercises, increase the students' motivation.

Fig. 6. Case 2 environment setup and instructions

3.3   Case 3 (Kinmen County)

In case 3, there are two participants with special needs in kindergarten at Kinmen county. In Fig. 7.left, the participant need to wear backrest to support body stability, In Fig. 7.right, the participant belongs to severely handicapped, atrophy. The kid could not be sit or stand, need parents to hold his body, the Jar-to-Happiness in the class as a stimulus, because the feedbacks could design as their course needs, also support their fine motor skills training.

Fig. 7. Case 3 environment setup and instructions in Kinmen County

3.4   Case 4 (Nantou County)

Participants of case 4 are Nantou junior high school student with cerebral palsy and Nantou kindergarten child. In Fig. 8.left, he lack the motivation in study, the special education teacher found he like the ONE PIECE (日语：ワンピース) series, and let it in the pause mode, when the participant throw something in the hole, the video will be in play mode, it would be a reinforce device on his fine motor skills training. In Fig. 8. right, the participant is a kid in kindergarten. There belongs relatively few resources in Nantou, the special education teacher design teaching materials via PowerPoint and setup in play mode, when the kid throe coin in the Jar-to-Happiness, the kid receive the dynamic feedback. Because there are not enough interactive teaching materials in Nantou educational environment, it could support kids have the opportunity to enjoy interactive effects.

Fig. 8. Case 4 environment setup and instructions in Nantou County

3.5   Case 5 (Penghu County)

The participants in case 5 are students Penghu elementary school. The Penghu or Pescadores Islands are an archipelago of 90 islands and islets in the Taiwan Strait.

Case 5 is the mathematics teaching scene of the special education class in elementary school at Penghu. Figure 9.left, the teacher design teaching materials combined Jar-to-Happiness via the counting course to train hand-eye coordination and gripping exercises. The special education teacher divided into high/medium/low groups according to students' ability, with different learning goals. As long as each gacha or coin is dropped, the PowerPoint presentation will play and give the sound feedback as 1, 2, 3... for low group, high group students throw 10 dollar coins that could be receive the feedback as 10, 20, 30...., throw50 dollar coins in the jar will receive the feedback sound as 50, 100, 150......, Fig. 9.left, the kid did not have enough patience and willingness in learning Mandarin phonetic symbols, the special education teacher design visual and auditory teaching materials, and let the kid operate the Jar-to-Happiness by himself, the teacher setup the game rule is when he watch the screen show some Mandarin phonetic symbols, he must try to spelling and speak loud, then he can throw a ball in to the jar to checkout that is his answer correct or not, although the operate process just like press computer keyboard space key or click the left mouse button, but the special education teacher give us the feedback: the kid like the Jar-to-Happiness as an interactive device and let him interested to try to used Jar-to-Happiness with interactive teaching materials in the spelling course.

Fig. 9. Case 5 environment setup and instructions in Penghu County

3.6   Case 6 (Special Olympics Players Training-Tainan City)

Case 6 is the roller skating training process from Taiwan Special Olympics coaches training special Olympic athletes in national special school. The Special Olympics World Games are an international sporting activity for participants with intellectual disabilities, and other disabilities. Special Olympics is the world's largest sports organization for children and adults with intellectual disabilities and physical disabilities. The coach serving in national special schools, his team participant skates in this study,

Because there are many training programs for roller skating, it could be help sensory integration for people with mental disabilities, stimulate the vestibule, control emotion, exhaust strong energy, improve leg shape and other issues, strengthen muscle strength and endurance, mental exercise, develop the courage to fall and still take the challenge, thus, roller skating as one of the important teaching subjects in special school.

Figure 10 shows that the coach took the relevant roller skating video and edited it into a computer, before each unit practice, the athletes throw a ball to start the video on play mode, after watching the relevant roller skating video, practice exercises to complete the action. It could be improve the one-way training, increase the willingness of athletes to learn the skills independently.

Fig. 10. Case 6 environment setup and instructions in Taichung County

3.7   Case 7 (Tainan City)

Case 7 is an institution in Tainan, this institution provides professional team services (education, physical therapy, occupational therapy, speech therapy, social work, health management, etc.). This institution arrange for infants with retarded development, children with mental disabilities between the ages of three and six, and multiple disabilities, every infant has an individual education plan (IEP). The educational plan adopts collaborative teaching, with life integration experience as the core goal. Figure 11 shows that the process in the institution, the teacher adjusts the training according to his individual special needs to enhance the fine movements of the hands.

Fig. 11. Case 7 environment setup and instructions in Tainan City

3.8 Service Field

Beside Table 1 shows 16 workshops and deliver 515 units in Taiwan, in addition, the department head (Business department of product innovation and entrepreneurship/ National Taipei University) assisted 18 cases in Taoyuan area. Nantou area needs more recourses, their teacher applies for 9 more items. Miaoli county was also a teacher who support as a seed teacher after receiving 9 pieces and extent them in Miaoli. After that, we also send Jar-to-Happiness to Malaysia, Japan, Philippine and China. Figure 12 shows that the Jar-to-Happiness results of diffusion via google map. Figure 12 shows parts of the google map, this google map URL: https://goo.gl/FbEP1w.

Fig. 12. Service area and URL: https://goo.gl/FbEP1w

4   Discussion

4.1   Design Application-Oriented

A universal design allows users to adjust according to the special needs of different students, giving teachers more flexible application. Jar-to-Happiness could be combined with computer software and games, toys and other media, giving users the flexibility of teaching preparation and individual adjustment. It is a flexible interactive teaching device that has a theoretical basis and could be combined with practical needs. No modification required the computer or install programs, through operation practice, although growth is slow, it may create progressive results.

4.2   Teaching Skill Application

Teachers use the Jar-to-Happiness to train students to participate in learning activities, learn to express their needs, learn to wait, empathize, be patient, etc. Among them, one teacher's teaching skills included let a student with cerebral palsy to operate the device, enabling teaching materials could jump pages in order, allowing other classmates to participate in class, and increasing the self-confidence and achievement for the student.

In the teaching of communication skills, teachers train students to express their intentions through happiness gas tanks. In the teaching of communication skills, teachers train students to express their intentions through the Jar-to-Happiness, students could get the positive connection and practice with picture cards. In addition, teachers use the characteristics of the Jar-to-Happiness, let the video play repeatedly, training students to practice phonetic notation songs, it could be contribute to the training of communication skills.

4.3   Perceptual-Motor Training

Through movement, it could be increased students' fine movement and hand-eye coordination, in conjunction with the hand training movements recommended by occupational therapist, using multimedia feedback to increase student training motivation, and choose suitable holes for training depending on student needs. In addition, teachers use it to solve the problems for lack of concentration; Using the feedback to guide students to learn more difficult actions or things that they don't like, such as doing housework, etc. or use the feedback obtained after input to guide students to learn difficult movements or things they do not like, such as doing housework, etc. it could be also provide the opportunity to train the rehabilitation training.

Acknowledgement. This work was financially supported by the Ministry of Education, Taiwan, under the Grant of the talent cultivation program for smart living industry, Crowdfunding (https://www.flyingv.cc/projects/20964), McDonald's donated plastic cups as parts of device and lots of vouchers for free meal as crowdfunding's perks.

References

1. Shah, H., Maniar, A., Tailor, K., Patel, D., Patel, H.: An arduino micro-controller operated automobile air conditioning system. In: Kumar, M., Pandey, R.K., Kumar, V. (eds.) Advances in Interdisciplinary Engineering. LNME, pp. 263–275. Springer, Singapore (2019). https://doi.org/10.1007/978-981-13-6577-5_26
2. Philippart, V.Y., Snel, K.O., de Waal, A.M., Jeedella, J.S., Najafi, E.: Model-based design for a self-balancing robot using the arduino micro-controller board. In: 2019 23rd International Conference on Mechatronics Technology (ICMT), pp. 1–6. IEEE (2019)
3. Drost, S., de Kruif, B.J., Newport, D.: Arduino control of a pulsatile flow rig. Med. Eng. Phys. **51**, 67–71 (2018)
4. Mezouari, A., Elgouri, R., Alareqi, M., Mateur, K., Dahou, H.: Hlou, L: A new photovoltaic blocks mutualization system for micro-grids using an Arduino board and Labview. Int. J. Power Electron. Drive Syst. **9**(1), 98 (2018)
5. Botes, R., Zeeman, M.: Measuring computer science students' acceptance of arduino micro development boards as teaching tool. In: ECIAIR 2019 European Conference on the Impact of Artificial Intelligence and Robotics, p. 61 (2019)
6. Ding, Q., et al.: Motion games improve balance control in stroke survivors: a preliminary study based on the principle of constraint-induced movement therapy. Displays **34**, 125–131 (2013)
7. Sunehra, D.: Web based smart irrigation system using raspberry pi. Technology **10**(2), 55–64 (2019)
8. Giglia, G., Crisp, K., Musotto, G., Sardo, P., Ferraro, G.: 3D Printing neuron equivalent circuits: an undergraduate laboratory exercise. J. Undergrad. Neurosci. Educ. **18**(1), T1–T7 (2019)
9. Zahid, A., Krumins, V., De Witte, L., Zahid, A.: The development of innovation sharing platforms for low cost and do-it-yourself assistive technology in low and middle-income countries. In: Global Perspectives on Assistive Technology, p. 359 (2019)
10. Lopez, E., Garcia, J.: Educational robots with arduino: annotated prototypes. Educ. Robot. Context Maker Mov. **946**, 161 (2019)

The Impact of Social-Support, Self-efficacy and APP on MBI

Shu-Mei Lin[1]([⊠]), Liang-Ming Lo[2]([⊠]), Chia-Yi Liu[3]([⊠]),
Chao Liu[1]([⊠]), and Wen-Ko Chiou[4]([⊠])

[1] Graduate Institute of Business and Management,
Chang Gung University, Taoyuan City, Taiwan
victoria9Lin@gmail.com, 174673015@qq.com
[2] Department of Obstetrics and Gynecology,
Chang Gung Memorial Hospital, Taipei City, Taiwan
lmlo@cgmh.org.tw
[3] Department of Psychiatry, Chang Gung Memorial Hospital,
Taipei City, Taiwan
liucy752@cgmh.org.tw
[4] Department of Industrial Design, Chang Gung University,
Taoyuan City, Taiwan
wkchiu@mail.cgu.edu.tw

Abstract. Social-support, self-efficacy and APP were one of the advanced MBI. This article presents a structured literature review of 44 articles to elucidate the impacts of social support, self-efficacy, APP. We discuss (1) the MBIs in which social-support, self-efficacy, and APP operate; (2) social-support, self-efficacy, and APP as MBI design choices and (3) the implycations of MBI design choices on MBI performance output. The structure of this article is based on the MBI-PPD-APP model. Results of our literature review revealed that, social-support, self-efficacy, and APP are employed in a variety of applications. We also found that MBI design involves choices pertaining to MBI configurations, MBI relationship, social-support, self-efficacy, and the APP process. The MBI performance outputs which were found to be most influenced by social-support, self-efficacy, and APP included PPD (reduce), MBI phenomena (reduced), and MBI responsiveness (improved). We used the findings of our literature review to develop a conceptual framework, which includes 18 propositions and an agenda for research. Specifically, the goal of this research agenda is to existing knowledge about how social-support, self-efficacy, and APP impact MBI design. We expect that social-support and self-efficacy and APP will eventually lead to improve.

Keywords: Social-support · Self-efficacy · APP · MBI

1 Introduction

Mindfulness was defined by Kabat-Zinn et al. (Kabat-Zinn and Zinn 2001): as "paying attention in a particular way: on purpose, in the present moment, and non-judgmentally". Mindfulness is a type of practice derived from the Buddhist

© Springer Nature Switzerland AG 2020
P.-L. P. Rau (Ed.): HCII 2020, LNCS 12193, pp. 138–150, 2020.
https://doi.org/10.1007/978-3-030-49913-6_12

contemplative practices and traditions of Vipassana, which is characterized by awareness of the current state of the mind and body without judgment, elaboration, or
attachment (Haslam et al. 2012). Many scholars have embraced a two-component model
of mindfulness which includes self-regulation of attention and attending to the present
moment. Self-regulation of attention refers to bringing awareness to a point of full
attention to one's thoughts, feelings, and sensations. This includes maintaining sustained attention, keeping attention flexible, focusing on direct/current experience and
inhibiting elaborate processing. The second component, orientation to the present
moment, refers to the attitude or approach one takes in attending to the present moment
and is exemplified by curiosity, openness, and acceptance (Bishop et al. 2004). Mindfulness has also been conceptualized as having three core components: intention,
attention, and attitude; a specific mindfulness mechanism has been proposed (Shapiro
et al. 2006). In regarding to the Mindfulness Based Intervention (MBI)-Post-Partum
Depression (PPD)-Application Portal (APP) process relationship is shown in (Fig. 1).
We will discussed social-support and self-efficacy and app over subsequent sections.

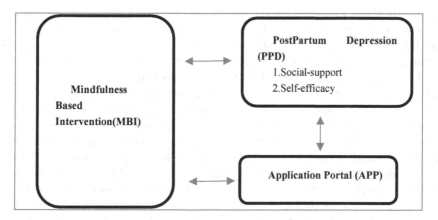

Fig. 1. The MBI-PPD-APP process relationship

2   Methodology

We performed both exploratory factor analysis and traditional 'narrative' reviews in
this study. We also completed a structured literature review to provide a solid theoretical foundation which can be used to inform future research (Price-Whelan et al.
2018). As recommended by Tranfield et al. (2003), in performing our literature review,
we employed a five-step approach. First, research questions were formulated. Second, a
search was conducted to identify relevant articles. Third, articles were selected and
assessed. Fourth, the results reported in the selected articles were analyzed and integrated and fifth, the information was applied as following:

2.1 Research Questions

The primary objective of this study was address using three research questions that were guided by the "cause and mediator and effect' model of the MBI-PPD-APP process relationship (Fig. 1).

2.2 Literature Search

To ensure that relevant articles were included in our literature review, we employed the following search terms were specified: 'MBI' and 'PPD' and 'APP'. In addition, their interchangeable terms were identified and connected by 'AND' and 'OR' searching engines. The university library Scopus was used and provided access to major online information sources and search engines such as Google Scholar and Directory of Open Access Journals. This resulted in the following information:

2.3 Selecting and Assessing Relevant Articles

According to Kabat-Zinn et al. (2001), mindfulness is defined as paying close attention of the present moment (Haslam et al. 2012); mindfulness has also been conceptualized as a direct current experience rather than full concentration or unconsciousness mindfulness-based skills (Tang et al. 2015), mindfulness related skill can be developed through scholarship or mindfulness-based interventions (MBI), Mindfulness have been developed by scholars to enhance these abilities through MBI may have effects on distal results, such as improved behavior or reduced psychopathological symptoms. Although the origin of mindfulness originally arose out of Buddhist philosophy (Grabovac et al. 2011), and is 2,500 years old, the earliest example of formal MBI research was mindfulness-based stress reduction (MBSR), MBSR was developed to help individuals learn to manage illness, pain, and stress. Other MBIs Based on the principles of MBSR have also emerged, including mindfulness-based cognition therapy (MBCT), which focuses on preventing the recurrence of depression. In recent years, mindfulness itself has gained attention as a method to reduce cognitive vulnerability to mental and emotional stress, and proposed a psychological experience of performance and implication based on specific behaviors (Bishop et al. 2002). The process consists of a two-part mindfulness model and each of these part is specified. Then, address the issues related to temporal stability and context specificity, and speculate on the concept and operational uniqueness of mindfulness. In general, MBI has been found to have a positive effect on both mental and physical health (Grossman et al. 2004; Khoury et al. 2013). Mindfulness-based intervention are increasingly employed to improve the behavioral, cognitive, and mental health outcomes of children and adolescents (Dunning et al. 2019). In this paper, we describe mindfulness using 7 measures proposed by Dunning et al. (2019). Applying MBI to improve the behavioral, cognitive, and mental health outcomes of children and adolescents (Dunning et al. 2019). Some researchers have adopted MBCT as an evidence-based treatment for unipolar depression (Hanssen et al. 2019). MBCT integrates the principles and practices of cognitive therapy into a mindfulness framework Clinicians from all backgrounds can use the tools of MBCT to help their patients maintain treatment benefits and potentially achieve remission as well. In practice, MBCT helps patients make simple but fundamental changes in the way they relate to the thoughts, feelings, and physical sensations that cause depression to recur. MBCT also provides a step-by-step guide to conscious practice and cognitive therapy as well as information to help patients understand mild states of sadness and prevent them from losing control. Included in MBSR is a clinical plan called mindfulness – based practice (MBP) that is designed to promote adaptation to medical disease (Bishop 2002). The use of MBSR has grown exponentially since it was first launched 20 years ago. Currently, there are an estimated 240 MBSR programs in North America and Europe, and new programs are being established each year; This trend has accelerated with the recent introduction of MBSR professional training program that can be completed at home. Indeed, this training program is likely to make the MBSR approach even more common. MBSR can be administered as a structured group plan that employs mindfulness meditation to relieve pain associated with physical and mental illness (Grossman et al. 2004). The program is non-religious and non-stubborn. It is a system-based program designed to increase awareness of how one experience s of psychological processes in the present moment. Over the past two decades, many research reports have provided evidence to support the utility of MBSR, suggesting that program can help a wide range of individuals with both clinical and nonclinical issues. Furthermore, cognitive changes which arise from a mindfulness practice mediate the effects of MBSR on spirituality. For example, the developing mindfulness-related skills has been found to increase meaning and promote inner peace, connection and personal growth in cancer patients. In addition, many researchers who explored negative behavior which arise from anxiety and attention-deficit/hyperactive disorder described impulsivity behavior (Dunning et al. 2019; Salem-Guirgis et al. 2019). Numerous researchers have also considered anxiety and stress (Cachia et al. 2016; Dunning et al. 2019), and many studies have discussed executive function (Price-Whelan et al. 2018; Dunning et al. 2019). Other studies introduced the concept of social support (Vaezi et al. 2019; Leahy-Warren 2012; Zimet 1988). There are a few years long from 1977 when Bandura first introduced the construct of self-efficacy with the seminal publication, "self-efficacy: Toward a Unifying Theory of behavioral change." A decade later (1981), Bandura published "Self-Efficacy", which situated the self-efficacy construct within a social cognitive theory of human behavior that diverged from the prevalent cognitivism of the day and embedded cognitive development within a socio-structural network of influences. A few decades later, other scholars expended the construct of self-efficacy (Vaezi 2019; Prasopkittikun and Vipuro 2008). The current study performed a literature review based on the 7 measures of mindfulness proposed by Dunning et al. (2019), Specifically, our literature review included the following topics: (1) MBP, MBCT and MBSR, (2) social behavior, (3) negative behavior, (4) depression, (5) anxiety/Stress, (6) executive function, (7) attention.

2.4   Analyzing and Integrating the Results

We selected 44 articles related to social-support, self-efficacy, and APP. These articles were coded and entered into a spreadsheet for analysis. The types of MBIs included in the analysis were MBT, MBCT and MBSR. The (input) MBI design choices were analyzed according to the definition of the MBI-PPD-APP elements: social-support and self-efficacy and APP. In the context of this study, "social-support" refers to MBI configuration choices; "self-efficacy" refers to MBI choices; "APP" refers to the choices related to social-support and self-efficacy within the MBI facilities. MBI performance outputs were analyzed according to who defines the social-support and self-efficacy and APP related MBI performance outputs.

2.5 Applying the Information

The coded information in the spreadsheet was used to analyze the relationships among the social-support and self-efficacy and APP design and MBI performance outcome (i.e. reduce or improve). We also used this information to develop a conceptual framework by formulating propositions and proposing a conceptual input-process-output model. Subsequently, we developed a research agenda, highlighting the potential area of MBI research that (1) related to proposition testing and (2) likely to facilitate the future roll-out of the full social-support and self-efficacy and app, the results are detailed over subsequent section.

3   Results and Discussion

In this following sections, we describe the conceptual framework we developed using the narrative results of the structured literature review.

3.1   Social-Support as MBI

This section explains the settings in which Social support thrives according to social – support literature. Social support can be conveyed through verbal and nonverbal communication, and through perceived or actual exchanges of physical or psychosocial resources, including information and knowledge (Morikawa et al. 2015), they are proposed these meta-analyses revealed that a combination of demographic, psychological, and cultural risk factors play important roles in the development of PPD in women (Vaezi et al. 2019). For example, the following factors were found to be strongly or moderately correlated with PPD: a personal history of depression (including prenatal and antenatal depression), prenatal and postnatal anxiety, stress related to childcare, an unsatisfying marital relationship, negative life events, certain baby characteristics, and importantly, low levels of social support (Haga et al. 2012; Vaezi et al. 2019). To explore the social support and health moved from mortality risk to morbidity risk, affecting pregnancy outcomes such as fetal health (e.g. preterm birth), infant health (e.g. low birth weight), and maternal health (e.g. postpartum depression). With regard to specific populations, in one study, Teen mothers reported receiving significantly less social support than did adult mothers. This was largely because they were less able to develop and maintain relationship with others (Kim et al. 2014). In Taiwanese fathers, PPD was also found to be high levels of social support (Gao et al. 2009). In the first mothers, relationships have also been found between social support, parental self-efficacy, and postnatal depression at 6 weeks post-delivery (Leahy-Warren et al. 2012).

Taken together, the aforementioned studies demonstrate that social support is close related to demographics. Furthermore, Bishop et al. (2004) proposed mindfulness influence people's attitudes towards the present as well as openness, and acceptance. Therefore, we can defined social support as a type of MBI (Table 1).

Table 1. Social-support literature

Topic	References
Past medical history of depression	Morikawa et al. (2015), Haga et al. (2012), Gao et al. (2009), Leahy-Warren et al. (2012)
Illness of baby (e.g. preterm birth, low birth weight)	Vaezi et al. (2019), Kim et al. (2014)
Teen mothers(15–19 years old)/ adult mothers (20+ years old)	Kim et al. (2014)

3.2 Self-efficacy as MBI

Self-efficacy is defined as the expectation that one can successfully perform a given behavior (Sherer et al. 1983). This section explains the settings in which self-efficacy thrives according to the self-efficacy literature. Self-efficacy can be conveyed through verbal and nonverbal communication, and through perceived or actual exchanges of physical or psychosocial resources. First-time mothers seem to be especially vulnerable to PPD. Other risk factors that have been repeatedly identified include low levels of social support (Gao et al. 2009) low self-esteem, being single, being a teenage mother, and a high level of breastfeeding Conversely, self-efficacy and high levels of social support are associated with less severe postpartum depressive symptom (Haga et al. 2012). Therefore, in developing health care policy and clinical guidelines, effective ways of increasing social support to enhance maternal self-efficacy need to be defined (Leahy-Warren et al. 2012). In one conceptualization, maternal maladjustments (i.e., feeling of depression, stress, anxiety, and unhappiness) and maternal self-efficacy were proposed to be consecutive mediators of the relationship between social support/family support and prenatal expectations (Mihelic et al. 2016). Proved to have implications for educational and counseling services offered to expectant women. Given that prenatal parenting expectations do not always align with real postnatal experiences, the best time to educate expectant mothers about parenthood and to manage unrealistic expectations is during pregnancy. Maternal self-efficacy is a crucial factor which facilitates a smooth transition into motherhood, particularly for primiparas (Shorey et al. 2015). The self-system houses the brain's cognitive and affective structures and is responsible for the following abilities: the ability to regulate one's own behavior, and the ability to engage in self-reflection (Pajares 1996). Much psychology research has focused heavily on how the mind works with regard to processing, organizing, and retrieving information. According to social learning theory, self-directedness operates through a self-system that comprises cognitive structures and subfunctions which are involved in perceiving, evaluating, motivating, and regulating behavior (Bandura 1981; 1982). Self-efficacy influences the emotions, thoughts, and actions that people have. With regard to motions, a low sense of self-efficacy is associated with depression, anxiety, and helplessness. Such individuals also tend to harbor pessimistic thoughts about their accomplishments and personal development (Schwarzer 1992). Self-esteem requires a global rating that fails to take into account that people are a process. Within Buddhist philosophy, suffering is understood to stem from attempting to maintain a static sense of self against a backdrop of constantly changing experiences (Thompson and Waltz 2008).

Bandura's theory (1981; 1982) and many research literature comprehensively believe that one can achieve a set goal and live a healthier, more effective, and more generally successful life; and Kabat-Zinn et al. (2001) argues that "focusing in a special way: purposeful, present and non-judgemental". Theory coincides, we can infer that self-efficacy is a type of as MBI (Table 2).

Table 2. Self-efficacy literature

Topic	References
Self-concept	Leahy-Warren et al. (2012), Mihelic et al. (2016), Shorey et al. (2015), Pajares (1996), Bandura (1981; 1982), Schwarzer (Schwarzer 1992), Sherer et al. (1983)
Self-esteem	Thompson and Waltz (2008), Haga et al. (2012), Gao et al. (2009)
Breastfeeding self-efficacy (BSE)	Haga et al (2012)

3.3 APP as MBI

This section explains the topics settings in which APP thrives according to APP literature. APP can be conveyed through verbal and nonverbal communication and through perceived or actual exchanges of physical or psychosocial resources, including information and knowledge. Wasil et al. (2019) proposed that mental-health-related smartphone applications (MH apps) can provide less stigmatizing treatment options, especially for individuals who prefer self-help-options. MH apps tend to be flexible and cost-effective, which has the potential to greatly increase the availability of evidence-based mental health treatment. For example, treatment via MH apps can be made available through workbooks, websites and digital therapies. Therefore, MH should facilitate more efficient and effective treatment of depression (Bakker et al. 2018). Some patients are unwilling or unable to attend face-to-face MBIs (van Emmerik et al. 2018). Additionally, in a number of countries, MBIs are not covered by most health insurance plans. Online (e-health) or smartphone-based (m-health) treatment options may help to overcome these challenges by allowing patients to receive treatment at their chosen time and place at little to no cost. Many of these smartphone apps are able to screen, monitor and even augment treatment for mood disorders, which has generated enthusiasm among not only patients and clinicians, but among technology companies, investors and healthcare regulators as well. APP relate to treatment for depression already comprise some of most commonly downloaded categories of health apps by the public (Torous et al. 2019). According to Buddhist philosophy, the goal of mindfulness are to "experience enlightenment", "perceive the true nature of reality", and to attain "compassion", "wisdom", and "insights into important fundamental truths… Which will finally lead to the ultimate goal of liberation" (Clarke and Draper 2020). Although there is currently no gold standard for the treatment of PPD, evidence from their meta-analysis indicated that interventions based in cognitive behavioural therapy (CBT) and MBCT can be effective at reducing repetitive negative thinking (RNT), even when administered by mobile apps. A recent systematic review and meta-analysis also cited strong evidence to support the use of mindfulness in treatment for depression. That study also reported that mobile apps can help beginners to learn meditation and other mindfulness practices in a short amount of time (Heckendorf et al. 2019; Rebedew 2018). The risk of developing chronic depression increases with successive depressive episodes, and even among patients who achieve clinical remission, residual depressive symptoms (RDS) following first-line antidepressant pharmacotherapy are common (Dimidjian et al. 2014). Mobile health technology (mHealth) provides promising tools which important health information and empower patients to take control of their own healthcare, because most people own and regularly use a mobile phone. Specifically, mHealth can be used to promote positive behavior changes that improve healthcare outcome (Schnall et al. 2016). Mobile devices have fundamentally changed teaching and learning practices, and these changes are displacing traditional teaching practices (Jahnke et al. 2020). Mindfulness interventions that employ mobile platforms are likely to be more accessible and less stigmatizing than conventional mental health treatments (e.g. antidepressants, cognitive behavioral therapy), especially among socio-economically disadvantaged individuals and adults who belong to a racial/ethnic minority (Burnett-Zeigler et al. 2018).

Research by the aforementioned scholars indicates that mobile health apps can be promote positive behavior changes, which should in turn reduce mental-health-related issues (Schnall et al. 2016). This previous research convincingly demonstrates that app-based interventions have the effect on mindfulness, so we defined them as a type of MBI (Table 3).

Table 3. APP literature

Topic	References
Randomized	Wasil et al. (2019), Bakker et al. (2018), van Emmerik et al. (2018)
Individual course of the study	Torous et al. (2019), Clarke and Daper (2020), Heckendorf et al. (2019), Rebedew (2018), Dimidjian et al. (2014), Schnall et al. (2016). Jahnke and Lei bscher (2020), Burnett-Zeigler et al. (2018)

3.4   Direction for Future Research

We will also developed a research agenda that encourages future research into the following 15 issues: (1) The benefits of MBP practice and training courses, the integration of MBP, (2) Decisions related to the replacement of MBP by MBCT; the effects of switch from MBP to MBCT on MBI, (3) The reduction PPD of MBSR when implementing MBP, and the impact of MBP designs, (4) The effects of disciplinary sanctions when switching from MBP to MBI on practice and training course, (5) The effects of dysregulation implementing MBSR on MBI and MBCT, (6) The effect of post-training from MBT to MBSR on externalizing relationships, (7) The effects of attention-deficit/hyperactive disorder improvements related to the MBI process-on MBP design decisions, (8) The effects of impulsivity behavior improve related to the MBI process on MBP design decisions, (9) The effect of stress level post practice of MBI on PPD, (10) The effect of anxiety through from MBI to MBSR on PPD, (11) The effect of stress level post practice of MBI on PPD, (12) The effects of trauma-informed improvements related to the MBP and MBCT, and MBSR processes, (13) The effects of improvements in mindfulness skills related to the MBP and MBCT, and MBSR processes, (14) The effect of attention post the MBP, (15) The impact of the APP on MBI based on PPD switches to MBSR to deal with the MBCT related, respectively.

4   The Proposition and Research Agenda

This paper based on Dunning et al. (2019) proposed 7 measures as: MBI, social behavior, negative behavior, depression, anxiety/stress, executive function, attention. In our literature review, we found that a number of researchers (i.e., Morikawa et al. 2015; Kim et al. 2014; Haga et al. 2012; Gao et al. 2009; Leahy-Warren et al. 2012; Vaezi et al. 2019) proposed 3 measures to defined social-support. Other researchers promoted the theory of self-efficacy (Mihelic et al. 2016; Shorey et al. 2015; Leahy-Warren et al. 2012; Pajares 1996; Bandura, 1981, 1982; Schwarzer 1992; Sherer et al. 1983; and Thompson and Waltz 2008; Haga et al. 2012; Gao et al. 2009). Finally, many researchers have noted the potential benefits of APP in mental health treatment (Wasil et al. 2019; Bakker et al. 2018; van Emmerik et al. 2018; Torous et al. 2019; Clarke and Draper 2020; Heckendorf et al. 2019; Rebedew 2018; Dimidjian et al. 2014; Schnall et al. 2016; Jahnke and Leibscher 2020; Burnett-Zeigler et al. 2018). Based on finding of our literature review, we developed the MBI-PPD-APP research agenda, which includes 18 themes based on 15 Proposition, shown as Fig. 2.

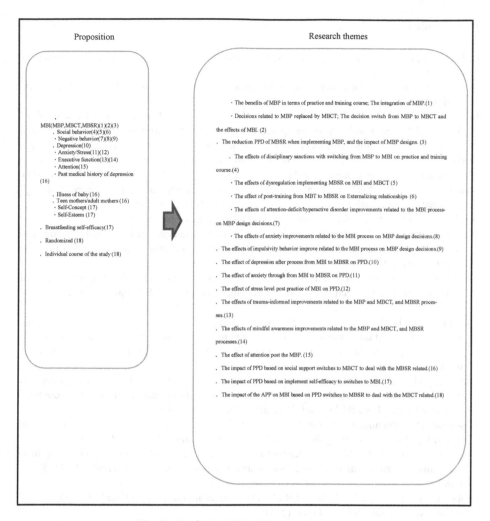

Fig. 2. The MBI-PPD-APP research agenda

5   Conclusion

This article consists of a structured literature review on social-support, self-efficacy and APP on MBI design, a conceptual framework, a research agenda for the roll-out of social-support and self-efficacy and APP on MBI. The main objective of this study was to increase performance about the impact that social-support, self-efficacy and APP have on MBI design. We were delivering a new agenda based on the previous foundation as the impact of PPD based on social-support and self-efficacy switches to MBCT to deal with the MBSR related.

References

Bishop, S.R., et al.: Mindfulness: a proposed operational definition. Clin. Psychol. Sci. Pract. **11**(3), 230–241 (2004)

Bishop, S.R.: What do we really know about mindfulness-based stress reduction? Psychosom. Med. **64**(1), 71–83 (2002)

Burnett-Zeigler, I.E., Waldron, E.M., Hong, S., Yang, A., Wisner, K.L., Ciolino, J.D.: Accessibility and feasibility of using technology to support mindfulness practice, reduce stress and promote long term mental health. Complement. Ther. Clin. Pract. **33**, 93–99 (2018)

Bakker, D., Kazantzis, N., Rickwood, D., Rickard, N.: A randomized controlled trial of three smartphone apps for enhancing public mental health. Behav. Res. Ther. **109**, 75–83 (2018)

Bandura, A., Schunk, D.H.: Cultivating competence, self-efficacy, and intrinsic interest through proximal self-motivation. J. Personal. Soc. Psychol. **41**(3), 586 (1981)

Bandura, A.: Self-efficacy mechanism in human agency. Am. Psychol. **37**(2), 122 (1982)

Clarke, J., Draper, S.: Intermittent mindfulness practice can be beneficial, and daily practice can be harmful. An in depth, mixed methods study of the "calm" app's (mostly positive) effects. Internet Interv. **19**, 100293 (2020)

Cachia, R.L., Anderson, A., Moore, D.W.: Mindfulness, stress and well-being in parents of children with autism spectrum disorder: a systematic review. J. Child Fam. Stud. **25**(1), 1–14 (2016)

Dimidjian, S., Beck, A., Felder, J.N., Boggs, J.M., Gallop, R., Segal, Z.V.: Web-based mindfulness-based cognitive therapy for reducing residual depressive symptoms: an open trial and quasi-experimental comparison to propensity score matched controls. Behav. Res. Ther. **63**, 83–89 (2014)

Dunning, D.L., et al.: Research review: the effects of mindfulness-based interventions on cognition and mental health in children and adolescents: a meta-analysis of randomized controlled trials. J. Child Psychol. Psychiatry **60**(3), 244–258 (2019)

Grossman, P., Niemann, L., Schmidt, S., Walach, H.: Mindfulness-based stress reduction and health benefits: a meta-analysis. Focus Altern. Complement. Ther. **8**, 500 (2004)

Gao, L.L., Chan, S.W.C., Mao, Q.: Depression, perceived stress, and social support among first-time chinese mothers and fathers in the postpartum period. Res. Nurs. Health **32**(1), 50–58 (2009)

Grabovac, A.D., Lau, M.A., Willett, B.R.: Mechanisms of mindfulness: a buddhist psychological model. Mindfulness **2**(3), 154–166 (2011)

Haga, S.M., Ulleberg, P., Slinning, K., Kraft, P., Steen, T.B., Staff, A.: A longitudinal study of postpartum depressive symptoms: multilevel growth curve analyses of emotion regulation strategies, breastfeeding self-efficacy, and social support. Arch. Women's Mental Health **15**(3), 175–184 (2012)

Heckendorf, H., Lehr, D., Ebert, D.D., Freund, H.: Efficacy of an internet and app-based gratitude intervention in reducing repetitive negative thinking and mechanisms of change in the intervention's effect on anxiety and depression: results from a randomized controlled trial. Behav. Res. Ther. **119**, 103415 (2019)

Hanssen, I., et al.: Exploring the clinical outcome of mindfulness-based cognitive therapy for bipolar and unipolar depressive patients in routine clinical practice: a pilot study. Int. J. Bipolar Disord. **7**, 18 (2019)

Jahnke, I., Liebscher, J.: Three types of integrated course designs for using mobile technologies to support creativity in higher education. Comput. Educ. **146**, 103782 (2020)

Khoury, B., et al.: Mindfulness based therapy: a comprehensive meta-analysis. Clin. Psychol. Rev. **33**, 763–771 (2013)

Kim, T.H., Connolly, J.A., Tamim, H.: The effect of social support around pregnancy on postpartum depression among canadian teen mothers and adult mothers in the maternity experiences survey. BMC Pregnancy Childbirth **14**(1), 162 (2014)

Leahy-Warren, P., McCarthy, G., Corcoran, P.: First-time mothers: social support, maternal parental self-efficacy and postnatal depression. J. Clin. Nurs. **21**(3–4), 388–397 (2012)

Mihelic, M., Filus, A., Morawaska, A.: Correlates of prenatal parenting expectations in new mothers: is better self-efficacy a potential target for preventing postnatal adjustment difficulties? Prev. Sci. **17**(8), 949–959 (2016)

Morikawa, M., et al.: Relationship between social support during pregnancy and postpartum depressive state: a prospective cohort study. Sci. Repo.rts **5**, 10520 (2015)

Price-Whelan, A.M., et al.: The astropy project: building an open-science project and status of the v2.0 core package. Astron. J. **156**(3), 123 (2018)

Pajares, F.: Self-efficacy beliefs in academic settings. Rev. Educ. Res. **66**(4), 543–578 (1996)

Prasopkittikun, T., Vipuro, N.: Assessing self-efficacy in infant care: a comparison of two scales. Asian Nurs. Res. **2**(3), 166–172 (2008)

Rebedew, D.: Five mobile apps for mindfulness. Fam. Pract. Manag. **25**(3), 21–24 (2018)

Schwarzer, R.: Self-Efficacy: Thought Control of Action. Routledge, Abingdon (1992). ISBN 1-56032-269-1

Shorey, S., Chan, S.W.C., Chong, Y.S., He, H.G.: Predictors of maternal parental self-efficacy among primiparas in the early postnatal period. West. J. Nurs. Res. **37**(12), 1604–1622 (2015)

Schnall, R., et al.: A user-centered model for designing consumer mobile health (mHealth) applications (apps). J. Biomed. Inf. **60**, 243–251 (2016)

Salem-Guirgis, S., et al.: MYmind: a concurrent group-based mindfulness intervention for youth with autism and their parents. Mindfulness **10**, 1730–1743 (2019)

Sherer, M., Adams, C.H.: Construct validation of the self-efficacy scale. Psychol. Rep. **53**(3), 899–902 (1983)

Shapiro, S.L., Carlson, L.E., Astin, J.A., Freedman, B.: Mechanisms of mindfulness. J. Clin. Psychol. **62**(3), 373–386 (2006)

Tang, Y.Y., Hölzel, B.K., Posner, M.I.: The neuroscience of mindfulness meditation. Nat. Rev. Neurosci. **16**(4), 213–225 (2015). https://doi.org/10.1038/nrn3916

Tranfield, D., Denyer, D., Smart, P.: Towards a methodology for developing evidence-informed management knowledge by means of systematic review. Br. J. Manag. **14**, 207–222 (2003)

Thompson, B.L., Waltz, J.A.: Mindfulness, self-esteem, and unconditional self-acceptance. J. Ration.-Emot. Cogn.-Behav. Ther. **26**(2), 119–126 (2008)

Vaezi, A., Soojoodi, F., Banihashemi, A.T., Nojomi, M.: The association between social support and postpartum depression in women: a cross sectional study. Women Birth **32**(2), e238–e242 (2019)

van Emmerik, A.A., Berings, F., Lancee, J.: Efficacy of a mindfulness-based mobile application: a randomized waiting-list controlled trial. Mindfulness **9**(1), 187–198 (2018)

Wasil, A.R., Venturo-Conerly, K.E., Shingleton, R.M., Weisz, J.R.: A review of popular smartphone apps for depression and anxiety: assessing the inclusion of evidence-based content. Behav. Res. Ther. **123**, 103498 (2019)

Zimet, G.: The multidimensional scale of perceived social support. J. Personal. Assess. **52**(1), 30–41 (1988)

Torous, J., Lipschitz, J., Ng, M., Firth, J.: Dropout rates in clinical trials of smartphone apps for depressive symptoms: a systematic review and meta-analysis. J. Affect. Disord. **263**, 413–419 (2019)

Haslam, S.A., Reicher, S.D., Levine, M.: When other people are heaven, when other people are hell: how social identity determines the nature and impact of social support. In: The Social Cure: Identity, Health and Well-being, pp. 157–174 (2012)

Kabat-Zinn, J., Zinn, J.K.: Mindfulness Meditation in Everyday Life. Published by Piatkus Books, London (2001)

Effects of Loving-Kindness Meditation on Mindfulness, Spirituality and Subjective Well-Being of Flight Attendants

Chao Liu[1]([✉]), Hao Chen[1]([✉]), Chia-Yi Liu[2], Rungtai Lin[3]([✉]),
and Wen-Ko Chiou[4]([✉])

[1] Graduate Institute of Business and Management, Chang Gung University,
Taoyuan City, Taiwan
victory666666@126.com, 174673015@qq.com
[2] Department of Psychiatry, Chang Gung Memorial Hospital,
Taipei City, Taiwan
liucy752@cgmh.org.tw
[3] Graduate School of Creative Industry Design,
National Taiwan University of Arts, New Taipei City, Taiwan
rtlin@mail.ntua.edu.tw
[4] Department of Industrial Design, Chang Gung University,
Taoyuan City, Taiwan
wkchiu@mail.cgu.edu.tw

Abstract. This study investigated (1) the effects of the loving-kindness meditation on mindfulness, subjective well-being (SWB), and spirituality and (2) the relationships between mindfulness, spirituality, and SWB. Methods: 98 flight attendants from Xiamen airlines in China were recruited and randomly assigned to the loving-kindness meditation training group (n = 49) or the waiting control group (n = 49). The loving-kindness meditation training group underwent an 8-week loving-kindness meditation training intervention, and the control group did not undergo intervention. The three main variables (SWB, mindfulness, and spirituality) were measured both before (pre-test) and after (post-test) the loving-kindness meditation training intervention. Results: In the experimental group, SWB and spirituality increased significantly (mean scores of SWB: 4.13 for pre-test and 5.38 for post-test; mean scores of spirituality: 3.85 for pre-test and 3.99 for post-test). (In the control group, no significant differences were observed for the three variables between the pre-test and post-test.) We also identified positive correlations between mindfulness, spirituality and SWB and observed that spirituality mediated the relationship between mindfulness and SWB. Conclusions: Our results indicated that loving-kindness meditation can have a positive impact on SWB and spirituality. However, the mechanisms which underlie the effects of the loving-kindness meditation on mindfulness, spirituality, SWB, and other psychological constructs require further elucidation.

Keywords: Loving-kindness meditation · Mindfulness · Spirituality · Subjective well-being

© Springer Nature Switzerland AG 2020
P.-L. P. Rau (Ed.): HCII 2020, LNCS 12193, pp. 151–165, 2020.
https://doi.org/10.1007/978-3-030-49913-6_13

1 Introduction

1.1 Loving-Kindness Meditation

The Loving-kindness meditation has been practiced for over 2500 years, yet its utility as a psychological intervention has only been explored recently (Hofmann et al. 2011). The aim of the loving kindness meditation (LKM) is to cultivate feelings of unconditional love, kindness, and acceptance (Salzberg 1995). When practicing traditional LKM, the practitioner directs loving-kindness, in a stepwise fashion, toward themselves, loved ones, acquaintances, strangers, and finally, all sentient beings (Galante et al. 2014; Hofmann et al. 2011; Salzberg 1995). Like mindfulness meditation (see Kabat-Zinn 1994), LKM is versatile; it can be practiced at any time and in a variety of postures (e.g., lying down, sitting, walking; see Hofmann et al. 2011; Salzberg 1995). Previous studies have demonstrated the therapeutic benefits of including the loving-kindness meditation in psychotherapy treatment, and these benefits have been observed in a number of different groups. For example, among the general population, the loving-kindness meditation has been found to reduce the negative emotions that parents have about their parenting abilities (Kirby and Baldwin 2018), reduce the negative emotions of adolescents (Kirby and Laczko 2017), reduce depression and anxiety among self-critical individuals (Shahar et al. 2015), and reduce the effects of post-traumatic stress disorder among veterans (Kearney et al. 2013; Kearney et al. 2014). For individuals who suffer from mental health issues, the loving-kindness meditation has been found to reduce depression in chronic depression patients (Schilling et al. 2018), reduce the negative emotions of schizophrenics (Johnson et al. 2009), and reduce depression and anxiety in individuals who suffer from borderline personality disorder (Graser and Stangier 2018; Keng and Tan 2018). In addition to studying the ability of the loving-kindness meditation to alleviate negative emotions, it is also important to (1) investigate whether loving-kindness meditation can increase happiness and (2) understand the mechanisms which underlie the benefits of the loving-kindness meditation from the perspective of positive psychology. Both mindfulness and spirituality are related to subjective well-being (Csikszentmihalyi 2013). However, only a few studies have investigated whether the loving-kindness meditation can increase mindfulness, spirituality and subjective well-being. Nonetheless, the research that has been conducted reported that, among adults, loving-kindness meditation increased mindfulness (Fredrickson et al. 2008; May et al. 2014; Sorensen et al. 2019), spirituality (Kristeller and Johnson 2005) and subjective well-being (Mohamed and Lewis 2016). The current study seeks to deepen this body of knowledge by investigating whether the loving-kindness meditation can increase mindfulness, spirituality, and subjective well-being of flight attendants from a positive psychology perspective.

1.2 Subjective Well-Being

Subjective well-being (SWB) primarily refers to how an individual perceives their quality of life, on both a cognitive and emotional level. In this sense, an individual's happiness or not determined by the actual events of their lives; happiness is determined by the individual's interpretation of these events and the cognitive and emotional responses they trigger (Edward Diener et al. 2002). There are two facets to SWB: emotional balance and life satisfaction. Emotional balance refers to the happy experience that occupies the comparative advantage compared with the unpleasant emotional experience, which is an overall and general evaluation of the individual's life. Emotional balance comprises both positive and negative emotions. However, these two dimensions are usually unrelated; they are relatively independent variables. Life satisfaction comprises an the perceptions an individual has about their life. As a cognitive factor, life satisfaction is independent of positive emotions and negative emotions. It is a more effective indicator of SWB (Diener et al. 1999). Subjective well-being is very important to physical, mental, and emotional health. For example, it has been found to have a positive impact on the physical abilities of the elderly, whereby higher levels of subjective well-being lead to greater physical abilities (Gildner et al. 2019). Conversely, subjective well-being negatively impacts depression and anxiety. Individuals with higher levels of subjective well-being have lower levels of depression and anxiety (Malone and Wachholtz 2018). Given the effects of subjective well-being on physical and mental health, it is important to investigate how this phenomenon enhances emotional and cognitive processes, both of which are related to mindfulness and spirituality (Csikszentmihalyi 2013).

1.3 Mindfulness

Mindfulness is defined as focusing purposeful, conscious, and non-judgmental attention/awareness to what is happening in the present moment. In other words, it involves being aware of what's going on in one's own consciousness and the surrounding environment without judging it, analyzing it, or reacting to it (Kabat-Zinn 2003). Previous research found that mindfulness can enhance subjective well-being among the elderly (Aliche and Onyishi 2019), among employees in the workplace, and among teachers. Mindfulness has also been found to positively impact the subjective well-being of college flight attendants, whereby higher levels of mindfulness led to higher levels of subjective well-being (Bajaj and Pande 2016; Ge et al. 2019; Schutte and Malouff 2011; Xu et al. 2016). Although there is much evidence to suggest that mindfulness has a positive impact on subjective well-being, research that explores the mechanism which underlies this relationship is limited. It is possible that spirituality can help explain the relationship between mindfulness and subjective well-being, and this topic deserves further investigation.

1.4 Spirituality

Spirituality is the connections that one pursues and experiences with the essence of life. It consists of three dimensions: connection with oneself, connection with others and nature, and connection with transcendent experiences (Meezenbroek et al. 2012). Studies have shown that spirituality can enhance the subjective well-being of the elderly (Stevens 2016; Kamitsis and Francis 2013; Lifshitz et al. 2019), and among adolescents (Cobb et al. 2015). Previous research has also determined that mindfulness can increase individual spiritual growth (Matiz et al. 2018). In investigating specific groups of people, researchers have found that mindfulness can enhance the spirituality of adolescents (Cobb et al. 2015), of patients with late cancer (Casula 2018; Labelle et al. 2015; Zernicke et al. 2016), and among husbands and wives in their marital relationship (Lord 2017). Finally, mindfulness was also found to positively impact the spirituality of psychotic patients (Da Silva and Pereira 2017). Taken together, these previous findings strongly suggest that individuals with a high degree of mindfulness experience higher levels of spirituality and thereby increase their subjective well-being.

1.5   Research Objective and Hypotheses

The primary objective of this study was to explore the effects of loving-kindness meditation on mindfulness, spirituality, and subjective well-being from a positive psychology perspective. The specific goals of this study included: (1) Investigating whether loving-kindness meditation can enhance mindfulness, spirituality and subjective well-being; (2) Investigating the direct and indirect relationships that exist among mindfulness, spirituality and subjective well-being; and (3) Elucidating the mechanisms which underlie these relationships.

Based on findings from previous research, we adopted the following assumptions:

Hypothesis 1a, The mindfulness score of participants should be significantly higher than in the post-test than in the pre-test.
Hypothesis 1b, The spirituality score of participants should be significantly higher in the post-test than in the pre-test.
Hypothesis 1c, The SWB score of participants should be significantly higher in the post-test than in the pre-test.
Hypothesis 2, Positive correlations exist between mindfulness, spirituality and subjective well-being.
Hypothesis 3, Spirituality mediates the relationship between mindfulness and SWB.

2   Methods

2.1   Participants

Participants in this study comprised 98 flight attendants from Xiamen Airlines in China. Of these flight attendants, 22 were male (22%). 44%, M = 29.26, SD = 6.12. The age of participants ranged from 21 to 40 years old. Participants were randomly assigned into one of two groups: the loving-kindness meditation training group (49 participants) and the waiting control group (49 participants). The two groups were not significantly different in terms of demographic characteristics (Table 1).

Table 1. Demographic characteristics of participants

	Total	LKM Meditation	Control Group
Age (SD)	29.26 (6.12)	30.14 (5.77)	28.37 (6.39)
Sex (%)			
Male	22.44	18.4	26.5
Female	77.56	81.6	73.5

No demographic characteristic was significantly different among the two groups.

2.2   Instruments

State Mindfulness Scale (SMS; Tanay and Bernstein 2013). This scale is used to measure participants' state mindfulness. The State Mindfulness Scale (SMS) was developed by Tanay and Bernstein (2013) (Tanay and Bernstein 2013) and contains 2 dimensions: body mindfulness, which involves an awareness of how the body feels and an awareness of sensations within the body; and psychological mindfulness, which involves an awareness of thoughts, images, and emotions that appear in consciousness. The body mindfulness dimension includes 15 items, and the psychological mindfulness dimension includes 6 items, for a total of 21 items. Participants answer questionnaire items of the SMS using a five-point Likert scale, whereby 1 means "not at all", and 5 means "very well". In the SMS, each subscale is individually scored, and the scores of the two subscales are summed to derive a total score. Previous studies have shown that the SMS has good validity (Botrel and Kubler 2019; Schindler et al. 2019). In the current study, the Cronbach's alpha value for the SMS was .95.

Spiritual Attitude and Involvement List (SAIL). This scale is used to measure the spirituality level of participants and contains 7 dimensions: meaning, trust, acceptance, caring for others, connection with nature, transcendence, and spiritual activity. The 7 dimensions include a total of 26 items. Participants answer questionnaire items of the SAIL scale using a six-point Likert scale, whereby 1 means "not at all", and 6 means "very well". Each subscale is individually scored, and the 7 subscales are summed to derive a total score. Previous studies have shown that SAIL has good validity (Jirasek and Hurych 2018; Thauvoye et al. 2018). In the current study, the Cronbach's alpha value for SAIL was .96.

The Positive and Negative Affect Scales (PANAS; Watson et al. 1988) **and Satisfaction with Life Scale (SWLS; Diener et al.** 1985). As noted, SWB is comprised of two parts: emotional balance and life satisfaction (Edward Diener et al. 2002). Therefore, the Positive and Negative Affect scale (PANAS), developed by Watson et al. (1998), is used to measure participants' positive and negative emotional experiences; and the Satisfaction with Life Scale (SWLS), developed by Diener et al. (1999) is used to measure participants' satisfaction with their lives.

PANAS contains 2 dimensions: positive emotional experiences and negative emotional experiences. Each dimension has 10 items, for a total of total 20 items. Participants answer using a five-point Likert scale, whereby 1 means "none at all", and

5 means "all the time". Each subscale is individually scored, and the two subscales are summed to derive a total score. Previous studies have shown that PANAS has good validity (Chen et al. 2019; Horwood and Anglim 2019). In the current study, the Cronbach's alpha value for PANAS was .97.

The SWLS includes 7 items, and participants answer using a seven-point Likert scale, whereby 1 means "strongly disagree", and 7 means "strongly agree". Previous studies have shown that that the SWLS has good validity (Gigantesco et al. 2019; Munoz-Rodriguez et al. 2019). In the current study, the Cronbach's alpha value for the SWLS was .95.

2.3   LKM Intervention

For the LKM intervention, participants were instructed to (1) sit or lay down with closed eyes and pay attention to their breath and body; (2) imagine receiving kindness, love, and compassion from a loving person; and (3) imagine sending those feelings, in a stepwise fashion, to themselves, their family and friends, their community, all people, and finally, all sentient beings. We also incorporated adaptations of LKM into the meditation program used in our study. For example, in session three, participants were encouraged to send loving-kindness toward a difficult person (i.e., a person who typically triggers negative feelings; see Salzberg 1995). In another session, participants were instructed to walk outside while sending loving-kindness toward people, animals, and nature in general. Participants were further asked to practice these formal meditations between sessions and to apply loving kindness skills in their workplace.

2.4   Procedure and Design

We posted recruiting advertisements at the BBS forum of Xiamen Airlines. Flight attendants who were interested in participating in our loving-kindness meditation research provided their registration information. We then randomly assigned 98 participants were to either the experimental group (i.e., the LKM intervention group, 49 participants) or the control group (i.e., the waiting group, 49 participants). The investigation was conducted by researchers who had 10 years of experience practicing LKM and 2 years of experience teaching meditation. The sessions (LKM or waiting) were conducted in a quiet, disturbance-free room, and each participant received 50 Chinese Dollars at the start of the investigation to strengthen their motivation. At the beginning of the investigation, each participant was told that they were participating in a personality-related study. Participants were then provided with instructions, and researchers confirmed that participants understood these instructions before continuing. Upon confirming that they understood the instructions, participants provided demographic data and completed the following questionnaires (pre-test): (1) State Mindfulness Scale (SMS); (2) Spiritual Attitude and Involvement List (SAIL); (3) The Positive and Negative Affect Scales (PANAS); and (4) Satisfaction with Life Scale (SWLS). The time required to answer each questionnaire was approximately 20 min. Participants then completed a 30 min loving-kindness meditation activity. The duration of the LKM intervention was 8 weeks. At the end of the intervention period, participants completed the same questionnaires again (post-test) and received another 50 Chinese Dollars as compensation. Finally, the true purpose of the study was explained to participants. This research was approved by the Huaqiao University Ethics Committee, and research protocols were carefully reviewed to ensure that they abided by the ethical guidelines of the China Psychological Association.

Mean values, standard deviations, and the Pearson correlation matrix were used to analyze data at the description level. Paired sample t-tests and SEM were used to analyze data at the inferential level. The sample size used in this research is equal to or larger than that used by previous studies. Data was analyzed using SPSS version 22, and the significance threshold was at $p < 0.05$.

3   Results

Our first hypothesis stated that loving-kindness meditation should increase mindfulness, spirituality, and subjective well-being. The results of our analysis, obtained using Paired sample t-tests, are shown in Fig. 1 and Table 2. We did not observe any significant differences between the pre-test and post-test for mindfulness. For spirituality, we did observe a significant difference between the pre-test and post-test; $t(48) = 2.13$, $p = 0.038$. We also observed a significant difference for subjective well-being between the pre-test and post- test; $t(48) = 5.75$, $p < 0.001$. As our results showed that the loving-kindness meditation significantly increased participants' spirituality and subjective well-being, Hypotheses 1b and 1c were supported.

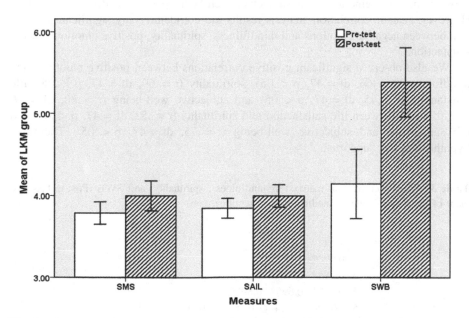

Fig. 1. Comparison of 3 scales before and after the loving-kindness meditation intervention.

White bars represent pre-test results; Black bars represent post-test results. Differences between the pre-test and post-test were significant for subjective well-being (SWB) and spirituality (measured by the Spiritual Attitude and Involvement List, SAIL). No significant differences were found between the pre-test and post-test were found for mindfulness (measured by the State Mindfulness Score, SMS). P < 0.05 SMS, State Mindfulness Scale; SAIL, Spiritual Attitude and Involvement List; SWB, Subjective well-being.

Table 2. Means and standard deviations for each measure pre- and post-loving-kindness meditation intervention.

Measure	Group	Mean (SD)			t	p
		Pre	Post	Post-Pre		
SMS	LKM	3.79(0.47)	3.99(0.63)	0.20(0.74)	1.98	0.053
	Control	3.78(0.49)	3.79(0.44)	0.01(0.46)	0.11	0.916
SAIL	LKM	3.85(0.42)	3.99(0.48)	0.15(0.49)	2.13	0.038
	Control	3.89(0.47)	3.85(0.43)	−0.45(0.48)	−0.44	0.661
SWB	LKM	4.13(1.49)	5.38(1.47)	1.25(1.51)	5.75	<0.001
	Control	4.09(1.51)	4.36(1.61)	0.27(1.31)	0.86	0.394

Hypothesis 2 stated that positive correlations should exist between mindfulness, spirituality and subjective well-being. The results of Pearson correlation analysis are shown in Table 3. Specifically, these results identified a significant negative correlation between negative emotions and subjective well-being ($r = -.56$, df = 47, p < .05). However, Pearson correlation analysis results did not identify any significant correlation between negative emotions and mindfulness, spirituality, positive emotions, or life satisfaction.

We also observed significant positive correlations between positive emotions and mindfulness ($r = .66$, df = 47, p < .05), spirituality ($r = .69$, df = 47, p < .05), life satisfaction ($r = .45$, df = 47, p < .05) and subjective well-being ($r = .80$, df = 47, p < .05); and between life satisfaction and spirituality ($r = .52$, df = 47, p < .05) and life satisfaction and subjective well-being ($r = .75$, df = 47, p < .05). Therefore, hypothesis 2 was supported.

Table 3. Pearson correlation matrix for mindfulness, spirituality, and SWB (Post-test assessment of the loving-kindness meditation intervention).

	1	2	3	4	5	6
1	1					
2	0.69**	1				
3	0.58**	0.70**	1			
4	0.66**	0.69**	0.80**	1		
5	−0.21	−0.24	−0.56**	−0.19	1	
6	0.33*	0.52**	0.75**	0.45**	−0.09	1

1, SMS; 2, SAIL; 3, SWB; 4, PA; 5, NA; 6, SWLS
*p < 0.05; **p < 0.01

The Sobel test was used to evaluate the mediating effect of spirituality on mindfulness and SWB. Results of the Sobel test showed that this mediating effect was significant ($Z = 3.43$, $p = 0.001$), indicating that mindfulness through spirituality to affect SWB. The standardized mediator effect size was $d = 0.402$. That is to say, each standard deviation increase of mindfulness will increase subjective happiness for 0.402 standard deviation through affecting spirituality.

4 Discussion

The primary objective of this study was to explore the effects of the loving-kindness meditation on mindfulness, spirituality, and subjective well-being from the perspective of positive psychology. The main goals of this study were to: (1) Investigate whether loving-kindness meditation can increase mindfulness, spirituality and subjective well-being; (2) Investigate the direct and indirect relationships between mindfulness, spirituality, and subjective well-being; and (3) Help elucidate the mechanism which underlies this relationship. The results of our research showed that: (1) The loving-kindness meditation significantly increased participant spirituality and subjective well-being scores. However, we did not find any significant differences between the pre-test and post-test in terms of mindfulness. (2) Positive correlations existed between mindfulness, spirituality, and subjective well-being. (3) As we expected, spirituality mediated the relationship between mindfulness and subjective well-being. Therefore, Hypothesis 1c, Hypothesis 2, and Hypothesis 3 were supported. These results are discussed in greater detail below.

4.1 Paired Sample t-Test

The loving-kindness meditation significantly increased the subjective well-being scores of participants. The explanation for this result is that, by sending loving-kindness to others, the practitioner creates a safe space in which they can experience calmness, satisfaction, love, and other positive emotions (Jazaieri et al. 2014). The loving-kindness meditation is based an emotional regulation strategy which involves focusing on the development positive emotions to distract attention away from negative emotions (Zeng et al. 2015). In focusing on the process of sending loving-kindness, immersion was produced, and feelings of selflessness were generated. This in turn generated positive cognition and improved life satisfaction (Weytens et al. 2014).

We also observed a significant difference between the pre-test and the post-test for spirituality score. The explanation which underlies this finding is that the loving-kindness meditation is a relatively independent meditation technique that attempts to help practitioners by encouraging them to treat both themselves and others with warm, compassionate emotions. This in turn improves the practitioner's ability to cultivate an accepting and open attitude, and ultimately, their spirituality. The loving-kindness meditation also helps dispel negative emotions and mental states. Distressed states of consciousness (such as hostility, greed, stress, and depression) are, in some sense, mental pollutants. Most mental pollutants are conditioned, maladaptive, and habitual responses to past experiences which typically lead to disturbing consequences. To adopt a benevolent attitude is to treat it in a warm and gentle way, and at least it will not make things worse. Loving-kindness meditation directly cultivates the four immeasurables: loving-kindness, compassion, appreciative joy, and equanimity. When these emotions are cultivated, prosocial attitudes are easily fostered. In fact, in developing the four immeasurables, a primary goal of the loving-kindness meditation is to counter negative, opposing emotions: anger, cruelty, jealousy, and obsession. By practicing the loving-kindness meditation and fostering a positive attitude towards oneself and others, practitioners also become likely to perform helpful acts more frequently, which in turn increases their spirituality (Condon et al. 2013).

4.2   Pearson Correlation Analysis

Our results identified a significant positive correlation between mindfulness and subjective well-being, and this correlation can be primarily explained by a significant positive correlation between mindfulness and positive emotions. Positive reappraisal is considered to be one of the important mechanisms by which mindfulness enhances positive emotions. Mindfulness allows the practitioner to respond to what is happening with a sense of detachment. Mindfulness can thus be said to promote accurate discernment. In other words, mindfulness helps create space between an individual and their circumstances, thereby allowing them to pause and choose between multiple coping strategies. Individuals with high levels of mindfulness almost always respond to feelings of uncertainty with a positive attitude. These individuals also tend to adopt healthy coping strategies, such as seeking social support, releasing negative emotions, and solving problem centers to enhance positive emotions. All of this serves to enhance subjective well-being (Lindsay and Creswell 2015).

In this study, we also observed a significant positive correlation between spirituality and subjective well-being. This finding can be primarily explained by the significant positive correlation that exists between spirituality and positive emotions. The underlying mechanism may be that, when an individual engages in spiritual practice, four specific areas of the brain become active. These areas have evolved over several years to promote positive emotions and cognition, which in turn promote subjective well-being (Nash and Newberg 2013; Newberg 2014; Yaden et al. 2017). When individuals have spiritually transcendent experiences, the body produces oxytocin, which promotes feelings of calmness, love, and connection. These feelings increase happiness and also increase the likelihood that an individual will engage in altruistic behaviors (Yaden et al. 2017).

Finally, we observed a significant positive correlation between mindfulness and spirituality. The explanation for this may be that mindfulness promotes a specific kind of cognition. In other words, by practicing mindfulness over the long-term, an individual's thinking gradually evolves from focusing only on the immediate self, to focusing on a larger and more permanent part of the self, to focusing on connection with other individuals, to linking the individual with a larger goal. All of this serves to increase the practitioner's spirituality (Cobb et al. 2015; Matiz et al. 2018).

4.3   Mediating Effects of Spirituality

As we predicted, spirituality was found to mediate the relationship between mindfulness and subjective well-being. Many new discoveries have indicated that mindfulness, empathy (Hofmann et al. 2011; Galante et al. 2014) and meditation lead to an increase in positive emotions, attention, and subjective well-being. These positive effects can be primarily explained by non-self concept. This is because mindfulness, compassion, and meditation create space between practitioners and their desires, and thereby reduce pain and distraction. This in turn leads to positive emotions, greater subjective well-being, and increased attention.

4.4   Contributions

This study makes several contributions to existing literature. First, we found that the loving-kindness meditation can not only reduce negative emotions such as depression and anxiety, it can increase subjective well-being and spirituality. Secondly, we found that mindfulness, spirituality, and subjective well-being are positively correlated and directly related. We further determined that spirituality is a key mediator involved in transforming mindfulness into positive emotions. Finally, we identified a link between mindfulness and subjective well-being through spirituality, thereby elucidating a more complete understanding of subjective well-being.

5   Conclusions and Directions for Future Research

This study employed experimental methods to investigate whether the loving-kindness meditation can increase mindfulness, spirituality, and subjective well-being. However, although some of our hypotheses were supported, our research used instruments such as the spirituality scale which were developed by Western scholars. Western society has primarily been influenced by Catholicism and Christian culture, while Chinese society has mainly been influenced by Confucianism, Taoism, and Buddhism. Therefore, spirituality may have cross-cultural issues. To overcome these issues, we suggest that future research develop a spirituality scale that is specifically designed for a Chinese context. In addition, this study only explored the influence of loving-kindness meditation on the promotion of mindfulness, spirituality, and subjective well-being. Future studies could fill existing research gaps by investigating the effects of the loving-kindness meditation on other aspects of positive psychology, which should open up other avenues by which to increase human happiness.

Note also that this study employed the group testing method. Although the researchers took great care in ensuring the rigor of the testing procedure, there were still some participants who did not follow instructions properly (for example, some participants answered the questions before they had listened to them in their entirety). Moreover, participants answered questions at different speeds, and participants who answered quickly sometimes interfered with participants who answered more slowly. We suggest that future research avoid group testing in order to reduce interference among participants. Finally, there may have been demographic bias in our study.

Specifically, all of our participants were flight attendants; which could limit the generalizability of our results. Our study also included a greater number of female participants than male participants, which may have biased our results and reduced the external validity of our research. Therefore, future research should seek to confirm whether the results of the current study can be extrapolated to other populations.

References

Aliche, J.C., Onyishi, I.E.: Mindfulness and wellbeing in older adults' survivors of herdsmen attack. The mediating effect of positive reappraisal. Aging Ment. Health, 1–9 (2019). https://doi.org/10.1080/13607863.2019.1602592

Bajaj, B., Pande, N.: Mediating role of resilience in the impact of mindfulness on life satisfaction and affect as indices of subjective well-being. Personal. Individ. Differ. **93**, 63–67 (2016). https://doi.org/10.1016/j.paid.2015.09.005

Botrel, L., Kubler, A.: Week-long visuomotor coordination and relaxation trainings do not increase sensorimotor rhythms (SMR) based brain-computer interface performance. Behav. Brain Res. **372** (2019). https://doi.org/10.1016/j.bbr.2019.111993

Casula, C.: Clinical hypnosis, mindfulness and spirituality in palliative care. Ann. Palliat. Med. **7** (1), 32–40 (2018). https://doi.org/10.21037/apm.2017.07.07

Chen, Q.S., Kong, Y.R., Niu, J., Gao, W.Y., Li, J.Y., Li, M.S.: How leaders' psychological capita influence their followers' psychological capital: social exchange or emotional contagion. Front. Psychol. **10** (2019). https://doi.org/10.3389/fpsyg.2019.01578

Cobb, E., Kor, A., Miller, L.: Support for adolescent spirituality: contributions of religious practice and trait mindfulness. J. Relig. Health **54**(3), 862–870 (2015). https://doi.org/10.1007/s10943-015-0046-1

Condon, P., Feldman Barrett, L.: Conceptualizing and experiencing compassion. Emotion **13**(5), 817–821 (2013)

Csikszentmihalyi, M.: Flow: The Psychology of Happiness. Ebury Publishing, London (2013)

Da Silva, J.P., Pereira, A.M.S.: Perceived spirituality, mindfulness and quality of life in psychiatric patients. J. Relig. Health **56**(1), 130–140 (2017). https://doi.org/10.1007/s10943-016-0186-y

Diener, E., Emmons, R., Larsen, R., Griffin, S.: The satisfaction with life scale. J. Personal. Assess. **49**, 71–75 (1985)

Diener, E., Suh, E.M., Lucas, R.E., Smith, H.L.: Subjective well-being: three decades of progress. Psychol. Bull. **125**(2), 276–302 (1999). https://doi.org/10.1037/0033-2909.125.2.276

Diener, E., Lucas, R.E., Oishi, S.: Subjective well-being: the science of happiness and life satisfaction. In: Snyder, C., Lopez, S.J. (eds.) Handbook of Positive Psychology, pp. 463–473. University Press, London (2002)

Fredrickson, B.L., Cohn, M.A., Coffey, K.A., Pek, J., Finkel, S.M.: Open hearts build lives: positive emotions, induced through loving-kindness meditation, build consequential personal resources. J. Personal. Soc. Psychol. **95**(5), 1045–1062 (2008). https://doi.org/10.1037/a0013262

Galante, J., Galante, I., Bekkers, M.J., Gallacher, J.: Effect of kindness-based meditation on health and well-being: a systematic review and meta-analysis. J. Consult. Clin. Psychol. **82**, 1101–1114 (2014)

Ge, J.J., Wu, J., Li, K.S., Zheng, Y.: Self-compassion and subjective well-being mediate the impact of mindfulness on balanced time perspective in Chinese college students. Front. Psychol. **10** (2019). https://doi.org/10.3389/fpsyg.2019.00367

Gigantesco, A., et al.: The relationship between satisfaction with life and depression symptoms by gender. Front. Psychiatry **10**. https://doi.org/10.3389/fpsyt.2019.00419

Gildner, T.E., Snodgrass, J.J., Evans, C., Kowal, P.: Associations between physical function and subjective well-being in older adults from low- and middle-income countries: results from the study on global ageing and adult health (SAGE). J. Aging Phys. Act. **27**(2), 213–221 (2019). https://doi.org/10.1123/japa.2016-0359

Graser, J., Stangier, U.: Compassion and loving-kindness meditation: an overview and prospects for the application in clinical samples. Harv. Rev. Psychiatry **26**(4), 201–215 (2018). https://doi.org/10.1097/hrp.0000000000000192

Hofmann, S.G., Grossman, P., Hinton, D.E.: Loving-kindness and compassion meditation: potential for psychological interventions. Clin. Psychol. Rev. **31**, 1126–1132 (2011)

Horwood, S., Anglim, J.: Problematic smartphone usage and subjective and psychological well-being. Comput. Hum. Behav. **97**, 44–50 (2019). https://doi.org/10.1016/j.chb.2019.02.028

Jazaieri, H., Mcgonigal, K., Jinpa, T., Doty, James R.: A randomized controlled trial of compassion cultivation training: effects on mindfulness, affect, and emotion regulation. Motiv. Emot. **38**(1), 23–35 (2014). https://doi.org/10.1007/s11031-013-9368-z

Jirasek, I., Hurych, E.: The perception of spiritual health differences between citizens and physicians in the Czech Republic. Health Promot. Int. **33**(5), 858–866 (2018). https://doi.org/10.1093/heapro/dax024

Johnson, D.P., Penn, D.L., Fredrickson, B.L., Meyer, P.S., Kring, A.M., Brantley, M.: Loving-kindness meditation to enhance recovery from negative symptoms of schizophrenia. J. Clin. Psychol. **65**(5), 499–509 (2009). https://doi.org/10.1002/jclp.20591

Kabat-Zinn, J.: Wherever You Go, There You Are: Mindfulness Meditation in Everyday Life. Hyperion, New York (1994)

Kabat-Zinn, J.: Mindfulness-based interventions in context: past, present, and future. Clin. Psychol.-Sci. Pract. **10**(2), 144–156 (2003). https://doi.org/10.1093/clipsy/bpg016

Kamitsis, I., Francis, A.J.P.: Spirituality mediates the relationship between engagement with nature and psychological wellbeing. J. Environ. Psychol. **36**, 136–143 (2013). https://doi.org/10.1016/j.jenvp.2013.07.013

Kearney, D.J., Malte, C.A., McManus, C., Martinez, M.E., Felleman, B., Simpson, T.L.: Loving-kindness meditation for posttraumatic stress disorder: a pilot study. J. Trauma. Stress **26**(4), 426–434 (2013). https://doi.org/10.1002/jts.21832

Kearney, D.J., McManus, C., Malte, C.A., Martinez, M.E., Felleman, B., Simpson, T.L.: Loving-kindness meditation and the broaden-and-build theory of positive emotions among veterans disorder. Med. Care **52**(12), S32–S38 (2014). https://doi.org/10.1097/mlr.0000000000000221

Keng, S.L., Tan, H.H.: Effects of brief mindfulness and loving-kindness meditation inductions on emotional and behavioral responses to social rejection among individuals with high borderline personality traits. Behav. Res. Ther. **100**, 44–53 (2018). https://doi.org/10.1016/j.brat.2017.11.005

Kirby, J.N., Baldwin, S.: A randomized micro-trial of a loving-kindness meditation to help parents respond to difficult child behavior vignettes. J. Child Fam. Stud. **27**(5), 1614–1628 (2018). https://doi.org/10.1007/s10826-017-0989-9

Kirby, J.N., Laczko, D.: A randomized micro-trial of a loving-kindness meditation for young adults living at home with their parents. J. Child Fam. Stud. **26**(7), 1888–1899 (2017). https://doi.org/10.1007/s10826-017-0692-x

Kristeller, J.L., Johnson, T.: Science looks at spirituality - cultivating loving-kindness: a two-stage model of the effects of meditation on empathy, compassion, and altruism. Zygon **40**(2), 391–407 (2005). https://doi.org/10.1111/j.1467-9744.2005.00671.x

Labelle, L.E., Lawlor-Savage, L., Campbell, T.S., Faris, P., Carlson, L.E.: Does self-report mindfulness mediate the effect of Mindfulness-Based Stress Reduction (MBSR) on spirituality and posttraumatic growth in cancer patients? J. Posit. Psychol. **10**(2), 153–166 (2015). https://doi.org/10.1080/17439760.2014.927902

Lifshitz, R., Nimrod, G., Bachner, Y.G.: Spirituality and wellbeing in later life: a multidimensional approach. Aging Ment. Health **23**(8), 984–991 (2019). https://doi.org/10.1080/13607863.2018.1460743

Lindsay, E.K., Creswell, J.D.: Back to the basics: how attention monitoring and acceptance stimulate positive growth. Psychol. Inq. **26**(4), 343–348 (2015). https://doi.org/10.1080/1047840x.2015.1085265

Lord, S.A.: Mindfulness and spirituality in couple therapy: the use of meditative dialogue to help couples develop compassion and empathy for themselves and each other. Aust. NZ J. Fam. Ther. **38**(1), 98–114 (2017). https://doi.org/10.1002/anzf.1201

Malone, C., Wachholtz, A.: The relationship of anxiety and depression to subjective well-being in a mainland chinese sample. J. Relig. Health **57**(1), 266–278 (2018). https://doi.org/10.1007/s10943-017-0447-4

Matiz, A., Fabbro, F., Crescentini, C.: Single vs. group mindfulness meditation: effects on personality, religiousness/spirituality, and mindfulness skills. Mindfulness **9**(4), 1236–1244 (2018). https://doi.org/10.1007/s12671-017-0865-0

May, C.J., Weyker, J.R., Spengel, S.K., Finkler, L.J., Hendrix, S.E.: Tracking longitudinal changes in affect and mindfulness caused by concentration and loving-kindness meditation with hierarchical linear modeling. Mindfulness **5**(3), 249–258 (2014). https://doi.org/10.1007/s12671-012-0172-8

Meezenbroek, E.D., et al.: Measuring spirituality as a universal human experience: development of the Spiritual Attitude and Involvement List (SAIL). J. Psychosoc. Oncol. **30**(2), 141–167 (2012). https://doi.org/10.1080/07347332.2011.651258

Munoz-Rodriguez, J.M., Serrate-Gonzalez, S., Navarro, A.B.: Generativity and life satisfaction of active older people: advances (keys) in educational perspective. Aust. J. Adult Learn. **59**(1), 94–114 (2019)

Mohamed, A.D., Lewis, C.: The efficacy of loving-kindness meditation on measures of subjective well-being in healthy young adults: preliminary data. Int. J. Psychol. **51**, 636–636 (2016)

Nash, J.D., Newberg, A.: Toward a unifying taxonomy and definition for meditation. Front. Psychol. **4** (2013). https://doi.org/10.3389/fpsyg.2013.00806

Newberg, A.B.: The neuroscientific study of spiritual practices. Front. Psychol. **5** (2014). https://doi.org/10.3389/fpsyg.2014.00215

Salzberg, S.: Lovingkindness: The Revolutionary Art of Happiness. Shambhala, Boston (1995)

Schilling, V., Lutz, W., Hofmann, S.G., Zimmermann, D., Wolter, K., Stangier, U.: Loving-kindness meditation for the treatment of chronic depression: treatment concept and results from a pilot study. Zeitschrift Fur Klinische Psychologie Und Psychotherapie **47**(3), 163–174 (2018). https://doi.org/10.1026/1616-3443/a000486

Schindler, S., Pfattheicher, S., Reinhard, M.A.: Potential negative consequences of mindfulness in the moral domain. Eur. J. Soc. Psychol. **49**(5), 1055–1069 (2019). https://doi.org/10.1002/ejsp.2570

Schutte, N.S., Malouff, J.M.: Emotional intelligence mediates the relationship between mindfulness and subjective well-being. Personal. Individ. Differ. **50**(7), 1116–1119 (2011). https://doi.org/10.1016/j.paid.2011.01.037

Shahar, B., et al.: A wait-list randomized controlled trial of loving-kindness meditation programme for self-criticism. Clin. Psychol. Psychother. **22**(4), 346–356 (2015). https://doi.org/10.1002/cpp.1893

Sheldon, K.M., Prentice, M., Halusic, M.: The experiential incompatibility of mindfulness and flow absorption. Soc. Psychol. Personal. Sci. **6**(3), 276–283 (2015). https://doi.org/10.1177/1948550614555028

Sorensen, S., Steindl, S.R., Dingle, G.A., Garcia, A.: Comparing the effects of Loving-Kindness Meditation (LKM), music and LKM plus music on psychological well-being. J. Psychol. **153**(3), 267–287 (2019). https://doi.org/10.1080/00223980.2018.1516610

Stevens, B.A.: Mindfulness: a positive spirituality for ageing? Aust. J. Ageing **35**(3), 156–158 (2016). https://doi.org/10.1111/ajag.12346

Tanay, G., Bernstein, A.: State Mindfulness Scale (SMS): development and initial validation. Psychol. Assess. **25**(4), 1286–1299 (2013). https://doi.org/10.1037/a0034044

Thauvoye, E., Vanhooren, S., Vandenhoeck, A., Dezutter, J.: Spirituality and well-being in old age: exploring the dimensions of spirituality in relation to late-life functioning. J. Relig. Health **57**(6), 2167–2181 (2018). https://doi.org/10.1007/s10943-017-0515-9

Watson, D., Clark, L.A., Tellegen, A.: Development and validation of brief measures of positive and negative affect: the PANAS scales. J. Personal. Soc. Psychol. **54**(6), 1063–1070 (1988)

Weytens, F., Luminet, O., Verhofstadt, L.L., Mikolajczak, M.: An integrative theory-driven positive emotion regulation intervention. PLoS ONE **9** (2014). https://doi.org/10.1371/journal.pone.0095677

Xu, W., Oei, T.P.S., Liu, X.H., Wang, X.M., Ding, C.: The moderating and mediating roles of self-acceptance and tolerance to others in the relationship between mindfulness and subjective well-being. J. Health Psychol. **21**(7), 1446–1456 (2016). https://doi.org/10.1177/1359105314555170

Yaden, D.B., Haidt, J., Hood, R.W., Vago, D.R., Newberg, A.B.: The varieties of self-transcendent experience. Rev. Gen. Psychol. **21**(2), 143–160 (2017). https://doi.org/10.1037/gpr0000102

Zeng, X., Chiu, C.P., Wang, R., Oei, T.P., Leung, F.Y.: The effect of loving-kindness meditation on positive emotions: a meta-analytic review. Front. Psychol. **6**, 1693 (2015)

Zeng, X., Chan, V.Y., Liu, X., Oei, T.P., Leung, F.Y.: The four immeasurables meditations: differential effects of appreciative joy and loving-kindness meditations on emotions. Mindfulness **8**(4), 949–959 (2017)

Zernicke, K.A., et al.: The ecalm trial: etherapy for cancer applying mindfulness. Exploratory analyses of the associations between online mindfulness-based cancer recovery participation and changes in mood, stress symptoms, mindfulness, posttraumatic growth, and spirituality. Mindfulness **7**(5), 1071–1081 (2016). https://doi.org/10.1007/s12671-016-0545-5

A Framework of Real-Time Stress Monitoring and Intervention System

Peixian Lu[1], Wei Zhang[1], Liang Ma[1(✉)], and Qichao Zhao[2]

[1] Department of Industrial Engineering, Tsinghua University, Beijing 100084,
People's Republic of China
liangma@tsinghua.edu.cn
[2] Kingfar Technology, No. 17 Building, No. 18, Anningzhuang East Road,
Haidian District, Beijing, China

Abstract. Stress is a universally experienced phenomenon in modern society. Stress influences the balance of Autonomous Nervous System (ANS). Studies have shown that cumulative stress in daily life can result in cardiovascular diseases and psychological or behavioral disorders, such as depression, and anxiety. Stress has also been investigated as a risk factor for reduced human performances, which in some situation, such as dangerous works or driving a car, may results in negative consequences. Therefore, in order to decrease the negative influence of stress, we proposed a framework for real-time stress measurement, monitoring and intervention. We used physiological responses detected by wearable sensors to measure stress in real time, including heart rate variability (HRV) and electrodermal activity (EDA). This framework can be used to measure and monitor stress in real time and makes it possible to provide corresponding intervention with smartphone for users under different stress levels.

Keywords: Stress monitoring · System framework · Stress intervention

1 Introduction

Stress is a universally experienced phenomenon in modern society and some special careers, such as policeman and pilot. Stress may be activated by different sources of stressors, such as physical stressors, psychological stressors, social stressors, and stressors that challenge cardiovascular and metabolic homeostasis [1]. According to the study of Fink [2], job stress is by far the major source of stress for American adults and has escalated progressively over the past few decades.

Stress influences the balance of Autonomous Nervous System (ANS) [3]. Studies have shown that cumulative stress in daily life can result in cardiovascular diseases [4] and psychological or behavioral disorders, such as depression, and anxiety [5]. Stress has also been investigated as a risk factor for reduced human performances, which in some situations, such as dangerous works or driving a car, may results in negative consequences [6]. Health problems caused by stress bring consequences to enterprises, where absenteeism, staff turnover [7] and tardiness increase, decreasing the production. The problem of "presenteeism" also arises, where employees attend their workplace,

P.-L. P. Rau (Ed.): HCII 2020, LNCS 12193, pp. 166–175, 2020.
https://doi.org/10.1007/978-3-030-49913-6_14

but they don't work at 100% of their capabilities. [8] According to the report of European Agency for Safety and Health at Work, the annual cost of absenteeism and presenteeism has been estimated at € 272 billion and the annual cost for loss of productivity at € 242 billion [9].

Therefore, in order to decrease the negative influence of stress, we proposed a framework of system to monitor stress and provide appropriate intervention. Traditional stress measures are mainly questionnaires based on several models, such as Demand–Control–Support model, Effort–Reward Imbalance model, and Person–Environment Fit model. Questionnaires measure stress according to the memory of users' experience for certain time other than the stress status in real time, which may make them miss some details for stress evaluation [10]. As a consequence, in this system, we used physiological responses detected by wearable sensors instead of questionnaires to measure stress in real time, including heart rate variability (HRV) and electrodermal activity (EDA) [8].

Different from other existing stress detecting system [11–13], we pay attention not only on stress monitoring, but also on stress intervention. In this framework, we provide appropriate stress intervention methods for different stress levels. According to our survey, there exist several stress intervention methods [14], such as: positive self-talk, spot checking and scanning, anchoring, cognitive rehearsal and desensitization, progressive muscle relaxation, imaginary and biofeedback, stress debriefing, visual-motor behavior rehearsal (VMBR), critical incident stress management (CISM), physical fitness, progressive relaxation, eye movement desensitization and reprocessing (EMDR). Considering applicability of the existing methods on smartphone APP and providing appropriate intervention methods for different stress levels, we need to select different methods for different levels of stress.

In this study, we proposed a system framework for real-time stress measurement, monitoring and intervention. This framework can be used to measure and monitor stress in real time and makes it possible to provide appropriate intervention with smartphone for users under high stress level.

2 System Architecture and Functions

In this study, we proposed a framework of real-time mental stress monitoring and intervention system. We designed main components and their information transmission method. For each major component, we designed its function and investigated common implement methods of some components, such as data collecting method, data analysis method, and stress intervention method. For data transmission method between each component, we designed different methods considering applicability and cost.

2.1 System Framework

The major function and process of this system is shown in Fig. 1. In this system, we use wearable sensors to collect user's physiological indicator data, including heart rate variability (HRV) and electrodermal activity (EDA). After data collection, we transmit the raw data to smartphone via Bluetooth, and then transmit them to cloud server through 4G network to process and analyze the data. Then, the analysis result will be transmitted to the smartphone through 4G network and displayed to user. According to different stress levels, this system will recommend different stress intervention methods to provide appropriate assistance. Key components and their major functions are shown in Fig. 2.

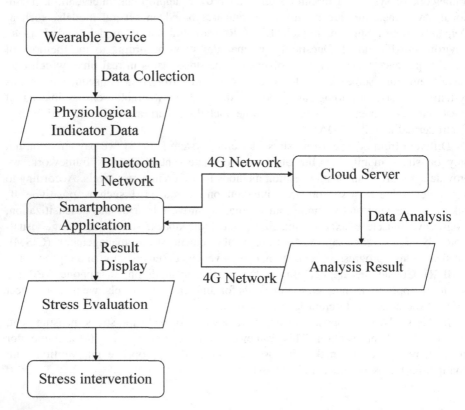

Fig. 1. Fundamental information transmission framework of stress monitoring and intervention system.

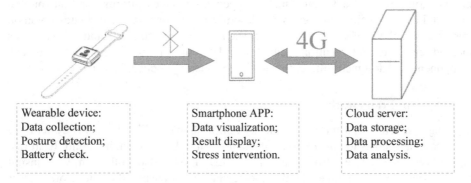

Fig. 2. Key components and their major functions in this system.

2.2   Stress Monitoring

Wearable Device
Considering the portability of wearable device, we designed it as a smart bracelet. This smart bracelet is used to detect physiological signals of user to provide information for mental stress monitoring. Main functions of this smart bracelet include: data collection, posture detection, and battery check (see Fig. 3).

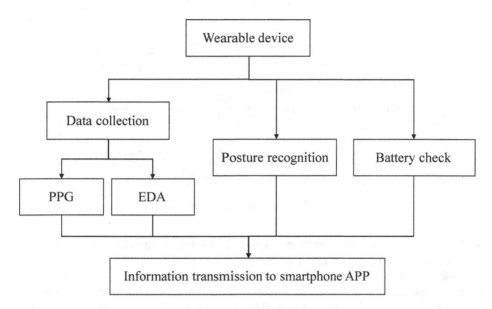

Fig. 3. Main functions of wearable device.

- Data collection: According to our investigation, the most common physiological indicators used for mental stress measurement are hormone levels, electrocardiogram (ECG), electroencephalogram (EEG), electrodermal activity (EDA), blood pressure (BP), skin temperature (ST), electromyogram (EMG), respiration, photoplethysmographic (PPG), pupil diameter (PD), eye gaze, and blinking [8]. Considering the detection point location of wrist, measurement feasibility of each indicator, and effect of mental stress measurement, we selected EDA and PPG (non-intrusively measurement signal of HRV) as detecting signals.
- Posture recognition: This function is to judge whether the user is in static status by using accelerator signal (ACC). If not, the data collected will be deleted to guarantee the accuracy of collected indicator data.
- Battery check: For long-time detection, we designed the battery life as 12 h. This function is designed to check the battery and warn user to charge it in time.

Smartphone APP

Functions of smartphone APP include main functions and secondary functions (see Fig. 4). Main functions of smartphone APP include: data visualization and result display for stress monitoring and stress intervention. Secondary functions include data transmission, register and log in, and personal settings.

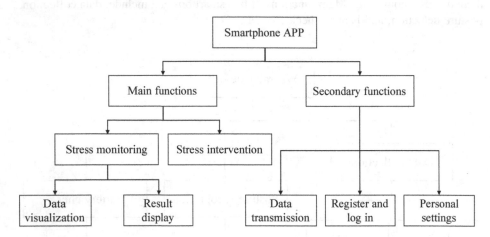

Fig. 4. Functions of smartphone APP.

- Data visualization: This function is designed to display the raw data to improve information transparency (see Fig. 5).
- Result display: This function is to give feedback of stress analysis result to user.
- Stress intervention: For different levels of stress, we recommend different methods to provide stress intervention. Detailed methods of stress intervention will be shown in Sect. 2.3.
- Data transmission: The smartphone APP should receive the raw data from wearable device and send it to the cloud server for data storage and analysis. What's more, it should receive the analysis result from the cloud server.
- Register and log in: For user management, this APP should provide register function for user without an account and require user to log in. Password request function should be provided to improve convenience for user.
- Personal settings: This module include common features of APP, such as: personal information setting, password modification, store path setting, help and feedback, and log out.

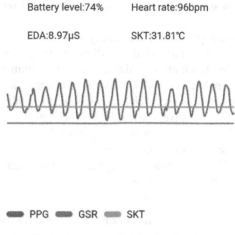

Fig. 5. Diagram of data visualization.

Cloud Server

Functions of cloud server include main functions and secondary functions (see Fig. 6). Main functions of cloud server include data storage and stress evaluation for stress monitoring. Secondary functions include data transmission and user management.

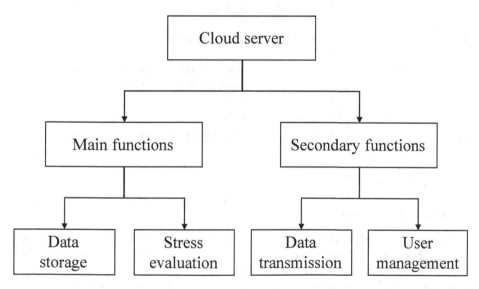

Fig. 6. Functions of cloud server.

- Data storage: All raw data received from smartphone APP will be stored in cloud server.
- Stress evaluation: Data processing and analysis for stress evaluation are implemented on the cloud server. The raw data will be processed and analyzed by model trained by appropriate algorithm. In order to select algorithm for model training of mental stress detection, we compared precision, indicator, and number of participants of common algorithms (see Table 1). Among these algorithms, we selected SVM algorithm for its extensive use and high precision.
- Data transmission: The cloud server should receive the raw data from smartphone APP and send back stress evaluation result.
- User management: This function is designed to store, search, and delete user account and their personal information.

Table 1. Comparison of mental stress detection algorithm [23].

Reference	Precision	Indicator	Classifier	Num of participants
[15]	83.3%	Breathe	k = 7 KNN	3
[13]	92.4%	ECG, GSR, ACC	Decision tree, SVM, bayes network	20
[16]	79.9%	ECG	Minimum distance classifier	6
[17]	93.5%	ECG, EMG, HRV, GSR, ST	KNN and Probabilistic Neural Network (PNN)	40
[18]	73%	ST, ECG, BP, GSR, Breathe	Decision tree	50
[19]	74.6%	RR intervals, HRV	- (Statistic analysis)	46
[20]	96%	EEG	Linear regression, support vector·machine, Naïve Bayes	42
[21]	89%	GSR	ANOVA test	45
[22]	92.75%	ECG, HRV	KNN, SVM	25
[23]	94.44%	Breathe	Three layer perceptron	43

Data Transmission

Data transmission among each component is implemented through Bluetooth network and 4G network (see Fig. 2).

- Bluetooth network is designed for data transmission between smart bracelet and smartphone APP, as these two components are always carried with user and distance between them is always smaller than 10 m.
- 4G network is designed for data transmission between smartphone APP and cloud server for the long distance between them.

2.3 Stress Intervention

Cumulative stress in daily life can result in cardiovascular diseases and psychological or behavioral disorders, such as depression, and anxiety. So, we need to provide stress intervention for user under stress. According to our survey, there exist several stress intervention methods. Considering applicability of the existing methods on smartphone APP and providing appropriate intervention methods for detected stress level, we select three types of methods for low, medium, and high level of stress (see Table 2).

- For low stress level, we selected articles and short videos relevant to stress intervention to provide knowledge for user. They can gain relevant knowledge and provide intervention for themselves spontaneously, such as singing, running, and writing.
- For medium stress level, we selected low-speed mini-games to provide external intervention, such as meditation, coloring and sand painting.
- For high stress level, we will provide professional consulting services for them.

Table 2. Method of intervention for different stress levels.

Stress level	Stress intervention method
Low	Relaxation class: relevant articles and short videos
Medium	Mini-games: coloring, meditation, and sand painting
High	Professional consulting services

3 Discussion

In this study, we proposed a system framework for real-time stress monitoring and intervention. Different from other existing stress detecting system frameworks, we integrate stress monitoring and corresponding stress intervention methods into a system. This system can help people with high stress risk, such as policeman and pilot, to monitor and intervene their stress in time.

In this framework, we chose physiological indicators to detect stress level using wearable smart bracelet. We can integrate other indicators into stress monitoring, as this framework has high extensibility. With development of technology, the detection of biochemical indicator can also be implemented on wrist, such as cortisol [24]. If we can obtain cortisol signal with wearable smart bracelet, the integration of biochemical indicator and physiological indicators may improve the precision of stress monitoring.

Except for detection of physiological signal, we can also integrate questionnaires into smartphone APP, such as Perceived Stress Scale, Stress Response Inventory, Life Event and Coping Inventory, Social Readjustment Rating Scale, Spielberger's Police Stress Survey, and Effort-Reward Imbalance Questionnaire. These questionnaires can be used to obtain self-assessment of their stress from different aspects. The assessment can provide a basis for recommending appropriate stress intervention method.

To implement this framework, there exist some difficult requirements to achieve the aim of real-time monitoring and intervention. First, data collection should be high-reliable and high-speed to guarantee the information input. Second, data analysis must be high-precision and high-efficient to provide rapid reliable response. Then, data transmission between each component should remain stable to avoid information loss. Finally, stress intervention module should be attractive enough to guarantee usage frequency of user.

4   Conclusion

In this study, we proposed a system framework for real-time stress measurement, monitoring and intervention. This framework can be used to measure and monitor stress in real time and makes it possible to provide appropriate intervention with smartphone for users under high stress level. With supplement of biochemical indicator and questionnaires, it will be more detailed for stress monitoring and more possible for appropriate stress intervention.

Acknowledgement. This study is supported by the Ministry of Science and Technology of the People's Republic of China (project number: 2017YFC0820200) and the Beijing Municipal Natural Science Foundation (project number: 9172008).

References

1. Pacak, K., Palkovits, M.: Stressor specificity of central neuroendocrine responses: implications for stress-related disorders. Endocr. Rev. **22**(4), 502–548 (2001)
2. Fink, G. (ed.): Stress: Concepts, Cognition, Emotion, and Behavior: Handbook of Stress Series, vol. 1. Academic Press, Cambridge (2016)
3. Kim, D., Seo, Y., Cho, J.: Detection of subjects with higher self-reporting stress scores using heart rate variability patterns during the day. In: 2008 30th Annual International Conference of the IEEE Engineering in Medicine and Biology Society, pp. 682–685. IEEE (2008)
4. Schubert, C., Lambertz, M., Nelesen, R.A., et al.: Effects of stress on heart rate complexity—a comparison between short-term and chronic stress. Biol. Psychol. **80**(3), 325–332 (2009)
5. Cohen, S., Kessler, R.C., Gordon, L.U. (eds.): Measuring Stress: A Guide for Health and Social Scientists. Oxford University Press on Demand, Oxford (1997)
6. Melillo, P., Bracale, M., Pecchia, L.: Nonlinear heart rate variability features for real-life stress detection. Case study: students under stress due to university examination. Biomed. Eng. Online **10**(1), 96 (2011)
7. Milczarek, M., González, E.R., Schneider, E.: OSH in figures: stress at work-facts and figures. Office for Official Publications of the European Communities (2009). https://osha.europa.eu/en/publications/reports/TE-81-08-478-EN-C_OSH_in_figures_stress_at_work
8. Alberdi, A., Aztiria, A., Basarab, A.: Towards an automatic early stress recognition system for office environments based on multimodal measurements: a review. J. Biomed. Inf. **59**, 49–75 (2016)
9. Hassard, J., Teoh, K., Cox, T.: Calculating the cost of work-related stress and psychosocial risks. Technical report, European Agency for Safety and Health at Work, Luxembourg (2014). http://dx.doi.org/10.2802/20493

10. Jimenez-Molina, A., Retamal, C., Lira, H.: Using psychophysiological sensors to assess mental workload during web browsing. Sensors (Switz.) **18**(2), 1–26 (2018). https://doi.org/10.3390/s18020458
11. Ahujaa, R., Bangab, A.: Mental stress detection in university students using machine learning algorithms. Procedia Comput. Sci. **152**, 349–353 (2019)
12. Cho, Y., Julier, S.J., Bianchi-Berthouze, N.: Instant stress: detection of perceived mental stress through smartphone photoplethysmography and thermal imaging. JMIR Mental Health **6**(4), e10140 (2019)
13. Sun, F.-T., Kuo, C., Cheng, H.-T., Buthpitiya, S., Collins, P., Griss, M.: Activity-aware mental stress detection using physiological sensors. In: Gris, M., Yang, G. (eds.) MobiCASE 2010. LNICST, vol. 76, pp. 282–301. Springer, Heidelberg (2012). https://doi.org/10.1007/978-3-642-29336-8_16
14. Patterson, G., Chung, T., Swan, I.: Stress management interventions for police officers and recruits: a meta-analysis. J. Exp. Criminol. **10**(4), 487–513 (2014)
15. Choi, J., Gutierrez-Osuna, R.: Using heart rate monitors to detect mental stress. In: Proceedings of the IEEE International Workshop on Wearable and Implantable Body Sensor Networks, pp. 219–223 (2009)
16. Boonnithi, S., Phongsuphap, S.: Comparison of heart rate variability measures for mental stress detection. In: Proceedings of the IEEE Computing in Cardiology, pp. 85–88 (2011)
17. Palanisamy, K., Murugappan, M., Yaacob, S.: Multiple physiological signal-based human stress identification using non-linear classifiers. Elektronika ir elektrotechnika **19**(7), 80–85 (2013)
18. Abouelenien, M., Burzo, M., Mihalcea, R.: Human acute stress detection via integration of physiological signals and thermal imaging. In: Proceedings of the 9th ACM International Conference on Pervasive Technologies Related to Assistive Environments, p. 32 (2016)
19. Salai, M., Vassányi, I., Kósa, I.: Stress detection using low cost heart rate sensors. J. healthc. Eng. **2016**, 13 (2016)
20. Subhani, A.R., Mumtaz, W., Saad, M.N.B.M., et al.: Machine learning framework for the detection of mental stress at multiple levels. IEEE Access **5**, 13545–13556 (2017)
21. Zangróniz, R., Martínez-Rodrigo, A., Pastor, J., et al.: Electrodermal activity sensor for classification of calm/distress condition. Sensors **17**(10), 2324 (2017)
22. Sriramprakash, S., Prasanna, V.D., Murthy, O.R.: Stress detection in working people. Procedia Comput. Sci. **115**, 359–366 (2017)
23. Fernández, J.R.M., Anishchenko, L.: Mental stress detection using bioradar respiratory signals. Biomed. Signal Process. Control **43**, 244–249 (2018)
24. Parlak, O., Keene, S.T., Marais, A., et al.: Molecularly selective nanoporous membrane-based wearable organic electrochemical device for noninvasive cortisol sensing. Sci. Adv. **4**(7), eaar2904 (2018)

Chinese Pain Descriptors Used by Medical Personnel: A Case Study in Beijing

Pei-Luen Patrick Rau[1], Zhi Guo[1], Runting Zhong[1,2(✉)],
and Soulki Kim[3]

[1] Department of Industrial Engineering, Tsinghua University,
Beijing 100084, China
[2] School of Business, Jiangnan University, Wuxi 214122, China
zhongrt@jiangnan.edu.cn
[3] Academy of Arts and Design, Tsinghua University, Beijing 100084, China

Abstract. Pain compels patients to visit doctors and is an inevitable topic of discussion between doctors and patients. The objective of the study was to investigate Chinese pain descriptors and explore their characteristics among 93 medical personnel in Beijing. This study used a questionnaire to collect Chinese pain descriptors used by medical personnel with more than two years of clinical experience. By qualitative analysis, 68 types of pain descriptors were identified from 801 descriptors and classified into 6 domains: *sensory, affective, intensity, cause, physical effect*, and *temporal*. *Sensory* pain descriptors were mentioned most frequently by the medical personnel (70.8%), whereas *affective* pain descriptors were mentioned least frequently (1.2%). The result revealed that medical personnel in Beijing seldom used affective descriptors, indicating that they tried to avoid their personal emotions when expressing pain. Based on the pain descriptors used by Chinese medical personnel, this study designed a visual pain assessment tool.

Keywords: Chinese culture · Doctor-patient communication · Pain · Pain assessment · Pain descriptors

1 Introduction

Pain compels patients to visit doctors and is an inevitable topic of discussion between doctors and patients. Pain descriptors are used to describe the pain experience. The use of appropriate pain descriptors can help a doctor accurately evaluate pain and improve communication with the patient. Numerous studies have examined pain descriptors in different cultural backgrounds. The McGill Pain Questionnaire (MPQ), a widely used pain measurement, contains 78 pain descriptors from the Dallenbach word list and the clinical literature [1]. A short-form of the McGill Pain Questionnaire (SF-MPQ) comprises 15 descriptors (11 sensory; 4 affective) as well as the Present Pain Intensity (PPI) index of the standard MPQ and a visual analogue scale (VAS) [2]. The SF-MPQ has been translated into Czech [3], Swedish [4], Greek [5], Korean [6], Thai [7] and Norwegian [8]. The SF-MPQ-2, an expanded and revised version of the SF-MPQ, was developed to provide a single measure of the major sensory and affective symptoms of

© Springer Nature Switzerland AG 2020
P.-L. P. Rau (Ed.): HCII 2020, LNCS 12193, pp. 176–190, 2020.
https://doi.org/10.1007/978-3-030-49913-6_15

both neuropathic and non-neuropathic pain [9, 10]. The SF-MPQ-2 was also translated and validated in Mandarin Chinese [11].

Pain descriptors are influenced by culture [12–14]. A pain descriptor that is prohibited by a culture will probably not occur; conversely, a permissible descriptor will be expressed [15]. According to Chen et al., Asian cancer patients hesitate to report pain, a behavior that may be related to the higher prevalence of undertreated pain among Asian cancer patients compared to North American and European patients [16]. Moore et al. developed a combination of qualitative and quantitative methods to describe the pain and pain coping perceptions of 25 Chinese, 25 Anglo-American and 35 Scandinavian subjects. The results revealed universal dimensions of pain, such as time, intensity, location, quality, cause and curability. More culture-specific dimensions included *suantong* described by Chinese as well as "real" and "imagined" pains described by Western subjects. These data indicated that the study methods used were sensitive to culture and that ethnicity may play a stronger role in the description of perceptions of pain than professional socialization [17]. A further study showed that similarities in the use of descriptors were observed within ethnic groups, whereas differences were observed between Chinese and American groups [18]. Tan explored pain description between hospitalized Chinese Canadian and non-Chinese Canadian school-aged child. The study found that Chinese children selected greater sensory words to describe pain compared to the non-Chinese children [19]. In addition, the Chinese children used less overt expressions in expressing feelings related to pain [19]. But a study suggests that Chinese displayed lower pain tolerance and reported higher SF-MPQ-Affective of pain compared to their Euro-Canadian counterparts [20]. Therefore, Chinese pain descriptors should not be directly translated from descriptors used in Western societies but require an exploration of how Chinese people use Mandarin Chinese to describe pain experience in the Chinese cultural context.

Several studies explored Chinese pain descriptors from patient's perspectives [21–24]. Rau et al. identified commonly used shoulder pain descriptors among rehabilitation patients, and found that female used more pain quality descriptors than male [21]. Chung et al. collected pain descriptors from 986 young adults who spoke Cantonese in Hong Kong. The pain descriptors were categorized according to nature, process, intensity, aggravating factors, accompanying symptoms and behavioral manifestation [23]. The results demonstrated that females use more pain descriptors than males, but the difference in the number of pain descriptors used by males and females was not significant [23]. The use of pain descriptors differed significantly among age groups and educational levels, and the number of descriptors used increased with increasing age and education level [23]. Females primarily used pain descriptors of nature type [23]. Whereas residents of Hong Kong use Cantonese, a dialect of Chinese, Mandarin Chinese is the most common dialect in the mainland China. Cantonese and Mandarin Chinese feature differences in pronunciation and underlying culture. Wang et al. collected 472 Chinese words from 507 Chinese adults in Beijing, who spoke Mandarin Chinese. The pain descriptors were categorized into four domains: sensory, intensity, affection and evaluation, and other [24]. Common pain descriptors were *distending, sore, cramp, pricking*, and *jumping* [24]. However, the studies [21, 23, 24] investigated pain descriptors used by general population and did not distinguish the characteristics of pain descriptors used by people with different occupations. The gap indicates a need to investigate pain descriptors used by people with different occupations, while the medical personnel are a representative case.

Doctor-patient communication in China has attracted increasing attention due to the deteriorating doctor-patient relationship in recent years [25]. According to a meta-analysis of observational surveys, the overall prevalence of workplace violence from 81,771 health-care professionals with available data was 62.4% [26]. The shortage of medical resources in China hinders visits to doctors, particularly skilled doctors in large hospitals, and patients who do have the opportunity to visit such doctors may have a very limited time to communicate with the doctors. In addition, low medical literacy of Chinese patient and poor communication skills of doctors leads to communication barrier [27]. But unlike many Western countries, Chinese patients did not want the relationship with doctor to be fully patient-centered [28]. In Chinese society, the doctor is perceived as a person of high social status [29]. Patients' responses to the decision-making and information dispensation were distinctively doctor-centered [28]. In order to get a better communication between doctor and patients in the limited consultation time, it is necessary to investigate pain descriptors used by medical personnel.

The objective of this study was to investigate Chinese pain descriptors used by medical personnel in Beijing. The results will enhance doctors' understanding of pain descriptors to improve communication with patients. This study also contributes to the understanding of cultural difference in pain expression.

2 Methods

2.1 Sample

The participants (n = 93, 75.3% female) were medical personnel recruited from a hospital located in Beijing, China. The average age was 34.0 ± 10.9 years. The age ranged from 18 to 72 years. The criteria for screening participants in the study were that 1) they should have more than 2 years of clinical experience and 2) use Mandarin Chinese as the primary language. Of the included personnel, 46 were doctors, and 46 were nurses (1 participant did not indicate his/her occupation). Approximately two fifths of the participants had a bachelor's degree or higher.

The study was approved by the Tsinghua University ethics committee. All participants provided written, informed consent and obtained monetary compensation for their participation.

2.2 Measure

A paper-pencil questionnaire was distributed to the participants. The questionnaire consisted of two parts. The first part was personal information about the participant, including gender, age, occupation, department, educational background, employment history, the most commonly used language, the second most common language, medical history, and pain treatment. The second part of the questionnaire investigated the pain experience and included the 28 types of pain used by Chung et al.'s study [23] and the types of pain listed in the "Classification of chronic pain" published by

International Association for the Study of Pain (IASP) [30]. The 28 types of pain could be found in Table 1. Participants were requested to choose the pain they experienced and evaluate the intensity and duration. Pain intensity was measured on a numerical rating scale of 1–5, with 1 indicating mild pain and 5 indicating extreme. Pain duration was measured on a category scale of 1–3, with 1 indicating constant pain, 2 indicating intermittent, and 3 indicating momentary. If the participants did not experience a specific type of pain, they were asked to choose 0. Furthermore, participants were requested to list words or phrases describing the pain they experienced, such as *pricking* or *sore*. The participants were also encouraged to list additional pain descriptors they knew to describe pain.

2.3 Pain Descriptor Analysis

The words and phrases recorded by the participants were coded and classified into domains by two researchers. Data were first coded and classified independently by each of the two researchers, and then the coding was compared. In the event of disagreement, the two researchers discussed their reasoning and reached a consensus.

The words and phrases were coded as pain descriptors, and the frequencies of their use for different types of pain were recorded. When a pain descriptor for a type of pain was mentioned by 1 participant, it was marked once. These pain descriptors were then classified into domains according to the properties of pain: *sensory*, which describes what the pain feels like; *affective*, which describes how bothersome or unpleasant the pain is; *intensity*, which describes the intensity of the pain; *cause*, which describes the cause of the pain; *physical effect*, which describes how the pain affect one's life; and *temporal*, which describes when or how often the pain occurs [23, 31].

3 Results

3.1 Medical Personnel's Pain Experiences

The descriptive statistics of the participants' pain experiences are presented in Table 1. The total number of pain descriptors was 801, of which 621 were based on real pain experience. The number of pain descriptors mentioned by each participant was 8.6 (SD = 6.7). The average pain intensity ranged from 1.5 (intercostal neuralgia) to 4.6 (labor pain).

Headache (74.2%), neck pain (61.3%) and stomachache (55.9%) were the three most common types of pain. 64.3% of the female participants had experienced menstrual pain, and all 19 female participants who had given birth had experienced labor pain.

Table 1. Descriptive statistics of participants' pain experiences (N = 93)

Type of pain	N (%)	Intensity		Duration (%)		
		M	SD	Constant	Intermittent	Momentary
Headache	69(74.2)	2.0	0.9	13.0	40.6	39.1
Neck pain	57(61.3)	2.1	0.9	19.3	35.1	38.6
Stomachache	52(55.9)	2.0	0.9	3.8	30.8	53.8
Toothache	47(50.5)	2.8	1.2	14.9	34.0	40.4
Sore throat	46(49.5)	2.2	1.0	13.0	26.1	50.0
Muscle soreness and pain	45(48.4)	2.1	1.1	15.6	40.0	40.0
Shoulder pain	44(47.3)	2.6	1.2	34.1	36.4	25.0
Backache	43(46.2)	2.3	1.0	23.3	46.5	25.6
Abdominal pain	39(41.9)	2.2	1.1	10.3	33.3	43.6
Muscular spasm (cramp)	33(35.5)	2.3	1.2	3.0	24.2	66.7
Lower extremity joint pain	25(26.9)	2.2	0.8	12.0	44.0	36.0
Ligament sprain	25(26.9)	2.5	1.1	44.0	24.0	32.0
Upper extremity joint pain	22(23.7)	2.0	0.9	13.6	31.8	45.5
Sciatica	14(15.1)	1.9	0.8	14.3	21.4	50.0
Surgical wound pain	14(15.1)	3.5	0.8	57.1	21.4	21.4
Chest wall pain	13(14.0)	1.8	1.1	0.0	38.5	61.5
Painful defecation	11(11.8)	1.9	0.9	0.0	45.5	45.5
Angina	8(8.6)	2.3	1.5	0.0	25.0	75.0
Intercostal neuralgia	8(8.6)	1.5	0.5	12.5	0.0	87.5
Trigeminal neuralgia	8(8.6)	2.3	1.3	0.0	12.5	87.5
Fracture	7(7.5)	2.7	1.6	28.6	14.3	28.6
Dysuria	5(5.4)	1.8	1.1	0.0	0.0	100.0
Palindromic rheumatism	3(3.2)	1.7	0.6	0.0	66.7	33.3
Post-herpetic neuralgia	3(3.2)	2.7	0.6	0.0	33.3	66.7
Pelvic pain	2(2.2)	2.5	0.7	0.0	50.0	50.0
Gout	1(1.1)	2.0	NA	0.0	0.0	100.0
Menstrual pain (N = 70 women)	45(64.3)	2.6	1.2	20.0	55.6	15.6
Labor pain (N = 19 women)	19(100)	4.6	0.8	36.8	31.6	26.3

Note: M = Mean, SD = standard deviation, NA = Not Applicable.

3.2   Identification and Classification of Descriptors

The 801 descriptors were classified into 68 types, which were divided into the 6 domains of *sensory*, *affective*, *intensity*, *cause*, *physical effect*, and *temporal*, as shown in Tables 2.

A total of 567 pain descriptors were identified as *sensory* descriptors, representing 70.8% of all descriptors. This domain included 36 types of descriptors, among which *pricking, sore, heavy, taut* and *distending* were most prevalent.

Only 10 pain descriptors were classified in the *affective* domain, representing 1.2% of the total descriptors. This domain included 5 types of descriptors.

A total of 64 pain descriptors were classified in the *intensity* domain, representing 8.0% of the total descriptors and including 10 types.

A total of 42 pain descriptors were classified in the *cause* domain, representing 5.2% of the total descriptors and including 7 types.

A total of 27 pain descriptors were classified in the *physical effect* domain, representing 3.4% of the total descriptors. This domain included 7 types of descriptors.

A total of 91 pain descriptors were classified in the *temporal* domain, representing 11.4% of the total descriptors and including 3 types.

Among the domains, *sensory* descriptors (70.8% of the 801 descriptors) were most prevalent among the descriptors mentioned by the medical personnel. *Affective* pain descriptors (1.2%) were the least prevalent.

Table 2. Frequency and classification of pain descriptors from medical personnel

Domain/code	N	%	Domain/code	N	%
Sensory	**567**	**70.8**	Bad mood	2	0.2
Pricking	55	6.9	Uncomfortable	2	0.2
Sore	55	6.9	Sad	1	0.1
Heavy	50	6.2	Feeling of impending death	1	0.4
Taut	48	6.0			
Distending	40	5.0	**Intensity**	**64**	**8.0**
Twitching	32	4.0	Horrible	28	3.5
Searing	30	3.7	Excruciating	9	1.1
Stuffy	29	3.6	Unbearable	7	0.9
Cramp	27	3.4	Common	5	0.6
Jumping	22	2.7	Very painful	5	0.6
Indistinct	17	2.1	Mild	3	0.4
Sharp	16	2.0	Extreme	2	0.2
Spasm	16	2.0	Bearable	2	0.2
Pressing	14	1.7	Bursting	2	0.2
Cutting	11	1.4	Hurt	1	0.1
Radiating	11	1.4			
Lacerating	10	1.2	**Cause**	**42**	**5.2**
Local	10	1.2	Painful movement	18	2.2
Dry	9	1.1	Pain made by effort	14	1.7
Drilling	9	1.1	Sudden pain	3	0.4
Explosive	6	0.7	Swelling	3	0.4
Numb	6	0.7	Inflammation	2	0.2
Pulsing	6	0.7	Pain in response to touch	1	0.1
Tugging	5	0.6	Tired	1	0.1

(*continued*)

Table 2. (*continued*)

Domain/code	N	%	Domain/code	N	%
Flashing	5	0.6			
String	5	0.6	**Physical effect**	**27**	**3.4**
Pinch	4	0.5	Stiff	7	0.9
Cold	4	0.5	Immobile	5	0.6
Pounding	3	0.4	Suffocating	4	0.5
Itchy	3	0.4	Harsh	4	0.5
Referred pain	3	0.4	Breaking cold sweat	4	0.5
Dizzy	2	0.2	Nausea	2	0.2
Kaka de tong	1	0.1	Difficulty sleeping	1	0.1
Torsion	1	0.1			
Tightening	1	0.1	**Temporal**	**91**	**11.4**
Reflex	1	0.1	Intermittent	57	7.1
			Constant	31	3.9
Affective	**10**	**1.2**	Momentary	3	0.4
Asthenia	4	0.5			

3.3   Domain Distribution

The distribution of the pain-domain descriptors is presented in Table 3. Pelvic pain was not mentioned in the collected data. For most types of pain, *sensory* descriptors were used most frequently. But for labor pain, *intensity* descriptors were most frequently used (50%), emphasizing how painful labor pain is. The second most frequently used descriptors varied. For example, toothache and menstrual pain were usually described by *intensity* descriptors, after *sensory* descriptors; whereas headache, stomachache and muscular spasm (cramp) were usually described by *temporal* descriptors. This illustrates that the descriptors selected to describe pain differ depending on the type of pain.

Table 3. Domain distribution of pain descriptors

Type of pain	Sensory	Intensity	Temporal	Cause	Physical effect	Affective
	N(%)	N(%)	N(%)	N(%)	N(%)	N(%)
Headache	84(80.0)	4(3.8)	15(14.3)	1(1.0)	1(1.0)	0(0.0)
Neck pain	42(76.4)	2(3.6)	3(5.5)	3(5.5)	4(7.3)	1(1.8)
Toothache	26(55.3)	12(25.5)	3(6.4)	5(10.6)	1(2.1)	0(0.0)
Trigeminal neuralgia	5(83.3)	1(16.7)	0(0.0)	0(0.0)	0(0.0)	0(0.0)
Sore throat	23(54.8)	3(7.1)	2(4.8)	11(26.2)	3(7.1)	0(0.0)
Angina	4(66.7)	1(16.7)	0(0.0)	0(0.0)	1(16.7)	0(0.0)
Chest wall pain	3(75.0)	0(0.0)	0(0.0)	0(0.0)	1(25.0)	0(0.0)
Intercostal neuralgia	2(100.0)	0(0.0)	0(0.0)	0(0.0)	0(0.0)	0(0.0)

(*continued*)

Table 3. (*continued*)

Type of pain	Sensory	Intensity	Temporal	Cause	Physical effect	Affective
	N(%)	N(%)	N(%)	N(%)	N(%)	N(%)
Backache	24(77.4)	2(6.5)	2(6.5)	2(6.5)	1(3.2)	0(0.0)
Sciatica	6(66.7)	1(11.1)	1(11.1)	0(0.0)	1(11.1)	0(0.0)
Stomachache	41(77.4)	2(3.8)	7(13.2)	0(0.0)	2(3.8)	1(1.9)
Abdominal pain	21(84.0)	2(8.0)	2(8.0)	0(0.0)	0(0.0)	0(0.0)
Upper extremity joint pain	13(56.5)	2(8.7)	4(17.4)	2(8.7)	1(4.3)	1(4.3)
Lower extremity joint pain	9(47.4)	2(10.5)	4(21.1)	4(21.1)	0(0.0)	0(0.0)
Gout	1(25.0)	1(25.0)	0(0.0)	1(25.0)	1(25.0)	0(0.0)
Muscular spasm (cramp)	16(51.6)	1(3.2)	9(29.0)	2(6.5)	2(6.5)	1(3.2)
Ligament sprain	13(61.9)	1(4.8)	4(19.0)	3(14.3)	0(0.0)	0(0.0)
Muscle soreness and pain	20(71.4)	0(0.0)	4(14.3)	4(14.3)	0(0.0)	0(0.0)
Fracture	1(50.0)	1(50.0)	0(0.0)	0(0.0)	0(0.0)	0(0.0)
Menstrual pain	22(78.6)	3(10.7)	3(10.7)	0(0.0)	0(0.0)	0(0.0)
Labor pain	7(31.8)	11(50.0)	3(13.6)	0(0.0)	1(4.5)	0(0.0)
Post herpetic neuralgia	3(100.0)	0(0.0)	0(0.0)	0(0.0)	0(0.0)	0(0.0)
Surgical wound pain	4(50.0)	3(37.5)	1(12.5)	0(0.0)	0(0.0)	0(0.0)
Shoulder pain	20(69.0)	2(6.9)	3(10.3)	2(6.9)	1(3.4)	1(3.4)
Painful defecation	2(50.0)	1(25.0)	0(0.0)	0(0.0)	1(25.0)	0(0.0)
Dysuria	3(100.0)	0(0.0)	0(0.0)	0(0.0)	0(0.0)	0(0.0)
Palindromic rheumatism	2(50.0)	1(25.0)	0(0.0)	0(0.0)	1(25.0)	0(0.0)

3.4 Common Descriptors

Table 4 presents the common pain descriptors for 27 types of pain (excluding pelvic pain). Those descriptors used with a frequency of greater than 10% for a particular type of pain were selected.

Some descriptors were used to describe more than one type of pain. For example, "heavy" was used to describe headache, neck pain, abdominal pain, menstrual pain and shoulder pain. "Sore" was used to describe neck pain, backache, sciatica, lower extremity joint pain, ligament sprain, muscle soreness and pain and shoulder pain. "Pricking" was used to describe trigeminal neuralgia, angina, chest wall pain, sciatica, post herpetic neuralgia, painful defecation and dysuria. These results suggest that these pain descriptors cannot be used to distinguish different types of pain.

Some descriptors appeared frequently for a particular type of pain. For example, "sore" was commonly used to describe neck pain (30.9%), backache (32.3%), and muscle soreness and pain (35.7%). "Heavy" was commonly used to describe menstrual pain (28.6%). "Cramp" was commonly used to describe abdominal pain (28.0%). The results suggest that these descriptors might have a high agreement rate among individuals.

Table 4. Common pain descriptors for 27 types of pain

Type of pain	N	Descriptors (percentage > 10%)
Headache	105	Heavy (21.0%), Taut (20.0%), Intermittent (11.4%)
Neck pain	55	Sore (30.9%), Taut (12.7%), Heavy (10.9%)
Stomachache	53	Cramp (17.0%), Searing (13.2%), Twitching (11.3%), Intermittent (11.3%)
Toothache	48	Horrible (12.5%), Drilling (10.4%)
Sore throat	43	Dry (20.9%), Painful upon movement (20.9%), Searing (16.3%)
Backache	31	Sore (32.3%), Taut (12.9%), Pressing (9.7%)
Muscular spasm (cramp)	31	Twitching (22.6%), Intermittent (19.4%), Spasm (12.9%)
Shoulder pain	29	Sore (20.7%), Taut (13.8%), Heavy (10.3%)
Muscle soreness and pain	28	Sore (35.7%), Constant (14.3%), Painful movement (10.7%)
Menstrual pain	28	Heavy (28.6%)
Abdominal pain	25	Cramp (28.0%), Heavy (16.0%), Distending (12.0%)
Upper extremity joint pain	23	Sharp (13.0%)
Labor pain	22	Horrible (22.7%), Excruciating (18.2%)
Ligament sprain	21	Constant (19.0%), Sore (14.3%)
Lower extremity joint pain	19	Sore (15.8%), Sharp (15.8%), Intermittent (15.8%), Horrible (10.5%), Painful movement (10.5%)
Sciatica	9	Distending (11.1%), Pricking (11.1%), Sore (11.1%), Sharp (11.1%), Local (11.1%), Radiating (11.1%), Bearable (11.1%), Intermittent (11.1%), Painful movement (11.1%)
Surgical wound pain	8	Lacerating (25.0%), Excruciating (25.0%), Searing (12.5%), Sharp (12.5%), Mild (12.5%), Constant (12.5%)
Trigeminal neuralgia	6	Flashing (33.3%), Pricking (16.7%), Numb (16.7%), Local (16.7%), Horrible (16.7%)
Angina	5	Pricking (20.0%), Stuffy (20.0%), Lacerating (20.0%), Cramp (20.0%)
Chest wall pain	4	Pricking (25.0%), Pressing (25.0%), Pounding (25.0%), Suffocating (25.0%)
Gout	4	Local (25.0%), Unbearable (25.0%), Painful movement (25.0%), Difficulty sleeping (25.0%)

(continued)

Table 4. (*continued*)

Type of pain	N	Descriptors (percentage > 10%)
Painful defecation	4	Distending (25.0%), Pricking (25.0%), Bursting (25.0%), Stiff (25.0%)
Palindromic rheumatism	4	Distending (25.0%), Taut (25.0%), Common (25.0%), Stiff (25.0%)
Post herpetic neuralgia	3	Pricking (66.7%), Flashing (33.3%)
Dysuria	3	Pricking (66.7%), Searing (33.3%)
Intercostal neuralgia	2	Sharp (50.0%), Jumping (50.0%)
Fracture	2	Distending (50.0%), Excruciating (50.0%)

3.5 Design of Visual Pain Assessment Tool

Based on the pain descriptors used by Chinese medical personnel, we designed a visual pain assessment tool, as Fig. 1 presented. The main interfaces included Personal information, location, nature, duration, and summary of the pain.

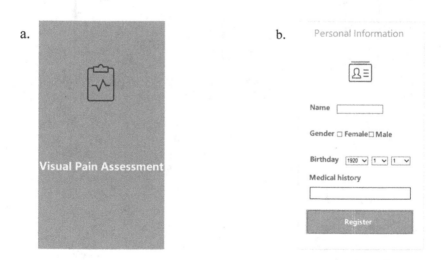

Fig. 1. (*continued*)

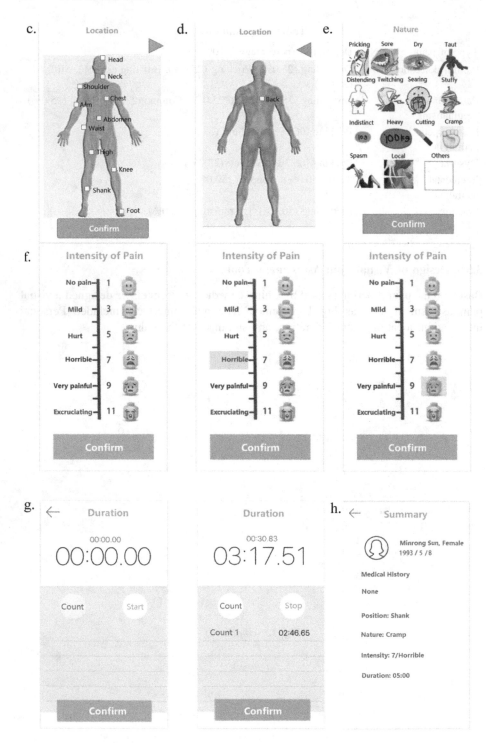

Fig. 1. Prototype of Visual Pain Assessment Tool. a. Home page; b. personal information; c. location-front; d. location-back; e. nature; f. intensity; g. duration; h. summary

4 Discussion

4.1 Affective Pain Descriptors Were the Least Frequent

This study identified 68 types of pain descriptors used by medical personnel from 801 descriptors and classified them into 6 domains: *sensory, affective, intensity, cause, physical effect*, and *temporal*. *Sensory* pain descriptors were mentioned most frequently by the medical personnel (70.8%), whereas *affective* pain descriptors were mentioned least frequently (1.2%). In Linl et al.'s study, the domain distribution is *sensory* (94%), *temporal* (22%), *affect* (16%), *spatial* (15%), *magnitude* (14%), *Interference/effect* (9%) and *other domain* (8%), respectively. Pain descriptors in *affective* domain used by medical personnel in this study were much less than those of Westerners [17, 31]. Chinese society is strongly influenced by Confucianism, which encourages stoicism [32]. Disclosure of negative emotion is not encouraged in Chinese culture for its capacity to disrupt group harmony and status hierarchies [33]. Chinese might replace affective expression with somatization as a safe means of expressing psychological discomfort to avoid losing face [34, 35]. Therefore, affective descriptors were not frequently used.

We also observed disparities in pain descriptors between medical personnel and Chinese patients. The mean number of pain descriptors mentioned by participant in this study is 8.6, larger than that of Chinese patients in Beijing (Mean = 0.93) [24] and Hong Kong (Mean = 3) [23]. This is not surprising because medical personnel have clinical experience. Regarding domain distribution, it is interesting to note that the using proportion of affective descriptors in medical personnel (1.2%) was less than those mentioned by Chinese patients (13.8%) in study [24]. It was found that medical personnel would focus on medical/technical tasks at hand rather than express their emotions because they may think dealing with the emotions is unprofessional, or too time-consuming [36, 37]. In China, doctors are under great time pressure to communicate with their patients, so they focus more on making the right decision for patients with the physical part of pain descriptors [27]. This discrepancy of pain descriptors between medical personnel and patients may lead to lack of empathy in physician-patient communication. It was found that Chinese patients indicated a desire for a doctor–patient relationship built on mutual understanding, and were particularly focused on being treated in a friendly manner and cared for in a manner that was considerate of their psychosocial context [28]. The result of this study suggests the necessity of promoting communication skills training for medical personnel in China via government healthcare promotion campaigns. Medical personnel should be aware of the discrepancies in pain descriptors between medical personnel and patients and use simple words or give sufficient explanation of professional terms (e.g. using metaphor) to promote patient understanding.

4.2 Limitations and Future Studies

This study is subject to limitations. First, the sample size is relatively small. Second, all participants in this study were from Beijing. The most common language used by all participants was Mandarin Chinese. In other areas of China, other dialects are commonly used in daily life. Language diversity was not considered in this study. Third, the classification of pain descriptors was determined by the authors and not the participants. Some descriptors were vague. To obtain a more accurate classification, in-depth interviews with participants may be needed to understand what these descriptors mean and in what context.

Future research could improve upon the present study in several ways. First, the pain descriptors in this study could be used as a blueprint for a pain assessment tool for the global Chinese population; the sensitivity and validity of such a tool in practice remains to be determined. Second, pain descriptors provided by patients could be collected for comparison with the descriptors used by medical personnel. Last, exploration of the influence of dialect on pain descriptors is also an interesting future topic.

5 Conclusion

This study investigated Chinese pain descriptors and explored their characteristics among 93 medical personnel in Beijing. By qualitative analysis, 68 types of pain descriptors were identified from 801 descriptors and classified into 6 domains: *sensory, affective, intensity, cause, physical effect*, and *temporal*. This study concluded that medical personnel in Beijing seldom used affective descriptors. The results provide insights on doctor-patient communication skills training in China. This study designed a visual pain assessment tool based on the pain descriptors used by Chinese medical personnel.

Acknowledgement. This study was funded by the National Natural Science Foundation of China (grant number 71661167006).

Conflicts of Interests. The authors declare that there is no conflict of interest.

References

1. Melzack, R.: The McGill pain questionnaire: major properties and scoring methods. Pain 1, 277–299 (1975)
2. Melzack, R.: The short-form McGill pain questionnaire. Pain 30, 191–197 (1987)
3. Solcová, I., Jakoubek, B., Sýkora, J., Hník, P.: Characterization of vertebrogenic pain using the short form of the McGill pain questionnaire. Casopís Lékařů Českých. 129, 1611 (1990)
4. Burckhardt, C., Bjelle, A.: A Swedish version of the short-form McGill pain questionnaire. Scand. J. Rheumatol. 23, 77–81 (1994)
5. Georgoudis, G., Watson, P.J., Oldham, J.A.: The development and validation of a Greek version of the short-form McGill pain questionnaire. Eur. J. Pain 4, 275–281 (2012)
6. Lee, H., Nicholson, L.L., Adams, R.D., Maher, C.G., Halaki, M., Bae, S.S.: Development and psychometric testing of Korean language versions of 4 neck pain and disability questionnaires. Spine 31, 1841–1845 (2006)
7. Kitisomprayoonkul, W., Klaphajone, J., Kovindha, A.: Thai short-form McGill pain questionnaire. J. Med. Assoc. Thail. 89, 846–853 (2006)

8. Strand, L.I., Ljunggren, A.E., Bogen, B., Ask, T., Johnsen, T.B.: The short-form McGill pain questionnaire as an outcome measure: test-retest reliability and responsiveness to change. Eur. J. Pain **12**, 917–925 (2008)

9. Dworkin, R.H., et al.: Development and initial validation of an expanded and revised version of the short-form McGill pain questionnaire (SF-MPQ-2). PAIN® **144**, 35–42 (2009)

10. Dworkin, R.H., et al.: Validation of the short-form McGill pain questionnaire-2 (SF-MPQ-2) in acute low back pain. J. Pain Off. J. Am. Pain Soc. **16**, 357–366 (2015)

11. Wang, J.L., Zhang, W.J., Gao, M., Zhang, S., Tian, D.H., Chen, J.: A cross-cultural adaptation and validation of the short-form McGill pain questionnaire-2: Chinese version in patients with chronic visceral pain. J. Pain Res. **10**, 121–128 (2017)

12. Coggon, D., et al.: Drivers of international variation in prevalence of disabling low back pain: findings from the CUPID study. Eur. J. Pain **23**, 35–45 (2018)

13. Young, J.R., Sih, C., Hogg, M.M., Anderson-Montoya, B.L., Fasano, H.T.: Qualitative assessment of face validity and cross-cultural acceptability of the faces pain scale: "revised" in cameroon. Qual. Health Res. **28**, 832 (2018)

14. Peacock, M.S., Patel, M.S.: Cultural influences on pain. Rev. Pain **1**, 6 (2008)

15. Kenny, A.: Wittgenstein. Harmondsworth, Pelican Books (1975)

16. Chen, C.H., Tang, S.T., Chen, C.H.: Meta-analysis of cultural differences in Western and Asian patient-perceived barriers to managing cancer pain. Palliat. Med. **26**, 206–221 (2012)

17. Moore, R., Miller, M.L., Weinstein, P., Dworkin, S.F., Liou, H.: Cultural perceptions of pain and pain coping among patients and dentists. Commun. Dent. Oral Epidemiol. **14**, 327–333 (1986)

18. Moore, R., Brødsgaard, I., Miller, M.L., Mao, T.-K., Dworkin, S.F.: Consensus analysis: Reliability, validity, and informant accuracy in use of American and Mandarin Chinese pain descriptors. Ann. Behav. Med. **19**, 295–300 (1997)

19. Tan, E.L.C.: Pain description of hospitalized Chinese Canadian and non-Chinese Canadian school-aged children (1995)

20. Hsieh, A.Y., Tripp, D.A., Ji, L.J., Sullivan, M.J.L.: Comparisons of catastrophizing, pain attitudes, and cold-pressor pain experience between Chinese and European Canadian young adults. J. Pain **11**, 1187–1194 (2010)

21. Rau, C.-L., et al.: Pain quality descriptors and sex-related differences in patients with shoulder pain. J. Pain Res. **11**, 1803 (2018)

22. Tsai, Y.-F., Tsai, H.-H., Lai, Y.-H., Chu, T.-L.: Pain prevalence, experiences and management strategies among the elderly in Taiwanese nursing homes. J. Pain Symptom Manag. **28**, 579–584 (2004)

23. Chung, W., Wong, C., Yang, J., Tan, P.: The use of cantonese pain descriptors among healthy young adults in Hong Kong. Acta Anaesthesiol. Sin. **36**, S1–S11 (1998)

24. Wang, L., Luo, A.-L., Zhang, Z.-X., Liu, L.-Y., Xu, Z.-H., Ren, H.-Z.: Investigation on the pain describing words in Chinese. Chin. J. Pain Med. **2**, 193–199 (1996)

25. Liu, X., Rohrer, W., Luo, A., Fang, Z., He, T., Xie, W.: Doctor–patient communication skills training in mainland China: a systematic review of the literature. Patient Educ. Couns. **98**, 3–14 (2015)

26. Lu, L., et al.: Prevalence of workplace violence against health-care professionals in China: a comprehensive meta-analysis of observational surveys. Trauma Violence Abuse **21**, 498–509 (2018)

27. Sun, N., Rau, P.-L.P.: Barriers to improve physician–patient communication in a primary care setting: perspectives of Chinese physicians. Health Psychol. Behav. Med. **5**, 166–176 (2017)

28. Ting, X., Yong, B., Yin, L., Mi, T.: Patient perception and the barriers to practicing patient-centered communication: a survey and in-depth interview of Chinese patients and physicians. Patient Educ. Couns. **99**, 364–369 (2016)
29. Tung, W.-C., Li, Z.: Pain beliefs and behaviors among Chinese. Home Health Care Manag. Pract. **27**, 95–97 (2015)
30. Merskey, H., Bogduk, N.: Classification of chronic pain: descriptions of chronic pain syndromes and definitions of pain terms. In: Taxonomy IAftSoPTFo. IASP Press, Seattle WA, USA (1994)
31. Linl, C.-P., Kupperl, A.E., Gammaitonil, A.R., Galerl, B.S., Jensenl, M.P.: Frequency of chronic pain descriptors: implications for assessment of pain quality. Eur. J. Pain **15**, 628–633 (2011)
32. Eleanor, H.: Developing a cultural model of caregiving obligations for elderly Chinese wives. West. J. Nurs. Res. **27**, 457–464 (2005)
33. Bond, M.H.: Emotions and their expression in Chinese culture. J. Nonverbal Behav. **17**, 245–262 (1993)
34. Kleinman, A.: Neurasthenia and depression: a study of somatization and culture in China. Cult. Med. Psychiatry **6**, 117–190 (1982)
35. Parker, G., Gladstone, G., Chee, K.T.: Depression in the planet's largest ethnic group: the Chinese. Am. J. Psychiatry **158**, 857–864 (2001)
36. Detmar, S.B., Muller, M.J., Wever, L.D., Schornagel, J.H., Aaronson, N.K.: Patient-physician communication during outpatient palliative treatment visits: an observational study. JAMA **285**, 1351–1357 (2001)
37. Hallenbeck, J.: Pain and intercultural communication. In: Moore, R.J. (ed.) Handbook of Pain and Palliative Care, pp. 19–34. Springer, New York (2003). https://doi.org/10.1007/978-1-4419-1651-8_2

Developing Empathy Towards Older Adults Through Emotional and Cognitive Enhancement

Pei-Lee Teh[1,2](✉) ⓘ, Motoki Watabe[1,2] ⓘ,
Annereena Ravichandran[1,2] ⓘ, and Kristel Tan[1,2] ⓘ

[1] School of Business, Monash University Malaysia, Bandar Sunway,
Selangor Darul Ehsan, Malaysia
{teh.pei.lee, motoki.watabe, annereena.ravichandran,
kristel.tan}@monash.edu
[2] Gerontechnology Laboratory, Global Asia in the 21st Century (GA21)
Platform, Monash University Malaysia, Bandar Sunway, Malaysia

Abstract. This paper aims to investigate impact of emotional and cognitive enhancement on improving the empathic aspects of young adults towards older adults. A sample of 90 young adults aged between 18 to 30 years was collected to test the research hypotheses. The results indicate that participants with either emotional or cognitive enhancement empathize lesser than those with both emotional and cognitive enhancement. Participants with both emotional and cognitive enhancement showed the highest level of empathy as with those without emotional, cognitive and both emotional and cognitive enhancement. These insights have important implications on the service sectors specifically towards serving and caring for an aging population in the midst of urbanization, globalisation and modernization. Young adults need to develop emphatic attitudes while providing service to the older adults as young adults are the future generation. The paper is concluded with a discussion on the findings, research implications and limitations.

Keywords: Young adults · Older adults · Emphatic attitudes · Emotional enhancement · Cognitive enhancement

1 Introduction

Global aging is occurring at an unprecedented rate. The world is experiencing a hike in the number and proportion of older adults in the population. The recent data from World Population Prospects: the 2019 revision [31] has revealed that by the year 2050, more than 15% of the people in the world will be over the age of 65 as compared to the 9% of people in the year 2019. This is a representation of the phenomenon known as population aging, represented by the United Nations (UN) as a process where the population of older adults becomes larger than the whole population [1]. Modernization has played a key role in the recent increase of human life expectancy [17]. An upturn in both physical and cognitive functionalities among the aging population has resulted in healthier and longer lives [30]. In parallel with modernization, drastic changes in economic and social

P.-L. P. Rau (Ed.): HCII 2020, LNCS 12193, pp. 191–199, 2020.
https://doi.org/10.1007/978-3-030-49913-6_16

advancement has crippled familial, social, cultural and social institutions. For instance, young people are more engrossed to seek for new opportunities and identities forgetting their sense of duty and commitment towards older adults [23].

Despite research [5, 29] stating that modernization has affected young adult's attitudes moulding them to become increasingly "me" oriented, the influence of these differences on intergenerational relationships has yet to be discovered [27]. This paper aims to bridge the perceived gap which exists among young and older adults. Older adults are easily overlooked and often discriminated by society due to misinformation, stigma and the false beliefs about aging [4, 20]. Older adults are often stereotyped and associated to negative behaviours and attitudes based on their perceived age [22, 23]. This phenomenon known as ageism is the most common form of prejudice which is often forgotten and easily overlooked by society [24]. The lack of attention to older adults is dominated by the presence of technology which contributes to an age-based digital device [7]. The intersection of age and technology is a major concern in the twentieth century as younger adults are moving too fast leaving older adults behind.

The challenges faced by older adults amidst modernization relates to factors such as the focus of Human Rights Act [18], lack of awareness amongst society towards older adults [22] and the lack of knowledge about the specific needs of older adults [14, 19]. This paper will focus on addressing the lack of awareness present amongst society particularly young adults towards the needs of older adults. In this day of age, young adults often dismiss older adult's contribution to society. Instead of treating older adults with appreciation and respect, older adults are often forgotten and perceived to be a burden. Young adults tend to forget that the simple act of paying attention would positively impact one's self and society. As the world is leaping into modernization, dealing with ageism is something which is unavoidable due to the unprecedented demographic shift. In the road to globalization, urbanization and modernization, it is imperative for young adults to be considerate and polite to individuals whose bodies and minds are aging as young adults would be leading the service sectors whose main consumers consist of older adults [6]. The ageing population needs affection and care from the existing young adults to generate value in service sectors which enhances health, well-being and social inclusivity among older people.

The concept of empathy has been discussed in literature [9, 13], yet there is still confusion as to what the word means and how it can be applied [32]. Empathy is the ability to place yourself in another person's shoes in pursue to better understand their feelings and experiences. Empathy can be simulated when a person is aware of another person's feelings. Contemporary researchers no longer consider empathy as a unitary concept conversely empathy is more commonly differentiated between two compo- nents - emotional and cognitive empathy [2, 8]. Emotional empathy refers to the sensations and feelings people receive in response to another person's emotions. On the other hand, cognitive empathy refers to the ability to identify and understand another person's emotions [2, 8]. Many young adults find themselves to be in roles which serve older adults, and thus emotional and cognitive empathy is critical to serve the aging population in sectors such as healthcare, education, communication and others. There is rationale to investigate emotional and cognitive empathy as a potential mechanism to improve the emphatic attitudes of young adults towards older adults.

It is vital for young adults to develop and fine tune their attitudes related to empathy, availability, understanding, interest and competence [6]. By being kind and showing compassion, the perceived gap between young and older adults can be overcome. This in return would be a step closer to reducing the challenges faced by the aging population. Researchers have been conducted on the global challenges of aging [28], more generally on older adults receiving poor treatment and service, health conditions and subjective age [21]. There has been a general lack of research on topics related to the empathic attitudes of young adults towards older adults resulting in the formation of an open research question. This study will examine the notion of empathy prioritizing the need of emotional and cognitive enhancement to increase the level of empathic attitudes among young adults towards older adults. Using an age simulation suit to ignite emotional enhancement and reading scenarios as cognitive enhancement, this paper will examine the emphatic attitudes among young adults towards older adults. In this study, findings are presented from a field experiment of young adults aged between 18 to 30 years old.

2 Literature Review and Research Hypotheses

Empathy depicts an essential role in human, social, and psychological interaction during all stages of life [8]. Given that the study of empathy is an ongoing area of major interest in various fields, this paper aims to examine the impact of emotional and cognitive enhancement on improving the emphatic attitudes of young adults towards older adults. This paper is built on social neuroscience literature to gauge a better understanding of empathy. Simulation Theory proposes that emotional empathy exists when a person notices another person experiencing an emotion [25]. Conversely, the person noticing another person simulates the same emotion in themselves to know first-hand what it feels like. On the other hand, the Theory of Mind proposes that cognitive empathy exists when a person is able to understand what another person is thinking and feeling based on rules of how one should think or feel [3]. This theory proposes the mental state of another person is determined by using cognitive thought processes.

To further strengthen this study, a three-component model of empathy is incorporated. This model entails an affective response to an individual, a cognitive response to identify the perspective of an individual and some regulatory mechanism taken into consideration by an individual [8, 9]. Literature suggest that empathy requires the ability to share emotional experience as well as to understand another person's experience [8]. These theories suggest that emotions during highly demanding activities impair cognitive processing efficiency [3]. In addition, simulation experience significantly influences the emotional state of the participants and potentially overwhelms their cognitive load [25].

According to the above discussion, we hypothesize that 1) emotional enhancement by simulating experience of older adult's physical difficulties would enhance empathy of young adults for older adults, and 2) cognitive enhancement (stimulus mentioning older adult's physical difficulties) would enhance empathy of young adults of older adults, too. In addition, combination of these two would have more effects than solo enhancement by each. Therefore, we propose the following five hypotheses. The first two are the main effect of emotion and cognitive enhancement. The rest of three are interaction effects of these enhancement.

H1: Young people who solely have emotional enhancement would develop a higher level of empathetic attitudes toward older adults compared to young adults without emotional enhancement.

H2: Young people who solely have cognitive enhancement would develop a higher level of empathetic attitudes toward older adults compared to young adults without cognitive enhancement.

H3: Young people who do not have the cognitive and emotional enhancement would develop a lower level of empathetic attitudes toward older adults compared to young adults with both emotional and cognitive enhancement.

H4: Young people who solely have cognitive enhancement would develop a lower level of empathetic attitudes toward older adults compared to young adults with both emotional and cognitive enhancement.

H5: Young people who solely have emotional enhancement would develop a lower level of empathetic attitudes toward older adults compared to young adults with both emotional and cognitive enhancement.

3   Research Method

3.1   Research Procedure

The experiment was conducted at the Gerontechnology Lab of Monash University Malaysia [11]. All research procedures are being performed in accordance with the university research ethics approval. Young adults aged between 18 to 30 years old was recruited to partake in this experiment. In order to obtain a better response, the young adults were recruited on a voluntary basis. The participant's anonymity was assured to be kept confidential. Each participant was given a token of appreciation worth MYR15 (USD3.58) per session as a sign of gratitude. Participants were given the choice to either keep the incentive given or donate to participating nursing/retirement homes.

The survey questionnaire was completed by 90 younger adults aged between 18 to 30 years old. The survey questionnaire included questions related to personal details and questions to identify level of empathic attitude. All questions were measured based on a 7-point Likert scale ('1' = 'strongly disagree', '7' = 'strongly agree'), adapted from prior studies [15, 26]. Emotional enhancement was achieved by wearing an age simulation suit. An age simulation suit offers the opportunity to experience the impairments of an older adult. The study was administered in two stages. On the other hand, cognitive enhancement was achieved by reading scenarios detailing daily activities. At the first stage, participants were briefed about the whole research and was requested to read and sign a consent form. Each participant was assigned a research code to conserve their anonymity and confidentiality.

At the second stage known as the experimental stage, the coded participants were randomly assigned to four different treatment groups. Control Group (without any enhancement) will answer the survey questionnaire. Cognitive enhancement participants were asked to read three scenarios detailing the daily activities of older people (cognitive enhancement), which include laundry, serving a meal and sorting coins. Emotion enhancement participants were requested to wear the age simulation suit (emotional enhancement) while completing daily activities such as laundry, serving a meal and sorting coins. Emotion and Cognitive enhancement participants were requested to put on the age simulation suit (emotional enhancement) while completing daily activities and asked to read three scenarios detailing daily activities of older people (cognitive enhancement). All participants were required to complete another survey questionnaire after completing their assigned tasks. The post manipulation survey has the same set of items on empathetic attitude.

3.2 Sample

The study had 90 participants with a balanced number of participants in gender (48 females and 42 males). Mean age was 24.61 (SD = 2.25). For ethnicity, Malay origin was 3.3%, Chinese origin was 68.9%, Indian origin was 11.1%, and Others were 16.7%. For majors, participants were from different background, namely engineering (14.4%), science (5.6%), art (2.2%), social science (7.8%), IT (4.4%), business (38.9%), medicine/nursing/pharmacy (13.4%) and others (13.3%).

3.3 Results

Reliability, Validity and Factor Analyses. The psychometric properties of the item measuring empathy are shown in Table 1. The Cronbach alpha had a value greater than 0.70. The composite reliability had a value greater than 0.80. This suggests that the items measuring constructs under study are reliable. In addition, the average variance extracted (AVE) for the construct is higher than the threshold value of 0.50 which suggest that convergent validity is established.

Table 1. Results if reliability and validity.

Construct	Item	Loadings	Cronbach's alpha	Composite reliability	Average Variance Extracted (AVE)
Empathy	E1: I believe I understand what it feels like to have problems associated with aging	0.905	0.773	0.901	0.819
	E2: I believe I can truly empathize with older people	0.905			

3.4   Experimental Findings

In order to test the hypotheses, ANOVA was performed with emotional enhancement and cognitive enhancement as independent variables, and difference of the scores on empathetic attitude between before manipulation and after manipulation.

ANOVA results show that the main effect of cognitive enhancement (control 0.224 vs. cognitive enhancement 0.660) is significant ($F (1, 86) = 7.08$, $p < 0.01$), and that of emotional enhancement (control 0.245 vs. emotional enhancement 0.659) is also significant ($F (1, 86) = 7.01$, $p < 0.01$), these results support H1 and H2.

The results also show that there is a significant interaction effects ($F (1, 86) = 5.31$, $p < 0.05$). As shown in Fig. 1, combination of the two enhancements has relatively large effects and simple main effect between no enhancement (0.217) and both enhancement (1.048) is significant ($p < 0.01$). H3 is supported. Comparison between both enhancement and solo cognitive enhancement is significant ($p < 0.01$), and between both enhancement and solo emotional enhancement is also significant ($p < 0.01$). Therefore, H4 and H5 are also supported.

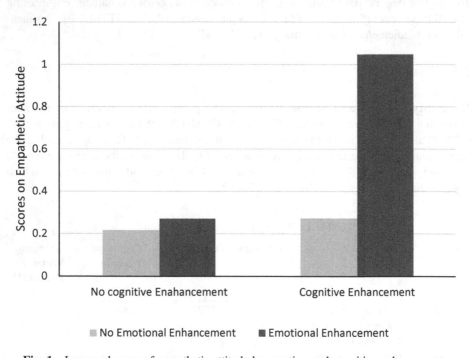

Fig. 1.   Increased score of empathetic attitude by emotion and cognitive enhancement.

4   Discussion and Conclusion

The aim of this study is to investigate the impact of cognitive and emotional enhancement to improve emphatic attitudes of young adults towards older adults. The empathy level of young adults was examined by wearing an age simulation suit for emotional enhancement while cognitive enhancement was examined by reading scenarios. The results show that emotional and cognitive enhancement are equally important to improve the emphatic attitudes of young adults towards older adults. The results indicated that the highest level of emphatic attitude was achieved by the group with both emotional and cognitive enhancement.

The findings of this study are aligned with literature findings. Healthcare literature suggest that the level of empathy amongst young adults is expected to increase through emotional enhancement of wearing an age simulation suit [10]. This study involved medical students in the field of geriatric medicine. It was concluded that student knowledge improved significantly after the simulation session was completed. A positive impact was achieved as the simulation session was able to change the perception of the medical students who wore the suit. On the other hand, young adult's level of cognitive empathy is expected to increase through cognitive enhancement of reading scenarios [16]. The results are consistent with healthcare literature which adopted the age simulation suit to mimic the effect of aging while studying the empathetic level of subjects towards older adults [12]. Hence, this study is imperative to bridge the existing perceived gap between young adults and older adults as well as to tackle the challenges faced by the aging population in various service-related sectors.

From a practical point of view, the findings will contribute to service sectors as the older adults are going to populate the service sector in the future. Prioritization should not only be given to patient centered care sectors, however sectors such as retail, banks, hotels, real estate, education, social work, media and others should adopt simulation devices in training their employees to treat older adults as equals. With findings showing that elements such as emotional enhancement and cognitive enhancement plays a significant role to improve emphatic attitude amongst individuals, steps should be taken to educate and raise awareness among young adults. In order to tackle challenges faced by older adults, individuals should come together with a receptive mind-set to explore new approaches in designing training programs as well as to adopt more creative methods to enhance service quality in various sectors.

There are two limitations in this study. First, the sample size for each group (treatment) is relatively small, which may not be representative of the population leading to bias results. In subsequent studies, the sample size will be increased to obtain more robust results. Second, the findings are based on self-reported data. The dependent variable empathy being self-reported may lead to bias scorings as participants may inflate the reported scores. To address this issue, the dependent variable will be studied in an objective manner. For instance, the frequency of actions of young adults interacting with older adults after wearing an age simulation suit will be collected for data analysis.

Acknowledgements. This research was supported by FMR Construction Sdn Bhd (BUS/FMR/07-2017/001), and Monash University Malaysia's School of Business, Gerontechnology Laboratory, Health and Well-Being Cluster, Global Asia in the 21st Century (GA21) Platform. The authors wish to express their appreciation for all the volunteers who participated in the study. Special thanks are due to Jeffery Yeow Teh Thiry for his help in data collection.

References

1. Ageing. https://www.un.org/en/sections/issues-depth/ageing/
2. Alicia, J.H., Stephanie, D.P.: The meaning in empathy: distinguishing conceptual encoding from facial mimicry, trait empathy, and attention to emotion. Cogn. Emot. **26**(1), 119–128 (2012). https://doi.org/10.1080/02699931.2011.559192
3. Astington, J.W.: The future of theory-of-mind research: understanding motivational states, the role of language, and real-world consequences. Child Dev. **72**, 685–687 (2001). https://doi.org/10.1111/1467-8624.00305
4. Barnes, L.L., de Leon, C.F., Lewis, T.T., Bienias, J.L., Wilson, R.S., Evans, D.A.: Perceived discrimination and mortality in a population-based study of older adults. Am. J. Public Health **98**(7), 1241–1247 (2008). https://doi.org/10.2105/AJPH.2007.114397
5. Bennett, S., Maton, K., Kervin, L.: The "digital natives" debate: a critical review of the evidence. Br. J. Educ. Technol. **39**, 775–786 (2008). https://doi.org/10.1111/j.1467-8535.2007.00793.x
6. Chen, A.K.M., Yehle, K., Plake, K.: Impact of an aging simulation game on pharmacy students' empathy for older adults. Am. J. Pharm. Educ. **79**(5) (2015). https://doi.org/10.5688/ajpe79565
7. Czaja, S.J., Lee, C.C.: The impact of aging on access to technology. Univ. Access Inf. Soc. **5**, 341 (2007). https://doi.org/10.1007/s10209-006-0060-x
8. Decety, J., Ickes, W.: The social neuroscience of empathy, pp. 1–16 (2009). https://ebookcentral-proquest-com.ezproxy.lib.monash.edu.au.   https://doi.org/10.7551/mitpress/9780262012973.001.0001
9. Decety, J., Meyer, M.: From emotion resonance to empathic understanding: a social developmental neuroscience account. Dev. Psychopathol. **20**(4), 1053–1080 (2008). https://doi.org/10.1017/S0954579408000503
10. Fisher, J.M., Walker, R.W.: A new age approach to an age old problem: using simulation to teach geriatric medicine to medical students. Age Ageing **43**(3), 424–428 (2014). https://doi.org/10.1093/ageing/aft200
11. Gerontechnology Laboratory. https://www.monash.edu.my/research/infrastructure/gerontechnology-laboratory
12. Groza, H.L., Sebesi, S.B., Mandru, D.S.: Age simulation suits for training, research and development. In: Vlad, S., Roman, N. (eds.) International Conference on Advancements of Medicine and Health Care through Technology; 12th–15th October 2016, Cluj-Napoca, Romania. IP, vol. 59, pp. 77–80. Springer, Cham (2017). https://doi.org/10.1007/978-3-319-52875-5_17
13. Hollan, D.: Author reply: the definition and morality of empathy. Emot. Rev. **4**(1), 83 (2012). https://doi.org/10.1177/1754073911421396
14. Morgan, J.M.: The computer training needs of older adults. Educ. Geronechnol.: Int. Q. **20**(6), 541–555 (1994). https://doi.org/10.1080/0360127940200601
15. James, T.P., Chad, B., Carole, B., John, O.B.: Aging game improves medical students' attitudes toward caring for elders. Gerontol. Geriatr. Educ. **15**(4), 45–57 (1995). https://doi.org/10.1300/j021v15n04_05
16. John, J.M.C., Gregory, J.M.: Reading and empathy. Read. Psychol. **38**(2), 182–202 (2017). https://doi.org/10.1080/02702711.2016.1245690
17. Kontis, V., Bennett, J., Mathers, C., Li, G., Foreman, K., Ezzati, M.: Future life expectancy in 35 industrialised countries: projections with a Bayesian model ensemble. Lancet **389**(10076), 1323–1335 (2017). https://doi.org/10.1016/S0140-6736(16)32381-9

18. Mégret, F.: The human rights of older persons: a growing challenge. Hum. Rights Law Rev. **11**(1), 37–66 (2011). https://doi.org/10.1093/hrlr/ngq050
19. Purdie, N., Gillian, B.L.: The learning needs of older adults. Educ. Gerontol. **29**(2), 129–149 (2003). https://doi.org/10.1080/713844281
20. Robbins, L.A.: The pernicious problem of ageism. Generations **39**(3), 6–9 (2015)
21. Rosowsky, E.: Ageism and professional training in aging: who will be there to help. Generations **29**(3), 55–58 (2005)
22. Rylee, A.D.: Stereotypes of aging: their effects on the health of older adults. J. Geriatr. **2015** (9) (2015). https://doi.org/10.1155/2015/954027
23. Santini, S., Tombolesi, V., Baschiera, B., Lamura, G.: Intergenerational programs involving adolescents, institutionalized elderly, and older volunteers: results from a pilot research-action in Italy. BioMed. Res. Int. **2018**(14) (2018). https://doi.org/10.1155/2018/4360305
24. Sargeant, M.: Ageism and age discrimination. In: Sargeant, M. (ed.) Age Discrimination and Diversity: Multiple Discrimination from an Age Perspective, pp. 1–15. Cambridge University Press, Cambridge (2011)
25. Shanton, K., Goldman, A.: Simulation theory. Wiley Interdisc. Rev.: Cogn. Sci. **1**(4), 527–538 (2010). https://doi.org/10.1002/wcs.33
26. Sze, J.A., Gyurak, A., Goodkind, M.S., Levenson, R.W.: Greater emotional empathy and prosocial behavior in late life. Emotion **12**(5), 1129 (2012). https://doi.org/10.1037/a0025011
27. Twenge, J.M.: The evidence for generation me and against generation we. Emerg. Adulthood **1**(1), 11–16 (2013). https://doi.org/10.1177/2167696812466548
28. Uhlenberg, P.: Demography is not destiny: the challenges and opportunities of global population aging. Generations **37**(1), 12–18 (2013)
29. Valkenburg, P., Piotrowski, J.: Youth and media. In: Plugged in: How Media Attract and Affect Youth, pp. 1–9. Yale University Press, New Haven and London (2017)
30. Van Hoof, J., Kazak, J.: Urban ageing. Indoor Built Environ. **27**(5), 583–586 (2018). https://doi.org/10.1177/1420326X18768160
31. World Population Prospects - Population Division - United Nations. https://population.un.org/wpp/
32. Zaki, J., Ochsner, K.N.: The neuroscience of empathy: progress, pitfalls and promise. Nat. Neurosci. **15**, 675–680 (2012). https://doi.org/10.1038/nn.3085

Developing the Interaction for Family Reacting with Care to Elderly

Yi-Sin Wu[1] , Teng-Wen Chang[2]([⊠]) , and Sambit Datta[3]

[1] Graduate School of Design, National Yunlin University of Science
and Technology, Douliu, Taiwan
Wu.rilla918@gmail.com
[2] Department of Digital Media Design, National Yunlin University of Science
and Technology, Douliu, Taiwan
tengwen@softlab.tw
[3] Curtin Institute of Computation, Curtin University, Perth, Australia
sambit.datta@curtin.edu.au

Abstract. This paper focus on the interaction design of a slow play for the family members, including multi-player experiences, interaction methods, user interface and accomplishment and scarcity. The interface used by the family member's side also affect the user's willingness to continue using it. Through the user task interface tests and interviews to summarize the following design guidelines that can be used for slow play in game—(1) have the meaning and it can unlock the accomplishment, (2) collaboration with strategic and (3) the tempting collection of uncertainty can improve player stickiness and satisfaction. Finally, this research develops a board-type puzzle game into an alternative form of play, is called "blindside".

Keywords: Interaction through play · Horticultural Interaction Game · User interface design · Interaction play elements

1 Introduction

In this paper, we are focus on the interaction design of a slow play for the family members, including multi-player experiences, interaction methods, user interface and accomplishment and scarcity, modify our past research—HiGame (Horticultural Interaction Game, Hi Game) [1]. As in the gamification belief of Hamari (2013): because games are fun, any service that uses the same mechanism should also prove to be more valuable and engaging [2]. We through analysis the game elements to develop an interactive play for family members with their parents who live alone. "Interaction through play" can encourage people to maintain many behaviors that are not easy to keep it in our lives. Such as drinking water, walking, reminding and even staying focused. Increasing user enthusiasm, community interaction, and productivity through interaction in games have been a hot topic in the past few years; gamification refers to using game elements in non-game systems to improve user experience and user engagement [3]. Due to the complex composition of the family's population, not only

© Springer Nature Switzerland AG 2020
P.-L. P. Rau (Ed.): HCII 2020, LNCS 12193, pp. 200–210, 2020.
https://doi.org/10.1007/978-3-030-49913-6_17

the potted plants of the elderly living alone need to be optimized, but the interface used by the family members also affect the user's willingness to continue using it.

Due to the complex composition of the family's population, not only the potted plants of the elderly who live alone need to be optimized, but the interface used by the family member's side also affect the user's willingness to continue using it. Through the user task test and interviews to summarize the following design guidelines that can be used for slow play in game—(1) have the meaning and it can unlock the accomplishment, (2) collaboration with strategic and (3) the tempting collection of uncertainty can improve player stickiness and satisfaction. Finally, this research develops a board-type puzzle game into an alternative form of play, is called "blindside".

1.1   Aging Population and Changes in Family Structures

Rapidly aging population is a common phenomenon in the demographic changes of countries around the world. With the trend toward fewer children, industrialization and urbanization promote population movements, the family structure is also rapidly changing. According to the explanation of the life cycle of a family in Taiwan's traditional cohabitation type, a newly-married couple first lived with their husband's parents, that is "a paternalistic extended family". Then they have their own family, that is nuclear family. Finally, when the husband's parents are gradually aging, they live with their parents again, that is transient extended family [4, 5].

However, according to the statistics of Taiwan's Ministry of the Interior, the ratio of elderly living with their children has been decreasing year by year, and the situation of elderly living alone has become more common. According to a report on the living conditions of elderly in 2017, the ideal living style for the elderly is living alone and living with their spouse only, the ratio is increased from 25.14% to 35.75% between 2013 and 2017; and declining willingness of older people to live with children from 2013 to 2017, the ratio is decreased from 65.72% to 54.34% [6].

1.2   Interaction Through Play and Eight Core Drives in Octalysis

As described in Sect. 1.1, promoting the connection between the elderly and their children to avoid the loneliness of the elderly is an important exploration in the future. In order to stimulate the user's feelings, motivations and investment levels, we conducted preliminary interaction design through Octalysis. According to the different methods can be applied to interactive games for the user's environment, requirements or needs, which can make interaction design more supportive of users [7]. Chou (2016) combined the game design theory, motivational psychology, action economics and summarized human behavioral motivations into eight core motivations, which were divided into positive motivations and negative motivations [8]. There are (1) Meaning, (2) Accomplishment, (3) Empowerment, (4) Ownership, (5) Social Influence, (6) Scarcity, (7) Unpredictability and (8) Avoidance (see Fig. 1).

These eight motivations are divided into positive motivation and negative motivation. Positive motivation includes meaning, accomplishment, and empowerment, it is about the interaction triggers. When the user's express creativity, the first and second core can be triggered. The negative motivations are scarcity, unpredictability and avoidance. If the user feels uncertain cause they don't know what will happen next, they will continue to wait for getting priority. It triggers the eighth core: avoidance. The traction of external and internal motivations will trigger each core motivation and increase user motivation. We used the Octalysis score in the Octalysis for design evaluation.

Fig. 1. Octalysis. User groups as the center to explore the core principles of good game design.

2   Analysis the Interaction Play Elements

When the family member's side is in multiplayer mode, the design of the play needs to be applicable for all ages (excluding the elderly). In this study, we are aggregated and analyzed the different type of game (1) the traditional table games that families in Taiwan often play at parties (2) it is having been popular in all ages and (3) it has the discussion in the App Store and Google play between 2017 to 2019. By disassembling the game features through the Octalysis, that can better understand the important elements that continue to play a game among family members.

2.1   Table Game and Digital Game for People of Different Ages

Most traditional table games are designed for the family. For example: Monopoly, Bridge, Go, Chess and Mahjong are typical representatives. Traditional table games are unique in that they use structured rules to define a field that can be using stimulating thinking and choice, players follow the rules to compete or cooperate with each other to win. Until today it is still a game type that many family and friends will play.

Facebook, the top social network globally [9]. It affects the form of social media and also indirectly affects people's lifestyles [10]. It has become a part of people's lives of all ages [7]. There are two classic games—Happy Farm and Candy Crush Saga, which are characterized by unlimited specific areas and it can interact with remote friends through computers or mobile phones. They are having different game architectures, as detailed below:

Happy Farm. Happy Farm is published in 2009, it made users into farmers [10, 11]. Users can grow crops or raise livestock and sell them to earn gold coins. They can also visit friend's farms or steal products. After the player taking care of the vegetable garden, their friends steal crops when they visit, therefore players have to go to their friends' farms to "steal vegetables". Interaction between friends and offensive and defensive battles is the key to making Happy Farm to be a popular game (see Fig. 2 left).

Candy Crush Saga. Candy Crush Saga is also one of Facebook's famous games published in 2012. It is a puzzle game with three to five as bases to eliminate candies and get scores [12, 13]. Each level has different unlocking requirements, players have to arrange the same type of candies in a row and detonate them, which will produce different effect powers. After completing the level under the rules, the player can go to the next level. At the beginning of the game will be provided five hearts. One failure will be deducted one heart at a time, and one will be increased one heart in 30 min. Players can also ask Facebook friends to repay their hearts. There is a level that requires a ferry ticket or key to pass. At this time, the player needs friends to help unlock it (see Fig. 2 right).

Fig. 2. Happy Farm (left). Player becames a farmer. They can grow crops or raise livestock and they can also visit friend's farms or steal their products. Candy Crush Saga (right). It is a puzzle game with three to five as bases to eliminate candies and get scores.

2.2 Best Mobile Games by Revenue and Downloads

SensorTower conducts data analysis through Mobile Apps every year. In its report on the world's highest revenue and downloads between 2017 to 2019 [14–16]. This study observes and discusses in two points: (1) stability: the game ranked in these three years steady in the leaderboard and (2) decline: it is decreased of downloads (see Fig. 3).

Stability. The Honor of Kings is a 5v5 multiplayer online combat technology game. Generally, players in the two teams compete with each other in the game. The goal of the game is through the teamwork and use of strategies to destroy the main castle of the opposing team. Each player will get a "hero" character by free choice or random distribution. Each hero has his own unique ability. In the game, he or she will increase the level with the experience value to unlock the hero skills. At the end of each game, players can get personal rewards, such as experience and gold; if the player has a hero used in the game, the proficiency of that hero will also be increased, and these values will be displayed on the player account instead of the hero. In addition, the game official will launch new heroes from time to time. If the player is very fond of the character, they can wear beautiful skin in the game after obtaining it through the purchase or lottery. Candy Crush Saga has been launched for eight years and still successfully ranked in the top five from 2017 to 2019. As the levels change from simple to difficult, the level map in the game will show the progress of friends, which can promote competition among players and keep them engaged.

Decline. Monster Strike is a catapult-hunting, encourages teamwork and has the strategic role-playing game. Players draw monster cards to get stronger monsters and cultivate the stars level. Each combat adopts a turn-based system, four monsters of your own can take turns to launch attacks through two operations, "Reflection" and "Through". During the battle, the player must pay attention to the relative of the attribute, water, fire, wood, light and darkness. Friendship skills are triggered by hitting a companion. When the player defeats a monster, they have a chance to get this monster. Puzzle & Dragons is a puzzle and battle game that combines role-playing and gem elimination. The mode of gem elimination is based on the design from Dungeon Raid, which is similar to gem cubes. Within a limited time through the eight directions to continues to move orb, the goal is to make the three or more orb of the same color to reach elimination. Each Orb represents different attributes. Eliminating orb of the same

Note: Does not include revenue from third-party Android stores in China or other regions.

Fig. 3. Top mobile games by revenue and downloads. This study observes stable games and decline games.

color will launch pets of this attribute to attack or restore their own health. The types of orbs are red fire attributes, green wood attributes, blue water attributes, yellow light attributes, purple dark attributes, and pink heart-shaped recovery orbs. Later, the game also added more attributes orbs that increase the difficulty of the game.

2.3   The Elements in Interaction Play

From the 2017 to 2019 game report comparing traditional games with the world's highest revenue and downloads, it is not difficult to find that although traditional games can use thinking skills, games lack vivid themes, and themed games are mostly dominated by luck (large Tycoon), you cannot use strategy to cultivate the characters used in the game. The once popular Happy Farm, because it did not add a new game method, although it ended in 2017, it also led to many similar farm-themed games, such as: LINE Bear Ranch, FarmVille, etc., and it is more real-time to play on mobile phone hardware, the elements of the game are also better.

From 2017 to 2019, the game report with the highest worldwide revenue and downloads found that most games have (1) a sense of mission to unlock achievements, (2) strategic collaborations, and (3) uncertain collections. Temptation, etc. can improve player adhesion and satisfaction (see Fig. 4). While two games like Monster Strike and Puzzle & Dragons have special operating methods, they actually cause game restrictions. The way to attract players can only rely on the introduction of new characters from time to time. When players buy new characters, they often have higher skills. Many of the old characters caused imbalance in the game, and over time the game was no longer attractive.

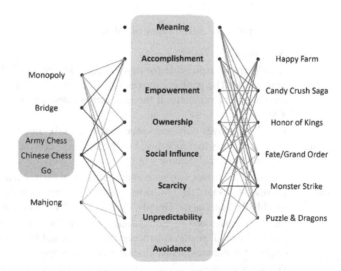

Fig. 4. Disassemble the Octalysis core of various games. The elements of these games are (1) have the meaning and it can unlock the accomplishment (2) collaboration with strategic and (3) the tempting collection of uncertainty can improve player stickiness and satisfaction. Those elements can improve user adhesion and satisfaction.

3 Design the Interaction for Play

After the discussion of Sect. 2, this study obtained the basic core motivation through the Octalysis, and the further established the game core of the family member's side. We calculate the Octalysis core of the current interactive design motivation, in the first, establish the game mechanism of HiGame next to the octagon frame, and assign a score of 0 to 10 to the core motivation, then square the score to get the core power score. Then add the eight-core power scores to the total score of the Octalysis. Each side of the octagon will expand or retract according to the strength of these interaction mechanisms. Either the side retracts or crosses the inside of the octagon, indicating that the side is very fragile, we need to modify the design. The final interaction design is described in Sect. 3.1.

3.1 The Blindside Game Mode: Situation and Gameplay

The game starts with the small lights that are connected to the potted plants in the morning. Through the infrared sensors around the potted plants, when the elderly approach the potted plants or small lights, the family members can know from the mobile phone that the elderly have got up. When the family members open the App interface, the unpreparedness mode will be immediately awakened.

The interactive interface will show two characters for each the family members to choose. There are seven types of roles—(1) Gardener, (2) Guard-warring statesman warrior, (3) Minister-brahma elephant, (4) Car-tank car, (5) Knight-MacGyver, (6) Cannon-Hummingbird and (7) soldier. A character has a fixed number and character traits (Table 1).

Table 1. Seven types of roles.

	Description
Gardener	The elderly is responsible for this role, it is key person in blindside game mode. The gardener moves only one space at a time, either horizontally or vertically. If the gardener is eaten, the blindside game is lost
Guard (Warring statesman warrior)	The Guard moves only one space at a time in the Jiugongge. Its character trait is low mobility, but the strongest defense, as the gardener's internal defense
Minister (Brahma elephant)	The Minister moves two spaces at a time diagonally, such as the Chinese character "田". Minister must stay within their own side, roughly the same as the Guards, used as a gardener's external defense
Car (Tank car)	The Cars moves one or more spaces horizontally or vertically provided that all positions between the original and final positions are empty. It is the most lethal character at long range
Knight (MacGyver)	The Knight moves two spaces horizontally and one space vertically, such as the Chinese character "日". It can move to eight directions; therefore, it is the most lethal character at close range, and it can use the skills to see the enemy's position every turn

(continued)

Table 1. (*continued*)

	Description
Cannon (Hummingbird)	If Cannon don't attack other characters during the period, it can move horizontally or vertically the unlimited distance in the same way as Car; However, in a capture move, there must be exactly one non-empty space in between the original and final position. Attacks are often used in conjunction with Car and Knight
Soldiers	The family members who selected this role can control three Soldiers of the movement position in each turn. The Soldiers move one space at a time. They can only go vertically one step in their area, and never go back. They can move horizontally when they reach the enemy area

The main purpose of attacking and preparing for war is to protect the gardener, in other words, to protect the elderly and the plants being planted. The family members use the above-mentioned role skills or position to block the enemy.

3.2 Accomplishment and Scarcity

Depending on (1) the character used, (2) defensive/attack success or failure, (3) the speed of the family's feedback, after the end of the blindside attack. Different items will be unlocked, the items divided into (a) seeds and (b) animals. And the unlocked items will be displayed in the cabinet of the game.

The interaction between seniors and physical pot plants is also a part of a mission that unlocks achievements. For example: if grandma takes care of the little tomato being planted every day, the time of care will be transmitted to the cloud database through the sensor. When the blindside game begins, the frequency of elderly's care will be converted into the defense power of the flower garden. This design is to make the elderly become the active players instead of passive caregivers.

4 Prototyping and Testing

Before the game is produced, we test the actual condition of the family member's game through prototype and test, which can be corrected before production. In order to make the interactive experience smoother, we have planned for the connection of the entity, the body and the space, the choice of game characters, the calculation of time and the scene (see Table 2).

Finally, the paper model was used for experiments. The focus group members included 56-year-old men, 54-year-old women and 27-year-old men (see Fig. 5). The interactive method is mainly based on task testing, supplemented by open interviews. Task testing includes: account login and connection, role selection and confirmation, role skills and movement, role cooperation and coordination, achievement unlocking, etc. The open interview is for interactive experiences, gameplay, achievement unlocking, and members of the focus group are invited to give suggestions for modification.

Table 2. More game details.

	Description
Concatenation	Account link via home phone
Select	When all the family members choose the role, the attack will begin immediately. The deadline for role selection is 9:00 every day. If children who didn't choose within the time, they cannot participate in this blindside game
Time	There is no limit to the speed at which everyone can give feedback. For example, if Dad takes a step forward by using a tank car at 10:00 am on Monday, the next is daughter's turn, she can use the skills of a Ministers at 2:00 pm on Wednesday, she can watch each other's character distribution. Complete this round
Scenes	The scene is divided into two parts: our side and the enemy side. The fog in the environment will disappear as the two sides get closer to each other. The fog will not appear again after it spreads. The use of Knights skills in the game can know the position of the enemy character in advance

Fig. 5. Task test. Researchers give task prompts, and subjects press each button on the model to complete each step.

5   Conclusion

In the first version of HiGame, only one family member can interact with the elderly, and the interaction methods are limited, it is a relatively monotonous interactive play. In this study, the Octalysis is used to analyze the design of multi-player experience, interaction methods, interaction interface and accomplishment and scarcity on the family side, this is in order to stimulate the family's willingness to use and further improve the effectiveness of HiGame with the elderly. This study conducted a paper model experiment using focus groups. The members included a 56-year-old male, a 54-year-old female and a 23-year-old male. There are two places need to be adjusted:

- **Time limits for character movement.** Because there is no time limit for family members to move characters in the game, which means that if the users didn't take the next step, it will affect the willingness of all players.
- **Where is the character can move?** Due to the Guards, Ministers and Knights had specific movements. Therefore, the focus group suggested in the test process that when the user moves the character, the system should be able to display the position where the character can be placed.

In the first interview, the researchers were found that 54-year-old women often played puzzle games on mobile phones, while 56-year-old men didn't have related operations experience, but they are had positive effects on interactive experiences, game methods, and achievement unlocking, it is displaying that people have a high acceptance of board puzzle games—Blindside. After the test, we have obtained suggestions from real users, in the next step, we will make high-fidelity models through Sketch and link them with HiGame's physical pot plants.

References

1. Wu, Y.-S., Chang, T.-W., Datta, S.: HiGame: improving elderly well-being through horticultural interaction. Int. J. Archit. Comput. **14**, 263–276 (2016)
2. Hamari, J.: Transforming homo economicus into homo ludens: a field experiment on gamification in a utilitarian peer-to-peer trading service. Electron. Commer. Res. Appl. **12**, 236–245 (2013)
3. Deterding, S., Sicart, M., Nacke, L., O'Hara, K., Dixon, D.: Gamification: using game design elements in non-gaming contexts. In: Proceedings of the 2011 Annual Conference Extended Abstracts on Human Factors in Computing Systems - CHI EA 2011 (2011)
4. Özbay, F.: Changes in the social and economic structure in rural areas. Changes in the Family in Turkey: Sociological Analysis, pp. 35–68 (1984)
5. Chang, G.-L., Chang, C.-O.: Transitions in living arrangements and living preferences among elderly: an analysis from family values and exchange. J. Popul. Stud. **40**, 41–90 (2010)
6. Jian, H.-J.: The orientation of welfare policies for the aged under the ageing population and changing household structure in Taiwan. Public Gov. Q. **7**(1), 96–101 (2019)
7. Bekker, T., Sturm, J., Eggen, B.: Designing playful interactions for social interaction and physical play. Pers. Ubiquit. Comput. **14**, 385–396 (2009)
8. Chou, Y.-K.: Actionable Gamification: Beyond Points, Badges, and Leaderboards. Business Weekly (2016)
9. Nielsen Wire: Global and social: Facebook's rise around the world. Markets and Finances. Nielsen Company (2012)
10. Wu, P.-C.: Addictive behavior in relation to the Happy Farm Facebook application. Soc. Behav. Pers. **41**, 539–554 (2013)
11. Wikipedia: Happy Farm page. https://www.wikiwand.com/en/Happy_Farm. Accessed 2008
12. Chen, C., Leung, L.: Are you addicted to Candy Crush Saga? An exploratory study linking psychological factors to mobile social game addiction. Telemat. Inform. **33**, 1155–1166 (2016)
13. ejinsight: Candy Crush killer? Facebook names best game page. http://www.ejinsight.com/20141211-Candy-Crush-killer-Facebook-names-best-game/. Accessed 2014

14. SensorTower: Top mobile games by revenue and downloads in 2017 (2018)
15. SensorTower: Top mobile games by revenue and downloads in 2018 (2019)
16. SensorTower: Top mobile games by revenue and downloads in 2019 (2020)

Culture, Learning and Communication

Say-It and Learn: Interactive Application for Children with ADHD

Sabeel Butt[1], Fazal E. Hannan[1], Mujahid Rafiq[1(✉)] ⓘ,
Ibrar Hussain[1] ⓘ, C. M. Nadeem Faisal[2] ⓘ, and Waleed Younas[1]

[1] The University of Lahore, 1 KM Defense Road Campus, Lahore, Pakistan
mujahid.rafiq@se.uol.edu.pk,
ibrar.hussain@cs.uol.edu.pk
[2] National Textile University, Faisalabad, Pakistan

Abstract. Attention Deficit Hyperactivity Disorder (ADHD) is the most common mental disorder in children. Commonly children with ADHD are treated through stimulant drugs that can be dangerous. Also, behavioral therapy sessions are carried out to help ADHD. No doubt it is useful for children, but these are hectic and expensive as well. Smartphone and tablet applications are widely used in healthcare and educational context. The objective of this study is to heighten the learnability of ADHD children using tablet apps. The developed app will provide endless opportunities for ADHD children. The objective is to help ADHD children in their learning activities via a friendly and interactive environment. The investigation is conducted by employing the proposed app using a sample of five children with ADHD to assess the applicability. A survey is conducted from the parents and caregivers of these children to measure the level of satisfaction and acceptance for learning content. The result demonstrates that the app is interesting, engaging, and improves learnability. Lastly, parents are satisfied and appreciated the design and functionality of "Say-it and learn."

Keywords: ADHD · Learning · Education · Communication · Interactive · Assistive technologies

1 Introduction

The usage of mobile apps is increasing every day, and people are trying to find a solution for daily life problems in the digital world. Digital advancements provide equal access and learning opportunities to people with disabilities [1]. ADHD is the most common mental disorder in children. Generally, it affects children between 3–9% [2]. Considering it a severe problem, we planned to address this issue through optimal design. Nowadays, children spend most of their time using devices; hence their treatment through mobile apps would be virtuous. ADHD children have difficulty in "paying attention" that disturbs their academic performance. That is why sometimes it also referred to as a "learning disorder" [3]. The researcher thus purposed the app to assist not only the students with ADHD but also their guardians.

Now a day's lots of apps are being developed to address the most common behavioral disorder ADHD that affects school-aged children between 3–9%. Most of

© Springer Nature Switzerland AG 2020
P.-L. P. Rau (Ed.): HCII 2020, LNCS 12193, pp. 213–223, 2020.
https://doi.org/10.1007/978-3-030-49913-6_18

these apps are just for the usage of ADHD children and meant for a single purpose with fewer functionalities. It is not a good gesture to practice such tools, so unless the child is perilous, all the children should be using the same app that could be a Game-based learning app. Considering ADHD a health issue, most people rely on medicines. Presently the improvement from medication is unquestionable as it transforms the ADHD children the same as their healthy classmates [4]. But we are giving an interactive app for learning with an active disorder. According, the medications for the treatment of ADHD children have side effects due to which the course of most treatment plans remains incomplete [5].

The goal current study is to motivate children and maintain their interest in the studies using the proposed app 'Say-it and Learn'. It is a tablet-based app with facial recognition techniques. Facial recognition will identify the different users of the game on the same gadget and save their performance accordingly. Children input their name on the startup and choose facial sign in. Then they can easily sign-in, and their profile is saved as they left it. This app offers to learn alphabets, counting, and shapes. The objects in the tasks are highlighted when an activity is being performed on them [6]. These objects are from the real-life, familiar to the children. Therefore, when encountered, such objects in the study can improve their performance. Apart from the tasks, the app offers tests for the self-evaluation of the children. Different tests are prepared on the topics they learned while performing tasks. Facial recognition along with the voice recognition technology in a kid's app is a treat for children that have focus problems and also a bonus for the normal children. The interactive learning with melodious music captures the interest of children is maintained. Children are also reminded by the app about different healthy activities e.g. drink water and milk, eat nuts, read books, play more and you're intelligent. These motivating phrases messages encourage children to behave in a well-mannered way. In this way, a medicine reminder can be set by the guardian, which reminds by a notification with a message e.g. Take your medicine dear. Such friendly reminders keep the children energetic.

Our brains have dopamine cells that are released, and they trigger the thinking ability as well as the attention of the person. The element of music in our system is for the purpose of improving kid's performance and making their mood better [5] because at the time of listening music the dopamine cells are released [7]. In a study, [8] investigated that ADHD children also have sleep problems. Therefore, the app also has a night mode and sleeping music. At night, the user can switch to night mode by simply clicking a button. In this mode, colors become light, and brightness is warm. It is one of the critical features of our app. 'Say-it and Learn' app offers game-based learning for both normal and ADHD children. We put emphasizes on the features we provide, considering the HCI principle of user study and user satisfaction.

The Paper is divided into multiple sub-section i-e. Related work, Design and Methodology, Evaluation and Results, and then finally the conclusion, limitation, and future work.

2 Related Work

Due to the effect of ADHD on the learning capability of the children [3], its diagnosis is taken very seriously. Most of the researchers work on the determination of this controversial psychological disorder [9]. According to a study conducted on Robotics in 2018, CAretaker RoBOt (CARBO) is a multi-sensory robot that not only the potential for diagnosis of ADHD but also fulfills the goals of Sensory Integration Therapy (SIT) [10]. Such developmental disorders are not recognized by their guardians as ADHD possess the element of inattention that is common in younger children. So to help in better understanding caregivers about ADHD children, a persuasive video, the game was designed [9].

Furthermore, this game helps to improve the life-quality of ADHD children. Another game, drawn to distraction [9], is a creative idea that enables the ADHD children to understand others. The negatively influenced and less productive parents were made to expand their vision about their children. It explains the attitude of ADHD children towards daily activities through animation. The development of assistive tools by the HCI experts has begun [11]. Chillfish tool is a biofeedback game that combines breathing exercises. This game relaxes the children and catches their attention [12].

Several researchers developed various apps that improve the ADHD students' performance in the classroom and also keeps the record of their performance. An example of one such app is iSelfControl [13]. It evaluates the behavior of individual students in the classroom and the staff. Then by aggregating the data, their progress is displayed. In this way, the behavioral changes in the students and the staff can be improved. Most apps do not calculate the behavior changes of the user that is not a practical approach for speedy therapy. The app also evaluates child improvement after a test. MOBERO [14], is another assistive technology that monitors the morning and bedtime routine of ADHD children and their guardians. Furthermore, it rewards the positive response that encourages them to make more effort every day. The sleep management issues [8] are also solved using these assistive tools. The researchers implemented a full-body driven game for the physical activity of the ADHD children [15]. The motive of the proposed app is to engage ADHD children in the game so that they repeat the tasks and increase their ability to focus. It is developed via iterative design and also provides audio feedback, so the children don't get bored while playing. Another learning app for ADHD children that is named e-tutor system [16] was developed for teaching Mathematics, basic hygiene practices, and language. It also followed the iterative design strategy, and its results showed that this app could be used as a supplementary tool for learning success. For critical review and comparison, the author divided the apps into different sub-categories, as shown in Table 1.

Table 1. ADHD application's categories and their explanation

Category name	Explanation
Educational	Helps the user in learning and academics
Guidelines	This category of application follow the design guidelines while designing the application
Motivation	These applications have tasks that motivate the users
Facial recognition	Applications that have facial recognition to sign-in
Reminder	User can add any task that needs to be done later in a reminder and application notifies the user about it
Music	Melodious classical and instrumental music is provided at the background
Quizzes	The app assesses user through quizzes
Report	It displays the score of the user in each quiz and measures the overall performance
Focus	An application that has the ability to maintain user's attention through any of its features
Voice recognition	It allows the user to operate through voice

3   Design and Methodology

The initial design of the app developed by adopting the design guidelines for ADHD children [6]. The developed also has sounds that help children in maintaining a calm mood [5] because, according to investigative reports, mostly ADHD children are impulsive, so this app enables them to keep calm [16]. We followed the user-centered design strategy [17] in developing 'Say-it and Learn' for children with attention Deficit Hyperactivity Disorder (ADHD). Similar design methodologies also used by these researchers [18–20]. This design process aids a lot in the designing of apps that depend most on the user study.

During the design process, we developed initial prototypes in many phases and evaluated these by ADHD professionals on a regular basis. Later on, we discussed with the consultants and another psychologist who has ADHD expertise. One of the HCI practitioners also supervised all our activities during the design process. During the development, researchers visited Asas International School in Islamabad (Pakistan) for a better understanding of the behavior of ADHD children. The visit was quite useful in understanding true user needs and also helpful in clarifying the technical requirements of the app. We discuss it with the employees of Roots & Wings Autism Center, Lahore, Pakistan to gather more information. The initial design was just for ADHD children, but after these visits, we decided to make it a neutral app in the access of every 4 - to 10-year children. ADHD students are already separated from others in many schools, which will not be proved effective vital for their speedy recovery.

According to the consultant, ADHD children need a variety of activities; otherwise, they get bored. These children cannot be forced to learn, they are handled politely, and their tasks are divided into different time intervals. Hence, the children don't get irritated and work with attentiveness. After gathering all the required information, we developed the final app. Figure 1 is showing the overall flow chart of the design process. Figures 2, 3, 4 and 5 is about the screenshots of the app, which is designed after completing the whole design process.

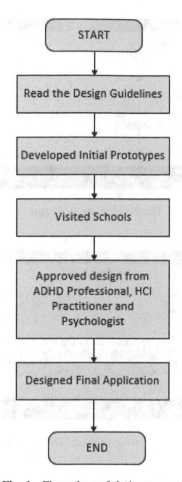

Fig. 1. Flow chart of design process

The developed app consists of 3 major modules. ^first^ is about learning English basic alphabets (A, B, C …), ^second^ about learning basic math's letter courting related exercises are involved, and the ^third^ or last module is basically about learning shapes. Different learning techniques and exercises are included in the app to evaluate the performance of children related to learning these things. Small exercises are involved at the end of each phase. In Fig. 2, the main menu presents options for the selection of an exercise. Choosing appropriate alphabets takes them to the next screen in Fig. 3. Then the user can learn the alphabets. Speech recognition allows children to repeat the alphabet with it. If a child doesn't sing along, then it continues to call alphabets on its own. It also encourages the child by popping friendly messages, e.g., say Z, Z for

Zebra, "Sing along, Join me." ADHD children also have sleep management issues that need to be addressed for their healthy living [8]. We also gave a night mode feature in this regard to provide ease as in MOBERO [14].

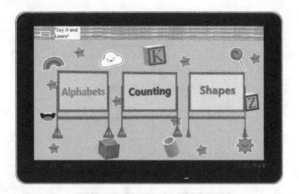

Fig. 2. Main menu of app

Fig. 3. App showing exercise related to alphabets

Following the design guidelines [6], the text is highlighted during its activity to avoid distraction issues while reading the text. Every exercise is interactive, and it engages the user very efficiently. From the tab on the top left corner, the user can choose to perform many other activities. Users can start a test on any topic. They can also check their scores from the scoreboard and has the option to change the music, change their username, or exit the game. Moreover, they can mute music whenever desired. Furthermore, the guardian or the participants can add a reminder. The app notifies the participants through a message or a ring. The quiz score is calculated in a database and displayed at the end of the exercise to the participants. Everyone has a separate record, saved in their profile.

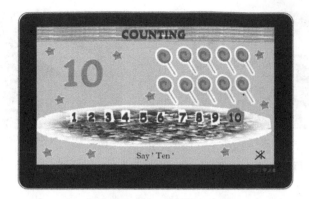

Fig. 4. Math's (counting) related exercise

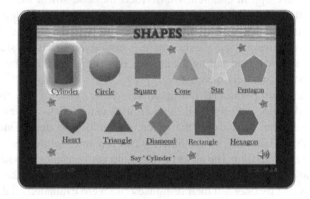

Fig. 5. Learning common shapes

4   Evaluation and Results

To evaluate the acceptance, and satisfaction of our proposed app, we engaged and observed 5 ADHD children having age (m = 6.4) years and their parents to measure overall satisfaction. 2 children were female, and the rest were males. Tablets were provided to the children individually and in turns (10 min/turn). All the children under observation were school-going with very little or no educational knowledge. All 5 children had a prior background of using a tablet at their home or in school. The response of the children after using the app was overwhelming, according to observers (1 consultant and 2 HCI experts). Figures 6 show that the child is learning shapers and doing counting related tasks. Faces of children kept private to ensure the privacy of children.

Child is learning shapes   Child is doing Math's (Counting) Exercise

Fig. 6. Actual participants (children) doing a real-time app

Two children were observed while using hand frees with their tablets. The remaining three children used the app without handsfree. In order to evaluate inter-activity regarding the app in children, we divided the assessment into two main portions. First is further divided into 5 tasks that are related to learning alphabets, shapes, and counting to the first exercise. In this phase, we observed the student's overall usage time of the app. And then, a post questionnaire is employed to get the student opinion. a consultant also assisted us in getting the answer from children this is because children were reluctant to give answers directly.

All the participants performed the activities easily. One of the children, while interacting with the app, performed all the activities using clicks however the other 4 children performed the tasks using the voice recognition system. One investigator observed the children carefully, where others write the notes while observing them for future improvement in design. The observations help the researchers to seek that which activity was enjoyed by participants. In post-survey evaluation, we asked the question to all participants one by one, and their responses (R) were evaluated on the basis of the 5-Likert scale. Questions (Q1–Q3) were about the overall preception? Q1: "Enjoyment in the app," Q2: "Colors are interactive," Q3: "Music in the app." Mean RQ1 = 4.00, mean RQ2 = 4.40, and mean RQ3 = 4.20. Two more questions (Q4, Q5) were asked and their responses (R) were measured in "Yes or No" (0 or 1). Q4: "You want this app again?" Q5: "Do you love this way of learning" Interestingly, mean RQ4, RQ5 = 100. The questionnaire statements were taken from literature [21–23] having acceptable Cronbach's alpha. All the children agreed that the app helped them to learn new things. The details of these results are given in Table 2.

Table 2. Details of result obtained

	N	Minimum	Maximum	Mean	Std. error	Std. deviation
RQ1	5	3	5	4.00	0.316	0.707
RQ2	5	4	5	4.40	0.245	0.548
RQ3	5	3	5	4.20	0.374	0.837

The researcher observed that those children who were not using hand frees, and they were also attentive. None of the children argued no to use the app, which shows that the app was not boring. Thus, the evaluation indicates that the app is useful in learning and engaging. The consultant involved in this process gave remarks that background music is quite relaxing and focusing and was very beneficial for children learning.

In the next phase of research, we requested parents and caregivers to allow the participants to use the app for the next 6 days under their observation/supervision, and on the 7th day, we inquired about the overall change that app brought in their child. All the families gave a positive response and explained that their children are progressing in respective subjects offered by the app. They were requested to rate the app for overall satisfaction. The question was, are you satisfied with learning using the proposed app [22–24]? The mean satisfaction rate was m = 4, which is quite acceptable in our case.

Detailed comparison of our app (based on categories mentioned in Table 1) and other famous apps are shown in Fig. 7.

Name of app	Educational	Guidelines	Motivation	Facial Recognition	Reminder	Music	Quizzes	Report	Focus	Voice Recognition
Say it & Learn	☑	☑	☑	☑	☑	☑	☑	☑	☑	☑
Math Ninja	☑						☑		☑	
MindNode									☑	
Audible	☑									
30/30	☑									
Unstuck	☑		☑						☑	
iReward Chart	☑		☑			☑				
Recap	☑			☑						
ADHD Alarm					☑					
ADHD Guide	☑	☑					☑			
ADHD Maze	☑	☑					☑			
ADHD Quiz		☑					☑			
ADHD Angel		☑				☑				

Fig. 7. Detailed comparison of our app and other app

5 Conclusion

The initial results demonstrate that the developed app is useful for children with ADHD. According to the observations, guardians, and teachers, the developed app highlighted the children's level of involvement compared to traditional methods of teaching. The proposed app is an initiative in designing and friendly that can also be used in clinics, schools, and homes as well. All of the professional and ADHD experts who tested the app, they agreed that user's needs are fulfilled with this app. Moreover, they validate 'Say-it and Learn' is an involving app which will be beneficial for all ADHD children in their academic activities.

6 Limitation

The authors acknowledged that the current study could be optimized by including the other technical aspects in the experimental setting and also by adding more participants to get more precise results. This work only focuses on school-going children who have some acquaintance with the English language, but the majority of children in Pakistan speak the Urdu language which may also affect the applicability. Therefore, the results might be will be different for participants having knowledge of the use of tablets or vice versa. So, in the future work of this app authors will try to minimize these limitations.

7 Future Work and Limitation

This research is an initial prototype of the complete system for ADHD to meet their learning needs. Future advancements will be made by getting live psychologists on a video call in the background. So they can monitor precisely the ADHD kid from their device and give feedback to their guardian. Furthermore, technical subjects will be added for learning, e.g., mathematics (addition, subtraction). This research can also be extended by adding more children to the detailed and optimized results. Thus, the small sample size considered as a limitation of current work that may affect the generalizability of the results. Future work will be submitted in the international journal of human-computer interaction.

Acknowledgment. We gratefully acknowledge the effort made by Asas International School and Roots & Wings Autism Center for providing us useful data. Special thanks go to Zahra Kalsoom (Consultant Psychologist) for giving us time and important advice. Also, thanks to all the participants of the survey and professionals involved in the research process.

References

1. Goodman, P.: 16 Advantages of Digital Technology. TurboFuture. https://turbofuture.com/computers/Advantages-of-Digital-Technology. Accessed 22 Oct 2019
2. nhs.uk: Attention deficit hyperactivity disorder (ADHD). https://www.nhs.uk/conditions/attention-deficit-hyperactivity-disorder-adhd/ Accessed 31 Oct 2019
3. Addiss.co.uk. http://www.addiss.co.uk/schoolreport.pdf. Accessed 17 Dec 2019
4. Blase, S.L., et al.: Self-reported ADHD and adjustment in college: cross-sectional and longitudinal findings. J. Atten. Disord. **13**(3), 297–309 (2009)
5. Nguyen, A.: Using classical music to increase productivity in elementary school students with attention deficit hyperactivity disorder (2014)
6. McKnight, L.: Designing for ADHD in search of guidelines. Designing for ADHD in Search of Guidelines, p. 30 (2010)
7. https://bigthink.com/robby-berman/music-can-help-you-be-productive-as-long-as-its-the-right-music. Accessed 21 Oct 2019
8. Konofal, E., Lecendreux, M., Cortese, S.: Sleep and ADHD. Sleep Med. **11**(7), 652–658 (2010)

9. Goldman, T.A., Lee, F.J., Zhu, J.: Using video games to facilitate understanding of attention deficit hyperactivity disorder: a feasibility study. Using Video Games to Facilitate Understanding of Attention Deficit Hyperactivity Disorder: A Feasibility Study, pp. 115–120. ACM (2014)

10. Krichmar, J.L., Chou, T.-S.: A tactile robot for developmental disorder therapy. A Tactile Robot for Developmental Disorder Therapy, p. 20. ACM (2018)

11. Sonne, T., Marshall, P., Müller, J., Obel, C., Grønbæk, K.: A follow-up study of a successful assistive technology for children with ADHD and their families. A Follow-up Study of a Successful Assistive Technology for Children with ADHD and their Families, pp. 400–407. ACM (2016)

12. Sonne, T., Jensen, M.M.: Chillfish: a respiration game for children with ADHD. Chillfish: A Respiration Game for Children with ADHD, pp. 271–278. ACM (2016)

13. Schuck, S., et al.: Designing an iPad app to monitor and improve classroom behavior for children with ADHD: iSelfControl feasibility and pilot studies. PLoS ONE **11**(10), e0164229 (2016)

14. Sonne, T., Müller, J., Marshall, P., Obel, C., Grønbæk, K.: Changing family practices with assistive technology: MOBERO improves morning and bedtime routines for children with ADHD. Changing Family Practices with Assistive Technology: MOBERO Improves Morning and Bedtime Routines for Children with ADHD, pp. 152–164. ACM (2016)

15. Hashemian, Y., Gotsis, M.: Adventurous dreaming highflying dragon: a full body game for children with attention deficit hyperactivity disorder (ADHD). Adventurous Dreaming Highflying Dragon: A Full Body Game for Children with Attention Deficit Hyperactivity Disorder (ADHD), p. 12. ACM (2013)

16. Supangan, R.A., Acosta, L.A.S., Amarado, J.L.S., Blancaflor, E.B., Samonte, M.J.C.: A gamified learning app for children with ADHD. A Gamified Learning App for Children with ADHD, pp. 47–51. ACM (2019)

17. Abras, C., Maloney-Krichmar, D., Preece, J.: User-centered design. In: Bainbridge, W. (ed.) Encyclopedia of Human-Computer Interaction. Sage Publications, Thousand Oaks, vol. 37, no. 4, pp. 445–456 (2004)

18. Sajjad, U.U., Shahid, S.: Baby + : a mobile application to support pregnant women in Pakistan. Baby + : A Mobile Application to Support Pregnant Women in Pakistan, pp. 667–674. ACM (2016)

19. Rahim, S.K.N.A., Nasrudin, N.H., Azmi, A.Z., Junid, R.A., Mohamed, Z., Abdullah, I.I.B.: Designing mobile application for dyslexia in reading disorder problem. Int. J. Acad. Res. Bus. Soc. Sci. **8**(1), 628–646 (2018)

20. Martin, E., Cupeiro, C., Pizarro, L., Roldán-Álvarez, D., Montero-de-Espinosa, G.: "Today I Tell" a comics and story creation app for people with autism spectrum condition. Int. J. Hum.-Comput. Interact. **35**(8), 679–691 (2019)

21. Gil-Gómez, J.-A., Manzano-Hernández, P., Albiol-Pérez, S., Aula-Valero, C., Gil-Gómez, H., Lozano-Quilis, J.-A.: USEQ: a short questionnaire for satisfaction evaluation of virtual rehabilitation systems. Sensors **17**(7), 1589 (2017)

22. Alqahtani, M., Mohammad, H.: Mobile applications' impact on student performance and satisfaction. Turkish Online J. Educ. Technol.-TOJET **14**(4), 102–112 (2015)

23. Digital.ahrq.gov. https://digital.ahrq.gov/health-it-tools-and-resources/evaluation-resources/workflow-assessment-health-it-toolkit/all-workflow-tools/questionnaire. Accessed 21 Dec 2019

24. Faisal, C.M.N., Gonzalez-Rodriguez, M., Fernandez-Lanvin, D., de Andres-Suarez, J.: Web design attributes in building user trust, satisfaction, and loyalty for a high uncertainty avoidance culture. IEEE Trans. Hum.-Mach. Syst. **47**(6), 847–859 (2017)

Museum Immersion Interactive Design:

Taking the Children Art Gallery Exhibition as an Example

Ching-Wen Chang[✉]

Graduate School of Creative Industry Design, National Taiwan University of Art,
Taipei City, Taiwan
lizchang@cycu.org.tw

Abstract. Art is the museum's collection, and education is the heart of the museum. The management of the museum is aimed at 3E: "Educate, Entertain, Enrich". In the 1960s, the theory of interaction was put forward. From the 1980s, museum exhibitions began to focus on audience participation. In the face of the challenges of the children's museum in new century, how should new strategies be used to transform resources? It is the subject of contemporary museums. Through cross-disciplinary cooperation in culture, entertainment, education and technology, using storytelling and cutting-edge technology, and adding Ecstatic experience to build a 4E model for future museum operations, that is, using the technology of immersive interactive devices, can better present the new look of the exhibits, generate a new dialogue mode, and highly enhance the joyful experience of the audience in contact with the exhibits.

In this study, through in-depth interviews with museum practitioners and expert consultations, the SHE curatorial design model for children's art gallery space are put forward, and they are actually applied to project planning. Then, by observing the museum audience experience, the narrative power of immersive interactive devices and the effects of cutting-edge technology are verified. Responding to and surpassing the concerns and needs of the parent-child audience of contemporary museums, inherited and followed in museum education.

Keywords: Discovery learning · Interaction theory · Immersive design · SHE design model

1 Introduction

The management of the museum is aimed at 3E: "Educate, Entertain, Enrich". Education gives rationality to visits, entertainment stimulates the motivation for exploration, and enriching museum experience is the primary concern of holistic operation [1]. The technological revolution is advancing with the times. In addition to iterating the museum's brand image, through storytelling and cutting-edge technology through cultural, entertainment, education and technology cross-domain cooperation, constructing a future museum visit model will be even more enjoyable (Ecstatic) experience, while driving innovative applications in education and experience. Here, especially the use of immersive interactive devices such as Augmented Reality (AR) and Virtual Reality

© Springer Nature Switzerland AG 2020
P.-L. P. Rau (Ed.): HCII 2020, LNCS 12193, pp. 224–236, 2020.
https://doi.org/10.1007/978-3-030-49913-6_19

(VR) can present a new look of the exhibits, generate a new dialogue mode, and highly enhance audience contact pleasant experience of exhibition.

The learning outcomes of the audience are mostly potential transformation experiences, such as changing the established thoughts or attitudes about things, paying more attention to certain things or phenomena, deepening their love or curiosity, and seeing the world from a more open perspective, etc. (Packer 2006) [2]. Children, however, are seen as the seed target for cultivating aesthetic experiences. Therefore, the application of digital technologies such as animation, games, somatosensory interaction, and operating experience to the planning of children's museum will further enable children to fully open their senses of sight, hearing, touch, and even sense of smell. With a sense of immersion, interaction, and theater, in the pleasant atmosphere of education and fun, enrich the wonderful experience of visiting the museum.

1.1 Theory of Interaction

In the 1960s, British pioneer of new media art Roy Ascott put forward the concept of interaction theory, thinking that creative works of art should take a completely open form of expression; designers should not only express their views unilaterally, but also participants are invited to enter the work; interact with the work and enjoy the creative and imaginative in-depth experience process [3].

1.2 Interactive Art Traits

The main characteristics presented by interactive art are: (1) Interactivity, which can be modified, simple, and feedback; similar to the exploration of toys; has the feeling, atmosphere, experience, and use of creating abstract emotional concepts Those who resonate. (2) Immersion, the viewer through the link, immersing the senses in the equipment like a full penetration. The user may equip virtual equipment to create a virtual reality like a dream. Therefore, how to design with the most direct interface and perfectly integrate with the work is the goal of interactive design. (3) Imagination and Creativity, through intellectual practice to complete a kind of idea that is different from the past, out of nothing, and unexpected whimsy, can generate original imagination and new creativity. (4) Hyper Media, which goes beyond the traditional narrative style of traditional media. As long as the cursor is moved to media such as sound, video, animation, movie graphics, and text, users can use the Hyperlink technology. Obtain cross-domain and interdisciplinary perceptions from sound, light, interactive programs, and even smell [4].

1.3 Immersive Experience

Over the past decade, neuroscience has uncovered a wealth of new information about our senses and how they serve as our gateway to the world. This splendidly accessible book explores the most intriguing findings of this research. With infectious enthusiasm, Dr. Rob DeSalle of the American Museum of Natural History illuminates not only how we see, hear, smell, touch, taste, maintain balance, feel pain, and rely on other less familiar senses, but also illustrates how these senses shape our perception of the world in aesthetics, art and music [5].

An immersive experience is "the perception of physical existence in a non-physical world." When it comes to virtual and augmented reality, this is twofold. This article will completely define what elements define an immersive experience and what steps you can take to improve your immersion in your next virtual or enhanced experience.

1.4   Immersive Element

Immersion depends on our sensory use, especially four of them: vision, sound, touch and smell. Virtual reality uses vision, sound, and touch.

1. Sight: Virtual reality headsets block peripheral vision (or use surround headphones to enhance it) to focus the wearer's attention on what happens directly in front of them. Augmented reality uses headphones or smartphone displays to add virtual elements to the real world.
2. Sound: Virtual reality headsets include sound-suppressing headsets, forcing the wearer to focus on the sounds of the virtual world. Augmented reality provides sound for everything that happens on the screen.
3. Touch: The accessory of the virtual reality headset provides tactile feedback to the wearer. Other examples of using touch include vibration and rumble when picking up an item or bumping with something in the virtual world. Due to the limitations of augmented reality technology, augmented reality rarely uses touch to increase immersion. All these different elements combine to create an immersive experience.

2   Literature Review

Gail Ringel, deputy director of the Boston Children's Museum, mentioned in the article "Designing for Children" that if the learning content set by the museum exceeds the understanding ability of children's audiences, even through interactive or fun learning methods, they cannot be miraculously learned [6].

Therefore, exhibition planning should start with understanding the capabilities of the audience. Rather than presume what children should learn, it is better to think about how to motivate their learning from their mental development stage; instead of setting museum exhibition goals, consider children's interests and needs. In addition, the museum's display goal should be to provide a comfortable and effective display for the audience and their families. To achieve this goal, it is recommended that the exhibition be designed so that the audience can choose and enjoy the visiting process independently to establish the museum's learning experience (William Crain) [7]. In view of this, combined with the intellectual ternary theory proposed by the American scholar Sternberg and the discovery learning theory of American psychology and educator Bruner, it is applied to the future curatorial design as the basis for the discussion of design architecture (see Fig. 1).

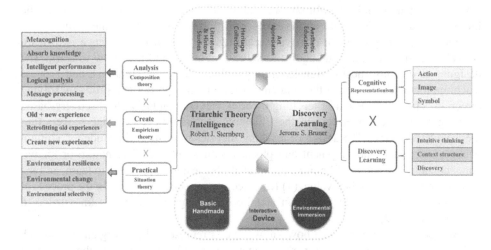

Fig. 1. Intellectual ternary and discovery learning applied to immersive interaction design

2.1   Triarchic Theory/Intelligence

American scholar Sternberg (1985) proposed the triarchic theory (intelligence), which is an intelligence theory oriented to information processing models. Contains three sub-theories: componential sub-theory, experimental sub-theory, and contextual sub-theory. The component theory explains the relationship between intelligence and the individual's inner world; it contains three basic information processing components: meta components, performance components, and knowledge acquisition components. Empiricism holds that intelligence should include two different types of information processing: novelty and automatization. Situation theory holds that intelligence is an individual's ability to adapt, change, and choose in real life and circumstances, and Situation theory is to explain the relationship between intelligence and the outside world [8].

Human intelligence is a complex formed by three different dimensions:

1. Componential intelligence: refers to the ability to memorize, discern, analyze, judge, and find out the answer to the question, the ability measured by the traditional intelligence test.
2. Experiential intelligence: refers to being good at getting inspiration and understanding from experience, thus forming personal creative ability.
3. Contextual Intelligence: the ability to respond to the needs of the environment only. People with high intelligence can adapt to their environmental requirements while adapting to their lives. They can also change the environmental conditions to achieve their goals.

2.2   Discovery Learning

American Psychology, educator Jerome Seymour Bruner's Discovery Learning it refers to human learning in an information-rich environment, by providing learners with sufficient but unorganized information, and then letting them actively discover the interrelationship between these messages and further understand the structure of knowledge. In the process of discovery learning, the role of the audience is to learn actively, so that they have the ability to solve problems and know how to learn. The designer or operator must design learning problems, learning situations, and provide teaching materials to guide the audience to find the appropriate problem solving direction. The development of teaching theories that are conducive to discovery-based learning requires consideration of the following factors: (1) Knowledge seekers (audiences) background: The design of teaching theories must meet the students' cultural background, mental development and physical constraints. (2) The nature of knowledge: consider the nature of knowledge, what skills the audience wants to learn, and the type of knowledge that they value. (3) Knowledge acquisition process: In the process of discovery learning, the audience can acquire knowledge and use this knowledge to solve problems [9].

Bruner was concerned with how knowledge is represented and organized through different modes of thinking (or representation). In his research on the cognitive development of children, Jerome Bruner proposed three modes of representation:

- Enactive representation (action-based)
- Iconic representation (image-based)
- Symbolic representation (language-based).

To the foundation of constructive learning theory established by Piaget, Jerome Bruner contributed important ideas regarding (a) modes of representation, (b) the importance of teaching and learning "optimal structure" (J.S. Bruner 1966), (c) the spiral curriculum, and (d) learning through acts of discovery in order to rearrange and transform what is learned "in such a way that one is enabled to go beyond the evidence so reassembled to additional new insights" (J.S. Bruner 1961) [10].

3 Research Methods

3.1 Interpretive Case Study: *"Reflections Along the River"* Exhibition, 2019

In recent years, the National Palace Museum has been committed to the implementation of digital collection and value-added programs in recent years. Through the progressive scanning technology, we can not only further study the details of ancient artifacts, but also break the boundaries of cultural relics that were difficult to get close to. The exhibition *"Reflections alone the river*: National Palace Museum with Weiwuying New Media Art Exhibition" will show the project that won the US Museum and Web GLAMi Awards - the virtual reality "UP the River During the Qingming Festival" series, and the VR and AI navigation equipment. There are also large-scale projection animations, which are more than ten meters long, and high-definition films produced by the National Palace Museum over the years. Through the digital display, the National Palace Museum will carry out new contexts and gestures. The exhibition space (see Fig. 2) and plan of the whole exhibition area as below (see Table 1).

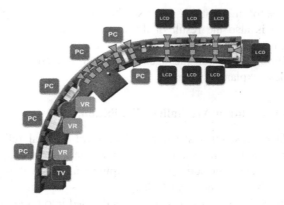

Fig. 2. The exhibition "Reflections along the River" whole space

Table 1. The plan of the whole exhibition "Reflections along the River" area design.

Area	Entrance Images	Time Tunnel	Full projection	Anime long scroll	VR
Content	Special Exhibition. Main Vision for Photo Spot. Introduce Curatorial Philosophy / Exhibition Introduction	Introduction to Ancient Painting Character Silhouette and Text Light and shadow design art	Playing on the canal. Appreciate the full picture.	Appreciate the whole ancient painting animation: "Up the River During Qingming"	Scenes and life in reality experience animation. "Hongqiao" "Feng Yi Ting" "Jinlanju"
Design	Immersive space	Interactive screen touch	Build a reduced version of Hongqiao	Multiple high-resolution projections	VR glasses interactive game
Digital Collection	Poster	Scan	Full Image Stitching	Animation	VR

Hooper-Greenhill (1994), a British museum scholar, pointed out that 10% of the memory obtained by visitors during the exhibition is through reading, 20% through hearing, 30% through viewing, 70% through personal participation, and 90% It is memorized by talking and doing at the same time [11]. Observe the dynamics of the audience's operations on the scene and discover that interactive exhibits are an important principle for modern museum displays. Of course, the dynamics of the exhibits can attract the attention of the audience, but the audience is really interested in the dynamics that they can participate in. Participatory dynamic display with the most display value is game-like participation; that is, the role of the audience in the display is not only the source of motivation, but also the guide of the display results. The audience's thinking is also the result of the display (Hambod 2000) [12, 13]. The knowledge learned in the game, or the thoughts experienced, are the goals of the museum. In addition, the lower the age, the higher the proportion of interactive exhibits, and the less explanatory text.

3.2   Case Object: Children Art Gallery Exhibition, 2020

The National Palace Museum has a rich collection of cultural relics and intensive research on cultural history, which can enable let audiences to enhance their experience of art appreciation and aesthetic education. In keeping with its spirit, the space planning of the entire area of the Children's Art Gallery is a 200 square meter narrow space. In addition to the parent-child friendly rest area, it is divided into three major areas: basic handwork, interactive device and environmental immersion. Allow visitors to learn the knowledge content of ancient artifacts of National Palace Museum through intuitive thinking, exploration and discovery, and situational structure. The exhibition whole space design (see Fig. 3) and the plan of National Palace Museum Children Art Gallery as below (see Table 2).

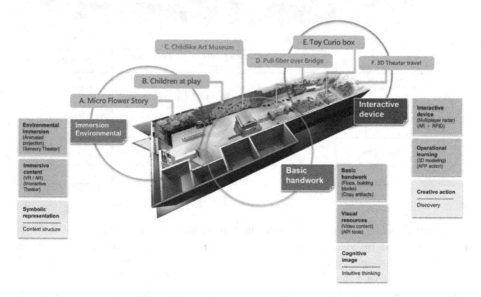

Fig. 3. The NPM Children Art Gallery Exhibition space design.

Table 2. The Storyboard plan of NPM Children Art Gallery Exhibition.

Area	Micro Flower Story	Children at play	Childlike Art Museum	Pull fiber over Bridge	Toy Curio box	3D Theater travel
Content	Use small trees, large flowers to make land-scapes.	Similar to Dunhuang frescoes, when the body touches the silhouette, a picture and explanation of dynamic toys will appear.	To understand-ing the twelve solar terms through Chinese painting, and also understanding the meaning of aesthetic education.	The boat can be moved slowly by using the track and the rope. It can carry children.	Children can take it out and put it on the lotus leaves in the next area for interactive experience.	The child stood in the theater as if walking into the painting. Just like it, it is the most fascinating place
Design	Environmental Immersive	Environmental Immersive	Basic Handwork	Basic Handwork	Interactive Device	Interactive Device
Digital Collection	Small Specimens Animated Projection	Multiplayer Radar Projec-tion	Poster/ Axis of rotation	Rail Drive	API Tool/ AR+RFID	APP Action/ 3D Modeling
Argument Basis	Intuitive Thinking	Cognitive Image	Symbolic Representation	Context Structure	Discovery	Creative Action
Cognition	Insight	Empathy	Interpretation	Communication	Awareness	Experience
Learning	Concentration/ Different view	Treat others well / Shared	Deep aesthetics	Cooperation/ Pass difficult	Stimulate imagination	Elegant / calm
Degree of difficulty	easy	median	median	hard	hard	easy

Immersive Experience Area. Use small trees (small specimens), large flowers (ani-mated projection) to make landscapes, and background music of flowers and plants, like entering a real courtyard. Let children understand the environment and atmosphere in Chinese painting, and have the opportunity to learn more about planting. Miniature specimens allow children to learn more about plants. Children's ability to zoom in and out is more focused, and the visual feast that dizzyingly gives children a deeper memory of the museum.

In addition, the theme murals of the exhibition will be operated in an atmosphere similar to Dunhuang murals. When the body touches the silhouette, a dynamic chil-dren's play screen and explanation will appear. The multi-person accurate interactive device is suitable for the whole class to play together, and the whole wall will become full color. Use the five senses to fully open to experience that ancient children are not the same as you. When all the black silhouettes are touched, the full-color *"Children at play*" will be presented as it is. It is very suitable for parent-child play or group cooperation. You can also learn to share and be kind to others by inducing empathy through cooperation.

Basic Handwork Experience Area. Flop Interactive Device. It can be experienced by many people, in addition to understanding the twelve solar terms through Chinese painting, and also understanding the meaning of aesthetic education. The whole pavilion is like a miniature aesthetic classroom, which can fully enjoy in the artistic aesthetics of Chinese painting.

Through the gazebo, you can reach the fiber bridge and cross the Hongqiao bridge. The boat can be moved slowly by using the track and the rope. It can carry children. In addition to the sound of ships, children can also play the trumpet sound that is made when the fiber is pulled by the fiber, and the parents can cosplay the cheering people. The vocal enthusiasm and modern prosperity allowed the scene to re-enact the most classic bridge section in the *"Up the River During Qingming"*.

Interactive Device Area. Various treasures are installed in Curio Box. Children can take it out and put it on the lotus leaves in the next area for interactive experience. Above the lotus leaf is equipped with AR (inductor) + RFID (induction point), when Jane is placed on the lotus leaf, the relevant introduction of the exhibits will be automatically played.

3D somatosensory theater, using *"Travelers Among Mountains and Streams"* and *"Early Spring"* for instant recitation. The child stood in the theater as if walking into the painting, it is the most fascinating place for immersive interactive devices. Here is the innermost part of the center of the theater. The left and right embracing exhibits in the area are swaying vividly like the sleeves of ancient people's clothes, removing the original theater partition and adding the elegance and calmness of ancient literati.

4   Results and Discussion

4.1   Learning Theory Applied to Interactive Devices

Looking at the planning of the whole district, we hope that children can use traditional basic hand-made devices such as flop cards, and still keep the quality and temperature of handwork while learning new knowledge. The interactive device of new technology application is a new generation of children's keen and even familiar vehicles, allowing participants to be curious and maintain the enthusiasm of absorbing new knowledge. By creating an immersive environment, children can directly receive the aesthetic baptism of the museum. Also, encourages children to grow up, they will be more willing and reflow to participate in the physical collection in the museum.

The micro flower story belongs to the learning area of image cognition and intuitive thinking; the change of proportion can promote intuitive memory. It also helps to absorb the concentration of new knowledge, and strengthens the adaptability of the environment by subverting the immersive environment of the old visual experience.

The Children at Play will provide a learning area for action cognition and exploration; under the premise of encouraging cooperation, it is expected to have a better group intelligent performance, and the ability to construct environment choices based on the black silhouette. Twenty-four solar terms and twelve aesthetic education in **the Childlike Art Museum** belong to the post-cognitive zone, which has a rich Aesthetics of the National Palace Museum. Each piece is an important symbol. By turning over the cards, explore the National Palace Museum database. At the same time, test your message processing skills and capabilities.

By playing the doll action of **the Toy Curio Box**, the children can explore and discover the value of traditional art. At the same time, by choosing the action of toys placed on the lotus leaves, they can further develop the information processing ability and experience the unique experience of old things and new play. The old and new experience creation experience, children can jump from the **3D Theater Travel** and merge into the painting. The new and old elements can be reconfigured so that children can learn the context structure and cultivate innovative narrative power in different role plays.

After experiencing full interactive devices and immersion in the environment, finally in the area of **the Pull fiber over the Bridge**, everyone can learn the wisdom of ancient people through motion cognition. If you can't automatically open the hull to pass like the Tower Bridge in London, then use your brain, hands on, work together to challenge contemporary artificial intelligence with ancient human wisdom. The old plus new experience allows the environment to change.

4.2   HE Exhibition Design Model

From the history of design development, the rise of human engineering after the Second World War in the 1950s continued into the rise of personal computers in the 1980s. The design of human-friendly interfaces and interactive interfaces based on human nature are more important. In the 21st century, the era of sensibility is coming. When we talk about cultural creativity's pleasure or experience, its interaction with "people" becomes more important [14, 15].

Therefore, in the **SHE** (Science-History-Education) Exhibition Design Model, the connotation of educational thinking is the basis of human nature. The immersive interactive designed through the three levels of cognition and the 4E (Educate, Entertain, Enrich, Ecstatic) spirit of museum management must be consistent with the museum audience experience and then constructed it has both immersive, theatrical, and interactive dimensions of science and technology applications. With the integration of STEAM (Science, Technology, Engineering, Art and Math), it achieves the core goal of SHE curation. (See Fig. 4).

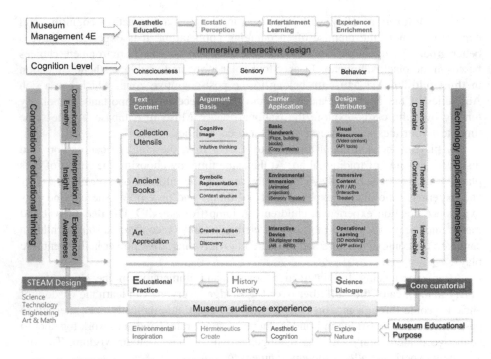

Fig. 4. SHE (Science-History-Education) design model for immersive interactive design

First of all, humanity-based educational thinking only takes into account the cultivation of empathy through communication, the discovery of insights through interpretation, and the cultivation of profound awareness through experience. Secondly, in the three levels of cognition, the details of text content, argumentation basis, carrier application, and design attributes are discussed in terms of consciousness level, sensory level, and behavior level. At this stage, it is necessary to consider whether the audience experience is in line with the museum's educational purpose: environmental inspiration, interpretation of creation, aesthetic cognition, exploration of nature, and whether immersive interactive design covers the spirits of aesthetic education, pleasure perception, entertainment learning, enriching experience, etc. Finally, the effect of technology application verification can reach immersion (desirable), theater Effects (continuable) and interactive (feasible) effects as a reference for subsequent corrections. The purpose of this framework is to enable STEAM (Science, Technology, Engineering, Art and Math) to be applied to design at the same time, and the curator can adhere to the core spirit of Science dialogue, History diversity, and Educational practice.

4.3   Evaluation of Immersive Interactive Devices and Discovery Learning

The immersive environment is a new trend of museum visits. The five senses are fully open, allowing participants can experienced (post) the experience (cognition) of others, and then translate the data into messages, which can be summarized as better absorbed knowledge. This is the learning model that uses experience and experience to classify and structure knowledge content. The National Palace Museum is a pioneer in the field of museums. In the creative planning of children's art gallery, it is especially necessary to consider the implementation plan of immersion, interaction and theater. This means a commitment built with children based on the prerequisites for sustainable development. In the future, after the actual opening and operation, the following topics should be further explored for audience research in order to strive for the improvement of the design of children's art space planning.

1. Whether it can help memory.
2. Whether the maximum learning transfer occurs.
3. Whether the audience has the opportunity to learn how to learn.
4. Whether to make the audience better understand the content of teaching aids and produce meaningful learning.
5. Whether the operation interface has reached the goal of keen and intuitive use.
6. Whether to increase the level of knowledge and pursuit of knowledge through game interaction.
7. Whether the audience can take the initiative to learn knowledge, have self-confidence, have the ability to solve problems, and have the ability to think.

5 Conclusion

Almost all participants believe that immersive interaction enhances their museum experience. Through in-depth interviews with visitors, it is found that the reasons why audiences like immersive interaction are: (1) The popularity of single-person interactive forms is higher than that of multi-person interactive forms; (2) The degree of discussion of immersive interactive devices is higher than that of physical hand-made devices; (3) Interactive devices can stimulate enthusiasm for learning; (4) Improving the interactive experience can effectively increase learning cognition.

Where there is no intention, display is not valid. The use of new technology has greatly facilitated cultural learning. Museum participants are guided by immersive interactive design, from traditional "Making" to open "Tinkering", to problem solving and "Engineering".

Through the analysis of museum audience experience and pleasant sensibility analysis, the combination of interactive technology and cultural connotation, with the museum and children's education concept as its purpose, is practically applied to the museum children's art gallery space creation plan. When art exhibits are not only placed in the museum's field, they can also use the business and art value-added of "culture plus digital" and "art plus technology" to open up cross-domain innovation experience, which is different from traditional new ones. The first-generation museum experience classroom let museums perpetually adhere to the fair injection of cultural resources and practice the future of communion and learning with the help of STEAM technology tools and SHE curatorial design modules.

References

1. Colleendilenschneider: What Influences Millennial Visitor Satisfaction Most. https://www. colleendilen.com/2018/12/05/influences-millennial-visitor-satisfaction-no-not-avocado-toast/. Accessed 05 Dec 2018
2. Packer, J.: Learning for fun: the unique contribution of educational, leisure experiences. Curator: Mus. J. **49**(3), 329–344 (2006)
3. Ascott, R.: Behaviourist art and the cybernetic vision. Cybernetica **9**, 247–264 (1966)
4. Lin, D., Pei-Hua, W.: A study in the context and the aesthetics of interactive art. Art J. **87**, 99–110 (2010)
5. DeSalle, R.: Our Senses: An Immersive Experience. Yale University Press, New Haven (2018)
6. Ringel, G.: Designing exhibition for kids: what are we thinking? Presented at the J. Paul Getty Museum Symposium. From Content to Play: Family-Oriented Interactive Spaces in Art and History Museums (2005)
7. Crain, W.: Forward to wood. In: Yardsticks, C. (ed.) Children in the Classroom Ages 4–14, 3rd edn. Northeast Foundation for Children, Inc, Turners Falls (2007)
8. Sternberg, R.J.: Behavioral and Brain Sciences, 7th edn. Cambridge University Press, New York (1985)
9. Bruner: Simply Psychology. McLeod, S.A. https://www.simplypsychology.org/bruner.html. Accessed 11 July 2019
10. Bruner, J.S.: The Process of Education, 2nd edn. Harvard University Press, Massachusetts (1961)
11. Hooper-Greenhill, E.: Museum and their Visitors. Routledge, London (1994)
12. Baode, H.: Exhibition Planning Theory and Practice. Pastoral Urban Culture Publishing, Taipei (2000)
13. Wang, C.-T.: A study on the production and design of interactive exhibitions in science museums. Technol. Mus. Rev. **10**(4), 73–88 (2006)
14. Lin, R.: Transforming Taiwan aboriginal cultural features into modern product design-a case study of cross cultural product design model. Int. J. Des. **1**(2), 47–55 (2007)
15. Lin, R.: A framework for human-culture interaction design-beyond human-computer interaction. In: International Symposium for Emotion and Sensibility 2008, June, 27–29, KAIST, Korea, p. 8 (2008). (Keynote Speech)

Developing Persona for the Chinese Learning Application for Foreigners in China on Mobile Devices

Zhe Chen[✉], Déborah Dauly, Sara Amaral, Rita Martinho,
Sandra Ruppel, Juho Toro, Yashuai Li, and Jichang Zhao

Beihang University, Beijing 100191, People's Republic of China
zhechen@buaa.edu.cn

Abstract. This study presented how to develop persona for the Chinese learning application on mobile devices. Two personas were developed according to the understanding of current products and previous studies. Target market analysis was used in developing the two personas for learning Chinese characters on mobile devices. Consequently, the two personas were designed for two target groups: the short-term visitors (e.g. exchanging students) and the long-term Cosmopolitans (e.g. professions in China). Other translation application and learning applications on mobile devices were also discussed and evaluated in this study. An interview was used to revise and improve the persona. Future research directions were discussed at the end, including location-oriented mode, rotation mode, and dark mode.

Keywords: Mobile application · Learning Chinese · International students

1 Introduction

1.1 Background

Chinese people use Chinese characters, which is different from alphabetical letters. For example, most alphabetical letters do not have meanings. Words (i.e. the combination of letters) have meanings. Chinese characters are much more complicated than alphabetical letters or words. Chinese characters do have a meaning and they also give us an indication of the pronunciation. Another difference is that there are only 26 letters in alphabet while there are more than 100000 different characters in China. 3000 to 6000 Chinese characters are frequently used in daily life. It is difficult to learn Chinese characters, especially for foreigners. That is why we want to design an English application that will help foreigner to learn Chinese characters. This application should be able to translate from Chinese to English and from English to Chinese. The goal will be to see what applications already exists, to look for a good method to learn Chinese characters and to propose the best application to learn Chinese characters. How can we improve the way of learning Chinese to make it more efficient and comfortable?

© Springer Nature Switzerland AG 2020
P.-L. P. Rau (Ed.): HCII 2020, LNCS 12193, pp. 237–249, 2020.
https://doi.org/10.1007/978-3-030-49913-6_20

1.2 Research Goal

The goal for the application is to provide mobile users with a comprehensive and in-depth learning application that is fast to use and focused on key sections to learn the practical use of Chinese language.

Key Features:

- Free dictionary: 5000 Chinese characters with stroke order demonstration and in-app training.
- Hand-writing input: In-engine recognition system for searching characters from the dictionary.
- Multiple Context for daily life use: comprehensive and practical packages with a list of key words provided with multiple example sentences and training.
- Hand-writing fonts: learn through examples how Chinese is written in reality.

In order to achieve this, the application will offer quick to load and practical packages of different environments where the users are likely to encounter Chinese language and written characters. This includes but is not limited to daily activities such as booking of a hotel, going to a restaurant or shopping and scenarios where more specific expertise on language is required such as taking a mortgage or sales negotiations. Moreover, as our own experience have demonstrated, more often than not these situations require reading and writing hand-written Chinese documents which is quite very different to reading or writing on an electric platform. To acknowledge this, the application will offer special hand-writing fonts in order to get our users more familiar with hand-writing styles and enhance their learning experience.

1.3 What is the Difference to Other Applications

In order to distinguish our application from others, we included the following characteristics:

- Learning how to write Chinese characters step-by-step;
- In-app drawing mode and training with strike order;
- Special packages for daily activities, for example: how to order food at a restaurant; how to say you want to try a different size of clothes when you go shopping, ask for directions when you go travelling; and so many others;
- Offline function to be able to study everywhere;
- Preparation mode for the HSK;
- Free.

1.4 Target Group

Designing our new application, we have to set up our future target groups, or who we expect to be our potential customers.

So first we set up some expectations about our customer. Due to the fact that our application will only be available in English, we assume that the consumer is English speaking. Another factor is the willingness to use mobile applications to learn a new language, because otherwise the consumer would not use our application. About the area the application can be used we consider that it can be used worldwide, where the people have access to the internet.

Taken all those expectations into consideration we set up two different target groups. Later we will transform the target groups into Personas.

Those Personas will represent a possible user of our application and should make it easier for us to have a better image of them. After conducting our interview, we will revise those personas and adjust them if necessary. Because those target groups and later on the personas are just assumptions, which need to be justified afterwards.

Target Group 1: Short-Term Visitors. Those customers, are short term visitors, which are either staying in China for a trip or are here for exchange. They wanted to learn some Chinese, to at least deal with some casual situations, like ordering food or asking for the direction. We expect them, to have no or little knowledge of the Chinese language and require having a basic level of Chinese at the end.

They have a need for support in casual situation and expect the application to be as easy as possible and offers as much information as necessary. They are not willing to pay a lot, caused by the fact that there are other competitors in the market, where they can easily go to.

Target Group 2: Cosmopolitans. Our second group are called the cosmopolitans. Those are not customers, who are travelling or studying short-term here in China, those are customers, who are staying here long-term. They are professionals, which are setting up there new living environment in China and already have prior expertise about Chinese language and culture. They require to gain an advanced level in Chinese, because of the fact, that they have to use it at the job, at official office, or the school of their children.

This group could be willing to pay for the application, the reason for that is, that they will be long term residents and would have more usage for the application then the short-term residents.

1.5   Research Question

Before starting to develop and design our application, we need to analyze the market and all the other existing applications. This way we can better understand what would make our application stand out from the others already available. To facilitate future work, we have come up with the following research questions:

- Are our target groups accurate? Do they really need a new application?
- What applications are already available?
- What features can we improve or add to our application that others aren't offering?
- What do users look for in an application like ours?
- What is the most convenient layout for our application?
- What technics can we incorporate in our app in order to help our users memorize Chinese characters more easily?
- Which are the most appropriate methods to use in the development of our app?

After we've answered all the questions above, we can then answer our main question and big goal:

How can we improve the way of learning Chinese to make it more efficient and comfortable?

2 Current Products

2.1 Overview of Translating Apps: Pleco and Google Translate

Both Google translate and Pleco are able to translate from any language to Chinese and the other way around. They offer different ways of translation, like scanning, translating pictures or drawing the characters. For Pleco it is required to be online, whereas in Google translator you can download certain language packages.

Google Translator. As shown in Fig. 1 the home screen offers different options to translate the text. There are various functions such as Camera, handwriting, conversation and last but not least voice translation. The biggest disadvantage of the usage of Google Translator in China is, that some functions are limited or not working caused by the internet restrictions in China. To get a competitive advantage for our application, we have to ensure, that our application does not face this problem as well and is usable all the time.

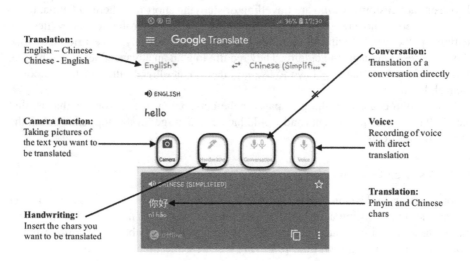

Fig. 1. Google Translator and its different functions [1]

Pleco Translate. Another application for translation is Pleco. It offers a wide range of functions, such as dictionary, show the chars and a step by step explanation how to draw the different characters stroke by stroke.

This application is especially useful, when you are trying to learn a word/char and do not know how to write them.

The biggest disadvantage is the fact, that there is a limited number where this step by step explanation is available (Fig. 2).

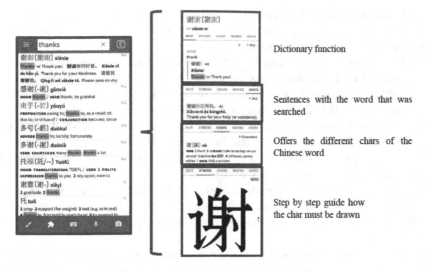

Fig. 2. Pleco and its different functions [2]

2.2 Comparison of Some Applications to Learn Chinese

Applications to Learn Chinese. Lots of application to learn Chinese exists. We quoted some of the most famous applications on the Table 1 below.

Table 1. Comparison of goals of applications to learn Chinese

Applications	Goal of the application
Skritter	Learn how to write Chinese character
FluentU	Learn Chinese with videos
Chinese Pod	Learning Chinese through podcasts
Memrise	Learn efficiently new vocabulary
Duolingo	Memorize vocabulary and learn grammar
The chairman's Bao	Read in Chinese

As we can see, all applications does not have the same goal. Of course, at the end, the objective is to learn Chinese but they use different methods. As we want our application to focus on the learning of the writing, Skritter seems to be the our biggest competitor. Let's focus about this application to know more about it and design a better application.

2.3 Literature Review

Hold and Interaction of Phone. In our application design, we are concerned of the ergonomic design of the mobile application. From our own experience, using the mobile device in our hand will become increasingly uncomfortable for the user the longer the device is being held in hands. One way to avoid is to take a user-oriented approach by studying how people actually prefer to use the mobile devices and to design our application interface according to this.

We have used secondary data to better understand how mobile users hold their devices. According to an observation of some 1300 users, the findings were the following: 49% were using the mobile device in one hand, 36% used another hand to support the device, and 15% of observed users used two hands [3–5].

The way that the users are holding the mobile device is important which needs to be addressed in the design of the user interface to meet the ergonomic design requirements. For example, the direct effect the different ways of holding the devices is the reach of the fingers and the accuracy of the touch.

The above picture demonstrates the accuracy of the touch when user is using thumb to control the display. In this we can see that the most accurate position for the controls are in the center of the display whereas the least accurate parts are in the corners of the mobile display.

In an ergonomically fit mobile design the primary content should be positioned somewhere in the center of the display which is the most accurate part for the touch. The secondary controls could be positioned at the lower end of the screen. Navigation between site sections should be smooth for the users, such as swipe function similar to that of the image gallery. Also, additional functions and controls can be placed behind menus so that users don't accidentally press them when there are multiple buttons close by in the less accurate parts of the screen.

Best Way to Learn Chinese Characters. In order to develop the best possible app for our users, we did some research on different ways to learn Chinese characters. Through this research, we discovered the key technics to make the Chinese learning experience more efficient and enjoyable.

Firstly, we discovered that, to learn Chinese characters fast, we first need to understand what exactly a Chinese character is. In modern Chinese, each character represents one mono-syllabic word, but most of words are composed of two or more characters. One important finding of this research is that some of the simpler characters are pictograms, or simplified representations of real-world things. For example, the character 木 (mù), which means "wood", looks just like a little tree, and the character 口 (kǒu), which means "mouth", it looks like an open mouth. Even though pictograms are very intuitive and may work for some characters, they can only get us so far, making them not the ideal way to learn Chinese characters. For example, it would be impossible to come up with symbols for "philosophy", "uncle", etc.

Through this research, we also discovered that most characters are built from several characters put together. For example, the character 木 (mù), the same mentioned before, reappears in 树 (shù), the character for "tree", and two 木 put together become 林 (lín), character for "forest" or "woods". These individual building blocks are called radicals, and around 200 of them make up all Chinese characters. This makes this technic very useful for our app, since that once our users have learned all the radicals, they have a solid foundation for breaking down any character they come across.

Another interesting characteristic we found out about Chinese characters is that most them not only have semantic (meaning) components, but they also have sound (phonetic) components. The phonetic component gives clues to the sound of the character. For example, all characters contain 林 (lín) plus one other radical, and they all share the same pronunciation.

After researching common characteristics among Chinese characters, we searched existing methods and techniques to help our users memorize them. We came across two interesting approaches that will certainly add value to our application. The first important method is Stroke Order, due to how memory muscle works. Studies have proven that our brain is able to automatically remember a complex sequence of movement. If strokes were written in a random order, they would be much harder to remember. For example, the character 国 (guó) means "country".

The second well known technic is Spaced Repetition System (SRS). SRS is a language learning method that allows users to periodically test themselves. Some people call this technic the flashcards of modern days, but it's actually an upgraded version. This is because SRS is automated by computer algorithms that tell users when they should review a certain card, based on how many times they got the correct answer. We thought that a convenient and fun way to incorporate this technic into our application is through quizzes, where the users will see questions they get wrong more frequently than ones they get right.

By incorporating in our application all the features gathered with this research, we can provide the best experience for our users.

HSK Test. The HSK test was launched by Hanban institution in an effort to better serve chinese language learners. It is an international standardized exam that tests and rates chinese language proficiency which assesses non-native chinese speakers' abilities in using the chinese language in their daily, academic and professional lives.

The structure of HSK consists of a writing test and a speaking test, which are independent of each other. There are six levels of writing tests, namely the HSK level I, HSK level II, HSK level III, HSK level IV, HSK level V, and HSK level VI. There are three levels of speaking tests, namely the HSK beginner level, HSK intermediate level, and HSK advanced level. During the speaking test, test takers' speeches will be recorded.

3 Methods

3.1 Interview

Before setting up the questions for the interview and the questionnaire, we decided to come up with personas related to our target group. The goal is that, once we finish making the interviews and analyzing the data, we would make small adjustments in the personas initially created. We set up personas according to:

- Age;
- Gender;
- Education experience;
- Mobile app used;
- Chinese proficiency;

Our first persona is Thomas, a man with 35 years old - Fig. 3. He is a consultant who just moved to China with basic knowledge of China and its culture. He did a gap year in Australia, has a bachelor and a master and is now setting up his career. He is a busy man and wants to reach a high proficiency level in Chinese.

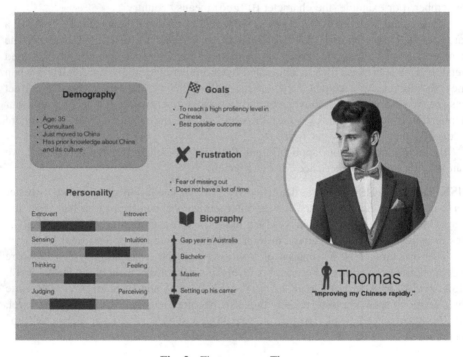

Fig. 3. First persona, Thomas

Our second persona is Lisa, a female with 23 years old - Fig. 4. She is an exchange student in China. She is only staying four months in China. She did a gap year in Australia after finishing high school. She has a bachelor and is now studying for her master. Her goal is not to become fluent in Chinese but to have some basic vocabulary to be able to communicate in daily life.

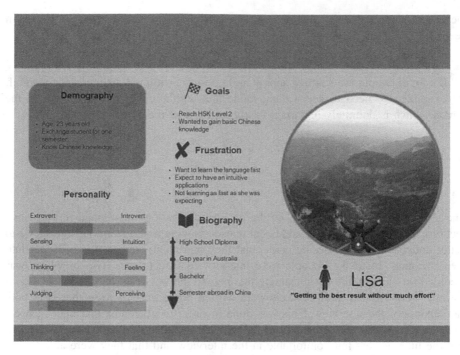

Fig. 4. Second persona, Lisa

After setting up the personas, we started planning our interviews.
We divided our interview in three sections:

- Section 1: Background information;
- Section 2: The applications used;
- Section 3: Environment and time.

In section 1, we collected some basic information about the people we were interviewing such as their gender, age, academic background and so on.

In section 2, we came up with the following question to help understand the process of learning a language and also the characteristics of a preferred application:

Do you use applications to learn new language?

- Which apps do you use?
- What do you like in these applications?
- What do you dislike?

Finally, in section 3, our goal was to find out and understand the problems concerning studying environment and time. In order to do so, in the last stage of our interview, we would ask the interviewees the following questions:

- Where do you use the application?

Some answers we can expect are 'silent Library' or 'crowded Bus', it is important to know where most people choose to use their learning applications in noisy or quiet location. Characteristics of the environment can greatly affect the ergonomic design needs.

- When/What time of the day?

If a lot of people use learning apps at night, this question will help us understand if, for example, we need to add a night mode and regulation of the brightness of the screen, which is definitely important for the comfort of the eyes.

4 Results

4.1 Conducting the Interview

The interview was carried based on the pre-made questions mentioned in the above sections. On top of this, some additional questions were asked from our interviews to better understand some specific points that they had mentioned, or to go deeper into their meaning. In total, 5 people were interviewed face to face, two of which was recorded on video while the remaining tree people did not grant permission to record the interview. Instead, their answers were written down on paper together with both participants of the interview. This was done in order to guarantee that their answers were comprehended correctly and was in line what they had said. Good care was taken that the interviewers felt comfortable in the interview and that they were able to talk freely in a friendly environment.

The place we set the interview was in a public café within the university campus and they lasted approximately half an hour or more each.

4.2 Analyzing Interview's Data

As for the applications used, the most common were PLECO, Hello Chinese and Google Translate, which all participant had actively used. Also, different video applications such as CCTV were used by most of the people participating in the interview. Upon asked about what they like in these applications, the common answers were the literal translation feature, interactive and fun design and the clear interface of the applications. These were highlighted by all the participants during the interview to some degree. The things that they did not like were advertisements & pop-up windows that are disturbing their use of the application and periodic notifications of upgrades to premium service. The applications are used not in a specific time of the day but instead are used every now and then: during breakfast, communing on bus/subway, during class breaks and in silent locations such as library.

Also, the interview was trying to understand the underlying motivation or need for using the language learning applications using Maslow's hierarchy of needs theory. Based on the common answers, we could conclude that most people wished to learn Chinese language in order to get a job of desire, which could fill a need for safety as it provides their future income, or even higher level of self-actualization as they wish to achieve their full potential in career, not only securing their place in the job market. Especially the basic and psychological needs was clearly seen by two of the interviews who were enthusiastic on talking about how a good command on Chinese language brings them closer to friends and connects them to new relationships with other individuals. Moreover, a longer conversation was had that goes well beyond this: one of the interview went on a long conversation about geopolitics and history and how the politics can escalate by the lack of understanding of other people and nations; the interview believed that having a command on a language not only brings connectivity between people but also grands ability to connect to their way of thinking as well. Indeed, the same person was worried of the economic development of his home region and the stability of the regions he wishes to immigrate to, because he wants to have a safe and stable ground to raise his future family.

4.3   Changes in the Personas

Before realizing the interviews, we created 2 personas: Thomas and Lisa. To create a buyer persona, we have to actually meet potential buyers and talk with them, this is what we did. After this we decided to make some changes. We decided to focus our personas on student because after discussion, a student and a business man are not that different to learn a new language. The difference that really matters in the duration of stay. People do not have the same objective with a short-stay in China and a long-stay, the goals are different. The main differences between our two personas is now the last of the stay. The application should be able to satisfy people staying a few weeks as well as people staying a few years.

Changes in Persona: Thomas. Thomas was our first persona. He was a consultant who just moved to China with basic knowledge. He was busy and wanted to reach a high proficiency level in Chinese (Fig. 5).

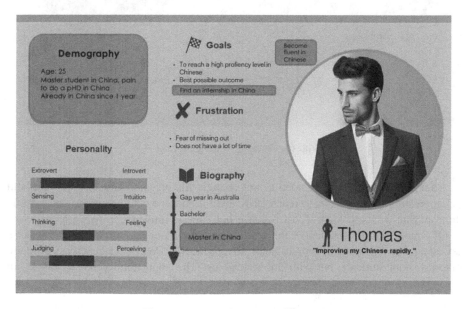

Fig. 5. Changes in persona Thomas

After the interviews, we decided to focus our target group on students and two types of student (study in China and Exchange student). Thomas is 25 years old. He is a master student who study in China and he plans to do a PhD here. He arrived in China one year ago and will stay several years in this country. We kept the same personality for the persona. Thomas still wants to reach a high proficiency level in Chinese and he also has the opportunity to have an internship in China. He should be able to communicate in Chinese, make him understand and should have some business vocabulary. So, this is something he will have to work on. He needs to become Fluent in Chinese. Frustration stays unchanged. He fears of missing out and he does not have a lot of time. Finally, the bibliography change: he is currently doing a master.

Changes in Persona Lisa. Our second persona is also a student but this time, it is an exchange student. Lisa is only here for four months. Her goal is not to become fluent in Chinese but to have some basis to be able to communicate in daily life and when she is traveling. Lisa represents very well some potential users of our application (Fig. 6).

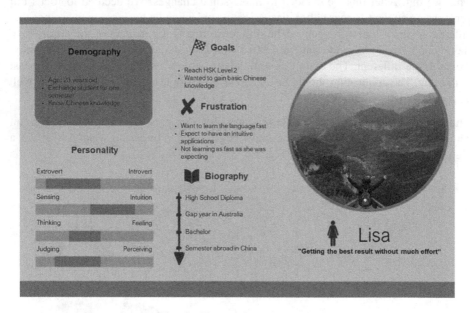

Fig. 6. Changes in persona Lisa

After evaluate data, we decided to not change this persona. Lisa is a 23-years-old exchange student who wants to reach HSK level 2 and wants to be able to speak basic Chinese. She wants to learn it fast because her time is limited.

Of course, not only students can use this application but they are our target because they are more likely to download such an application. We have here two different personas, both students, but with different goals. The application needs to satisfy all these goals.

4.4   Future Ideas to Improve Our Application

Location Related Packages Popping Up at the App. The idea is that our application will have location oriented hints, which package is especially useful for the location the consumer is be. This adjustment would have the effect that we have to use the location data of the user. As we know that many consumers are not willing to share their location data, we would have to make this future optional, so that every user can decide for herself/himself whether he wants to use that feature or not.

Rotation Mode of the Application. As many other competitors are offering a rotation mode, we want to improve our application, to make it more usable in more situations and set up an rotation mode. Due to this mode, we will be able to offer the consumer the opportunity to use the phone either horizontal or vertical.

Dark Mode for Usage During the Night. Nowadays we are spending more and more time in front of our mobile devices. Facing this tremendous usage of the mobile devices, our eyes are starting to feel dry and it sometimes even cause headaches, or neck pain. Trying to overcome those problems, we will set up a dark mode, that can be used while there is no or just a bit of light.

Acknowledgement. This study was supported by the National Nature Foundation of China grant 71601011, the social Science Foundation Beijing grant 16YYC040.

References

1. Google Translator Homepage. http://www.googletranslator.com. Accessed 31 Dec 2019
2. Pleco Translator Homepage. http://www.pleco.com. Accessed 31 Dec 2019
3. Hoober, S.: UXmatters. From How Do Users Really Hold Mobile Devices?. https://www.uxmatters.com/mt/archives/2013/02/how-do-users-really-hold-mobile-devices.php. Accessed 18 Feb 2013
4. Hoober, S.: UXmatters. From Design for Fingers, Touch, and People, Part 1. https://www.uxmatters.com/mt/archives/2017/03/design-for-fingers-touch-and-people-part-1.php. Accessed 6 Mar 2017
5. Koemets, R.: Weekdone. The Benefits of Dark Mode: Why should you turn off the lights?. https://blog.weekdone.com/why-you-should-switch-on-dark-mode/. Accessed 26 Dec 2019

Understanding Learning of Chinese Characters for International Students in China

Zhe Chen[(⊠)], Cynthia Kunda, Dennis Oweke, Bayo Komolafe,
Buyan-Erdene Badamsereejid, and Zhihong Zou

Beihang University, Beijing 100191, People's Republic of China
Zhechen@buaa.edu.cn

Abstract. This research paper has attempted to present the learning performance of Chinese characters for foreign students. Two consecutive experiments
were conducted in order to attain our objectives. A number of participants were
subjected to a short lecture using two different methods, "learning with mnemonic" and "learning with radical". This lecture was followed by a test to assess
the effectiveness of the learning. Despite the time and resource constraints that
could not allow the possibility of having more than two experiments, two
preliminary findings could be concluded: Firstly, learning curve of Chinese is
positively related to interest. That is, it was showed that interest of learning
Chinese as a factor affected the learning rate of Chinese characters among
foreign students. Secondly, teaching method was demonstrated to affect the
learning rate. For instance, participants performed better in mnemonic class than
in radical class. Limitations and future research were discussed in this research.

Keywords: Chinese learning · International students · Learning

1 Introduction

In the last decade, Chinese has been one of the most popular languages in the world as
China has become one of the most powerful countries in the world. Moreover, ever
since the open up the west policy was adopted in 1999 in China, when foreigners were
granted access to trade, live or school in china, learning Chinese has become more of a
necessity if not an advantage for foreigners.

However, the debate over "how difficult or easy learning Chinese characters are"
has been a subject matter for a couple of decades, thereby necessitating the need to
learn Chinese language and characters. Articles and journal available online all point to
the simplicity of Chinese characters. For instance, (Li Quan 2010) opined that saying
"Chinese characters is difficult to learn" is lack of convincing reason, and it is a false
proposition. Nathan Thomas (2019) in his own view declared that "Chinese individual
word is like brick that you are free to arrange in your own order and could be consider
easier than several western languages" while other researchers and scholars such as:
Cui Yonghua (2008), Leixin Su and Zhu Zeng (2015) were all of the opinion that
learning and remembering Chinese characters are not as difficult as it seems or as
preached.

© Springer Nature Switzerland AG 2020
P.-L. P. Rau (Ed.): HCII 2020, LNCS 12193, pp. 250–258, 2020.
https://doi.org/10.1007/978-3-030-49913-6_21

However, the testimony of several foreign and Chinese students has been that the character is one of the most difficult things a man can learn. Furthermore, in his article, Nathan Thomas established that Chinese character are made up of the same collection of elements known as radical and once familiar with a few categories, the rest stop looking alien and start to make more sense. However, first-hand experience and testimonies of students all seems to be on the contrary; as learning the character is perceived to be an endless foray. Although several researchers as discussed have attempted to disprove the ideology of perceiving learning Chinese character as a difficult task, but very few if not none has attempted to understudy the learning curve of Chinese characters for foreigners.

It is on this note that this research has attempted to understudy the learning curve of Chinese characters for foreign students. Therefore, the aim of this study is to investigate the learning curve of Chinese characters for foreign students, and the main objectives shall include:

- Determining the learning curve of Chinese characters for foreign students;
- Determining the correlation or variation in the learning curve of the samples (if any);
- Identifying the factors that are responsible for the correlation or variation between the learning curves of the sample (if any).

2   Literature Review

Plenty articles and journal available online have discussed this topic and have provided mechanism or means of enhancing learning Chinese characters by foreigners or non-native users. Among such include: Björn Liljeqvist (2014) in his article titled "How to memorize Chinese characters" though relies on the research conducted at Stellenbosch University in Sweden, state the two major ways of enhancing the learning process of Chinese characters, which are the people-placing Mnemonic and the Spaced Repetition System.

The first effective method, mnemonic is any learning technique that aids information retention or retrieval in human memory, according to the dictionary. It makes use of elaborative encoding, retrieval cues, and imagery as a specific tool to encode any given information in way that allows for efficient storage and retrieval. To apply this principle, according to the research, for each character, a little scene is created, like an image or a story that contains certain elements. The objects in the scene correspond to the graphics of the character. In each scene there is a person too, giving us a hint about the pronunciation.

The second effective method, the space repetition system, according to the article was first proposed in the book Psychology of Study by Prof. C. A Mace in 1932 and tested in 1939 by H.F Spitzer on sixth-grade students in Iowa who were learning science facts, this method is an evidence-based learning technique that is usually performed with flashcards in which newly introduced and more difficult flashcards are shown more frequently while older and less difficult flashcards are shown less frequently in order to exploit the psychological spacing effects.

To support this methodology, Jeremiah Daneil de la Rouviere (2013) in his study titled "Chinese Radicals in Spaced Repetition Systems: a pilot study on the acquisition of Chinese characters by students learning Chinese as a foreign language" established that "Spaced repetition systems are especially beneficial for learning the substantial number of new vocabulary items necessary when setting out to learn a new language. The spacing effect has been shown to be a cognitive phenomenon in which the spacing of repetitions of vocabulary items improves students' ability to recall these items". Among several space repetition systems available, Björn Liljeqvist (2014) suggested The Ten-Minute Rule saying "The best way to use the time when memorizing characters is 20:10:5; spend twenty minutes memorizing characters using the PPM system. Then take a ten-minute break. Then spend five minutes testing yourself, that you still remember the characters. The "Ten Minute Rule" refers to the ten-minute break that is absolutely essential for learning. Skip the ten-minute break, and you will be wasting your time. During the break, you must not think of what you just learned. Do something else, drink water, check facebook, play a game, whatever".

Contrary to the view of the previous writers is Liangchuan Sun. In his own view, he emphasized the understanding of characters radical first before attempting to learn the characters as this will not only enhance learning but help retention. He said "As a prerequisite, users need to have a basic understanding of Chinese characters' composition and structures for a thorough comprehension. This method is different from the existing approaches as it helps broaden learners' vocabulary beyond its textbooks".

Several other articles that are not mentioned in this paper have discussed this topic.

3   Methodology

In order to attain our objectives, we shall conduct an experiment with the help of a number of international students that are currently learning Chinese for the first time. In this research paper, the methods used are:

- Mnemonic
- The radicals.

3.1   Sample Size and Population

The experiment population size is the international students in Beihang University. A group of twelve students with different countries were selected, to which 20 carefully selected Chinese characters were taught using the above-mentioned methods. The characters selected are ones that we are certain the participants have not learned in class before.

Mnemonic. In this method, we came up with 10 characters that would be affiliated or linked to something the participants were familiar with. For example, the Chinese character "人" which means "person" looks somebody walking, hence making it easier to remember how to write the character.

Each of the 10 characters was explained to the participants after which they were asked to re-write the characters while being timed. We determined the number of characters written and the time taken by each participants to write the characters. The characters used in this experiment were: 众, 串, 苗, 田, 人, 飞, 火, 马, 网, 高.

The Radicals. This method mainly emphasizes the understanding of characters radical first before attempting to learn the characters as this will not only enhance learning but help retention. Because it is important that users have a basic understanding of Chinese characters composition and structures for a thorough comprehension. Each radical of the characters was taught and properly explained to the participants for 1 h. Then the participants were asked to re-write the characters.

3.2 Questionnaire Design

As the participants arrived in the classroom, well aware of the experiment objectives, they were given a questionnaire that includes their basic information (the ones listed in the table above) and a number of rating questions that are to be answered by the participants individually before starting the experiment.

Gender	Region of origin	Period of stay in China	Level of study
Male: 50%	Asia: 33.3%	Below a year: 75%	83%: Masters
Female: 50%	Africa: 33.3%	Above a year: 25%	17%: Bachelor
	Europe: 33.3%		

This well-structured questionnaire, that included 13 questions, was used to evaluate the level of interest the participants had towards learning Chinese. The questionnaire was a 3-Likert Scale where "Very Useful = 2", Useful = 1 and "Non-Useful = 0". A high score by the participants, typically 75% indicates a high level of interest. 45% would indicate a mild interest in Chinese while any figure below 11 would indicate no interest in learning Chinese Characters.

To determine the reliability of the questionnaire, we used the "Crombach Alpha" coefficient to assess the reliability of the questions in eliciting the participant's interest. The reliability test revealed Crombach Alpha Coefficient $\alpha = 0.81$.

3.3 Experiment Design

The experiment was conducted in two stages, the first stage included the participant's level of interest being determined using the mentioned questionnaire. The participants were then grouped in to two groups, group A and B; such that we had two participants from aforementioned regions fall into group A & B. For example, we had two Europeans participants in each group.

Group A was then taught 20 Chinese characters using Mnemonics and radicals and tested, then group B was taught and tested as well using the same two methods. We then collected data; number of characters remembered and time taken to write the characters. We then plot the graph of the characters remembered using both methods against region.

4 Results

This experiment included male and female adult students learning Chinese language for the first time. The participants' origins varied from Asia, Africa to Europe. The biggest half of the participants had been in China for a period of less than a year. The participants' level of study varied from graduate to undergraduate school. The summarized basic information about the participants is listed in the table below (Table 1):

Table 1. Basic information of the participants

Region	Country	Language spoken	Mnemonic score	Time	Radical score	Time	Interest
Asia							
Sample 1	Turkey	3	7	3.05	4	4.12	50.00%
Sample 2	Pakistan	5	10	2.18	6	2.43	76.90%
Sample 3	Indonesia	2	6	3.18	5	2.12	84.60%
Sample 4	Pakistan	4	10	2.1	9	3.29	50.00%
		Average	8.25	2.6275	6	2.99	65.40%
Africa							
Sample 1	Zambia	2	10	5	3	4.18	69.20%
Sample 2	Nigeria	2	6	4	2	4.12	53.80%
Sample 3	Ghana	2	4	5	1	3.3	38.50%
Sample 4	Liberia	2	7	4.52	4	4.18	53.80%
		Average	6.75	4.63	2.5	3.945	53.80%
Europe							
Sample 1	Armenia	3	9	2.48	7	4.16	50.00%
Sample 2	Ukraine	4	6	3.18	4	3.24	65.40%
Sample 3	Russia	2	8	2.56	6	4.24	57.70%
Sample 4	Russia	2	6	5.12	4	3.48	53.80%
		Average	7.25	3.335	5.25	3.78	56.70%

The results obtained from the questionnaire evaluation indicated that the participants from Asia displayed the highest level of interest in learning Chinese with the average interest rate of 65.4%, followed by the Europeans, while the African samples displayed the lowest level of interest in learning Chinese language.

4.1   Performance Based on Sample Group

The final results obtained by the experiment were used the draw the learning curve of Chinese characters. The red graph shows the performance of the participant when they were taught using mnemonic, while the blue graph represents the performance of the participants after they were taught using radical. This graph represents the average remembering ability of the participants.

From Fig. 1, it is revealed that participants from Asia write an average correct character of 8.25/min after being taught using Mnemonic. In contrast, the group has a lower performance of 6 correct characters per minute after being taught using Radicals. African participants had an average of 6.75 correct characters per minute after being taught using mnemonic and 2.5/min when tested after radical class. Finally, the European wrote an average of 7.25 correct characters and 5.2 Correct characters per minute after Mnemonic and Radical class respectively.

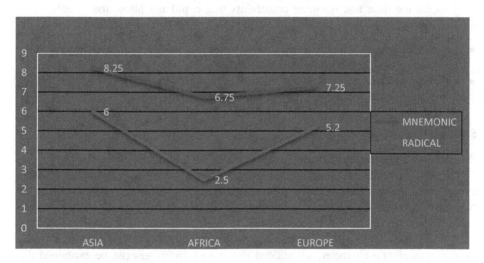

Fig. 1. Performance of using mnemonic and using radicals (Color figure online)

Aside the fact that the Asian participants had some background with method of learning relating to characters, Interest was also observed to be related to general performance of the participants. For instance, Average interest rate of Asian participants was the highest among the three group and so was their performance. European participants have the second highest level of interest and so the performance. African participants on the other hand has the lowest interest rate and so was their performance the lowest among the three group. As a result of this, the interrelation between interest level of participants and their performance were individually measured using Correlation. The result of the result of the test is presented below.

4.2 Relationship Between Interest and Participants' Performance

The correlation coefficient of level of interest and Performance is   (Approx. 0.24). According to Kubinger, Rasch and Šimeýkova (2007) A Correlation Coefficient reveal no statistical relationship between the variables. Further, when a positive relationship is established, , then, a negative relationship is established.

Hence, from above, a correlation coefficient of   reveals a positive relationship between interest level of participants and their performance.

5   Conclusion

This research paper has attempted to present the learning curve of Chinese characters for foreign students. Two consecutive experiments were conducted in order to attain our objectives. A number of participants were subjected to a short lecture using two different methods, mnemonic and radical; followed by a test to assess the effectiveness of the methods. Although the constraints, nevertheless, the following:

Despite the time and resource constraints that could not allow the possibility of having more than two experiments, the following could be concluded:

- Learning curve of Chinese is positively related to interest. That is, interest as a factor affect the learning rate of Chinese characters among foreign student
- Teaching method is also a factor that affect the learning rate. For instance, participants performed better after mnemonic class than radical.

5.1   Research Constraint

While conducting this experiment, we noticed the following limitations:

Time Constraint: the study of a learning curve is one that explores the learning evolution of participants over a long period of time in order to determine whether the hypothesis or methods are actually effective or not, but in our case, this study being a class project, we did not have enough time to do so.

Not all characters can use mnemonic to be explained: as this method uses imagery to help remember a character, we noticed that not all characters can be explained this way, only a limited number of them.

Resources Constraint: it was not an easy task to get a venue to accommodate our participants, however this was even easier than getting the volunteering participants to attend the experiment as everyone has their different occupations.

5.2   Recommendation and Further Study

Having considered the learning curve of Chinese characters among foreign students with the above results. It is important to recommend further study into the relationship between teaching method (Most especially Mnemonic) and performance.

For instance, if further study proves that mnemonic is more effective than existing teaching methods, the method can further be adopted with materials provided on more characters.

Acknowledgement. This study was supported by the National Nature Foundation of China grant 71601011, the social Science Foundation Beijing grant 16YYC040.

Appendix

Appendix A. What are your feelings about Chinese as a language?

No	Questions
1	Chinese is a language with a rich vocabulary
2	Chinese is a very difficult language
3	Chinese is a language where pronunciation is very important
4	Chinese is a language with a lot of grammar
5	Chinese is a beautiful language
6	Chinese is an amazing language to learn
7	Chinese is a boring language to learn

Appendix B. In what situation would Chinese be useful for you.

No	Questions
1	Teaching or learning something in school
2	Making new friends
3	Watching Chinese movies
4	Communicating with friends
5	Buying something
6	Listening to music
7	Reading instruction in cosmetic product
8	Chatting with foreigner
9	Speaking to your lecturer
10	Taking Chinese Examination (HSK)
11	Continuing study in University
12	Job interview
13	Receiving email
14	Knowing popular idol
15	Searching for something on the internet
16	Operating computer
Others	Please Explain:

Appendix C. Have you ever used the following medium in studying Chinese? If yes, how useful were they?

No	Activities
1	Practicing conversation from a book or internet
2	Free conversation with native speakers
3	Free conversation with other learners of Chinese
4	Memorizing Chinese vocabulary lists
5	Google Translator/Baidu
6	Studying the Chinese Radical

References

Thomas, N.: Extracted via (2019). https://www.fluentu.com/blog/chinese/2017/10/31/is-chinese-hard-to-learn/

Su, L., Zeng, Z.: Theory Pract. Lang. Stud. **5**(12), 2545–2549 (2015)

Quan, L.: A reexamination of Chinese characters: are they really hard to learn. Lang. Teach. Linguist. Stud. **2**, 30–35 (2010)

de la Rouviere, J.D.: Chinese radicals in spaced repetition systems: a pilot study on the acquisition of Chinese characters by students learning Chinese as a foreign language (2013)

Sun, L.: Radical; A learning system for Chinese Mandarin characters. extracted via (2013). https://repository.library.northeastern.edu/files/neu:rx915j987/fulltext.pdf. Accessed 11 Nov 2019

Liljeqvist, B.: How to memorize Chinese characters; extracted via (2014). http://www.braingain.se/wpcontent/uploads/2013/10/Memorizing_Chinese.pdf. Accessed 11 Nov 2019

https://www.hackingchinese.com/the-real-challenge-when-learning-characters/

https://www.hackingchinese.com/phonetic-components-part-1-the-key-to-80-of-all-chinese-characters/

Cultural Engagement and Interactive Communication: A Study on the Implementation of New Media on Museum's Digital Interpretations

Chih-Yung Aaron Chiu[1]([⊠]) and Deng-Teng Leo Shih[2]

[1] National Tsing Hua University, No. 101, Section 2, Kuang-Fu Road,
Hsinchu 30013, Taiwan
aaronchiu88@gmail.com
[2] China University of Technology, No. 56, Section 3, Xinglong Road,
Wunshan District, Taiepi 116, Taiwan

Abstract. Museology is undergoing a sea change in the digital era. Studying new technologies or pioneering experiments on digital art alone is far from enough for us to fully grasp such a revolutionary change. As a matter of fact, the influence of digital technology is so pervasive that it is extended over almost all aspects of the society and even leads to cultural reorientation. To the extend, we can see an accelerating trend towards creating works of art with digital media technology, an innovative tool that also occupies a crucial role in the maintenance, preservation, and display of art institutions' collections. Against this background, this paper attempts not only to identify the latest development of this trend by case studies, but also to investigate how digital technology helps preserve and perpetuate traditional arts and crafts, so as to provide suggestions on reducing the preservation costs and increasing the perpetuation efficiency. In addition, by reference to the results of the case studies and the analysis of professionals' experiences, this paper seeks to explore the possibilities of facilitating cultural exchange and interactive communication with digitalized display and innovative transformation. This paper concludes with reflections on some cultural issues concerning the application of digital media technology to museum collection display.

Keywords: Cultural engagement · Interactivity · Digital technology

1 Introduction

Museology is undergoing a sea change in the digital era. Studying new technologies or pioneering experiments on digital art alone is far from enough for us to fully grasp such a revolutionary change. As a matter of fact, the influence of digital technology is so pervasive that it is extended over almost all aspects of the society and even leads to cultural reorientation. Therefore, the museological turn is manifested in multiple dimensions, such as place (space), community, culture, and technology [1]. In his article "Manifesto for a New Museum," Peter Weibel pointed out that art museums must try to

© Springer Nature Switzerland AG 2020
P.-L. P. Rau (Ed.): HCII 2020, LNCS 12193, pp. 259–269, 2020.
https://doi.org/10.1007/978-3-030-49913-6_22

cooperate with science and technology if they want to survive the future. This argument was perfectly exemplified by the emergence of techno art, in which many media artists use tools surprisingly similar to those adopted by physicists and engineers [2]. Swept along on this wave, the digital culture has become an essential element in social, cultural, artistic, and economic dimensions. Digital technology has transmuted the achievements of traditional cultures and arts into the forms that meet the requirements for archiving or display. Whatever form they may take, the transdisciplinary integration within the contemporary knowledge system has made media technology a unique medium for artistic creation. Besides, the whole process from production to collection and exhibition bears the signature of digital interaction and participation.

We can see an accelerating trend towards creating works of art with digital media technology, an innovative tool that also occupies a crucial role in the maintenance, preservation, and display of art institutions' collections. Against this background, this paper attempts not only to identify the latest development of this trend by case studies, but also to investigate how digital technology helps preserve and perpetuate traditional arts and crafts, so as to provide suggestions on reducing the preservation costs and increasing the perpetuation efficiency. In addition, by reference to the results of the case studies and the analysis of professionals' experiences, this paper seeks to explore the possibilities of facilitating cultural exchange and interactive communication with digitalized display and innovative transformation. This paper concludes with reflections on some cultural issues concerning the application of digital media technology to museum collection display.

2   Media Technology and Museums

The rapid development of digital media and new technologies have dramatically affected museums' traditional roles in exhibition, collection, restoration, and education. Electronic media have established a continuing existence in museums of science, technology, natural history, and art since the 1980s, which was primarily because the curators of these museums tried to attract a greater number of visitors by adopting new interactive technologies in exhibitions. Corporate sponsors and donors have shown their keen interest in new media. Museum visitors, especially the young generation, have also made a beeline for interactive exhibitions and deemed such interaction as a major part of their museum experiences. Curators advocating the use of digital technology claimed that interactive display is relatively flexible so that it offers an alternative solution to the presentation of complicated ideas and processes. These interactive technologies (e.g. interactive touchscreen, computer game, large screen installation, TV wall with various images, digital information center, smart badge, 3D animation, and virtual reality) have collectively constructed the so-called digital museum system. These technologies have substantially altered museums' physical characters. Nowadays, museums transcend the physical confines of time and space via the Internet, making their online databases accessible for virtual visitors, and allowing them to interact with the exhibits in an innovative way.

Introduced by André Malraux in 1947, the term "*musée imaginaire*" refers to "a collection of digitally recorded images, sound files, text documents and other data of historical, scientific, or cultural interest that are accessed through electronic media" [3]. Today's digital museums not only go beyond traditional communication and interaction with visitors, but also utilize the resources in a more agile manner. To seamlessly connect media technology with museums, we need to promote, position, and strengthen the role of "digital application" in terms of strategy, practice, technique, and theory, so as to graft "technology" onto "content" as well as to mediate and integrate the two parts. Digital application is a "superimposed third-party profession" that responds accordingly to the introduction of digital technological innovation into museums' traditional contents and functions. The projection-like technology of edge blending and warping also contributes to the seamless integration and augmentation of digital "content + technology." Moreover, digital application is a crucial third pillar supporting the structure and development of museum technology. The importance of digital application is clearly highlighted here.

3 Digital Application: The Wide Applications of Display Technology

In terms of technology, aesthetics, and associated concepts, digital media technology has become a "visual interpretive program" dedicated to tackling the following questions. In what way and form can artistic images be represented? How can the chosen form of representation be connected with museums' constituent elements, works of art, and exhibition design? What implications should be embedded in the conveyed information and displayed images? How can the meaning of a museum's collection be redefined to create a perfect fusion of the displayed images and the other elements in the exhibition when creators blend digital media technology into the given forms of the exhibits [4]? In sum, digital archive is an active management technology that ensures the constant accessibility of museums' digital contents.

What content interpretation attempts to produce is the major achievement of the guidance on display technology—"interpretive planning," which emphasizes that interpretation should meet the needs of transdisciplinary content transformation and conform to the actual situation of introducing technology into display (even though "interpretation" is a term more suitable for describing the exhibition content design technique) in view of the inexorable trend towards presenting exhibition contents with technologies in a transdisciplinary fashion. Research materials that underpin exhibitions are crucial contents. However, some technical issues (e.g. data decipher, content interpretation, and transmedia storytelling) still need to be resolved if one is going to present these materials in the digital form. The issues arising from flourishing display technology further highlight the significance of interpretative planning, a task that entails the specialty of content analysis and design, digital literacy, as well as the ability to direct or coordinate proper digital forms.

Accordingly, a museum can employ a two-pronged strategy that involves technology display and display technology. The former refers to the introduction and display of advanced or daily life technologies, while the later focuses on the instrumentality of technologies, urging the museum to rethink traditional values and the roles they play, as well as the ways to enhance visitors' experiences and the museum-visitor relationship [5]. As museums have become an important part of our digital life, voices from the outside world beyond the museums have been made heard so that museums must find a faster and more effective way of communication to maintain a healthy relationship with their visitors and communities. That is why museums have meta-morphosed from collection-oriented into visitor/user-oriented operation [6]. The applications of new media and digital technology in contemporary museum collection, restoration, and exhibition are summarized as follows:

3.1 Museum Collection Presented in the Form of Techno Art

The combination of contemporary thinking with new media has fundamentally chan-ged the one-on-one relationship between creators and their oeuvres as well as the entire creative process. "Re-creation," namely reinterpreting original works of art, not only embodies the spirit of contemporary culture, but also facilitates modern people to perceive, interpret, and re-create arts. For instance, carried along on the tide of digi-talization, the National Palace Museum has undertaken the Digital Archives Project, devoting itself to the promotion of transboundary (i.e. culture and technology) coop-eration, transdisciplinary art, and social education. Besides, the project has introduced relevant technologies, audiovisual media, and artistic digitalization. Its achievements in associated projects and transboundary cooperation have also garnered international reputation.

Other examples include the kinetic installation of dynamic display by Taiwanese artist Tien-Chang Wu at the 2015 Venice Biennale, and "A Reform of Lotus Pond in Zuoying—Multi-Sensory Interactive Exhibition in Virtual Reality" at the National Taiwan Museum of Fine Arts (NTMoFA) that transformed traditional static presen-tation of paintings into technological display. The question as to how we can employ a "contemporary technology," which can exert its effect only in a specific era, to pre-serve, archive, and then restore and represent originals in an effective and artistic fashion has become a radical challenge to digital art.

3.2 Online Display

A museum's online display requires the establishment of a content management system and a distinct database. People tend to use museum databases for historical search. However, the design of ordinary databases is not aimed at playing tricks, rekindling memories, or encouraging users to search in a retrospective manner. Instead, the raison d'être of data is to run certain application programs, and the role of algorithms is to predict and optimize its future functions. To put it another way, museum databases give prominence to historical memories, and the pieces of information they collected and stored are not passive data but potential materials for creators to produce more contents [7]. The most telling example is "Points of Departure: Connecting with Contemporary Art," a project carried out by the San Francisco Museum of Modern Art (SFMOMA) in 2001. It created a stimulating environment for visitors to experience contemporary art with the interactive model developed collaboratively by MIT, the Ideal Integration in San Francisco, and the Compaq Computer Corporation in Silicon Valley. It was SFMOMA's first time to use SmartTables that combine touch table with interactive computer screen for introducing each gallery and the works therein. Meanwhile, it was also the museum's first time to adopt PDA as the multimedia guide, whereby the visitors could view artists explaining their own works by clicking on the thumbnails. The museum's another experiment allowed the visitors to hang works in a virtual gallery via "Make Your Own Galley" on the interactive kiosk. "Point of Departure" won the 2002 Gold MUSE Award for the best use of new technologies in an art museum setting [8].

The Europeana Collections is a prime example as well. Built on Europe's rich heritage, the website has not only gathered the digital contents of European galleries, libraries, museums, archives, and audiovisual collections, but also made these cultural resources easily accessible to the users whether for work, study or fun [9]. In 2011, the Rijksmuseum started to cooperate with the Europeana Collections, making its public domain images and metadata accessible through the latter's web portal [10]. In addition, the M+ Museum of Visual Culture is an emerging institution dedicated to digital archive, digital display, and online curating. It is under construction and will soon become a new contemporary visual art center in Hong Kong's West Kowloon Cultural District. What the M+ has so far is not so much a physical museum as the compact M+ Pavilion hosting small-scale exhibitions and communicating its vision. Nevertheless, the M+ has operated actively in the form of a museum since 2012, and its online activities have become its main focus at the current stage. In 2018, the M+ not only released its bilingual story platform to build up its niche audience on social media, but also participated in a series of museum-related events around the world. Digitalized online display not only enables museums to share and interact with audiences around the globe, but also stimulates, encourages, and supports many creative communities.

3.3 Interactive Display

Interactivity gives birth to various forms of browsing and ways of combination, making the admiration of works of art no longer just a pure psychological operation. An increasing number of museums (incl. the Metropolitan Museum of Art, the Virtual Museum of Canada, and SFMOMA) have allowed their visitors to create personalized digital collections, whereby the visitors can repeatedly admire the works in their collections on an irregular basis. Some museums also allow their online visitors to download the images of exhibits into personal galleries, add captions, and share with other online visitors. Digital technology not only affords interaction between museums and their visitors, but also offers the latter new routes to engagement, interpretation, and experience. The enormous potential of digital technology in changing the visitor-exhibition relationship speaks for itself [11].

As technology advances every day, museums have taken different forms (e.g. digital museums, integrated museums, and open museums) that not only reshaped their social images, but also modified visitors' way of participation. Such formal change of museums is characterized by interactive multimedia display and the popularization of interactive multimedia exhibitions. For example, the National Palace Museum adopted digital technology to create the digital version of *Up the River during Qingming*, which was nothing if not aesthetically impressive. In 2015, the NTMoFA presented "Decoding the Treasure Trove: An Exhibition of Collection and Conservation" that addressed three main themes, including "Interpretation of Collection: The Formation of Taiwanese Art," "Looking into Collection: Art Preservation and Maintenance," and "Linkage of Collection: Extension and Application." This exhibition featured the display of its distinguished collection, the environment control of its collection repository, the preservation and maintenance of its collection, the application of scientific detection, and the scenario display of restoration process. In particular, it combined interactive technology with a masterpiece designated as national treasure in its rich collection—Lin Yu-Shan's Asian gouache painting *Lotus Pond*—to create a VR version of this enthralling painting, thereby immersing the viewers in the lyrical atmosphere and offering them multi-sensory experiences.

After renovation, the Cooper Hewitt Smithsonian Design Museum has reopened and devoted itself to modern interactive art. To this end, the museum developed the "Cooper Hewitt Pen" in collaboration with a Taiwanese technology firm for the visitors to collect and share its exhibition information. The smart-pen consists of two main technologies. The first is the conductive material used in its nib and the touch screen interacting with it. The second is the near-field communication interface of the interactive screen. The pen even allows the visitors to view the information of the exhibits they collected during the tour on the high-definition interactive table. This function turns the visitors into their own curators who can design their own exhibitions. After collating the collected works and associated information, the visitors can store their "exhibitions" on a cloud database and will receive the corresponding collect symbol and code. Then the visitors can access their own "exhibitions" by entering the code on the website cooperhewitt.org/you at home.

Digital archive databases and special exhibition research data provide profound contents for digital guide service. By means of mobile screens, these contents open up new opportunities for the visitors to actively explore the information of exhibits, which not only allows the viewers to admire the exhibits in different ways, but also grants them a wider scope of options on related knowledge.

3.4 Virtual Presentation

VR and AR are the most common interfaces adopted by museums for virtual presentation. As digital technology and social media flourish every day, the Internet has been construed as a virtual "third place," which not only meets the criteria of personalization, accessibility and comfortability, but also satisfies the public needs for social intercourse. In 2012, the California Association of Museums issued its foresight research report titled "Museums as Third Place," in which "virtuality" was included as one of the key characteristics of a third place. In fact, an online/virtual museum has transcended the limitations of traditional visitor participation. It is not so much a cyber-colony of physical museums as a digital existence with complementary functions, because all the interactive mechanisms, games, videos, 3D simulations, forums, and community management that online/virtual museums provide can supplement or enhance the visitors' viewing experiences.

The objectives shared among online/virtual museums (e.g. remote, alternative, differential demand, and pre-visit) have been attained in the current environment underpinned by advanced digital technology, popularized digital devices, and improved cultural literacy. The creative, highly amusing digital interactive design with a low entry threshold, the growing participation of digital service users, and the efforts of digital museums, have collectively transmuted the unapproachable archives stored in the form of readme file in obscure corners of databases into the subjects of searching and browsing as well as the contents for entertainment and interaction via smartphones. These digital knowledge/information service designs are tantamount to a significant landmark in the history of digital technology. Anyway, to fulfill knowledge exchange, the underlying principle for museums is to select and present proper contents to visitors, through which enjoyable cultural experiences can be created [12].

3.5   3D Scanning and 3D Printing

3D scanning and database systems have become necessary commodities for museums to enrich the public understanding of their collections. Some museums have embarked on the 3D scanning of their collections. By virtue of 3D scanning and 3D printing, artifacts' details can be preserved and presented in the form of digital sculpture. Photogrammetry, a 3D photo modeling technology, can transform real-time graphic big data into hyper-realistic 3D digital files by algorithms. Then the files are styled through parameter adjustments and 3D fusion, and finally combined with full-color 3D modeling technology to fit them into real-life scenes. A surreal atmosphere is thus created. Photographers become sculptors. Photo modeling and digital sculpture will spur revolutionary innovations of digital cameras.

The Museum of Pure Form is undertaking an experiment of sharing and displaying 3D information. In 2004, it scanned a whole set of sculpture database. It also developed installations of its collection, allowing the visitors to interact with the works by using 3D digital technologies such as stereo vision, virtual cave technology, and haptic devices [13]. Established by the Smithsonian Institution in 2013, Smithsonian X 3D platform provides the 3D open-source files of its collection (incl. data area, browsing interface, as well as augmented information files of texts, images and audiovisuals) for online appreciation, education, and valued-added development. More important, it extends the use of digital artifacts to real classrooms by dint of 3D printing files. In her keynote speech at the 7th International Euro-Mediterranean Conference, Diane Zoric, the director of the Smithsonian's Digitization Program Office, introduced the Smithsonian Museum's Digital-First Strategy. The Smithsonian X 3D platform on the one hand tries to increase and connect the digitalized information of its collection with linked open-data, and on the other hand continues using value-added applications of AR, MR and VR to enlarge, represent, and immerse digital artifacts in a realm interlaced by the virtual and the real.

3.6   Immersive Projection Display

To attract more visitors, contemporary alternative museums have utilized software to merge different projections seamlessly into a huge one and transform the exhibition space into an immersive field with images as the contents of display. The "MORI Building Digital Art Museum: Epson teamLab Borderless" featured a total of 50 interactive exhibits created by enlisting 520 computers and 470 projectors in a space covering more than 33,058 m^2. Its five interconnected exhibition areas constituted a completely immersive, gorgeous digital art space. The sense of immersion brought by the museum's interactive projections did allow the visitors to enjoy the borderless aesthetic beauty visually and somatosensorily. The content design and technology design of an exhibition involve the accumulation of relevant literature and practical experiences about the traffic flow, content design, interactive installation, and multimedia display, so that digital application and display can produce narratives that are appealing to visitors.

The Culturespaces, a world-renowned curatorial team and a pioneer of AMIEX (art and music immersive experience), was in charge of the software and hardware design for the three inauguration exhibitions of the Atelier des Lumieres in 2018. The special exhibition featuring the works by Gustav Klimt was the most eye-catching. It projected the images of Gustav Klimt's paintings with more than 140 projectors in the exhibition space covering 3,300 m^2, thereby immersing the visitors in the alluring brushstrokes, colors, images, and figures created by Klimt. Following the Gustav Klimt Exhibition, the Van Gogh Show took place on February 22, 2019, which was curated by the Culturespaces and executed by the Danny Rose Studio.

These professional light art curatorial firms, be they the teamLab or the Culturespaces, have proved their market value, though the teamLab focuses on techno-art, whereas the Culturespaces accentuates immersive audiovisual exhibitions. Leaving their scale and technology aside, the two firms demonstrate the commercial value and value-added applications of "culture plus digital" and "art plus technology." Art is by no means confined to museums and galleries.

4 Conclusions

Many museums have introduced portable electronic tour guides since the 1950s. Visiting museums has also become a source of social experience. Therefore, grasping the exhibition contents that visitors would like to share has constituted a real challenge to museums. In her "post-museum" discourse, Eilean Hooper-Greenhill argued that museums, as cultural institutions emerging with modernization, can no longer act like before, namely treating themselves as the only place capable of imparting knowledge and truth. She proposed the approach of visual culture, providing the contents of education and learning by focusing on the way of "display." As one of the core functions of museums, display per se is a presentation of visual arts at the material dimension. This approach aims to trigger richer and more diverse imagination and discussion about museum display. In addition, archiving, also a core function of museums, is a manifestation of our material civilization. However, the archived exhibits do not speak for themselves. Their meanings are produced within their respective contexts through the interpretive strategy of curating. What the visitors see, identify, grasp, or interpret is structured by their own knowledge backgrounds. Michel Foucault's concept of "gaze" refers to the experience of knowing things by viewing. We can use it to question the boundaries between the visible and the invisible, as well as between the describable and the unspeakable [14].

This paper offers synthetic suggestions concerning the application of digital media technology in the following four dimensions: (1) the display and re-creation of digital archive; (2) the introduction of digital technology into research and development; (3) the practice of display technology; and (4) the digital preservation and application of new media art. We conducted several interviews with professionals in this field. All of them agreed that innovation is absolutely necessary whether in terms of digital technology R&D or application.

1. Jay Tseng, the director of Ultra Combos, claimed that we know nothing but mere formality about digital technology. People tend to grasp it from the keywords such as AI, AR, or VR. However, digital technology should be understood as flowing and replete with possibilities. It can reorganize the world, and its applications are limitless. It should not be confined to the concepts of these keywords.
2. Tsun-Hung Tsai, an assistant professor at the Shih Chien University, pointed out that information security tends to be ignored in the process of digitalization. In fact, once digital data leak out, there is no way to get them back. Therefore, museums or galleries should be very cautious about security leak when they attempt to apply digital data for further promotion or platform construction.
3. Kudo Takashi from the teamLab highlighted the idea of boundary-crossing. In his opinion, the teamLab has never been perplexed by the issues concerning the balance among technology, art, and market. It treats digital technology as a tool and art as the content. The teamLab believes that art proposes questions and design delivers answers, which is exemplified by its exhibition venue in which no sign of exit is provided so that the visitors have to engage in finding their own answers.
4. Ulanda Blair, a curator from the M+, also adopted a cautious stance towards the museum application of technology which should be meaningful, reflective and critical.

In general, all these interviewees are capable of cultural content thinking (at least attending simultaneously to content and technology). According to their practical experiences, these experts prefer cultural practice with externalities, which is similar to Friedrich Kittler's idea of "cultural techniques." They employ technologies to sustain culture, while cultural practice is embedded in the context of cultural techniques. In terms of digital application and its functions, these professionals place a higher priority on representation's condition (technology) than on its meaning (content).

Kei Arai, a professor at the Tokyo University of the Arts, said bluntly that the rapid development of contemporary digital technology has not only attracted considerable attention of galleries and museums around the world, but also prompted them to explore its potential for application. Arai also pointed out that the application of digital technology to the restoration, preservation, and display of traditional arts must lay greater emphasis on cultural education than on display of spectacles, and should not habitually cater to the fashion of the day. Digital technology empowers people to increase their human potential, and ergo its application should set great store by the parts unable to be seen in ordinary exhibitions, such as the underlying textures, compositions, and structure of exhibits. Diane Wang, the digital program producer of the M+, made it clearly that contemporary museums and galleries must adopt a three-pronged strategy in response to the impact of new media and digital technology.

Firstly, they should improve their abilities to utilize technologies and facilitate inno-vation, so as to establish a sound, powerful foundation (e.g. database, and art evalu-ation system). Secondly, they should build a data structure that allows their users to retrieve information and conduct technological experiments. Thirdly, they need to prepare themselves for more responsive, dynamic application of technologies, which will in turn enable museums and galleries to keep up with the latest trends.

The experts we interviewed for this study are active in digital engineering and techno-art. Based on their astute observations and extensive experiences of the plan-ning, R&D, implementation, and innovation of large-scale digital projects and pro-grams, these experts shared their insights and made many valuable suggestions about many issues, including "the valued-added application of digital archive," "virtual museum," "display technology development," "AI and big data application," "3D printing," "new media art archiving and documentation," "the introduction and application of AR and VR devices," "3D scanning," "digital tools and experiences," "digital strategy and organizational policy," "the design of digital participation," "the introduction of user experiences," "the technologies of new media art preservation and maintenance," and "the balance between technicality and artistry." To sum up, when applying innovative technologies, be it AI, AR, MR, VR, IoT, 5G, or cloud computing, museums and galleries must use digital technology to design "emotive projects" that feature not so much objects as stories and underpin the interaction among virtual characters, real visitors, and objects. Furthermore, apart from connecting online experiences with on-site ones, museums and galleries should render their activities before, during, and after exhibitions coherent, and make a unique blend of tangible and intangible experiences, insofar as to create a captivating hybridization of 2D planes and 3D spaces, in which the narrative frameworks for social and emotional engagement can be developed.

Work Cited

1. Susana Smith Bautista: Museums in the Digital Age: Changing Meanings of Place, Community, and Culture, p. 7. AltaMira, UK (2014)
2. Bast, G., Carayannis, E.G., Campbell, D.F.J. (eds.): The Future of Museums. ARIS, p. 50. Springer, Cham (2018). https://doi.org/10.1007/978-3-319-93955-1
3. Styliani, S., Fotis, L., Kostas, K., Petros, P.: Virtual museums, a survey and some issues for consideration. J. Cult. Herit. **10**, 520–528 (2009)
4. Thomas, S., Mintz, A.: The Virtual and the Real: Media in the Museum, p. 5. American Association of Museums, Washington, D. C. (1998)
5. Chen, M.-T., Chu, Y.-M.: Science and technology exhibition planning: from the viewpoint of interpretation of technology. Technol. Mus. Rev. **4**(17), 27–56 (2013)
6. Giannini, T., Bowen, J.P. (eds.): Museums and Digital Culture. SSCC, pp. 63–64. Springer, Cham (2019). https://doi.org/10.1007/978-3-319-97457-6
7. Pepi, M.: Is a Museum a Database?: Institutional Conditions in Net Utopia. e-flux. https://www.e-flux.com/journal/60/61026/is-a-museum-a-database-institutional-conditions-in-net-utopia/. Accessed 15 July 2019
8. Susana Smith Bautista: Museums in the Digital Age: Changing Meanings of Place, Community, and Culture, p. 105. AltaMira, Plymouth (2014)

9. Ko, C.-R.: The Experience from the Rijksmuseum: The Decision-making Process of Opening its Collection to the Public (2015). http://creativecommons.tw/blog/20151113. Accessed 9 Jan 2017

10. Pekel, J.: Democratising the Rijksmuseum. https://pro.europeana.eu/files/Europeana_Professional/Publications/Democratising%20the%20Rijksmuseum.pdf. Accessed 9 Jan 2017

11. Jewitt, C.: Digital technologies in museums: new routes to engagement and participation. Des. Learn. **5**, 74–93 (2012)

12. Carrozzino, M., Bergamasco, M.: Beyond virtual museums, experiencing immersive virtual reality in real museums. J. Cult. Herit. **11**, 452–458 (2010)

13. Sportun, S.: The future landscape of 3D in museums. In: Levent, N., Pascual-Leone, A. (eds.) The Multisensory Museum Cross-Disciplinary Perspectives on Touch, Sound, Smell, Memory, and Space (Plymouth, pp. 331–340. Rowman & Littlefield, UK (2014)

14. Hooper-Greenhill, E.: Museums and the Interpretation of Visual Culture, p. 49. Routledge, London (2000)

References

1. Bast, G., Garayannis, E., Campbell, D.: The Future of Museums. Springer, Switzerland (2018). https://doi.org/10.1007/978-3-319-93955-1

2. Bautista, S.: Museums in the Digital Age: Changing Meanings of Place, Community, and Culture. AltaMira, Plymouth (2014)

3. Carrozzino, M., Bergamasco, M.: Beyond virtual museums, experiencing immersive virtual reality in real museums. J. Cult. Herit. **11**, 452–458 (2010)

4. Chen, M.T., Chu, Y.M.: Science and technology exhibition planning: from the viewpoint of interpretation of technology. Technol. Mus. Rev. **4**(17), 27–56 (2013)

5. Giannini, T., Bowen, J.: Museums and Digital Culture: New Perspectives and Research. Springer, NY (2019). https://doi.org/10.1007/978-3-319-97457-6

6. Hooper-Greenhill, E.: Museums and the Interpretation of Visual Culture. Routledge, London (2000)

7. Jewitt, C.: Digital technologies in museums: new routes to engagement and participation. Des. Learn. **5**, 74–93 (2012)

8. Ko, C.R.: The Experience from the Rijksmuseum: The Decision-making Process of Opening Its Collection to the Public. http://creativecommons.tw/blog/20151113. Accessed 9 Jan 2017

9. Pekel, J.: Democratising the Rijksmuseum. https://pro.europeana.eu/files/Europeana_Professional/Publications/Democratising%20the%20Rijksmuseum.pdf. Accessed 9 Jan 2017

10. Pepi, M.: Is a Museum a Database?: Institutional Conditions in Net Utopia. https://www.e-flux.com/journal/60/61026/is-a-museum-a-database-institutional-conditions-in-net-utopia/. Accessed 15 July 2019

11. Sportun, S.: The future landscape of 3D in museums. In: Levent, N., Pascual-Leone, A. (eds.) The Multisensory Museum Cross-Disciplinary Perspectives on Touch, Sound, Smell, Memory, and Space, pp. 331–340. Rowman & Littlefield, Plymouth (2014)

12. Styliani, S., Fotis, L., Kostas, K., Petros, P.: Virtual museums, a survey and some issues for consideration. J. Cult. Herit. **10**, 520–528 (2009)

13. Thomas, S., Mintz, A.: The Virtual and the Real: Media in the Museum. American Association of Museums, Washington, D. C. (1998)

Applied the Technology Acceptance Model to Survey the Mobile-Learning Adoption Behavior in Science Museum

Cheng-wei Fan[(⊠)]

Department of Digital Media Art, School of Art and Design,
Fuzhou University of International Studies and Trade, Fuzhou, China
fanchengwei@fzfu.edu.cn

Abstract. The purpose of study is to propose and verify that the extended technology acceptance model can be applied to explain and predict the acceptance of mobile learning in museum. In the study, we try to review and establish the relationship between the external variables and user's attitude and behavior in museum mobile learning system. According the relationship between the external variables and user's attitude and behavior, we will do the investigation in our museum for the m-learning system exhibition. We have finished the detail investigation and find the constructs relationship between the external variables and user's attitude and behavior in museum.

Keywords: Extended technology acceptance model · Mobile learning · External variables

1 Introduction

The concept of mobile learning was proposed by Revans from England in 1982 which has been more than 25 years (Revans 1982). Revans offers an iterative model, successively alternating experience and preparation/reflection, which is a useful paradigm for mobile learning (McDermott et al. 2000). However, scholars perceive mobile learning in different ways. The following section contributes to various explanations of mobile learning by international scholars: m-learning is e-learning through mobile computational devices: Palms, Windows CE machines, even your digital cell phone (Quin 2001). Mobile learning is a context-based learning by using mobile technology medium and is learner-centered. The flexibility of mobile learning in a proper location allow learners to interact with other learners and instructors and conduct technology-learning, content learning or context-based learning that is proactive, instant, distant/approximate, individual or group-centered. Moreover, learner will experience meaningful knowledge construction through this process (Young et al. 2005). Mobile learning is defined as any educational provision where the sole or dominant technologies are handheld or palmtop devices (Traxler 2005).

    The primary goal of this study was to enhance our understanding of user acceptance of m-learning in museum. This study addressed the ability to predict museum visitors' acceptance of m-learning in terms of individual difference as stipulated by the extended

© Springer Nature Switzerland AG 2020
P.-L. P. Rau (Ed.): HCII 2020, LNCS 12193, pp. 270–280, 2020.
https://doi.org/10.1007/978-3-030-49913-6_23

technology acceptance model (TAM2). The TAM2 is to explain perceived usefulness and usage intentions in terms of social influence and cognitive instrumental processes. Because m-learning technology is still in its development stage in museum, the crucial motivational variables that affect its adoption by museum visitors need to be explored.

2   Related Literature

2.1   Technology Acceptance Model

The Technology Acceptance Model (TAM) is an information systems theory that models how users tend to accept and use a technology. The model suggests that when users are presented with a new software package, a number of factors influence their decision about how and when they will use it, the two main issues: Perceived usefulness (PU) - This was defined by Fred Davis as "the degree to which a person believes that using a particular system would enhance his or her job performance". Perceived ease-of-use (PEOU) - Davis defined this as "the degree to which a person believes that using a particular system would be free from effort" (Davis 1989) (Fig. 1).

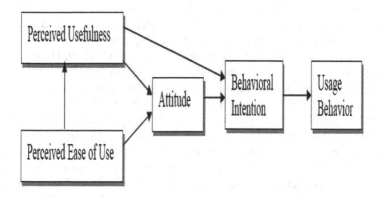

Fig. 1. Technology acceptance model (Davis 1989)

TAM is one of the most influential extensions of Ajzen and Fishbein's theory of reasoned action (TRA) in the literature. It was developed by Fred Davis and Richard Bagozzi (Bagozzi et al. 1992; Davis et al. 1989). TAM replaces many of TRA's attitude measures with the two technology acceptance measures—ease of use, and usefulness. TAM has discovered strong relationships between individual differences and IT acceptance (Agarwal and Prasad 1999; Venkatesh 2000). The Technology Acceptance Model (TAM) has served as basis for past researches on IS dealing with behavioral intentions and usage of IT (Adams et al. 1992; Davis et al. 1989; Gefen and Straub 1997).

As a well-recognized theoretical basis for studying user acceptance, TAM proposes that user's perceptions of a system's ease of use and usefulness can influence how quickly and efficiently users will adopt the new technologies. Thus, according to TAM, the easier a technology is to use, and the more useful it is perceived to be, the more positive the user's attitude and intention towards using the technology. Consequently, the usage of the technology increases. Recently, researchers have explored personal and situational factors that influence users' perceptions. One such factor is the user's perception of his/her computer self-efficacy, i.e., proficiency at using technology (Igbaria and Iivari 1995; Compeau and Higgins 1995; Venkatesh and Davis 1996; Venkatesh 2000).

2.2   The Extended Technology Acceptance Model (TAM2)

While users' perceptions of computer self-efficacy have been shown to be important in their system perceptions, knowledge workers need both computer and task proficiency to apply a workplace system efficiently and effectively in performing their jobs. Thus, their perceptions of self-efficacy related to both computer technology and the under-lying task are likely to affect their perceptions about the system and their intentions to use it as intended by the system developers. Earlier research on the diffusion of innovations also suggested a prominent role for perceived ease of use. Tornatzky and Klein (1982) analyzed the adoption, finding that compatibility, relative advantage, and complexity had the most significant relationships with adoption across a broad range of innovation types. Several researchers have replicated Davis's original study (Davis 1989) to provide empirical evidence on the relationships that exist between usefulness, ease of use and system use (Adams et al. 1992; Davis et al. 1989; Hendrickson et al 1993; Segars and Grover 1993; Subramanian 1994; Szajna 1994). Much attention has focused on testing the robustness and validity of the questionnaire instrument used by Davis. Adams et al. (1992) replicated the work of Davis (1989) to demonstrate the validity and reliability of his instrument and his measurement scales. They also extended it to different settings and, using two different samples, they demonstrated the internal consistency and replication reliability of the two scales. Hendrickson et al. (1993) found high reliability and good test-retest reliability. Szajna (1994) found that the instrument had predictive validity for intent to use, self-reported usage and attitude toward use. The sum of this research has confirmed the validity of the Davis instru-ment, and to support its use with different populations of users and different software choices. Segars and Grover (1993) re-examined Adams et al.'s (1992) replication of the Davis work. They were critical of the measurement model used, and postulated a different model based on three constructs: usefulness, effectiveness, and ease-of-use. These findings do not yet seem to have been replicated.

Venkatesh and Davis extended the original TAM model to explain perceived usefulness and usage intentions in terms of social influence and cognitive instrumental processes. The extended model, referred to as TAM2, was tested in both voluntary and mandatory settings. The results strongly supported TAM2 (Venkatesh and Davis 2000) (Fig. 2).

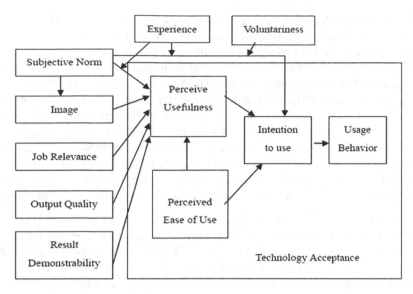

Fig. 2. TAM2 (Venkatesh and Davis 2000)

2.3   External Variables

Although TAM is a model applicable to a variety of technologies (Adams et al. 1992; Chin and Todd 1995; Doll et al. 1998), it has been criticized for not providing adequate information on individuals' opinions of novel systems (Mathieson 1991; Moon and Kim 2001; Pereay Monsuwe et al. 2004). Davis (1989, p. 985) observed that external variables enhance the ability of TAM to predict acceptance of future technology. In other words, the constructs of TAM need to be extended by incorporating additional factors. Choosing additional factors depends on the target technology, main users and context (Moon and Kim 2001). Job relevance and result demonstrability seemed to play important role, but there were also cases where these were not perceived. Result demonstrability seemed to be extremely important when judging whether or not to continue using system. Subjective norm did not present itself in the form it was introduced in TAM2, but when superior did suggest experimenting using web based course tools it did take place at least in one case. Image and output quality were noticeable, but seemed not to be critical factors. All factors introduced in TAM2 were noticeable at least in some degree, but in none of the cases were all factors clearly present at the same time. These findings suggest that there seems to be personal differences in approaches towards technology. Wang et al. (2003) noted that variables relating to individual differences play a vital role in the implementation of technology. To understand user perception of M-learning, this study integrated four individual difference variables and try to set up the first level constructs, namely "learning motivation, job relevance, learning efficiency and user characteristics" into the proposed TAM2 model. Those four constructs are captioned behind.

Learning Motivation: Mobile Learning is not only a technology that has to be introduced but a whole concept which also requires changes in the museum exhibition to work fast and efficiently. Especially in combination with assured information delivery and just in time learning there is no clear dividing line between intranet-knowledge management systems and mobile learning environment. There are many theories of learning, some apparently more applicable to informal learning in general and to museums in particular, some seemingly more relevant to the use of digital technologies. Many of the best-known models provide useful insights, at least into identifying issues worthy of consideration. According to Falk and Dierking (1997) individual interest is one of the major factors that influence a visit to a museum. "Personal history and values play a major role in museum-going as well". The individual interest is seen as an example of intrinsic learning motivation, and it has been found to influence user acceptance importantly.

Job relevance: Effects of this new technology and a way of work and learning have not earned as much attention as they might deserve. Computing technology has been a major force for change in organizations for over 30 years and throughout that time there has been little evidence that developers of user applications are able to predict or plan organizational outcomes (Eason 2001). One can not deny that when implementing a new system into organization, it quite likely produces consequences which could not be predicted. About the m-learning system in museum, we try to understand whether the factor have the important effect to accept the novel technology.

Learning efficiency: The most valuable function of mobile device is to provide the description content of the exhibit items. Mobile device also allows the visitor to record the content they previously viewed and provide the apparatus of self-reflection and recall memories. It is evident that internet search engine and interactive Q&A will allow the visitors to self-examine the learning efficiency in museums. Hiebert et al. (2002) assert that 'teachers rarely draw from a shared knowledge base to improve their practice' nor do they routinely use research-based knowledge to inform their work, and concurrently draw attention to the assumption that researcher's knowledge could be of value to teachers in its generalized and trustworthy character whilst the knowledge teachers use is often considered craft knowledge, characterized more by its concreteness and contextual richness than its generalization ability and context independence. One viewpoint from the cognitive learning theorist is that new knowledge is learned by the merging of previous knowledge with new information (Hannafin and Peck 1988). In a similar view, Brandt (1997) agrees that learners construct knowledge by making sense of experiences in terms of what is already known. So this study treats learning efficiency as a new variable in the TAM2.

User characteristic: When looking the results using theoretical framework from TAM, it can be quite unarguably said that perceived usefulness does play more important role than perceived ease of use. Venkatesh and Morris (2003) did suggest that this is a male dominant way of thinking, but this study does not make that clear difference between genders and personal priority knowledge of mobile device. This is quite obvious when listening stories about difficulties encountered when taking m-learning systems into use for the first time. This study treats genders and personal priority knowledge as a new variable.

Mobile learning behavior and mobile learning adopting behavior: Recently, in order to supply the widely learning opportunity, museums start to invite the mobile multimedia device to expand their service. These kinds of device can be tracked from the PDA model modified like Zaurus, Psion, and Apple Newton. The Apple Newton, or simply Newton, is an early line of personal digital assistants developed and marketed by Apple Computer from 1993 to 1998. There were a number of projects that used the Newton as a portable information device in cultural settings such as museums. For example, Visible Interactive created a walking tour in San Francisco's Chinatown but the most significant effort took place in Malaysia at the Petronas Discovery Center, known as Petrosains. It's purpose is to reinforce the visiting experience for exhibition in museum by multimedia of text, graphic, sound and animation. When we observe the visitor's behavior of using mobile device in museum, we can find the reason why visitors want to use them is strong relationship with the exhibition style in museum. For example, if the exhibition is high interactive, hands-on operation, they will ignore the mobile device to help them getting more information for learning. Because they are so busy to focus how to operate and play the exhibition, then they will tend to ignore some mobile advice in science museum. But, it's different kinds of user attitude in history and art museum. As usual, the art and history museum exhibition is focusing on the fine art works or history objects and has less hands-on exhibition and caption, so the visitor is tend to use it to access more information when they visit art or history museum. Although the TAM is widely applied to many areas in user behavior and user adopting behavior, it also need to be redefined how the system to work when we apply the mobile learning system in science museum exhibition.

3   Research Method and Hypotheses

This study is to discover the m-learning system user's attitude and behavior in museum. The issue includes the application of information technology and education theory. Therefore, except for integrating the TAM2 into the base of study, we also synthesis related education theory to study and evaluate the learning attitude and satisfaction level for m-learning users. Meanwhile, the mediate variables will accord to the factors of Perceived usefulness (PU) and Perceived ease-of-use (PEOU) which mentioned in TAM2. However, the both of factors of information technology and education theory are inclined to the learning cognition and ignore the subject factors. So this research will include the learning motivation, job relevance, learning efficiency and user characteristics to build the relationship between the Perceived usefulness and Perceived ease-of-use. As shown in Fig. 3, the proposed TAM2 includes four external variables. These four constructs may significantly affect existing TAM variables. In addition, other relationships between the constructs by the TAM2 are also presented (Venkatesh and Davis 2000). The next section describes in detail all hypotheses concerning the relationships among the variables in the model.

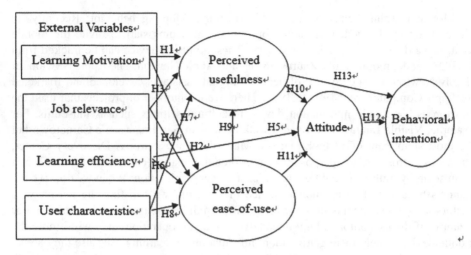

Fig. 3. The extended TAM model

3.1 Learning Motivation

Learning Motivation has not been tested previously, but it relates to users' personal awareness of mobility value. Mobility enables users to receive and transmit information anytime and anywhere (Anckar and D'Incau 2002; Coursaris et al. 2003; Hill and Roldan 2005; Ting 2005). The mobility associated with time-related needs will encourage users to adopt mobile technology since enhanced accessibility in the museum is expected to affect hands-on interaction exhibition and high levels of engagement. Hence, visitors who perceive the value of mobility also understand the uniqueness of M-learning in museum and have a strong perception of its usefulness. In other words, perceived mobility value has a positive effect on the perceived usefulness of M-learning. Therefore, this work treats Learning Motivation as a direct antecedence of perceived usefulness and perceived easy-of use.

H1. Learning Motivation has a positive effect on perceived usefulness on mobile learning in museum.
H2. Learning Motivation has a positive effect on perceived easy of use on mobile learning in museum.

3.2 Job Relevance

The concept of Job relevance adapted from Davis et al. (2000) means that users feel helpful for their work from the instrumental value of using M-learning. Prior studies on technology acceptance behavior examined the effects of Job relevance on perceived ease of use (Venkatesh 2000; Venkatesh et al. 2003; Yi and Hwang 2003).

H3. Job relevance has a positive effect on perceived usefulness on mobile learning in museum.
H4. Job relevance has a positive effect on perceived ease of use on mobile learning in museum.

3.3 Learning Efficiency

There is a causal relationship between Learning efficiency and attitude. When users feel that M-learning is easy of use, it will in turn enhance their perception of M-learning. Some research showed that attitudinal outcomes, such as happiness, pleasure, and satisfaction, result from the enjoyable experience (Childers et al. 2001; Moon and Kim 2001; Heijden 2003; Yu et al. 2005). These findings indicate that Learning efficiency highly correlates with the users' positive attitudes.

H5. Learning efficiency has a positive effect on attitude on mobile learning in museum.
H6. Learning efficiency has a positive effect on perceived ease of use on mobile learning in museum.

3.4 User Characteristic

User Characteristic of gender and priority knowledge has not been tested previously, but it relates to user difference and ability to new technology.

H7. User Characteristic has a positive effect on perceived usefulness on mobile learning in museum.
H8. User Characteristic has a positive effect on perceived ease of use on mobile learning in museum.

3.5 Perceived Ease of Use, Perceived Usefulness, Attitude, and Behavioral Intention

TAM delineates the causal relationships between perceived usefulness, perceived ease of use, attitude and behavioral intention to explain users' acceptance of technologies. Perceived easy of use is hypothesized to be a predictor of perceived usefulness. Additionally, attitude is determined by two salient beliefs, namely perceived usefulness and perceived ease of use (Davis 1989). Finally, behavioral intention is determined by perceived usefulness and attitude.

The influence of perceived ease of use on perceived usefulness, TAM posits a strong direct link between perceived ease of use and perceived usefulness. If all other factors are equal, users are likely to consider a technology to be more useful if they perceive that it is easier to use (Brown and Licker 2003; Bruner and Kumar 2005; Hu et al. 1999; Igbaria and Iivari 1995). Therefore, perceived ease of use is likely to have a direct effect on the perceived usefulness of the construct.

H9. Perceived ease of use has a positive effect on perceived usefulness on mobile learning in museum.

3.6 The Influence of Perceived Ease of Use and Perceived Usefulness on Attitude

The attitude toward using a given technology is the overall evaluation that predicts a user's likelihood of adopting that emerging technology. Past research indicates that

C. Fan

attitude is influenced by both Perceived easy of use and Perceived usefulness components (Childers et al. 2001; Dabholkar and Bagozzi 2002; Mathieson 1991; O'Cass and Fenech 2003). Thus, that attitude is positively influenced by Perceived usefulness and Perceived easy of use is proposed here.

H10. Perceived usefulness has a positive effect on attitude on mobile learning in museum.
H11. Perceived ease of use has a positive effect on attitude on mobile learning in museum.

3.7 The Influence of Perceived Usefulness and Attitude on Behavioral Intention

In TAM, behavioral intention is influenced by both Perceived usefulness and Attitude. This relationship has been examined and supported by many prior studies (Adams et al. 1992; Davis et al. 1989; Hu et al. 1999; Venkatesh and Davis 1996, 2000). Therefore, this study presents the following hypotheses.

H12. Attitude has a positive effect on behavioral intention on mobile learning in museum.
H13. Perceived usefulness has a positive effect on behavioral intention on mobile learning in museum.

4 Result and Analysis

Interviews showed that people adapt and use technology in different ways. Original reasons for taking unfamiliar new technology into use did also vary. The heterogeneity of users was quite evident, although there were no real borders between different disciplines in adapting new technology. There might have been some special requirements for the actual ways of technology use in teaching though (Jyri 2004). The study is trying to construct the new extended technology acceptance model for museum m-learning. Until now, we have the study model and will design the questionnaire for investigate the items used to construct each variable which were mainly adopted from the study.

5 Conclusion

In the past, the learning method in museums is to present a real object or a model to the audience. However, the learning stops after visitors leave the museum. The advanced internet technology gives birth to online virtual museums which present the exhibit items digitally, distinguishing it from traditional museums which feature exhibitions, education, research and archive. Online museums thus allow learners to browse and learn through computers at home with no time limit but are restrained by the immobility of the bulky computers. Nevertheless, the development of small size mobile device, along with wireless internet technology, the assistance provide by mobile device further extends the functions of museums regardless of the location and significantly enhances learning efficiency.

The pilot study is trying to establish the relationship between the external variables and user's attitude and behavior in the museum's mobile learning system. The study is still under construction and later we will do the investigation in target museum for the m-learning system exhibition. After that, we will finish the final in our paper to show the detail relationship between the external variables and user's attitude and behavior.

References

Adams, D.A., Nelson, R.R., Todd, P.A.: Perceived usefulness, ease of use, and usage of information technology: a replication. MIS Q. **16**, 227–247 (1992)

Agarwal, R., Prasad, J.: Are individual differences germane to the acceptance of new information technologies? Decis. Sci. **30**(2), 361–391 (1999)

Bagozzi, R.P., Davis, F.D., Warshaw, P.R.: Development and test of a theory of technological learning and usage. Hum. Relat. **45**(7), 660–686 (1992)

Brown, I., Licker, P.: Exploring differences in internet adoption and usage between historically advantaged and disadvantaged groups in South Africa. J. Glob. Inf. Technol. Manage. **6**(4), 6–22 (2003)

Bruner II, G.C., Kumar, A.: Applying T.A.M.: to consumer usage of handheld Internet devices. J. Bus. Res. **58**, 553–558 (2005)

Childers, T., Carr, C., Peck, J., Carson, S.: Hedonic and utilitarian motivations foronline retail shopping behaviour. J. Retail. **77**(4), 511–535 (2001)

Chin, W., Todd, P.: On the use, usefulness, and ease of use of structural equationmodelling in MIS research: a note of caution. MIS Q. **19**, 237–246 (1995)

Compeau, D.R., Higgins, C.A.: Computer self-efficacy: development of a measure and initial test. MIS Q. **19**(2), 189–211 (1995)

Coursaris, C., Hassanein, K., Head, M.: M-Commerce in Canada: an interaction framework for wireless privacy. Can. J. Adm. Sci. **20**(1), 54–73 (2003)

Dabholkar, P., Bagozzi, R.: An attitudinal model of technology-based self-service:moderating effects of consumer traits and situational factors. J. Acad. Mark. Sci. **30**(3), 184–201 (2002)

Davis, F.D.: Perceived usefulness, perceived ease of use, and user acceptance of information technology. MIS Q. **13**(3), 319–340 (1989)

Doll, W.J., Hendrickson, A., Deng, X.: Using Davis's perceived usefulness andease-of-use instrument for decision making: a confirmatory and multigroup invarianceanalysis. Decis. Sci. **29**(4), 839–869 (1998)

Eason, K.: Changing perspectives on the organizational consequences of information technology. Behav. Inf. Technol. **20**(5), 323–328 (2001). https://doi.org/10.1080/0144929011083585

Falk, J.H., Dierking, L.D.: School field trips: assessing their long-term impact. Curator **40**(3), 211–218 (1997)

Gefen, D., Straub, D.W.: Gender differences in the perception and use of e-mail:an extension to the TAM. MIS Q. **21**(4), 389–400 (1997)

Hannafin, M., Peck, K. : The Design Development and Evaluation of Instructional Software. MacMillian Publishing, New York (1988)

Heijden, H.: Factors influencing the usage of websites: the case of a generic portal in the Netherlands. Inf. Manage. **40**(6), 541–549 (2003)

Hendrickson, A.R., Massey, P.D., Cronan, T.P.: On the test-retest reliability of perceived usefulness and perceived ease of use scales. MIS Q. **17**, 227–230 (1993)

Hill, T.R., Roldan, M.: Toward third generation threaded discussions for mobile learning: opportunities and challenges for ubiquitous collaborative environments. Inf. Syst. Front. **7**, 55–70 (2005). https://doi.org/10.1007/s10796-005-5338-7

Hu, P.J., Chau, P.K., Liu Sheng, O.R., Tam, K.Y.: Examining the TAM using physicianacceptance of technology. J. MIS. **16**(2), 91–112 (1999)

Igbaria, M., Iivari, J.: The effects of self-efficacy on computer usage. Omega Int. J. Manag. Sci. **23**(6), 587–605 (1995)

Jyri, N.: Reflections on technology acceptance in higher education (2004). http://is2.lse.ac.uk/asp/aspecis/20040115.pdf. Accessed 5 Dec 2006

Mathieson, K.: Predicting user intentions: comparing the TAM with the theory of planned behaviour. Inf. Syst. Res. **2**(3), 173–91 (1991)

McDermott, K.J., Nafalski, A., Gol, O.: Active learning in the University of South Australia. Front. Educ. Conf. **1**(18–21), 18–21 (2000)

Moon, J.W., Kim, Y.G.: Extending the TAM for a world-wide-web context. Inf. Manage. **38**(4), 217–230 (2001)

O'Cass, A., Fenech, T.: Web retailing adoption: exploring the nature of internet users' web retailing behavior. J. Retail. Consum. Serv. **10**, 81–94 (2003)

Quin, C.: Mlearning: mobile, wireless, in – your-pocket learning. LiNE Zine (2001)

Revans, R.: The Origins and Growth of Action Learning. Chartwell Bratt, Sweden (1982)

Segars, A.H., Grover, V.: Re-examining perceived ease of use and usefulness: a confirmatory factor analysis. MIS Q. **17**, 517–525 (1993)

Subramanian, G.H.: A replication of perceived usefulness and perceived ease of use measurement. Decis. Sci. **25**(5/6), 863–873 (1994)

Szajna, B.: Software evaluation and choice: predictive evaluation of the technology acceptance instrument. MIS Q. **18**(3), 319–324 (1994)

Ting, R.Y.L.: Mobile learning: current trend and future challenges. In: Proceedings of the Fifth IEEE International Conference on Advanced Learning Technologies (ICALT 2005)

Tornatzky, L.G., Klein, R.J.: Innovation characteristics and innovation adoption-implementation: a meta-analysis of findings. IEEE Trans. Eng. Manag. EM **29**, 28–45 (1982)

Traxler, J.: Mobile Learning: It's Here but Where Is It? (2005). http://www2.warwick.ac.uk/services/cap/resources/ineractions/archive/issue25/traxler/. Accessed 5 Dec 2006

Venkatesh, V.: Determinants of perceived ease of use: integrating control, intrinsic motivation, and emotion into the technology acceptance model. Inf. Syst. Res. **11**(4), 342–365 (2000)

Venkatesh, V., Davis, F.D.: A model of the antecedents of perceived ease of use: development and test. Decis. Sci. **27**(3), 451–481 (1996)

Venkatesh, V., Davis, F.D.: A theoretical extension of the technology acceptance model: four longitudinal field studies. Manag. Sci. **46**(2), 186–204 (2000)

Venkatesh, V., Morris, M.G., Davis, G.B., Davis, F.D.: User acceptance of information technology: toward a unified view. MIS Q. **27**(3), 425–478 (2003)

Wang, Y., Wang, Y., Lin, H., Tang, T.: Determinants of user acceptance of Internet banking: an empirical study. Int. J. Serv. Ind. Manage. **14**(5), 501–519 (2003)

Yi, M.Y., Hwang, Y.: Predicting the use of web-based information systems:self-efficacy, enjoyment, learning goal orientation, and the technology acceptance model. Int. J. H-C Stud. **59**(4), 431–449 (2003)

Young, S.C., Chung, C.H., Liu, I.F.: An overview of integration of mobile technologies into teaching and learning settings. Instr. Technol. Media **73**, 62–76 (2005). (in Chinese)

Yu, J., Ha, I., Choi, M., Rho, J.: Extending the TAM for a t-commerce. J. Inf. Manage. **42**(7), 965–976 (2005)

Designing and Developing a Sandbox-Style Tangible AR for Geoscience Learning

Chia-Yu Hsu, Weijane Lin$^{(\boxtimes)}$ 🆔, and Hsiu-Ping Yueh 🆔

National Taiwan University, No. 1, Sec. 4, Roosevelt Road,
Taipei 10617, Taiwan
vjlin@ntu.edu.tw

Abstract. Considering the potential of sandbox-style tangible augmented reality and its enabling technologies to improve users' engagement, this study intends to design and develop a tangible AR environment for students' geoscience learning in museums. With reference to the basic functionality of a tangible AR, and the possibilities of AR to support meaning making for science learning, this study firstly developed a sandbox-style tangible AR environment to enable basic interactivity. And the school curriculum of geoscience for the local community in Taiwan was then referred in order to develop the instructional plans with the sandbox TAR. Finally, there were four AR learning packages in total completed with expert teachers' review. These four lessons consisted of different infusion of tangible AR elements that allowed learners to search, connect, collect and generate geographical information. A preliminary user testing with 5 college students were conducted to confirm the quality of system instruction and the functionality of the system.

Keywords: Augmented reality · Tangible AR · Sandbox-style TAR

1 Introduction

Museums as informal learning environment to include learners of various disciplines and levels, have gained significant attention from both the research and practices of education [1, 2]. How to manage the learning materials, how to cooperate appropriate technology in exhibition and education have become important concerns for museums. Combing tangible user interface (TUI) and augmented reality (AR) technology, recently tangible augmented reality has been used in displays in exhibitions [4, 5]. Tangible AR using sandbox allows users to control both real and virtual objects with their bare hands to obtain real time feedbacks. For the applications of geoscience, for instance, sandbox-style TAR enables learners to shape various landforms and understand their structures at the same time. Apart from traveling to real fields, students can also create a field indoors by sandbox-style TAR [3, 6–8].

With sandbox-style TAR in museums, it is possible for visitors to experience the outdoor setting in a simulated yet instructional environment, and it also extends the physical entities of museum artifacts and buildings to a boundless and resourceful learning environment. Stimulated by the aforementioned potentials which is regarded as an effective way to interest students in science learning. Its quality, hence, plays a

© Springer Nature Switzerland AG 2020
P.-L. P. Rau (Ed.): HCII 2020, LNCS 12193, pp. 281–290, 2020.
https://doi.org/10.1007/978-3-030-49913-6_24

critical role, and the effects which sandbox-style TAR possess would be important and worthy of exploration. Stimulated by the aforementioned background, this study intends to design and develop a tangible AR environment for students' geoscience learning in museums.

2 Literature Review

2.1 Sandbox-Style Tangible AR

Since tangible AR is a kind of AR whose user interface is tangible [4], its development is aligned with tangible user interface [9]. Sandbox-style TAR comes into use in the form of a sandbox with a projector and a depth camera hanging above. The continuous, kinetic materials such as sand or clay in the sandbox give users more flexibility in manipulation [10]. Considering people's instinct to explore the world by touching, tangible user interface allows users to control digital information directly rather than using media like mice and key-boards which are necessary in other modern user interfaces [11]. The materials in sandbox-style tangible AR need to imply positions information so that the information can be controlled while users are manipulating the materials. And then the projector will give feedback once changes are sensed by the depth camera, making it possible for users to manipulate virtual objects in AR [12].

Basically in a sandbox-style tangible AR environment, the manipulation is that users change positions of materials and see feedback directly projected in the sandbox. The team of Tangible Landscape, however, has enabled other more modes of interaction and types of feedback [8]. In their original design of Tangible® [8], there are six kinds of interaction and they can be further classified into three categories based on the similarity between modes. First, what users can do in category one is change the form of materials whether they use their bare hands or tools, which is the basic design of sandbox-style TAR. And the second category allows users to place several markers such as pins, patches or outlines on the materials; different markers have their own functions (e.g.: river, forest…etc.). The third category includes the interaction that users establish viewpoints in the sandbox, in which external monitors are necessary.

The current ways how sandbox-style presents feedback can be divided into two. Users can get feedback either from the surface of materials or from a monitor aside [8]. The former is the common way to present feedback, serving as the basic setup of sandbox-style TAR; however, the latter, for certain purposes, can simulate what virtual or analog objects will look like in reality on a monitor equipped. Users who intend to experience the third category of sandbox-style TAR's modes of interaction will get corresponding feedback only if there is a monitor displaying changes of viewpoints.

Recognized by its positive effects, sandbox-style TAR is used to train a variety of abilities. For one, users acquire such basic skills as students use to understand topography. Users show their better abilities to read contour lines via sandbox-style tangible AR. On the other hand, ones are more likely to have difficulties when using planar materials [13, 14]. For another, users also undergo drills in engineering. And in the study of [8], the results suggest that work made by users trained with sandbox-style TAR tend to be of higher quality than that made with either analog or digital methods.

In view of the above, it implies that the purposes of sandbox-style TAR involve both theoretical and practical aspects. And its users are mainly aimed at college students or above. The user studies which have been conducted so far show that college subjects gain positive experience from sandbox-style TAR [8, 13, 14], while other researches discussing TAR's application indicate that it is of the design of intuitive manipulation and can be easily accessed [4]. The state that few studies have dealt with other groups of users doesn't seem to be consistent with such original intention, however.

2.2 Learning with Sandbox-Style Tangible AR

In the research of [15], the factors influencing students' motivation in science learning are divided into six constructs: self efficacy, active learning strategies, science learning value, performance goal, achievement goal and learning environment stimulation. In this research, we focus on the last one given sandbox-style TAR's role of a pedagogic medium, which can be a stimulus in a learning environment.

TAR generally features four attributes, namely tactile richness, manipulability, real-time computational analysis, and multiple access points [4, 8, 12–14]. Via tactile contact, users can feel material qualities. Manipulability allows users to carry out manipulation by their own volition and learn by doing. Real-time computational analysis refers to the immediate and relevant information tangible augmented reality generates after computational analysis. Multiple access points enable all users of tangible augmented reality to see what's going on and get their hands on the central objects of interest. The combination of manipulability and real-time computational analysis, in particular, reflects the essence of constructivism, which considers that human learn from the accumulative experience of observing, interpreting and processing. And such learning theory has been recognized in geoscience education [5]. That is, tangible augmented reality can be an ideal medium of learning geoscience: users may have various interpretations following their observation on the information given by the system, and then they can process what has been done accordingly. Several empirical studies, in correspondence, have indicated its positive effects on geoscience learning [8, 13, 14].

Several characteristics of sandbox-style TAR promote students' motivation to participate in the class based on the construct of learning environment stimulation in [15] 's questionnaire. Exciting and changeable content and opportunities to join discussions can be facilitated via sandbox-style TAR's tactile richness and multiple access points respectively. Manipulation out of students' volition can lead to less pressure from teachers, and system's real-time feedback draws students' attention on what they have done. Sandbox-style TAR promotes students' learning motivation. In addition, the level where students engage in the class is considered to increase when they get interested or motivated [15]. That is, the more sandbox-style TAR motivates its users, the more the users get engaged in learning by manipulating the device, which can be another beneficial effect of sandbox-style tangible AR.

Regarding the learning effectiveness, previous studies have indicated that high levels of both motivation and engagement can lead to students' greater achievements [15]. In most countries around the world, geoscience basically shares the same syllabus with science [3]; students' achievements in geoscience, thus, are evaluated in a way similar to those in science, which are judged from three aspects: attitude, process and knowledge [16–18]. Among the three aspects, different levels of knowledge of a certain scientific concept, including knowing, understanding or applying [18], are regarded as a common indicator implying students' achievements in many studies as well as in studies about sandbox-style tangible AR's learning effects [8, 13, 14]. With a unique environment, sandbox-style tangible AR's learning effects, however, should involve wider aspects, which has rarely been dealt with in previous studies yet.

Therefore, this study attempts to discover other possibilities and would like to put emphasis on the aspect of process because learning by doing/manipulating, one of sandbox-style tangible AR's characteristics, is believed to improve this kind of achievement. The aspect of process tackles students' scientific process skills, referring to the abilities to facilitate a scientific study [16]. With reference to the curriculum guidelines for primary and secondary education of science and technology in Taiwan, five scientific process skill are emphasized and included: observing, comparing & classifying, organizing & relating, generalizing & inferring and interpreting. Stimulated by the aforementioned issues, the purpose of this study is to explore sandbox-style tangible AR's effects on learners who visit a museum. In the literature review above, studies have confirmed that sandbox-style TAR does have positive learning effects, yet several questions still remain unknown.

3   Method

Based on the literature review, this study intends to design and develop a tangible AR environment for students' geoscience learning in museums. With reference to the basic functionality of a tangible AR, and the possibilities of AR to support meaning making for science learning, this study firstly developed a sandbox-style tangible AR environment to enable basic interactivity. And the school curriculum of geoscience in general, and topographic maps in specific, in both local and global communities [19, 20] was then referred in order to develop the instructional plans with the sandbox TAR. Finally, there were four lessons in total completed with expert teachers' review. These four lessons consisted of different infusion of tangible AR elements that allowed learners to search, connect, collect and even generate. A preliminary user testing with 5 college students were conducted to confirm the system instruction and functionality.

Instruments: The system is constructed on the platform and framework of ARSandbox, developed by Oliver Kreylos in University of California, Davis, U.S.A. The sandbox in use of this study is 75 cm(L) × 60 cm(W) × 160 cm(H) with 20 kg kinetic sand loaded. Microsoft Kinect Xbox 360 ® was set up to sense the surface change and transmit the data back to the Linux server. An ultra short throw projector with high luminous flux of 3000 lm was set on top of the sandbox to project visual information. The final system outlook is shown as Fig. 1 and Fig. 2. Physical objects as markers, including thumbtacks, shovels, flags, rulers and blocks were also distributed for users to conduct manipulations like indicate, measure and shape.

Fig. 1. The experiment setting of this study.

Fig. 2. The ARSandbox used in this study

4 Results

With references to the school curriculum of topographic maps [19, 20], there were four instructional plans of typographic maps developed to coordinate with the ARSandbox (see Table 1). The instructional objectives of all lesson plans were to acquaint learners with topographic maps, and these four lesson plans distinguished from each other by their required manipulation tasks of searching, connecting, collecting and generating, respectively.

Table 1. Learning goals of the experimental instructional plans

ID	Main learning tasks	Goals of learning
1	Searching	Search specified features on 3D landforms
2	Connecting	Connect 3D landforms with topographic maps
3	Collecting	Collect outlook information of two spots to create a profile
4	Generating	Generate a building solution with reference to the topographic maps

In the searching tasks, learners were asked to seek possible water flows and watersheds from a landform with a topographic map (see Fig. 3). In the connecting tasks, learners needed to shape a terrain according to a given topographic map (see Fig. 4). For collecting tasks, learners were asked to judge the visibility of an assigned spot from three alternative reservoirs by collecting the information of heights and profiles of the landform (see Fig. 5). And in the generating tasks, learners needed to determine where to build a dam with evaluating the available information such as slope, catchment area, and cost of construction, all provided by the system (see Fig. 6).

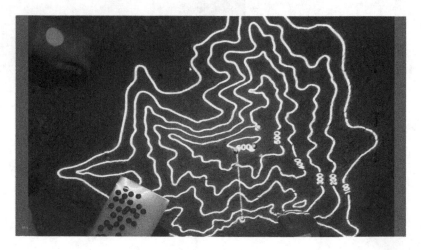

Fig. 3. Searching

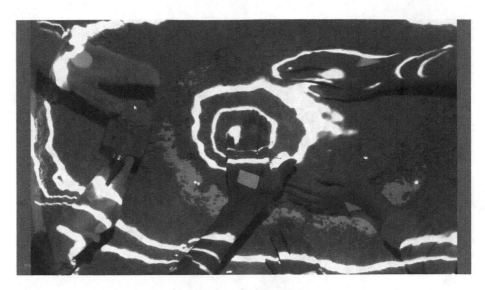

Fig. 4. Connecting

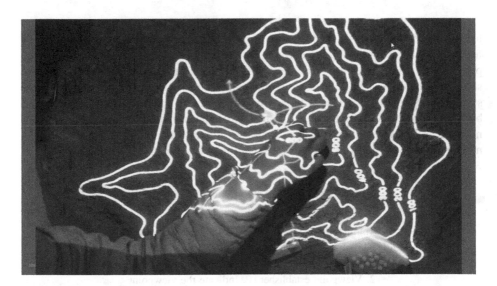

Fig. 5. Collecting

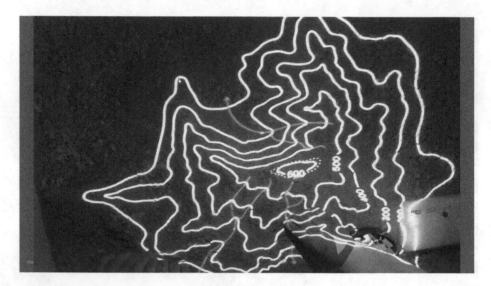

Fig. 6. Generating

These four lesson plans were reviewed by 2 subject experts of geoscience education to ensure the validity and independency of each lesson plan. Dynamic and immediate feedbacks were projected to the surface of sand when users activated the raining by putting their hands over the box. Static and real time instruction and feedback were shown on the display in front of the participants. In order to ensure the user flow and system functionality, 5 college students were invited to use the sandbox with their behaviors observed and recorded. The results of the user testing informed the technological affordance of the physical markers, and the modification of the physical markers and their functions were made accordingly as shown in Table 2.

Table 2. Physical markers used in each lesson plan

Lesson plan	Physical markers	Functions
1 Searching	Thumbtacks in colors	Indicate water flows and watersheds
2 Connecting	Shovel	Model and shape the sand
3 Collecting	1. Thumbtacks in colors 2. Viewpoint establisher 3. Flags	1. Indicate spots 2. Indicate the viewpoint 3. Check the visibility
4 Generating	1. Thumbtacks in colors 2. Ruler 3. Blocks	1. Show landform information 2. Measure distance between two points 3. Indicate the dams

5 Conclusion

This study reported our design and development of a series of geoscience learning materials using ARSandbox. The four AR learning packages of topographic maps with careful instructional design were developed and assessed by subject experts to ensure the validity of the content as well as the interactivity of the system. From the interviews with the users in pilot study, it was also proved that the learning tasks of manipulation engaged the participants and motivated their problem solving skills. With the instructional plans ensured, in our future works, the user studies will be conducted with a larger population of high school students who are learning geoscience.

References

1. Behrendt, M., Franklin, T.: A review of research on school field trips and their value in education. Int. J. Environ. Sci. Educ. **9**(3), 235–245 (2014)
2. Griffin, J.: Research on students and museums: looking more closely at the students in school groups. Sci. Educ. **88**(1), S59–S70 (2004)
3. King, C.: Geoscience education: an overview. Stud. Sci. Educ. **44**(2), 187–222 (2008)
4. Billinghurst, M., Kato, H., Poupyrev, I.: Tangible augmented reality. In: ACM SIGGRAPH ASIA, vol. 7 (2008)
5. Nawaz, M., Kundu, S.N., Sattar, F.: Augmented reality sandbox and constructivist approach for geoscience teaching and learning. World Acad. Sci. Eng. Technol. Int. J. Soc. Behav. Educ. Econ., Bus. Ind. Eng. **11**(6), 1613–1616 (2017)
6. Azuma, R.T.: A survey of augmented reality. Presence Teleoper. Virt. Environ. **6**(4), 355–385 (1997)
7. Milgram, P., Kishino, F.: A taxonomy of mixed reality visual displays. IEICE Trans. Inf. Syst. **77**(12), 1321–1329 (1994)
8. Millar, G.C., et al.: Tangible landscape: a hands-on method for teaching terrain analysis. In: Proceedings of the 2018 CHI Conference on Human Factors in Computing Systems, p. 380. ACM (2018)
9. Ishii, H.: The tangible user interface and its evolution. Commun. ACM **51**(6), 32–36 (2008)
10. Ishii, H., Ratti, C., Piper, B., Wang, Y., Biderman, A., Ben-Joseph, E.: Bringing clay and sand into digital design—continuous tangible user interfaces. BT Technol. J. **22**(4), 287–299 (2004)
11. Ishii, H., Ullmer, B.: Tangible bits: towards seamless interfaces between people, bits and atoms. In: Proceedings of the ACM SIGCHI Conference on Human factors in computing systems, pp. 234–241 (1997)
12. Reed, S.E., et al.: Shaping watersheds exhibit: an interactive, augmented reality sandbox for advancing earth science education. In: AGU Fall Meeting Abstracts (2014)
13. Woods, T.L., Reed, S., Hsi, S., Woods, J.A., Woods, M.R.: Pilot study using the augmented reality sandbox to teach topographic maps and surficial processes in introductory geology lab. J. Geosci. Educ. **64**, 199–214 (2016)
14. Richardson, R., Sammons, D., Delparte, D.: Augmented affordances support learning: comparing the instructional effects of the augmented reality sandbox and conventional maps to teach topographic map skills. J. Interact. Learn. Res. **29**(2), 231–248 (2018)
15. Tuan, H.L., Chin, C.C., Shieh, S.H.: The development of a questionnaire to measure students' motivation towards science learning. Int. J. Sci. Educ. **27**(6), 639–654 (2005)

16. A Study on the Change of Scientific Competence of Senior Students in Elementary School from Natural Subject's Outdoors Teaching. https://hdl.handle.net/11296/9ucxwf. Accessed 27 Aug 2018
17. Studies on the Outdoor Education in Relation to the Scientific Achievements and Attitudes of Fifth Grade Students. https://hdl.handle.net/11296/uwg7ut. Accessed 27 Aug 2018
18. Lawless, K.A., Brown, S.W.: Multimedia learning environments: issues of learner control and navigation. Instr. Sci. **25**(2), 117–131 (1997)
19. K-12 Education Administration, Ministry of Education. Curriculum Guidelines of 12-Year Basic Education. https://cirn.moe.edu.tw/Upload/file/946/70456.pdf. Accessed 27 Dec 2019
20. Woods, T.L., Reed, S., et al.: Pilot study using the augmented reality sandbox to teach topographic maps and surficial processes in introductory geology labs. J. Geosci. Educ. **64** (3), 199–214 (2016)
21. Millar, G.C., Tabrizian, P., et al.: Tangible landscape: a hands-on method for teaching terrain analysis. In: Proceedings of the 2018 CHI Conference on Human Factors in Computing Systems, vol. 380 (2018)

Cultivate Deeper Cross-Cultural Context into Foreign Language Teaching

Shu-Hua Hsueh[(⊠)] and Mei-Jin Hsiao

Fuzhou University of International Studies and Trade, No. 28,
Yuhuan Road, Shouzhan New District, Changle District 350202, Fujian,
People's Republic of China
Katherinepaloma03@gmail.com

Abstract. Nowadays, the Internet is not only a new invention of information technology but also an advanced tool to learn foreign language in our globalized world. Learning foreign language has been widespread globally and being part of our modern life. Furthermore, language learning should focus more on cultural part besides of language itself. This paper reviews several notions of language and culture, then move to intercultural competence in foreign language classroom. Besides, there is a big difference between the traditional and modern foreign language teaching now. As Hinkel mentioned that second language learners should be familiar with fundamental learning second cultural concepts and constructs, otherwise, they cannot make the best of their educational, professional and vocational opportunities. Being a foreign language teacher in the modern world, we should be aware of "the learning of culture is an integral part of language learning and education because culture crucially influences the values of the community, everyday interaction, the norms of speaking and behaving, and the sociocultural expectations of an individual's roles". (Hinkel 2014) However, under the explosion of information, language learning is not only to learn the grammar, vocabulary and four skills- listening, speaking, reading and writing, therefore, this paper will provide further discussions about cultural awareness, intercultural teaching and suggestions for cultivating deeper cross-cultural teaching in foreign language classroom.

Keywords: Communicative competence · Foreign language teaching · Cultural teaching · Communicative language teaching · Intercultural teaching · Cross-cultural experience

1 Introduction

In the era of globalization and internationalization with frequently interpersonal communication, particularly after the arising of internet, our world has been changed dramatically in all aspects such as science, technology, economy and social system. On the world of Internet, we interact easily and frequently with people from different countries and cultures. It means that we have already been doing many cross-cultural activities every day. And learning foreign language acts like a bridge to connect all of the people in the world doing these activities.

© Springer Nature Switzerland AG 2020
P.-L. P. Rau (Ed.): HCII 2020, LNCS 12193, pp. 291–299, 2020.
https://doi.org/10.1007/978-3-030-49913-6_25

The main purpose of learning a foreign language is not only to learn how to speak the language fluently but also to learn how to communicate properly with the people of the target language. Nowadays, the communicative competence is globally emphasized in language teaching and learning. Saville-Troike (1982, p. 6) offered a "definition of what it means to be able to communicate and included both social and cultural knowledge in addition to linguistic knowledge in her description and outlines a wide range of linguistic, interactional and cultural phenomena that contribute to being communicatively competent". (Saville-Troike 1982 cited in Foley and Thompson 2003). In a word, language and culture are the two important tools to reach the communicative competence.

Traditionally, in Eastern countries foreign language teaching concentrated on linguistic learning such as vocabulary, grammar while paid little attention on the culture terms. But what parts of culture should be taught in classroom? Tylor (1920, p. 9), a nineteenth-century anthropologist, first defined culture as "that complex whole which includes knowledge, belief, art, morals, law, custom, and any other capabilities and habits by man as a member of a society". So, culture is not a single term in language teaching but a process of language teaching. It is not limited in the literature, poem and arts but should cover all aspects of culture in the target language.

As Shemshadsara (2012) stated the view of teaching culture "is a means of developing an awareness of, and sensitivity towards, the values and traditions of the people whose language is being studied." The key point is to realize what aspects of culture should be taught and how to incorporate them into foreign language teaching context. As a foreign language teacher in China, the author encountered the problems of teaching foreign language without mentioning much culture things in classroom. Most of Foreign language teachers concentrate on vocabulary and grammar analyzing during the limited teaching time. Naturally, the language learning and measurement coverages are the same without any cultural knowledge.

2 Notions on the Link Between Culture and Foreign Language

Foreign Language Teaching is always linked with culture. There is no doubt that the researchers who advocate the existence of a close link between language and culture and indicate that teaching language automatically entails teaching culture (Brown 1987; Buttjes 1990; Jiang 2000; Gao 2006, cited in Hawkar 2016). It is impossible to teach foreign language without mentioning any culture in the classroom.

The relationship of Culture and Language described by Brown (1994, p. 165) as follows:

"A language is a part of a culture and a culture is a part of a language; the two are intricately interwoven so that one cannot separate the two without losing the significance of either language or culture." Language and culture should belong to each other, students learn a foreign language along with culture things such as foods, religion and customs. Culture teaching will make language learning more vivid and meaningful.

Jiang expressed her opinions on the relationship of language and culture by three interesting metaphors as below:

From a philosophical view:

language + culture - > a living organism

flesh blood

Language and culture makes a living organism; language is flesh, and culture is blood. Without culture, language would be dead; without language, culture would have no shape.

From a communicative view:

Language + culture - > swimming (communication)

swimming skill water

Communication is swimming, language is the swimming skill, and culture is water. Without language, communication would remain to a very limited degree (in very shallow water); without culture, there would be no communication at all.

From a pragmatic view:

language + culture - > transportation (communication)

vehicle traffic light

Communication is like transportation: language is the vehicle and culture is traffic light. Language makes communication easier and faster; culture regulates, sometimes promotes and sometimes hinders communication." (Jiang 2000, p. 328).

Indeed, language cannot act itself without culture involving in. Language is a vehicle for people to get to communicate one another in different culture.

Hinkel's view of culture. There are two layers:

–the visible culture	The visible culture refers to literature, the arts, the architecture, and the history of a particular people. That's what people mention about their own culture things and normally comes with the styles of dress, cuisine, customs, festivals, and other traditions.
–the invisible culture	meant that sociocultural beliefs and assumptions that most people are not aware of and thus cannot examine intellectually. (Hinkel 2014, p. 396)

So, whenever we mention culture teaching, it should include the sociocultural beliefs and assumptions in which people believe and think appropriately.

According to Marczak, culture has always been constituted an element of foreign language teaching. However, it has mostly involved transmission of declarative, factual knowledge, which teachers relayed to learners from the position of a 'knower'. Therefore, intercultural teaching, which is advocated today (Byram 1997, 1998, 2003, 2008, cited in Marczak 2010), shifts the teaching of culture towards the development of skills of observation, empathy for otherness, and the ability to adopt behavior which would help one function appropriately in intercultural situations.

3 Cultural Awareness and Intercultural Communication in Foreign Language Classroom

According to Mingyu, Foreign Language Teaching in China is getting more and more popular and has gone through several reforms, but the teaching result has been unsatisfactory.

> "The students have strong and good language skills. But their social and intercultural communication skills are poor. College English teaching is a typical example. Our research has found that grammatical sensitivity has a significant impact on their cross-cultural communication and language learning activities among foreign-language learners who are native speakers of Chinese. After research, we can say that the means of making words, extending sentences and reading paragraphs can effectively test the grammatical sensitivity of Chinese learners. With the continuous development of the social environment, the means of learning continue to improve. Intercultural communication skills of foreign language learners change and affect the result of learning the language."(Mingyu 2019)

In Mingyu's research, it demonstrated that grammatical sensitivity has been influenced by cross-cultural communication. Therefore, Cultural Awareness and Intercultural Competence are two important aspects and should be integrate into Foreign Language Classroom.

3.1 Cultural Awareness

Kuang (2007) claims that the definition of Cultural Awareness as seeing both the positive and negative aspects of cultural differences and understanding the thinking ways and life style of people from other cultures. As a foreign language teacher, it is essential to deliver this basic understanding and thinking of cultural awareness to foreign language learners. With this kind of awareness, learners will open their mind to perceive and accept automatically culture difference or culture shock while they encounter the different culture.

Also, Tolinson and Masuhara (2004) claim that an increased cultural awareness helps learners broaden the mind, increase tolerance and achieve cultural empathy and sensitivity. According to Tomalin and Stempleski (1993), cultural awareness encompasses three qualities:

– awareness of one's own culturally-induced behavior
– awareness of the culturally-induced behavior of others
– ability to explain one's own cultural standpoint (p. 5)
  (cited in Shemshadsara (2012))

These three qualities of cultural awareness will enhance teachers to prepare cross-culture context and students will form a basic foundation for students to learn culture in foreign language classroom.

3.2 Intercultural Communication

After being aware of cultural empathy and sensitivity, language educators addressed that foreign language learning should increase students' intercultural competence

(IC) which would give themselves the opportunities to realize relationships between different cultures, mediate across cultures, and critically analyze cultures including their own (Chapelle 2010, cited in Moeller et al. 2015).

Robinson (1985) was one of the first in the field of second language education to argue that instead of treating culture as a collection of static products or facts that may be presented to learners in different terms, it should be taught as a process, that is, as a way of perceiving, interpreting, feeling and understanding. This perspective gives the opinion on the culture as part of the process of living and being in the world, the part that is necessary for understanding the meaning of target culture. (Robinson 1985, cited in Shemshadsara Z. 2012).

So, culture teaching is a dynamic teaching in classroom. Schulz proposes that the teaching of intercultural competence should include developing awareness of variables that affect communicative interactions, recognizing stereotypes and evaluating them, and developing awareness of types of causes for cultural misunderstandings between members of different cultures. He suggested that a culture-learning portfolio allows teachers to assess students' progress over time based on specific objectives. Also these portfolios can be related to students' individual interest and encourage critical reflection and self-evaluation and, especially important in the area of cultural learning, the use of multiple sources of evidence (Schulz 2007, p. 18, cited in Moeller et al. 2015).

Mingyu (2019) demonstrated that Intercultural Communication Theory is like Current Perspective which is viewed as a hallmark of an independent and mature discipline. Intercultural communication makes language teaching experts recognize that language teaching should include cultural aspects. Foreign language communication is hence moving to intercultural communication. An important criterion for measuring foreign language talents is to see whether they have the abilities of cultural cognition and intercultural communication.

Facing the changing world of teaching foreign language, Kuang (2007) suggests that teachers should prepare themselves with the following two things:

1. Understanding the cultural differences, especially the differences in the deep structure of different cultures.
2. Becoming flexible in intercultural communication since we need to adopts the elements of one culture to another. It's very important to avoid bringing cultural prejudice into foreign language class.

All in all, Ugur (2012) concluded that communicative language teaching and the competences involved in it seem to comprise the last broadly conceived, systematized and implemented pedagogy. It can be discussed whether learning about a culture along with the language is a must but as it would be hard to deny the fact that cultural awareness would facilitate interpersonal communication, the communicative approach especially with its component of sociolinguistic competence can be mentioned to be the first to take the cultural dimension of language learning into demonstrable consideration.

4   Suggestions of Cultivating Deeper Cross-Cultural Context into Foreign Language Teaching

There are three suggestions to cultivate deeper cross-cultural context in foreign language classroom when teachers and students engage in foreign language teaching and learning.

Firstly, Foreign Language Teachers should have established themselves the sense of cultural awareness. Their cultural knowledge for language teaching is very crucial to students. Even though, today's students are able to access all kinds of cultural resources, they still need their teachers to guide and monitor them to select and screen out what they need to learn or know during studying foreign language.

As Moeller (2015) describe the role of foreign language teachers as below:

"In such a learning environment the role of the teacher changes from one of authority figure or expert who delivers knowledge to one who facilitates, guides, and supports student learning. The teacher assumes greater responsibilities in designing and supporting individual and personalized learning tasks. This has tremendous implications for teacher educators and teacher trainers to act as agents of change as they foster language learning through the use of public pedagogy and critical media literacy".

Therefore, with well cultural awareness, teachers must act as teaching guides, supporters which are very different from traditional role model. They need to communicate with students deeply and understand what their problems are in language learning. Then, teachers can provide good teaching plans for students in foreign language classroom.

Secondly, students should equip their own cultural knowledge before learning foreign language culture.

Intercultural knowledge is already being a must taught section in Foreign Language teaching. By nurturing cross-cultural experience, students learn ethnic, racial, social class, and arts of the target language. But before that, students need to learn well about their own culture first. Byram (1997) discourses that, in interpreting experiences of a new culture and constructing new cultural meanings, one tends to relate the new culture to one's own native culture. Indeed, the knowledge one has about cultures – including especially one's own culture – serves as a "resource for learning new cultures" (Liddicoat and Scarino 2013, cited in Chan and Klayklueng 2018). In other words, learning a foreign culture should begin from knowing well about their own culture.

By using their own culture as a base, they expand cultural knowledge into understanding foreign language culture.

Marczak (2010) indicates intercultural teaching should focus on two culture systems: the learner's native culture and the target one. And these two cultures interact in the foreign language classroom. Therefore, intercultural teaching encourages the learner to gain additional insight into their own native culture.

Thirdly, intercultural teaching environment should be arranged on the foreign language teaching practice.

Having a developed understanding of cross-cultural awareness, teachers will be able to incorporate culture related topics into their teaching plans. But, how do they incorporate these topics into their teaching practice? This needs a well arranged environment to provide a great opportunity for students to become familiar with a certain culture and bring versatility into the foreign language classroom. Even though, there is no authentic context, teachers still can immerse culture in classroom based on the holiday. For example, teachers may use role play to introduce the holiday Thanksgiving in China. As Thanksgiving is celebrated in USA, Chinese students don't know why people celebrate it in USA. Teachers may create a drama about Thanksgiving and assign students to play different roles. By doing so, Chinese students will access to the internet to search the origin of this holiday and understand American culture and the reason why Americans celebrate it.

5 Conclusion

In the modern era, English functions mostly is like a lingua franca, i.e. a tool for international communication, which does not necessarily involve native speakers (Komorowska 2006). The current trend on learning English as second language, people don't emphasis much on British English or American English, but mention to Global English. The purpose of learning English is not to speak like a native speaker, yet it is to speak English appropriately. Therefore, the discussion of cultural contents in Foreign Language Teaching needs to consider the influence of globalization because it raises the problem of what culture to be taught and whose culture is the target culture. Considering an English-as-a-lingua-franca situation, a Chinese speaker might communicate with a Korean speaker using English as a medium.

Although, some of the reading context are about foreign society or geography. The deeper insight of cultural knowledge such as universal categories of human behavior and procedures should be mentioned (Sun 2013). According to Celce-Murcia and Olshtain (2000), in language learning and usage, pragmatic and cultural competence are closely related, and both require learners to "use language in socio-culturally appropriate ways" (p. 20). For example, learning how to persuade or convince others or how to schedule an appointment with proper communicative target language should be basic things in language learning. Xue (2014) concluded that "cultural teaching is an appropriate and feasible way to develop college students' intercultural communication competence.... and at present, communicative language teaching (CLT) is widely adopted by the foreign language teachers, especially English teachers, in China."

However, the main purpose of language teaching should focus on how to facilitate students to speak and act appropriately in target language. The deeper social cultural knowledge settings are necessary in classroom in which students will learn the target culture based on their own culture. In a word, students will be inspired by the experience of different cultures and fulfill the goal of language learning in the modern world.

References

Acevedo, M.V.: Department of Curriculum and Instruction, University of Massachusetts-Boston, 100 Morrissey Boulevard, Boston, MA 02125, USA. In: Brown, H.D., (ed.) Principles of Language Learning and Teaching, 3rd edn. Prentice Hall Regents, Englewood Cliffs (1994)

Byram, M.: Teaching and Assessing Intercultural Communicative Competence. Multilingual Matters, Clevedon (1997)

Chan, W.M., Klayklueng, S.: Critical and cultural awareness and identity development: insights from a short-term Thai language immersion, National University of Singapore, Singapore. Electron. J. Foreign Lang. Teach. **15**(Suppl. 1), 129–147 (2018). © Centre for Language Studies National University of Singapore

Foley, J., Thompson, L.: Language Learning: A Lifelong Process. Distributed in the United States of America by Oxford University Press Inc., New York (2003)

Hawkar, A.A.: Does teaching language automatically entail teaching culture? Int. J. Lang. Linguist. **2**(4), 258–262 (2014)

Hsin, C.: Language and culture in foreign language teaching (2008). http://www.leeds.ac.uk/educol/documents/178899.pdf

Jiang, W.: The relationship between culture and language. ELT J. **54**(4), 328–334 (2000)

Komorowska, H.: Intercultural competence in ELT syllabus and materials design. Scripta Neophilologica Posnaniensia vol. VIII, pp. 59-83 (2006)

Kuang, J.F.: Developing students' cultural awareness through foreign language Teaching. Sino-US English Teaching, USA, Dec 2007, vol. 4, No. 12 (Serial No. 48) (2007). ISSN: 1539-8072

Kumagai, Y.: The Effects of Culture on Language Learning and Ways of Communication: The Japanese Case. Master's Capstone Projects. 80 (1994). https://scholarworks.umass.edu/cie_capstones/80

Marczak, M.: New trends in teaching language and culture. In: Komorowska, H., Aleksandrowicz-Pędich, L., (eds.) Coping with Diversity, pp. 13–28. Szkoły Psychologii Społecznej (2010)

McConarchy T.: L2 pragmatics as 'intercultural pragmatics': Probing sociopragmatic aspects of pragmatic awareness (2019). https://doi.org/10.1016/J.PRAGMA.2019.02.014

Published: 2019-10 Journal of Pragmatics Journal homepage. www.elsevier.com/locate/pragma

Mingyu, Z.: Correlation Study on Grammatical Sensitivity Test Indexes in Intercultural Communication Revista de cercetareşiintervenţiesocială, vol. 65, p. 26 (2019)

Moeller, A.K., Catalano, T.: Foreign Language Teaching and Learning. Faculty Publications: Department of Teaching, Learning and Teacher Education. 200 (2015)

Richard, C., Robertson, A., Mahony, Ipromote learners' intercultu: Intercultural language learning: the Indonesian for Teachers Initiative (InTI) experience. Lang. Intercult. Commun. **19**, 357–370 (2018). https://doi.org/10.1080/14708477.2018.1545778

Shemshadsaraw, Z.G.: Developing Cultural Awareness in Foreign Language Teaching www.ccsenet.org/elt English Language Teaching, vol. 5, no. 3, Published by Canadian Center of Science and Education 95 (2012)

Sun, L.: Culture Teaching in Foreign Language Teaching, Theory and Practice in Language Studies, vol. 3, no. 2, pp. 371–375 (2013). ISSN 1799-2591

Tomalin, B., Stempleski, S.: Cultural Awareness. Oxford University Press, Oxford (1993)

Tomlinson, B., Musuhara, H.: Developing cultural awareness. MET **13**(1), 1–7 (2004)

Ugur, R.C.: WCES 2012 Intercultural communicative competence in ELT. Procedia Soc. Behav. Sci. **46**, 3445–3449 (2012)

Xue, J.: Theory Pract. Lang. Stud. **4**(7), 1492–1498 (2014)

Zhang, X., Zhou, M.: Interventions to promote learners' intercultural competence: a meta-analysis. Int. J. Intercult. Relat. **71**, 31–47 (2019). https://www.elsevier.com/locate/ijintrel

An Intelligent Platform for Offline Learners Based on Model-Driven Crowdsensing Over Intermittent Networks

Shin'ichi Konomi[1(✉)], Lulu Gao[2], and Doreen Mushi[3]

[1] Faculty of Arts and Science, Kyushu University, 744, Motooka, Nishi-ku,
Fukuoka 819-0395, Japan
konomi@artsci.kyushu-u.ac.jp
[2] Graduate School of Information Science and Electrical Engineering,
Kyushu University, 744, Motooka, Nishi-ku, Fukuoka 819-0395, Japan
[3] Institute of Educational and Management Technologies, The Open University
Tanzania, Dar es Salaam, Tanzania

Abstract. Despite the continuous growth of global Internet users, almost 4 billion people do not use the Internet. The offline population includes people who live in developing regions or rural aging communities. In this context, we propose a learning-support platform for learners without an easy, reliable, and affordable means to access digital learning environments on the Internet. Unlike existing systems that provide little support for efficient educational data collection from offline learners, our proposed platform combines delay-tolerant networking mechanisms and active learning-based model-driven crowdsensing techniques to deliver learning materials and collect educational data efficiently.

Keywords: Developing regions · Older adults · Crowdsensing · Educational data · DTN · Active learning · Predictive analytics · Learning analytics

1 Introduction

Digital learning-support environments such as learning management systems (LMS), electronic portfolio systems, and digital textbooks are increasingly used in various schools and online courses [45]. They can facilitate learning activities in and outside classrooms, and their exhaust data can be used to perform *learning analytics*, which is the measurement, collection, analysis and reporting of data about learners and their contexts, for purposes of understanding and optimizing learning and the environments in which it occurs. Such a data-centric approach also allows for a potential use of early prediction about learners [17].

Although digital learning environments can facilitate and enrich learning experiences as exemplified in various learning analytics projects in countries including Japan, it is very difficult for people without Internet connectivity to use such environments [28]. Older adults who do not use the Internet cannot access digital learning environments easily. The same is true for people living without reliable and affordable Internet infrastructure in developing regions including some Tanzanian communities.

© Springer Nature Switzerland AG 2020
P.-L. P. Rau (Ed.): HCII 2020, LNCS 12193, pp. 300–314, 2020.
https://doi.org/10.1007/978-3-030-49913-6_26

In rural marginal villages with most inhabitants being senior citizens, it may be extremely difficult for them to find someone who can help solve their technical problems with digital technologies and the Internet. In addition, people without access to digital learning environments would not be able to get evidence-based feedback from a system or an instructor due to the lack of required data for learning analytics. Because of these issues, the advances in digital learning-support technologies arguably widen the educational gap between the connected and the not connected.

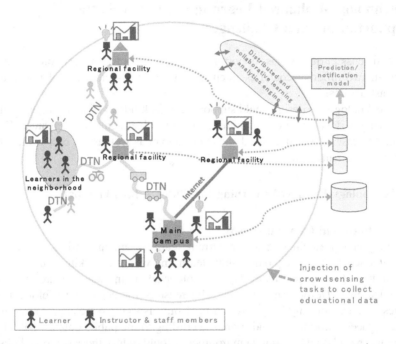

Fig. 1. Overview of the proposed platform. The illustration shows a school that has a main campus and three regional facilities. The main campus is connected to one of the regional facilities via the Internet. The other two regional facilities are not connected to the Internet. Learning contents and educational data are transmitted to and from these two regional facilities via delay-tolerant networking involving vehicles and pedestrians as "slow transporters of data."

Researchers have proposed technical solutions to deliver digital learning contents for teachers and learners in developing regions. However, existing proposals without intelligent and efficient data collection mechanisms cannot easily support evidence-based pedagogical approaches involving learning analytics. In this paper, we discuss a novel learning-support platform that integrates delay-tolerant networking (DTN) mechanisms and model-driven crowdsensing techniques to deliver learning materials and collect educational data (see Fig. 1). Staff members or volunteers at each regional facility serve as crowdsensing workers who collect educational data from learners by using a web form, a camera, etc. on their mobile devices.

The platform we propose could support various offline learners including people in developing communities and older adults. We thus look into the case of the super-aged society of Japan as well as the case of developing communities in Tanzania. Our platform employs active learning to collect useful educational data in an intelligent and efficient manner. The data are shared across different regional facilities and the main campus via DTN, thereby enabling a variety of analysis and visualization. Instructors, students, and other stakeholders can thus explore actionable insights for improving teaching and learning based on data.

2 Technology-Enhanced Learning: Current Status, Opportunities and Challenges

We next discuss current status, opportunities and challenges of technology-enhanced learning in two different countries, focusing on critical sociotechnical issues around ICT infrastructures.

The technology we design could support various kinds of offline learners including people living in developing communities as well as older adults in rural areas. We thus look into the case of the super-aged society of Japan as well as the case of developing communities in Tanzania.

2.1 Technology-Enhanced Learning for Older Adults in Japan

Current Status and Opportunities
Technology-enhanced lifelong and recurrent learning are increasingly perceived as important since they can help older adults learn knowledge and skills that can improve their quality of life. Indeed, many Japanese older adults in their 60's are interested in lifelong learning. Despite such interest, the reasons for not doing lifelong learning activities include not only busyness and cost but also lack of relevant opportunities, facilities, places, information, and friends according to the public opinion poll in Japan [7]. Internet-based digital learning environments could reduce these perceived obstacles substantially.

It is a relatively new idea to use learning analytics to understand and support older learners in lifelong learning scenarios [22]. Analyzing activities of older learners can be useful for improving learning materials and tools as well as providing relevant feedback to learners, instructors, and other stakeholders.

Challenges
Older and economically deprived people in rural areas cannot easily use Internet-based digital learning environments. Only about 68%, 47%, and 20% of people in their 60's, 70's, and 80's use the Internet, respectively, according to the survey conducted by the Japanese government in 2017. Other statistics show that the percentage of individuals using the Internet are much smaller for low income families and in rural areas.

Although digital learning environments and learning analytics can open up unexplored opportunities for older adults to improve their quality of life, lack of Internet connectivity for certain relevant population as well as the scarcity of "learning log" data about older learners make it difficult to pave the way for the future in which *all* is benefitted from digital learning technologies.

2.2   Technology-Enhanced Learning in Tanzania

Current Status and Opportunities

The need for deploying technology in improving the quality of education has been a prioritized agenda in both governmental and institutional levels in Tanzania. The government recognizes that quality education is fundamental for attainment of national sustainable development and it has been making substantial efforts in making sure that the target is realized. One way of supporting this was the formulation of National ICT Policy (United Republic of Tanzania, 2016) which (through its objectives), clearly stipulates the intent to use ICT to improve the quality of education delivery in all fields.

E-learning is a permanent agenda in the country and in response to this, the education sector, from primary to tertiary level, has been embarking on finding avenues of integrating ICT in teaching and learning activities. In the case of higher education sector, universities have put in place ICT infrastructure, corresponding mediums and developed virtual learning environments to enhance learning experiences and access to content. The rise of mobile technology is also a significant contributor to the demands pertaining to e-learning development.

The developments in e-learning in Tanzania have so far brought a plethora of advantages including improved access to learning materials, self-paced and flexible learning, reduced educational costs and improved teaching and learning practices. The current status of e-learning in Tanzanian higher education sector is in its fundamental stages with ample room for potential development. There has been an increasing deployment of virtual learning environments, to engage in online teaching and learning at both distance and on-campus institutions. Universities are acquiring learning management systems and invest in supplementing technologies such as mobile learning to ensure students get access to learning materials. However, further developments such as learning analytics and game-based learning are under exploited.

Information service in Tanzania is operated from the National Fibre Optic Cable Network named the National ICT broadband Backbone (NICTBB); and two submarine cables namely Eastern Africa Submarine Cable System (EASSY) and Southern and Eastern Africa Communication Network (SEACOM). The broadband provides leased connection to Mobile network operators, internet service providers, local television and radio stations and data service providers [31].

Challenges

Despite the policies and initiatives to establish the ICT infrastructure, the e-learning sector in Tanzania is still faced with problems: As in other African countries, the key challenges facing e-learning implementation include poor ICT infrastructure, lack of facilities and lack of internet connectivity. According to World Bank, by 2017 only 16% of total Tanzanian population has access to the internet as compared to Japan which is at 91%. There is a huge gap in terms of urban and rural access to ICT Services. In rural areas problems such as lack of reliable electricity and limited access to computers intensify the issues exponentially. For the case of the Open University of Tanzania which provides service through 30 regional centers across the country, this problem has been evident. Most students from remote areas do not have access to the internet and hence cannot access resources in Moodle [30]. In this regard, students have been supported by interactive CDs that are equipped with learning materials. Furthermore, lack of skilled human resources, technical skills and motivation amongst academic staff are identified as challenges as well.

3 Related Works

3.1 Technologies for Supporting Education in Developing Regions and Rural Areas

Researchers have proposed technologies for supporting education in developing regions. Brewer et al. discussed applications of intermittent, delay-tolerant networking (DTN) technologies for the education of children in developing regions. The applications they propose include a local content repository where students and teachers can store and retrieve digital stories, games, and other digital content that they create by using easy-to-use authoring tools. This application requires only intermittent networking for each school. Parikh and Lazowska discuss mobile applications that suit requirements of rural regions. In particular, they propose a framework called CAM, which support paper-based navigation and offline interaction using barcodes and mobile cameras [34]. They describe several applications of CAM, ranging from microfinance and healthcare to a type of local knowledge repository. The Digital Study Hall system [50] exploits intermittent networking technology, thin-client displays, and educational content repository to support usage scenarios such as lecture capture and replay, homework collection and feedback, and question-answer sessions in resource-starved village schools in rural India. However, these proposals do not support the collection of learning activity data, which makes it difficult to enable evidence-based pedagogical approaches in developing regions.

The rise of mobile technology in developing regions creates opportunities to develop novel e-learning environments. Mobile phones allow for bidirectional communication with learners, and thus we can collect data from learners by using interactive mechanisms such as mobile crowdsourcing. Several projects have deployed mobile crowdsoucing environments in developing regions. For example, Singh et al. developed an SMS-based prototype that provides real-time notification and information gathering capabilities [47]. Gupta et al. developed a mobile crowdsourcing platform that exploits SMS, making it accessible from a low-end mobile phone [13]. Their platform allows participation by people who do not own high-end mobile phones, thereby offering employment opportunities to low-income workers. There are many smartphone users in developing regions. Open-source tools such as Open Data Kit (ODK) [5] enables flexible and powerful data collection using web forms, cameras, microphones, sensors, GPS, and databases. ODK allows for an asynchronous means of data transfer, thereby supporting pervasive crowdsensing regardless of the availability of Internet connectivity. These mobile crowdsourcing technologies could be extended and integrated with digital learning environments. However, existing systems often incur too much burden on crowdworkers without intelligent mechanisms to minimize human labor, which makes it difficult to realize a successful crowd-powered evidence-based digital learning environments.

3.2 The Uses of Educational Data and Machine Learning for the Improvement of Learning

In recent years, the advancement of the machine learning technology has made large impacts in many fields, and some researchers have applied it in education to extract hidden information behind the learning behavior. For example, behavioral data of studetns can be used for dropout rates prediction, performance prediction, and course recommendation, etc. The historical data of students can be collected in a certain dimension, and we can predict dropout rates so that teachers can assist students in time, or predict students' performance to identify their weaknesses and suggest methods for improvements.

Again, teachers can promptly take measures to help students who have a high possibility of dropout continue their studies for a better future if we can predict student's dropout risk. Nicolae-Bogdan combined the data from the MaCom Lectio system and public online dataset as the datasets and applied machine learning methods in these datasets to predict dropout risks [39]. Random forest-based prediction achieves an accuracy of 93.47% in their experiments, showing that machine learning can effectively predict the high-school student's risk of dropout. Rovira et al. have also demonstrated the power of machine learning techniques in dropout prediction [36]. Sansone has shown that teachers can get more information from student's high-dimensional data and could use machine learning algorithms to effectively predict the risk of dropout of high school [38]. Dekker et al. have found techniques to improve the prediction of dropout without additional data about the students [9]. Lee and Chung used synthetic minority oversampling techniques (SMOTE) and ensemble approaches to get balanced samples and then evaluated the performance of random forest, boosted decision tree, random forest with SMOTE, and boosted decision tree with SMOTE, indicating that boosted decision tree is optimal [24]. Santana et al. used four classifiers to predict the dropout risk of online education students, which Tan and Shao also proved, and the results show that the SVM algorithm is optimal [37, 48]. Mduma et al. review the prediction of dropout method and suggested that, in developing countries, the prediction of dropout should also take school level factors into consideration [29].

There have been many studies on the prediction of students's performance. Sekeroglu et al. utilize two data sets to predict and classify the performance of students, respectively [42]. They use five machine learning techniques and their preliminary experimental results show that student's performance can be predicted and classified. Similarly, Pojon used logistic regression, decision tree, and Naive Bayes to predict the performance of students using two public datasets, suggesting that machine learning can effectively predict student's performance [35]. Belachew applied neural net, naïve Bayesian and SVM to the collected transcript data (i.e., final GPA and grades in all courses) of students at Wolkite University, and suggested that Naïve Bayesian have higher performance [2]. Khan et al. used a decision tree algorithm to predict the final score of each student in a programming course [21]. Elbadrawy applied a linear regression model in student performance prediction [10]. Qazdar et al. proposed two models based on machine learning method at H.E.K high school in Morocco to predict student performance in the next semester and the national exam results [32]. Zohair has proved that student's performance can be predicted with a small dataset, and also shown the efficiency of SVM when the size of a dataset is small [1]. Kaur et al. used a machine learning approach or machine learning classification method to predict student academic performance [20]. Livieris et al. used two semi-supervised learning approaches to predict student's performance and suggested that semi-supervised approaches can significantly improve the classification accuracy in the final examinations [26]. Kalles applied machine learning algorithms to predict the performance in the final exams of the student in distance learning [18].

Despite the developments in modern learning-support techniques such as predictive analytics, little work has been done on the integration of such techniques with the technological and social contexts in developing regions and rural areas.

4 Crowdsensing Educational Data

Educational data about learners, teachers, learning contents and contextual factors can be used to visualize, analyze and predict patterns of educational successes and failures. Systems can provide resources for reflecting on the past, present and future of educational environments to induce actionable insights. They can also recommend relevant information or provide pertinent advice for learners and teachers automatically or with some help from human experts.

Employing visualization, prediction, and recommendation techniques based on students' activity log data can help reduce dropouts as well as improve students' performance and satisfaction. For instance, effective intervention based on learning analytics can cut dropout rates, change students' behaviors, and improve students' performance [40].

Our experiences with learning analytics in university environments [33] suggest some of the attributes that can be used to analyze and predict dropouts and academic performance:

- Demographic information
- Attendance
- Scores of quizzes
- Submissions of assignments
- Access logs of learning materials
- Learning journals
- Responses to surveys (e.g., course evaluation surveys)
- Grades

Educational data can be collected at different places and at different times as learners may engage in self-paced learning as well as classroom-based learning. Thus, we can also consider contextual attributes such as location and time.

These types of information can be collected easily if all students use personal computers, high-speed Internet, and digital learning environments. In learning environments where students may use analog and/or offline media such as standalone personal computers, mobile phones without broadband networking, and even sheets of paper, the above types of information could be collected if we can leverage the power of human computation effectively. Instructors, assistants and volunteers can use their mobile devices to digitize the information on analog and/or offline media by using web forms and mobile cameras, and inject the digitized data into a delay-tolerant communication infrastructure. This can be understood as a type of crowdsensing that involves instructors, assistants and volunteers as crowdworkers. Apparently, making this approach successful requires minimization of the workload of crowdworkers.

5 Minimizing the Workload for Data Collection

To collect educational data successfully based on crowdsensing, it is critical to minimize the workload of crowdworkers. In this section, we propose an approach to urge crowdworkers to collect data from appropriate samples (i.e., learners), which can minimize the collective workload of all crowdworkers.

5.1 Model-Driven Crowdsensing

To minimize the workload, we exploit the general idea to reduce the costs of data collection, including human labor and mobile battery consumption, by optimizing collective behaviors of crowdworkers based on a model of the target environment. In our previous project called cooperative Human Probes [49], we have introduced a mechanism that minimizes battery consumption of mobile phones in urban crowdsensing scenarios by reducing sensing frequency in a cooperative manner. In addition, we proposed a crowd replication technique [14] that allows a small number of volunteers to collect human activity data efficiently based on a sampling strategy that is aware of an existing model of the target space. The model triggers dynamic instructions on crowdwoekers' smartphones, which can drive the behaviors of crowdworkers. Crowd replication can be considered as a type of mode-driven crowd sensing, which relies on cluster sampling where the physical entry points of the space are interpreted as clusters and random sampling is applied within each entry point to minimize bias to the distribution of user demographics. This approach can mitigate possible biases that are often difficult to avoid and understand with crowd sensing methods while minimizing crowdworkers' workload. In order to employ a similar approach for educational data, we devise an intelligent sampling mechanism based on active learning.

5.2 Active Learning

Active learning is a modern method in machine learning, aiming to reduce the sample size (namely the dataset), complexity, and increase the accuracy of the data tasks as much as possible with less data. The key hypothesis of active learning is that the learning mechanisms will be more intelligent if the learning algorithm can actively choose the most significant unlabeled data. An active learner will query only a small number of valuable unlabeled instances to be labeled by an oracle (or annotator) to automatically enlarge the labelled dataset, in an intelligent manner [43].

There are three main scenarios that have been studied of active learning, *membership query synthesis*, *stream-based selective sampling* and *pool-based sampling* [19, 43, 52]:

- In *query synthesis*, any unlabeled instance can be queried by an active learner, including the model-generated although it may have no practical meaning and cannot be labeled by human annotator. While the other scenarios do not have this problem that cannot be labelled, because the learner must query the instances of what it thinks important from the actual input pool.
- In *stream-based selective sampling*, the unlabeled instances will be query sequentially by the learner [25]. And the learner will decide whether the instance be annotated or not.
- In *pool-based sampling,* a large number of unlabeled instances are assumed to be available. In this kind of scenario, the learner should rank the entire unlabeled instances according to an informativeness measure, that is the pool of unlabeled instances, and then, query the most informative one [25]. The main difference between pool-based sampling and stream-based selective sampling is that the former should evaluate all unlabeled data before select query, while the latter just query the instance in sequence [44].

The measure of informativeness evaluation is vital in all active scenarios, and can be parted into four groups [3, 19, 46]:

- *Uncertainty selection*, which would query the most uncertain instance on the prediction of the current model.
- *Query by committee*, which query the most disagreeing instance of the committees' prediction. Each committee member is a different model based on the current training set.
- *Expected objective change*, which query the instance that could make the maximizing impact on the objective. For example, maximizing model change, maximizing the generalization error reduction, maximizing the output variance reduction.
- *Data-centered method*, which query the most representative of the most informative instance.

5.3   Active Learning-Based Crowdsensing

It can be seen that active learning and crowdsourcing are the key technologies for optimizing data collection and processing, and many researchers have conducted a lot of studies on the ways to integrate them [12]. Although existing studies have certain achievements on classification tasks, regression-based prediction tasks are rarely considered. In addition, there are fewer studies on crowdsourced data acquisition tasks than labelling tasks.

Lease suggest that crowdsourcing, with active learning, may provide new insights for better focusing annotation effort on the examples that will be most informative to the learner to accelerate model training, as well as reduce cost of annotation vs. traditional annotators [23]. Costa et al. propose two methods of combining crowdsourcing and active learning. The two methods were tested with Jester data set, a text humor classification benchmark, and the result shows promising improvements [8].

Crowdsourcing systems sometimes assign a task to multiple crowdworkers to control the quality of accomplished tasks. Techniques to deal with such redundancy can impact the collective workload of crowdworkers.

In the crowdsourcing scenario of active learning, many researches are conducted on the multi-annotator. Because of the carelessness and knowledge limitation in the target domain, the annotations generated by multiple crowdworkers can be noisy. In spite of the noisiness, Hsueh et al. have demonstrated that its performance is better than a single non-expert annotator for modeling [16]. Therefore, in active learning-based crowd-sourcing, many strategies to estimate and select the most suitable annotator as the oracle without experts were studied by researchers and many noise-robust schemes with unknown ground truth, which could iteratively evaluate the label quality and chose the most informative instance to query, were proposed [11, 27, 51, 53].

Again, conventional approaches rarely consider regression-based prediction tasks and data acquisition, which are important to minimize the workload for collecting and predicting educational information. We next describe our active learning-based sampling strategy for collecting and predicting educational information.

5.4   Sampling Strategy for Collecting and Predicting Educational Information

For the prediction of student performance, we can easily obtain plenty of students' learning data through various Internet-based methods in developed countries. However, in developing regions and rural areas without reliable network connections, such data could not be collected easily. As we discusses earlier, interactive CDs are mailed physically to learners across Tanzania without a systematic environment for collecting educational data from learners in remote areas. Collecting data from remote learners would enable prediction of their performance and thereby providing appropriate learning contents and feedback.

Distance learning students are located in different regions (the Open University of Tanzania provides learning service in 30 regional centers across the country). Crowdworkers including instructors, assistants and volunteers may use a mobile data collection tool to capture students' learning log data, however, it is prohibitively costly to collect data from all students. When we opt for collecting samples rather than entire population, a question is which samples to select for the quality of educational data and the effectiveness of relevant performance prediction.

Active learning can find the most informative data to improve the performance of prediction model. Therefore, we apply active learning in student's data collection in developing regions and rural areas to solve the problems raised above. We assume that a certain amount of data has been collected and a preliminary model of student performance prediction has been generated. The students whose information will effectively improve the performance of the model are s^*. We propose the process of finding s^* as follows:

1. The existing dataset $\mathcal{D}$ is clustered, and the $\mathcal{C} = \{c_1, c_2 \ldots, c_n\}$ are the result. Let $S_{c_i}(i \in [1, n])$ be the student who produce the data of category c_i.

2. $\mathcal{D}^{c_i}$ represents the dataset of category c_i. k samples extracted according to the data density from each $\mathcal{D}^{c_i}$ marked $\mathcal{D}_j^{c_i}(j \in [1, k])$. Gaussian noise is added to each $\mathcal{D}_j^{c_i}$, $\mathcal{D}_j^{c_i\prime} = \mathcal{D}_j^{c_i} + \lambda_j^{c_i}$, and make up the new dataset $\mathcal{D}^{c_i\prime}$.
3. The new dataset $\mathcal{D}^{c_i\prime}$ will be added to $\mathcal{D}$ to form a new dataset $\mathcal{D} \bigcup \mathcal{D}^{c_i\prime}$, and new prediction models will be re-trained in $\mathcal{D} \bigcup \mathcal{D}^{c_i\prime}$.
4. Compare the models with the original model, and we can find the class c^* that has the most influence on the model. We then obtain $s^* = S_{c^*}$.

6   Preliminary Data Collection Form

Figure 2 shows our preliminary data collection form that exploits Open Data Kit [5] to upload and visualize educational data on a cloud server. It records contextual information (location and time) as well as student's demographic information (ID, gender, age) and feedback (perceived difficulty and satisfaction, and comments). It can also capture student's handwritten learning journal entries. All of the data can be captured offline without requiring internet connectivity. The captured data will be uploaded to a server when the device becomes online.

Fig. 2. Preliminary data collection form that exploits Open Data Kit to upload and visualize educational data on a cloud server.

7   Conclusion and Future Work

Despite the continuous growth of global Internet users, almost 4 billion people do not use the Internet. In this context, we have discussed a learning-support platform for learners without an easy, reliable, and affordable means to access digital learning environments on the Internet.

Our proposed platform integrates delay-tolerant networking (DTN) mechanisms and active learning-based model-driven crowdsensing techniques to deliver learning materials and collect educational data efficiently.

Our future work includes the formative evaluation of the platform, including its preliminary mechanisms and tools, based on a user-centered approach involving stakeholders in Tanzania and Japan. We also intend to consider mechanisms for remedying cold start problems in predictive analytics.

Acknowledgement. This work was supported by JSPS KAKENHI Grant Number 17K00117.

References

1. Abu Zohair, L.M.: Prediction of Student's performance by modelling small dataset size. Int. J. Educ. Technol. Higher Educ. **16**(27) (2019). https://doi.org/10.1186/s41239-019-0160-3
2. Belachew, E.B., Gobena, F.A.: Student performance prediction model using machine learning approach: the case of wolkite university. Int. J. Adv. Res. Comput. Sci. Softw. Eng. **7**(2), 46–50 (2017)
3. Bernard, J., Zeppelzauer, M., Lehmann, M., Müller, M., Sedlmair, M.: Towards user-centered active learning algorithms. Comput. Graph. Forum **37**(3), 121–132 (2018)
4. Brewer, E., et al.: The case for technology in developing regions. IEEE Comput. **38**(6), 25–38 (2005)
5. Brunette, W., Sudar, S., Sundt, M., Larson, C., Beorse, J., Anderson, R.: Open Data Kit 2.0: a services-based application framework for disconnected data management. In: Proceedings of the 15th Annual International Conference on Mobile Systems, Applications, and Services (MobiSys 2017), 440–452 (2017)
6. Cabinet Office of Japan: White Paper on Aging Society in 2019. (in Japanese) https://www8.cao.go.jp/kourei/whitepaper/w-2019/html/zenbun/index.html. Accessed 22 Nov 2019
7. Cabinet Office of Japan: Public Opinion Poll on Lifeong Learning. (in Japanese). https://survey.gov-online.go.jp/h20/h20-gakushu/index.html. Accessed 31 Jan 2020
8. Costa, J., Silva, C., Antunes, M., Ribeiro, B.: On using crowdsourcing and active learning to improve classification performance. In: International Conference on Intelligent Systems Design and Applications (ISDA 2011), pp. 469–474 (2011)
9. Dekker, G.W., Pechenizkiy, M., Vleeshouwers, J.M.: Predicting students drop out: a case study. In: Proceedings of the 2nd International Conference on Educational Data Mining (EDM 2009), pp, 41–50 (2009)
10. Elbadrawy, A., Studham, S., Karypis, G.: Personalized multi-regression models for predicting students performance in course activities. In: Proceedings of 5th International Conference on learning analytics and knowledge (LAK 2019), pp. 16–20 (2015)
11. Fang, M., Yin, J., Tao, D.: Active learning for crowdsourcing using knowledge transfer. In: Proceedings of the Twenty-Eighth AAAI Conference on Artificial Intelligence (AAAI'114), vol. 3, pp. 1809–1815 (2014)

12. Gilyazev, R.A., Turdakov, D.Y.: Active learning and crowdsourcing: a survey of annotation optimization methods. Program. Comput. Softw. **44**(6), 476–491 (2018)
13. Gupta, A., Thies, W., Cutrell, E., Balakrishnan, R.: mClerk: enabling mobile crowdsourcing in developing regions. In: Proceedings of the Conference on Human Factors in Computing Systems (CHI 2012), pp. 1843–1852 (2012)
14. Hemminki, S., Kuribayashi, K., Konomi, S.I., Nurmi, P.T., Tarkoma, S.: Crowd replication: sensing-assisted quantification of human behaviour in public spaces. ACM Trans. Spat. Algorithms Syst. (TSAS) (2019). Article No. 15
15. Hilbert, M.: Big data for development: a review of promises and challenges. Dev. Policy Rev. **34**(1), 135–174 (2016)
16. Hsueh, P.Y., Melville, P., Sindhwani, V.: Data quality from crowdsourcing. In: Proceedings of the NAACL HLT Workshop on Active Learning for Natural Language Processing, Boulder, Colorado, pp, 27–35 (2009)
17. JiWon, Y.: Identifying significant indicators using LMS data to predict course achievement in online learning. Internet Higher Educ. **29**, 23–30 (2016)
18. Kalles, D., Pierrakeas, C.: Analyzing student performance in distance learning with genetic algorithms and decision trees. Appl. Artif. Intell. **20**(8), 655–674 (2006)
19. Kangkang, L., Xiuze, Z., Fan, L., Wenhua, Z., Alterovitz, G.: Deep probabilistic matrix factorization framework for online collaborative filtering. IEEE Access **7**, 56117–56128 (2019)
20. Kaur, A., Umesh, N., Singh, B.: Machine learning approach to predict student academic performance. Int. J. Comput. Sci. Eng. (IJRASET) **6**(4), 734–742 (2018)
21. Khan, I., Al Sadiri, A., Ahmad, A. R., Jabeur, N.: Tracking student performance in introductory programming by means of machine learning. In: Proceedings of 4th MEC International Conference on Big Data and Smart City (ICBDSC 2019), pp. 1–6 (2019)
22. Konomi, S., et al.: Towards supporting multigenerational co-creation and social activities: extending learning analytics platforms and beyond. In: Streitz, N., Konomi, S. (eds.) DAPI 2018. LNCS, vol. 10922, pp. 82–91. Springer, Cham (2018). https://doi.org/10.1007/978-3-319-91131-1_6
23. Lease, M.: On quality control and machine learning in crowdsourcing. In: Proceedings of the 11th AAAI Conference on Human Computation (AAAIWS'11 2011), pp. 97–102 (2011)
24. Lee, S., Chung, J.Y.: The machine learning-based dropout early warning system for improving the performance of dropout prediction. Appl. Sci. **9**(15), 1–14 (2019)
25. Liu, D., Liu, Y.: An active learning algorithm for multi-class classification. Pattern Anal. Appl. **22**(3), 1051–1063 (2019)
26. Livieris, I.E., Drakopoulou, K., Tampakas, V.T., Mikropoulos, T.A., Pintelas, P.: Predicting secondary school students' performance utilizing a semi-supervised learning approach. J. Educ. Comput. Res. **57**(2), 448–470 (2019)
27. Liyue, Zh., Sukthankar, G., Sukthankar, R.: Incremental relabeling for active learning with noisy crowdsourced annotations. In: 2011 IEEE Third International Conference on Privacy, Security, Risk and Trust and 2011 IEEE Third International Conference on Social Computing, Boston, MA (PASSAT/SocialCom 2011), pp. 728–733 (2011)
28. Mathew, H.: Bridging the digital divide with off-line e-learning. Dist. Educ. **39**(1), 110–121 (2018)
29. Mduma, N., Kalegele, K., Machuve, D.: A survey of machine learning approaches and techniques for student dropout prediction. Data Sci. J. **8**(14), 1–10 (2019). https://doi.org/10.5334/dsj-2019-014
30. Moodle. https://moodle.org/. Accessed 28 Dec 2019
31. NICTBB. Status of the NICTBB and Prospects for local contents development in Tanzania. http://www.nictbb.co.tz/news.php. Accessed 28 Dec 2019

32. Qazdar, A., Er-Raha, B., Cherkaoui, C., Mammass, D.: A machine learning algorithm framework for predicting students performance: a case study of baccalaureate students in Morocco. Educ. Inf. Technol. **24**, 3577–3589. https://doi.org/10.1007/s10639-019-09946-8 (2019)

33. Okubo, F., Yamada, M., Oi, M., Shimada, A., Taniguchi, Y., Konomi, S.: Learning support systems based on cohesive learning analytics. In: Emerging Trends in Learning Analytics, pp. 223–248. Brill, Leiden (2019)

34. Parikh, T.S., Lazowska, E.D.: Designing an architecture for delivering mobile information services to the rural developing world. In: Proceedings of the 15th International Conference on World Wide Web, pp. 791–800. ACM Press, New York (2006)

35. Pojon, M.: Using Machine Learning to Predict Student Performance. Faculty of Natural Sciences Software Development of University of Tampere (2017)

36. Rovira, S., Puertas, E., Igual, L.: Data-driven system to predict academic grades and dropout. PLoS ONE **12**(2), 1–21 (2017)

37. Santana, M.A., Costa, E.B., Neto, B.F.S., Silva, I.C.L., Rego, J.B.A.: A predictive model for identifying students with dropout profiles in online courses. In: Proceedings of CEUR Workshop, p. 1446 (2015)

38. Sansone, D.: Beyond early warning indicators: high school dropout and machine learning. Oxford Bull. Econ. Stat. **81**(2), 456–485 (2019). https://doi.org/10.1111/obes.12277

39. Şara, N. B., Halland, R., Igel, C., Alstrup, S.: High-school dropout prediction using machine learning: a Danish large-scale study. In: Proceedings of the 23rd European Symposium on Artificial Neural Networks, Computational Intelligence and Machine Learning (ESANN 2015), pp. 319–324 (2015)

40. Sclater, N., Mullan, J.: JISC briefing: learning analytics and student success – assessing the evidence. In: Effective Learning Analytic (2017)

41. (2017). http://repository.jisc.ac.uk/6560/1/learning-analytics_and_student_success.pdf

42. Sekeroglu, B., Dimililer, K., Tuncal, K.: Student performance prediction and classification using machine learning algorithms. In: Proceedings of 8th International Conference on Educational and Information Technology (ICEIT 2019), pp. 7–11 (2019)

43. Settles, B.: Active learning literature survey. University of Wisconsin-Madison Department of Computer Sciences (2009)

44. Settles, B.: Active Learning: Synthesis Lectures on Artificial Intelligence and Machine Learning. Carnegie Mellon University (2012)

45. Shailendra, P., et al.: Online education: worldwide status, challenges, trends, and implications. J. Global Inf. Technol. Manag. **21**(4), 233–241 (2018)

46. Shuji, H., Peiying, H., Peilin, Z., Steven, C.H.H., Miao, C.: Online active learning with expert advice. ACM Trans. Knowl. Disc. Data **12**(5), 1–22 (2018). https://doi.org/10.1145/3201604

47. Singh, A., Li, Y., Sun, Y., Sun, Q.: An intelligent mobile crowdsourcing information notification system for developing countries. In: Proceedings of Machine Learning and Intelligent Communications (MLICOM 2016), pp. 139–149 (2017)

48. Tan, M., Shao, P.: Prediction of student dropout in E-learning program through the use of machine learning method. Int. J. Emerging Technol. Learn. **10**(1), 11–17 (2015)

49. Thepvilojanapong, N., Konomi, S., Tobe, Y.: A study of cooperative human probes in urban sensing environments. IEICE Trans. Commun. Spec. Sect. Fundam. Issues Deployment Ubiquitous Sen. Networks, **E93-B**(11). 2868–2878 (2010)

50. Wang, R., et al.: The digital study hall. Computer Science Department, Princeton University, Technical report TR-723-05 (2005)

51. Welinder, P., Perona, P.: Online crowdsourcing: rating annotators and obtaining cost-effective labels. In: 2010 IEEE Computer Society Conference on Computer Vision and Pattern Recognition - Workshops, San Francisco, CA, pp. 25–32 (2010)
52. Xu, Q., Zheng, R.: When data acquisition meets data analytics: a distributed active learning framework for optimal budgeted mobile crowdsensing. In: Proceedings of IEEE Conference on Computer Communications (IEEE INFOCOM 2017), Atlanta, GA, pp. 1–9 (2017). https://doi.org/10.1109/infocom.2017.8057034
53. Yan, Y., Rosales, R., Fung, G., Dy, J.G.: Active learning from crowds. In: Proceedings of the 28th International Conference on Machine Learning (ICML 2011), pp. 1161–1168 (2011)

The Current Situation of AI Foreign Language Education and Its Influence on College Japanese Teaching

Tzu-Hsuan Kuo[(✉)]

Fuzhou College of Foreign Languages and Trade, Fuzhou, Republic of China
kaku322@gmail.com

Abstract. With the rapid development of artificial intelligence (AI), the development of AI technology is bound to have an important impact on foreign language education. Therefore, under the foreign language teaching system, "AI + Education" has become a new trend of current research and can improve the teaching efficiency of college foreign language education. Therefore, AI has gradually become the focus of foreign language education. At present, AI mainly plays four roles in the world: learning partner, student, AI teacher and classroom teacher.

However, through the development of "AI + Education", Japanese education is not only applied in pre class, classroom, after class, extracurricular, examination and other teaching environments, but also brings profound changes to Japanese teaching.

The purpose of this thesis is to analyze the current application of AI in foreign language teaching and its influence on College Japanese teaching, as well as the role-playing and future challenges. It can provide reference ideas and experience for College Japanese education in the development of AI teachers and the construction of dual teacher classroom. Its research methods are data search and induction, and in terms of the impact on Japanese teaching, questionnaire survey is used to analyze the relevance of its data. The results of the analysis are helpful to understand the application and current situation of students' AI + education. Furthermore, effective improvement strategies will be provided, which will contribute to the development of foreign language teaching and Japanese education in the future.

Keywords: Artificial intelligence · Japanese teaching in colleges and universities · Intelligent teaching system · Network teaching · Foreign language teaching

1 Literature Discussion

The traditional Japanese teaching method focuses on the basic theory education, too much emphasis on the Japanese grammar teaching, and the students who are trained have strong ability to take the test, but the Japanese Listening and speaking ability is weak, which is difficult to adapt to the needs of the test. Under the background of the Internet Age, the Japanese teachers should make full use of the Internet connection and

© Springer Nature Switzerland AG 2020
P.-L. P. Rau (Ed.): HCII 2020, LNCS 12193, pp. 315–324, 2020.
https://doi.org/10.1007/978-3-030-49913-6_27

information-based teaching methods to give full play to the main position of the students, actively guide, and make Students actively learn knowledge, strengthen skills, and cultivate students' comprehensive abilities in listening, speaking, reading and writing.

Some representative references about AI AI application in foreign language teaching. Yu and Wang (2019) explained in detail the definition of "knowledge outsourcing" and the definition based on four layers of knowledge outsourcing. Chen, Huang, Zeng (2019) explained the functions and roles of AI in the world, and gave great help to the four challenges AI teachers will face in the future, such as technical, application, acceptance, ethical judgment and future development direction. Gao (2019) mentioned in the research on the role orientation and transformation of teachers in the context of AI that the role of practical teachers changed from lecturer to tutor, from single leader to collaborative learner. The emergence and development of song (2019) information technology has provided many teaching tools for the education industry, such as PPT, pictures, videos and other content display by the original abstract teaching content in a specific way in front of students. Zhou (2019) explained clearly the application analysis and ways of network resources in Japanese teaching. Yu (2018) proposed that under the background of AI Artificial Intelligence in the future, teachers, as the main participants of school curriculum reform, must provide accurate preparation for students. It must be consistent with personalized talent training and ability improvement. First of all, we must pay more attention to the cultivation of core quality oriented talents. It should be the core and focus of human teachers' attention to change from knowledge system oriented teaching, to the cultivation of core literacy, to the application of situational socialization of students' creative ability, aesthetic ability and collaborative ability. Secondly, we should pay more attention to the cultivation of the thinking mode of man-machine combination. Using the thinking mode of man-machine combination to significantly improve the productivity of education, education can achieve the large-scale coverage of everyone, and can achieve the personalized development matching with.

2   The Current Situation of "AI + JAPANESE TEACHING" and the Application and Presentation of "KNOWLEDGE OUTSOURCING"

"In December 2015, Xi Jinping attended the second world Internet Conference and made an important speech. At the meeting, China Internet development foundation established "China Internet + alliance" with relevant enterprises. This series of policy background and situation marked the real arrival of China's "Internet +" era. In addition, Yu Weiguo, Secretary of the CPC Fujian Provincial Committee, put forward "a higher starting point to promote the construction of a new Fujian" on April 17, 2019, during the inspection of the work of the provincial government, which said that the development of Fujian's digital economy has stepped into a fast lane. According to the data, at present, the total digital scale of the country has exceeded 130 million yuan, forming a digital economic development grid with software and information technology service industry, communication service industry as the growth point, big data, Internet of things, cloud computing, mobile Internet, artificial intelligence, etc. as the breakthrough population.

Therefore, we should attach importance to Internet economic thinking in economic development. At the same time, foreign language education should conform to the trend of the new era and cultivate more useful talents for our country. The era of "Internet +" is such an era. It has been integrated into all aspects of our life and has a great impact on our study and life. Therefore, under the background of "Internet +" and "Ai +" era, the current situation of foreign language teaching, how to conform to the trend and integrate with the reality, is worth us to sort out and analyze. Therefore, the use of network resources in foreign language teaching has three importance: first, network learning resources are very rich, students can choose freely, which can greatly improve the learning efficiency of students, and promote them to form a good habit of independent learning. 2 Network resources make Japanese teaching more impressive, including images, audio, video, animation, etc. teachers can step-by-step teaching, and gradually cultivate students' foreign language literacy. At the same time, students can also deeply study foreign language structure. In the learning of these resources, we should play a subjective initiative. Acquire rich foreign language knowledge and arouse students' strong interest and enthusiasm. Three, network resources originally belong to modern information technology, which is different from traditional teaching. It is more innovative and meets the needs of modern education. Teachers can implement targeted teaching to cultivate the ability and quality of each student. It can be seen that the application of Internet resources in foreign language teaching is very important.

In this case, due to the limited ability and capacity of individual learning time information processing, it will be more difficult for a single individual to cope with the exponential and growing information and obtain the content to meet the needs of individual development. Under the inevitable pressure, the change of the traditional way of knowledge will inevitably result in the outsourcing of knowledge. Therefore, we need to think with the help of intelligent devices to adapt to the new way of life in the environment of information upheaval. Therefore, the concept of "knowledge outsourcing" in the era of artificial intelligence and its significance and development status.

Yu and Wang (2019) pointed out in the definition and meaning of "knowledge outsourcing", the emergence and wide application of intelligent technology and intelligent equipment have brought opportunities for the change of human knowledge mode. Intelligent equipment has gradually become an important tool to assist human thinking and knowledge, and the thinking mode of man-machine combination will also become the basic thinking mode for human beings to adapt to society in the information age, which can assist human beings to adapt to the society The basic direction of the transformation of human thinking direction is to break through the limit of individual knowledge, control the complex situation beyond the level of individual knowledge, deal with the massive information beyond the ability of individual knowledge, and deal with the behavior evolution beyond the speed of individual knowledge. Because the core of the direction of thinking and knowledge with the help of external devices is to outsource the lack of human knowledge ability to external intelligent devices, it is defined as "knowledge outsourcing". From the perspective of foreign language teaching, foreign language learning is the process of establishing a social knowledge link between individuals and external networks. The link moves from a pure human perspective to a dual perspective of human and knowledge. The link process includes two types of nodes: social network relationship node and knowledge network relationship node. Through this node as content sharing, the negotiation and exchange of foreign language learning can realize the connection, aggregation, sublimation and creation of knowledge, and then extend the brain of a single individual to realize the promotion of the depth of knowledge. As a knowledge scaffold for foreign language learners to expand the breadth and depth of learning, it can provide support for learning from different perspectives. Its cognitive outsourcing can be divided into four types: one is the outsourcing of connecting computing information: the functions of growing information memory, storage, processing, supplement and auxiliary. 2. Outsourcing of connected perceptual information: strengthen the recognition of learning image, voice, emotion and perception. Third, outsourcing of connected cognitive information: it emphasizes the function of computing, reasoning and analyzing the complex information behind the perceptible transaction. 4. Outsourcing connecting social networks: an important way for individuals to interact directly and indirectly to promote domain accumulation and social development, and to promote deep-seated exchange, sublimation and feedback of knowledge.

3   The Role and Function of "AI+" in Japanese Teaching

The role and function of "Ai +" in Japanese teaching is to construct specific Japanese teaching work under the framework of human-computer cooperative teaching, give full play to the work of Japanese teaching and show the cooperation with Japanese learners and promote the development of students' all-round learning, practice the tacit understanding of Japanese efficient teaching, and show the core value of AI as the two main bodies of artificial intelligence and human brain intelligence Value. Therefore, Yu and Wang (2019) play four main roles: one is AI agent, two is AI assistant, three is teachers and AI partner.

1. AI agent is a low-level collaboration, which means replacing the real teachers' intelligent style of dealing with low-level, monotonous and repetitive work, and using calculators to deal with simple things. For example, grading, assignment, examination paper, grading, score statistics, lesson preparation, parents' feedback, etc. These tasks are highly repetitive and regular, with low intellectual input, but they need to spend a lot of time and energy, make teachers overwork, affect teachers' satisfaction and identity to their work, and even affect teachers' teaching, professional development, and the creativity of education.
2. AI assistant means that Japanese teachers can use AI to deal with mechanical repetition automatically, which can greatly improve work efficiency, and can deal with problems with complete rules. However, the process of education is also the process of emotional interaction and creation besides knowledge transfer. Japanese learners' subjective feelings, emotional experiences, etc. have an important impact on learners' subjective feelings, emotional experiences, etc. on learning results.

However, AI agent can not analyze the problem by combining the emotional experience and life experience of learners, which makes it difficult to make a precise and comprehensive interpretation of the meaning behind the evaluation report of Japanese learners, and then it is difficult to provide adaptive solutions, which is the bottleneck of AI agent. In this case, Japanese teachers should intervene to play a guiding role in the machine, let AI act as a Japanese teacher assistant, enhance the intelligence and intelligence of AI in dealing with affairs through the education intelligence of Japanese teachers, so as to improve the efficiency of Japanese teachers in dealing with teaching and educating people. Therefore, the AI assistant is a Japanese teacher's use of AI to improve the normal work efficiency. It is the embodiment of low intelligence in AI. With the help of its perceptual intelligence, it can process the teaching and learning data collected. The Japanese teacher provides meaning and interpretation for the data, and the teacher will enhan.

3. AI teachers are super Japanese teachers who combine human and computer. At this time, AI has cognitive intelligence, which can significantly enhance the ability of teachers in perception and knowledge, break through the limit of teachers' individual knowledge, and make Japanese teachers have greater educational creativity. Traditional Japanese teachers emphasize the design of teaching, the teaching of content, the evaluation and feedback of learning. In the era of artificial intelligence, knowledge is no longer the only standard to measure Japanese learners. The cultivation of corresponding problem-solving ability, the improvement of creativity, the shaping of social interaction ability, and the correct guidance of mental and physical health are all important aspects of Japanese teachers' work, such as educating people, facing the typical problems such as fighting, early love, over worship of stars and so on in the process of children's growth Often because they don't understand the characteristics of pedagogy, psychology, social science and other knowledge behind the problem, they can't start, or just teach or intervene rudely, which is not conducive to the healthy growth of children. In the face of such a complex Japanese teaching work, teachers need to have the ability to make correct decisions according to the analysis of teaching development and laws, and then promote teaching management and education quality improvement.

4. AI partner is the most advanced human-computer collaboration mode. At this time, AI has social intelligence, and can interact with human Japanese teachers in a social way. At the same time, AI's creativity and autonomy reach the level of human Japanese teachers. It can independently communicate with human Japanese teachers in an equal way, and Practice co evolution and mutual promotion. When AI's intelligence and autonomy are further enhanced and enter the era of strong artificial intelligence or super artificial intelligence, AI will become a socialized and independent individual with independent consciousness and independent problem-solving partner of AI Japanese teachers and human Japanese teachers. AI will no longer rely on the problem-solving rules designed by human Japanese teachers, but can be an individual with social intelligence and human day The acquisition of new rules in communication and coordination provides new services. Therefore, as the highest form of human-computer collaboration, AI partner's socialized intelligence

is the vision of AI technology development. It will still rely on a large number of social and cultural interaction data, and no longer rely on human summarized data interaction rules and patterns. Therefore, human Japanese teachers should not only cooperate with machines, but also guide the development of machine intelligence. As a kind of outsourcing of social intelligence, machines can help and promote human beings according to their reasonable needs. It will also show different expressions of joy, anger, sadness, joy and so on because of human guidance. This kind of behavior and human is a kind of partnership and an intelligent machine with emotional life, rather than a lifeless intelligent machine.

4   The Importance of AI Artificial Intelligence Resources Application to Japanese teaching

From the role and function of "Ai +" in Japanese teaching, we can see that the reasonable use of network resources is very important for Japanese teaching. Schools must plan carefully and build a good learning environment so that AI can interpret its functions. It has three unique advantages in foreign language teaching. First, AI intelligent resources generated through network resources belong to modern information technology, which is different from the traditional teaching mode. It is innovative and adapts to the needs of modern education. Second, AI teaching makes Japanese learners more intuitive, including images, music, video, animation, etc. teachers can gradually cultivate students' Japanese literacy step by step. Three AI learning is very rich, students can choose freely, which can greatly improve the learning efficiency of students and promote them to form a good habit of independent learning. In addition, the use of AI intelligent resources can enhance students' listening ability while learning Japanese. In the traditional way of listening teaching, students' Japanese listening is generally weak, and the incomplete listening system makes foreign language learning unable to break through and slow progress. In order to improve students' listening ability, we should make full use of AI intelligent resources to train students in Japanese and gradually develop their listening ability. At the same time, students need to actively communicate with teachers to fill their own learning loopholes. So as to practice the comprehensive and balanced development. The resources and contents of AI intelligence are very rich and extensive. Teachers should consciously choose to help students with foreign language listening training and testing with the help of rich and diverse teaching resources. In combination with students' individual characteristics, they should carry out various teaching courses to improve their listening ability.

In addition, because of AI resources, improve students' Japanese reading skills, reading and writing as an important part of learning Japanese, students must fully understand and master the basic reading ability. In the classroom, teachers can use AI teaching to improve students' Japanese reading literacy and help them to learn comprehensive Japanese knowledge. For example, teachers can organize students to watch micro courses for one-to-one reading training. At the same time, the school can set up an organization to arrange Japanese listening exercises in class according to the time and times of the curriculum, so as to effectively enhance students' reading ability. What is the meaning of asking students questions through AI intelligent resources? At the same time, teachers provide Japanese reading skills and methods to master correct Japanese reading skills.

Using AI intelligent equipment can improve the spoken Japanese level. In the training of spoken Japanese, because there is no environment to communicate with foreigners, it is always the most difficult. Therefore, teachers can use the diversity of AI intelligence to improve students' oral Japanese level. Therefore, teachers can use the diversity of AI resources on the Internet to provide an opportunity platform for Japanese communication and expression. Also through AI platform, set up listening practice, let students listen more and understand more properly every day. Teachers can also use AI for Japanese video endorsement or interview practice, download software and app, etc. Interactive teaching and application of Japanese at any time.

Therefore, network AI learning is a necessary tool for future development. Practice teaching effect through teaching and communication. Through the above analysis, we know that AI intelligence is very important for Japanese teaching and learning. In the course of Japanese learning in the future, it can be imagined that the application of AI Artificial Intelligence is becoming more and more popular and developed. The use of AI is not only around every aspect of our lives. Especially in the study of various subjects, we should rely on his support and assistance. Therefore, in addition to the development of Japanese education, it is also necessary to have a better active use and understanding. Therefore, it can be predicted that the relationship between AI and foreign language teaching is mutually enhanced and shaped. The mutually evolved AI can not only enhance the teaching ability of Japanese teachers, but also enhance the educational wisdom of AI. Therefore, in this mutually reinforcing development and evolution, Japanese teachers will face the challenges of AI's technicality, usability, acceptability and ethics. In Japanese teaching, AI teachers have the superficial ability to provide learners with personalized learning experience, and can also liberate human teachers, so that human teachers can get rid of heavy, repetitive and monotonous lectures and homework correction work. We should pay more attention to the research of innovation and enter a new era of innovation and breakthrough.

It can be imagined that in the future, the relationship between AI and Japanese teachers is mutually reinforcing, shaping and advancing.

In this way, AI can enhance the ability of Japanese teachers to carry out educational work, and Japanese teachers can also enhance the educational wisdom of AI. In this mutually reinforcing development and evolution, the following three core types of Japanese education may emerge. 1. The change of the focus of Japanese teacher's work: in the future, the focus of teacher's work in the era of human-computer cooperation is not only the traditional "preaching, teaching and solving puzzles", but also the need to stimulate students' curiosity and imagination, cultivate creative critical thinking, so as to achieve individualized and accurate education for students. The core value of teachers is not only the development of subject knowledge and professional skills, but also the cultivation of teachers' core literacy, such as humanistic background, responsibility, national identity, cross-cultural communication and aesthetic appreciation. The teacher's responsibility is not to irrigate knowledge, but to help students to dig out everyone's superficial quality, to become the spiritual tutor of students, to play a wise role in cultivating students' wisdom, helping students to become talents and enlightening students' minds. Human Japanese teachers will not be replaced, but cooperate with artificial intelligence teachers to undertake teaching tasks, and show their unique advantages in the process of human-computer cooperation. In the future, Japanese teachers will be able to provide reports of diagnosing students, and explain and treat the functions of their programs in combination with artificial intelligence technology. Therefore, in the future, Japanese teachers will have a more detailed and individualized division of labor. The individualized problems will be completed by human teachers, and the common and simple repetitive problem. 2. The change of teachers' working style. In the era of artificial intelligence, teachers' working style will change greatly, most of the knowledge teaching will be undertaken by artificial intelligence, more of which is the design of learning, urging, encouraging and accompanying, more of which is the emotional communication between teachers and students. The future education environment is a combination of virtual and real environment supported by artificial intelligence. There are thousands of learning services online and offline. Different AI supports students' free combination and teachers play different roles, such as learning service design, learning companionship, emotional motivation, learning problem diagnosis and transformation, learning guidance student cliff development planning, planning and design of social activities, etc. The main work style of teachers will change in time and quality. The future work of teachers will become (1) design and development of learning services. (2) Personalized guidance. (3) Organization of comprehensive learning activities. (4) Social network connection guide. (5) Diagnosis and improvement of learning problems. (6) Mental health management and counseling. (7) Physical health monitoring and promotion. (8) The influence of faith and value. (9) Development assessment and improvement. (10) The influence of cliff development planning. (11) Peer help professional growth. (12) The final account of human-computer education. (13) AI education service ethics supervision. Teachers' social coordination has changed. Social division of labor or social coordination is the external manifestation of production relations. Efficient social division of labor is an important way to simplify labor, improve work efficiency, and promote productivity change. However, the change of technology driven work style and the large-scale improvement of work efficiency will lead to the incongruity between traditional social division of labor and production relations, and then lead to the change of social division of labor. The industrialization revolution has promoted the large-scale and refined social division of labor, which makes the role of teachers as knowledge imparters more and more prominent, and the category of teachers' knowledge inheritance more specific: with the impact of artificial intelligence on the field of educational reception, the social division of teachers needs to be further changed. In the future (1) teachers' social division of labor is more and more detailed, and teachers' responsibilities are more and more professional. (2) The work of teachers has changed from the simple coordination of individuals to the large-scale coordination of groups. (3) The process of teachers' work is more and more smooth, and the boundary is more and more fuzzy. (4) The cooperative objects of teachers' work are more and more diverse, and human-computer cooperation has become the mainstream instead of human cooperation.

5   Empirical Analysis of "AI + JAPANESE TEACHING"

Based on the explanation and analysis of the above related theories, the author tries to interview ten experts who are engaged in Japanese teaching by oral way. There are five parts in the questionnaire. The first part is the basic information: including gender, age, years of Japanese teaching. The second part is the current situation of "Ai + Japanese Teaching": including whether there is any way of using artificial intelligence in teaching, and what is its situation?. The third part uses the content of the third chapter to access whether artificial intelligence actually includes the main roles and functions of the four AI agents, two AI assistants, three AI teachers and AI partners. The fourth part is the interaction and influence between AI and teachers in the future. The results are as follows: the first part of the basic information: male teachers (3 persons), female teachers (7 persons). Age: 40–50 years (5 persons), 50–60 years (5 persons). Teaching years of Japanese: 5–10 years (6 persons), more than 10 years (4 persons).

The second part is the current situation of "Ai + Japanese Teaching": all the teachers use AI to engage in teaching and auxiliary teaching. Among them, 8 teachers think it is necessary to use this way to interact in listening and speaking. Moreover, the students' ability of listening and speaking has been improved in a short period of time due to AI teaching, and they are also more dare to speak and face unclear questions. At the same time, AI teaching courses are being implemented and developed in these teachers' schools.

The third part of AI includes four parts in practice: the main roles and functions of AI agent, AI assistant, AI teacher and AI partner. In terms of the role of agent and assistant teachers, the five young teachers think it is possible, but the older teachers don't agree with it. They think AI can't replace teachers' intentions and feelings. At the same time, the data and data of AI must be input by teachers in advance to respond correctly. But it is feasible in the roles and functions of AI teachers and AI partners. In particular, it is very appropriate to input the theoretical knowledge before teaching and partner role-playing.

The fourth part is the interaction and influence between AI and teachers in the future. All the teachers agree that it is necessary for the future cooperation of human-computer teaching. Because it can achieve the effect of division of labor and coordination. It's true that basic theoretical information can also be properly input. Let AI teachers replace human teachers in teaching. And it can make students do more practice and response, and at the same time, it can reduce the burden of human teachers, make more interaction with students and carry out teaching development and research. For teachers, the coordination between AI and teachers is very important and can help students improve the number and practice of listening, speaking, reading and writing. Therefore, Japanese teachers agree that AI + Japanese teaching is the trend of future development, and also encourage Japanese teachers to break through personal factor learning and AI interaction. Develop vivid, lively and creative Japanese teaching.

6 Conclusion

In the process of the integration of artificial intelligence and education, with the increasing ability of artificial intelligence in helping teachers to solve problems such as teaching design, teaching implementation, after-school guidance, intelligent evaluation, intelligent teaching and research, individual reflection, etc., machines will gradually replace the cooperative teachers, listening and evaluating teachers in traditional teaching and become the most important working partners of teachers. Therefore, this study suggests that teachers engaged in foreign language teaching and Japanese Teaching in the future should actively cooperate with and develop online teaching and Ai Ai Ai teaching courses. In the face of the needs of the vast number of learners, we should break through the traditional teaching methods, develop situational intelligent teaching, develop a lively and organized teaching system for students, and achieve accurate teaching. Teachers will become students' companions in the learning process to meet students' personalized needs and development. To encourage students to have situational knowledge and to be able to really put themselves into the real correspondence when learning a foreign language. Therefore, the future "Ai + foreign language teaching" and "Ai + Japanese Teaching" are the development trend, and every foreign language learner and foreign language teacher must learn and develop.

References

1. Li, J.: Discussion on the micro course teaching mode in Colleges and universities in the era of "Internet +". China higher Education Research (2017)
2. Du, S., Wang, X.: Discussion on the reform of curriculum teaching structure in the era of "Internet +". Education Discussion (2017)
3. Liu, G., Li, J., Liang, H.: China Higher Education Research (2016)
4. Zhou, Y.: Integration of "Internet +" and higher education. Research on Practical Language Teaching in Contemporary Education (2016)
5. Chen, J., Zhao, J.: Professional Development of University Teachers under "Internet + education". Education Theory and Practice (2016)
6. Yu de, Y.: The construction of teacher education curriculum resources under the background of "Internet +". Education Theory and Practice (2016)
7. Ma, X.: deconstruction of teachers' professional development in the era of "Internet +". Modern Educational Technology (2016)
8. Wei, Z.: Research on problems and countermeasures of teaching and learning in China's universities in the era of "Internet +". Master's thesis of Xi'an University of Technology (2018)
9. Sun, di.: Research on Teachers' role cognition in classroom teaching under the background of "Internet +", master's thesis of Zhejiang Normal University (2015)
10. Berge, Z.L.: Facilitating computer conferencing: recommendations from the field. Educ. Technol. 35(1), 15–30 (1995)
11. OECD: Staying Ahead-In-service Training and Teacher Professional Development (1998)
12. Boyer, E.L.: Scholarship Reconsidered. Carnegie Foundation and Jossey Bass, San Francisco (1990)

Creativity Initiative: Design Thinking Drives K12 Education from a Future Thinking

Yin Li and Zhiyong Fu[✉]

Tsinghua University, Beijing, China
liyinl9@mails.tsinghua.edu.cn,
fuzhiyong@tsinghua.edu.cn

Abstract. This paper analyzes the practical effects and problems of current design thinking activities in the field of education. By investigating the basic characteristics of current design thinking activities involved in k12 education in China. On the basis of this data analysis, this paper uses MLP and CLA tools to comb out a guiding framework for the development of young people's innovation ability driven by design thinking. This framework shows the opportunity, function and significance of design thinking in China's educational innovation and development in the next five years from four levels of Litany, System, Worldview and Metaphor. This paper also points out that this framework is developing dynamically. In the follow-up "Creativity Initiative" project research and practice, it continues to develop and iterate based on the input of new data and new factors.

Keywords: Design thinking · K12 education · Multi level perspective · Casual layered analysis · Futures studies

1 Introduction

1.1 Background

At present, China attaches great importance to the cultivation of young people's innovative talents. As early as 2009, the Ministry of Education issued the outline of the national medium and long-term education reform and development plan (2010–2020), which clearly pointed out that the reform of talent training system should be carried out and the concept of talent training should be updated. Tsinghua University released the Blue Book of China Maker Education in 2015 [1], which proposed 6 major challenges faced by China's innovative education at that time. Among them, how to coordinate the efforts of all parties to form a talent training pattern with multiple participation is the core challenge. According to the OECD index 2019 [2], it is expected that 67% of the 24–35-year-old young people in China will receive higher education for the first time. This directly reflects China's desire and demand for innovative talents in the future. With the rapid arrival of the era of artificial intelligence, these new technologies and ecological changes have had a profound impact on the future development of China's education. These trends make the exploration and discovery of future oriented innovative education very urgent in China [3].

© Springer Nature Switzerland AG 2020
P.-L. P. Rau (Ed.): HCII 2020, LNCS 12193, pp. 325–337, 2020.
https://doi.org/10.1007/978-3-030-49913-6_28

Education is a long-term development and undefined problem [4]. This kind of problem belongs to the "system problem" in the large-scale social technology system, so new solutions and pathways are needed [5]. How to use design thinking to solve education problems and let design drive innovation has been the consensus of many countries and organizations [6]. The Design Council proposed how design can promote the impact of science and technology research in education and accelerate the innovation and upgrading of the education industry [7]. IDEO has helped Peru design and build a new school system INNOVA schools. With the core goal of cultivating students' independent learning ability, it provides teachers with online curriculum resources, supporting multi-functional teaching space, and integrating business models. Until now, the system-designed comprehensive program has been the most ambitious private education project in Latin America [8]. Afterwards, IDEO launched a design thinking tool for educators, which aims to help more teachers cultivate more creative young people through design thinking and accumulate the underlying strength for social innovation [9].

1.2 Motivation and Research Problem

In the past, the term "design thinking" was generally regarded as "using the feelings and methods of designers" to solve problems [10]. Today, after decades of development, design thinking has been widely used in education, business and other fields, and plays an important role in promoting talent innovation, technological innovation and other aspects [11]. The future-oriented characteristic of design thinking will enhance human adaptability to a rapidly changing future world, and it is also a reflection of human future value and competitiveness in the era of artificial intelligence [12].

Design thinking is entering the field of education in China, and more schools have begun to teach design thinking courses and train teachers. Many education stakeholders are beginning to realize that educational innovation requires an influential, efficient, and widely adopted innovation method [13]. This method should be able to be integrated into all levels from society to education [14]. Individuals and teams can use it creates breakthrough ideas. At the same time, more and more designers also realize that they should teach design methods to those who never think they are designers, let them use these methods to solve a wider range of problems [15].

This paper explores how design can extend from the traditional realm to education. How to design a future education framework that can continuously iterate, give design more education-driven innovation, empower design thinking as a method and tool to empower young people, and cultivate their future-oriented interdisciplinary learning ability [16]. Cultivating creative talents with design thinking is a new way for design to involve education innovation [9, 17]. The extension of design from concept to practice is the core issue of this paper.

2 Research Method

This research, with the support of Tsinghua University's Art and Technology Innovation Base, conducts a survey of the current state of Chinese design thinking from the beginning of 2019. It collects data and information through quantitative questionnaires, in-depth interviews, desk research and other methods to sort out the development and application of Chinese design thinking.

This paper also looks at the opportunities of design thinking in the future development of Chinese education. Inayatullah sohail mentioned six core frameworks [18, 19] in his futurology works, which provide us with a theoretical basis for development from practice. Futurology tries to help individuals and organizations understand the process of change, so that we can actively create a better and happy future. Among them, there is an important method in deepening the future framework, Casual Layered Analysis (CLA). This study attempts to derive the development and application of design thinking in China five years later through CLA combined with current survey data.

Facing the complicated problem of how to use design thinking to cultivate the innovative ability of young people, system-level tools and methods are needed. So how to create system-level change? Multi Level Perspective (MLP) is a theory that can explain the transformation of human society and technology system (Socio-technical system) [20]. With the help of MLP tools, based on the current and future analysis, this paper sorts out a guiding framework for design thinking to drive the development of young people's innovative ability.

This study designed and implemented the Tsinghua University "Creativity Initiative" Maker Challenge in 2019. Through the tools and methods of design thinking, the students were guided to carry out problem discovery and prototype creation. This activity is the starting point for verifying the framework proposed above, and will continue to develop and iterate based on new data and new factor inputs in subsequent research and practice.

3 Exploration and Validation

3.1 An Analysis of the Development of Design Thinking in Chinese Adolescents

The application field of design thinking in this survey is mainly focused on K12 education. The final collection of effective samples includes 334 samples of design thinking-related practitioners (corporate employees, K12 educational institution employees, college teachers). There are nearly 20 entrepreneurs and experts.

In recent years, the popularity of design thinking in China is increasing, and it seems to be a popular word in the field of education. The public began to have a vague sense of design thinking. The results of this survey show that 64.6% of the relevant practitioners think that the development of domestic design thinking is in the preliminary stage of exploration. In the field of education, more and more schools and youth education institutions are beginning to explore the training mode of design thinking to empower innovative talents, but the teaching level and teaching quality are uneven, ranging from shallow methodological learning to core design thinking ability training. Involved; compared with foreign countries, the current domestic government departments' attention to design thinking needs to be improved, and related policy support is still relatively lacking.

What is the effect of the development of teenagers' design thinking education?
Based on empathy, stimulate creative potential and improve comprehensive ability.
The results show that the most outstanding thing that teenagers' design thinking education can stimulate students' ability is exploration ability and innovation ability, and the proportion of recognizing the improvement effect of this ability reaches 72.4%. Secondly, it is believed that design thinking contributes to the cultivation of observation ability, problem finding ability and empathy, accounting for 69.0%, 69.0% and 65.5% respectively. As the first link in the design thinking process, empathy is the basis for building other abilities. The establishment of empathy can make children more easily think from the perspective of others, so as to improve their observation ability, problem finding ability and other related abilities.

In addition to the cultivation of the above abilities, it is easy to feel the improvement of some basic abilities in teenagers' daily life and learning, especially based on the exploration of themselves, people and things around them and the society, so as to establish self-confidence, social participation literacy and the ability to believe in themselves to change the world. The results showed that 69.0% of them accepted the design thinking education, 65.5% of them accepted the design thinking education, and 62.1% accepted the design thinking education (see Fig. 1).

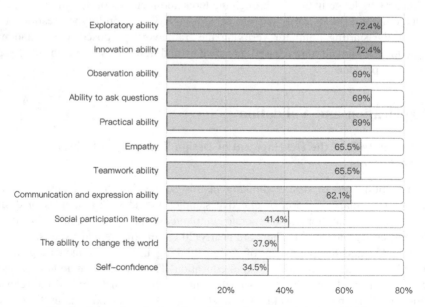

Fig. 1. Improving the learning ability of teenagers' design thinking.

Parents have a better evaluation of the effect of design thinking education, and the recognition of ordinary teachers is average. According to the survey results of the parents of the students, it is found that the parents are satisfied with the learning effect of the design thinking education of the teenagers, and the satisfaction evaluation of the learning effect is 77.2 points (see Fig. 2). From the feedback of parents, they can obviously feel the improvement of their children's ability, such as being able to use empathy to communicate with their parents and actively find ways to solve the inconvenience in their grandparents' lives; children can also feel their own changes, such as being liked by their teachers and classmates; however, teachers who are not engaged in design thinking teaching generally have low recognition of design thinking 17.7% of ordinary teachers are not willing to integrate design thinking into their own teaching.

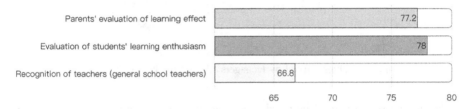

Fig. 2. Recognition and effect evaluation of teenagers' design thinking.

At present, most educational institutions usually use the ability evaluation form to record and evaluate the learning effect of students, but the way to evaluate the ability through quantitative indicators is not scientific enough, and it needs to improve the evaluation of learning effect through qualitative dimensions such as behavior observation.

What are the problems faced by teenagers' design thinking education?
Social education institutions lack of their own teaching resources, lack of standard teacher training system and corresponding software and hardware support. At present, the problems faced by young people in the field of design thinking education are, on the one hand, the shortcomings of the educational institutions themselves. 82.8% of the practitioners believe that the current teachers with design thinking ability and teaching experience are insufficient; 58.6% of the practitioners said that there are currently some The youth training institutions named after design thinking have not cultivated design thinking skills in the actual teaching process, which is also one of the problems existing in the education supply side. In addition, it is difficult to evaluate the effect of teaching is also a place to be improved, with 51.7% of practitioners I think this is the main problem; other deficiencies include the lack of teaching materials, the lack of teaching facilities and equipment, and the lack of related theoretical research in education and teaching (see Fig. 3).

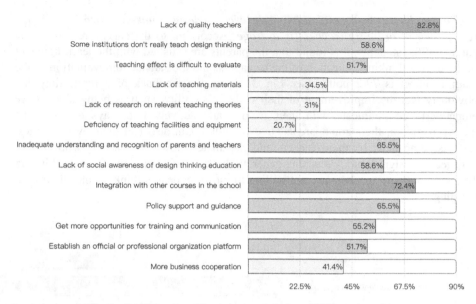

Fig. 3. Problems faced by teenagers' design thinking education.

The current social and educational environment does not have enough recognition of design thinking. On the other hand, the problem is mainly due to the lack of acceptance and recognition of design thinking in the overall social and educational environment. Nearly 60% of practitioners believe that most parents, teachers of other disciplines, and the general public have insufficient awareness and understanding of design thinking education; Another 48.3% of the practitioners believe that the difficulty in changing traditional education concepts and teaching models is also a barrier to the development of youth design thinking education.

Is it possible to enter the national education standard and curriculum system in the future? Is education policy skewed? Innovative methods of design thinking entering China's education standards and national curriculum system will greatly promote development. Promoting the development of youth design thinking education inside and outside the school requires the joint help of all parties. First, 72.4% of practitioners believe that design thinking teaching should not be isolated from the curriculum system, and only be taught as a separate course. Design thinking is integrated and should be integrated with other courses; secondly, 65.5% Of practitioners believe that relevant policy support and guidance is very important; 55.2% of practitioners hope to get more opportunities for communication and training; 51.7% of practitioners hope that relevant departments can establish official organization platforms; 41.4% of practitioners Cooperate with more enterprises, and help the widespread dissemination of young people's design thinking through business.

3.2   MLP Trends and Outlook

Based on the teaching effects and problems found in the above survey, this study attempts to use MLP for trend analysis. This theory allows one to understand how a mainstream paradigm is shaped, and also gives designers the opportunity to find breakthrough points that change the mainstream paradigm. Through design to reinforce and connect related Niche to replace the mainstream paradigm. This paper attempts to deduce design thinking as a new innovative education method through the MLP model and intervene in the mainstream education paradigm in the future. Paths are deduced from three levels: Niche, Regime, and Landscape (see Fig. 4).

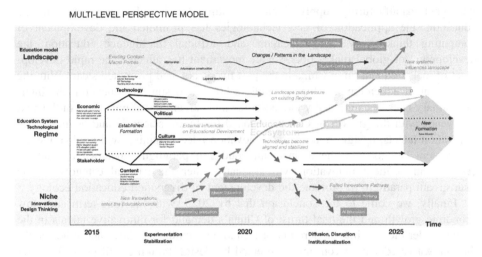

Fig. 4. A way of design thinking in Education by MLP.

Landscape. It represents the macro-economic trend of China at present and in the next five years. China's economy will gradually enter a plateau in the next 5 years. China's demand for future innovative talents has continued to drive China's large-scale investment in educational innovation [21].

Regime. It represents the mainstream education paradigm and mainstream education ecosystem in China. This educational paradigm will be influenced by six categories: economy, science and technology, politics, culture, stakeholders and content. For example, economy, national education funds, family education investment, the scale of non-profit organizations and the coverage rate of free education have a profound impact on the mainstream education paradigm in the economic category. The development of information technology, Internet technology, Internet of things technology and teaching aids represents the profound promotion of technology to the mainstream education paradigm. National political stability, national prosperity, military influence and national education policy all have a profound impact on the mainstream education paradigm from the perspective of the political top. National education level, family education and teachers' dignity reflect the cultural category of the mainstream education paradigm. Curriculum system, teacher training, school construction, selection mechanism and evaluation mechanism constitute the core content of the mainstream education paradigm. Finally, six categories of mainstream education paradigm are constructed together with government education officials, education bureaucrats, higher education system, k12 education system, private education system, social organizations and education company ecology [22, 23].

Niche. It represents the education paradigm used by people who are not satisfied by the mainstream education. It is mainly embodied by the educational methods and methods with innovation as the prominent feature. In the past 20 years, with the rapid development of China's manufacturing industry, it has been at the core of the global intelligent manufacturing supply chain, promoting the rise of engineering thinking education; the application of new technologies has promoted the development of computing thinking, VR/AR education, and artificial intelligence education; the development of global maker open-source movement has affected the rapid development of maker education in China in the past five years, and promoted steam With the integration of education in Chinese public schools and subject education, the interdisciplinary Niche has gradually moved to the mainstream paradigm stage. In the next five years, with the growth of China's demand for future scientific and technological innovation talents, design thinking and innovation talents training will gradually enter the content category of the mainstream education paradigm; meanwhile, student-centered and critical innovation will gradually enter the cultural category of the mainstream paradigm to promote the development of diversified education ecology.

Finally, we come to the conclusion that by 2025, with the long-term and slow economic growth and the dual thrust of China's demand for innovative talents in the future, under the continuous iteration of technology, culture, politics and other fields, the innovative education concept represented by design thinking will gradually enter the main paradigm of China's education.

3.3   CLA Analysis and Vision

Based on the trends and prospects analyzed by the MLP above, we continue to use CLA tools for analysis and vision. the theory of Causal Layered Analysis, a practice of organizational, social and civilizational change, seeking to transform the present and the future through deconstructing and reconstructing reality at four levels. Because China's planning is based on 5 and 10 years as the basic time unit, for example, China is about to enter the fourteenth five-year plan (2021–2025). Therefore, this paper has combed and analyzed the four levels of Litany, System, Worldview, and Metaphor from the current and 2025 dimensions.

As shown in the Table 1, in Litany layer, the current state focuses on three general descriptive factors, e.g. "Lack of effective evaluation of the effects of design thinking education on adolescents". In the future, it will be reflected in two general descriptive factors: "Integration of multiple education forms" and "Design thinking is one of the basic contents of Youth Education".

Table 1. Design Thinking in K12 education by CLA.

Layer	Current	2025
Litany	Parents recognize the impact of design thinking on adolescents Lack of professional design thinking teachers in off-campus training institutions Lack of effective evaluation of the effects of design thinking education on adolescents	Integration of multiple education forms Design thinking is one of the basic contents of Youth Education
System	K12 Design Thinking Curriculum System and Evaluation Method for Teenagers Comprehensive teacher training system Design institutions and universities open resources and platforms to connect youth design thinking education (providing projects, platforms, professional tools and method training, professional designer sharing, etc.) Curriculum system enters the mainstream curriculum system category	Integrating design thinking into daily education of family and school Closely combined with moral education and daily behavior norms of teenagers Perfect evaluation system of design thinking and integration of students' personal comprehensive information One of the assessment contents of national innovative talent selection mechanism
Worldview	More empathetic More young people pay attention to social innovation Caring for the society and paying attention to all classes	Lifelong learning, critical innovation, ubiquitous learning and change are everywhere
Metaphor	Reshape the purpose of education and implement the training of design thinking ability	A strong youth is a strong China

In the systematic layer, the current status focuses on "K12 Design Thinking Curriculum System and Evaluation Method for Teenagers", "Curriculum system enters the mainstream curriculum system category" and other systematic factors. The future situation will focus on the systematic factors such as "Integrating design thinking into daily education of family and school", "One of the assessment contents of national innovative talent selection mechanism".

In the worldview layer, the current awareness focuses on the factors of "More young people pay attention to social innovation" and "Caring for the society and paying attention to all classes ". The future consciousness is embodied in "Lifelong learning, critical innovation, ubiquitous learning and change are everywhere." Factors.

At the metaphor layer, we come to the conclusion that "Reshape the purpose of education and implement the training of design thinking ability". In the future, the metaphorical factor of "A strong youth is a strong China".

As a whole, it can be concluded that the social recognition of design thinking is constantly improving, and it has become one of the basic quality training contents for teenagers. With the promotion of social recognition of design thinking, people will gradually realize the important value of empathy, the ability to find and solve problems brought by design thinking, and the important role of design thinking in cultivating students' basic literacy. In the future, design thinking education will gradually move forward to basic education, providing systematic innovation education for primary and secondary school students based on design thinking, such as innovation courses, creative maker space, specialized teacher training, etc., so as to train students to become talents of innovation and entrepreneurship, and then fully adapt to the development requirements of the future society and the needs of the construction of an innovative country.

3.4   Creativity Initiative (CI) Framework Design

Based on the design and conception of CLA, relying on the art and science and technology innovation base (ATI) of Tsinghua University, this paper plans a CI project for the next five years, and verifies the guiding framework design above through this project. The CI includes education vision, innovation tool base, activity platform, collaborative environment and other contents at different levels [24]. The core content of the activity platform is the evaluation and evaluation system. The process of each activity will generate a large number of personal data of students participating in the activity, and obtain the ability map of each child in the process of pretest, process and final evaluation (Fig. 5).

Fig. 5. At the event, students use design thinking tools to make prototypes.

In November 2019, the CI project launched a verification practice. A total of 251 people from 53 middle schools across the country participated in the event. A complete set of video and audio recording equipment (as shown in the figure) is applied in this activity to record and analyze students' behavior patterns in different stages of the activity, including semantic analysis of team discussion, interaction frequency between them, similarity between prototyping and conceptual design. By recording the process of behavior, we observed that students can use design thinking tools for team thinking and collaboration, and the design thinking tools provided can support the divergent process of students' early creativity. Combined with the analysis of data, we can see that the ability map generated in the activity has an effective corresponding relationship with the design thinking tools used, which is helpful to demonstrate the effectiveness of design thinking in the innovation activities for the improvement of young people's innovation ability. While on the whole, the establishment and evaluation of the students' ability map will continuously verify the preliminary results of the CLA framework design above and iterate. Of course, we also found that there is inconsistency between the direct use of design thinking tools and the production process. The future improvement direction is proposed for the research (Fig. 6).

Fig. 6. Process review and final review.

It is proved that it is feasible to apply design thinking to the cultivation of innovation ability through the CI project. Through follow-up surveys in the following three months, this study collected effective feedback from more than 100 students in more than 60 schools, supporting the project's planning and vision.

4   Discussion and Future Work

Through the verification and analysis of MLP, CLA and Ci, this paper gives the author some enlightenment on the future development of design thinking. In the past, designers helped change education and were limited to designing easy-to-use campuses and services. But in the future, in an information society that emphasizes digital production capabilities, helping students become more creative and gaining innovative capabilities will be even more important. It is necessary to use design thinking as a tool and method to empower more young people, educate stakeholders, and explore how to effectively acquire future-oriented ability learning.

Faced with such a complex future situation, what scenarios need to be further explored to support new approaches to sustainable development?

Integration System. The design thinking teaching platform of the system can support multiple contents, general standards and docking resource output standards.

Education Innovation Platform. The establishment of national innovative talent training mode and standard, and the diversification of evaluation mechanism and talent selection.

Systematic Design Tool. It can support content output and delivery at all levels under the framework of FIEF. And help education stakeholders to promote localization of programs.

Collaborative Environment. Link online and offline. Artificial intelligence empowers schools of the future.

Future research will continue to iterate this framework through more design practices, linking and enhancing more environments and tools. Try to enrich the connotation and extension of the design discipline with more designers and groups, as well as effective ways to apply to different practice areas. Use the power of design to influence society.

5 Conclusions

Based on the analysis of the current situation of design thinking in China's k12 education field and the verification and design with CLA and MLP tools, this paper draws a guiding framework for design thinking to drive the development of youth's innovative ability. and predicts the development of design thinking in China's young people's innovation education in the next five years. With the continuous verification of the follow-up Creativity Initiative practice projects and the continuous enrichment of the data in the framework level, the path of design thinking involved in educational innovation will be constantly revised. This framework can provide a top-level design method and approach for more education stakeholders to explore the future innovative talents training with design thinking. It extends the research and practice field of design.

Acknowledgment. This paper is supported by Tsinghua University Teaching Reform Project (2019 autumn DX05_01), Construction of Online Educational Tools and Evaluation System Based on Design Thinking. Thanks to Tsinghua University ATI in the research of design thinking data. Thanks for the support of the Institute of service design, Academy of Arts & Design, Tsinghua University.

References

1. The blue book of China's maker education. https://www.tsinghua.edu.cn/publish/thunews/9654/2016/20160322085808927938023/20160322085808927938023_.html
2. OECD: "China", in Education at a Glance 2019: OECD Indicators, OECD Publishing, Paris (2019). https://doi.org/10.1787/7c9859c1-en
3. Simandan, D.: Wisdom and foresight in Chinese thought: sensing the immediate future. J. Fut. Stud. **22**(3), 35–50 (2018)
4. Buchanan, R.: Wicked problems in design thinking. Des. Issu. **8**(2), 5–21 (1992). [Crossref]
5. Schon, D.: Educating the Reflective Practitioner: Toward a New Design for Teaching and Learning in the Professions. Jossey-Bass, San Francisco (1987)
6. Brown, T.: Change by Design: How Design Thinking Transforms Organizations and Inspires Innovation. Harper Collins, New York (2009)

7. Design Council: "Innovation: The Essentials of Innovation" (2009). http://www. designcouncil.org.uk/en/About-Design/Business-Essentials/Innovation/. Accessed 18 Aug 2009
8. RIVERDALE, IDEO: Design thinking for educators [EB/OL], 11 March 2017. http://media. wix.com/ugd/04245b_f2620b574493595d39b357cc2c84028b.pdf
9. Design Thinking for Educators [EB/OL], 30 November 2016. http://www. designthinkingforeducators.com/about-toolkit/
10. Rowe, P.: Design Thinking. MIT Press, Cambridge (1987). 1998
11. Kimbell, L.: Rethinking design thinking: Part I. Des. Cult. 3(3), 285–306 (2015). https://doi. org/10.2752/175470811X13071166525216
12. Simon, H.: The Sciences of the Artificial, 3rd edn. MIT Press, Cambridge (1969). 1996
13. Lawson, B.: How Designers Think: The Design Process Demystified, 4th edn. Architectural Press, London (1980). 2005
14. Kolko, J.: Thoughts of Interaction Design. In: Chapter II management complexity of data, information, knowledge, wisdom, 2 edn., p. 46 (2012)
15. Zhiyong, F., Xia, Q.: Possession tool: design preferable future with humane assistant and diegetic prototype. In: IASDR (2019)
16. Dubberly, H.: A proposal for the future of design education. The Design Education Manifesto (2011)
17. Brown, T., Wyatt, J.: Design thinking for social innovation. Dev. Outreach 12(1), 29–43 (2010)
18. Inayatullah, S.: YouthBulge: demographic dividend, time bomb, and other futures. J. Fut. Stud. 21(2), 21–34 (2016)
19. Inayatullah, S.: Six pillars: futures thinking for transforming. Foresight 10(1), 4–21 (2008)
20. Irwin, T.: Transition design: a proposal for a new area of design practice, study, and research. Des. Cult. 7(2), 229–246 (2015)
21. OECD: Four Future Scenarios for Higher Education. Higher Education to 2030 (2008)
22. Moultrie, J., Nilsson, M., Dissel, M., Haner, U.-E., Janssen, S., Van der Lugt, R.: Innovation Spaces: Towards a Framework for Understanding the Role of the Physical Environment in Innovation (2007)
23. Huber, G.: Synergies between organizational learning and creativity & innovation. Creat. Innovat. Manag. 7(1), 3–9 (1998)
24. Zhiyong, Fu: The Design Theory and Research Framework for Public Service in Social Media Age. DMI, China (2011)

Asynchronous Co-eating Through Video Message Exchange: Support for Making Video Messages

Kanako Obata[1], Yuichi Nakamura[1]([✉])(iD), LongFei Chen[1], and John Augeri[2]

[1] Academic Center for Computing and Media Studies,
Kyoto University, Sakyo, Kyoto, Japan
{obata,yuichi}@media.kyoto-u.ac.jp
[2] Université Numérique Paris Ile-de-France, 90 Rue Tolbiac,
75634 Paris cedex 13, Paris, France
john.augeri@unpidf.fr

Abstract. Co-Eating, *i.e.*, eating meals in the company of other people, has been widely recognized as good for both physical and mental health. However, the chances of co-eating have drastically decreased for families living separately and for older people living alone. To cope with this problem, we propose a framework of "asynchronous co-eating" that enables virtual co-eating through video message exchanges, which does not necessarily require people to eat simultaneously. This framework is aimed to maintain frequent communication between family members and promote ordinary types of co-eating when possible. To make this process easy for both older people and their distant family members, we designed a video message exchange scheme with an omnidirectional camera and a topic recommendation mechanism. With preliminary experiments, we obtained results that suggest our framework has the potential to be beneficial.

Keywords: Co-eating · Communication support · Health and mental care · Gerontology

1 Introduction

It is widely acknowledged that co-eating, i.e., eating meals with other people, particularly those with whom we have close relationships, is good for both physical and mental health [1]. Co-eating provides good opportunities for communication among families, friends, and other members of the community for introducing, educating, and maintaining food and dietary cultures [2–4]. Furthermore, co-eating allows for participants to be mutually aware of one another and potentially helps maintain good dietary habits and health by encouraging people to consume sufficient nutrition, but not too much [5,6]. In recent years, however, chances of co-eating have been decreasing due to the increasing number of small families and people living alone; solitary eating is often seen among older people.

© Springer Nature Switzerland AG 2020
P.-L. P. Rau (Ed.): HCII 2020, LNCS 12193, pp. 338–348, 2020.
https://doi.org/10.1007/978-3-030-49913-6_29

With this in mind, our research is aimed at providing virtual co-eating opportunities through the use of information and communication technology (ICT), and consequently helping to cope with the social problems of older people living alone and families living separately. Supporting communication while eating has much potential for alleviating some of these social problems, because eating and taking time to eat is essential for every person. During meals, people are often relaxed and have enough time to think of other people, especially family members.

As part of previous research on this topic, Tokunaga, et al. proposed a framework of co-eating through video conference [7]. They did experiments wherein two groups of family members living separately—on one side, older parents and on the other, their son or daughter and his/her partner and children-each ate their meals while watching and chatting with each other. The results of this experiment revealed that the older participants' quality of life was much improved, in particular their pleasure and interest in life due to their curiosity about discovering new things to serve as topics for conversation.

Although this type of simultaneous co-eating has many benefits, we often have difficulties for sharing time in this way. Family members living separately usually have different schedules, with, for example, older people tending to eat early in the evening and working people more likely to have quick meals later at night. As a result, it is often challenging for each group to adjust their time and way of eating. Surely, therefore, we need ideas on how to fill the gap between synchronous co-eating and eating alone.

To this end, we propose a framework of "asynchronous co-eating" that enables virtual co-eating through video message exchanges, which does not require people to eat simultaneously. This framework is not intended to replace synchronous co-eating, but to ease the difficulties of simultaneous eating, maintain communication, and promote ordinary types of co-eating when possible. Moreover, asynchronous co-eating also stimulates communication among family members who live together but have different schedules and do not regularly have meals together.

2   Video Message Exchange for Co-eating

Our scheme of asynchronous co-eating is organized as follows. Suppose that X and Y are partners, each of them has a mobile device that can record video messages, upload or download them to or from cloud file servers, and replay downloaded video messages. Using these functions, X and Y record video messages as illustrated in Fig. 1.

- X or Y records video messages with the device and uploads them to a cloud folder they share. Messages can be captured while executing everyday activities at home or anytime and anywhere.
- X or Y downloads messages from their counterpart and views them while they have their meal. Video responses also can be recorded while watching downloaded messages.

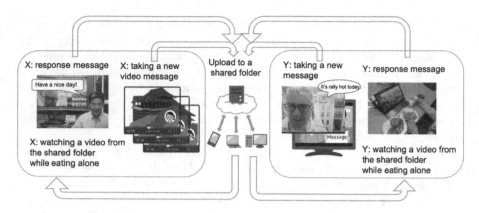

Fig. 1. Framework of asynchronous co-eating

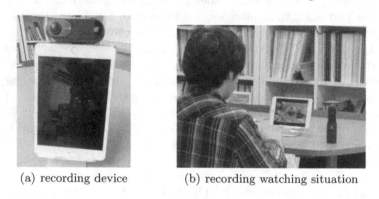

(a) recording device   (b) recording watching situation

Fig. 2. Video recording device with omnidirectional camera attached

Thus, both X and Y can upload a new video message and reply to their partner's messages. Viewing video messages and possibly replying to them while eating is the crux of our framework for asynchronous co-eating. We assume that one of the most important users of this system would be older people living apart from their children or intimate individuals and the another type of users would be persons between 20 to 60 years old who have busy work lives. Therefore, we need to consider some problems caused by their living styles and differences.

Usability:
- The device and user interface needs to be suitable for use by elderly people and while eating.
- The process should not require undue time and efforts for daily use.

Communication:
- Motivation for making video messages is necessary because older people tend to have fewer events and changes in their lives compared to younger individuals. It is possible that their messages could potentially contain complaints about their lives or environments.

- Suppression of complaints and unpreserved expressions is necessary as these kinds of messages often cause worry or annoyance, which further discourages video message communication.
- To compensate for the lack of real-time interactions, responding is encouraged.

The problems of usability are primarily dealt with via the design of the device and its software.

3   Design and Challenges

One of the challenges of this research was assisting users, especially older people, to create good-quality video messages. To facilitate this, we designed the message acquisition scheme as follows:

- The communication device is equipped with an omnidirectional camera that takes images of not only what the operator or sender wishes to shoot but also of how the person behaves while recording the video (Fig. 2). This is significant because we often feel that seeing the face of the family member is as important as it is to see what they are shooting.
- The length of video messages is deliberately kept short, e.g., 30 s or 1 min, making both recording and watching easy.
- We also designed a topic selection assistance function that makes it easier for users to choose topics that are interesting and/or acceptable to their counterparts; this is enabled by aggregating the preferences of both sides and introducing random selections.

As mentioned above, because the face of the operating person, i.e., the message sender, is important to the message receiver, we need to detect the face and ensure that it is properly included in the final, edited video. For this purpose, we implemented a face tracking program that detects a face and tracks it with the Kalman filter based on a common face detection software [8].

Figure 3 illustrates examples of image composition from omnidirectional videos. (a) is a panoramic view that is most similar to a captured video, (b) is a horizontally merged view of the front and the back view, (c) is a frontal view with the face superimposed, for which the size and position can be changed, and (d) is a merged view wherein the front and back view are vertically aligned. For (b) and (d), an omnidirectional video is split into both front and back views based on the position of the camera's operator face, which is then merged horizontally or vertically. For (c), the area of the image around the detected face is superimposed in the front view. Because each of these views has advantages and disadvantages, we asked participants for subjective impressions for them. The results are shown in a later section.

(a) panoramic view

(b) split-and-merge view (horizontal)

(d) split-and-merge view
(vertical)

(c) superimpose view

Fig. 3. Videos edited to show the face of the person recording it

4   Support for Topic Selection

Candidates for potential topics were arranged into the following groups:

(i) Topics on which the sender (the person recording) can easily make a message.

(ii) Topics that the receiver (the person viewing) is interested in.

(iii) Topics on current or seasonal events.

(iv) Requests for responses to previous messages.

Group (i) contains topics on hobbies, meals, family histories, etc., which encourage the sender to record the message. A small number of topics dealing with health problems and complaints on current problems, which may discourage

Table 1. Topic selected in the experiments

	Without roulette	With roulette
Health condition	11(8%)	6 (5%)
Weather	7 (5%)	5 (4%)
Daily activity	62 (45%)	25 (20%)
Family-related topic	8 (6%)	2 (1.6%)
Events	7 (5%)	4 (3%)
Current news	10 (7%)	2 (1.6%)
Others	32 (23%)	-
Chosen topic by the counterpart	0	56 (45%)
Response to a previous message	0	25 (20%)

communication, can be included. Group (ii) comprises topics that the receiver wants to see or hear from the sender. These topics are suggested by the receiver beforehand. It is difficult for both the sender and receiver to choose a potential topic every time in Group (iii), for which the system provides based on news and other public sources. Group (iv) accelerates dense communication on some topics and gives a feeling of interactive communication.

The sender may feel that he/she is forced to use the selected topic if an actual topic is simply specified. Our system intends to reduce this feeling of being forced by introducing randomness using a roulette. The sender uses the roulette to randomly select a topic from the above-mentioned topic groups. We expect that both the sender and receiver will be more comfortable without feeling the responsibility of choosing a topic.

5   Preliminary Experiments

Topic Selection

We asked five participants to record video messages on five topics each day for at most ten days. We asked the participants to record video messages based on their arbitrary choices in the first experiment. Chosen topics are listed in the left column of Table 1. Dominant topics were health conditions, weather, daily activity, current news, events, family-related, etc. Without specified topics, the participants mostly tried to find something new in everyday life, which was sometimes a considerable burden. In fact, this caused one participant to drop out without completing the task.

We asked the participants to record video messages with the topic suggested by the roulette in the second experiment. The number of topics recorded per day and the period for which they were recorded were the same as in the first experiment. Topic groups were selected based on the method mentioned in the previous section, taking into consideration the topics chosen in the first experiment. Chosen topics are listed in the right column of Table 1. Distribution of the topics was roughly controlled by the candidates and randomness. As a result, "response to a previous message" is chosen at a rate of 20%.

Table 2. Comparison of with and without roulette

	Without roulette	With roulette
New findings	17 (12.4%)	34 (27%)
Complaints	14 (10%)	6 (4.8%) mostly light (not serious)

Table 3. Evaluation of video messages (how interesting it is)

Score	Without roulette	With roulette
1 (not interesting)	0	0
2	11 (8%)	1 (1%)
3 (neutral)	95 (69%)	55 (44%)
4	29 (21%)	55 (44%)
5 (quite interesting)	2 (1.5%)	14 (11%)

Concerning the content of the video messages, we asked the participants what new thing did they learn about their counterparts. This evaluation did not concern the topic content, but rather the characteristics, ideas, daily life, or anything else about the message senders. Table 2 demonstrates the comparison of the first and second experiments. The proposed method apparently has benefits for eliciting new information that family members did not have beforehand. It also suppresses serious complaints that may worry the receivers. Table 2 shows that the number and quality of complaints decreases when using this method.

Another feature of this proposed method is that it occasionally leads to message content that the receiver does not expect. For example, one participant asked about "animals," considering this to mean a pet, but he received a message concerning a mosquito and its bites. This type of unexpected message exchange contributes to the sharing of new information among families.

As another aspect of content evaluation, we asked the participants to evaluate video messages based on how interesting they were. Table 3 compares the results of the first and second experiments; scores are marked from 1 (nothing interesting) to 5 (quite interesting). It can be seen that the proposed method made messages more acceptable to the receivers.

As for the difficulty in making video messages, we asked the participants to score it between 1 (easy) and 5 (difficult). The result suggests that the proposed method makes the task easier (Table 4).

Table 4. Difficulty in making video messages (Figures in the two columns on the right indicate the number of participants)

Score	Without roulette	With roulette
5 (difficult)	1 (dropped out)	0
4	2	1
3 (neutral)	2	1
2	0	0
1 (easy)	0	2

Table 5. Comments on topic selection

– It is difficult to find fresh topics every day by myself
– Topic selection makes me notice that my daily life lacks variety and tends to be trivial
– It was easy for me to make video messages on the specified topics chosen by the roulette
– Choosing topics by myself is easier
– Making video messages is like writing in a diary.
– The topics need to be more varied
– I wish to record messages based on some topics that were not chosen

Table 6. Impressions and comments on the scheme

– It is easier to record a video message than talk on the telephone or face-to-face
– It is easier to view a video message than to talk on the telephone or face-to-face
– I noticed everyday things a bit more carefully because I needed to make a message for someone
– Recording video messages is fun, as if I am chatting with a friend
– It is difficult to talk to a camera
– I hesitate to record video messages in a crowded space
– To watch daily messages is more fun than I previously expected. Even ordinary content can be interesting and fun
– Seeing the face of the sender is often more important than what they are saying and makes for good content in itself

Table 5 indicates the comments given by the participants. It suggests that the proposed method makes topic selection easier. However, one participant felt it would be easier to choose a topic on his own. It may be necessary to increase the rate of a roulette result of "free topic," to allow users to arbitrarily select topics.

We also need to consider topic variations, and how the users expect them. Table 6 also shows the impressions and comments on the entire scheme of asynchronous co-eating. The comments suggest that our scheme has considerable advantages.

Video Composition

To clarify the characteristics of possible video compositions, we asked the participants to state their impressions after viewing the edited message videos. Table 7 presents viewers' common impressions. For the comparison, baseline video compositions were also considered, i.e., ordinary composition with the camera pointing at a target and taking a "selfie."

The impressions were practically what we expected. Ordinary video compositions without the message sender in the frame or "selfie" lack information and do not stimulate responses. Among the composition from omnidirectional video, the split-and-merge view and the superimposed view were better received than

Table 7. Impressions and comments on the image compositions. Actual samples are presented in Fig. 3.

Panoramic view, e.g., Fig. 3 (a)
– Difficult to view and understand the scene
– It has unpleasant distortion
– Looks like a mirror
– This may be unsuitable or difficult for older people to view as it requires skills
Split-and-merge view, e.g., Fig. 3 (b), (d)
– Easy to understand where and how the person recording the message is
– It is mostly good if the message sender is not moving fast
– It is sometimes confusing if both the front and back views are similar, e.g., Fig. 4(a)
– It stimulates replying because it is easily understandable
Superimposed view, e.g., Fig. 3 (c)
– It feels like a television screen
– A larger image of the message sender is preferred. Faces in samples are too small, e.g., Fig. 3 (c)
– Want to see the body and clothes
– It is mostly good if the message sender is not moving fast
– Difficult to see what the sender is looking at if he/she frequently turns the head, e.g., Fig. 4(a). – The superimposed face stimulates response
Baseline (ordinary shot and selfie), e.g., Fig. 4 (a) and (b)
– Easy to watch, but boring (both)
– Want to see the sender's face/body (the case of ordinary view)
– Want to see the surrounding environment (both)

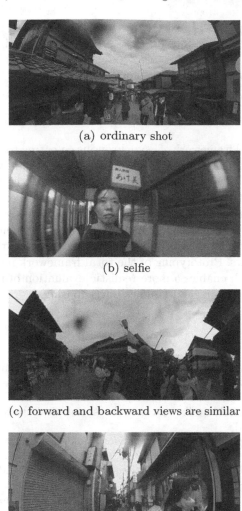

(a) ordinary shot

(b) selfie

(c) forward and backward views are similar

(d) difficult to find gazing target

Fig. 4. Supplemental samples for the impressions in Table 7

the panoramic view. The panoramic view could contain a lot of information of the sender's surroundings; however, images captured this way were extremely distorted and the sender's face was too small. This made viewing videos captured in this view difficult and weakened the feeling of interaction on the part of the receiver. Therefore, we consider both the split-and-merge and superimposed views to be the primary candidates of video composition in our model.

That said, it may also be true that what constitutes suitable composition and editing can differ depending on the situations and environments wherein videos are captured, and, of course, according to personal preferences. We need to further investigate automatic video composition.

6   Summary

We introduced a novel framework of asynchronous co-eating to stimulate communication with loved ones for older people and separated family members. First, we discussed the problems preventing eating together and the idea of video message exchange targeting virtual co-eating. Second, we present the scheme and design of our asynchronous co-eating system, concentrating on device design and the support for topic selection. Our preliminary experiments indicated good potential of our scheme, although we need systematic evaluation with a higher number of participants. Prototyping of the total framework must be undertaken in the future, in which enables a more realistic evaluation of the system with a variation in the older people and families participating.

References

1. Healthy Eating Habits: Benefits Of Eating Together With Family And Friends. https://www.flavoursholidays.co.uk/blog/healthy-eating-habits-why-eating-with-friends-and-family-keeps-you-young/. Accessed 27 Jan 2020
2. Bossard, J.: Family table talk – an area for socialogical study. Am. Sociol. Rev. **8**(3), 295–301 (1943)
3. Gahagan, S.: Development of eating behavior: biology and context. J. Dev. Behav. Pediatr. **33**(3), 261–71 (2012)
4. Dunbar, R.: Breaking bread: the functions of social eating. Adapt. Hum. Behav. Physiol. **3**, 198–211 (2017)
5. Nakata, R., Kawai, N.: The "social" facilitation of eating without the presence of others: self-reflection on eating makes food taste better and people eat More. Physiol. Behav. **179**, 23–29 (2017)
6. Tokunaga, H., Mukawa, N., Kimura, A.: Structural differences of eating behavior between solitary eating and co-eating. J. Integr. Stud. Dietary Habits **27**(3), 167–174 (2017)
7. Konno, H., Tokunaga, H., Mukawa, N.: Influence of video-mediated co-eating communication between elderly parents and their independent child on meal satisfaction and quality of life. IEICE SIG-HCS **117**(29), 265–270 (2017). (In Japanese)
8. Bulat, A., Tzimiropoulos, G.: How far are we from solving the 2D & 3D Face Alignment problem? (and a dataset of 230, 000 3D facial landmarks). In: International Conference on Computer Vision (2017). http://arxiv.org/abs/1703.07332

Improving Memory Recall and Measuring User Ability Through Gamified Techniques with 'Chatty': An E-Learning Application for Foreign Languages

Hyeyeon Park[1]([✉]), Jacob D. Burke[1], Volny Blin[2], and Harris Chrysanthou[1]

[1] Tsinghua University, Beijing 100082, China
loolphy@gmail.com
[2] Institut National des Sciences Appliquées de Lyon, 69100 Lyon, France

Abstract. We aim to create a more efficient online, or E-learning, environment that will promote participation and enhance the learning speed of foreign languages. The goal is to explore interests and features that can be incorporated in an educational platform which transitions users from a state of explicit learning to implicit learning. This method calls upon the study of intrinsic motivations and identification of needs for different target audiences. Our deliverable is a prototype application called "Chatty", where users with unique personas can practice and improve foreign languages together. We turned typical practices for learning languages such as communicating with others, asking and answering questions, giving and receiving critical feedback, and participating in grammar activities into an enjoyable and meaningful gamified experience. Next, we measured the ergonomic design of the Chatty app through a user ability test based on the Goal, Question, Metric (GQM) model. By measuring the time to complete six unique tasks in Chatty, our sample study yields geometric means to complete each task within 50 s. The geometric mean is a meaningful measurement to predict the median population times to complete a task within Chatty; therefore, we find that our application is intuitive and efficient. Lastly, we tested our gamified environment's ability to improve a user's memory recall for new language material. With 95% confidence, our experiment results show that users who took a grammar test in Chatty's gamified environment were better able to recall the tested material later on. This means that gamification shows promise for improving memory recall in users learning new languages. Though our app is aimed at the study of foreign languages, gamification can be applied to other various industries and future studies should be considered. Access to the prototype can be granted upon emailed request.

Keywords: E-learning · Online learning · Language application · Learning language · Gamification · Gamified learning · Gamified learning language · Application design · App design · Human centered design · User interface design · UI design · User experience design · UX design · Service design · Explicit learning · Implicit learning · Intrinsic motivation

© Springer Nature Switzerland AG 2020
P.-L. P. Rau (Ed.): HCII 2020, LNCS 12193, pp. 349–366, 2020.
https://doi.org/10.1007/978-3-030-49913-6_30

1 What Is Gamification

At first glance, gamification contains the word "game." This instantly leads the public to associate gamification as all play with no work. However, in gamification, "a game is only a tool to accomplish specific goals in a non-gaming area" [4]. In our project, that area is education. Historically, gaming and education have long been separated. Not until the 1970's has gamification been introduced to the classroom in basic ways [3].

Today, gamification is the combination of modern gaming aspects with established teaching methods; therefore, with rapid increases in technology, the benefits for educational gamification are endless. Some examples of modern gaming aspects include rules of play which follow a story, achievements, rewards, challenges and goals, badges, personalized avatars, point scoring with summarized leaderboards for competition, and more [5]. The objective of gamification is to accelerate the learning curve [2] through more engaged and implicit learning. However, implicit learning is more complex than simply changing the names of grades and assignments to "points" and "quests" [1]. It requires an in-depth approach for recognizing user needs and personas.

Other than implicit learning, there are extra reasons to implement gamification in traditional learning environments. Because the gamified learning environment is often digital, it incorporates multi-media inputs which require a fundamental understanding of technology [2]. This means that users must have basic technological skills and use those in combination with critical thinking processes. In addition, it offers something the real world cannot: a modeled environment. Modeled environments create opportunities for users to solve problems in a safe and recoverable atmosphere. Also, it enables connections and access to resources users would not conventionally have. In the field of language learning, this is especially useful since users can now connect with anyone from various cultural and language backgrounds in the gamified environment. This creates an opportunity for teamwork, which is fundamental in learning. Lastly, gamification should be implemented because it can not only be applied to language learning but also to any other educational setting.

2 Understanding Users

Primary users are the people who actually interact with a system. They then become main users since they are the ones playing and learning from the gamified system. In addition, there are secondary users. These are individuals who do not actually use the system but still have influence over the primary user. Secondary users are usually buyers (such as a parent for their child) or other decision makers like an app designer, developer, and more.

Within a primary user, there are several characteristics to consider for designing the E-learning platform. These include personality, cognitive functions required, motivation, generational differences, and user lifestyle [6]. Considering these characteristics of the primary user can take a gamified application to the next level. For example, what cognitive processes are used in language learning specifically as opposed to learning arithmetic [7]? What motivates a user to learn a language versus learning about the arts? Are the lifestyles of language learners on the go, in a formal setting, or in their personal free time? After answering these basic questions about the user, there are three analysis methods to consider when designing the gamified experience: user analysis, task analysis, and context analysis.

The **user analysis** is the "first step to create a rich multi-faceted player persona" [8]. People differ in terms of behavior and motivation [12] so there are three subcategories to characterize the user analysis: cognitive model, role model, and persona model.

Cognitive Model. Cognitive Model focuses on the individual cognitive processes within a user's head. This model is related to how an individual user understands the system while using the system and how the user learns to operate the system. This idea directly relates to the combination with basic technological understanding. Other cognitive functions include adaption to challenges, associative memory, and the locomotion of the neural network. This model does not apply to Chatty as it requires brain mapping for optimal results.

Role Model. Role Model focuses on the relationship between the user and the system. It can be described as a set of the user's behavior that characterizes the relationship between the user and the system. Relationship types can include those for banking security, pure gaming, communication, information storage, etc. In Chatty, the role model function is that of language learning.

Persona Model. Role Model refers to a typical and hypothetical person created to represent various types of users who may use a digital product or service. It addresses that "the first step in player centered design is to create persona model". By modeling an expected persona, the design process for Chatty is simplified for our app prototype purpose and expected needs of the app can be better designed [8].

Task Analysis. Task Analysis considers how users perform a task using a product or service. It is the process of figuring out what tools and actions users need to achieve their goals and what knowledge they should have in order to do so. The general research approach is meant to be used in different case scenarios [10] while evaluating the hierarchy of tasks, sequence or progression throughout the gamified environment, and workflow (moving in and out of different sections depending on app complexity). Between theory and real-world applications, "the integration of scenario-based activities provides a strong bridge" [9] between the user and the target material. There are 5 task analysis methods.

- **Hierarchical task analysis (HTA):** Divide one job into several tasks, divide each task into subtasks, and identify the hierarchical structure of the job.
- **Scenario**: Can be a small story. A description of the user's specific experience using the system.
- **Sequence model analysis**: A sequential description of the process by which the user performs detailed tasks.
- **Job analysis**: Not a process of analyzing the progress of a user's specific task, but of analyzing what happens throughout the day or month.
- **Workflow analysis (or Business process analysis):** A piece of work is collaborated on by several people and their interactions to complete the task is studied.

Context Analysis. Context Analysis contains the process of analyzing information that can characterize the environment in which users are using the system. The table below summarizes the three contexts which surround the user. *Physical context* does not reflect socio-cultural values, but only judges the mechanical considerations of the app. *Social context* evaluates and interprets the various values related to the situation. *Cultural context* is cultural tendency of people. "The design process consists of two major iterative steps, the context analysis (User-Centered Design) and the iterative conception of the gamification experience" [11] (Table 1).

Table 1. Elements of Context Analysis.

	Physical Context	Social Context	Cultural Context
Time element	Using time Using day Using season	Working time Time pressure	Time perception Time orientation
Location element	Space organization, Congestion, Flow	Home or workplace privacy	Power distance
Other element	Light, noise, temperature, dust	Power Social hierarchy Division of labor Standard and policy	Uncertainty avoidance Controllability

3 Matching Players with Motivation

Motivation generally refers to a force that drives people to act and can vary not only in the level but also in type. There are two types: extrinsic motivation and intrinsic motivation (authentic motivation). Intrinsic motivation is generated from within, meaning learners actively seek to gain more knowledge for some personal reason [17]. For example, a user chooses to download Chatty so they can practice a foreign language for an upcoming trip abroad. Communicating with others make people feel good about themselves, thus the motivation is intrinsic. On the other hand, extrinsic motivation comes from an external source to either receive an award or avoid punishment. This key difference means people with intrinsic motivation often express more excitement, interest and persistence. In addition, one task can have both extrinsic and intrinsic motivation. For Chatty, we implement gamified extrinsic motivations such as rewards, points, and level ups in combination of intrinsic motivations such as positive grammar feedback to avoid future embarrassment. After identifying motivation, the types of different users in a gamified environment are summarized in the table below (Table 2).

Table 2. Types of players.

Achievers	Socializers	Explorers	Killers
Players who focus on measurable outcomes	Get to know people through interactive layouts	Keen to explore apps, discover new areas and features	Competitive and Dominant Players

For each of these player types, they each have different motivations for the reason they've started playing. Six basic motivations are as follows [18]:

- Social interaction or network
- Fantasy or role playing
- Passing time/escapism
- Self-presentation, social influence
- Entertainment
- Challenge/competition

When learning material, it has been researched that students recall information at success rates of 10% when they read it, 20% when they hear it, 30% when they see it (visual presentation), and 50% when they observe others doing it live. But when learners do the job themselves, learning success is categorized at 90% [19]. Thus, intrinsically motivating users to 'do the job themselves' is an ultimate goal of Chatty so that maximum learning efficiency is allowed.

4 Methodology to Design Chatty

Analysis models, primary vs. secondary users, player classifications, motivation types, and reasons for playing constitute the design decisions for a gamified app. For Chatty, the persona model within the user analysis method was chosen. By first creating a persona, goals and scenarios can be defined to make Chatty relevant to the hypothetical user. The below figure summarizes the created persona for Chatty (Fig. 1).

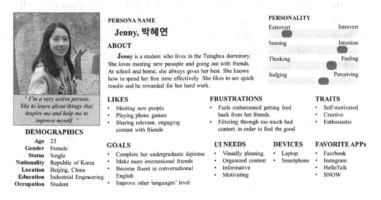

Fig. 1. Persona model designed for Chatty.

5   Introduction to Chatty

In short, Chatty's main gamified function is to ensure players are motivated to use a selected learning language in order to gain points and badges within the app. These increases can raise their experience level to unlock bonus features in the game section, or uniquely personalize their profile avatar. Users can even increase app functions such as chat room capability and the number of possible learning languages. More use of the app equals better app function. In addition, we set rules for entering chatrooms and learning new languages to make the gamified experience somewhat exclusive, encouraging users to up their profile status (Fig. 2).

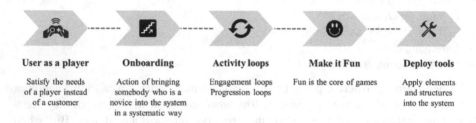

User as a player	Onboarding	Activity loops	Make it Fun	Deploy tools
Satisfy the needs of a player instead of a customer	Action of bringing somebody who is a novice into the system in a systematic way	Engagement loops Progression loops	Fun is the core of games	Apply elements and structures into the system

Fig. 2. Gamification process for designing Chatty [13–16].

5.1   Registration Section

The registration process is the user's first experience with Chatty. Chatty requires a minimum amount of information to get started learning a language and communicating with others.

Fill out Information and Choose Nationality and Language. The user first inputs birth date and gender. Because Chatty is a gaming educational application, it does not require an actual picture. Users can choose their avatar to portray themselves. The users select nationality and native language. Nationality flag is displayed at the bottom left of the avatar to create intimacy when users meet or talk with the same nationality. Also, it helps show the diversity of users in the app. Mother tongues are automatically assigned a crown. The crown means there is no level to go up anymore. The learning languages can go from bronze medals to gold medals. Users can teach other users using their native language. By default, a new user can select two learning languages. Users can add 3rd and 4th learning languages by using XP and Coins obtained from app usage (Fig. 3).

Fig. 3. Creating an account.

5.2 Profile Setup Section

The main purpose of the profile section is to check the information entered by the user at the time of registration along with current user status. No further modifications are possible, only verification. Level represents the total XP users have earned using "my learning languages" in chats, games, and QA. Badges are the result of earning special achievements in games, chats or Q&A. Coins can also be earned in games or chat (Fig. 4).

Fig. 4. My profile summary.

5.3   Chatrooms Section

Table 3. Summary of chatroom section.

Online learning	Gamified experience
Talk with people from all over the world	Level up to increase user's public rooms quota
Select user language	
Learn new vocabulary by joining various topics	Earn coins to join public rooms
Give and receive feedback on messages	
Create public rooms and share user experience	
Create private rooms and invite members	

Main Page. The page My Chat Rooms represents the cornerstone of the application. The user can consult the rooms he has joined and also join or create new unique rooms. Each room is characterized by a topic, a language, a number of participants and a timer. Two different types of rooms are available (Table 3):

- *Public rooms* can be joined by anyone for a specific amount of coins. A user can only join a limited number of public rooms at once. The increase of the quota is linked to the user's level. A user not active after 1 day is considered a deserter and is automatically ejected from the chat to avoid ghost rooms.
- *Private rooms* can only be joined with a specific password in order to chat only with people the user wants to. He can join as many private rooms as he wants for free. The room can have either a limited or unlimited duration depending on its initial parameters.

The chat interface is very similar to other interfaces users would find in a chatting app. However, in addition to sending messages, the user can also give feedback about other's messages. Giving someone a thumbs down is a good way to aware a member of an eventual language mistake and does not penalize him. On the contrary, a thumbs up can be used to congratulate a member about the quality of a message and reward that user by increasing the XP gauge (Fig. 5).

Joining and Creating Chat Rooms. In the same way as for the main page, the list of pages can be filtered. Restrictions such as type of room language or category can be applied for a targeted search. Create a room allows the user to start a topic of choice and share it with the community or only with specific members. The creation of a room requires the input of all initial parameters including a name of the topic, a type of room, a set of three categories and a duration (Fig. 6).

Fig. 5. Public chatroom example.

Fig. 6. Creating and joining chatrooms.

5.4 Q&A Section

Table 4. Summary of Q&A section.

Online learning	Gamified experience
Ask questions	Gain XP interacting in Q&A section
Select user language	Level up when gaining likes for comments and
Learn new vocabulary	questions
Give feedback on	
questions/answers	

Main Page. The user can view all the questions asked through the Question Feed displayed on the front page. In addition, the user can create a question using the plus icon on the top right corner and choose the desired language of this section. Each question is characterized by a topic that acts as a filtering system for users to better locate questions in the future. Thumbs up, thumbs down, and answering posted questions are all ways to interact and gain XP while helping/practicing with others (Table 4).

Create a Question. New questions allow the user to start a question of choice and share it on the Q&A section of Chatty. The creation of a question requires the input of all initial parameters including a question topic, question content and a set of three categories (Fig. 7).

Fig. 7. Creating a new question.

5.5 Games and Challenges Section

Table 5. Summary of games and challenges section.

Online learning	Gamified experience
Learn grammar and vocabulary	Play fun games
	Play single mode or multiplayer
	Unlock new games
	Earn coins by winning games
	Earn coins by realizing challenges

Games. Games focus on specific aspects of a language like grammar or vocabulary but within a gamified environment. Games can be played in the language of users' choice, single or multiplayer, and the selected difficulty; all which will impact the amount of the reward. A click on the Play button directs the player to a waiting page. The app finds a playing partner if the selected mode is multiplayer. This game imagined for this prototype is built around the idea of a Connect Four: if the player gives a correct answer, they place a token on the grid and score increases (Table 5 and Fig. 8).

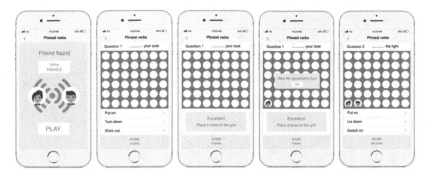

Fig. 8. Grammar game demo.

Challenges. Challenges are daily or monthly tasks to accomplish in order to receive coins. The page displays the list of current challenges and their related coin reward. They encourage the user to progress through the app and be active in the community. Gradually, the difficulty of challenges increases with the user's level. By constantly raising the difficulty and increasing the amount of reward, the user remains stimulated.

5.6   Shop Section

Table 6. Summary of shop section.

Online learning	Gamified experience
New chatting languages open new learning opportunities within the app New games are fun and effective: combining proven teaching points into entertaining pre-existing game ideas More chat rooms allow the user more diverse opportunities to practice	Unlockable content: - All purchases require a minimum XP - Available purchases require Coins XP and Coins are earned in other learning areas of the app Avatar add-ons create personalization

Languages. In Shop Languages, currently owned languages are displayed along with the corresponding level in each. For adding new languages, the app sets XP requirements for each additional language. If the user has enough XP, they are shown a list of options to choose from. The prototype contains a handful of languages, but the goal in a future application will be to contain all major languages (Table 6 and Fig. 9).

Fig. 9. Buying additional learning languages.

Games. In Shop Games, users can select from multi or single player options. Each games' name, information button, and difficulty are displayed in a clear and aesthetic manner. The game's instruction, XP requirement, and coin cost have purposefully been placed in the information popup. Next to each game is a "play" button. It provides a shortcut for the user to go directly to a game and resume learning.

Avatars. In Shop Avatar, users can personalize their photo with different accessories and styles. Here the user's extrinsic motivation is really driven, allowing them to set themselves apart from others with unique add-ons. In each option, the XP level and coins required are displayed. After purchasing an avatar add-on, the profile photo and status bar will be updated to show the new item. Under the style tab, users can opt to change their avatar completely.

Chats. In Shop chats, users are shown the rooms they already participate in. Again, we see the ergonomic feature of ease to transition. A "Go Chat" button encourages the user to resume chatting. Similar to Shop Languages, users can try to increase their chat room quota. The baseline number of chatrooms available to new users is 2. Using XP and coins to buy an additional chatroom, the user can increase the number of topics available to practice their learning languages in (Fig. 10).

Fig. 10. Personalizing and updating avatar.

6 Experiments

Two experiments were designed to test Chatty's overall efficacy and user ability. We tested N = 50 users from 6 countries with 25 males and 25 females. The app prototype is created mainly in English with a design framework emphasizing the use of clear icons so that users from different backgrounds can participate. The experiments were conducted simultaneously for each individual user with the process described below.

6.1 Experimental Process

Memory Experiment (Part A). With purpose unknown, divide users into two groups and issue a simple multiple-choice English grammar test. The questions in each group are identical with the only difference being the method of test taking. Each test has 4 questions (Fig. 11).

1) **Group 1**: Test via paper.
2) **Group 2**: Test via Connect 4 game programmed in Chatty.

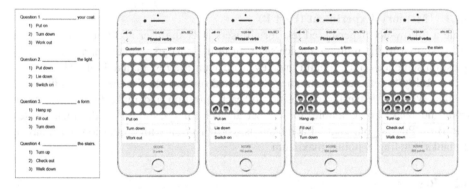

Fig. 11. Normal paper test versus gamified Chatty test

User Ability Experiment. This experiment serves two functions:

1) **Function 1:** Measures user experience (UX) and user interface (UI) of Chatty with 6 timed tasks.
2) **Function 2:** With the purpose of the previous English test (Memory Experiment A) unknown, distract the user with another task so that their working memory focuses on a new topic.

Table 7. List of tasks used in user ability experiment

Task
1. Buy Chinese language as a new learning language in the app, and how much did it cost? 购买中文作为一种新的学习语言（learning language），你花费了多少金币？
2. Check your user ID. 检查你的用户ID。
3. How many questions are posted in the question feed? 问题摘要（question feed）中展示了多少个问题？
4. Create new room with the following criteria. 遵循以下标准创建一个新房间：Room type: Private; Language: English; Category 1: Arts; Category 2: Arts Movements; Category 3: Impressionism; Duration: 1 day.
5. How many friends do you have on the app? 在这个app中，你有多少个朋友？
6. Buy your avatar an army hat. 为你的人物形象（avatar）在商店中购买一顶军帽（army hat）.

6.1.1 Memory Experiment (Part B)

Issue a follow-up, paper-based test for all users after the user ability experiment. The test is similar to the multiple-choice segment in memory experiment part A except the question sentences only contain one key word with the rest blanked out. This test the users' ability to remember what they were tested on. We require the users to fill in the blanks. We only leave the preposition of each question and make two blanks at the front and back. For example, the correct answer for question 1 in the memory test Part B is "Put on your coat." Each blank is worth 1 point with 4 questions each having 2 blanks, totaling 8 points maximum.

6.2 Results

Memory Experiment Results. At-test was performed with 95% confidence to see if there is any significant difference between the memory experiment part B results for the two different groups. Our hypothesis is that the group who takes the Part A test through the gamified Chatty app will perform better on memory test Part B than those who take the part A test by paper.

$$H_0 : \mu_{chatty} > \mu_{paper} \tag{1}$$

$$H_A : \mu_{chatty} \leq \mu_{paper} \tag{2}$$

The N = 50 users are divided into 25 observations, with each observation having a pair of users from each separate test group (Chatty v. paper). In these results, the null hypothesis states that the mean Part B test result from users in the Chatty group is higher than the mean Part B test result from users in paper-based test group. Because the p-value is less than 0.046, we reject the null hypothesis at the 0.05 significance level and conclude the gamified computer-based learning method in Chatty is more effective than the paper-based learning method.

User Ability Experiment Results. Whenever a user downloads a new app, they are unfamiliar with its processes and design. Therefore, the layout and structure of a new app must be intuitive in order for a user to accomplish whatever comes to mind. The Goal, Question, Metric (GQM) model is a hierarchal structure for software user ability. Goals are at the top level of the model and state the purpose and object for measurement. Questions break a goal down into several subcomponents which can then be measured specifically as metrics [21].

For our purposes, the goal is to make Chatty ergonomically designed so that users can navigate quickly and easily in the app. This goal can then be broken down into several questions (6 tasks) to accomplish. Finally, the metric used is the time measurement in seconds to complete each task. It can be said that a faster time to accomplish a task correlates to better app design. Hussain et al. [20] developed a framework for measuring mobile phone application usability based on this GQM model. In this framework, goals are broken down into three subcategories: effectiveness, efficiency, and satisfaction. The goal of user efficiency is similar to Chatty's goal for users to be able to navigate quickly and easily. This shows that out experimental method of measuring time to complete a task is a valid approach for testing user ability in Chatty.

Table 8. Results for time to complete task

Task	1	2	3	4	5	6
Mean	46.69	9.59	8.13	53.91	8.54	19.28
Median	37.45	9	7.32	48.88	5.94	16.4

Table 8 summarizes the average and median times it took all 50 users to complete each of the tasks from Table 7. We can see that all 6 tasks are completed within a minute, on average. These results are promising, but a benchmark is lacking since different apps will have different task completion times. Currently, there is no industry standard for how long it should take a user to complete a task. The overall goal is to minimize this time for the population. Sauro et al. [22] explains that "task times in usability tests tend to be positively skewed (longer right tails) due users who take an unusually long time to complete the task." This phenomenon is shown for some users who take 2–3 min to complete certain tasks in Chatty.

Due to there being no industry standard benchmark and an ease for right skewness, analysis for a new app's usability test should be aimed at estimating the population's usability performance. This estimation can be gathered by using sample tests to predict the population's median test performance. Medians are reliable for eliminating negative effects from outliers, since it is the middle most value. Sauro et al. used Monte Carlo simulations to compare different types of sample means' ability for predicting the population median. They conclude that "when providing an estimate of the average task time for small sample studies, the geometric mean is the best estimate of the center of the population (the median)" [22]. The geometric mean differs from normal mean calculations in that it is the nth root of the product of n numbers. The geometric mean is more appropriate for timed figures since it compounds each element. Other means compared were arithmetic, winsorized, harmonic, trim-top, and trim-all (Table 9).

Table 9. Geometric mean results for user ability test

Task	1	2	3	4	5	6
Geometric Mean	37.69	8.89	7.61	49.28	7.03	17.22

Based on this research, it can be concluded that the median task times for the future population of all Chatty users can all be accomplished within 50 s, 10 s faster than the arithmetic mean.

7 Conclusion

Chatty is an online platform where users can learn and improve their foreign languages. Chatty connects learners from all levels, cultures, and backgrounds so that they can communicate freely and efficiently. The goal of Chatty is to create implicit learning where users are fully engaged and do not realize how much they are learning. Chatty accomplishes this great teaching method through some unique qualities:

- **Group Participation**: Lessens the pressure of 1 on 1 communication, provides a friendlier atmosphere for users to speak in, and enforcing chatroom quotas which ensure topic rotation.
- **Instant Feedback**: Live peer evaluation within chatrooms grows the user's confidence.
- **Question Boards**: Language and culture questions can be asked and answered with certainty. This creates an exchange between users and leaves no topic left unanswered.

Lastly, Chatty is a *gamified experience*. It meets gamification standards with avatar personalization, badges, unlockable content, fun and relevant games, customized chat topics, and more. The main goal of educational gamification is to accelerate the learning curve of its users. From the experimental process we can see this application has hope in doing so by providing a fun, valuable, and flexible platform for users to grow with.

The app prototype's ergonomic design was measured through a user ability test based on the Goal, Question, and Metric (GQM) model. By measuring the time to complete six unique tasks in Chatty, the sample study yields geometric means to complete each task within 50 s. The geometric mean is a meaningful measurement to predict the median population times to complete a task within Chatty; therefore, we find that our application is intuitive and efficient and could easily be used by the population. Lastly, we tested Chatty's ability to improve a user's memory recall for new language material via gamification methods. With 95% confidence, experiment results show that users who took a grammar test in Chatty's gamified environment were better able to recall the tested material later on. This means that gamification shows promise for improving memory recall in users learning new languages.

References

1. Kingsley, T.L., Grabner-Hagen, M.: Gamification: questing to integrate content knowledge, literacy, and 21st-century learning. J. Adolesc. Adult Lit. **59**(1), 51–61 (2015). https://doi.org/10.1002/jaal.426
2. Buck, M.F.: Gamification of learning and teaching in schools a critical stance. Int. J. Media Technol. Lifelong Learn. **13**(1), 35–54 (2017). https://files.eric.ed.gov/fulltext/ED573768.pdf
3. Ling, L.T.: Meaningful gamification and students' motivation: a strategy for scaffolding reading material. Online Learn. J. **22**(2), 141–155 (2018). https://doi.org/10.24059/olj.v22i2.1167
4. Çeker, E., Özdamlı, F.H.: What "Gamification" is and what it's not. Eur. J. Contemp. Educ. **6**(2), 221–228 (2017). https://doi.org/10.13187/cjced.2017.2.221
5. Wiklund, E., Wakerius, V.: The Gamification Process: A framework on gamification. Master thesis, Jonkoping University, Sweden (2016)
6. Kim, J.: Human Computer Interaction. Ahngraphics, Seoul (2012)
7. Urh, M., Vukovič, G., Jereb, E.: The model for introduction of gamification into e-learning in higher education. Procedia-Soc. Behav. Sci. **197**, 388–397 (2015). https://doi.org/10.1016/j.sbspro.2015.07.154
8. Kumar, J.: Gamification at work: designing engaging business software. In: Marcus, A. (ed.) DUXU 2013. LNCS, vol. 8013, pp. 528–537. Springer, Heidelberg (2013). https://doi.org/10.1007/978-3-642-39241-2_58
9. Stott, A., Neustaedter, C.: Analysis of gamification in education. Surrey, BC, Canada **8**, 36 (2013). http://clab.iat.sfu.ca/pubs/Stott-Gamification.pdf
10. Dubois, D.J., Tamburrelli, G.: Understanding gamification mechanisms for software development. In: Proceedings of the 2013 9th Joint Meeting on Foundations of Software Engineering, pp. 659–662 (2013). https://doi.org/10.1145/2491411.2494589
11. Mora, A., Riera, D., Gonzalez, C., Arnedo-Moreno, J.: A literature review of gamification design frameworks. In: 2015 7th International Conference on Games and Virtual Worlds for Serious Applications (VS-Games), Skovde, Sweden, pp. 1–8 (2015). http://doi.org/10.1109/VS-GAMES.2015.7295760
12. Kankanhalli, A., Taher, M., Cavusoglu, H., Kim, S.H.: Gamification: a new paradigm for online user engagement. In: Proceedings of International Conference on Information Systems, ICIS 2012, vol. 4, pp. 3573–3582. International Conference on Information Systems, ICIS 2012, Orlando, FL, US (2012). http://pdfs.semantischolar.org/1a3a/6cee15d4464a33d735349ff92db113308962.pdf
13. Radoff, J: Game On: Energize Your Business with Social Media Games. Wiley, Hoboken (2011). https://doi.org/10.2501/IJA-30-5-916-917
14. Zicherman, G., Cunningham, C.: Gamification by Design: Implementing Game Mechanics in Web and Mobile Apps. O'Reilly Media, Sebastopol (2011)

15. Julius, K., Salo, J.: Designing gamification. University of Oulu (2013). http://jultika.oulu.fi/files/nbnfioulu-201306061526.pdf
16. Werbach, K., Hunter, D.: For the Win: How Game Thinking Can Revolutionize Your Business. Wharton Digital Press, Pennsylvania (2012)
17. Lee, J., Lee, M., Choi, I.H.: Social network games uncovered: motivations and their attitudinal and behavioral outcomes. Cyberpsychol. Behav. Soc. Network. 15(12), 643–648 (2012). https://doi.org/10.1089/cyber.2012.0093
18. Kalmpourtzis, G.: Educational Game Design Fundamentals: A Journey to Creating Intrinsically Motivating Learning Experiences. AK Peters/CRC Press (2018). https://doi.org/10.1201/9781315208794
19. Subramony, D.: Dale's cone revisited: critically examining the misapplication of a nebulous theory to guide practice. Educ. Technol. 43(4), 25–30 (2003)
20. Hussain, A., Kutar, M.: Usability Metric Framework for Mobile Phone Application (2009). https://pdfs.semanticscholar.org/52c5/b1bd37509acdb203e9b1bbc951e1f6319e09.pdf
21. Basili, V.R., Caldiera, G., Rombach, H.D.: The Goal Question Metric Approach (1994). https://www.cs.umd.edu/users/mvz/handouts/gqm.pdf
22. Sauro, J., Lewis, J.: Average task times in usability tests: what to report? In: Conference on Human Factors in Computing Systems, pp. 2347–2350 (2010). https://doi.org/10.1145/1753326.1753679

Cognitive and Computational Aspects of Intercultural Communication in Human-Computer Interaction

Marcel Pikhart[(⊠)]

Faculty of Informatics and Management, University of Hradec Kralove,
Hradec Kralove, Czech Republic
marcel.pikhart@uhk.cz

Abstract. Human-computer interaction is the foundation of basically all fundamental communication practices which are underway in today's global world of interconnectedness. The areas included are mostly business, corporate and managerial communication, social media communication patterns and practices, various kinds of intercultural communication, etc. Human-computer interaction is also massively implemented in modern educational strategies, such as e-Learning, blended learning, hybrid learning and mLeaning. These two areas, i.e. business and learning processes, are heavily influenced by current trends in ICT and all aspects are influenced by new communication paradigms. The new communication paradigms are both cognitive and computational. Analog communication has been vastly abandoned and substituted by modern communication tools, means and processes. These cognitive and computational aspects must be taken into consideration so that we can optimize our communication patterns. The paper highlights the importance of intercultural aspects in human-computer interaction and communication. The research shows that the awareness of this topic is still not sufficient and tries to highlight its importance. The paper also provides pragmatic solutions for global digital communication patterns and strategies which could be implemented in the data transfer through visualization in websites. This way of optimizing is necessary for any human-computer interaction so that it will remain competitive and sustainable in the global world of interconnectedness.

Keywords: HCI · Human-computer interaction · Communication · Business communication · Intercultural communication · e-Learning · Hybrid learning · Blended learning · mLearning · Interculturality · Digital communication

1 Introduction

The recent unprecedented changes in the global world of interconnectedness [1–4] have brought various challenges in human communication that is now predominantly human-computer interaction-based communication (facilitated nowadays more and more through various social media and platforms such as Facebook, Twitter, Instagram, and with the use of business emails, presentations, etc. for everyday digital managerial, business and corporate communication) [5–7].

© Springer Nature Switzerland AG 2020
P.-L. P. Rau (Ed.): HCII 2020, LNCS 12193, pp. 367–375, 2020.
https://doi.org/10.1007/978-3-030-49913-6_31

These changes, initiated by internationalization, globalization and the ubiquitous use of information and communication technology in business and everyday communication practices, are responsible for a set of new approaches associated with modern communication tools and techniques. These aspects are already very much reflected for instance in modern teaching methodologies such as e-Learning, mLearning, blended learning, hybrid learning, etc. [8–13], and naturally, also in business communication based on these modern tools which are indispensable from current business communication [14–18].

This kind of computer-human interaction, i.e. using electronic tools in the learning process and business communication are both characterized by several aspects. One of the most important, and paradoxically the most neglected, is interculturality, or transculturality, which combines both cognitive and computational aspects. Cognitive aspects deal with values and categories our brain processes, and computational is how these values and categories are processed through digital communication means in any kind of human-computer interaction.

The global world can be defined by many features and characteristics, however, interculturality is certainly the most crucial despite the fact that it is still rather forgotten by information and communication experts and departments. Despite the urgent need to realize and implement interculturality in both e-Learning and business communication, we still lack its intentional presence and utilization in either of these platforms.

The paper focuses on both e-Learning and business communication as the author comes from the university which uses e-Learning in tutoring its international students of management. The paper claims that these two areas can work in synergy, exactly in the same way as the global world around us – i.e. the unique combination of ICT and business. These two areas are not only connected as isolated entities, but they present an environment of cooperation and a source of mutual enrichment.

The importance of machine learning, deep learning, computational linguistics and other current trends implemented in human-computer interaction clearly show the increased utilization of these modern trends in various aspects of human-computer interaction [19–21]. They are also a very important driver for innovation [22, 23] and can be widely implemented in educational platforms [8, 10–13, 24]. This kind of HCI, i.e. the utilization in smart devices in the learning process has seen many benefits that are well described by numerous research [25–38]. The research clearly shows the benefits and also stresses the importance of implementing these trends in e.g. e-Learning. We can see that e-Learning without artificial intelligence is still available in our universities and this presents a serious threat to our educational system which could slowly become obsolete and old-fashioned, i.e. not efficient and not attractive to the users.

However, all these processes, i.e. business, educational, communicational, and, basically, any kind of human-computer interaction, are always based on interculturality because they are executed in the global world of digital interconnectedness. It means that any kind of communication, human-computer interaction and data transfer in the global world, which is always and naturally culturally specific, i.e. it bears particular patterns which are embedded in the given culture and the users use them as a point of reference which creates the meaning for them, is done in peculiar combination of cognitively specific symbols through the means of digital media.

To realize cultural differences is a crucial aspect for the creators of various on-line courses as more and more students come from all over the world to use these tools. It is very similar in business studies because without the proper understanding of inter-culturality, we cannot succeed in the global village. Some aspects of interculturality have been implemented in user interface and business communication, but there are many of them to be investigated and described so that they can be further developed and used properly.

The cognitive aspects of communication define communication as a culturally-based set of tools and processes which work basically like the software of mind which influences all communication processes. Human-computer based interaction can, therefore, be likened to two various platforms (i.e. cognitive and computational) upon which this communication process is done. Culture and interculturality only add various aspects that alter the communication channels significantly if we, as the users of human-computer interaction, do not realize that, then a significant part of the communication is inevitably distorted or lost.

We must not forget that also in data representation, e.g. in websites, the model of information transfer is culturally specific, i.e. it is encoded, encrypted in the form of language used in the website and the user has to decode the message which the website contains. This process is well-known from communication science and must not be forgotten by information and communication specialist, website designers and creators.

2 Research Methodology

2.1 Research Design

The research was conducted in two areas: first, the university students, and second, several small and medium enterprises. The idea was to analyse both two areas, i.e. the university students and business practitioners, and compare the results. We supposed that the results yielded by the research would be rather different and maybe even contradictory because the former group are the students of ICT and the latter is the ICT practitioners.

Qualitative research was conducted at the Faculty of Informatics and Management at the University of Hradec Kralove, the Czech Republic, in its foreign students into the importance of interculturality in e-Learning platforms and in several Czech SMEs doing business globally. The research was conducted in 2019 during the Summer School of the University, which is July and August 2019. The participants came mostly from China, Hong-Kong and Taiwan. They all took part in the course of Intercultural business communication tutored by the author of this paper. The total number of respondents was 37, both male and female, age from 21 to 25.

The researched small and medium enterprises (SMEs) (also in summer 2019) were the Czech small and medium sized enterprises doing business globally. Their management (the total number was 18 respondents) had to answer the same questions as the university students. Their age was between 34 to 65.

The data collection process was in the form of a questionnaire with the first group (i.e. the university students) and guided interviews with the second one (i.e. the managers of the Czech SMEs).

The research focused on how much both the students and the management of SMEs realize the importance of interculturality in human-computer interactions, i.e. in e-Learning platforms and electronic business communication, respectively. The idea was to analyse their approach to the importance of cultural issues in various data platforms, such as company websites, e-Learning tools, e-Learning apps, etc.

2.2 Research Question

How much will the international students from Asia and the Czech managers of small and medium enterprises be aware of the importance of intercultural issues in global management, business and learning? How much importance will they attribute to the issue of interculturality in various aspects of human-computer interaction, such as company websites, dynamic platforms, apps, e-Learning tools, etc.?

2.3 Hypothesis

The research hypothesis is that the awareness in neither of the groups will be significant and that the respondents in both groups will be generally untouched by the issue despite the current research into interculturality in business, managerial and corporate communication and its utilization in various ICT and digital communication platforms.

2.4 Research Importance

The research findings will be important for the creators of curricula and various on-line learning platforms and for business practitioners who use modern communication tools on a daily basis for their business communication. As described above, those who are responsible for these items do not realize the importance of interculturality in ICT and business communication, and also the students of business and ICT lack a significant notion about the complexity of the issue.

Cognitive and computational aspects of human-computer interaction are crucial in several areas of human endeavor. Namely, business, communication and education. In the global business activity, the processes are, naturally, intercultural, such as communication and education which are conducted in the global environment. To be able to succeed in this global context, we cannot forget about this aspect, and human-computer interaction practices must take it into consideration if we want to keep it competitive and sustainable.

2.5 Research Findings

The research findings are as follows:

- 67% of the students do not realise the importance of interculturality in e-Learning platforms and business communication
- 45% of the managers of SMEs do not realise the importance of interculturality in business communication

- 34% of the students cannot see any relevance of interculturality in ICT and HCI
- 27% of the managers of SMEs cannot see any relevance of interculturality in ICT and HCI.

The results clearly show the differences in these two groups. The students, despite their lack of practical experience, are more aware of the relevance of the topic. It is probably caused by their everyday contact with technologies that are operating globally and bear intercultural aspects into consideration. However, the SMEs managers are less aware of the topic due to their lack of experience with the issue. Their lack of awareness of this issue can be crucial for their international business encounters and, potentially be very risky for their business communication practices in the future.

However, after the course of Intercultural business communication, the numbers have changed significantly. The same research (informal control research) was conducted again at the end of the course whose aim was to improve their awareness of the topic and equip them with communication strategies they could implement in their professional expertise, both business and informational (ICT). Finally, after the course, the students acknowledged the importance of intercultural issues in the global world of business and information technology.

The differences in these two groups of respondents, i.e. the students and the managers, were mostly influenced by their age. The students were Generation Z, i.e. the digitally savvy and well-equipped generation, however, the managers were mostly middle-aged generation, in their 40s and older, who still lack the hands-on experience with the global business communication despite the fact that these companies do business globally, but on a rather limited scale.

The research proved that the awareness of the importance of interculturality issues in ICT and business communication is very low and both the students and the managers were surprised how much this lack of information can influence human-computer interaction processes.

2.6   Research Question Solution

The research question focused on how much the two researched groups will be aware of the importance of the given topic. Despite the relevant literature and research into this area, the real awareness is rather limited, it is not missing totally, but is it more or less intuitive, based on some suppositions and personal feelings.

This approach is, naturally, not sufficient and can cause significant problems.

2.7   Research Hypothesis Confirmation

The research hypothesis has been, thus, confirmed by the research, i.e. the awareness in neither of the groups is significant and that the respondents in both groups are, generally, untouched by the issue despite the current research into interculturality in business, managerial and corporate communication and its utilization in various ICT and digital communication platforms.

2.8 Limitations of the Research

The research was conducted on a small scale of Asian students (34) and Czech managers (18), however, the paper claims the results can be generalized and are replicable.

The research does not need to be repeated on a larger scale as these results are sufficient for the basic information about the situation. It should be rather followed up with practical and pragmatic steps.

3 Practical Implications

The research findings will be helpful both for ICT area and business studies because they clearly navigate through the wild area of human-computer interaction which for the time being lacks significantly relevant guidance.

There are, basically, two general approaches to this issue that could be implemented in ICT. They will improve information transfer and global communication practices. They could be applied in website creation, data representation, information transfer, etc. These two approaches are as follows:

– First, culturally specific, and
– Second, culturally neutral.

The first means creating culturally specific messages, i.e. websites which apply the principles peculiar to the given culture. This would mean the geographical localization of the website. This approach is used in many international companies already.

The second, which is more modern, is based on minimalistic website and information representation, which will provide culturally neutral information in basically any culture, and this approach can be used globally without any particular cultural aspect. The benefit is that the minimalistic website will be attractive to the global audience without any negative connotations which are present in the first model. However, this model can seem sterile and not very attractive.

4 Conclusion

The paper attempts to draw our attention to the importance of intercultural issues in business, education and also in ICT. All these areas are massively influenced by this aspect due to the wide-spread globalization and ignoring this topic poses a threat to our communication strategies. By ignoring it, we cannot succeed and our competitiveness in the global market is also heavily reduced.

Cognitive aspects of human communication and all the cultural aspects of it are crucial not only from a psychological point of view but they create both an opportunity and a threat to our communication patterns in the global digital world. This paper attempts to bring this issue to the attention of ICT practitioners who are responsible for data transfer optimization and any kind of human-computer interaction in companies.

The research showed that the topic, despite its urgency, is still neglected and this matter should be discussed in more detail to keep our business and educational institutions competitive and sustainable.

Acknowledgements. The paper was created with the support of SPEV 2020 at the Faculty of Informatics and Management of the University of Hradec Kralove, Czech Republic. The author would like to thank the student Ales Berger for his help when collecting the data of the research.

References

1. Pikhart, M.: Intercultural business communication courses in European Universities as a way to enhance competitiveness. In: Soliman, K.S. (eds.) Proceedings of the 32nd International Business Information Management Association Conference (IBIMA), 15–16 November 2018 Seville, Spain, pp. 524–527. International Business Information Management Association (2018) ISBN: 978-0-9998551-1-9
2. Pikhart, M.: Multilingual and intercultural competence for ICT: accessing and assessing electronic information in the global world. In: Choroś, K., Kopel, M., Kukla, E., Siemiński, A. (eds.) MISSI 2018. AISC, vol. 833, pp. 273–278. Springer, Cham (2019). https://doi.org/10.1007/978-3-319-98678-4_28
3. Pikhart, M.: Technology enhanced learning experience in intercultural business communication course: a case study. In: Hao, T., Chen, W., Xie, H., Nadee, W., Lau, R. (eds.) SETE 2018. LNCS, vol. 11284, pp. 41–45. Springer, Cham (2018). https://doi.org/10.1007/978-3-030-03580-8_5. Print ISBN: 978-3-030-03579-2, Electronic ISBN: 978-3-030-03580-8
4. Pikhart, M.: Communication based models of information transfer in modern management - the use of mobile technologies in company communication. In: Soliman, K.S. (ed.) Proceedings of the 31st International Business Information Management Association Conference (IBIMA), 25–26 April 2018 Milan, pp. 447–450. International Business Information Management Association (IBIMA) (2018). ISBN: 978-0-9998551-0-2
5. Pikhart, M.: Sustainable communication strategies for business communication. In: Soliman, K.S. (ed.) Proceedings of the 32nd International Business Information Management Association Conference (IBIMA), Seville, Spain, 15–16 November 2018, pp. 528–53. International Business Information Management Association (2018). ISBN: 978-0-9998551-1-9
6. Pikhart, M.: Current intercultural management strategies. The role of communication in company efficiency development. In: Proceedings of the 8th European Conference on Management, Leadership and Governance (ECMLG), pp. 327–331 (2012)
7. Pikhart, M.: Communication based models of information transfer in modern management – the use of mobile technologies in company communication. In: Innovation Management and Education Excellence through Vision 2020. IBIMA 2018, pp. 447–450 (2018)
8. Klimova, B.: Teacher's role in a smart learning environment—a review study. In: Uskov, V. L., Howlett, R.J., Jain, L.C. (eds.) Smart Education and e-Learning 2016. SIST, vol. 59, pp. 51–59. Springer, Cham (2016). https://doi.org/10.1007/978-3-319-39690-3_5
9. Klimova, B.: Assessment in the e-Learning course on academic writing – a case study. In: Wu, T.-T., Gennari, R., Huang, Y.-M., Xie, H., Cao, Y. (eds.) SETE 2016. LNCS, vol. 10108, pp. 733–738. Springer, Cham (2017). https://doi.org/10.1007/978-3-319-52836-6_79

10. Klímová, B., Berger, A.: Evaluation of the use of mobile application in learning English vocabulary and phrases – a case study. In: Hao, T., Chen, W., Xie, H., Nadee, W., Lau, R. (eds.) SETE 2018. LNCS, vol. 11284, pp. 3–11. Springer, Cham (2018). https://doi.org/10.1007/978-3-030-03580-8_1

11. Klimova, B., Poulova, P.: Mobile learning and its potential for engineering education. In: Proceedings of 2015 I.E. Global Engineering Education Conference (EDUCON 2015), pp. 47–51. Tallinn University of Technology, Tallinn (2015)

12. Klimova, B., Poulova, P.: Mobile learning in higher education. Adv. Sci. Lett. **22**(5/6), 1111–1114 (2016)

13. Klimova, B., Simonova, I., Poulova, P.: Blended learning in the university English courses: case study. In: Cheung, S.K.S., Kwok, L.-F., Ma, W.W.K., Lee, L.-K., Yang, H. (eds.) ICBL 2017. LNCS, vol. 10309, pp. 53–64. Springer, Cham (2017). https://doi.org/10.1007/978-3-319-59360-9_5

14. Pikhart, M.: Electronic managerial communication: new trends of intercultural business communication. In: Innovation Management and Education Excellence Through Vision 2020, IBIMA 2018, pp. 714–717 (2018)

15. Pikhart, M.: Managerial communication and its changes in the global intercultural business world. In: Web of Conferences (ERPA 2015). vol. 26 (2016)

16. Pikhart, M.: Intercultural linguistics as a new academic approach to communication. In: Web of Conferences (ERPA 2015), vol. 26 (2016)

17. Pikhart, M.: Implementing new global business trends to intercultural business communication. In: Procedia Social and Behavioral Sciences. ERPA 2014. vol. 152, pp. 950–953 (2014)

18. Pikhart, M.: New horizons of intercultural communication: applied linguistics approach. In: Procedia Social and Behavioral Sciences, ERPA 2014, vol. 152, pp. 954–957 (2014)

19. Alpaydin, E.: Machine Learning, The New AI. MIT Press, Cambridge (2016)

20. Buckland, M.: Information and Society. MIT Press, Cambridge (2017)

21. Clark, A., et al.: The Handbook of Computational Linguistics and Natural Language Processing. Blackwell, Chichester (2010)

22. Simonova, I., Poulova, P.: Innovations in data engineering subjects. Adv. Sci. Lett. **23**(6), 5090–5093 (2017)

23. Simonova, I., Poulova, P.: Innovations in enterprise informatics subjects. In: Auer, M.E., Guralnick, D., Uhomoibhi, J. (eds.) ICL 2016. AISC, vol. 544, pp. 583–590. Springer, Cham (2017). https://doi.org/10.1007/978-3-319-50337-0_56

24. Klimova, B.: Assessment in the e-Learning course on academic writing – a case study. In: Wu, T.-T., Gennari, R., Huang, Y.-M., Xie, H., Cao, Y. (eds.) SETE 2016. LNCS, vol. 10108, pp. 733–738. Springer, Cham (2017). https://doi.org/10.1007/978-3-319-52836-6_79

25. Wu, Q.: Learning ESL vocabulary with smartphones. Procedia Soc. Behav. Sci. **143**, 302–307 (2014)

26. Wu, Q.: Designing a smartphone app to teach English (L2) vocabulary. Comput. Educ. (2015a). https://doi.org/10.1016/j.compedu.2015.02.013

27. Wu, Q.: Pulling mobile assisted language learning (MALL) into the mainstream: MALL in broad practice. PLoS ONE **10**(5), e0128762 (2015)

28. Sung, Y.T., Chang, K.E., Liu, T.C.: The effects of integrating mobile devices with teaching and learning on students' learning performance: a meta-analysis and research synthesis. Comput. Educ. **94**, 252–275 (2016)

29. Tayan, B.M.: Students and teachers' perceptions into the viability of mobile technology implementation to support language learning for first year business students in a Middle Eastern university. Int. J. Educ. Lit. Stud. **5**(2), 74–83 (2017)

30. Teodorescu, A.: Mobile learning and its impact on business English learning. Procedia Soc. Behav. Sci. **180**, 1535–1540 (2015)
31. Tingir, S., Cavlazoglu, B., Caliskan, O., Koklu, O., Intepe-Tingir, S.: Effects of mobile devices on K–12 students' achievement: a meta-analysis. J. Comput. Assist. Learn. **33**(4), 355–369 (2017)
32. Miller, H.B., Cuevas, J.A.: Mobile learning and its effects on academic achievement and student motivation in middle grades students. Int. J. Schol. Technol. Enhanced Learn. **1**(2), 91–110 (2017)
33. Muhammed, A.A.: The impact of mobiles on language learning on the part of English foreign language (EFL) university students. Procedia Soc. Behav. Sci. **136**, 104–108 (2014)
34. Oz, H.: Prospective English teachers' ownership and usage of mobile device as m-learning tools. Procedia Soc. Behav. Scie. **141**, 1031–1041 (2013)
35. Males, S., Bate, F., Macnish, J.: The impact of mobile learning on student performance as gauged by standardised test (NAPLAN) scores. Iss. Educ. Res. **27**(1), 99–114 (2017)
36. Mehdipour, Y., Zerehkafi, H.: Mobile learning for education: benefits and challenges. Int. J. Comput. Eng. Res. **3**(6), 93–101 (2013)
37. Lopuch, M.: The effects of educational apps on student achievement and engagement (2013). http://www.doe.virginia.gov/support/technology/technology_initiatives/eLearning_back pack/institute/2013/Educational_Apps_White_Paper_eSpark_v2.pdf. Accessed 2 Mar 2018
38. Luo, B.R., Lin, Y.L., Chen, N.S., Fang, W.C.: Using smartphone to facilitate English communication and willingness to communicate in a communicative language teaching classroom. In: Proceedings of the 15th International Conference on Advanced Learning Technologies, pp. 320–322. IEEE (2015)

Secure Agents for Supporting Best-Balanced Multilingual Communication

Mondheera Pituxcoosuvarn[1]([⊠])(iD), Takao Nakaguchi[2], Donghui Lin[1](iD),
and Toru Ishida[3]

[1] Department of Social Informatics, Kyoto University, Kyoto, Japan
`mondheera@ai.soc.i.kyoto-u.ac.jp`
[2] Kyoto College of Graduate Studies for Informatics, Kyoto, Japan
[3] The School of Creative Science and Engineering, Waseda University, Tokyo, Japan

Abstract. There are technologies that support intercultural collaboration by allowing people to communicate more easily across the barriers of culture and language. However, sometimes user-sensitive information needs to be accessed. In best-balanced machine translation, a method that recommends the languages and machine translation services that should be used to assist multilingual group communication, user test scores must be disclosed to generate the language recommendations. There are various methods that can protect the data (test scores) and methods that allow simple statistic calculations, however, no existing method supports the complex calculations needed by the best-balanced machine translation method. This paper emphasizes the importance of user privacy in intercultural collaboration. We provide the initial idea and show how user test scores can be protected while supporting the recommendation system. We introduce a detailed example to discuss the design of a suitable user interface.

Keywords: User privacy · Multilingual communication · Secured implementation

1 Introduction

In intercultural collaboration, language differences are often a huge barrier. Machine translation (MT) has become a powerful tool to overcome these language barriers [4]. MT can be used as interpretation-rich chat system, where the users chat in their own language or their preferred language to another user who might not be able to use the same language(s) [8,12]. There are many MT services available with varied quality, but sometimes users' foreign language skill can yield better communication if the MT quality is too low. Our previous work proposed best-balanced machine translation (BBMT), a method that helps to identify the best language combination and the best language services [7]. Since it is difficult for humans to decide what languages should be used by a group of

© Springer Nature Switzerland AG 2020
P.-L. P. Rau (Ed.): HCII 2020, LNCS 12193, pp. 376–388, 2020.
https://doi.org/10.1007/978-3-030-49913-6_32

people who speak different languages with different levels of proficiency, BBMT suggests what languages should be used in multilingual communication given a set of known machine translation services. In order to implement BBMT, the quality of MT services and users' language test scores, i.e. TOEIC, TOEFL, must be disclosed and shared with a central BBMT server.

However, many users will not feel comfortable with sharing their language scores and forcing them to do so might give a negative impression of BBMT. As well as other personal information, it is important to protect the confidentiality of test scores as is evidenced by the many organizations that emphasize the privacy of test scores. For example, Education Testing Service (ETS), a non-profit organization that administers international tests, including, TOEFL, and TOEIC, pays close attention to confidentiality. Their policy requires private information, including score data, to be kept confidential unless there is the informed consent of the individual is given. The Family Educational Rights and Privacy Act (FERPA) of the United State also requires written permission from the students' parent or eligible student before any data from a student record can be released including test scores [13].

Given the importance of preventing test scores from being disclosed, we address here a key issue with the previous version of BBMT, its process requires the distribution of test scores, which violates the confidentiality of users' sensitive data.

Various methods exist to protect user privacy [5,11,15]; however, nnone are suitable for BBMT. Most of the existing methods can protect the data itself and simple statistical calculations. They do not work for BBMT since BBMT requires fairly complex calculation procedures.

This paper provides the initial idea and presents an example of how user test scores can be protected while being subjected to complex calculations. In addition, this paper also discusses how to design a user interface based on BBMT, as we would like to emphasize the importance of privacy in intercultural collaboration.

2   Related Work

Currently, a number of methods can be used to protect data. For example, K-anonymity [11] is commonly used to enforce data privacy, in particular for data publishing; it usually involves data suppression and generalization. Different types of data will have different characteristics, and so different security methods might be needed. For instance, student test scores also have their own characteristic, Yi [15] presented a method to publish test scores in a location-based service while protecting student's privacy with K-anonymity.

Cryptography has been used to help protect user privacy. Private data can be leaked, especially when the data is online. There are studies that use encryption to protect confidentiality, for example, Popa et al. [9] proposed a system called CryptDB; it uses encrypted database queries to protect sensitive data. Their idea is to execute SQL queries on encrypted data and link encryption keys to user passwords so that even the database admin cannot access the data.

Many times the data must be protected but also processed. Studies have examined the use of the data without violating data privacy. [5] proposed a method based on min max normalization transformation that can protect the privacy of data in data mining services. In addition to protecting user's data, Yokoo et al. [16] proposed a method to protect agent's private information with distribution techniques. They use a public key encryption scheme that allows the information to be computed cooperatively while making it impossible to link the data back to the agents.

Using raw data encryption and decryption is not enough to make user scores invisible from the other agents, since the data manipulation schemes can be very complex and there is a chance that another agent can guess a user's language level. Existing methods to protect data privacy while allowing the data to be processed and utilized, but each was designed for a specific type of data and specific application. For example, data suppression is not suitable if the computations must be performed on the raw data, but it is useful for data publication services. None of the existing methods can keep language score data private while making best-balanced calculation possible.

There are researchers have been working on security and privacy in various areas of HCI [6,10]. For example, Bauer et at. [1] studied the effects of awareness program on information security in banks, and Caviglione [3] studied human awareness of security and privacy threats in smart environments. As awareness and the importance of user privacy have not been discussed in intercultural collaboration, our goal is to emphasize the importance of user privacy in this field.

3   User Language Score in Best-Balanced Machine Translation

In this section, we describe how BBMT employs user language scores to provide language recommendations.

Figure 1 shows a situation wherein it is difficult to decide what language and what service should be used. There are three users: user J, user C, and user K. They have different mother languages and they have different levels of English skill. User J has limited English skill. So, when they decide to chat using English, user J cannot actively participate in the conversation. If they user MT and if the translation between Chinese language and Korean language is poor, user J can participate actively using the native language but user C and user K might have trouble reading the poorly translated messages. With more users, it would be even more difficult to decide the languages that should be used. To solve this problem, BBMT asks users to send their language scores to a central BBMT server, called here the *Optimizing Agent*, to generate a recommendation of the most suitable language to be used. In this example, the best language combination should be for user J to use Japanese language while user C and user K speak in English.

3.1   Language Combination

BBMT selects the best-balanced languages by first listing all possible combinations of languages. Let ja, ko, and zh represent Japanese Korean, and Chinese language and $C_i = (L_J, L_K, L_C)$. Combination C_i specifies the user/language pairing Each combination C_i contains the language used by user $J(L_K)$, user $K(L_K)$, and user $C(L_C)$. From the user profiles in Fig. 1, when there could be eight possible language combinations, C_1 to C_8 as follows:

$$C_1 = (ja, ko, zh)$$
$$C_2 = (ja, ko, en)$$
$$C_3 = (ja, en, zh)$$
$$C_4 = (ja, en, en)$$
$$C_5 = (en, ko, zh)$$
$$C_6 = (en, ko, en)$$
$$C_7 = (en, en, zh)$$
$$C_8 = (en, en, en)$$

With MT, combination C_1 is generally used when everybody uses their native languages. C_8 indicates the situation wherein English is used by all users, in this case it means no translation is needed. The recommendation in Fig. 1 is C_4 so user J uses Japanese and the others user English.

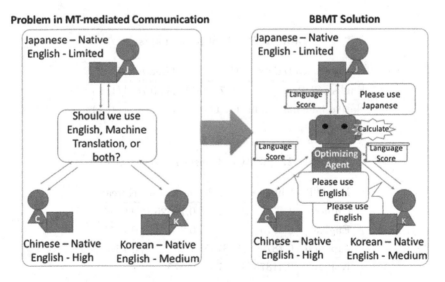

Fig. 1. A problem in MT-mediated communication and a solution with BBMT.

3.2 Quality of Message

Based on an existing work [2], BBMT uses user language scores and MT quality to calculate a value called quality of message (QoM).

$$QoM(P_i, MT_{i,j}, P_j) = WritingSkill(P_i, L_i) \times Accuracy(MT_{i,j}) \times ReadingSkill(P_j, L_j) \quad (1)$$

From Eq. (1) QoM is calculated by multiplying writing skill in language L_i of user P_i by MT quality achieved when translating the original message language into the receiver's language, and the product is then multiplied by receiver P_j 's reading skill of language L_j. Since QoM from P_i to P_j is not equal to the QoM from P_j to P_i, the two QoM values are averaged before use in the next step of the calculation.

3.3 Selecting Best-Balanced Language Combination

To select the best balanced language combination, all QoMs must be calculated and the data used in this calculation includes user language score and MT quality. Table 1 shows that the language skill is given by $(ReadingSkill, WritingSkill)$ and consists of values in the range of 0 to 1. Human-evaluated MT quality, in Table 2, also ranged from 0 to 1. 1. When no translation is needed, for example from Chinese to Chinese, the quality is set to 1.

Table 1. Profile of participants

Language skill/User	User J	User K	User C
English Skill	(0.75, 0.5)	(1, 0.75)	(1, 1)
Native Language Skill	(1, 1)	(1, 1)	(1, 1)

Table 2. Quality of translation services

From/To	Chinese	English	Japanese	Korean
Chinese	1	0.6625	0.75625	0.6625
English	0.5875	1	0.7	0.7375
Japanese	0.7875	0.88125	1	0.75
Korean	0.41875	0.5875	0.675	1

To demonstrate the calculation, we use the language skills in Table 1 and MT quality in Table 2 to calculate average QoM (AvgQoM) for every combination, as shown in Table 3. Table 3 shows AvgQoM from C_1 to C_8 for each user communication pair.

The combination with Pareto optimal AvgQoM is selected as BBMT output. In this case, C_4 is the only Pareto optima since it is impossible to make one AvgQoM better without making another AvgQoM worse. As a result, BBMT selects the language combination C_4, which recommends user J to use Japanese, and user K and user C to use English when conversing.

If there is more than one Pareto optima, the combination with the least variance among its AvgQoMs is selected.

4   User Language Score Protection

Because the original BBMT process requires that a central server collect all user language scores, we describe a method of computing BBMT without destroying user privacy.

There are two key ideas. First, the calculation tasks are divided into small pieces and distributed to different agents, so none of them can know or guess the full information. Second, when a part of the data that contains test score information must be transmitted to permit processing, it is encrypted with a public key. The agent with the private key to decrypt the data must not be able to relate decrypted test score to the score owner.

Figure 2 shows how BBMT can be computed without disclosing user scores. For BBMT, test score information exists in QoMs and AvgQoMs. Instead of

Table 3. An example of AvgQoM Table.

Combination	Language and average QoM between two users		
	User J - User C	User C - User K	User K - User J
C_1	ja-zh	zh-ko	ko-ja
	0.7125	0.5406	0.7719
C_2	ja-en	en-ko	ko-ja
	0.7906	0.625	0.7719
C_3	ja-zh	zh-en	en-ja
	0.7125	0.5703	0.7906
C_4	ja-en	en-en	en-ja
	0.7906	0.875	0.7906
C_5	en-zh	zh-ko	ko-en
	0.4047	0.5406	0.4688
C_6	en-en	en-ko	ko-en
	0.75	0.625	0.4688
C_7	en-zh	zh-en	en-en
	0.4047	0.5703	0.5312
C_8	en-en	en-en	en-en
	0.75	0.875	0.5312

having a centralized *Optimizing agent* to perform the calculation, AvgQoM calculation is done by the personal agents or on the user's computers. This version sets *Process Managing Agent(PMA)* to create the list of possible language combinations, in the previous example the combinations C_1 to C_8. Next, PMA tries to collect all AvgQoM for every combination. For each AvgQoM, PMA will send a request to one of the user's *Personal Agent (PA)* randomly. AvgQoM calculation is computed by two PAs and the calculation is divided into two parts.

4.1   AvgQoM Calculation

To calculate AvgQoM between user k and user j in combination C_8 when everybody use English, PMA sends a request contains necessary information including a reference ID, language that user K uses in combination C_8, next agent to send the calculation result to, and language that user J uses in combination C_1. Using this example, PMA asks the *Personal Agent* of user K (PA_K) to perform the first part of the calculation. This first requires the agent to compute two values by using the public key to do multiplication. Given that MT quality is disclosed to every agent, the first value is calculated by multiplying user k's English writing skill by the MT quality, in this case from English to English, meaning no real MT used so MT quality is 1 (perfect translation). The second value is calculated by multiplying user k's English reading skill by the same MT quality. With the information in Table 1 and Table 2, the first raw value should be 0.75 multiplied by 1 which results 0.75 and the second raw value should equal to 1 (1 multiplied by 1). However, these values are calculated with the private key so they are encrypted. The encrypted values are sent to the next agent, *Personal Agent* of user j (PA_J).

After receiving two pieces of encrypted AvgQoM, PA_J multiplies the first value with user j's English reading skill using its public key. If this value is not encrypted the raw value should be 0.75 multiplied by 0.75 which equals 0.5625. The second value is calculated by multiplying the received value, 1, with the English writing skill of user J which yields 0.5. These values cannot be seen even by PA_J, who performs the calculation since it does not have the private key needed for decryption. These two values are added together also using the public key, and the result, called encrypted AvgQoM, is sent back to PMA.

This simple example shows how AvgQoM is calculated without releasing raw user scores. To select the best-balance combination, PMA needs to send many calculation request to collect all the encrypted AvgQoM for every combination. If AvgQoM is not encrypted, PMA would accumulate exactly the same data as in Table 3. Since the AvgQoMs sent to PMA are encrypted, it can make a table filled with encrypted AvgQoM values.

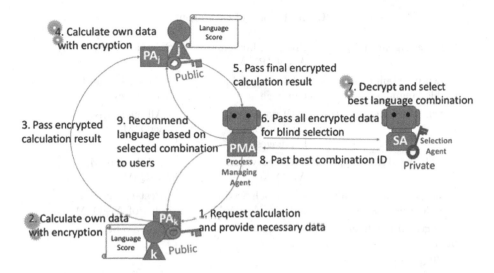

Fig. 2. A process to compute BBMT without disclosing user language score

4.2   Selecting Best-Balanced Combination

Because PMA knows the entire process and knows the users, it cannot have the private key. If this agent has the private key and thus the raw AvgQoM, if an AvgQoM is very low and MT quality is also very low, it can guess that both users for whom AvgQoM was calculated, have very low language skill. For this reason, another entity is needed to hold the private key. We also assign the selecting task to this agent and call it $SelectionAgent$ (SA).

Before passing the table information to SA, PMA removes all data that could be associated with users, such as user names and language combinations, before sending it to SA. SA sees only encrypted values. Its task is to decrypt those values with private keys and select the row with Pareto optimal QoM. Even though SA can see the raw AvgQoM value, it knows nothing about those AvgQoMs such as combination, language, or score owner.

5   Privacy Protection Effect

We set the security requirement to be, no agent other than user's PA can see or guess the user's test score.

To prove that privacy is protected, we will make security argument using the view of each agent, as shown in Table 4. In secure computing, *view* of an agent contains information that is visible to each agent. Here, we assume that each agent is Honest-but-Curious (HbC), that is, the agent follows the steps of the protocol but tries to learn as much information as possible [14].

Table 4. View of each agent

Personal Agent (PA)	Process Managing Agent (PMA)	Selection Agent (SA)
- Own user language usable language	- All user usable language	- Public key and private key
- Own user language score	- All possible combination of languages	- All encrypted AvgQoM
- Public key for encryption	- All encrypted AvgQoM	- All decrypted AvgQoM
- Encrypted value that include other's score	- Best-balanced row index of AvgQoM	- Best-balanced row index of AvgQoM
- Suggested language to be used	- MT quality	- MT quality
- MT quality		

If a PA becomes an HbC adversary, it should not be able to determine the test score of any other user. From the view, PA has own user language score but has encrypted data from another PA. The encrypted data contains the value of the other's test score multiplied by MT quality. Since the data is encrypted, a PA who receives this data cannot see the raw value.

Next we consider PMA as an HbC adversary; this agent has user language list and language combination. However, AvgQoM values sent to this agent are encrypted. Without the private keys, it is impossible to see the test scores.

SA is the only agent that holds the private key of the user. If this agent knows the raw AvgQoM of a pair of users, it could guess the language scores. For example, if AvgQoM is close to 0, both users must be bad at the language(s). However, SA does not know the language nor whose scores the AvgQoM was calculated from. It has only AvgQoM, which cannot be linked back to language combinations or users.

Using view of each agent, we can conclude that our security requirement is satisfied. However, the natural leakage of information cannot be prevented, regardless of how secure the system is. For example, a malicious PA can joins the system many times and change its data input little by little. It can look for the change in recommended language result and become able to estimate the level of language ability of another user.

6   Interfaces Design

Using multi-agent and secure computation alters the process of calculation, however, the user might aware that their test score was not sent from their computers. To create this awareness, we propose a user interface design that implements BBMT.

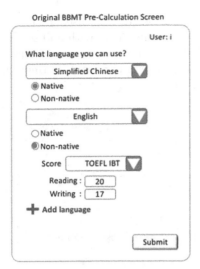 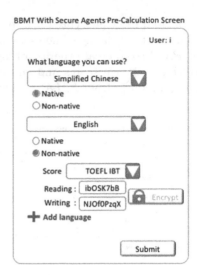

Fig. 3. User interface of the original BBMT and suggested interface for privacy-awared calculation

The left interface in Fig. 3 shows the original user interface of BBMT. The user is asked to select his/her language(s) using drop-down list. Then, whether his/her level is native or non-native. If the level is non-native, the interface will show another drop-down for the user to select an exam he/she took and ask for reading and writing scores. If the user speaks many languages, is it possible to click the plus symbol to add more languages. After all the data is entered, the user clicks on the submit button and all data is sent to the central *Optimizing Agent.*

To increase security awareness and improve users' attitude toward to the system, our interface proposal is shown on the right side of Fig. 3. An encryption button is added so the user can clearly see that the data is encrypted. After inputting the reading and writing scores, clicking on the encrypt button, the start of the encrypted data appears instead of the actual scores. The real encrypted data could be very long and only the first part of the data is visible to the user. The user can clearly see that the original score is encrypted and it could create different attitude toward the system.

This interface is simple for the user; however, in the implementation, the encryption process must be altered, depending on the encryption technic and tools. In the proposed computation method, encryption before receiving the calculation request might be complicated. For example, the test score is needed to be multiplied by all MT quality of every available MT services, since we do not know what language the other users or the future user will use.

An alternative interface that would make the calculation process less complicated requires two steps. The two-step interface includes pre-calculation and calculation. User language scores are required in the second step, so the data does not need to be encrypted before the calculation. In this case, the first step asks only for the languages the user can use to communicate with and sends the list to PMA so to create the list of all possible combinations. The second step of entering language scores and encrypting the scores can be performed after receiving a request from PMA, as shown in Fig. 4.

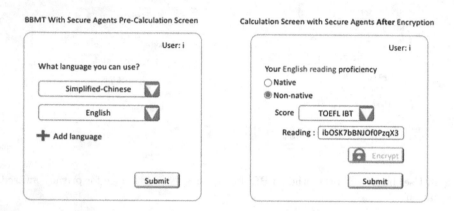

Fig. 4. User interface of 2-step interface calculation

While this 2-step interface prevents unnecessary calculations, multiplying user language scores by all MT quality values listed in the system, it could increase the user's burden as the user must assist in all subsequent computations of AvgQoM if necessary.

7   Conclusion

Best-balanced machine translation (BBMT) was proposed to select the languages and MT services best suited to each instance of MT-mediated communication. The original method requires users to disclose their language test scores to a central server, but many users will be uncomfortable with disclosing their language scores. To assure user privacy in intercultural collaboration, this paper described our initial idea and gave an example of how BBMT can be performed without creating a security risk. We applied a multi-agent approach and cryptography to create a privacy-aware version of BBMT. Our method allows BBMT to be computed while preventing any agent from seeing the test scores of any other agent.

We validated the method by considering each agent as an adversary and used agent views to ensure that no adversary has enough information to know or guess user language scores.

We proposed two user interface designs and discussed their advantages and weaknesses. The interfaces can be used in the privacy-aware version of BBMT to create awareness of data security and improve the user attitude toward BBMT.

Acknowledgments. This research was partially supported by a Grant-in-Aid for Scientific Research (A) (17H00759, 2017–2020) and (B) (18H03341, 2018–2020) from Japan Society for the Promotion of Science (JSPS). We thank Prof. Masayuki Abe for providing insight and expertise in secure computation used in this research.

References

1. Bauer, S., Bernroider, E.W.N.: The effects of awareness programs on information security in banks: the roles of protection motivation and monitoring. In: Tryfonas, T., Askoxylakis, I. (eds.) HAS 2015. LNCS, vol. 9190, pp. 154–164. Springer, Cham (2015). https://doi.org/10.1007/978-3-319-20376-8_14
2. Bramantoro, A., Ishida, T.: User-centered QoS in combining web services for interactive domain. In: 2009 Fifth International Conference on Semantics, Knowledge and Grid, pp. 41–48. IEEE (2009)
3. Caviglione, L., Lalande, J.-F., Mazurczyk, W., Wendzel, S.: Analysis of human awareness of security and privacy threats in smart environments. In: Tryfonas, T., Askoxylakis, I. (eds.) HAS 2015. LNCS, vol. 9190, pp. 165–177. Springer, Cham (2015). https://doi.org/10.1007/978-3-319-20376-8_15
4. Ishida, T., Murakami, Y., Lin, D., Nakaguchi, T., Otani, M.: Language service infrastructure on the web: the language grid. Computer **51**(6), 72–81 (2018)
5. Jain, Y.K., Bhandare, S.K.: Min max normalization based data perturbation method for privacy protection. Int. J. Comput. Commun. Technol. **2**(8), 45–50 (2011)
6. Papastergiou, S., Polemi, N., Karantjias, A.: CYSM: an innovative physical/cyber security management system for ports. In: Tryfonas, T., Askoxylakis, I. (eds.) HAS 2015. LNCS, vol. 9190, pp. 219–230. Springer, Cham (2015). https://doi.org/10.1007/978-3-319-20376-8_20
7. Pituxcoosuvarn, M., Ishida, T.: Multilingual communication via best-balanced machine translation. New Gener. Comput. **36**(4), 349–364 (2018)
8. Pituxcoosuvarn, M., Ishida, T., Yamashita, N., Takasaki, T., Mori, Y.: Machine translation usage in a children's workshop. In: Egi, H., Yuizono, T., Baloian, N., Yoshino, T., Ichimura, S., Rodrigues, A. (eds.) CollabTech 2018. LNCS, vol. 11000, pp. 59–73. Springer, Cham (2018). https://doi.org/10.1007/978-3-319-98743-9_5
9. Popa, R.A., Redfield, C., Zeldovich, N., Balakrishnan, H.: CryptDB: protecting confidentiality with encrypted query processing. In: Proceedings of the Twenty-Third ACM Symposium on Operating Systems Principles, pp. 85–100. ACM (2011)
10. Prettyman, S.S., Furman, S., Theofanos, M., Stanton, B.: Privacy and security in the brave new world: the use of multiple mental models. In: Tryfonas, T., Askoxylakis, I. (eds.) HAS 2015. LNCS, vol. 9190, pp. 260–270. Springer, Cham (2015). https://doi.org/10.1007/978-3-319-20376-8_24
11. Sweeney, L.: Achieving k-anonymity privacy protection using generalization and suppression. Int. J. Uncert. Fuzz. Knowl. Syst. **10**(05), 571–588 (2002)
12. Takasaki, T., Murakami, Y., Mori, Y., Ishida, T.: Intercultural communication environment for youth and experts in agriculture support. In: 2015 International Conference on Culture and Computing (Culture Computing), pp. 131–136. IEEE (2015)
13. U.S. Department of Education: Family educational right and privacy act (2018)
14. Wang, J., Kissel, Z.A.: Introduction to Network Security: Theory and Practice. Wiley, Singapore (2015)

15. Yi, T., Shi, M., Hong, Z.: Privacy protection method for test score publishing. In: 2015 7th International Conference on Information Technology in Medicine and Education (ITME), pp. 516–520. IEEE (2015)
16. Yokoo, M., Suzuki, K., Hirayama, K.: Secure distributed constraint satisfaction: reaching agreement without revealing private information. In: Van Hentenryck, P. (ed.) CP 2002. LNCS, vol. 2470, pp. 387–401. Springer, Heidelberg (2002). https:// doi.org/10.1007/3-540-46135-3_26

CIAM: A New Assessment Model to Measure Culture's Influence on Websites

Surbhi Pratap$^{(\boxtimes)}$ and Jyoti Kumar

Department of Design, Indian Institute of Technology Delhi, New Delhi, India
surbhi.pratap@gmail.com, meetjyoti@gmail.com

Abstract. Literature has reported user's culture to be an influencing factor towards the user experience of a website and hence it contributes to its rejection or uptake. It has also been reported that different cultures exhibit specific user interface preferences. However, there has been limited work to develop operational models that can assess the cultural inclination of a website design, which contributes to its user experience. This paper proposes an assessment tool called CIAM (Culture's Influence Assessment Model) through deriving observable user interface elements and mapping them to prevalent culture models. The proposed markers of culture's influence on a website were derived by a creative extension of reported work in literature and then was applied on 16 websites of 8 countries by 5 industry experts. It was found that the CIAM based assessment of websites was congruent with cultural dimensions of the 8 countries. In view of these findings, this paper argues that CIAM can be a useful tool when cultural disposition of a website needs to be assessed.

Keywords: Culture models · Assessment tool · Cultural influences · User interface elements

1 Introduction

The past decade has seen several studies highlighting the importance of factoring in user's culture while designing interactive products. Studies indicate that cultural characteristics are partially responsible towards rejection or slower uptake of a system [1]. Literature has also reported variations in specific user interface preferences across cultures [2]. It is noted that localization of user interface is essential to match the cultural characteristics for a good website experience [3]. It is also reported that interfaces designed for users from a specific country were perceived more attractive [4], and improved the work efficiency of those they were intended for [5]. A rapid increase in the presence of persuasive technologies in digital products which are designed to modify human behaviour and responses is recounted [6] and is used in studies to show that prior experiences and individual's sense of self in a social context have an effect on

© Springer Nature Switzerland AG 2020
P.-L. P. Rau (Ed.): HCII 2020, LNCS 12193, pp. 389–408, 2020.
https://doi.org/10.1007/978-3-030-49913-6_33

his subsequent behaviour without conscious awareness [7]. Cross-cultural research also shows that in order for persuasion to be most effective, it is often necessary to draw upon important cultural themes of the target audience [8]. Different cultures produce different artefacts and environments and similarly artefacts when consumed by multitudes of people may influence or even create new cultures [3, 9]. With this premise, this paper argues that operational tools and models that measure the influence of culture on an HCI product are relevant.

Culture models of Hofstede, Hall and Schwartz have been extensively used to develop frameworks for adaptation of culture on web communication [10, 11], user experience and user interface aspects [12, 13]. However, there is little literature on adaptation of Nisbett's culture model on user interface aspects. Some studies have used Nisbett's culture model to understand the implications of cultural difference on user cognition and aesthetic perception [14–16]. Most studies use a country-based definition of culture and propose design categories or suggest direct user interface adaptations related to a culture dimension. There has been limited work to develop operational models that can assess the influence of culture using visible user interface elements using more than one culture model even though it is noted that combining two or more culture models is more effective than using only one [17]. This paper develops a tool to assess the cultural disposition of a website using visible user interface elements. Since culture influences the user experience of a website, firstly observable user interface elements were identified from 5 layers of user experience using Garett's framework. Secondly, studies from literature were adapted to map these user interface elements to culture models of Hofstede, Hall and Nisbett. Finally, a metric called the Culture Influence Assessment Model(CIAM) is proposed to assess a website design through observable user interface elements. This metric is used by 5 UX designers to assess 16 military and educational websites of 8 countries. The findings suggest that CIAM can successfully assess the cultural disposition of a website design.

2   Methodology for Development of CIAM

The methodology used to develop the proposed 'Culture's Influence Assessment Model' (CIAM) in this paper consisted of three steps. In the first step, user interface elements were identified, in the second step, the identified user interface elements were mapped onto cultural models and in the third step, a metric for assessment of cultural influence on websites was developed. Details of each step has been presented in the following three subsections. Figure 1 illustrates this methodology in a schematic.

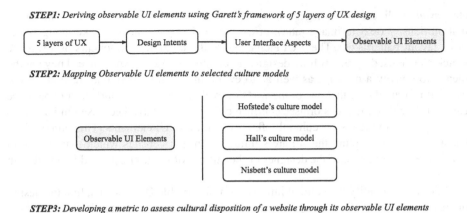

STEP1: Deriving observable UI elements using Garett's framework of 5 layers of UX design

5 layers of UX → Design Intents → User Interface Aspects → Observable UI Elements

STEP2: Mapping Observable UI elements to selected culture models

Observable UI Elements

Hofstede's culture model

Hall's culture model

Nisbett's culture model

STEP3: Developing a metric to assess cultural disposition of a website through its observable UI elements

Observable UI Elements — *assessed for* → Culture's influence on UI elements — *develops metric for* → UI Markers for website evaluation

Fig. 1. Schematic diagram of the methodology used to develop CIAM

2.1 Deriving Observable User Interface Elements from Garett's UX Model

First step in development of CIAM was to identify User Interface (UI) elements from websites so that based on these elements an individual can assess the cultural aspects in the website. For this purpose, a model of User Experience (UX) design proposed by Garrett was chosen [18]. This section discusses Garrett's model and derivation of UI elements based on this model.

Garett has described the five layers as a way to build UX in websites, namely, Strategy, Scope, Structure, Skeleton and Surface. It has been argued by Garett that from UX 'strategy' to the 'surface', UX develops in 'layers' where each intermediary layer progresses from abstract 'strategy' to more concrete 'surface'. The 'strategy' layer defines the strategy of the website, which is a response to the business goals and the user needs for that product. The 'scope' layer specifies functional and content requirements of the product. This includes services, features and facilities. The 'structure' layer defines the information architecture (the workflow and the hierarchy) of the product. The 'skeleton' layer defines the navigation, layout and arrangement of elements and the 'surface' layer defines the tangible elements like buttons, text, illustrations etc. Garett's 'elements of user experience' has been used widely for assessment of UX [19, 20] and it was felt by authors to be also useful to the cultural assessment process.

As each of these 'layers' is 'designed' with an 'intent' by a 'human' UX designer, thereby there is a possibility of culture's influence in selection of these UI elements. This paper has looked into this possible 'design intent' being influenced by the culture of the 'designer' or the 'design process' at each layer of UX.

In this paper, the term 'UI elements' has been used to refer to the 'surface' layer of the website consisting of the visible elements. The 'UI elements' of a website may include *graphical markers* like colours, orientation, saturation, geometrical elements etc.; *symbols* like fonts, images, icons, animation etc.; *regional markers* like information density (text to image ratio), grids, etc. and *surface markers* like navigational flow, layout patterns etc. These UI elements are the tangible components of a website which can be used by the website designer to create 'intended' experience. They are the means to convey a message as well as to evoke the desired emotional response from users. It is argued here that one of the ways of evaluation of a website's user experience can be to identify the types of user interface elements that have been used in its design and map them to the visible cultural influences on these UI elements. This process thus has a potential to capture the culture's influence in the websites which may be resent either due to the culture of the designer or the culture of the user captured by the design process.

In order to identify the cultural influence on observable UI elements, first the design intents at each layer of UX design process needs to be mapped. Figure 2 illustrates how the five layers of user experience are schematized into design intents and finally to observable user interface elements (OUI) and Table 1 presents the mapping.

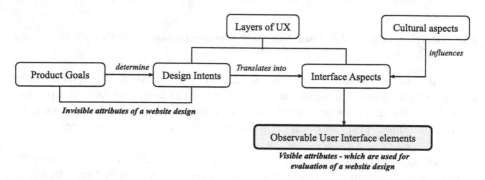

Fig. 2. Schematic diagram depicting how OUI are translated from the 5 layers of UX

Table 1. Deriving observable user interface elements from Garett's UX model

UX layer	Design intent	Interface aspect	Observable UI elements
Strategy	Persuasion - through representation/ exaggeration	Image selection	- Images that evoke a coveted emotion. - Montages/collages to create an effect
	Generation of interest-through first impression or building up learnability	Layout	- Information density - Minimal layout
		Navigation	- Navigation designed for user control - Shortcuts for repeat users

(continued)

Table 1. (*continued*)

UX layer	Design intent	Interface aspect	Observable UI elements
Scope	Motivation - through content - Establish context for user discretion	Text content	- High text to image ratio - Use of slogans/callouts/captions
		Iconography	- Visual correlation between graphic elements - Emphasis on symbols, certification, stamps
		Image selection	- Images celebrating youth - Images depicting conformity
Structure	Task flow - establish access control - navigation for user control	Navigation	- Contextual navigation - Task flows for user control - Direct access to nested items - Membership/sign up requirement
		Iconography	-Visible buttons that activate after signup - Use of wizards as help/support
		Social access	- Accented affiliations to outside groups - Easy sharing to social networking sites
		Text content	- Friendly messages - Chat support
Skeleton	Guide the user - through visual cues - using design principles	Navigation	- Nested/flat navigation
		Colour scheme	- Semantic colour scheme - high/low contrast colours
		Text content	- Fonts to organize content
		Layout	- Use of grids to categorize content - Use of Gestalt's principles to organize content
Surface	- Create a brand identity - Enhance the visual experience	Colour scheme	- Saturated/pastel palette - Monochromatic/Polychromatic - Colour scheme depicting a 'brand'
		Text content	- Fonts to depict a brand identity - Fonts for visual ease
		Iconography	- Ornamental icons - Icons of a 'brand'

As observable in Table 1, the first column enlists the five layers of UX as proposed by Garrett. The second column examines some of the possible design intents behind each layer. The third column classifies the user interface aspects through which these design intents could be achieved. These are then categorized into observable user interface elements which are finally visible to the user. Essentially this table derives the visible attributes of a website design from the 'invisible' design intent behind the website. After having identified the OUI elements, next they were mapped against the cultural models which is described in the next sub-section.

2.2   Mapping Culture Dimensions into Observable User Interface Elements

Literature has reported models and frameworks for adaptation of culture on web communication [11, 21], user experience and user interface aspects [12, 13, 22]. It is observed that most of the studies on culture's influence on websites have used one of the prevalent culture models like that of Hofstede, Hall or Schwartz [59]. It has also been argued that combining two or more culture models is more effective than using only one [17].

Nisbett's model of culture is another model which has been less reported to be used for website assessments though studies have reported its implication on user cognition and aesthetic perception [15, 16, 23–25]. It is argued here that Nisbett's model needs to be used for culture's assessment as this model takes the viewpoint of cultural differences on cognitive functions [26] and cognitive functions are primary to the UX while using a website [26, 27]. Hence, this paper has used Nisbett's model along with Hofstede's and Hall's. Three culture models of Hofstede, Hall and Nisbett and their implications on user interface aspects are discussed in the following three subsections.

Culture Models
Hofstede's Culture Dimensions
Hofstede [28] developed a theory of cultural dimensions using factor analysis to examine the results of a world-wide survey of employee values by IBM in the 1960s and 1970s. The original theory proposed four dimensions (later extended to six dimensions) along which cultural values could be analysed:

- Individualism-Collectivism IDV;
- Uncertainty Avoidance UA;
- Power Distance (strength of social hierarchy) PD
- Masculinity-Femininity (task orientation versus person-orientation) MAS.
- Long-Term Orientation LTO
- Indulgence - Self-Restraint IND [29].

Despite being criticized for its national concept and other shortcomings [30, 31], this model has been successfully applied in the field of HCI [29] and because of its empirical verification, is reported to be one of the most extensively applied and validated in a variety of cultural contexts [32]. There is a significant body of literature available on application of Hofstede's model in study of culture's influence on websites. Therefore for the authors of this paper, it was easier to develop a mapping of identified user interface aspects of the cultural dimensions by creative extension of the reported influences of culture on website design. Table 2 presents user interface aspects derived from related works against the reported literature based on which the mapping was developed.

Table 2. User interface aspects based on Hofstede's culture dimensions

Culture dimension	User interface elements	References
Power Distance - PD	Structured access to information Emphasis on symbols, authority, expertise, certification, stamps Prominence to leaders vs citizens Importance of security & barriers to access Social roles used to organize information. (like a section not visible to all, but only to a member)	[11, 33]
Individualism vs Collectivism - IDV	Images/Motivation based on personal achievements vs. socio-political success (A star on your uniform vs Flag over a summit) Argumentative rhetoric vs Community slogans Youth focused vs Aged in images and ease of reading the website content. Truth(facts) vs Relationships (social morality) Emphasis on change (focus on new things introduced vs using traditional expertise) Giving personal info out in the open vs protection of individual's info and hiding behind a group	[11, 33, 34]
Masculinity vs Femininity - MAS	Traditional distinctions on gender, age and family are marked upfront. Quick results for tasks to be achieved - gives a sense of mastery of the tool Navigation oriented to control rather than support (ease of mastery in use) Attention gained through competitions, games rather than poetry & visuals Graphics, Sound & animations are more focused to be utilitarian rather than pleasant.	[11, 33, 34]
Uncertainty Avoidance - UA	Simple and minimal designs with limited and clear choices Attempts to forecast results on established patterns Navigation designed for user to be in control - you are clear where you are on the website at any given point Help options clearly given to reduce errors. Redundant cues like colour, typo, sound used to reduce ambiguity, even if those cues don't have any relation with one another.	[11, 33, 34]
Long Term vs Short Term Time Orientation - LTO	Content focused on facts rather than practice. Rules are a source of credibility and information rather than relationships/authority Immediate gratification	[33, 34]

Hall's Theory on Cultural Context

Hall describes a culture's style of communication to distinguish it [35]. High-context cultures are those in which the rules of communication are primarily transmitted through the use of contextual elements (i.e., body language, a person's status, and tone of voice) and are not explicitly stated. This is in direct contrast to low-context cultures, in which information is communicated primarily through language and rules are explicitly spelled out. He developed this on his theory of Proxemics or the relationship of one with the space around himself and the way one defines the concept of time - Monochronic or Polychronic [36, 37].

Literature has reported studies which have analysed web design aspects based on Hall's theory of context, [32, 38–42], but they do not offer an objective framework to interpret it to observable user interface aspects. In this paper, the authors have examined Hall's theory of communication, interpreted the features of high context and low context cultures for a website user and then correlated them to user interface elements identified from related works in literature. Table 3 presents the identified user interface aspects derived from related works on the effect of Hall's cultural theory on website designs.

Table 3. User interface aspects based on Hall's cultural theory

Culture context	User interface aspects	References
High context cultures	Implicit messages are accepted. Figure & Ground seen together User will blame self for not understanding the website, so will put in effort to navigate to nested items More graphical/subtle cues to communicate Loyalty & Bonding with community will work Flexible layout Entire process of navigation is more important than the final result Can do multiple things at a time Distraction by elements will be forgiven Promptness is not so important Can share space Less concern for material focused security	[11, 43, 61]
Low context cultures	Direct and clear messages sent The website will be blamed for not being user friendly, so user will lose interest if (s)he finds a workflow tedious Clear content with instructions Individual rewards will be preferred Highly organised layout Final outcome is more important than process Can do only one thing at a time Design should make it easier to concentrate on one task at a time Promptness is very important Ownership of space is very important Security of 'owned' things - account/personal layout etc. is important	[11, 43]

Nisbett's Culture Theory

Nisbett has proposed that human behaviour and intelligence is not hard wired, rather a function of their socio-cultural environment and people use different tools to understand the world around them and hence their cognitive processes vary from each other [44]. He explains how ecology and economy shape the social structure which determines the cognitive process of an individual (Fig. 3).

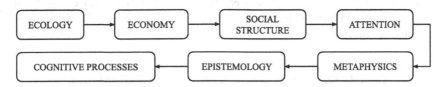

Fig. 3. Nisbett has proposed a schematic model of influences on cognitive processes

The theory proposes that due to different ecological and geographical environment, people from Asian cultures and those from the western cultures think in fundamentally different ways. The westerners focused more on the individual and their achievements. Their focus was on understanding the fundamental nature of everything, including the essence of individuals. This explained why they propounded more scientific theories. They would focus on categories with defined attributes and preferred rules and logic to separate a structure from its context. In contrast, Asians had a collectivist approach, where the emphasis was on how individuals could contribute to the society. The group was greater than the individual. They would see things in entirety, not as absolute and would prefer experience based knowledge and allow for multiple perspectives. This explained their rich tradition of philosophies and preference to predict events based on experiential learning. Figure 4 elucidates this theory.

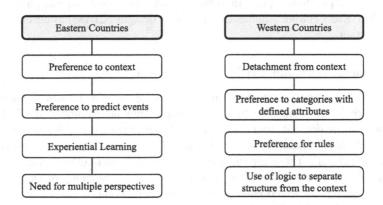

Fig. 4. Schematic of how easterners and westerners think differently according to Nisbett's theory

Nisbett's culture theory explains the effect of culture on cognition, which is an important aspect of HCI design [45]. However, it has mostly been explored to report cultural difference in perception of aesthetics, perception of object in a context and visual information processing [14, 46–50].

In this paper, inferences were taken out from related works in literature on Nisbett's theory on how cultural differences influence cognition, visual information processing, perception of aesthetics, perception of an object in a context. Next, these were examined from the perspective of a website user and user interface aspects were identified which are influenced by geography and culture of the user. The inferences are as presented in Table 4.

Table 4. User interface aspects based on Nisbett's cultural theory

Culture	User interface aspects	References
Western	- Navigation helps in control of individual elements - Visual focus on individual elements (even if they do not necessarily correlate) - Clear categories with defined attributes - First time right approach - preferred to be clear the first time	[14, 34, 47]
Eastern	- Navigation helps to put things in context - Visual focus on relationships between elements (buttons, fonts, colors, etc.) - Blurred categories - Experience learnability - repeated use(familiarity) can make the website easier to use	[14, 34, 47]

As observed in the previous sub-sections, this paper has adapted studies from literature on culture models of Hofstede, Hall and Nisbett [11, 14, 33, 34, 43, 47, 61] and derived user interface aspects from them. Using the above mapping, a metric was developed to assess culture's influence on website designs (CIAM) as described in the next sub-section.

2.3   Developing the Culture Influence Assessment Model

This section describes the development of CIAM (Culture's Influence Assessment Model) which is the main objective of this paper. For development of CIAM, first aspects of UI were derived from Garrett's UX design framework. Also, observable UI elements were listed against each aspect and each layer of UX design framework (as presented in Table 1). These aspects were then mapped onto cultural models (as presented in Table 2, 3 and 4). In this section, the process for mapping of Observable UI elements to the three selected cultural models has been done.

Table 5 displays the mapped UI elements against the three cultural models. The mapping was developed by creative extension of the research reported in literature as presented in the three tables above (Table 2, 3 and 4). Table 5 thus is a collation of specific Observable UI elements against the specific features of the cultural models. For example, in Table 5, row number 1, the interface aspect of 'Image selection' which a UX designer decides at a 'strategic level' with a specific 'design intent' (as presented in Table 1) may choose to present the image of 'individuals' rather than 'groups of people' on the website, which is a marker of 'Individuality' in Hofstede's model, represents 'Western orientation' in Nisbett's model and 'Low Context' in Hall's model.

Table 5. Mapping observable UI elements to culture models of Hofstede, Hall and Nisbett

Interface aspect	CIAM code	Observable user interface elements	Hofstede's culture model	Nisbett's model	Hall's model
Image selection	A1	Images celebrating youth, individuals	IDV	West	Low
	A2	Images of leaders, head of institution	PD | COL	East	High
	A3	Images depicting tradition, social order	PD | COL | UA		High
	A4	Images of groups of persons, families	PD | COL	East	High
	A5	Images depicting clear gender roles	MAS		
	A6	Animations or montages to create an effect	FEM		High
Color scheme	B1	Semantic color scheme	IDV | UA		
	B2	High contrast/saturated/bright colors	MAS | COL	East	High
	B3	Monochromatic color scheme	IDV		
	B4	Color scheme depicting a 'brand'/tradition	COL		High
Icons/graphic elements	C1	Visual correlation in graphic elements	UA		
	C2	Emphasis on symbols, certification, brand	PD | COL | UA	East	High
	C3	Ornamental icons	FEM		
	C4	Visible buttons that activate after sign up	Low UA | LTO		
	C5	Use of wizards as help/support	PD | MAS | UA		High
Layout	D1	Use of grids to categorize content	PD| UA | MAS | LTO	West	Low
	D2	Use of Gestalt's principles to organize content	UA		
	D3	Low information density at first level	MAS | STO		Low
	D4	Minimal layout	MAS | UA	West	Low

(*continued*)

Table 5. (*continued*)

Interface aspect	CIAM code	Observable user interface elements	Hofstede's culture model	Nisbett's model	Hall's model
Navigation	E1	Navigation designed for user exploration	MAS | UA		
	E2	Opening in the same browser window			Low
	E3	Direct access to nested items/sidebars/menus	PD		High
	E4	Membership/sign up requirement	Low UA		
	E5	Shortcuts for repeat users	LTO	East	
Text content	F1	Fonts to depict a brand identity/tradition	UA		
	F2	Vision statements/testimonials	PD		
	F3	Friendly messages	UA | MAS | Low PD	West	
	F4	Chat support	COL | UA		Low
	F5	Free trials/downloads/toll free support	UA | MAS		Low
	F6	High text to image ratio	FEM | IDV		Low
	F7	Use of slogans/callouts for social actions	PD | COL		High
Social links	G1	Links to outside groups/subscriptions/newsletters	COL | UA		

(PD = High Power Distance, COL = Collectivist, IDV = Individualistic, UA = High Uncertainty Avoidance, MAS = High Masculinity, FEM = High Femininity, LTO = Long Term Orientation, STO = Short Term Orientation)

Once this table (now called CIAM) was developed, it was decided to give CIAM to 6 expert UX designers to be used in the process of assessment of culture's influence on websites. For this, first a questionnaire was created where each expert was asked to rate a website design for each observable UI element identified in CIAM. A total of 8 military and 8 university websites were given to each expert for assessment. The process of culture's influence assessment on a website using CIAM is described in the next section.

3   Assessment of Military and University Websites Using CIAM

The technique used for the assessment of culture's influence on a website design using CIAM was content analysis by 6 expert UX designers of homepages of 8 military and 8 public university websites.

Content Analysis. Content analysis [51] has been reported to be a technique for analysing values, norms of behaviour and other elements of a culture [52–54]. A review of 60 studies done in the past 15 years reports content analysis as the primary method to investigate cultural values and markers on websites [60].

The Importance of the Homepage of a Website. The homepage of a website has been referred to in literature as the face of the company [55] responsible to create the first impression on the user which strongly influences the user's decision of browsing the site [56]. It serves as the central point of navigation where visitors may refer back to from any page of the website [57].

Related Work in Literature. While cultural influence on website designs has been studied in literature, it has been reported that 72% of these studies were done on company and e-commerce websites and 28% included government websites like banking, university, ministry, railways. There is little literature available on assessment of cultural influence on military websites. This paper argues that while websites like tourism, entertainment etc. are designed for user engagement, most institutional websites are designed to provide information and e-commerce websites are designed to persuade the buyer to make a purchase and then generate trust for repeated purchases. Military websites, however are designed to target citizens to attract and persuade them to invest a lifetime towards the nation [58]. Similarly, public university websites are designed to attract potential students towards commitment of their golden years of learning to that particular institute. It can be argued thus that both military as well as university websites are designed to persuade as well provide information to the users. Also, in both these kinds of websites, displaying the identity of the nation or the university is an important aspect and hence the cultural influence would play an important part in the design of website user experience. There is minimal research available in the literature on cultural aspects of both these kinds of websites. In the light of this argument, this paper reports the assessment of 8 military and 8 public university websites from eastern and western countries using CIAM.

Sampling of Websites. Hofstede's dimensions were used to identify four culturally similar and geographically close countries, each from the East and the West. Geographical proximity has a significant influence on culture as brought out by Nisbett. The nations chosen in the East were India, Nepal, Bangladesh and Sri Lanka. These nations are in geographic proximity to each other in South/South-East Asia. The nations chosen in West were France, Italy, Spain and Switzerland. All of them are neighbouring western European nations whose cultures, languages, and social identities share many similarities. The French, Italians and Spanish people can be considered culturally related because their religious values, languages, immigrant influences, business practices and lifestyles are similar (Hettinger 2008). All the four nations from the east are 'high-context' while all the four nations from the west are 'low-context' according to Hall's culture theory.

3.1   Methodology

CIAM was used to assess 16 websites by six expert UX designers. The experts were asked to rate the occurence of each of the 32 observable UI elements identified in CIAM on the homepage of 8 military websites and 8 university websites on a rating scale of 1 to 5 (1 being the lowest and 5 being the highest) as presented in Fig. 5. Thus, an expert analysed a total of 512 (16 × 32) observable UI elements. Six experts analysed the same set of websites.

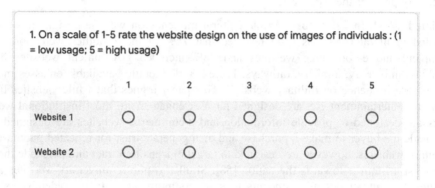

Fig. 5. Sample rating scale based on CIAM given to experts

Inter-rater reliability between the six experts was checked for a total of 3072 responses using Cronbach alpha. Table 6 presents the values for Cronbach alpha two types of websites:

Table 6. Inter-rater reliability scores for the 6 experts who rated the websites using CIAM

University websites	Value	Military websites	Value
Total no. of experts	6	Total no. of experts	6
Total no. of questions	256	Total no. of questions	256
Sum of variance for each question	257.44	Sum of variance for each question	268.44
Variance of total scores for each expert	6761.2	Variance of total scores for each expert	7545
Cronbach alpha value	0.966	Cronbach alpha value	0.968

Table 6 shows that the Cronbach alpha values was high and thus the inter-rater reliability between the experts was high. This implies that usage of CIAM gave good agreement between the experts.

3.2 Assessment Findings

The mode of ratings given by six experts was used to determine the cultural disposition of the websites. For some of the CIAM questions, the mode of ratings given by all the experts were similar for all the selected websites. This could be due to the presence of common UI elements in the sample websites. Such CIAM questions were excluded from the final analysis to avoid ambiguity in results. The ratings for the remaining questions clearly showed a difference between the observable UI elements of websites. For each military and university website which represented a specific country, high and low range of values was estimated and plotted against the high and low values of Hofstede's cultural dimensions. The ranges taken for the mode of assessment ratings given by the six experts were: 1–3 = Low; 4–5 = High. The ranges taken from Hofstede's cultural dimensions for comparison with expert ratings were: 10–50 = Low; 51–90 = High. The results are presented in Table 7 and 8. It can be observed in Table 7 and 8 that the websites ratings given by the experts using CIAM has matched with Hofstede's Cultural Dimensions. In the military websites, for five dimensions for eight countries, there was only one discrepancy each for Power Distance, Individualism, Uncertainty Avoidance and Masculinity. However, for the dimension of Long Term Orientation, the ratings did not match for 4 out of 8 websites. In the university websites, there was only one discrepancy each for Individualism and Uncertainty Avoidance and two for the dimension of Long Term Orientation.

Similarly, for each military and university website which represented a specific country, high and low range of values was estimated and plotted against the high and low context cultures according to Hall's theory. The results are presented in Table 9 and 10. As can be observed in Table 9 and 10, the assessment of the military websites by experts were in congruence with the cultural contexts of the sample countries according to Hall's theory. As shown in Table 9, there were a few exceptions like France and Italy, which were rated as being high context for 2 OUI elements each in military websites and as being low context for nine OUI elements. But it is argued here that this is because in Hall's cultural context theory, these two countries lie near the center in the range where countries are plotted between being low context and high context [59]. For the university websites, there was an exception of the university website of Switzerland which was rated as being low context for 10 OUI elements but high context for 2 OUI elements.

It is therefore argued here that the CIAM based assessment of websites is giving a good estimate of cultural dispositions expressed in the websites. While CIAM looks into the user interface elements, Hofstede's model had looked into the organisational behavioural patterns while Hall's model had looked into the communication patterns and sense of space and time. This paper had derived the user interface elements based on the literature and took assessments of websites on the user interface elements. The findings of this paper therefore suggest that there are cultural dispositions expressed in the websites UI elements which can be assessed using CIAM.

Table 7. Ratings of military websites of 8 countries assessed using CIAM and high and low values of their respective Hofstede's Dimensions (HD)

Country	PD		IDV		UA		MAS		LTO	
	CIAM	HD	CIAM	HD	CIAM	HD	CIAM	HD	CIAM	HD
SriLanka	High	High	Low	Low	Low	Low	**High**	Low	**High**	Low
India	High	High	Low	Low	Low	Low	High	High	Low	Low
Nepal	High	High	Low	Low	Low	Low	Low	Low	High	
Bangladesh	High	High	Low	Low	High	High	High	High	Low	Low
France	**Low**	High	High	High	**Low**	**High**	Low	Low	**Low**	**High**
Spain	Low	Low	**High**	**Low**	High	High	Low	Low	High	High
Italy	Low	Low	High	High	High	High	High	High	**Low**	**High**
Switzerland	Low	Low	High	High	High	High	High	High	**Low**	**High**

Table 8. Ratings of university websites of 8 countries assessed using CIAM and high and low values of their respective Hofstede's Dimensions (HD)

Country	PD		IDV		UA		MAS		LTO	
	CIAM	HD	CIAM	HD	CIAM	HD	CIAM	HD	CIAM	HD
SriLanka	High	High	Low	Low	Low	Low	Low	Low	**High**	Low
India	High	High	Low	Low	Low	Low	High	High	Low	Low
Nepal	High	High	Low	Low	Low	Low	Low	Low	High	
Bangladesh	High	High	Low	Low	High	High	High	High	Low	Low
France	Low	Low	**Low**	**High**	High	High	Low	Low	High	High
Spain	Low	Low	High	High	**Low**	**High**	Low	Low	High	High
Italy	Low	Low	High	High	High	High	High	High	**Low**	**High**
Switzerland	Low	Low	High	High	High	High	High	High	High	High

Note: PD = Power Distance; IDV = Individualism; UA = Uncertainty Avoidance; MAS = Masculinity; LTO = Long Term Orientation; HD = Hofstede's Dimensions range; CIAM = Range of ratings given by experts using CIAM

Table 9. Ratings of military websites assessed using CIAM mapped with Hall's and Nisbett's cultural models

CIAM code	Low context cultures *Western countries*	High context cultures *Mostly Eastern countries*
A1, A2	Switzerland, Italy, Spain	Nepal, Bangladesh, India, SriLanka, **France**
A3, A4, A6, B2, B4, D1, D3, D4, F7	France, Switzerland, Italy, Spain	Nepal, Bangladesh, India, SriLanka
C2, F6	France, Switzerland, Spain	Nepal, Bangladesh, India, SriLanka, **Italy**

Table 10. Ratings of university websites assessed using CIAM mapped with Hall's and Nisbett's cultural models

CIAM code	Low context cultures *Western countries*	High context cultures *Mostly Eastern countries*
A1, A2, A3, A4, B2, B4, C2, D1, D3, F7	Switzerland, Italy, Spain, France	Nepal, Bangladesh, India, SriLanka
A6, D4	France, Italy, Spain	Nepal, Bangladesh, India, SriLanka, **Switzerland**

4   Conclusion

The observations of this study indicate that the proposed Cultural Influence Assessment Model (CIAM) can be used to assess the culture's influence on websites and can give an indication towards its cultural dimension and the communication context of the culture it belongs to.

The tool however does not identify how those cultural influences were formed. Whether they are a result of the designer's culture or if they are an indicator of a good user centred design process, where the designer has designed the website for users of specific cultures. There may also be external factors like the cultures of the authorities and leaders who take the final call on the design before it is released. Also, there is a need for further work using the tool proposed in this paper called CIAM on a variety of websites to gauge the difference that cultural dispositions create in different types of websites. For example an e-commerce website may show a different cultural disposition than a matrimonial website or a tourism website. The tool can also pave the way for further studies where guidelines can be made for UX designers for user centred website design which factors in the user's culture during the design process.

References

1. Cyr, D., Bonanni, C., Bowes, J., Ilsever, J.: Beyond trust. J. Glob. Inf. Manag. **13**, 25–54 (2005)
2. Marcus, A.: Culture class versus culture clash. In: HCI and User-Experience Design. HCIS. Springer, London (2015). https://doi.org/10.1007/978-1-4471-6744-0_2
3. Rau, P.L.P. (ed.): CCD 2015. LNCS, vol. 9181. Springer, Cham (2015). https://doi.org/10.1007/978-3-319-20934-0
4. Corbitt, B., Thanasankit, T.: A model for culturally informed web interfaces. Internet Management Issues (2002)
5. Smith-Jackson, T.L., Resnick, M.L., Johnson, K.T.: Cultural Ergonomics: Theory, Methods, and Applications. CRC Press, Boca Raton (2013)
6. Fogg, B.J., Fogg, G.E.: Persuasive Technology: Using Computers to Change What We Think and Do. Morgan Kaufmann, Burlington (2003)
7. Cash, P.J., Hartlev, C.G., Durazo, C.B.: Behavioural design: a process for integrating behaviour change and design. Des. Stud. **48**, 96–128 (2017)

8. Khaled, R., Barr, P., Fischer, R., Noble, J., Biddle, R.: Factoring culture into the design of a persuasive game. In: Proceedings of the 20th Conference of the Computer-Human Interaction Special Interest Group (CHISIG) of Australia on Computer-Human Interaction: Design: Activities, Artefacts and Environments - OZCHI 2006 (2006)
9. Sato, G.Y., Barthes, J.-P., Chen, K.-J.: Following the evolution of distributed communities of practice. In: 2008 7th IEEE International Conference on Cognitive Informatics (2008)
10. Fletcher, R., Melewar, T.C.: The complexities of communicating to customers in emerging markets. J. Commun. Manag. **6**, 9–23 (2002)
11. Singh, N., Matsuo, H.: Measuring cultural adaptation on the web: a content analytic study of U.S. and Japanese web sites. J. Bus. Res. **57**, 864–872 (2004)
12. Reinecke, K., Bernstein, A.: Tell me where you've lived, and i'll tell you what you like: adapting interfaces to cultural preferences. In: Houben, G.-J., McCalla, G., Pianesi, F., Zancanaro, M. (eds.) UMAP 2009. LNCS, vol. 5535, pp. 185–196. Springer, Heidelberg (2009). https://doi.org/10.1007/978-3-642-02247-0_19
13. Marcus, A.: Cross-cultural user-experience design for work, home, play, and on the way. In: SIGGRAPH Asia 2014 Courses on - SA 2014 (2014)
14. Masuda, T., Gonzalez, R., Kwan, L., Nisbett, R.E.: Culture and aesthetic preference: comparing the attention to context of East Asians and Americans. Pers. Soc. Psychol. Bull. **34**, 1260–1275 (2008)
15. Nisbett, R.E.: Intelligence and How to Get It: Why Schools and Cultures Count. W. W. Norton & Company, New York (2010)
16. Cohen, A.B., Varnum, M.E.: Beyond east vs. west: social class, region, and religion as forms of culture. Curr. Opin. Psychol. **8**, 5–9 (2016)
17. Baack, D.W., Singh, N.: Culture and web communications. J. Bus. Res. **60**, 181–188 (2007)
18. Garrett, J.J.: Elements of User Experience, the: User-Centered Design for the Web and Beyond. Pearson Education, Pearson Education (2010)
19. Joshi, A., Medh, P.: Heuristic evaluation of e-learning products extended garrett's model of user experience. J. Creat. Commun. **1**, 91–104 (2006)
20. Wu, X., Wang, C.: Research on designing the official websites of trade shows based on user experience. J. Conv. Event Tour. **17**, 234–246 (2016)
21. Fletcher, R.: The impact of culture on web site content, design, and structure. Int. J. Inf. Commun. Technol. Educ. **10**, 259–273 (2006)
22. Li, H., Sun, X., Zhang, K.: Culture-centered design: cultural factors in interface usability and usability tests. In: Eighth ACIS International Conference on Software Engineering, Artificial Intelligence, Networking, and Parallel/Distributed Computing (SNPD 2007) (2007)
23. Nisbett, R.E., Nisbett, R.E., Norenzayan, A.: Culture and Cognition. Stevens' Handbook of Experimental Psychology (2002)
24. Masuda, T., Gonzalez, R., Kwan, L., Nisbett, R.E.: Culture and aesthetic preference: comparing the attention to context of East Asians and Americans. Pers. Soc. Psychol. Bull. **34**(9), 1260–1275 (2008). https://doi.org/10.1177/0146167208320555
25. Solomon, R.C., Deutsch, E.: Culture and modernity: east-west perspectives. Philos. East West **43**, 565 (1993)
26. de Oliveira, S., Nisbett, R.E.: Culture changes how we think about thinking: from "human inference" to "geography of thought". Perspect. Psychol. Sci. **12**, 782–790 (2017)
27. Johnston, V., Black, M., Wallace, J., Mulvenna, M., Bond, R.: A framework for the development of a dynamic adaptive intelligent user interface to enhance the user experience. In: Proceedings of the 31st European Conference on Cognitive Ergonomics - ECCE 2019 (2019)
28. Hofstede, G.H., Hofstede, G.: Culture's Consequences: Comparing Values, Behaviors, Institutions and Organizations Across Nations. SAGE, Thousand Oaks (2001)

29. Marcus, A., Baumgartner, V.-J.: A practical set of culture dimensions for global user-interface development. In: Masoodian, M., Jones, S., Rogers, B. (eds.) APCHI 2004. LNCS, vol. 3101, pp. 252–261. Springer, Heidelberg (2004). https://doi.org/10.1007/978-3-540-27795-8_26

30. McSweeney, B.: Hofstede's model of national cultural differences and their consequences: a triumph of faith - a failure of analysis. Hum. Relat. **55**, 89–118 (2002)

31. Myers, M.D., Tan, F.B.: Beyond models of national culture in information systems research. J. Glob. Inf. Manag. **10**, 24–32 (2002)

32. Singh, N., Zhao, H., Hu, X.: Cultural adaptation on the web: a study of American companies' domestic and Chinese websites. J. Global Inf. Manage. (JGIM) **11**(3), 63–80 (2003). https://doi.org/10.4018/jgim.2003070104

33. Reinecke, K., Minder, P., Bernstein, A.: MOCCA - a system that learns and recommends visual preferences based on cultural similarity. In: Proceedings of the 15th International Conference on Intelligent User Interfaces - IUI 2011 (2011)

34. Marcus, A., Gould, E.W.: Crosscurrents: cultural dimensions and global web user-interface design. Interactions **7**, 32–46 (2000)

35. Hall, E.T.: Beyond culture. Anchor (1977). https://books.google.com/books/about/Beyond_culture.html?hl=&id=8EhKtQEACAAJ

36. Lipman, A., Hall, E.T.: The hidden dimension. Br. J. Soc. **21**, 353 (1970). https://doi.org/10.2307/589150

37. Hall, E.T.: The Silent Language (1969). https://books.google.com/books/about/The_Silent_Language.html?hl=&id=a_2QvgAACAAJ

38. Fink, D., Laupase, R.: Perceptions of web site design characteristics: a Malaysian/Australian comparison. Internet Res. **10**, 44–55 (2000)

39. Goyal, N., Miner, W., Nawathe, N.: Cultural differences across governmental website design. In: Proceedings of the 4th International Conference on Intercultural Collaboration - ICIC 2012 (2012)

40. Usunier, J.-C., Roulin, N., Ivens, B.S.: Cultural, national, and industry-level differences in B2B web site design and content. Int. J. Electron. Commer. **14**, 41–88 (2009)

41. Cho, C.-H., Cheon, H.J.: Cross-cultural comparisons of interactivity on corporate web sites: the United States, the United Kingdom, Japan, and South Korea. J. Advert. **34**, 99–115 (2005)

42. Chun, W., Singh, N., Sobh, R., Benmamoun, M.: A comparative analysis of Arab and U.S. cultural values on the web. J. Glob. Mark. **28**, 99–112 (2015)

43. Wurtz, E.: Intercultural communication on web sites: a cross-cultural analysis of web sites from high-context cultures and low-context cultures. J. Comput.-Mediat. Commun. **11**, 274–299 (2005)

44. Nisbett, R.E.: The Geography of Thought: How Asians and Westerners Think Differently - and Why. Hachette, UK (2011)

45. Harris, D. (ed.): EPCE 2017. LNCS (LNAI), vol. 10276. Springer, Cham (2017). https://doi.org/10.1007/978-3-319-58475-1

46. Miyamoto, Y., Nisbett, R.E., Masuda, T.: Culture and the physical environment: holistic versus analytic perceptual affordances. Psychol. Sci. **17**(2), 113–119 (2006). https://doi.org/10.1111/j.1467-9280.2006.01673

47. Nisbett, R.E., Miyamoto, Y.: The influence of culture: holistic versus analytic perception. Trends Cogn. Sci. **9**, 467–473 (2005)

48. Ji, L.J., Peng, K., Nisbett, R.E.: Culture, control, and perception of relationships in the environment. J. Pers. Soc. Psychol. **78**, 943–955 (2000)

49. Kitayama, S., Duffy, S., Kawamura, T., Larsen, J.T.: Perceiving an object and its context in different cultures: a cultural look at new look. Psychol. Sci. **14**, 201–206 (2003)

50. Boduroglu, A., Shah, P., Nisbett, R.E.: Cultural differences in allocation of attention in visual information processing. J. Cross Cult. Psychol. **40**, 349–360 (2009)
51. Kassarjian, H.H.: Content analysis in consumer research. J. Consum. Res. **4**, 8 (1977)
52. Cho, B., Kwon, U., Gentry, J.W., Jun, S., Kropp, F.: Cultural values reflected in theme and execution: a comparative study of U.S. and Korean television commercials. J. Advert. **28**, 59–73 (1999)
53. Chan, K., Cheng, H.: One country, two systems: cultural values reflected in Chinese and Hong Kong television commercials. Int. Commun. Gaz. **64**, 385–400 (2002)
54. Lin, C.A.: Cultural values reflected in Chinese and American television advertising. J. Advert. **30**, 83–94 (2001)
55. Nielsen, J., Tahir, M.: Homepage Usability: 50 Websites Deconstructed. Turtleback, USA (2001)
56. Okonkwo, U.: Sustaining the luxury brand on the Internet. J. Brand Manag. **16**, 302–310 (2009)
57. Brinck, T., Gergle, D., Wood, S.D.: Designing Web Sites that Work: Usability for the Web. Morgan Kaufmann, Burlington (2002)
58. Wilson, P.H.: Defining military culture. J. Mil. Hist. **72**, 11–41 (2007)
59. Hall, E.T., Hall, M.R.: Understanding Cultural Differences: Germans. French and Americans. Nicholas Brealey, London (2000)
60. Moura, F.T., Singh, N., Chun, W.: The influence of culture in website design and users' perceptions: three systematic reviews. J. Electron. Commer. Res. **17**(4), 312–339 (2016)
61. Ahmed, T., Mouratidis, H., Preston, D.: Website design guidelines: high power distance and high context culture. Int. J. Cyber Soc. Educ. **2**(1), 47–60 (2009). ATISR. Retrieved January 27, 2020

Contrastive Study on User Satisfaction of Weibo and Instagram Common Users

Huijun Qin[✉][iD]

School of Digital Media and Design Arts, Beijing University of Posts
and Telecommunications, Beijing 100876, China
usaginomifi@qq.com

Abstract. Both Instagram and Weibo are among the most popular social platforms for young Chinese. In view of the common ground that they are both basing on photo sharing social functions, this paper tries to analyze the differences between their user satisfaction, then provide reference value for domestic social product design. To investigate the user satisfaction of the two products, user interviews were conducted to collect the pre-options of the questionnaire, and the Single Ease Question (SEQ) and Net Promoter Score (NPS) question were applied to design questionnaire. Results of user interviews are qualitatively analyzed, results of questionnaire are quantitatively analyzed. The results show that: the satisfaction level of certain tasks and the NPS level of Weibo are significantly lower than that of Instagram, satisfaction levels of Weibo on other tasks don't show significant differences comparing to that of Instagram. Positive correlation of the satisfaction level and the NPS level is revealed in both Instagram and Weibo. While the satisfaction level of some tasks show negative correlations with their respective frequency of use. Respective paired T-tests within gender levels, educations levels, and age levels were conducted. However, some of the results differ from the conclusion of overall analysis. After interpreting all the results, specific advice for Weibo and even domestic social media product have been concluded at last.

Keywords: Social media · User satisfaction · Weibo · Instagram

1 Introduction

Newly emerged social applications have enabled new ways of information spreading, communication, and social participation, with their participative, interactive, open, and transparent features [1]. In China, the development of the civil society sector has been greatly influenced by the advancement in information technology, particularly the Internet [2–4]. According to the data, social media has surpassed search engines and become the largest source of Internet traffic, accounting for 46% and 40% respectively [5]. Weibo is one of the largest social network platforms in China, comparing to instant messaging apps like WeChat and Tencent QQ, Weibo mainly focuses on information and entertainment. The 2018 Weibo User Development Report shows, Weibo's monthly active users were 462 million in the fourth quarter of 2018, keeping an increase of 70 million for three consecutive years [6].

© Springer Nature Switzerland AG 2020
P.-L. P. Rau (Ed.): HCII 2020, LNCS 12193, pp. 409–423, 2020.
https://doi.org/10.1007/978-3-030-49913-6_34

As is known to many, Instagram has been blocked in mainland China, while Chinese youngsters still hold great interests using it, which forms a weird phenomenon that many young Chinese and their friends own Instagram accounts though rarely use it. In June 2018, Instagram's main mobile photo sharing network reached 1 billion monthly active users, up from 800 million on September 2; there are 400 million active Stories users every day in the world. Since Instagram is popular among all over the world, it seems that culture differences are dismissed in the Instagram app. Weibo published the function of "Weibo Story" by referring to Instagram's Ins story function. However, Weibo stories are not as successful as Ins stories landing on Instagram, which indicates that cultural differences may still effects on Weibo instead of Instagram. Research on the differences of Weibo and Instagram can not only provide guidance to social media product design, but also reveal the cross-cultural causes behind the satisfaction level of the two products. Though Chinese belong to the groups of context-dependent and holistic perceptual processes, and show higher tolerance of overwhelming information [7], this situation may have changed because of the dynamic nature of culture. Since many common users of the two products have a well-educated English learning background, and might have been abroad for short or long periods, multicultural effects can be the cause of their preference for Instagram. Considering the information on Instagram is much less and much more concentrated than that of Weibo (e.g. browse certain content on Instagram by searching hashtags, while on Weibo, searching by key words are more common), thus a preference for concentrated and high fidelity information/pictures may exists among the Chinese common users of these two products.

Contrastive studies on cross-cultural effects to satisfaction level can serve as references of this research. At the present stage, the goal of this study is to investigate the differences in common users' satisfaction levels of Weibo and Instagram, refine advice for domestic product design.

2   Literature Review

Xie et al. did a comparison between WeChat and Facebook user Motivation, experience and NPS (Net Promoter Score) among Chinese people living overseas by conducting a triangulation research approach with an online survey and follow-up interviews [8]. They first captured basic usage metrics of both applications, including frequency of use, daily length of use, total count of "friends", and length of ownership of the accounts. Then they measured user motivations while using both Facebook and WeChat based on the questionnaire Lien and Cao [9] designed to examine the effects of psychological motivations (entertainment, sociality, and information). Their third section measured the user satisfaction regarding the overall experience, and other aspects of WeChat and Facebook that provide physical/visual pleasures, physiological pleasures, and ideological and social pleasures [10]. This included "look and feel", "security", "positive attitude", and "cultural connectedness" aspects of both applications. In addition, a Net Promoter Score (NPS) question was asked to measure user loyalty. Huang et al. [11] focused on three dimensions of social media usage, including satisfaction, perceived trust and privacy [12], extent of use, and the reasons to use or not to use functions in social media. They did the comparison between Facebook and WeChat by delivering online survey consisting of the Single Ease Question (SEQ), questions of perceived trust and privacy, questions of extent of use, and questions about the reasons to use or not to use functions.

The researches mentioned above both compared WeChat to Facebook by the means of user interview and online survey. Though the researches introduced before have investigated the existing differences and their possible reasons between WeChat and Facebook, they didn't propose design advice or solutions for domestic social media product design. Thus this study tries to refine advice for domestic product through comparing Instagram and Weibo. Satisfaction level evaluation by user interviews and online questionnaires are chosen to be the most suitable means. Sauro et al. [13] introduced many questionnaires to quantify the user experience, some of them are ideal for the study, such as the QUIS, PSSUQ, ASQ, HQ etc. While considering of the implementability and validity, Single Ease Question (SEQ) and Net Promoter Score (NPS) were chosen to design the questionnaire.

Single Ease Question (SEQ) is a useful and simple version of this idea that has been experimentally validated and demonstrated as reliable, valid, and sensitive. The SEQ asks the user to rate the difficulty of the activity they just completed, from Very Easy to Very Difficult on a 7-point rating scale [14]. NPS stands for Net Promoter Score which is a metric used in customer experience programs. NPS measures the loyalty of customers to a company. NPS scores are measured with a single question survey and reported with a number from −100 to +100, a higher score is desirable. It measures customer perception based on one simple question: "How likely is it that you would recommend [XXX] to a friend or colleague?" Respondents give a rating between 0 (not at all likely) and 10 (extremely likely) and, depending on their response, customers fall into one of 3 categories to establish an NPS score. Promoters respond with a score of 9 or 10 and are typically loyal and enthusiastic customers. Passives respond with a score of 7 or 8. They are satisfied with the present service but not happy enough to be considered promoters. Detractors respond with a score of 0 to 6. These are unhappy customers who are unlikely to use the product again, and may even discourage others from using the product. To calculate the final NPS score, just subtract the percentage of Detractors from the percentage of Promoters. For example, if 10% of respondents are Detractors, 20% are Passives and 70% are Promoters, your NPS score would be 70–10 = 60 [15].

Hofstede's Cultural Model is widely used to study cross-cultural phenomena between different countries, which implements five cultural dimensions of power distance, individualism, masculinity, uncertainty avoidance, and long term orientation [16]. Hofstede's advocates have established a substantial base of work describing which UI aspects are influenced by certain dimensions and their different score ranges. Reinecke et al. summarized the influence of Hofstede's dimensions on UI preferences by literature reviewing, which can help improve UI design for specific cultural group [17]. Thus knowing the performance of China in Hofstede's Cultural Model helps explain the results of questionnaires, as well as refine advice for Weibo and other domestic products. According to Hofstede's official website [18] for comparing countries in the five dimensions mentioned above, China is a country at high power distance level, masculinity level and long term orientation level (see Table 1), Chinese value showing respect to seniors and superiors, caring for the weak, hardworking for better life, and taking long period to accomplish a goal. Besides, Chinese rated low at individualism and uncertainty avoidance (see Table 1), which indicates that Chinese people often see themselves as part of a group, collective interest is prior to individual's, and tolerate uncertain, ambiguous, and unstructured circumstances.

Table 1. Performance of China in Hofstede's cultural model

Dimension	Score
Power distance	80
Individualism	20
Masculinity	66
Uncertainty avoidance	30
Long term orientation	87

3   Methodology

The goal of the present stage of study is to provide reference value for domestic social product design by telling and analyzing the differences of satisfaction level between Instagram and Weibo. To achieve this goal, target user interviews were firstly done to characterize the habits and motivations to use Weibo and Instagram. Through the interviews, the pre-options of designing the satisfaction evaluation questionnaire was refined, which are the 6 popular common tasks users will operate when using Instagram and Weibo. 7 common users were recruited and got equal amount of monetary rewards after the interviews. The interviews were conducted in the same school office, and were restricted of time. Records of the interviews were taken in both literature and voice recording.

After collecting the 6 main common tasks users usually operate as materials, the 3 hypothesis of the study and the 7-point Likert scale questionnaire was designed. It consists of 6 SEQs of Weibo, 6 SEQs of Instagram, 1 NPS question of Weibo, 1 NPS question of Instagram, and two questions which required the users to rate the six tasks of Instagram and Weibo by frequency of usage. The questionnaire is delivered by online survey link, the responses of non-common users of both Instagram and Weibo were determined as invalid questionnaires, each participant was rewarded by a random amount of monetary incentive added to the end of the questionnaire.

The statistics obtained by the questionnaires were imported into the SPSS software to process. Since the survey of Instagram and Weibo was conducted on the same group of users (common users of both Instagram and Weibo), two-tailed t-tests for paired two sample were used to examine the difference of satisfaction level between the two products at a holistic level and at three classified level, i.e. the gender levels, the education levels, and the age levels. Pearson correlation analysis were implemented to analyze the correlation of satisfaction level between different tasks and the NPS of the product. Moreover, independent T-tests were used to explore the difference within different gender groups, education level groups, and age groups. After interpreting all the results, specific advice for Weibo and even domes-tic social media product have been concluded at last.

4 User Interviews

The interviews focused on the popular tasks, motivations of use, frequency of use, and accumulated time of use. 7 common users who use the two products every day or every other day were recruited and got equal amount of red packets after the interviews. The interviews were conducted in the same school office, and were restricted of time. Records of the interviews were taken in both literature and voice recording.

After the interviews, 6 main common tasks were refined and used to design the questionnaire (see Table 2). The numbering of the 6 main tasks followed the frequency rankings, which were resulted by questionnaire responses (see Sect. 5.).

Table 2. 6 main common tasks of Instagram and Weibo usage

	Main tasks
Task 1	Browsing certain contents
Task 2	Discovering or searching
Task 3	Posting
Task 4	Browsing posts of friends and respond
Task 5	Browsing posts of mine
Task 6	Checking and replying to messages

Regarding the results of user interviews, the hypotheses of this research are listed below:

Hypothesis 1: The NPS level of Instagram is higher than that of Weibo.

Hypothesis 2: The satisfaction level of Instagram is higher than that of Weibo.

The information on Instagram is much less than that of Weibo. Though Chinese belongs to the groups of context-dependent and holistic perceptual processes [19], a preference of Instagram still exists to attract Chinese users.

Hypothesis 3: There is a positive correlation between the NPS level and the satisfaction level of the tasks.

5 Questionnaires

Take the 6 main common tasks concluded in 4., the 7-point Likert scale questionnaire was designed. It consists of 6 SEQs of Weibo, 6 SEQs of Instagram, 1 NPS question of Weibo, 1 NPS question of Instagram, and two questions which required the users to rate the six tasks of Instagram and Weibo by frequency of usage. The questionnaire is delivered by online survey link, the responses of non-common users of both Instagram and Weibo were determined as invalid questionnaires, each participant was rewarded by a random amount of monetary incentive added to the end of the questionnaire.

5.1 Analysis of All Responses

The total number of responses is 2532, the number of valid questionnaires is 2301. 64% of the respondents are male, 36% are female. 37% of the respondents are with bachelor degree, 6% are with degrees of master or above, 26% are with college degree, 25% are high school/secondary school/technical school students (see Fig. 1). Besides, respondents who were born in 1990s took 48%, those born in 2000s took 21%, and those born in 1980s took 24% (see Fig. 2).

Fig. 1. Descriptive result of education level

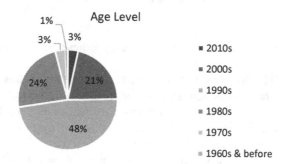

Fig. 2. Descriptive result of education level

Usage frequency rankings of 6 tasks are the same for both Weibo and Instagram (see Fig. 3), their ratings are distributed from 1 (=very frequent) to 7 (=not frequent at all). The numbering of the 6 main tasks followed the results of frequency rankings, Task 1 (Browsing certain contents) is the most frequent task among 6 tasks, Task 6 (Checking and replying to messages) is the least frequent. Rankings of SEQ ratings of Weibo and Instagram are not the same, but similar. A 7-point Likert scale from 1 (=extremely difficult) to 7 (=extremely easy) was applied in SEQ rating. Ratings of Task 1 (Browsing certain contents) are the highest and ratings Task 3 (Posting) are the lowest for both products (see Fig. 4). NPS score of Instagram is 36.55, which is higher than the 31.73 of Weibo (see Table 3). Therefore, the design of posting function of both products may need improvement, though Task 3 (Posting) ranked the third of usage frequency while last of satisfaction.

Table 3. NPS scores of Weibo and Instagram

	Weibo	Ins
Promoters	1187	1247
Passives	652	646
Detractors	457	406
NPS	31.73	36.55

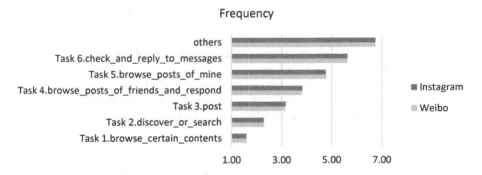

Fig. 3. Descriptive result of task usage frequency

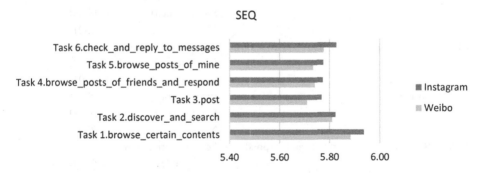

Fig. 4. Descriptive result of Task Single Ease Question (SEQ)

To test Hypothesis 1 and Hypothesis 2, t-tests were conducted to investigate the difference between Instagram and Weibo in users' satisfaction. The t-tests for paired two sample of the 6 tasks are shown in Table 4. According to the results, the satisfaction level of Task 1 (Browsing certain contents), Task 3 (Posting), Task 6 (Checking and replying to messages), and the NPS level of Weibo are significantly lower than that of Instagram, satisfaction levels of Weibo on other tasks don't show significant differences comparing to that of Instagram. Hypothesis 1 is proved and part of Hypothesis 2 is proved. In addition, T-test on task frequency of Weibo and Instagram doesn't show significant difference.

Table 4. Paired T-test on the 6 main tasks

Task	t	Sig. (2-tailed)
Task 1. Browsing certain contents	−2.316	0.021
Task 2. Discovering or searching	−0.550	0.583
Task 3. Posting	−2.383	0.017
Task 4. Browsing posts of friends and respond	−1.356	0.175
Task 5. Browsing posts of mine	−1.606	0.108
Task 6. Checking and replying to messages	−2.014	0.044
NPS	−3.935	0.000

To test Hypothesis 3, Pearson correlation analysis were implemented to analyze the correlation of satisfaction level between different tasks and the NPS of the product. Table 5 shows the results of Pearson correlation analysis of Weibo, Table 6 shows the results of Pearson correlation analysis of Instagram. Positive correlation of the satisfaction level and the NPS level is revealed in both Instagram and Weibo for all the 6 tasks.

Table 5. Pearson correlation analysis between SEQ and NPS of Weibo

Weibo – SEQ		Weibo – NPS
Task 1. Browsing certain contents	Pearson correlation	.587**
	Sig. (2-tailed)	0.000
	N	2301
Task 2. Discovering or searching	Pearson correlation	.640**
	Sig. (2-tailed)	0.000
	N	2301
Task 3. Posting	Pearson correlation	.570**
	Sig. (2-tailed)	0.000
	N	2301
Task 4. Browsing posts of friends and respond	Pearson correlation	.637**
	Sig. (2-tailed)	0.000
	N	2301
Task 5. Browsing posts of mine	Pearson correlation	.593**
	Sig. (2-tailed)	0.000
	N	2301
Task 6. Checking and replying to messages	Pearson correlation	.633**
	Sig. (2-tailed)	0.000
	N	2301

**. Correlation is significant at the 0.01 level (2-tailed).

Table 6. Pearson correlation analysis between SEQ and NPS of Instagram

Instagram - SEQ		Instagram - NPS
Task 1. Browsing certain contents	Pearson correlation	.650**
	Sig. (2-tailed)	0.000
	N	2301
Task 3. Posting	Pearson correlation	.604**
	Sig. (2-tailed)	0.000
	N	2301
Task 5. Browsing posts of mine	Pearson correlation	.598**
	Sig. (2-tailed)	0.000
	N	2301
Task 2. Discovering or searching	Pearson correlation	.654**
	Sig. (2-tailed)	0.000
	N	2301
Task 4. Browsing posts of friends and respond	Pearson correlation	.642**
	Sig. (2-tailed)	0.000
	N	2301
Task 6. Checking and replying to messages	Pearson correlation	.620**
	Sig. (2-tailed)	0.000
	N	2301

**. Correlation is significant at the 0.01 level (2-tailed).

Some negative correlations between the satisfaction ratings and usage frequency ratings has been found (see Table 7). The satisfaction ratings of Task 3 (Posting) on Weibo, Task 3 (Posting) on Instagram, Task 5 (Browsing posts of mine) on Instagram

Table 7. Negative correlations

		Weibo. seq. Posting
Weibo. freq. Posting	Pearson correlation	−.073**
	Sig. (2-tailed)	0.000
	N	2301
		Ins. seq. Posting
Ins. freq. Posting	Pearson correlation	−.042*
	Sig. (2-tailed)	0.042
	N	2301
		Ins. seq. Browse posts of mine
Ins. freq. Browse posts of mine	Pearson correlation	−.043*
	Sig. (2-tailed)	0.041
	N	2301
		Ins. NPS
Ins. freq. Browse posts of mine	Pearson correlation	−.047*
	Sig. (2-tailed)	0.026
	N	2301

show negative correlations with their respective usage frequency ratings. Given that "1" represents "very frequent" in rating task frequency, and represents "extremely difficult" in rating SEQ, they are actually positive correlations. Negative correlation is also found between the frequency rating of Task 5 (Browsing posts of mine) on Instagram and its NPS score.

5.2   Comparison at Gender Level, Education Level, and Age Level

Independent T-test conducted between male and female respondents shows, SEQ and NPS ratings from female users are significantly higher than that from male users (see Table 8), which indicates a deviation that females prefer to give more positive rating on user satisfaction and NPS.

Independent T-test conducted between respondents with college or above degree and college or below degree shows, SEQ and NPS ratings from users who are qualified with college or above degree are significantly higher than that from users who are qualified with college or below degree (see Table 8), which reveals a preference for giving positive ratings from users with higher educational background.

Selecting the responses which were submitted from those whom were born in 2000s, 1990s, and 1980s, then dividing them into three groups by age level, i.e. the 2000s group, the 1990s group, and the 1980s group. Independent T-tests were conducted among the three groups (see Table 8). The result shows, SEQ and NPS ratings from the 2000s group are significantly lower than that from 1990s and 1980s, which reveals a preference for giving negative ratings from users who were born in 2000s.

Moreover, NPS ratings, SEQ ratings of Task 1 (Browsing certain contents) and Task 5 (Browsing posts of mine) from the 1990s group is significantly lower than that from the 1980s group, so is SEQ ratings of Task 4 (Browsing posts of friends and respond) on Weibo and Task 3 (Posting) on Instagram.

The results above present a preference for giving more positive ratings by female respondents and the respondents who have college or above degrees. In addition, those who were born in 2000s prefer to give more negative ratings compared to its counterparts. Therefore, respective paired T-tests within gender levels, educations levels, and age levels were conducted to investigate different conclusion from the result in Sect. 5.1 (see Table 9).

When analyzing all the responses, NPS score of Weibo is significantly lower than that of Instagram. While when analyzing the responses at classified levels, NPS score of the two products in users who have college or below degrees and users born in 2000s don't have significant difference.

The satisfaction rating of Task 1 (Browsing certain contents) on Instagram is significantly higher than that on Weibo in male users and users who have college or above degrees, which is partially consist with the analysis result of all responses.

The satisfaction rating of Task 3 (Posting) on Instagram is significantly higher than that on Weibo when analyzing all data, while when dealing with the classified data, preference of Task 3 (Posting) on Instagram is only found within the 1980s group.

The satisfaction rating of Task 6 (Checking and replying to messages) on Instagram is also higher at the holistic aspect, but only the results from the users who have college or above degrees and the users born in the 1980s are the same.

Table 8. Significant results of independent T-test at gender levels, education levels, and age levels

Task	Gender Level	Education Level	Age Level		
	Male vs. Female	College or above vs. College or below	2000s vs. 1990s	1990s vs. 1980s	2000s vs. 1980s
Weibo. seq. Browse certain contents	-**	+**	-**	-**	-**
Weibo. seq. Posting	-**	+**	-**	—	-**
Weibo. seq. Browse posts of mine	-**	+**	-**	-**	-**
Weibo. seq. Discover and search	-**	+**	-**	—	-**
Weibo. seq. Browse posts of friends and respond	-**	+**	-**	-**	-**
Weibo. seq. Check and reply to messages	-**	+**	-**	—	-**
Weibo. NPS	-**	+**	-**	-**	-**
Ins. seq. Browse certain contents	-**	+**	-**	-**	-**
Ins. seq. Posting	-**	+**	-**	-**	-**
Ins. seq. Browse posts of mine	-**	+**	-**	-**	-**
Ins. seq. Discover and search	-**	+**	-**	—	-**
Ins. seq. Browse posts of friends and respond	-**	+**	-**	—	-**
Ins. seq. Check and reply to messages	-**	+**	-**	-**	-**
Ins. NPS	-**	+**	-**	-**	-**

"-**" stands for significantly lower at the 0.01 level (2-tailed).
"+**" stands for significantly higher at the 0.01 level (2-tailed).
"—" stands for no significant difference.

Furthermore, satisfaction rating of Task 5 (Browsing posts of mine) on Instagram is significantly higher than that on Weibo within the respondents who have college or above degree and who were born in 1990s.

Table 9. Significant results of paired T-test at gender levels, education levels, and age levels

Male	Weibo vs. Instagram	t	Sig. (2-tailed)
	seq. Browse certain contents	−2.121	0.034
	NPS	−3.011	0.003
Female	Weibo vs. Instagram	t	Sig. (2-tailed)
	NPS	−2.603	0.009
Edu - College or below	Weibo vs. Instagram	t	Sig. (2-tailed)
	seq. Check and reply to messages	−2.092	0.037
Edu - College or above	Weibo vs. Instagram	t	Sig. (2-tailed)
	seq. Browse certain contents	−2.475	0.013
	seq. Browse posts of mine	−1.994	0.046
	NPS	−3.649	0.000
Age - 2000s	Weibo vs. Instagram	t	Sig. (2-tailed)
	freq. Browse posts of mine	2.057	0.040
	seq. Check and reply to messages	−2.448	0.015
Age - 1990s	Weibo vs. Instagram	t	Sig. (2-tailed)
	seq. Browse posts of friends and respond	−2.105	0.035
	NPS	−3.727	0.000
Age - 1980s	Weibo vs. Instagram	t	Sig. (2-tailed)
	seq. Posting	−2.295	0.022
	seq. Check and reply to messages	−1.965	0.050
	NPS	−2.068	0.039

6   Discussion and Conclusion

According to the results in Sect. 5.1, the satisfaction level of Weibo on Task 1 (Browsing certain contents), Task 3 (Posting), Task 6 (Checking and replying to messages), and the NPS level of Weibo are significantly lower than that of Instagram, Hypothesis 2 is proved and part of Hypothesis 1 is proved. Positive correlation of the satisfaction level and the NPS level is revealed in both Instagram and Weibo for all the 6 tasks, Hypothesis 3 is also proved. The format of contents display, posting function, checking and replying function might need redesign for Weibo. The three aspects are all highly related to the task flows which deal with complicated and overwhelming information, no matter it is from the Internet or the user himself/herself. Since the information display on Instagram is more concentrated and simply constructed, which suits the habit of those avoid uncertainty and emphasize individualism [17], the original conclusion of Hofstede that Chinese are highly collectivists may be biased to some extent. For domestic product design, new study of individualism, recognition, and aesthetics of their target Chinese users is needed, because it will not only tell what transformation of recognition and aesthetics there is in Chinese, and why it happened.

In addition, the satisfaction level of Task 3 (Posting) on Weibo, Task 3 (Posting) on Instagram, Task 5 (Browsing posts of mine) on Instagram show negative correlations with their respective frequency of use. That is to say, the more frequent the task is operated, the higher its satisfaction level is, since "1" represents "very frequent" in rating task frequency, and represents "extremely difficult" in rating SEQ. Negative correlation is also found between the frequency rating of Task 5 (Browsing posts of mine) on Instagram and its NPS score. That is, the more frequent Task 5 is operated on Instagram, the higher its NPS score is. Therefore, improving the posting function of Weibo will do good to promote the satisfaction level of the function, thus boost the usage frequency of the function as well.

On the basis of the results in 5.2, NPS ratings, SEQ ratings of Task 1 (Browsing certain contents) and Task 5 (Browsing posts of mine) from the 1990s group is significantly lower than that from the 1980s group, so is SEQ ratings of Task 4 (Browsing posts of friends and respond) on Weibo and Task 3 (Posting) on Instagram. The satisfaction rating of Task 5 (Browsing posts of mine) on Instagram is significantly higher than that on Weibo within the respondents who have college or above degree and who were born in 1990s. Task 1, Task 5, and Task 3 are all highly individual tasks, only Task 4 is a half-individual and half-collective task. Thus there may be a possibility that the 1990s group is more individualist, given that those whom were born in 1990s are mostly the only child in his/her family. Further research needs to be done to investigate whether individualism can explain the preference for the four tasks, and whether the 1990s group is more individualist.

Moreover, NPS scores among users who have college or below degrees and users born in 2000s don't express significant difference, while being higher educated and elder, the NPS score of Instagram is significantly higher. It seems that Instagram is more prevailed in users who are elder and with higher degrees. The influence to cultural dimension performance of education level and education methodology behind this is worth to explore.

Furthermore, the satisfaction rating of Task 1 (Browsing certain contents) on Instagram is significantly higher than that on Weibo in male users and users who have college or above degrees. Since Task 1 is the most frequently operated task for both products, male users and users who have college or above degrees are more fond of using Instagram to browse the contents they focus. This might be caused by the quality of contents, while also might be caused by the preference for the schemes of information presenting, which is affected by uncertainty avoidance and individualism [17].

In conclusion, firstly, the satisfaction level of Weibo on Task 1 (Browsing certain contents), Task 3 (Posting), Task 6 (Checking and replying to messages), and the NPS level of Weibo are significantly lower than that of Instagram. Secondly, there is positive correlation between the satisfaction ratings and the NPS score of both Weibo and Instagram, which means the two indices explains each other. Thirdly, differences of satisfaction ratings exist at gender levels, education levels, and age levels, further research of their causes at cultural dimensions need to be done. Lastly, advice for Weibo and domestic products have been concluded (see Table 10).

Table 10. Advice for domestic products

1	Updated study of Chinese cultural performance, recognition, and aesthetics of target users is needed to give reference value for design
2	The format of contents display, posting function, checking and replying function might need redesign for Weibo
3	Improving the posting function of Weibo will do good to promote the satisfaction level of the function, thus boost the usage frequency of the function as well
4	Applying designs that individualists prefer to products for the 1990s group or the highly educated users might be good
5	Even if the target users are from the same cultural group, thoroughly study of their respective cultural performance can help improve design

There are still a lot of limitations of this research, such as couldn't conduct the survey by using a more precise questionnaire and lack of attention to the user interviews. Also, responses collected from users recruited online are not fully convincible, since there was no moral restrict mechanism like face-to-face distributing and retrieving, respondents might had cheated in order to get the incentive, e.g. pretended to be a common user of Weibo and Instagram. Besides, users need VPN to log in Instagram in mainland China, which affects the usage scenario and usage frequency, thus might had exerted some biasing influence on the generalization of the results. Furthermore, cross-cultural effects on the satisfaction level of users have not been investigated, which needs further research.

References

1. Campbell, D.A., Lambright, K.T., Wells, C.J.: Looking for friends, fans, and followers? Social media use in public and nonprofit human services. Public Adm. Rev. **74**(5), 655–663 (2014)
2. Tai, Z.: The Internet in China: Cyberspace and Civil Society. Routledge, New York (2006)
3. Yang, G.: The co-evolution of the Internet and civil society in China. Asian Surv. **43**(3), 405–422 (2003)
4. Yang, G., Calhoun, C.: Media, civil society, and the rise of a green public sphere in China. China Inf. **21**(2), 211–236 (2007)
5. Tan, T., Zhang, Z.: The current situation, development and trends of social media in China. Editor. Friend **01**(1003–6687), 20–25 (2017)
6. The 2018 Weibo User Development Report. http://data.weibo.com/report/reportDetail?id=433. Accessed 31 Jan 2020
7. Nisbett, R.E., Peng, K., Choi, I., Norenzayan, A.: Culture and systems of thought: holistic versus analytic cognition. Psychol. Rev. **108**(2), 291–310 (2001)
8. Xie, C., Putrevu, J.S.H., Linder, C.: Family, friends, and cultural connectedness: a comparison between WeChat and Facebook user motivation, experience and NPS among Chinese people living overseas. In: Rau, P.-L.P. (ed.) CCD 2017. LNCS, vol. 10281, pp. 369–382. Springer, Cham (2017). https://doi.org/10.1007/978-3-319-57931-3_30
9. Lien, C.H., Cao, Y.: Examining WeChat users' motivations, trust, attitudes, and positive word-of-mouth: evidence from China. Comput. Hum. Behav. **41**, 104–111 (2014)

10. Jordan, P.W.: Designing Pleasurable Products: An Introduction to the New Human Factors. CRC Press, Boca Raton (2002)
11. Huang, H., et al.: International users' experience of social media: a comparison between Facebook and WeChat. In: Rau, P.-L.P. (ed.) CCD 2018, Part I. LNCS, vol. 10911, pp. 341–349. Springer, Cham (2018). https://doi.org/10.1007/978-3-319-92141-9_26
12. Yang, H.: Young American consumers' online privacy concerns, trust, risk, social media use, and regulatory support. J. New Commun. Res. **5**, 1–30 (2013)
13. Lewis, J., Sauro, J., Sauro, J.: Excel and R companion to "Quantifying the user experience–practical statistics for user research, 2nd edn. Measuring Usability LLC, CO, Denver (2012)
14. Lewis, J.R.: IBM Computer Usability Satisfaction Questionnaires: Psychometric Evaluation and Instructions for Use. International Journal of Human-Computer Interaction **7**(1), 57–78 (1995)
15. Reichheld, F.F.: The one number you need to grow. Harv. Bus. Rev. **81**(12), 46–55 (2003)
16. Hofstede, G.: Culture's Consequences: Comparing Values, Behaviours and Organisations Across Nations, 2nd edn. Sage Publications, London (2001)
17. Reinecke, K., Bernstein, A.: Knowing what a user likes: a design science approach to interfaces that automatically adapt to culture. Manage. Inf. Syst. Q. **37**(2), 427–453 (2013)
18. COMPARE COUNTRIES. https://www.hofstede-insights.com/product/compare-countries/. Accessed 31 Jan 2020
19. Nisbett, R., Miyamoto, Y.: The influence of culture: holistic versus analytic perception. Trends Cogn. Sci. **9**(10), 467–473 (2005)

Explore the Appeal of Social Media in Aesthetics Communication Among Different Culture

Kai-Shuan Shen[1(✉)], Kuo-Hsiang Chen[2], and Yen-Tao Liu[1]

[1] Fo Guang University, Jiaoxi 2624, Yilan County, Taiwan, ROC
ksshen319@gmail.com
[2] Fuzhou University of International Studies and Trade,
Changle District 350202, Fujan, People's Republic of China

Abstract. The way social media in aesthetics communication changes the traditional model of marketing revolutionarily. This type of communication generally uses many delicately designed images online to activate consumers' interests and improve the appeal of products. The success of the novel type of online communication motivates my study. Besides exploring the Kansei factors which affect social media in aesthetics communication, the marketing of net aesthetics is novel and worth exploring additionally. In addition, different culture causes different results of aesthetics communication in social media and needs to be explored. This study aims to explore the successful cases of product marketing through net aesthetics communication on the basis of Kansei Engineering. In the aspect of methodology, the study uses EGM (Evaluation Grid Method) to determine the appeal elements and characteristics of social medial in aesthetics communication. In addition, the study uses Quantification Theory Type I to measures the weights of individual appeal factors and characteristics. Hence, experts' points of views are obtained through in-depth interviews and consumers' opinions from different culture are collected through questionnaire survey so all of their preferences to aesthetics communication in social media can be disclosed. This study will determine that the semantic structure of appeal from different culture shows the hierarchy of the relationship among appeal factors, the reasons for users' preferences, and the specific characteristics of net aesthetics of products. In addition, appeal factors will be affected in varying degrees by particular reasons and characteristics. Then, in the aspects of marketing strategies for media in aesthetics communication, the study drafts the strategies of communication and the winning principles for social media in aesthetics communication on the basis of the literature and results of this study. Then, the study can provide important information for researchers who are interested in net aesthetics communication and marketing, and also contribute to the field of integrating media and product design.

Keywords: Kansei engineering · EGM · Quantification Theory Type I · Social media · Aesthetics communication · Media design · Web communication · Visual communication · Product design

© Springer Nature Switzerland AG 2020
P.-L. P. Rau (Ed.): HCII 2020, LNCS 12193, pp. 424–433, 2020.
https://doi.org/10.1007/978-3-030-49913-6_35

1 Introduction

Social media in aesthetics communication could be one of the most popular way of marketing. This type of communication takes advantage of a social media user's behaviors in daily life, such as uploading pictures for online check-in. Hence, aesthetic pictures, conveying various activities, such as a wonderful journey, a cool visit, a colorful live, and a desirable fashion, can be shared and distributed based on social media users' psychology of envy. While doing the type of online activities through social media, users actually promote products or brands for sellers freely (Fig. 1).

Fig. 1. The example of social media in aesthetics communication

The focus of this research was to explore social media in aesthetics communication from the users' motivations with different culture. More specifically, the focus of this research was to discover how the appeal of social media in aesthetics communication can drive user emotions and determine user motivation.

2 Review of the Literature

2.1 Social Media Influencer Marketing

A celebrity plays an important role in influencer marketing because he has a huge amount of influences on social media. Two types of celebrities, including Instagram and traditional celebrity, were studied how they had influence on source trustworthiness, brand attitude, envy and social presence [1]. This study also proved that influencer marketing was effective on consumers. In addition, how influencer marketing has influence on consumer behavior was studied [2].

The study proved that the selection of information sources which affected consumers' online purchase decisions strongly changed by culture [3]. This also means that culture had huge influence on the use of information sources to affect purchase decisions, including social media. Furthermore, social media plays an important role in the success of influencer marketing. Hence, the issue how culture differences affect consumers' motivation on influencer marketing, which is practiced by social media in aesthetics communication, motivates the researcher to probe this study.

2.2   Kansei Engineering

Kansei engineering is used to study the styling and design specification of products based on users 'emotions. Hence, the relationship between an impression and characteristics of styling could be explored through a subjective evaluation, which were carried out by semantic differential methods and analyzed by using multivariate analysis [4]. Kansei engineering was applied to explored the appeal of social media in aesthetics among different cultures in this study. The theory of Kansei engineering was realized through the Evaluation Grid Method (EGM) and the Quantification Theory Type I in this study.

2.3   Evaluation Grid Method EGM

Sanui and Inui [5] developed the EGM based on the repertory grid method derived by Kelly's personal construct theory [6]. The EGM is used to visualize user' requirements so users' impressions and design specification of social media in aesthetic communication could be disclosed in a hierarchy form.

2.4   Quantification Theory Type I

Quantification Type I Method, as a quantitative tool, was used to analyze the importance of the appeal factors, reasons and characteristics of the interaction which was formed through influencer marketing in this study. More specifically, Quantification Type I Method could measure and quantify the upper-l and lower-level items using the importance levels from the original evaluation items. Quantification Theory Type I can statistically predict the relationship between a response value and the categorical values using multiple linear regression methods [6]. Moreover, in the field of design, the weights of the factors of users' preferences can be evaluate using Hayashi's Quantification Theory Type I [7, 8].

3   Research Objectives

This study attempted to explore the appeal of social media in aesthetics communication among different culture. Hence, the researcher tried to construct the semantic hierarchy diagram to show the appeal of social media in aesthetics communication. The design characteristics and user motivations of social media in aesthetics communication could be disclosed in this semantic hierarchy diagram. Then, users' preferences from various culture for social media in aesthetics communication could be determined through statistical analysis.

4   Research Methods

In order to explore the appeal of social media in aesthetics communication among different cultures, emotion-based Kansei Engineering was used to probe the appeal of social media in aesthetics communication among different cultures. Furthermore, this study could be realized through two phases. In the first phase, this study would establish common evaluation principles of aesthetics communication among different cultures based on the technique of EGM (Evaluation Grid Method). In the second phase, this study would use the established common evaluation principle to survey users among different cultures and analyzed the questionnaire survey using Quantification Theory Type I. The further explanations are listed below:

In the first phase, the EGM was used for the determination of the common evaluation principles of aesthetics communication among different cultures. Hence, the Kansei words, containing design characteristics and emotional concepts, had to be widely collected through two approaches, including article reviews and expert interviews. The former approach was conducted through examining related articles, which focused on reviewing social media in aesthetics communication. In addition, authoritative magazine, professional books and web sites which were appropriate sources for the collection of Kansei words about social media in aesthetics communication. The latter approach was conducted through interviewing professionals who had expertise in social media in aesthetics communication, such as marketing specialist, social media designer, and experienced users.

All the Kansei words collected from article examinations and expert interviews were processed based on the technique of the EGM. Hence, the Kansei words were arranged from abstract to specific concepts. In this study, the abstract concepts were more emotional and named as "upper-level" language, such as "desirable"; the specific concepts were more professional and named as "lower-level" language, such as "a spectacle image". Then, each "upper-level" language would have it corresponding "lower-level" language.

5 Analysis and Results

"Motivated sharing" and "credible and reliable" were determined as the two original evaluation items. The corresponding "upper-level" concepts of "motivated sharing" included "desirable" and "accessible searching". Furthermore, the corresponding "lower-level" concepts of "desirable" comprised "beautiful tourist sights", "the tourist experience", "a spectacle images", "taking a pictures at a graffiti wall", "free publicity photos", "qualitative contents". Then, the corresponding "lower-level" concepts of "accessible searching" consisted of "a clear index for taking the spectacle picture", "organized graphics in text", "search Engine Optimization (SEO)", and "searching for more contents and detail".

5.1 Evaluation Grid Method (EGM)

Table 1 shows the order of occurrences of the vocabulary from the EGM hierarchical chart. The decisions regarding the upper-level and lower-level words were also based on the EGM statistics, as shown in Table 2. Table 2 shows the original impressions of the two selected according to the number description in the EGM hierarchical chart and their reasons, which were included in the questionnaire. Table 3 shows the setting and structure of the questionnaire, including the original evaluation items, the upper-level words, and the lower-level words.

Table 1. The ranking from the hierarchical diagram by the number of times the descriptions appeared

Original images	Upper level (reasons)	Lower level (specific attributes)
Motivated sharing 8	Word-of-mouth 8	A clear index for taking the spectacle picture 18
Credible and reliable 7	Desirable 7	Organized graphic in text 13
Wonderful 6	Authoritative 7	Beautiful tourist sights 12
Cool 5	Accessible searching 5	A spectacle images 10
Colorful 4	Recommended 4	A maven's (someone who owns professional knowledge) opinions 10

Table 2. The best four "original images and reasons" selected from the hierarchical diagram by the higher number of times they appeared

Classified	Original images	Reasons (upper level)
First	Word-of-mouth 8	Influential friends' recommendations 7 Blogger's recommendation 5 Close to daily life 5
Second	Desirable 7	Beautiful tourist sights 12 A spectacle images 10 Taking a pictures/at a graffiti wall 8
Third	Authoritative 7	A maven's (someone who owns professional knowledge) opinions 10 The participation of Key Opinion Leader (KOL) 9 Celebrity experience 7
Forth	Accessible searching 5	A clear index for taking the spectacle picture 18 Organized graphics in text 13 Search Engine Optimization (SEO) 8

Table 3. The setting of the level-based construction of questionnaire

Level of questionnaire	The first level	The second level	The third level
The type of question	Original evaluation item	Upper level	Lower level
The example of a question subject	Credible and reliable	Authoritative	The participation of Key Opinion Leader (KOL)

The interview contents were recorded in a hierarchical format, as shown in Fig. 2 and Fig. 3. Figure 2 is the hierarchical chart of the answers from a 28-year-old male expert who participated in the interview, including the upper-level and lower-level words, and the relationship between the upper-level and lower words. Figure 2 shows the hierarchical chart obtained by the researchers after recording and collating the responses of all the experts after EGM interviews.

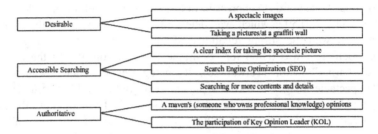

Fig. 2. Hierarchical chart of a 28-year-old male expert participating in the interview

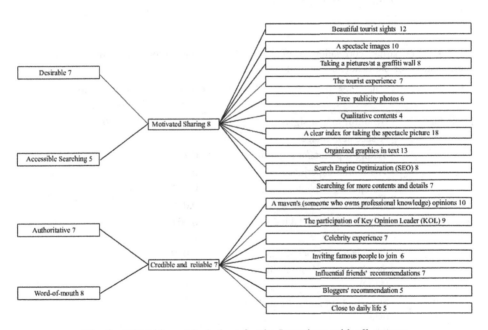

Fig. 3. EGM hierarchical chart for the Interviews with all experts

5.2   Quantification Theory Type I

The following statistical analysis was based on the results of the questionnaire survey from users with different cultures, including Taiwanese and non-Taiwanese. The primary appeal of social media in aesthetics communication was that it is "motivated sharing", and its upper-level word evaluation items included "desirable" and "accessible searching". This indicated that when the social media in aesthetics communication left consumers with an impression of being "motivated sharing", they would choose the above two upper-level words to express it. In this study, the coefficient of determination was (R^2) = 0.842 & 0.592, which was determined by the results of the quantitative analysis and showed the strong reliability of the survey tools. The highest partial correlation coefficient was 0.906 for "desirable", which contributed the most to the "motivated sharing" factor (Taiwanese). Its categories included "beautiful tourist sights", "a spectacle images", "taking a picture/at a graffiti wall", "the tourist experience", "free publicity photos", and "Qualitative contents". Table 4 shows the narrative statistics of each item, which revealed that "taking a picture/at a graffiti wall" and "a spectacle images" had the strongest attraction (category score = 0.148) for "desirable"; in addition, "beautiful tourist sights" had the most negative attraction (category score = −0.202) for "desirable" (Table 4).

Table 4. The partial correlation coefficients, the category scores and the coefficient of determination for the factor of "motivated sharing" (Taiwanese)

Items	Categories	Category scores	Partial correlation coefficients
Desirable	Beautiful tourist sights	−0.202	0.906
	A spectacle images	0.148	
	Taking a picture/at a graffiti wall	0.148	
	The tourist experience	−0.041	
	Free publicity photos	−0.061	
	Qualitative contents	0.018	
Accessible sharing	A clear index for taking the spectacle picture	0.061	0.070
	Organized graphics in text	−0.059	
	Search Engine Optimization (SEO)	−0.019	
	Searching for more contents and details	0.111	
C	0.841		
R=	0.918		
R^2=	0.842		

Table 5. The partial correlation coefficients, the category scores and the coefficient of determination for the factor of "motivated sharing" (Non-Taiwanese)

Items	Categories	Category scores	Partial correlation coefficients
Desirable	Beautiful tourist sights	−0.154	0.748
	A spectacle images	0.100	
	Taking a picture/at a graffiti wall	0.082	
	The tourist experience	−0.060	
	Free publicity photos	0.015	
	Qualitative contents	−0.065	
Accessible sharing	A clear index for taking the spectacle picture	0.003	0.224
	Organized graphics in text	0.008	
	Search Engine Optimization (SEO)	−0.024	
	Searching for more contents and details	0.046	
C	0.858		
R=	0.770		
R^2=	0.592		

The second attraction element was "credible and reliable", which included the upper word evaluations of "authoritative", and "word-of-mouth". In this study, based on the quantitative category analysis results, the coefficient of determination (R^2) was determined to be "0.735", which also showed that the survey tools have strong reliability. The highest partial correlation coefficient was 0.849 for "authoritative" (Table 7), which indicated that it contributed the most to the "credible and reliable" factors. "authoritative" contained "a maven's (someone who owns professional knowledge) opinions", "the participation of Key Opinion Leader (KOL)", "celebrity experience", and "inviting famous people to join". Table 6 shows the category of each item, among which "the participation of Key Opinion Leader (KOL)" had the strongest appeal for "authoritative". "inviting famous people to join" had the most negative appeal for "authoritative".

Table 6. The partial correlation coefficients, the category scores and the coefficient of determination for the factor of "motivated sharing" (Taiwanese)

Items	Categories	Category scores	Partial correlation coefficients
Authoritative	A maven's (someone who owns professional knowledge) opinions	−0.017	0.797
	The participation of Key Opinion Leader (KOL)	0.133	
	Celebrity experience	0.083	
	Inviting famous people to join	−0.191	

(*continued*)

Table 6. (*continued*)

Items	Categories	Category scores	Partial correlation coefficients
Word-of-mouth	Influential friends' recommendations	0.055	0.488
	Blogger's recommendation	−0.044	
	Close to daily life	−0.044	
C	0.861		
R=	0.840		
R²=	0.705		

Table 7. The partial correlation coefficients, the category scores and the coefficient of determination for the factor of "motivated sharing" (Non-Taiwanese)

Items	Categories	Category scores	Partial correlation coefficients
Authoritative	A maven's (someone who owns professional knowledge) opinions	−0.009	0.849
	The participation of Key Opinion Leader (KOL)	0.130	
	Celebrity experience	0.035	
	Inviting famous people to join	−0.156	
Word-of-mouth	Influential friends' recommendations	0.041	0.413
	Blogger's recommendation	−0.017	
	Close to daily life	−0.026	
C	0.854		
R=	0.857		
R²=	0.735		

6 Discussion and Conclusions

This study determined that the semantic structure of appeal from different culture showed the hierarchy of the relationship among appeal factors, the reasons for users' preferences, and the specific characteristics of net aesthetics of products. The two appeal factors "motivated sharing" and "credible and reliable" were evolved from the four "upper-level" concepts, including "desirable", "accessible searching", "authoritative" and "word-of-mouth". The two appeal factors reflected that the popularity of social media in aesthetics communication could be ascribed to the two appeal factors. The two appeal factors also indicated consumers aggressively shared their experience in social media and had credible and reliable influence on their friends or fans. In addition, the four "upper-level" concepts, as consumers' motivations, drove their using social media in aesthetics communication. Furthermore, the four "upper-level" concepts means that consumers realized social media in aesthetic communication through "accessible searching" for the "desirable" and had authoritative influence on friend or fans through the "word-of-mouth" way. The results of this study also shows user from different culture could be motivated through varied extents of the design elements of social medial in aesthetics communication.

References

1. Jin, S.V., Muqaddam, A., Ryu, E.: Instagamous and social media influencer marketing. Mark. Intell. Plann. **37**(5), 567–579 (2019)
2. Kádeková, Z., Holienčinová, M.: Influencer marketing as a modern phenomenon creating a new frontier of virtual opportunities. Commun. Today **9**(2), 90–105 (2018)
3. Goodrich, K., Mooij, M.D.: How "social" are social media? A cross-cultural comparison of online and offline purchase decision influences. J. Mark. Commun. **20**(1–2), 103–116 (2014)
4. Jindo, T., Hirasago, K.: Application studies to car interior of Kansei engineering. Int. J. Ind. Ergon. **19**(2), 105–114 (1997)
5. Sanui, J., Inui, M.: Phenomenological approach to the evaluation of places: a study on the construct system associated with the place evaluation (1). J. Architect. Plann. Environ. Eng. **367**, 15–22 (1986). (in Japanese)
6. Kelly, G.A.: The Psychology of Personal Constructs, vol. 1–2. W. W. Norton, New York (2003)
7. Iwabuchi, C., et al.: Data Management and Analysis by Yourself, pp. 180–185. Humura Publishing, Tokyo (2001)
8. Sugiyama, K., Novel, K.: The Basic for Survey and Analysis by Excel: A Collection of Tool for Planning and Design, pp. 51–62. Kaibundo Publishing, Tokyo (1996)

Investigating Culture as a Precedent Factor for Dual Social Network Site Use and Social Capital Development

Chien Wen (Tina) Yuan[(✉)]

Graduate Institute of Library and Information Studies,
National Taiwan Normal University, Taipei, Taiwan
tinayuan@ntnu.edu.tw

Abstract. This study investigated how culture influences East Asian users' relation-ship development and group identification on a home-country social net-work site (SNS) and Facebook and how social capital development across sites is shaped by these factors. An online survey (N = 335) among Chinese and Korean international students in the U.S. was conducted, and structural equation modeling was used to analyze the data. The current study complements existing literature in several aspects. First, while previous studies posit that cultural values have majorly accounted for home-country-site use, our study shows cultural values also influence international people's Facebook use. Then we show the pattern of social capital development is similar across Facebook and Renren/Cyworld for both bonding and bridging social capital. Light-weight SNS-enabled social interactions such as commenting or liking others' posts are sufficient, in contrast to meaningful relationship engagement and group formation for both types of social capital. Last, our results suggest bonding social capital is more valued by users.

Keywords: Social network sites · Cross-cultural communication · Social capital · Measurement invariance model · Structural equation modeling

1 Introduction

Social network sites (SNSs), like Facebook, are handy tools for their users to develop and maintain social connections. They make searching potential friends or connecting with old and new friends much easier, as social networks of all kinds are laid out on the sites in a way that makes users feel connected (Binder et al. 2009; DiMicco et al. 2008; Ellison et al. 2011). SNSs are especially helpful for people relocated to a new place, such as international students (Choi et al. 2011), because they can help transcend time and space for managing distant and close or new and existing social connections. From a social capital perspective, these social relationships can be leveraged for tangible and intangible resource access, or called social capital; scholars usually categorize social capital into two types: social trust and support, or bonding social capital, that come from close relationships, and information diffusion and opportunities, or bridging social

© Springer Nature Switzerland AG 2020
P.-L. P. Rau (Ed.): HCII 2020, LNCS 12193, pp. 434–446, 2020.
https://doi.org/10.1007/978-3-030-49913-6_36

capital, from distant connections (Putnam 2000). In other words, one of the strengths of SNSs is to maintain bonding social capital and develop bridging social capital (Ellison et al. 2007).

Much previous research on SNSs has implicitly assumed that people use a single SNS (usually Facebook) to manage their social relationships and develop social capital (e.g., Ellison et al. 2007; Lampe et al. 2006; Lin et al. 2012). For example, SNS literature that focused on American users' Facebook use found that Facebook use largely contributes to users' bridging social capital (e.g., Ellison et al. 2007). Cross-cultural SNS studies compared how Americans used Facebook with how users from eastern countries used a local SNS and pointed out that bridging social capital may be more valued by users from the western cultures and bonding social capital by users from the eastern cultures (e.g., Choi et al. 2011; Kim et al. 2011). However, users actually manage a wide variety of SNSs for different purposes at the same time (Yuan and Fussell 2017). Similarly, in the case of international students in the U.S., bonding and bridging social networks may be split across two or more SNSs instead of on a single site. These students may have used a local SNS based in their home country (e.g., China's Renren or Weibo, Korea's Cyworld, Japan's Mixi, Russia's Vk.com, etc.) that includes networks of friends who share the same cultural values and speak the same native language. This makes it valuable for keeping using the local site so as to maintain connections with friends from home. At the same time, engagement in a global SNS such as Facebook may be important for creating and maintaining connections with new friends and acquaintances in the U.S. or from other countries.

Unlike juggling around multiple but different sites like Facebook, Youtube, and LinkedIn, using two sites of similar purposes but different network components, one being local and the other global, may present some dilemmas for international students. For example, if there is limited time available for socializing, time spent on one site will lead to less time on the other. Less time spent on either site may lead to reduced social capital resources on that site (Qiu et al. 2013).

Much previous cross-cultural research on SNS use adopted a between-study design to compare American users' Facebook use with international users' local site use (e.g., Choi et al. 2011; Ji et al. 2010; Qiu et al. 2013; Shin 2010; Zhou 2011). Such study design overlooks the fact that users often see the needs to juggle between two or more SNSs of similar purposes but different network components for social connections and social capital resources. Studies started to use a within-study design that investigates the situation where international people may need to adopt a home-country site and Facebook to manage friends from different countries and found that they indeed leveraged networks on both sites for bonding and bridging capital (e.g., Yuan and Fussell 2017). The current study complements previous ones and investigates how culture, as a precedent variable, influences international people's social interaction and social capital development on a home-country site and Facebook.

We surveyed 335 international students from China and South Korea who studied in the U.S. and used either Renren (China) or Cyworld (Korea) in addition to Facebook. We examined how cultural values influence their social interaction and social capital development on a home-country site and Facebook. Our general hypothesis was that cultural values may be positively associated with people's practices of social interaction and group identification on their home country site where social networks of similar culture and language coexist and therefore more social capital resources are accumulated on the site in contrast to Facebook. We found that site per se did not work as social identity label because our participants engage in similar activities on the home-country site and Facebook. Collectivistic culture itself accounts for the similar interaction pattern across sites. Then, we found that users did not engage in meaningful relationship and group activities using SNSs. Last, we found that users develop both bonding and bridging social capital from the social connections they have on the sites but bonding social capital is more valued by users.

2   Related Work

2.1   Culture and SNS Use

Cross-cultural psychology suggests that culture may shape people's behaviors, such as communication norms and styles (Gudykunst 1998). Individuals internalize the norms and values and construct shared perceptions, or cultural values, about their social environments and how they engage in interactions. Individualism-collectivism has been recognized as one of the major dimensions of cultural variability (Triandis 1986; Hofstede 1980). Western individualistic cultures (e.g., that of the U.S.) communicate in a direct and precise manner with ample and accurate information delivered and they tend to emphasize the individual's goals, whereas eastern collectivistic ones (e.g., that of China and of Korea) interact indirectly and pay more attention to interpersonal dynamics as well as the specific communication context. In collectivistic cultures, the group goals have precedence over individual goals (Gudykunst 1998; Triandis 1986; Hofstede 1980).

The same interaction pattern was found true in mediated social contexts such as SNSs (Recabarren et al. 2008). Cross-cultural SNS research posits that SNSs are culturally bounded and reflect specific norms and values. Practices on SNSs appear to be different between American-based SNSs and Asian-based SNSs: SNS users from collectivistic cultures value in-group bonds and identification and engage in relationship-oriented activities, like chatting with friends, seeking social support, and forming dense social networks, for bonding social capital (Choi et al. 2011; Kim and Yun 2007). Users from individualistic cultures, like American users, value connecting with acquaintances on Facebook and gain bridging social capital (Ellison et al. 2007). It is less discussed in the literature how individuals' cultural values influence users to behave in a western mediated context versus an eastern one to fulfill users' relational needs. Our study complements prior research by investigating culture's impacts on Chinese and Korean users' behaviors on a global or western SNS, Facebook, and a local or eastern site, Renren for Chinese users and Cyworld for Korean users. We use two dimensions, relationship development and group identification, to discuss SNS use, both of which reflect cultural values and in turn contribute to social connections and social capital development.

2.2   A Social Identity Perspective: Relationship Development and Group Identification

Social identity is middle ground between self-conception and group processes, which can be conceived as individual's sense of belonging to certain social groups as well as the identification of group membership (Tajfel 1978). Social groups can be all kinds and sizes, ranging from demographic categories like national or cultural groups to ad-hoc and task-oriented groups in a team, that provide their members with a shared identity to guide people's beliefs and behaviors and distinguish ingroup members from outgroup ones (Hogg et al. 2004). When social identity of a certain group becomes more salient than the others, the associated set of values and attitudes may prompt people to conduct identity-related behaviors. Different groups may compete with one another for positive cognitive and emotional distinctiveness (Tajfel 1978). Meanwhile, it is also important to discuss how social influence of groups is derived: people develop shared group norms as part of their social identity through interaction and relationship development with fellow group members (Turner 1982).

Drawing on social identity perspective, we propose that both relationship development and group identification are two important conceptual components to examine influences of different social groups (Hogg 2003). The two components serve as different explanatory functions regarding how cultural values may influence users' behaviors on Facebook and users' home-country sites.

Despite that SNSs support development and maintenance of multiple relationships, users may not weigh their relationships with different cultural groups similarly on SNSs. For example, international students in the U.S. report a sense of social obligation towards those from the same home country, especially in the face-to-face, informal social settings (Yuan et al. 2013). However, they may adapt to the individualistic culture when they interact with American networks (Choi et al. 2011). A local site that consists of networks of similar culture and language may prompt users to engage in activities beneficial to social capital development because much emphasis is placed on social relationships in collectivistic cultures, so in-group members have intense interactions and stronger bonds with one another. On the other hand, a global site may yield fewer related activities and social capital resources because in individualistic cultures, where people are more independent, ties to the group may be weaker and social interactions relatively temporary and voluntary (Triandis et al. 1988). Drawing on social identity perspective, collectivistic cultural values may work as a salient trigger for users to engage in more relational activities on a home-country site. Therefore, we hypothesize that culture influences users' social relationship development on Renren/Cyworld and Facebook, specifically with higher intensity on Renren/Cyworld than on Facebook.

H1: Collectivistic culture will have a positive association with relationship development on Renren/Cyworld more than on Facebook.

From a social identity perspective, people's social categories, such as nationality and culture, affect how they position themselves in a social context. People affiliate with groups to derive self-evaluation (Tajfel 1978) and develop in-group identification and distinction from out-groups (Hogg et al. 2004). People from collectivistic cultures approach the groups similar to themselves or would agree to them (McPherson et al. 2001), which contributes to the commitment to the group. Their identification with their original cultural group could be salient when compared with the newly adopted one or the one comprising people from different cultures. Therefore, we predict that collectivistic culture will influence Chinese and Korean users to develop group identification with social networks on Renren/Cyworld. Social networks on Facebook comprise cross-cultural networks, and Chinese and Korean users' group identification will be lower.

H2: Collectivistic culture will have a positive association with group identification on Renren/Cyworld more than on Facebook.

The socio-technical affordances of SNSs support relationship development among acquaintances and close friends through developing interconnected social networks (Ellison et al. 2007). The motivation of developing social relationships drives users to engage in relationship-driven activities and develop understanding about one another, such as browsing friends' pages, leaving comments, or "Liking" their status updates (Ellison et al. 2011). Given that culture is reflected in people's interpersonal communication styles and relationships are more valued in collectivistic cultures in contrast to instrumental motivations in individualistic cultures (Gudykunst 1998; Triandis et al. 1988), it may be the case that activities related to relationship development on Renren/Cyworld are more significant factors in connecting with friends than they would be on Facebook.

H3: Users' relationship development on Renren/Cyworld will be more positively associated with social connection with friends than on Facebook.

People's group identification elicits emotional involvement and senses of belongingness and membership towards their social networks (Tajfel 1978). It also drives people's active interaction with their group members. Given that collectivistic culture plays a role in motivating people's identification with in-group members, we hypothesize such group identification will contribute to social connection with one's group on Renren/Cyworld more than on Facebook.

H4: Users' group identification on Renren/Cyworld will be more positively associated with social connection with friends than on Facebook.

SNSs sustain maintaining bonds with close friends, expanding ties with acquaintances, and connecting with otherwise unlikely relationships with friends' friends (latent ties) (Ellison et al. 2011). It has been established that, from tightly structured relationships constructed by close friends and family members, users can obtain bonding social capital, whereas from loosely structured networks constructed by acquaintances or latent ties, bridging social capital is derived (Putnam 2000). Renren/Cyworld may be a source of bonding social capital, because previously constructed networks and close friends are active on the site, whereas Facebook may be a source of bridging capital because of the diversity of its users and potential for gaining instrumental help. Therefore, we hypothesize:

H5: Connection with friends on Facebook will be positively associated with higher bridging social capital on Facebook.

H6: Connection with friends on Renren/Cyworld will be positively associated with higher bonding social capital on Renren/Cyworld.

3 Method

3.1 Research Target and Survey Design

We focus on East Asian international students (N = 335: 196 Chinese, 139 Korean) who have existing relationships at home they need to maintain but are also motivated to develop new social networks in a Western cultural context, the U.S. We compare the use of their home-country sites (Renren or Cyworld) and Facebook.

We conducted an online survey study using Qualtrics. Recruitment was through social media, including Facebook and participants' home-country site. Average respondents were female (Chinese: 51.5%; Korean: 47%) and college undergraduate (Chinese: 69.4% had a bachelor's degree; Korean: 78.7%), whose ages ranged from 18 to 41 years old (Chinese M = 24.5, SD = 3.25; Korean M = 25.04, SD = 3.52). To participate in the study, respondents must be at least 18 years old, have Facebook and Renren/Cyworld accounts, and have lived in the U.S. less than five years (Chinese M = 2.96; Korean M = 3.67).

The survey was conducted in English. There were two parallel sets of survey items: one about participants' use of Facebook and the other Renren or Cyworld. The wording of each question was the same, and only the target site changed for different sub-sets of the survey. We randomized the survey order to reduce order bias. All survey items were drawn from previously validated scales. Responses were given on a 5-point Likert scale (1 = strongly disagree; 5 = strongly agree). See Table 1 for the means, standard deviations, correlations, and reliability and validity measures associated with the variables.

3.2 Measures

Collectivistic Culture. We selected three sub-components of Gudykunst et al.'s (1998) measure to operationalize collectivistic culture: interpersonal sensitivity (5 items, e.g., "I qualify my language when I communicate"), precise communication (4 items, e.g., "I openly show my disagreement with others"), and indirect communication (6 items, e.g., "I convey difficult messages to others indirectly").

Group Identification. Dimensions about group identification were drawn on previous validated scales include subjective norms (13 items, e.g., "Most people that have influence on my behavior think that I should participate in <SNS>"), cognitive social identity (3 items, e.g., "My personal image has an overlapping with <SNS>"), affective social identity (4 items, e.g., includes "I feel a strong feeling of membership in FB"), and evaluative social identity (6 items, e.g., "I am an important member of <SNS>") (Zhou 2011).

Relationship Development. We adapted Choi et al. (2011) to gauge seven dimensions of relationship development: interdependence (3 items), breadth (2 items, e.g., "My communication with those who I interact with on <SNS> ranges over a wide variety of topics"), depth (5 items, e.g., "I feel I could confide in those who I interact with on <SNS> about almost anything"), code change (4 items), predictability (4 items), commitment, (3 items, e.g., "I would make a great effect to maintain my relationship with those who I interact with on <SNS>"), and network convergence (3 items).

Connection with Friends. Scales from Ellison et al. (2011) were adapted to assess respondents' social connections with people from their own country (4 items) and from other countries (9 items) on each SNS.

Social Capital. We drew on Ellison et al. (2007) to measure bonding social capital, which includes four dimensions, emotional support, access to scarce resources, mobilizing solidarity, and out-group antagonism (10 items, e.g., "When I feel lonely, there are people on <SNS> I can talk to"). There are also 10 items for measuring bridging social capital, which contains four dimensions, outward looking, network diversity, diffused reciprocity, and a sense of connectedness (e.g., "Interacting with contacts on <SNS> makes me interested in what people unlike me are thinking").

3.3   Analysis

The hypothesized model was examined as a second-order model with structural equation modeling (SEM) using Mplus 7.4. The analyses were run in maximum likelihood estimation with robust standard errors (MLR) and conducted in the following steps (Kline 2011). First, we averaged the observed predictors into their correspondent latent variables to indicate the sub-dimensions of each second-order factor. Then, we constructed our measurement model for confirmatory factor analysis using the latent variables (see Table 1).

Since the study looks at the respondents' Renren/Cyworld and Facebook use and we used identical measures for these sites, we performed multi-group measurement invariance model comparisons (Vandenberg and Lance 2000) to examine the extent to which the psychometric properties of our indicators are generalizable across sites (home-country site was set as reference group) (see Table 2). For measurement invariance model comparisons, we pursued the following steps. First, a configural invariance model (1) was initially specified to test if the factors measured across sites have the same factor structures. It had a good fit, and thus a series of model constraints were then applied in successive models to examine potential decreases in fit resulting from measurement non-invariance. Next, the metric invariance model (2) investigated if the factor loading was the same for each factor across sites. The results showed that partial metric invariance model in which we freed the constraints of the following three latent variables, subjective norms, connection with one's own group, and emotional support (2a), did not result in a significant decrease in fit relative to the configural model. Then, we proceeded to examine whether the factors had the same item intercepts at the same absolute level of the trait across sites in scalar invariance model (3). Again, partial scalar model in which the intercept for interdependence and access to share scarce resources (3a) were allowed to differ between sites, resulting in a good-fitting model. We used the partial scalar invariance model (3a) for measurement model modification. A sequence of model modifications was pursued in an effort to improve the overall measurement model (4). After it reached a model fit with adequate convergent and discriminant validity, we removed non-significant covariances, which further improved the model (4a). We then proceed to construct the structural relational model. The original hypothesized model (5) converged after we allowed covariance between latent variables for home-country sites and Facebook.

Table 1. Descriptive results of each factor and correlations.

Descriptive results	M	SD	AVE	CR	1	2	3	4	5	6
1. Cultural Values	3.84	.47	.58	.81	**.76**					
2. Group Identification	3.71 (3.80)	.64 (.53)	.42 (.41)	.86 (.85)	.78***	**.65/.64**				
3. Relationship Development	3.75 (3.80)	.58 (.52)	.28 (.26)	.93 (.92)	.78***	.96***	**.53/.51**			
4. Connection with Friends	4.01 (4.20)	.83 (.63)	.51 (.35)	.67 (.52)	.73***	.95***	.96***	**.71/.59**		
5. Bonding Social Capital	3.75 (3.81)	.66 (.58)	.36 (.30)	.81 (.75)	.72***	.97***	.98***	.96***	**.60/.55**	
6. Bridging Social Capital	3.81 (3.86)	.66 (.54)	.33 (.30)	.79 (.71)	.64***	.84***	.84***	.88***	.88***	**.57/.55**

Note: $^+p < .10$ $^*p < .05$ $^{**}p < .01$ $^{***}p < .005$ $^{****}p < .001$
Square root of AVE in diagonal to indicate discriminant validity; CR to indicate composite reliability

Through our analysis, we ensured the observed differences between sites reflect actual differences in the variability of the constructs but not in sites. Third, the relationships between the two sites and the identified factors were examined with the structural relation model. The final structural relation model reached a good fit with $\chi 2$ [391] = 318.64, p = .997; RMSEA = .00, CI [.00, .00]; CFI = 1.00; SRMR = .028.

4   Results

The summary of the hypothesis testing results is reported in Fig. 1. H1 stated that collectivistic culture would be more positively associated with relationship development on Renren/Cyworld than on Facebook. The positive association between cultural value and relationship development is significant on both Facebook ($\beta = .79, p = .001$) and Renren/Cyworld ($\beta = .78, p < .001$). H1 was partially supported. Similarly, the result of H2 confirmed that collectivistic cultural values would have a positive association with group identification on Facebook ($\beta = .70, p < .001$) and Renren/Cyworld ($\beta = .78, p < .001$); H2 was partially supported.

Table 2. Model fit indices.

Summary of fit indicators

Model	χ^2 value	χ^2 DF	χ^2 p-value	CFI	RMSEA estimate	RMSEA lower CI	RMSEA higher CI	RMSEA p-value	SRMR	TRd	Δdf	p-value
1. Configural Invariance Model	814.62	474	<.0001	.96	.046	.04	.05	.87	.04	–	–	–
2. Metric	847.19	492	<.0001	.96	.046	.04	.05	.87	.05	32.45	18	.019
2a. Partial Metric	818.84	489	<.0001	.96	.045	.04	.05	.93	.04	4.72	15	.994
3. Scalar	846.10	504	<.0001	.96	.045	.04	.05	.94	.04	30.05	30	.463
3a. Partial Scalar	835.53	502	<.0001	.96	.045	.04	.05	.96	.04	18.97	28	.899
4. Final Measurement Model	310.71	390	0.9988	1	0	0	0	1	.03	–	–	–
4a. Final Measurement Model_Revised	347.58	411	0.9897	1	0	0	0	1	.03	38.02	21	.013
5. Final SR Model	318.64	391	0.997	1	0	0	0	1	.03	2.26	1	.132

Note:
Mplus provides tests of the goodness of fit for the overall model, including a non-significant χ^2 goodness-of-fit index that shows the data is not different from the proposed model, the root mean square error of approximation (RMSEA, <.5), the confidence interval of RMSEA (CI, lower bound < .5; higher bound < .10), the Comparative Fit Index (CFI, >.9), and the standardized root mean square residual (SRMR, <.8)[34].

H3 posited that relationship development would be more positively associated with connection with friends on Renren/Cyworld than on Facebook. It was neither supported on Facebook ($\beta = .35, p = .77$) nor on Renren/Cyworld ($\beta = .42, p = .87$). H3 was not supported. H4 was not supported because group identification was neither associated with connection with friends on Facebook ($\beta = .44, p = .72$) nor on Renren/Cyworld ($\beta = .40, p = .88$).

H5 proposed that connection with friends on Facebook would be positively associated with greater bridging capital. The hypothesis was supported on Facebook ($\beta = .92, p < .001$) but also on home-country sites ($\beta = .88, p < .001$). H6 proposed that connection with friends on Renren/Cyworld would be associated with higher bonding social capital. It was supported on Facebook ($\beta = 1.07, p < .001$) and home-country sites ($\beta = 1.09, p < .001$).

5   Discussion

Our study extends earlier work by showing that collectivistic culture influences SNS use on both home-country site with existing networks and Facebook with diverse, new contacts. Since we used a within-study design to compare culture's influences on users' behaviors on a home-country site and Facebook, we found that there exist more similarities than differences between home-country site and Facebook regarding the links between culture and relationship development/group identification. The result does not support what prior studies suggested that relationship development was only valued in East Asian users' home-country sites or users switched behaviors towards different social networks across sites (e.g., Choi et al. 2011). Instead, culture carries the influence across sites on users' social interactions with different cultural/linguistic networks (H1). From a social influence perspective, our results indicate that collectivistic culture influences group behaviors on both home-country sites and Facebook (H2).

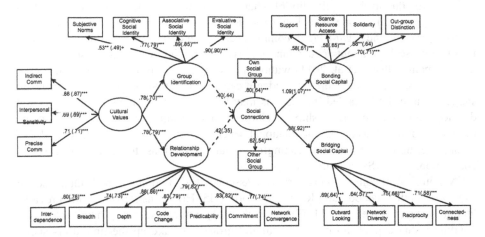

Fig. 1. Standardized results of the final model (Facebook results in the parentheses) with χ2 [391] = 318.64, p = .997; RMSEA = .00, CI [.00, .00]; CFI = 1.00; SRMR = .028 [Note: Covariances not shown in the figure].

Extending social identity perspective, our results from H1 and H2 suggest that users from eastern cultures engaged in SNSs, whether it is local or global, the same way as there is no discrepancy in the two explanatory factors in terms of how cultural values influence users' SNS practices across sites. Our participants do not change their relational interactions nor group identification just because they were on different online mediated social network platforms. In other words, their own sets of cultural values prevail; social network sites of different network components do not elicit competing social identities.

Our study evidenced no substantial differences in relationship development on home-country sites and Facebook. Our participants practiced culturally specific norms and patterns of online interactions irrespective of which sites they used. This calls into question the generalizability of prior cross-cultural SNS research that compared American and East Asian users. Our study suggests that a holistic approach looking at the same group of users' relational behaviors across sites may be more appropriate. Instead of adjusting to different cultural norms on different sites, our respondents' sustainable behaviors across sites reflect the internalization of collectivistic culture and social identity. However, we did not distinguish with "which" network our participants interacted on both sites. It may be possible that the participants follow the collectivistic cultural norms and interact with people from the same country on SNSs. Future study should unpack the components of social network on SNSs to further understand the interaction targets and identify sources of social capital.

Beyond our expectation and what previous studies suggested, neither relationship development nor group identification had a significant association with social connections with social networks on both Facebook and Renren/Cyworld (H3, H4). One possible explanation is that, while SNSs help manage diverse social networks, users do not rely on SNSs for maintaining social relationships or tightening group identification.

This may be due to the availability of other one-on-one communication tools, such as WeChat (from China) or Kakao Talk (from Korea), in respondents' home countries. It is also possible the *light-weight* communication functions like "Liking" or social information seeking about acquaintances provides sufficient contexts for social capital development (Ellison et al. 2011) without requesting users to engage in intense relational engagement or develop group identification with networks on SNSs. Our result suggests these SNS-enabled interactions may be sufficient channels for social capital development; intense relationship development and group identification may not be necessary for users to appropriate relational benefits from their networks. It is worthy of comparing light-weight with meaningful social interactions for establishing social connections on SNSs in future studies.

Making social connection is positively associated with bonding and bridging social capital on both Facebook and Renren/Cyworld (H5, H6), consistent with the previous literature (e.g., Choi et al. 2011; Ellison et al. 2011). Some researchers have argued that bonding social capital in one's own cultural group can take up the time users spend socializing online (Binder et al. 2009), reducing interaction with acquaintances on Facebook and developing bridging social capital. However, our results indicate that bonding and bridging social capital are developed on both Facebook and Renren/Cyworld. Further, we extend previous literature by showing that the regression coefficient for bonding social capital was higher than that for bridging social capital on both Facebook and Renren/Cyworld, which suggests that our respondents use SNSs to maintain their strong social connections back home and obtain new bonding social capital in the U.S.

There are several limitations in this study. First, our data was cross-sectional so cannot be used to make any causational statements about our findings. In addition, since social networks change over time, a longitudinal study of relationship development would offer valuable insight. We have to note that the adoption of Renren and Cyworld has been on the decline throughout the years since we collected our data. Nevertheless, what we tried to evidence is the phenomenon and underlying cultural mechanisms of social interactions, social relationship building, and social capital accumulation where a home-country site and a globally adopted site were used at the same time. Last, we did not focus on distinctions among different social groups with whom users interact in this current study. It should be included to tease apart the sources of bonding and bridging social capital in future study.

6 Conclusion

This study extends previous research by adopting a within-study design to investigate users' home-country site and Facebook use. Cultural value was included as a precedent variable that influenced users' relational activities and group identification, which work as explanatory factors contributing to users' social connection development for social resources like bonding and bridging social capital. Despite that home-country site consists of networks which share similar culture and language and Facebook diverse cultures and non-native language, our study found that site per se did not work as social identity label because our participants engage in similar activities on the home-country site and Facebook. Collectivistic culture itself accounts for the similar interaction patterns across sites. Then, we found that users did not engage in meaningful relationship and group activities using SNSs. Last, we found that users develop both bonding and bridging social capital from the connections they have on the sites, a result different from previous cross-cultural research that adopts a between design. We also confirmed that bonding social capital is more valued by users.

References

Binder, J., Howes, A., Sutcliffe, A.: The problem of conflicting social spheres: effects of network structure on experienced tension in social network sites. In: Proceedings of the SIGCHI Conference on Human Factors in Computing Systems, pp. 965–974 (2009)

Choi, S.M., Kim, Y., Sung, Y., Sohn, D.: Bridging or bonding? A cross-cultural study of social relationships in social networking sites. Inf. Commun. Soc. 14, 107–129 (2011)

DiMicco, J., Millen, D.R., Geyer, W., Dugan, C., Brownholtz, B., Muller, M.: Motivations for social networking at work. In: Proceedings of the 2008 ACM Conference on Computer Supported Cooperative Work, pp. 711–720, November 2008

Ellison, N., Steinfield, C., Lampe, C.: Connection strategies: social capital implications of Facebook-enabled communication practices. New Media Soc. 6, 873–892 (2011)

Ellison, N., Steinfield, C., Lampe, C.: The benefits of Facebook "friends:" social capital and college students' use of online social network sites. J. Comput. Mediated Commun. 12, 1143–1168 (2007)

Gundykunst, W.B.: Individualistic and collectivistic perspectives on communication: an introduction. Int. J. Intercult. Relat. 22, 107–134 (1998)

Hofstede, G.: Culture's Consequences: International Differences in Work-Related Values. SAGE Publications, Beverly Hills (1980)

Hogg, M.A.: Social identity. In: Leary, M.R., Tangney, J.P. (eds.) Handbook of Self and Identity, pp. 462–479. Guilford, New York (2003)

Hogg, M.A., Abrams, D., Otten, S., Hinkle, S.: The social identity perspective intergroup relations, self-conception, and small groups. Small Group Res. 35, 246–276 (2004)

Ji, Y.G., Hwangbo, H., Yi, J.S., Rau, P.P., Fang, X., Ling, C.: The influence of cultural differences on the use of social network services and the formation of social capital. Int. J. Hum. Comput. Interact. 26(11–12), 1100–1121 (2010)

Kim, Y., Sohn, D., Choi, S.M.: Cultural difference in motivations for using social network sites: a comparative study of American and Korean college students. Comput. Hum. Behav. 27(1), 365–372 (2011)

Kim, K.H., Yun, H.: Cying for me, Cying for us: relational dialectics in a Korean social network site. J. Comput. Mediated Commun. 13, 298–318 (2007)

Kline, R.B.: Principles and Practice of Structural Equation Modeling. Guilford Press, New York (2011)

Lampe, C., Ellison, N., Steinfield, C.: A Face (book) in the crowd: social searching vs. social browsing. In: Proceedings of the 2006 20th Anniversary Conference on Computer Supported Cooperative Work, pp. 167–170, November 2006

Lin, J.H., Peng, W., Kim, M., Kim, S.Y., LaRose, R.: Social networking and adjustments among international students. New Media Soc. 14(3), 421–440 (2012)

McPherson, M., Smith-Lovin, L., Cook, J.M.: Birds of a feather: homophily in social networks. Annu. Rev. Sociol. 27, 415–444 (2001)

Putnam, R.D.: Bowling Alone: The Collapse and Revival of American Community. Simon and Schuster, New York (2000)

Qiu, L., Lin, H., Leung, A.K.Y.: Cultural differences and switching of in-group sharing behavior between an American (Facebook) and a Chinese (Renren) social networking site. J. Cross Cult. Psychol. **44**(1), 106–121 (2013)

Recabarren, M., Nussbaum, M., Leiva, C.: Cultural divide and the Internet. Comput. Hum. Behav. **24**, 2917–2926 (2008)

Shin, D.H.: Analysis of online social networks: a cross-national study. Online Inf. Rev. (2010)

Tajfel, H.E.: Differentiation Between Social Groups: Studies in the Social Psychology of Intergroup Relations. Academic Press, London (1978)

Turner, J.C.: Towards a cognitive redefinition of the social group. In: Tajfel, H. (ed.) Social Identity and Intergroup Relations, pp. 15–40. Cambridge University Press, Cambridge (1982)

Triandis, H.C.: Collectivism vs. individualism: a reconceptulization of a basic concept in cross-cultural psychology. In: Bagley, C., Verma, G.K. (eds.) Personality, Cognition, and Values: Cross-Cultural Perspectives of Childhood and Adolescence, pp. 60–95. University of Calgary Press, Calgary (1986)

Triandis, H.C., Bontempo, R., Villareal, M.J., Asai, M., Lucca, N.: Individualism and collectivism: Cross-cultural perspectives on self-in-group relationships. J. Pers. Soc. Psychol. **54**, 323–338 (1988)

Vandenberg, R.J., Lance, C.E.: A review and synthesis of the measurement invariance literature: Suggestions, practices, and recommendations for organizational research. Organ. Res. Methods **3**, 4–70 (2000)

Yuan, C.W., Fussell, S.R.: A tale of two sites: dual social network site use and its influence on social network development. Comput. Hum. Behav. **74**, 83–91 (2017)

Yuan, C.W., Setlock, L.D., Cosley, D., Fussell, S.R.: Understanding multilingual communication. In: Proceedings of the 2013 27th Anniversary Conference on Computer Supported Cooperative Work (2013)

Zhou, T.: Understanding online community user participation: a social influence perspective. Internet Res. Electron. Netw. Appl. Policy **21**(1), 67–81 (2011)

Culture and Creativity

Parametric Mechanism of Computer Aided Craft Design: Taking Wooden Crib as an Example

Kung-Ling Chang[✉]

Department of Crafts and Design, National Taiwan University of Arts,
New Taipei City, Taiwan
kling@ntua.edu.tw

Abstract. Computer aided design usually refers to the use of drawing. This study has a discussion on digital and craft design, which is based on the advantages of parametrization. The discussion of parametrization is about the integration of design conditions, manufacturing problems, and checking the safety problems in the crib, the results show that the parametrization of design conditions and modeling logic is helpful to check the practical problems as an evaluation mechanism. The advantages stem from the concept of the visualization program in Grasshopper (GH), which is a parametric tool works with the interconnected components to make definitions and get modeling results. The GH visual program is easy for designers to understand without programming languages, and carry on design editing, modification, and extract data for fabrication and evaluation, contributing to the customization of craft design.

Keywords: Parametric modeling · Evaluation mechanism

1 Introduction

Dynamic feedback is one of the main features of parametric design; it is able to get results immediately after modification of design conditions. There are some parametric experiences and examples in some 3D software, such as the command of array in AutoCAD, the user can get rectangular array or polar array after select an object and enter the numbers of items, between, rows etc. Further, you can change numbers again or drag the point or arrow grips for adjusting and then the figure results will also change immediately.

In response to the trend of maker movement, some software and free tools have developed many simple features for specific purposes for makers, such as Slicer, Parametric Patterns Designer, Sketch Chair, Pepakura Designer. Some of them unfold the 3D models and automatically calculates the flaps for joint; some can slice and convert 3D models into 2D patterns that can be cut flat. Nevertheless, the above software is all restricted in some specific purposes, even if you can adjust the numbers or make some choices. If a designer wants to change the connection method of joint, it is never be able to change; in other words, the designer at this point is a parametric user with only choice, not a designer yet (Fig. 1).

© Springer Nature Switzerland AG 2020
P.-L. P. Rau (Ed.): HCII 2020, LNCS 12193, pp. 449–462, 2020.
https://doi.org/10.1007/978-3-030-49913-6_37

Fig. 1. 2D cut layout with slicer

Based on the above, some software has provided a basic parameter experience by adjustable mechanism. Further, the parameter experiences have given rise to the motivation of re-customization for this research. The so-called re-customization doesn't just refer to the basic choices of adjustable mechanism and can't change the defined options and default conditions. This study takes Grasshopper software (GH) as a research tool because of the open source features of its components. The relationship among the components in Grasshopper is to link components together to produce an effect. It is called visual programming and associative modeling. Therefore, it's easy for designers to carry on editing and modification.

In the feature of dynamic feedback in GH, different parameter conditions can get the results immediately after modification. Designers can compare different design conditions at the same time (Feasible Solutions). Therefore, a wide range of design conditions will be able to be parameterized as design options for users, such as material size, joint size, limitations, and forming conditions etc. Parametrization changes the object modeling into parametric modeling.

In the respect, this research focuses on the benefits of parametrization for craft design. As the previous discussed about dynamic feedback, parametric modeling doesn't need to redraw as object modeling when the design conditions are changed, it's quite different from object modeling. In the field of parametric modeling, the design conditions and design results are interdependently as loops, it's also called "associative modeling".

Furthermore, the parametric modeling provides a logic graphic thinking that allows a designer to conceive, evolve and organize his design ideas based on the linking approach of components in GH. In terms of associative modeling, the relationships between components and the output data are supposed to give more information and applications. And in this way, this research gets an opinion on the evaluation mechanisms for the design results before manufacturing. Therefore, some options of design conditions must be set up at the beginning of design, including the conditions of manufacturing, when the design is completed, the result needs be tested by evaluation mechanism. Through the design and manufacture of the crib, the purposes of this study as follow: first, set up the evaluation mechanism, and second, to explore the parametrization aspects of craft design, which is called parametric mechanism.

2 Literature Review

2.1 Parametric Design

"Parameters" are involved with varieties of conditional options and variables; there are some interactive relationships among them. For example, the height of a floor is associated with the steps of a staircase and the height of a step. When the height of a floor is not changed, and the height of each step is increased, the total number of steps will be reduced, and the number, length and slope of the railings will change. It is an easy example such as Form-Z software that provides the command tool of staircase to produce a 3d model. In addition, some 3d software provides scripting language, but designers are limited by the difficulty of scripting language, so the design process is not easy as traditional computer drawings. The traditional computer drawings in this research refers to the object models which are intuitively to move, pull, split or trim objects without strictly definitions, and get the results directly. However, this research has acquired a benefic way with visual programming in GH, and it is easier for designers instead of the complex scripting language. It's a get-started tool for the understanding of parametric design [7].

Grasshopper is a graphical algorithm editor that is included with Rhino version 6 and integrated with Rhino 3d's modeling tools. On GH's canvas, there are components connected together with wires to form a definition for generating tasks (models) in Rhino's canvas. GH definitions are the set of rules and instructions among components, each component requires input parameters along the left side, and then providing data, geometries, vector, and so on to obtain the results along the right side. Some parts of the definition group can be assembled to create a new component called cluster, it can be renamed, change icon, and then modify the new component as user definition [1]. Depending on the specific purpose, a designer has the potential to define his own components without having to fully understand the scripting language.

2.2 Parametric Modeling and Object Modeling

Object modeling refers to the computer-aided drafting; it is a traditional practice of drawing geometry and objects directly. It obtains the model through intuition rather than from reasoning. Therefore, object modeling also called direct modeling. Direct modeling creates geometry rather than features so it supports that conceptual effort where the designer doesn't want to be tied down with features and their interdependencies and the impact that making a change might have [2]. In contrast, parametric modeling need to define clear questions to form a feature, such as set values, data, geometry, range, etc. All design procedures and activities are related to another one. The following figure (Fig. 2) and point of views on parametric modeling can be used to understand the difference:

1. Parametric Design Schema should be formulated and explored as a comprehensive theoretical framework to support design [6].
2. It asks architects to start with the design parameters and not preconceived or pre-determined design solutions [4].

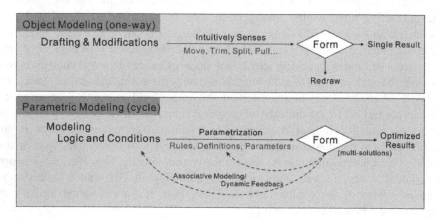

Fig. 2. Comparing parametric modeling with object modeling

Although parametric modeling doesn't have the intuitive tendency on drawing, but the advantages and visual features have prompted designers to start working with parametric modeling. Nowadays, it is difficult to find CAD software that has no parametric mechanism. Many of the CAD applications currently in circulation today, employ the parametric approach to 3D modeling [8]. In the case of Rhinoceros3D, Rhino possesses both parametric modeling and object modeling, and objects in object modeling can be imported into GH as reference objects. It is also an advantage for designers. In this study, the most direct difference is that the design modification is more efficient and accurate.

2.3   Properties of the Parametric Design

Summing up the features of the parametric design including the parametrization of design conditions, feasible solutions, associative modeling, and dynamic feedback, further, there are some properties that are associated with them. Professor Chen [3] has proposed six properties of the parametric design, which are showed in the following Table 1:

Table 1. Properties of the parametric design

Properties of the parametric design	
1. Management of conditional parameters	Figure out the relationship between design conditions: The relationship between materials, limitations, funds, benefits and model
2. References to shape grammars	Producing similar design cases based on established cases: Applying the established cases with shape grammar and parameterize it
3. Continuous differentiation	Developing design conditions into parametric models: When the design conditions are changed, it doesn't need to redraw
4. Feasible solutions	Providing solutions and choices of different design conditions: More comparisons between feasible solutions
5. Animate form	The evolution and sequence of forming process: To observe animate form through timer
6. Digital fabrication	Simulating practical problems of manufacture: Producing more details and members of complex forms

Source: Chen [3]

3 Parametric Mechanisms

As a new tool that is different from the object modeling, the forming of the parametric mechanisms has thinking outside the box of one-way requirements to get model results. The three aspects of parametric mechanisms have its origins in conditional parameters. It is based on the first property of the management of the design conditions as shown in Fig. 3. Parametric modeling should not only be a tool for form development, but also the key for parametrization as a parametric design, which improve the rankings above the concept of computer aided drawing.

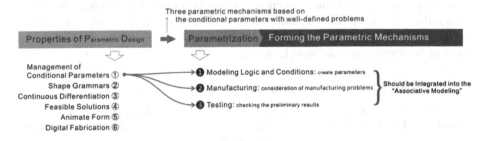

Fig. 3. The origin of the three aspects

Based on the interconnected components in GH, there are a lot of geometries, vectors, and data in the relationships. Parameterization can capture different information and data from the right side of components at different stages. Taking the component of <Evaluate Length> as an example, there are three kinds of output data in the right side for captured by panel as Fig. 4, or taking output data into another component to form a definition for generating tasks as Fig. 5. In this sample, it can get the coordinate location, direction, and length. It is helpful to the management of wood size, quantity, cutting length, and shows the advantages of how parameterization could form a modeling logic. The management and parameterization of design conditions is the first aspect of parametric mechanisms.

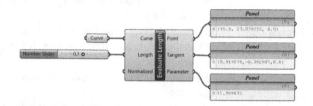

Fig. 4. Capturing the output data by panels

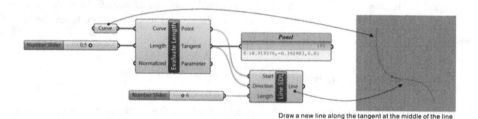

Draw a new line along the tangent at the middle of the line

Fig. 5. Draw a new line along the tangent at the middle of the line

The second aspect is about associative modeling and dynamic feedback, it is not only convenient for object modification, but also related to manufacturing, and is one of the parametric mechanisms. All design modifications are related to the final output and can be repeatedly tested and contrasted with practical issues.

In the parametric modeling, as long as the height coordinates of objects are found through the relationship between components, the height difference will be calculated as a testing work and the design results can be evaluated. The evaluation is the third aspect of parametric mechanisms (Table 2).

Table 2. Parametric mechanisms in the aspects of craft design process

1. Parameterize the design conditions and modeling logic	Management of design conditions: Integrating various conditions and information to form a definition as a modeling logic
2. Consideration of manufacturing problems	Improve the manufacturing process: Material preparation, cost saving, lofting, output, nesting, labeling, and assembling
3. Checking the preliminary results	Checking the design results: Test and avoid human error

3.1   Conditions

Size Selection of Mattress. The size of the mattress is the most important prerequisite for design, which directly affects the length and width of the crib, the distance of the posts and the interval of the railings. When the selected size of the mattress is different, all component sizes and joints will be reset. Take Fig. 6 as example, this project have set up the data based on the sizes of commercial mattresses, and input the data into <list item>, <list item> as a data filter with a slider for user selection. The user selects the length and width through the sliders for generate following tasks. This selection is a 70 * 130 U.S. mattress.

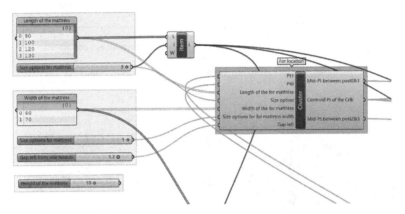

Fig. 6. Options of the parameters for mattress size

Height of the Deck Frame. The height of the deck frame of crib involves many factors, such as: If the frame is too high, then the safety height of the railing will not be enough. The railing should be higher than the chest when baby is standing. If the crib will be next to parents' bed, the height needs to be matched with the adult mattress. In addition, the height of the deck frame should not be adjusted above or below the side board of the crib. If the deck frame is too high, mattress can't be fixed by the side boards. If the deck frame is too low, mattress will be lower than the side board cover and exposed. The Relationship between them is shown in Fig. 7. The height difference for mattress fixing is an automated calculation of a <cluster> definition (Fig. 8). The above cases are the conditions of the parameterization, in the process of the parameterization should be related, when a parameter value changes, the other values and results also change.

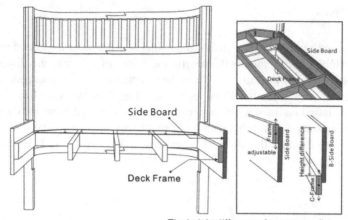

Side Board

Deck Frame

The height difference for mattress fixing
is an automated calculation of component definitions.

Fig. 7. Relationship between frame and side board

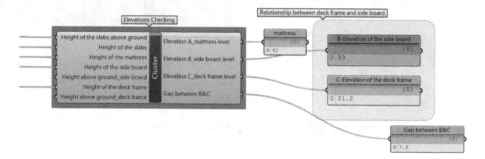

Fig. 8. The cluster component for the high-control checking

Specifications of the Material. The wood size used in the crib is the pre-set data of the existing wood specifications at the beginning. The sizes of tenon knifes have also been loaded into the option of 7°, 9.5°, and 14° depending on the tool sold on the market (Fig. 9).

Fig. 9. Materials and tool specifications

3.2 Manufacturing

The assistance of manufacturing, including templates, measurement, and statistics for lofting or jigs making. Some special shape requires template to replicate and lofting for milling; obtaining measurement information can know the angle and depth of material for cutting, and make jig to aid production; statistics can calculate the quantity, length, classification or extract specific information for various types of wood. In addition, the component number (labeling) and layout (nesting) for output are also the applications of measurement and statistics (Table 3).

Table 3. The assistance for manufacturing process

	Description	Application	Image
Lofting	Templates for lofting	1. Templates cutting 2. Outlines printing by laser on wood surface 3. Divide the hole position	
Measurement	Information for lofting, such as length, angle	The assistance for jigs making	
Statistics	1. Using panels to convert file formats for Excel, Google documents 2. Using the series of <list> components for data extracting	Applications of quantity, sorting, measuring, extract data and so on 1. Sorting and induction of irregular dimension 2. Materials preparation 3. Mark the cutting position	

3.3 Checking

Design results can be limited in a range, such as the height of the deck frame is defined a definite confine with the side board. If it is not easy to set the safety limit, then the final checking should be set to confirm the safety.

All of the information and conditions have been integrated in the parametric modeling, such as the slats are no more than 2–3/8 in. (6 cm) apart, corner posts are no more than 1/16 in. (1.5 mm) high [5]. The interval of railings is less than 6 cm, hands and feet won't get stuck; the gap between slats of the crib is 7 mm, so that the fingers will not be caught; the bed posts are not protruding, avoiding hooking up the baby's clothes.

Some options are not open for safety reasons, including changes in railing length, quantity, and radius that may affect safety. Therefore, the design finally set up some test for checking, as shown in Fig. 10, to avoid the result of customization is not safe.

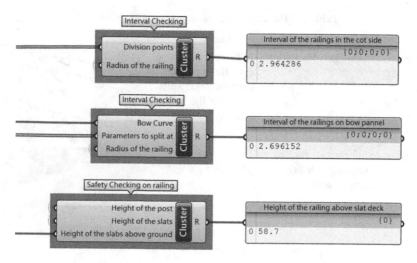

Fig. 10. Safety checking on the interval and height of railings

4   Results and Discussion

4.1   Basic Information and Drawing of the Crib

1. Design and manufacturing: Author of this Study
2. Functionality: Crib
3. Size Information: L158 * W79 * H88 cm
4. Drawing of the Crib (Fig. 11):

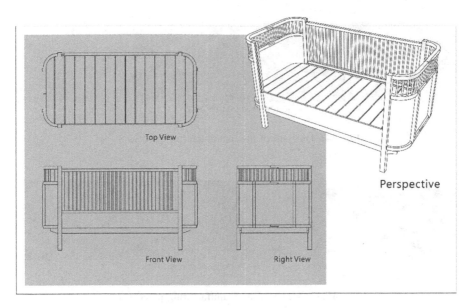

Fig. 11. Views of the crib

4.2   Process of Manufacturing

See Figs. 12, 13, 14 and 15.

template cutting and mortise milling

Fig. 12. Diagram of the manufacturing process 1

component production and assembly testing

Fig. 13. Diagram of the manufacturing process 2

mortises and tenons making

Fig. 14. Diagram of the manufacturing process 3

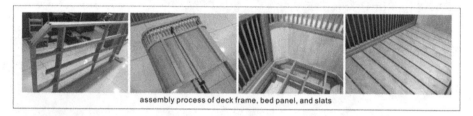

assembly process of deck frame, bed panel, and slats

Fig. 15. Diagram of the manufacturing process 4

4.3 Discussion

One of the results of this study is the setting of evaluation mechanism, which gives feedback on the whole, and contributes to the exploration of parametric mechanisms, such as the following three points:

1. from the Parametrization of Conditions to Solution Mechanism
   Based on the well definition and integration of conditions, different solutions can be developed according to different demand objectives as a solution mechanism. Hence, besides the design conditions, the strict rules need to be set up into the solution mechanism. The rules come with the survey, calculation, investigation, and then get the solution or feedback to the redefinition of rules. The mechanism is related to the properties of "Continuous Differentiation" and "Feasible Solutions", which works with optimization and rule definition.
2. from the Parametrization of Manufacturing to Fabrication Mechanism
   The manufacturing problems including the variables of the actual material thickness, proportion division, quantity, and so on. Besides the manufacturing problems, the assembly problems are also the need to respond to practical problems when the model is completed, such as similar parts need to be numbered to distinguish and automatically layout for cutting. All the parameters need to be set to form the fabrication mechanism.
3. from the Parametrization of Testing to Evaluation Mechanism
   When the design is complete, basic testing is required. Besides the functional demand, aesthetics, and avoid human error, safety checks in every part of the crib are even more important. Hence, the property of "Feasible Solutions" will provides the feedback of test data immediately after each modification. The integration of the

evaluation mechanism should be considered to lead the parametric modeling more than a tool for form finding.

4. Feedback and Reflection

The three parametric mechanisms come from the management of conditional parameters (first property of parametric design) with well-defined problems into the issues of design conditions, manufacturing, and testing. After the stage of testing, the evaluation mechanism gives some feedback into the three parametric mechanisms and provides the basis for the parameter modifications. For example, if the interval of the railings is too large in the evaluation mechanism, then the restrictions can be added with the conditional parameters as a feedback. The feedback will make the setting of the evaluation mechanism more complete.

The relationship between parametric mechanisms and properties is not the development of one-way line as the beginning, and in the overall terms, it can be seen that the issues of "continuous differentiation", "feasible solutions", and "digital fabrication" are closely related to the development of craft design in parameterization. Finally, all the feedbacks are taken back into the conditional parameters as a new cycle for modifying the parametric mechanisms. It is shown in Fig. 16.

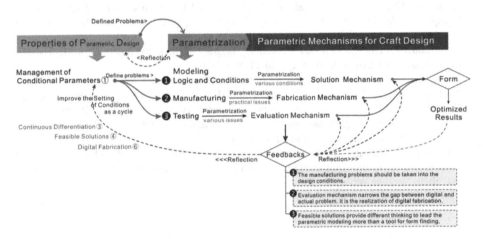

Fig. 16. Framework of the parametric mechanisms

5 Conclusion

This study brings the advantages of feasible solutions, real-time modification and feedback into the traditional craft design. In addition to the efficiency of solution comparison, lofting, calculation and material preparation, the data and relationship in the associative modeling are available for extended application, such as the setup of evaluation mechanism. In the orientation of extensibility and operability, the evaluation mechanism can be called "the seventh property of parametric design" proposed in this study for craft design.

Computer aided craft design is not only drawing, simulation and alternative manual. Compare traditional computer drawing with parametric design, there are more advantages in the parameter integration, providing the assistance throughout the design and manufacturing process. Take a good productive mechanism with parameterization to provide customization, material management, and short run production. In the follow up study, it can include the database of detail processing, accessory options, and the calibration parameters for different techniques and equipment.

References

1. Bai, Y.S., Gao, Y.H.: Parametric nonlinear design. Huazhong University of Science and Technology, Wuhan (2018). (in Chinese, semantic translation)
2. Brunelli, M.: Parametric vs. Direct Modeling: Which Side Are You On? (2017). https://www.ptc.com/en/cad-software-blog/parametric-vs-direct-modeling-which-side-are-you-on. Accessed 15 Jan 2020
3. Chen, C.C.: The significance and application of parametric design in the process of architecture design. National Science Council research report (No. NSC101-2221-E032-065), unpublished (2012). (in Chinese, semantic translation)
4. Karle, D., Kelly, B.: Proceedings of the 31st Annual Conference of the Association for Computer Aided Design in Architecture (ACADIA). University of Calgary, Alberta, Canada (2011)
5. Kidshealth.org: Household Safety: Preventing Injuries in the Crib (2019). https://kidshealth.org/en/parents/safety-crib.html. Accessed 21 Nov 2016
6. Oxman, R., Gu, N.: Theories and models of parametric design thinking. In: Proceedings of the 33rd Education and research in Computer Aided Architectural Design in Europe Annual Conference (eCAADe). Vienna University of Technology, Vienna, Austria (2015)
7. Tang, T.W., Peng, Z.Q.: Grasshopper mania I: parametric graphics. Tamkang University, Taipei (2015). (in Chinese, semantic translation)
8. Tutorial45: Understanding the Difference between Parametric and Non-Parametric CAD Modelling (n.d.). https://tutorial45.com/parametric-vs-nonparametric-models/. Accessed 15 Jan 2020

Research on the Utilization of Unconventional Materials in Fashion Styling

Tuck Fai Cheng[1,2(✉)], Yanru Lyu[1], Cheng Hsiang Yang[1], and Po-Hsien Lin[1]

[1] Graduate School of Creative Industry Design,
National Taiwan University of Arts, New Taipei City 22058, Taiwan
lyuyanru@gmail.com, yjs.amo@gmail.com,
t0131@ntua.edu.tw
[2] Graduate School of Applied Cosmetology, HungKuang University,
Taichung City 43302, Taiwan
kenneth1831@hk.edu.tw

Abstract. The use of unconventional materials as a fashion design has become a trend in recent year. Based on the "Alienation" [1] and "Aesthetic Experience" theories [2]. This article discusses the use of hot-melt adhesives as unconventional material in the fashion styling design. 9 items(sub-factors) from "Material Characteristics", "Material Experience", "Model Shaping", "Technological Innovation", "Fashion Cultivation", "Unique Enchantment", "Visual Effects", "Qualia Design" [3] and "Taste Cultivation", to evaluate the degree of the "Creative Performance" and "Satisfaction" of hot-melt adhesives in design works. The results of related research through quantitative analysis after questionnaire surveys showed that the sub-factor of "Material Experience" is the highest scores from 9 items. Simultaneously, 9 items are distributed into 3 factors of "Creativity Thinking", "Image Medium", and "Taste Aesthetic", showed that the affection of the "Creative Performance" is the factor of "Taste Aesthetic ", and for the degree of the "Satisfaction" is "Image Medium". Besides, the "Visual Effects", "Material Experience" and "Model Shaping" are the first three important ranking to the design works. Among the three questionnaire participants' backgrounds (graduates, undergraduate classmates including creators), the full scores (5.00) was given by the creator's themselves for the hot-melt adhesives evaluation. In the other hand, their undergraduate classmates gave the lowest scores (3.92), while the graduate students gave the medium scores (4.25). Mean of three groups was 4.19. Hot-melt adhesives as a non-mainstream creative and design material, it provides an aesthetic reference for related industries.

Keywords: Unconventional materials · Fashion styling · Hot-melt adhesive

1 Introduction

The use of unconventional materials as a fashion design has become a trend in recent year. An internationally renowned and experienced wearable art competition –*The World of Wearable Art (WOW) Awards Competition of New Zealand* [4], gives an opportunity for designers around the world to be innovative, originality to create the

© Springer Nature Switzerland AG 2020
P.-L. P. Rau (Ed.): HCII 2020, LNCS 12193, pp. 463–472, 2020.
https://doi.org/10.1007/978-3-030-49913-6_38

unimaginable and also to push the boundaries of creativities to challenge the conventional and creative expectations of fashion styling design. In order to explore how unconventional materials were turned into visual experiences and mental ideas, "Alienation" and "Aesthetic Experience" theory will be used as connections between creative motivation sources was employed in this study to develop the questionnaire. Based on it, this study examined the unconventional materials used in fashion styling design as final project artworks of college students from HungKuang University [5], Taiwan. Through an approach of style analysis, 9 items were selected after consulting with experts, It concluded as "Material Characteristics", "Material Experience", "Model Shaping", "Technological innovation", "Taste Cultivation", "Unique Enchantment", "Visual Effects", "Qualia Design" and "Taste Cultivation", to evaluate the factor degrees of "Creative Performance" and "satisfaction" in the design works.

The results of the study were expected to reinforce theoretical support for unconventional materials used, especially hot-melt adhesives in fashion styling design. Therefore, the research purpose can be briefly described as follows:

1. Explore the cognition and preference of hot-melt adhesive materials in fashion styling design.
2. Explore the creative multiple applications and performance of hot-melt adhesive as media for the concept of "Body becomes the exhibition field".
3. Explore the value of hot-melt adhesive to provides an aesthetic references for related industries (Fig. 1).

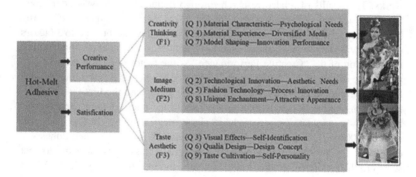

Fig. 1. The evaluation of "Creative Performance" and "Satisfaction" in design works

2   Literature Review

2.1   Alienation Theory

Herbert Marcuse is one of the important alienation thinkers of the Frankfurt School. In his "*One-Dimensional Man*" [1], mentioned the concept of "Artistic Alienation" about the ability of art to change the individual's perception and consciousness from the inside through the aesthetic transformation of the form and content of the artwork, to reach a qualitative world that was suppressed and distorted by the established reality "Sensed and Seen" in the individual's heart.

Another book Marcuse, called *"The Aesthetic Dimension"* [6] disclosed the Art-Perception emancipation theory, emphasized the internal aspects of individual subjectivity: the aspects of passion, imagination, and conscious. And advocated that the liberation is possible because of these internal Outward to External realization. Marcuse called such a transformation process as aesthetic "Sublimation" or "Stylization". More precisely, the transformation caused by art begins with the transformation of personal sensibility, imagination, and rationality: by becoming an aesthetic form and giving an artistic reality, art gives people a new perception. Hot-melt adhesives as unconventional material in fashion styling tried to emerge a revolution in design perception, to avoid "One-Dimensional Society" from "Assimilation" [6]. "Alienation Theory" can be supported to extend the analysis including the subcultural phenomena.

2.2   Aesthetic Experience Theory

Hekkert based on the original aesthetic experience map of Leder et al. (2004), proposed the perception model of aesthetic pleasure as shown in Fig. 2, showing the emotional state of aesthetic experience, from the self-operational work to the aesthetic judgment of the perceiver (Aesthetic judgment) or aesthetic experience pleasure, The process of which starts with perceptual analysis, implicit information integration, explicit classification, and cognitive mastering [7]. After the evaluation, an aesthetic judgment or aesthetic pleasure experience is produced. This model clarifies the perception of aesthetic pleasure and is deeply influenced by personal past experience. The schematic relationship between fashion styling design [8] and theoretical framework of aesthetic experience can be also shown in Fig. 2.

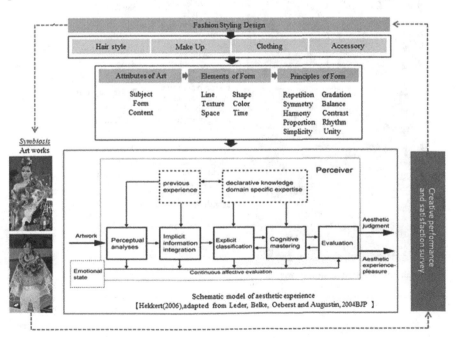

Fig. 2. Converted schematic diagram of the relationship between fashion styling design and theoretical framework of aesthetic experience from Leder et al.

3 Research Methodology

3.1 Research Process

This research was based on the graduation project of undergraduate students` works (styling show on 2019.12.01) of Applied Cosmetology Department [1] of Hungkuang University, Taiwan. An online questionnaire was developed to examine the standard of the Creative Performance and the Satisfaction of using hot-melt adhesives as the main physical materials to being transformed by the designer into appearance materials or appearance design works. A total of 55 questionnaires had been returned (Table 1).

After obtaining the data required for style analysis, a statistical technique of multiple regression analysis was employed to explore and evaluate the significance of these relations in degrees of Creative Performance and the Satisfaction of the design works [3].

Table 1. *Symbiosis,* the hot-melt adhesives works

Design Works	Designer Statement	Materials/ Participants
Details of hot-melt adhesive after creation.	In this beautiful new world, everything is equal. A community of its own was developed in which lives are inseparable. Taking marine corals as inspiration and spindrifts as imprints, the counter-attack and fusion of spray curves conceived the birth of the new generation of marine aesthetics and the new blooming of beautiful images. "Symbiosis" interprets the self-worth established by the development of the association with the ocean, and the multiple and peaceful coexistence of all beings.	Appearance main material : Hot-melt adhesive(HMA) Designers: Ching Chen, Yu-Pei Lin, Ting -Yu Kao Shu-Jung Wu, Jz-Han Shu. Models: Well-Kang Sun, Siou-Yan Hong . Project Supervisors Tuck-Fai Cheng, Pei-Ti ,Shih. Date/venue: 2019.12.1 Hung Kuang University, Taiwan

3.2   Research Framework

This research framework mainly illustrates how the case study could be used to develop the process to reach the conclusion. The figure illustrates the 9 items (questions) in the questionnaire content (from F1 to F9). The purpose was to decode the coding of the designer or creator's work to audiences. The decoding process was to understand the conversion from the technical level of the work to the semantic level, to reach the effectiveness to get the meaning. In addition, it also involved from the emotional material, through the aesthetic process, to create the emotional image and finally aesthetic experience would be obtained. Meanwhile, 9 items (questions) in the questionnaire were used to have further analysis (Fig. 3).

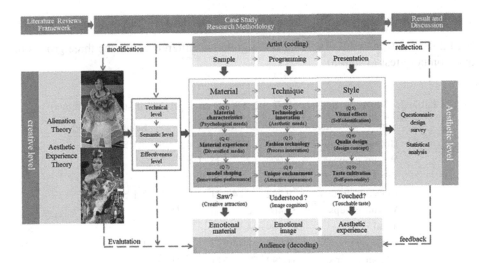

Fig. 3.   Research framework for case study

3.3   Research Stimuli

These 9 sub-factors as a test to discuss the topic, were being consultation with experts and scholars. The participants of questionnaire were composed of graduate and undergraduate students. Moreover, the undergraduate students were divided into creator and non-creator groups in same the class. A total of 55 participants completed the questionnaire.

4   Results and Discussions

4.1   Analysis the Degree of Preference

This study analyzed participants' impression towards design works. Evaluation was used on the degrees of 9 sub-factor demonstrated in the design works. A preference and mean scores were for evaluating overall impression and the outcome was shown in

Table 3. The first rank was technological innovation for aesthetic needs (Q4), and the last would be Self-personality for Taste Cultivation (Q9) (Table 2). Descriptive statistics showed that degree of Creative Performance (4.22) is lower than Satisfaction (4.24) (Table 9).

Table 2. The ranking degree of preference

Rank	1	2	3	4	5	6	7	8	9
Question	Q4	Q7	Q5	Q1	Q2	Q3	Q6	Q8	Q9
Mean scores	4.40	4.35	4.33	4.16	4.16	4.13	4.11	4.09	4.02

4.2   Variation Analysis for Three Groups of Students

F1, F2, F3, M (Mean, Q1 ~ Q9) showed significant differences for the three groups of questionnaire test (Table 3).

Table 3. Variation analysis of F1, F2, F3 for three groups of students (Anova)

	Source of variation	SS	Df	MS	F	Scheffe method
F1	Between groups	6.281	2	3.141	7.423***	3.1 > 2
	Within groups	22.002	52	.423	(.001)	
	Total	28.283	54			
F2	Between groups	9.242	2	4.621	6.972**	3.1 > 2
	Within groups	34.467	52	.663	(.002)	
	Total	43.709	54			
F3	Between groups	8.034	2	4.017	6.570**	1 > 2
	Within groups	31.792	52	.611	(.003)	
	Total	39.826	54			
M	Between groups	7.752	2	3.876	7.507**	1.3 > 2
	Within groups	26.846	52	.536	(.001)	
	Total	34.598	54			

N = 55 **p < 0.01 ***p < 0.001

4.3   T Test of the Effect Gender

Gender differences slightly different for F1, F2, F3. In other words, the average score of male was generally higher than the average score of female but not up to par (Table 4).

Table 4. T test of the effect gender on F1, F2, F3 in the study sample (N = 55)

Variable	Item	N	M	SD	t
Gender	Female	49			
	Male	6			
	F1	49	4.24	.726	−1.734
		6	4.78	.544	−2.173
	F2	49	4.14	.900	−1.375
		6	4.67	.816	−1.485
	F3	49	4.03	.845	−1.261
		6	4.50	.937	−1.162

4.4 Construct Validity for F1, F2, F3

Construct Validity for F1, F2, F3, showed that communalities was higher than .5. The eigenvalue was higher than 1.0, factor loading was higher than .7, % of variance was higher than 50%. This conclusion showed that the way to constitute F1, F2, F3 from Q1 to Q10 is acceptable (Table 5).

Table 5. Construct validity for F1, F2, F3

Sub-scale	Item	Factor Loading	Communalities	Eigenvalue	% of variance
F1	Q1, Q4, Q7	.909, .877, .916	.826, .769, .840	2.435	81.166
F2	Q2, Q5, Q8	.972, .955, .939	.944, .912, .882	2.738	91.275
F3	Q3, Q6, Q9	.948, .929, .956	.898, .863, .913	2.674	89.144

4.5 Reliability Analysis

From this reliability analysis, the whole scale of F1, F2, and F3 values were .967 and α deletion of Q4 (.972) in 9 items might decreased the reliability, but only little impact the normalized Cronbach' α value (.971). For the overall reliability analysis, the Cronbach α and the average value of F1, F2, and F3 were all together greater than 0.9. Therefore, this reliability analysis was reliability predictive (Table 6).

Table 6. Summary for reliability analysis

Subscale	Item	α if item deleted	α
F1	Q1, Q4, Q7	.967, .972, .969	.969
F2	Q2, Q5, Q8	.966, .967, .965	.966
F3	Q3, Q6, Q9	.967, .966, .967	.967
Whole scale			.967

4.6 Multiple Regression Analysis on Creative Performance

The F1, F2 and F3 in the multiple regression analysis model to Creative Performance showed that F value of the overall regression model reached 60.316 (p < .05), which showed that a significant correlation between the independent and dependent variables. Produced R^2 = .780, F = .883, suggested a statistically significant association between independent variables and the dependent variable (p<.05). As could be seen in Table 7, F3 (Taste aesthetics) scales had significant positive regression weight, indicated the design works with higher scores on the F3 was expected to have the strongest significant to Creative Performance (Table 7).

Table 7. Multiple regression analyses with fundamental relations as the dependent variable (creative performance)

Dependent variable	Independent variable	B	SE	β	t
Creative performance	F1	.273	.185	.244	1.475
	F2	.270	.163	.300	1.657
	F3	.347	.166	.369	2.089*
	R = .883			R2 = .780	F = 60.316***

*p < 0.05 **p < 0.01 ***p < 0.001

4.7 Multiple Regression Analyses on Satisfaction

The F1, F2 and F3 in the multiple regression analysis model to Satisfaction showed that F value of the overall regression model reached 81.171 (p < 0.01), which showed that a significant correlation between the independent and dependent variables. Produced R^2 = .827, F = .909, suggested a statistically significant association between independent variables and the dependent variable (p < 0.01). As could be seen in Table 9, F2 (Image medium) scales had significant positive regression weight, indicated the design works with higher scores on the F2 was expected to have the strongest significant to Satisfaction (Table 8).

Table 8. Multiple regression analyses with fundamental relations as the dependent variable (satisfaction)

Dependent variable	Independent variable	B	SE	β	t
Satisfaction	F1	.273	.174	.230	1.566
	F2	.498	.154	.521	3.239**
	F3	.186	.157	.186	1.186
	R = .909			R2 = .827	F = 81.171***

*p < 0.05 **p < 0.01 ***p < 0.001

4.8 The First-Three Ranking Among 9 Optional Questions

Ranking of the first-three important among 9 Optional Questions were Q3, Q4 Q7. Although Q2 did not carry out the top three, it still obtained the important role (Table 9).

Table 9. The first-three ranking among 9 optional questions

Top three picks	1	2	3
Ranked 1st	Q3	Q5	Q2
Ranked 2nd	Q4	Q6	Q2
Ranked 3rd	Q7	Q4	Q2
Degree of creative performance	4.22		
Degree of satisfaction in the design works	4.24		

4.9 Second Questionnaire Survey for Group 2 (Non-creator Classmates)

A second multiple selection Questionnaire to discover the reasons for failing to give full marks as below. Make-up problem is the main disadvantage (55.6%), the less would be hair-style (25.9%), clothing problem(18.5%), etc. (Fig. 4).

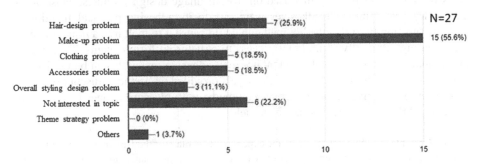

Fig. 4. Reasons for failing to give full marks from Group 2 (non-creator classmates)

5 Conclusions and Suggestion

This research selected 9 items(sub-factors) from "Material Characteristics", "Material Experience", "Model Shaping", "Technological Innovation", "Taste Cultivation", "Unique Enchantment", "Visual Effects", "Qualia Design" and "Taste Cultivation", to evaluate the degree of the "Creative Performance" (4.22) and "Satisfaction" (4.24) of hot-melt adhesives in design works. The results of related research through quantitative analysis after questionnaire surveys showed that the sub-factor of "Material Experience" (4.40) is the highest scores from 9 items.

Simultaneously, 9 items are distributed into 3 factors of "Creativity Thinking", "Image Medium", and "Taste Aesthetic", showing that the affection of the "Creative Performance" is the factor of "Taste Aesthetic ", and for the degree of the "satisfaction" is "Image Medium". Besides, the "Visual Effects", "Material Experience" and "Model Shaping" are the firs-three important ranking to the design works from 9 sub-factors. Among the three questionnaire participants` backgrounds (graduates, undergraduate classmates including creators), mean of three groups for Q1 ~ Q9 demonstrated that the full scores (5.00) was given by the creator's themselves for the hot-melt adhesives design works` evaluation in the same class. Besides, undergraduate classmates gave the lowest scores (3.92) and graduate students gave the medium scores (4.25). The reason had showed in Table 3. Mean of three groups (F1, F2, F3 or Q1 ~ Q9) was 4.19

The result can be used as a reference for subsequent performance research in hot-melt adhesive. F1, F2, F3 showed significant differences for the three groups of questionnaire test. Through variation analysis, T Test of the Effect Gender, the average score of male was generally higher than the average score of female, but not up to par. Construct Validity for F1, F2, F3 tested could be acceptable. Reliability Analysis was reliability predictive. Multiple Regression Analyses on "Creative Performance" and "Satisfaction" had showed the strongest significant for the research. The First-Three Ranking among 9 Optional factors (Q1 ~ Q9), which is the most important factors of design for unconventional material used, especially for hot-melt adhesive were "Visual Effect", "Material Experience" and "Model Shaping".

Among the many unconventional materials to engage in image creation, hot melt adhesive was one of the few that used on overall image design products. Most of the reasons for using hot melt adhesives were due to its adhesive physical function to aesthetic function [9]. Only the hot melt gun could cause it to melt into a liquid or semi-liquid, through difficulty of molding process to structuring form designs. Through the questionnaire survey we concluded that hot-melt adhesive materials can be used as the material or design in fashion styling industry. It provided an aesthetic discussion of the application of unconventional materials as a media with pleasure images [9] under the concept of "Body becomes the aesthetic field".

Acknowledgements. Special thanks to the experts and scholars of the Creative Industry Design, Gradual school of National Taiwan University of Arts for their assistance and suggestions in this article.

References

1. Marcuse, H.: One-Dimensional Man, 1st edn. Beacon Press, Boston (1964)
2. Hekkert, P.: Design aesthetics: principles of pleasure in design. Psychol. Sci. **48**(2), 157–172 (2006)
3. Yen, H.Y., Lin, P.H., Lin, R.: Qualia characteristics of cultural and creative products. J. Kansei **2**(1), 34–61 (2014)
4. WOW. https://www.worldofwearableart.com/. Accessed 31 Jan 2020
5. ETToday NEWS. https://www.ettoday.net/news/20191204/1592904.htm. Accessed 31 Jan 2020
6. Marcuse, H.: The Aesthetic Dimension: Toward a Critique of Marxist Aesthetics, 1st edn. Beacon Press, Boston (1979)
7. Blijlevens, J., Thurgood, C., Hekkert, P., Chen, L., Leder, H., Whitfield, T.W.: The aesthetic pleasure in design scale: the development of a scale to measure aesthetic pleasure for designed artifacts. Psychol. Aesthet. Creat. Arts **11**(1), 86–98 (2017). https://doi.org/10.1037/aca0000098
8. Ocvirk, O.G., Stinson, R.E., Wigg, P.R., Bone, R.O., Cayton, D.L.: Art Fundamentals Theory and Practice, 8th edn. McGraw-Hill Education, New York (1997)
9. Hsieh, T.S.: Introduction to The Art. Wer Far Books, Taipei (2004)
10. Hsiao, K.A., Chen, Y.P.: Cognition and shape features of pleasure images. Des. J. **15**(2), 1–17 (2010). https://doi.org/10.6381/JD.201006.0001

Applications of Asian Abstract Imagery in Modern Fabric Design

Feng-Tzu Chiu[⊠]

School of Art and Design, Fuzhou University of International Studies and Trade,
Fujian, China
ftchiu@fzfu.edu.cn

Abstract. The purposes of this study include: (1) integrating Asian aesthetics and western fashion, forming a unique fabric deign encompassing multiple cultures and design languages, (2) re-thinking and investigating the design of needle punched felt based technique, with Asian culture elements, on fabric design, (3) investigating the painting style of the famous Chinese French painter, Wou-Ki Zao, and the application of his color concept into modern fabric design.

The research process was divided into four stages: (1) Studying the painting style of Wou-Ki Zao, identifying his most famous artworks, and analyzing the unique characters of his artworks. (2) Analyzing ancient felting technique, studying its applications on modern crafts and designs, and applying needle punched felting technique to create fabrics resembling oil-painting. (3) By employing the creation framework and processes, extracting key colors and then applying in modern fabric design, and (4) Examining this works of fabric design and discussing the opportunities in continuing the development in this fashion design.

The results show that (1) Master Zao made cross-cultural art and aesthetic easier to be understood and enable the West to understand and appreciate Asian art and painting. (2) Many concepts such as abstract and concrete, art and fashion, sense and sensibility, old and modern, east and west, appear to be opposite, but are complimentary. As Kandinsky, master of abstract painting, described the elements of painting: Painting is not unintentional but intimately related, and all phenomena have dual nature, external and internal. When applying needle punched felt technique on painting, abstract patterns of people, objects, locations, and things are created. The compositions were based on the simple elements of painting, color, lines and shapes. Although the painting seems to be abstract in appearance, but the expression is concrete at its core. (3) A series of abstract painting-like fabric designs were developed to demonstrate an inclusion of concrete and external, and abstract and internal in the same art works. The fabric designs are touchable and fashionable, but also full of invisible cross-cultural aestheticism. (4) These two-dimensional fabric works can be further used in the three-dimensional fashion design, expanding the applications of cross-cultural art design.

Keywords: Asian · Abstract imaginary · Cross-cultural · Needle punched felt · Modern fabric design

© Springer Nature Switzerland AG 2020
P.-L. P. Rau (Ed.): HCII 2020, LNCS 12193, pp. 473–490, 2020.
https://doi.org/10.1007/978-3-030-49913-6_39

1 Introduction

The difference between fashion design in industry and academia is similar to that between fashion and modern art. In particular, fashion strongly relies on business mechanisms, requiring the balance between business and art.

In facing the fashion platform with many international buyers, the author always thinks about how to find the balance between perception-oriented art and ration-orientated fashion. The author is trying to integrating Asian aesthetics and western fashion, forming a unique fabric deign encompassing multiple cultures and design languages.

1.1 Design Process Diagram

Diagram 1 shows the design processes of this study.

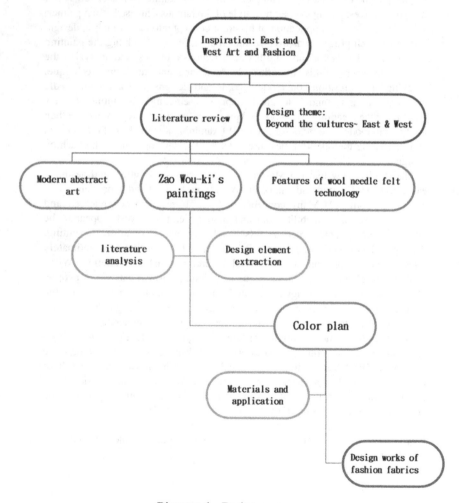

Diagram 1. Design processes.

2 Literature Review

2.1 Modern Abstract Art

In the book of History of Art, Jason (2004) mentioned "Abstraction usually means analysis and simple means to observe the processes or results. Its literal meaning is disintegrating reality and digesting things.

Abstract art usually represents those art work, in the 20th century, with no concrete and symbolic functions nor real-form paintings or sculptures. Abstractionism does not represent those art works created by someone or some periods of time. Instead, it formed from being direct or indirect inheritance of cubism and different art movements, and can be divided into two categories.

Perceptual Abstraction represented by Kandinsky (Fig. 1).

Fig. 1. Kandinsky, YELLOW-RED-BLUE, 1925. Musée d'Art Moderne de la Ville de Paris 1.27 m × 2 m (Color figure online)

Rational abstraction in Mondrian geometry (Fig. 2).

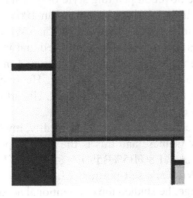

Fig. 2. Mondrian, composition of red; yellow and blue, 1930. 20 × 20 in. N.Y. (Color figure online)

No matter rational or perceptual abstractionism, they both replied on primary colors, red; yellow and blue, as the painting elements. Most artworks are made from two major elements, shapes and colors. Through effective organization and composition, they can be self-expressed, without any assistance from language and symbols.

2.2 Modern Western Art and Traditional Culture: Artistic Inspiration from Chinese French Painter Zhao Wou-Ki

"Western" is a rather general name. "Western" seems to have specifically referred to Europe, especially Western Europe. Since the nineteenth century, hundreds of genres and numerous artists have appeared. Modern western art history is a history of keeping challenging the peaks of art, making art appreciators especially pleasant (Jiang Xun, History of Western Art 2003, p. 2).

Master Zhao Wou-Ki was born in the east and trained with western painting skill. After absorbing the spirit of western painting skill, he brings his painting style back to his own cultural (Figs. 3, 4, 5 and 6). This unique combination of eastern and western painting and culture make him to be internationally recognized for his art achievement. Among the many artists, his extraordinary background and experience inspire the author about how to apply that into fashion design.

Master Zhao is a famous Chinese French painter. He was born in Beijing in 1921. In 1935, he was admitted to the Hangzhou Art College (HZAC), majoring in oil painting at the school. After the victory of the War of Resistance Against Japan, he held a personal art exhibition in Shanghai in 1947. In that exhibition, he was challenged with "You did not study in western. Why you draw western painting?" Therefore, in 1948, as advised by the Dean Lin Fengmian of HZAC, he went to Paris to study painting.

After his study in Paris, he started to travel around the world and later came back to Paris to continue his painting. At that period of time, he integrated western abstract painting skill and Chinese freehand style and ethereal imagery together, making oil painting very Chinese. The novel oil painting style of thin slash ink and dry brushwork attracted many people in his exhibitions in more than 100 countries.

When the "60-year Retrospective exhibition of Zhao Wou-Ki" was held in Beijing and Shanghai in 1999, Chinese art circle was shocked and inspired. French President, Schuck at that time, wrote foreword for the exhibition and mentioned that "Zao Wou-Ki understands the sensibility of our two nations. He integrated the two cultures together, making it belong to both China and France. His art has absorbed the essence of the cultures of our two countries."

Zhao said "Although I chose France as my nationality, my source of creation is from China. My interior is very Chinese and this is the most important thing" (Wikipedia, http://zh.wikipedia.org/zh-hk/%E8%B5%B5%E6%97%A0%E6%9E%81).

In the book of "Zao Wu-Kai's self-portrait, Master Zhao mentioned that when he explored art in his young age, he studied the conventional academic classes, challenged the traditions, and felt that he was caged by traditions. Therefore, he started to study oil painting. He gave up all Chinese interests, and is always looking for something, missing and coming back, and never stop trying." (Zao Wou-Kai's self-portrait p. 28, 1996)

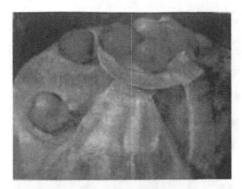

Fig. 3. Zhao Wou-Ki, still life 1935–36 oil painting

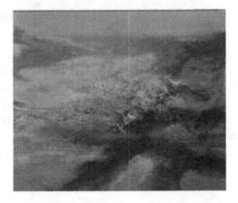

Fig. 4. Zhao Wou-Ki, 21. 2. 72. 40F oil painting F.W Aish, Paris

Fig. 5. Zhao Wou-Ki, 26. 8. 78. 100F oil painting (Coll. Particulière, Paris, Ex. Pierre Matisse Gallery, N.Y.)

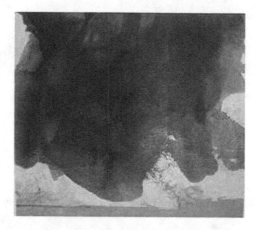

Fig. 6. Zhao Wou-Ki, 22. 6. 91. 150 × 162 cm oil painting

His personal character of keeping thinking and self-exploring in painting and art made his artworks very novel and appreciated. After 60 years of painting, his artworks were well recognized and collected by many art galleries around the world. He realized that the element of eastern ink has strong influence on his painting, and is an important component to make people appreciate his artworks. Therefore, it is not surprised that he said he have re-hugged Chinese tradition (Fig. 7).

"For me, leaving China is for walking into China again" (*Zao Wou-Kai's self-portrait* p. 155, 1996).

Fig. 7. Zao Wou-Kai with his Chinese painting, 1989

Master Zao made cross-cultural art and aesthetic easier to be understood and enable the West to understand and appreciate Asian art and painting.

2.3   Development and Application of Wool Felt

Felt is probably the oldest fabric known in human history. Wool or related animal hairs, such as camel hair and goat hair, are unique in that there are countless scaly tissues on the surface of their fibers. These scaly tissues (see Fig. 8) will swollen in humid and heat condition. After continuous pressure and water, the hooks inside will be tightly tangled and intertwined, forming a strong felt, which is called "felting".

Fig. 8. Wool fiber surface is scaly.

In general, wool felting can be divided into three methods:

(1) **Wet felting.** After laying wool on the design board, add warm water or alkaline soapy water, and knead the wool to form a tangled felt. This method can be repeated multiple times with indirect painting methods such as oil painting (Figs. 9, 10 and 11).

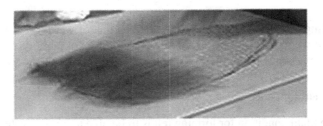

Fig. 9. Wool fibers spread on board

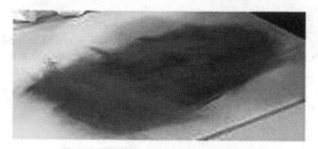

Fig. 10. Multiple layers of wool fibers

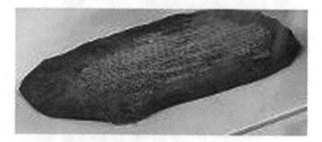

Fig. 11. Constantly wet felting wool fibers to form a felt

(2) **Needle felting.** With a special wool needle (see Fig. 12), the grooves on the needle help the wool to be punctured continuously, and the fiber surface scales are entangled to form a layer. This method can be added directly at any time, as is the direct painting method of juxtaposition and color mixing.

Fig. 12. The appearance of felting needle

(3) **Full felting.** The basic principle is the same as that of wet felting, except that the unformed wool fiber is transformed into a style of wool fabric. Knitted or woven fabrics are acceptable, but the wool content must be more than 50%.

2.4   Wool Felting Tools

The most important condition for forming felt is to be able to humidify, heat, pressurize and agitate wool fibers. If the equipment used can cause these conditions, it can be used as a tool for felting.

Because the watering tools and waterproof cloth for wet felt are easy to use with general household products, such as water spray bottles, water basins and cling film for, the tools for needle felting technology are more specialized, especially the felting needle

(Fig. 13), The combination of different numbers and the thickness of the needles will have different operating speeds and results (Fig. 14).

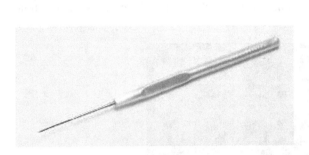

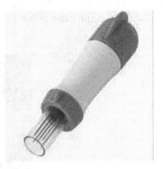

Fig. 13. Single wool felting needle

Fig. 14. 5 wool felting needles kit

When thinking about how to make a large fabric of wool needle felt, machines are often used to replace the manual works, in particular, the most labor-intensive work, quickly and continuously poking the wool up and down with needles. Figure 15 shows an machine that can be used in the creation of wool felting fabric.

Fig. 15. SiRUBA electric needle felt machine

2.5   Felt Test Swatch

The design and application of wool felt fabrics are based on the needle felt technique similar to the oil painting "parallel blending" technique (Fig. 16). After that, the wool fibers of different colors cannot replace oil paints to make mixed color changes, but in the process of creating color screens, However, the thickness and position of the color fibers can be adjusted at any time through the laying of various types of wool felt. This can produce subtle color shades and hue changes. It is also necessary to use the electric needle felt machine (Fig. 17), so the area of fabric creation corresponding to time also has a lethal degree of freedom, and can better grasp the real-time color inspiration and emotional impression display (Fig. 18). These are hindered by the influence of humidity on the color of the fur during the application of the wet felt technique. It is difficult to adjust the color in real time, so it is not used in this research and creation.

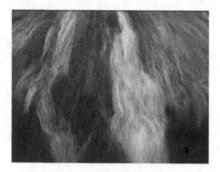

Fig. 16. The image of color wool fibers juxtaposition and display

Fig. 17. Aided by the electric needle felt machine

Fig. 18. Test result for ideal wool felt

3 Results and Discussion

Investigating the painting style of the famous Chinese French painter, Zao Wou-Ki, and the application of his color concept into modern fabric design.

Chinese French painter Zhao Wou-Ki's has unique style in his paintings, which can often inadvertently convey the emotion of the east, but also has the charm of western abstraction. His painting comprises of the lightness like Chinese painting ink, and the western multi-color objects. The author's intention is to make her needle felt wool work into a texture level like western oil painting, and to design the fabrics with an integration crosses the eastern and western cultures.

"Many concepts such as abstract and concrete, art and fashion, sense and sensibility, old and modern, east and west, appear to be opposite, but are complimentary. As Kandinsky, master of abstract painting, described the elements of painting: Painting is not unintentional but intimately related, and all phenomena have dual nature, external and internal. When applying needle punched felt technique on painting, abstract patterns of people, objects, locations, and things are created. The compositions were based on the simple elements of painting, color, lines and shapes. Although the painting seems to be abstract in appearance, but the expression is concrete at its core.

3.1 Design Theme

This fashion design theme is "Look at something" (Cross culture ~ East and West)" (see Fig. 19), and is based on Zao Wou-ki's abstract painting style of oil painting works (see Figs. 20, 21 and 22.). For examples, the unique properties include the blue and black with oriental ink, the gray, white and western abstraction, and the three primary colors of stippling form the dynamic vision of high chroma or the slow flowing colors that are coordinated as a whole to medium to high lightness. The oil paint and

Fig. 19. Fashion theme board

canvas in the famous oil paintings are general, and the fabric design is completed by the wool felt craftsmanship, achieving both the western fashion appearance and the eastern artistic spirit.

3.2   The Elements of Design Theme

(1) **Color plan.** Key colors: Figs. 20, 21 and 22 show that in the extracted paintings, the blue, black, gray, white of the ink and the bright hues in the middle are the key colors for the fabrics (Figs. 23 and 24).

Fig. 20. Zao Wou-Kai, 21. 2. 72. 40F, oil painting (Color figure online)

Fig. 21. Zao Wou-Kai, 15. 4. 86. 162 × 150 cm, oil painting (Color figure online)

Fig. 22. Zao Wou-Kai 21. 9. 89. 114 × 195 cm, oil painting (Color figure online)

Key colors:

Fig. 23. Key colors/dark blue/purple blue/red/yellow/grey/white (Color figure online)

Color proportion:

Fig. 24. Color bar for proportion

(2) **Texture and material application.** Texture: All the wool materials were used to transform Zao Wou-ki's paintings sometimes heavy, and sometimes light and elegant oil paints (see Fig. 25), turning them into thick or fibrous wool felt creation fabrics (Figs. 26 and 27.)

Fig. 25. Zhao Wou-Ki 1997, oil painting

Fig. 26. Thick needle felting fabric

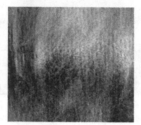

Fig. 27. Thin needle felting fabric

Material 1: The summer wool (see Fig. 28) is the foundation cloth for light weight felting fabrics.

Material 2: The dark blue woolen wool (see Fig. 29) is the foundation cloth for heavy weight felting fabrics.

Fig. 28. Summer wool cloth   **Fig. 29.** Woolen wool cloth (Color figure online)

Material 3. New Zealand's top 100% Ultra-fine Merino wool fiber, fiber fineness: 18 μ. Its super soft hand feel allowed the wool needle felt to remain a soft feel after many times of needle felting. This is mostly used in creation of the main background color, which can be adjusted in color brightness (Fig. 30).

Fig. 30. 100% Ultra-fine Merino wool fiber, black/DK. blue/white (Color figure online)

Material 4. Mercerized Merino wool (100% Top-Merino wool fiber), fiber fineness: 22 μ. Its soft feel, remained after many times of needle felting, makes this material be used to create a large area of the main color wool (Fig. 31).

Fig. 31. 100% Top-Merino wool fiber, black/green blue/white/red (Color figure online)

Material 5. New Zealand Merino wool blended silk (80% Merino 20% silk), fiber fineness: 22 μ. The material is smooth and soft, with unique color and rich sense of layer. This is often used to assist the main hue to create a richer color tone (Fig. 32).

Fig. 32. 80/20 Top-Merino wool/Silk, red/orange/green/blue (Color figure online)

Material 6. Mercerized wool (100% fine-merino wool), fiber fineness: 25 μ. This type of wool fiber is thin and long, showing a natural silky luster. The feel after needle felting will be more solid. Therefore, this is usually selected for the lighter pastel colors to create different color tones (Fig. 33).

Fig. 33. 100% fine-Merino wool, pink/Lt. yellow/Lt. blue/Lt. purple (Color figure online)

Material 7. General wool (100% merino wool), fiber fineness: 30 μ. After needle felting, this wool has a harder feel. This material was mostly chosen for vivid colors to create accent colors (Fig. 34).

Fig. 34. 100 Merino wool, Bt. red/orange/golden yellow/Bt. blue/grape purple (Color figure online)

3.3 Wool Felting Design Fabrics

A series of abstract painting-like fabrics (See Figs. 35 and 36) were developed to demonstrate an inclusion of concrete and external, and abstract and internal in the same art works. The design fabrics are touchable and fashionable, but also full of invisible cross-cultural aestheticism.

Every piece of needle punched felt fabric is like an abstract painting, shows the external essence of one body and two sides as well as the internal perceptual call. It is a fashion fabric that can be felt and seen.

The colors of wool felting fabrics will vary due to the influence of the position and thickness of the wool. Like oil painting, no matter how careful you are when making it, it is not possible to be the same. It is difficult to draw exactly the same picture, so each fabric created is unique.

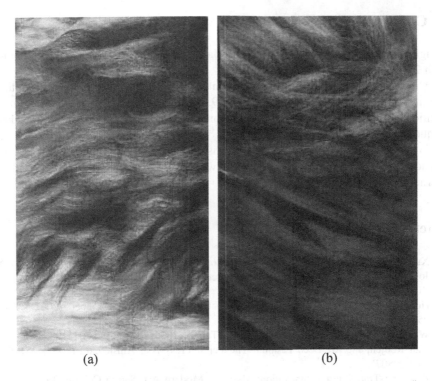

Fig. 35. (a) Impression of distant mountains, 24″ × 45″; (b) Impression of tsunami, 24″ × 45″

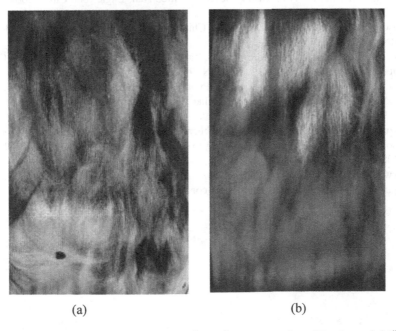

Fig. 36. (a) Impression of towards the sun, 24″ × 45″; (b) Impression of flaming red, 24″ × 45″ (Color figure online)

4   Conclusions

Design thinking beyond cross-culture for these needle punched felts can be applied from 2D fabrics to 3D clothing designs.

This painting-like fabric works will continue to be used as a follow-up clothing design, such as the image board in Fig. 19. The fashion style is different from the traditional female curve figure in the 1920s and going to present three-dimensional and unique wearable art.

In addition to presenting the characteristics of artistic painting on fabrics, this creation explores and presents the creative works of Asian culture in a cross-cultural international fashion language.

References

1. Xun, J.: Introduction to Art. Sanlian Bookstore Press, Beijing (2000). ISBN: 7108014351
2. Jones, S.J.: Fashion Design, 2nd edn. Laurence King Publishing, London (2005). ASIN: B00NBK8K7Q
3. Hong, Z.X.: Absolute Sexuality. Times Culture Publishing, Taipei (2001). ISBN: 9571332925
4. Wang, S.: History of Fashion. Artist Press, Taipei (2006). ISBN: 9867034198
5. Van Roojen, P.: Art Deco Fashion. The Pepin Press BV, Amsterdam (2007). ISBN-10: 946009807X
6. Zeng, S.: Tradition and Innovation: Myths of Modern Art. San-yi Culture, Taipei (2002). ISBN: 9579900558
7. Janson, H.W., Janson, A.F.: History of Art. Prentice Hall, Englewood Cliffs (2004). ISBN-10: 0131195654
8. Janson, H.W.: History of Art, Zeng Yun's Chinese Translation. You-shi Press (1913–1982). ISBN: 9789575300494
9. Zao, W.-K., Ma, K.: Translated by Liu Li, Zao Wou-ki's Self-Portrait (Traditional Chinese Edition). Artist Press, Taipei (1996). ISBN: 9579500517
10. Xun, J.: Meditation on Beauty. Lion Art Publishing, Taipei (2003). ISBN: 9574740625
11. Dickins, R.: Translated by Zhu Huifen, What About Modern Art. Sanyansha (2006). ISBN: 978-986-7581-46-4
12. Pizzuto, J.J.: Fabric Science. Fairchild Publications, New York (2009). ISBN: 0870055712
13. Wool Felt Hand-made Museum: Learning to Make Wool Felt. Suzaku Culture Publishing (2008). ISBN: 9789866780394
14. www.style.com
15. http://www.feltmaking.com.tw/shop/shop_content.php?coID=402

Research on the Cognitive Differences of Different Types of Interactive Artworks

Yang Gao[1(✉)], Jun Wu[2], and Rungtai Lin[1]

[1] Graduate School of Creative Industry Design,
National Taiwan University of Arts, New Taipei City, Taiwan
Lukegao1991@gmail.com, rtlin@mail.ntua.edu.tw
[2] School of Journalism and Communication, Anhui Normal University,
Wuhu, People's Republic of China
junwu2006@hotmail.com

Abstract. Interactivity is a hot topic today and an important medium for people to perceive art. Art has many possibilities for interaction, the impact of different types of interaction on audience's perception needs to be explored. In this research, three artworks with different interactive forms in the art exhibition "Big Stuff" are used as the object of study. Using the communication theory proposed by Dr. Rungtai Lin and Ms. Sandy Lee, the research uses questionnaires with three levels, the "technical level", "semantic level" and "effect level" to explore: the cognitive differences based on three different forms of interaction: mechanical interaction, experiential interaction and creative interaction. The research finds that: 1. Different audiences of different genders, ages, educational backgrounds and professions have shown similar differences in the evaluation of the three types of interactive artworks. 2. The audience's preference for interactive forms cannot determine the audience's preference for artworks. 3. Experiential interaction has the widest impact, followed by mechanical interaction, and finally, creative interaction, which is consistent with the order of preference of works.

Keywords: Artworks · Interaction · Cognitive differences

1 Introduction

Contemporary public art focuses on topicality, participation, interaction and experience [1]. In recent years, artists of urban public sculptures have paid more attention to the interaction with the public, besides, paying attention to artistry and uniqueness. Public sculptures with "interaction" have become more and more popular among people [2]. Interactivity has also become an important medium for people to perceive installation art [3]. Howard Gardner emphasized in his research: the interactivity can stimulate the understanding ability of different learning individuals and greatly deepen the memory [4]. It can be seen that interactivity can positively affect the audience's perception. Studies have shown that interactions affect viewers' perceptions by triggering a sense

© Springer Nature Switzerland AG 2020
P.-L. P. Rau (Ed.): HCII 2020, LNCS 12193, pp. 491–502, 2020.
https://doi.org/10.1007/978-3-030-49913-6_40

of pleasure, as well as by increasing audience's recognition of the work [5]. However, the way of interaction is not unique [6]. The audience's cognitive differences in different forms of interactive artworks are the content of this article.

This research uses three artworks with different interactive forms in the art exhibition "Big Stuff" as materials. Based on the communication theory proposed by Dr. Rungtai Lin and Ms. Sandy Lee, through the questionnaire survey, we hope to achieve the following three goals: 1. to understand whether the different interaction forms of artworks will cause viewers' cognitive differences. 2. to understand the cognitive differences caused by different interaction forms of artworks; 3. and to understand the reasons for the differences.

2 Literature Review

2.1 The Concept of Interactive Art

Interactive art is an interactive form of artistic expression, which is an art form closely related to art and technique, works and audience, creators and audience [6]. Interactive art invites people to touch or enter the field of works at close range, making no boundary between the work and the audience [7]. This invitation is an artists' use of human behavioral psychology to organize or produce a certain participatory content, attracting viewers to become part of the work. This form of art treats human participation as part of the whole art, only when the audience participates in it can it be complete and have artistic value [2].

The forms of art interaction can be divided into three categories: mechanical interaction, experiential interaction and creative interaction. Among them: mechanical interaction refers to the space reserved by the creator on the work for the audience, allowing the audience to touch and operate. Experiential interaction is more about allowing the public to participate in the work and change the original form of the work. Creative interaction refers to the participation of the public in the process of creation of the work [6].

2.2 Three Interactive Artworks

The artworks in this research come from the art exhibition "Big Stuff". The exhibition is a researcher's personal art exhibition, which was held in 2019 at the Forbidden Academy Wuyishan Branch. A total of 5 interactive artworks were on display. This research selected 3 of them to correspond to three types of interaction: "Reading" (creative interaction), "Audiobook" (experiential interaction), and "Best companion" (mechanical interaction).

"Reading" is an art performance, a game that takes place between the artist and the audience. The rule is that the audience proposes the name of a children's game (such as Hide and Seek), and then the artist finds the corresponding text in the book (The Interpretation of the Dream), tears it off and collages it on the paper to repay the audience (Fig. 1).

"Audiobook" is an installation composed of 800 pages of paper bubbles, they are neatly arranged on the ground. When stepped on, they will make a crackling sound (Fig. 1).

"Best companion" is an installation consisting of a yellow round table and two spotlights, the table stands on the ground. One lamp shines on the round table to form a yellow and bright round platform and the shadow of the round platform on the ground. The other lamp is lit up from one side of the round table, when the audience approaches, the figure (shadow) will appear behind him (Fig. 1).

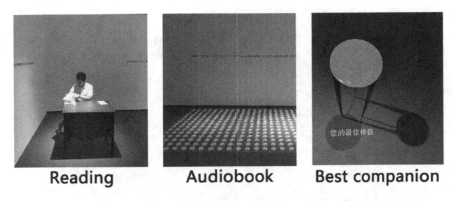

Reading   **Audiobook**   **Best companion**

Fig. 1. Reading, audiobook and best companion (Color figure online)

2.3   Art Aesthetics and Cognition

Reber et al. (2004) proposed that in order to make the evaluation of artworks must first understand the communication between the artist and the audience, it is not only a need in the social context, but to understand the emotional cognitive experience between the creators and the viewers as well [8]. The artist proposes the creative idea internally transformed and presents the work in an external form (encoding process), and the work will be understood and appreciated by the audience (decoding process), forming a positive communication between the artist and the audience. As far as the theory of communication is concerned, successful communication needs to have three levels, namely the technical level, the semantic level and the effect level [9]. Corresponding to the three levels of artistic creation, it can be interpreted as the perception of the audience (technical level) of the appearance to form the perception of shape, the awareness (semantic level) of connotation to form the sense of meaning, reaching (effect level) the emotional relations to produce the inner feeling [10]. Scholar Wilbur also put forward his views on the communicating process: the communicator first encodes the information, and then decodes the information after received by the other party in order to achieve the cognitive effect. It is important that the sender and receiver have a common range of experience in both the encoding and decoding stages. Only in this way can the two communicate and generate consensus [11].

Based on the above theory, this study draws a cognitive model of interactive sculpture (Fig. 2). On the left is the artist's encoding process, and on the right is the viewer's decoding process. The encoding process goes from bottom to top, the artist first decides the desired artistic effect, then plans the way to achieve the effect and chooses the appropriate technique and materials, and finally completes the artistic work. What goes from the top to the bottom is the decoding process, the viewer first obtains the perception of the shape of the work, and then forms the meaning of the work through the analysis of the appearance. At last, the reflection on the shape and meaning of the work produces an inner feeling. The message in the middle shows the common perception of viewers and artists.

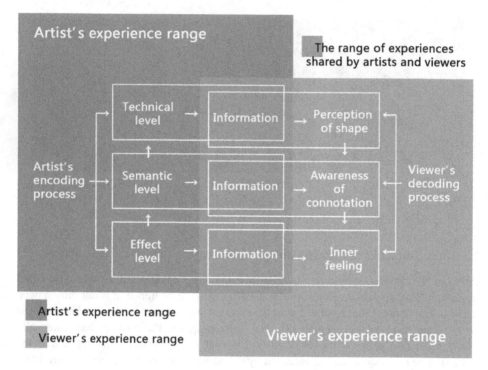

Fig. 2. Cognitive model of interactive sculpture (Reference of: Lin R and Wilbur)

3   Research Method

3.1   Research Process

This research is aimed at the audience who participated in the "Big Stuff" art exhibition held in Wuyishan, China in 2019. Through a questionnaire survey, we explored the audience's cognitive differences to three artworks with different forms of interaction: "Reading", "Audiobook" and "Best companion." A total of 64 valid questionnaires were collected.

There were 30 males and 34 females; 46 people were under 35, 12 people were 35–50, and 6 were over 50; 25 people related to fine arts, 19 people related to design, 20 people in other majors; 30 people with bachelor's degree or below, 34 people with master's degree or above. Based on the questionnaire information, this research is divided into three stages: the first stage is set up to test the reliability of the questionnaire and evaluates its validity; the second stage to comprehend the impact of differences in audience's basic information on cognition; the third stage to understand the influence of interaction types on the cognitive effect of works. The research process is shown in Fig. 3.

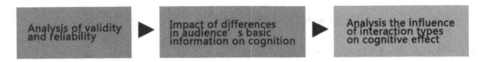

Fig. 3. The study process

3.2 Questionnaire Design

The questionnaire contains 35 questions, which are divided into two parts: basic information and work cognition. The basic information includes: gender, age, professional background, and educational qualification. The cognitive part of the work uses 5-points scale to understand the audience's attitude towards the three artworks.

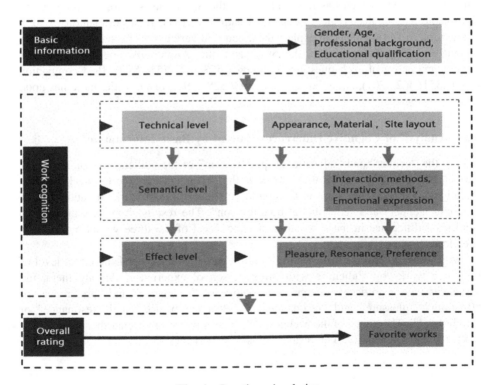

Fig. 4. Questionnaire design

The questions are divided into three levels: the technical level, the semantic level and the effect level. The technical level includes: appearance, material selection and site layout; the semantic level includes: interaction methods, narrative content and emotional expression; the effect level includes: degree of pleasure, degree of resonance and degree of preference. Besides, the choice of favorite works is added as a general review (Fig. 4).

4   Analysis and Discussion of Results

4.1   Analysis of Validity and Reliability

The test of the reliability of the questionnaire is to explore the internal consistency of the various facets of the scale and the reduction of the Cronbachα coefficient of different part after the deletion of a single question, as a reference for selecting the question and the reliability of the scale. The questionnaire analysis found that the Cronbachα coefficient was .958. The overall correlation of the evaluation of each facet and content single question is from .580–.768, and the "α coefficient after deletion" is from .955–.957. It can be seen that the internal consistency between the choices is high and the choices are reasonable. An analysis of the validity of the three works separately shows that the KMO coefficients are: Reading (.923), Best companion (.856), Audiobook (.899), which has high value, and the Sig value is .000, reaching strong significant. The characteristic values are: Reading (6.131), Best companion (5.463), Audiobook (6.144), which can explain the amount of variation of preset use of Reading (68.119%), Best companion (60.695%), and the Audiobook (68.266%). Factor load/commonality of each question: Reading (.553–.873/755–.895), Best companion (.680–.851/.462–.701), Audiobook (.726–.893/.528–.797), this questionnaire has good structure validity.

4.2   Analysis of Cognitive Differences Caused by Basic Information

Taking the "gender" and "educational qualification" of the audiences as independent variables and the effect level of the work as the dependent variable to check whether there is a significant difference in the cognitive effect of the artworks by audiences of different "gender" and "educational qualification". The results show that there is no significant difference in the evaluation of effect level of the three works by different "gender".

Meanwhile, there is a significant difference in the evaluation of the effect level of the three works by audiences with different school experience. Among them, the audiences have significant differences in degree of "resonance" and "preference" of "Reading"; "pleasure" and "resonance" of "Best companion" and "resonance" of "Audiobook". The scores of the bachelor's degree or below are higher than those of the master's degree or above. The results are shown in Table 1.

Table 1. Difference of the effect level by different educational qualification

Artworks	Factors	Educational qualification	N	M	SD	T	Sig
Reading (Creative interaction)	Resonance	Master's degree or above	34	3.18	.936	−2.278*	2 > 1
		Bachelor's degree or below	30	3.77	1.135		
	Preference	Master's degree or above	34	3.21	1.067	−2.785**	2 > 1
		Bachelor's degree or below	30	3.93	1.015		
Best Companion (Mechanical interaction)	Pleasure	Master's degree or above	34	3.38	.922	−2.866**	2 > 1
		Bachelor's degree or below	30	4.03	.890		
	Resonance	Master's degree or above	34	3.53	1.022	−2.302*	2 > 1
		Bachelor's degree or below	30	4.03	.718		
Audiobook (Experiential interaction)	Resonance	Master's degree or above	34	3.56	1.078	−2.714**	2 > 1
		Bachelor's degree or below	30	4.20	.805		

*$p < .05$ **$p < .01$ (1: Master's degree or above, 2: Bachelor's degree or below)

An analysis of differences in the cognitive effects of works between audiences with different "professional background" and "ages" shows that there is no significant difference in the evaluation of effect level of the three works by different "professional background". However, the cognitive effects of audiences of different "ages" are significantly different. The elder age group's evaluation of the three works' effect level are significantly higher than the lower age group. The results are shown in Table 2.

Table 2. Difference of the effect level by different age

Works	Factors	Source	SS	DF	MS	F	Scheffe
Reading (Creative interaction)	Pleasure	Between groups	9.220	2	4.610	5.385**	3 > 2 > 1
		Within group	52.217	61	.856		
		Total	61.437	63			
	Resonance	Between groups	16.591	2	8.295	9.155***	3 > 2 > 1
		Within group	55.268	61	.906		
		Total	71.859	63			
	Preference	Between groups	9.870	2	4.935	4.562*	3 > 2 > 1
		Within group	65.989	61	1.0817		
		Total	75.859	63			
Best companion (Mechanical interaction)	Pleasure	Between groups	6.750	2	3.375	4.037*	3 > 2 > 1
		Within group	51.000	61	.836		
		Total	57.750	63			
	Resonance	Between groups	8.582	2	4.291	5.829**	3 > 2 > 1
		Within group	44.902	61	.736		
		Total	53.484	63			
	Preference	Between groups	9.071	2	4.536	5.715**	3 > 2 > 1
		Within group	48.413	61	.794		
		Total	57.484	63			
Audiobook (Experiential interaction)	Pleasure	Between groups	8.348	2	4.174	5.027**	3 > 2 > 1
		Within group	50.652	61	.830		
		Total	59.000	63			
	Resonance	Between groups	11.350	2	5.675	6.609**	3 > 2 > 1
		Within group	52.384	61	.859		
		Total	63.734	63			
	Preference	Between groups	10.586	2	5.293	5.886**	3 > 2 > 1
		Within group	54.851	61	.899		
		Total	65.437	63			

* $p < .05$ ** $p < .01$ *** $p < .001$. (1: <35 years old, 2: 36–50 years old, 3: >50 years old)

4.3 Analysis of Cognitive Differences Between the Three Works

The analysis on the differences of the "interactive forms" and the three factors of effect level shows that the audience's evaluation of the "interactive methods" of the three artworks: experiential interaction (Audiobook) is higher than creative interaction (Reading) than mechanical interaction (Best companion), while the evaluation of "pleasure" and "preference" of works: "Audiobook" is higher than "Best companion" than "Reading". The data are shown in Table 3.

Table 3. Difference between the three works

Factors	Source		DF	MS	F	Scheffe
Interactive method	Between groups	8.469	2	4.234	4.386*	"Audiobook" > "Reading" > "Best companion"
	Within group	182.484	189	.966		
	Total	190.953	191			
Pleasure	Between groups	10.292	2	5.146	5.458**	"Audiobook" > "Best companion" > "Reading"
	Within group	178.188	189	.943		
	Total	188.479	191			
Preference	Between groups	9.698	2	4.849	4.610*	"Audiobook" > "Best companion" > "Reading"
	Within group	198.781	189	1.052		
	Total	208.479	191			

$*p < .05$ $**p < .01$ $***p < .001$.

4.4 Correlation Analysis of Cognitive Effects and Influencing Factors

Using the six factors of the technical level and semantic level of the work as independent variables and the three factors of the effect level as dependent variables, the correlation between the effect level and the technique level as well as the semantic level was analyzed through multiple regression. The results show that:

The "preference" of the work "Reading" is significantly related to "narrative content" and "emotional expression"; "resonance" is significantly related to "emotional expression"; "pleasure" is significantly related to "material selection" and "emotional expression". The "preference" of the work "Best companion" is significantly related to "material selection" and "emotional expression"; "resonance" is significantly related to "interaction form" and "narrative content"; "pleasure" is significantly related to "material selection" and "interaction form." The results are shown in Table 4. The "preference", "resonance" and "pleasure" of the work "Audiobook" are all significantly related to the "interaction form", and the "resonance" is also significantly related to "narrative content" and "emotional expression".

Judging from the influence of the "interactive form", the "preference" and "pleasure" of "Reading" are not significantly related to the "interactive form" of the work. The audience's "resonance" and "pleasure" of the "Best companion" are significantly related to the "interactive form" of the work. The audience's "preference", "resonance" and "pleasure" of "Audiobook" are significantly related to the "interactive form" of the work.

Table 4. Correlation analysis of cognitive effects and influencing factors

Works	Effects	Factors	B	β	T
Reading (Creative interaction)	Preference	Narrative content	.281	.257	2.101*
		Emotional expression	.321	.299	2.570*
	R = .845 Rsq = .714 F = 23.685***				
	Resonance	Emotional expression	.319	.305	2.170*
	R = .763 Rsq = .582 F = 13.245***				
	Pleasure	Material	.277	.270	2.287*
		Emotional expression	.394	.409	3.186**
	R = .808 Rsq = .653 F = 17.889***				
Best companion (Mechanical interaction)	Preference	Material	.325	.313	2.033*
		Emotional expression	.415	.382	2.991**
	R = .771 Rsq = .594 F = 13.904***				
	Resonance	Interactive method	.347	.359	3.524***
		Narrative content	.339	.334	2.699**
	R = .804 Rsq = .647 F = 17.404***				
	Pleasure	Material	.431	.414	2.911**
		Interactive method	.309	.307	3.043**
	R = .748 Rsq = .559 F = 12.813***				
Audiobook (Experiential interaction)	preference	Interactive method	.555	.439	3.430***
	R = .813 Rsq = .661 F = 18.522***				
	Resonance	Interactive method	.364	.291	2.970**
		Narrative content	.352	.327	2.929**
		Emotional expression	.383	.349	3.075**
	R = .895 Rsq = .800 F = 38.096***				
	Pleasure	Interactive method	.498	.415	3.366***
	R = .828 Rsq = .685 F = 20.696***				

*$p < .05$. **$p < .01$. ***$p < .001$.

5 Conclusion and Suggestion

This research is one of a series of studies on the impact of sculpture interaction on art cognition, and explores the influence of different forms of interaction on cognition. The results show that:

1. Audiences with different genders, ages, educational qualification and professional background show similar differences in the evaluation of artworks in different forms of interaction. There is no significant difference in the perception of each work by different genders or professional background. It can be seen that although interactive art has received attention, it is still a new art concept for China. Related knowledge and theories have not yet been popularized, and related art courses are rarely offered, as a result, there is no significant difference between the audiences of the different gender and professional background. The audiences of the elder age group have significantly higher evaluations of the three works than the younger age group. It can be seen that the older audience's love of art is not lower than that of the younger audience, and they even show more enthusiasm for the art than the younger people. Audiences with bachelor's degree or below have a higher evaluation of the three works than those with master's degree or above. This shows that audiences with a master's degree or above have more stringent evaluation criteria for art than those with a bachelor's degree or below.
2. In terms of audience's evaluation of the three types of interaction form, experiential interaction (Audiobook) is higher than creative interaction (Reading) than mechanical interaction (Best companion). However, the audience's degree of preference for the work: Audiobook (experiential interaction) is higher than the Best companion (mechanical interaction) than Reading (creative interaction). It can be seen that the audience's preference for interactive forms does not determine the audience's preference for artworks.
3. Creative interaction has no significant impact on the cognitive effect of artistic works. Mechanical interaction has a significant influence on the degree of resonance and pleasure. Experiential interaction has a significant impact on the degree of preference, resonance and pleasure. As far as the sphere of influence on the cognitive effect of artistic works is concerned, the experiential interaction has the widest impact, followed by mechanical interaction, and finally, creative interaction, which is consistent with the order of preference of works.

The audience's cognitive differences in interactive art are complex. This research only discusses the impact of interaction on the effect level, while the experience of audience and artists has not been considered. Hoping that future research can continue to explore in this section and the influence of interactivity on artistic cognition will be discussed in more depth.

References

1. Dingyu, W., Haochen, W.: Feasibility exploration of interactive public art intervention in subway space. Fine Arts Res. **2**, 111–112 (2016)

2. Yali, W., Qiumei, Z.: "Interactivity" analysis of urban public sculpture. Furniture Interior Decoration **3**, 88–89 (2014)
3. Dongliang, H.: Interactive study of installation art in contemporary urban space. Beauty Times: City **1**, 80–81 (2018)
4. Caulton, T.: Hands-On Exhibitions: Managing Interactive Museums and Science Centres. Routledge, London (1998)
5. Yang, G., Wang, I.-T., Lo, H., Lin, R.: Research on the influence of interactivity on the aesthetic cognition of art. In: Rau, P.-L.P. (ed.) HCII 2019. LNCS, vol. 11576, pp. 592–601. Springer, Cham (2019). https://doi.org/10.1007/978-3-030-22577-3_43
6. Feng, W.: Exploration of public art interaction in the context of new technology. J. Nanjing Univ. Art Fine Art Des. **1**, 146–148 (2010)
7. Meecham, P., Sheldon, J.: Modern Art: A Critical Introduction. Routledge, London (2005)
8. Reber, R., Schwarz, N., Winkielman, P.: Processing fluency and aesthetic pleasure: is beauty in the perceiver's processing experience? Personality Soc. Psychol. Rev. **8**(4), 364–382 (2004)
9. Lin, R., Sandy, L.: Poetic Charm and Painting Elegance - Sharing of Experiences in the Beauty of Xianyun. National Taiwan University of the Arts, New Taipei (2015)
10. Lin, R., Qian, F., Wu, J., Fang, W.-T., Jin, Y.: A pilot study of communication matrix for evaluating artworks. In: Rau, P.-L.P. (ed.) CCD 2017. LNCS, vol. 10281, pp. 356–368. Springer, Cham (2017). https://doi.org/10.1007/978-3-319-57931-3_29
11. Wilbur, S.: How Communication Works. In: Schramm (ed.) The Process and Effects of Mass Communication, Urbana, I11, pp. 4–8. The University (1954)

A Case Study of Applying 'Black Humor' to Ceramic Art Performance

Mei-Ling Hsu[1]([⊠]), Wen Ting Fang[2], Po-Hsien Lin[1], and Rungtai Lin[1]

[1] Graduate School of Creative Industry Design,
National Taiwan University of Arts, New Taipei City, Taiwan
g910504@gmail.com, t0131@ntua.edu.tw,
rtlin@mail.ntua.edu.tw
[2] Shanghai Dianji University, Shanghai, People's Republic of China
f_wenting@163.com

Abstract. The aim of this study is to explore a concept of "black humor" applying into art performance through a case study of a ceramic art exhibition. Nine ceramic art works are used as the stimulus material, and 122 subjects participated in this study. 34 male subjects and 88 female subjects came from web community. After a questionnaire evaluation of each art work, the scores are analyzed and discuss. The results showed that the "black humor" applying in art performance can be understood by audience that provides the valuable information to the artist for creating the performance art and worthy of further research. Eventually, the findings of this study can give an insight into the cognition of "black humor" for artists.

Keywords: Black humor · Ceramic works · Performance art · Cognitive ergonomics

1 Introduction

Foreword People can choose different life styles, which is also an expression of life tastes and values. Although the life style and the way of showing living tastes chosen by each person are different, they are all values of life; their value is not counted to be high or low and good or bad, which depends entirely on personal feelings and experience. However, life always holds a common point of view, no matter what lifestyle you choose; when people encounter difficulties in life or are not satisfactory, they still have to live! For instance, after the typhoon, the prices of vegetables rise, people feel inconvenient in life when ponding water does not flow away. We always comfort ourselves by using "life is always going on!", which seems to fill us with joy when finding happiness in suffering; if we encounter a worse or unfortunate event, in addition to finding happiness in suffering, we also ridicule ourselves for a moment, which some people call "black humor." (www.britannica.com). The Encyclopaedia Britannica interprets "black humor" as a kind of desperate humor, trying to draw people's laughter as a response to human beings' apparent helplessness and absurdity in life. In short, black humor reveals the absurd nature of society and life with exaggeration and irony,

P.-L. P. Rau (Ed.): HCII 2020, LNCS 12193, pp. 503–515, 2020.
https://doi.org/10.1007/978-3-030-49913-6_41

and deliberately confronts tragic events with a relaxed and ridiculous attitude (www. encyclopedia.com). The most typical black humor: Someone who was sentenced to a gallows pointed to the gallows asking the executioner before going on the gallows: "Are you sure this is strong?" [9, 11].

Many artists use "black humor" as a theme to express the plight of people's lives in novels, comics or other artistic forms [1]. For instance, people love "desserts", knowing clearly that sweets are harmful to their health, but they can't resist the dilemma; there are a group of female artists in Taiwan who use desserts as the theme and use different media to create colorful works; such as the artists, Su Zihan, Chen Qiujin and Wang Liangyin. The works created by Su Zihan in 105 "Miniature City Memories" are a series of rich dessert-like works that describe people and urban settlements with urban styles created by composite media. Chen Qiujin's works show beautiful and delicious paintings with a delicate image of sweets transmitted through brushes; the fruit and delicious desserts coupled with delicate lace tablecloths depict gorgeous visual deliciousness. However, Wang Liangyin is good at using acrylic paints to draw the understanding of desserts created by the layers of sweetness, of desserts, creating a dripping effect that triggers associations with failure and destruction. These desserts seem to be true or false, and their attractive appearance often makes it impossible for the readers and listeners to distinguish between true and false. With the artists' craftsmanship, the taste that originally belongs to tongue will be transformed into visual enjoyment. These dessert-based works of art, which are both real and inedible, are typical black humors that are ironic and seeking pleasure under adverse circumstances. The artists have created a series of artistic works with ridiculous vision and staggered scenes. Through the artistic works, the contradictions and disputes between ideals and reality are presented [3]. The strong contrast has pointed out the dilemma between a dream of happiness and the desires unable to be realized. For example, the huge ice cream created by virtue of ceramics exudes a seductive coldness, which makes one tempted to get close to licking on a hot summer day [2]. In the attractive sweet works, a close look will reveal many soldiers armed to the teeth standing on the front and attack aggressively; the ice cream is enlarged to a human in size, but the soldier is reduced to a tiny figure, which satirizes the life of one soldier as small as an ant. However, soldiers are sacrificed needlessly in order to fight for the desire to possess [3, 12].

2 Literature Review

2.1 Black Humor

Black humor is a literary genre that emerged in the United States in the 1960s. Most of them described the cynical cynicism of nobodies in their predicament, and set off their eccentric behaviors using some ridiculous events, revealing the characters' pessimism, distress and helplessness while ridiculing. The rise of black humor showed its specific era background. At that time, after the end of the Korean War, on one hand, the United

States suffered from social unrest and frequent labor-management conflicts. On the other hand, under the influence of McCarthyism, the entire society permeated with depression. In the early 1960s, the United States was involved in the Vietnam War again. The defeat of the War made the anti-war sentiment in the country high, and the situation became turbulent, resulting in social chaos. In the context of the incomprehensible society, a "black" humor of thought was generated to make fun of, attack and satirize the reality. According to the definition of black humor, it must have the following characteristics: (1) it has a humorous trait that makes people laugh; (2) it has a black ridiculous trait that is hopeless and absurd. Since many writers wrote a large number of novels related to black humor, they became a significant genre in modernism. Nowadays, black humor is not limited to literature. In the fields of art and film and so on, black humor has become an art thinking that can not be ignored [13] (Fig. 1).

Figure 2 illustrates the transformation process of black humor. The "protagonist" or "event" that has been stereotyped in real society, through the "taunt and funny" conversion in black humor, urges the audience to perform "the main character" or "event". The sense of "humorous and amusing" discovers the truth of "plot conflict" and also stimulates the audience's attention to "unusual". In addition, when socially recognized values are continuously deconstructed and reconstructed in life, black humor will make the audience understand the meaning of its life value; when the event results, the cruel reality will be presented in a relaxed and humorous "music in pain" way. While alive, the hard-necked spirit of "no fear of adversity" was expressed while making people laugh, which inspired the audience to deliberately or unconsciously. Because of these characteristics, the "bent postbox" is so fascinating to the audience, which is also a form of storytelling with a strong plot such as black humor, which can give the audience thought-provoking meaning.

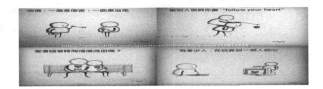

Fig. 1. The comic works illustration of black humor

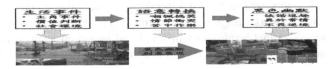

Fig. 2. "bent postbox" illustrates the transformation process of black humor.

2.2 The Cognitive Process Model of Black Humor

With regard to the cognitive model of black humor, as far as communication theory is concerned, the conversion and cognitive process of the bent postbox in Fig. 2 includes three levels: technical level (see it?), semantic level (understand it?), and effect level (touched?). First, the audience perceives the appearance representation of the "technical level", then understands the meaning and connotation of the "semantic level", and finally reaches the emotional connection of the "effect level". [4, 6]. These three levels correspond to the artistic creation of artists, and the coding process is to generate "black humor" through "life events" and via "semantic conversion". For the readers and listeners, the decoding process is (1) whether the readers and listeners see the sensory impression of appearance perception produced; (2) whether the readers and listeners understand the thinking mode of meaning cognition; (3) whether the readers and listeners are moved to realize the psychological activity of inner feeling. In other words, for readers and listeners, there are three key steps to understand the meaning of black humor: attracting attention (recognition), correct recognition (understanding) and profound emotion (reflection), as shown in Fig. 3 [10]. Recognition as situational awareness indicates whether artistic works are sufficient to attract the audience; understanding as mood awareness indicates whether the audience can understand the meaning of its information as a psychological feeling and whether the audience can be deeply moved by the artistic works [4–6].

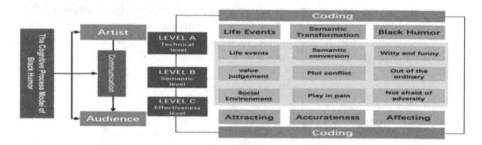

Fig. 3. The cognitive process model of black humor

From the perspective of cognitive ergonomics, Fig. 3 also conforms Norman [7] to the proposed design concept models, including design model, user model and system impression, which represent the artist's thinking model, the audience's cognitive model, and the artistic works, respectively. Norman [8] further points out three levels of the design process: instinct level, behavior level and reflection level, which represent the readers and listeners' aesthetic experience, meaning experience and emotional experience, respectively, and explain the changes in the cognition mood of the readers and listeners during the communication process in Fig. 3.

A well created black humor must reach the three levels of communication and cognition shown in Fig. 3: technical level, semantic level and effect level. The successful communication process should ensure that the readers and listeners complete the decoding process. There are three links in the horizontal and vertical directions; the horizontal axis is the progressive process of the readers and listeners' perception of the situation to the meaning of experience; and the vertical axis is the in-depth process from the outside to the inside; both of them jointly build a cognitive model of "black humor". This study combines communication, cognitive theory, and aesthetic experience through literature review, and proposes a black humor experience cognitive model (Fig. 3), which is the basis for subsequent evaluation of black humor cognition [4–6].

2.3 Black Humor from the Ceramics Exhibition of the Eater Soldiers Series

The art creator used a unique perspective to see the ridiculous qualities from the unpleasant reality. The black humor reality is manifested through the works, making people feel hopeless and helpless, and at the same time, it still sends out an understanding smile, so as to ease the inexplicable life anxiety and suffocating depression. For instance, artist Hsu Chia-Yu [2] created the Eater Soldiers series, which extended a desire for appetite to the desire for war and aggression, and conveyed the concept of anti-war with black humor. Hsu Chia-Yu 's Eater Soldiers series is witty and ironic, of which ceramics are counted as ice cream to symbolize people's desires, and the ants on the ice cream are transformed into soldiers, which is a mockery and a hint that the artist conveyed the concept of anti-war through the huge ice cream sculpture and small toy soldiers. In addition, desserts are metaphorized as a symbol of desire, but the ants are transformed into soldiers, mocking them for being silly and also mocking themselves. The work takes away the cruel war, and only mentions fight and desire, reality and absurdity. War is ruthless, starting with endless desire. On the other hand, the weaknesses of human plunder and possession are also found out, and this is the rationalization of the plunder process from zero to one. When simulating a real object, the size and proportion of the actual object are changed, causing ridiculous visual chaos and dislocation of the scene, reflecting the cruelty of human competition and desire expansion.

Table 1. Eater soldiers series artwork photos and statement

Artwork photos		statement
	1.	Sweet Ice Cream (taunting finding happiness in suffering) It takes the homonym of sise in Chinese, and blessing, pay, longevity, and happiness with good luck are loved by ordinary people.
	2.	Double-collapsed Soldier's Cream (taunting the terrorist attack) Originating from the terrorist attacks of 9/11, it has the ice cream's shape metaphor of the twin towers collapsed. The bloated cream shape directly points to people's greed and desire, and the twin towers arise from desire.
	3.	Soldiers' Ice Cream (taunting the dignitaries and cravings) The sweet ice cream pile symbolizes the craving power of the capital society.
	4.	Cream of landing soldier (taunting away from the war) The most violent war in recent history Normandy War is selected as the background. ﹑
	5.	Attacking Soldier's Cream (taunting the temptation of interest) In front of delicious muffin ice cream, heroic soldiers swarmed up, desperately attacked, and intended to siege the city slightly for their own possession, but they did not know where they stood at a high point, they would find that the gorgeous and rich muffin ice cream is just a piece of waste.
	6.	Inverted Soldier's Cream (taunting retrograde power)) Ice cream is used to imply power, the swelling sweet cream and crisp and sweet tube are metaphor of the bloated power which is very fragile indeed, and such a reversed mode implies that power will fall down in the end one day for justice, time, or other factors.
	7.	Escaper Cake (taunting terrible sweets) A piece of delicious red ice cream seems from a distance to be a "cherry", but it is a bloody skull only by a close look, which means that the sweet and delicious chocolates like "dead soldiers" scattered over the wilderness.
	8.	Poppy Soldier's Cake (taunting sweet drugs) Green fruit is made from poppy seed bodies by means of rollover. It is ironic that the current society is flooded with drugs. Poisonous poppy seeds are poisoning the world.
	9.	Cake for Soldier Writing Love Letter (taunting war and death) (size: 25x25x10cm) This is an anti-war work. A letter written by a soldier to his lover in the battlefield shows the helplessness and sadness of the soldier who did not want to fight but sacrifice.

3   Research Methods

In this study, the black humor experience cognitive model in Fig. 3 was used as a research framework to explore how artists create through black humor, and to study how ordinary readers and listeners understand and recognize the creative concepts of artists and understand the connotation of black humor [4–6]. Stimulus samples are the nine works listed in Table 1. First, the participants were asked subjectively to assess the degree of understanding of the author's creative idea (1–100 points), then the participants were asked to evaluate the black humor related works of the works and finally, the subj participants ects were asked to objectively evaluate the extent to which others may understand the creative idea (1–100 points). The form of the questionnaire is shown in Table 2. After assessing 9 works, the participants were asked to answer the following questions: (1) Which of these works do you think is the most "ridiculous" creative? (2) Which of these works do you think is the most "humorous" creative? (3) Which one do you like the most?

Table 2. Questionnaire design for evaluation on black humor works

2.   Escaper Cake (Size: 24X12X12cm)

A piece of delicious red ice cream seems from a distance to be a "cherry", but it is a bloody skull only by a close look, which means that the sweet and delicious chocolates like "dead soldiers" scattered over the wilderness. The "Escaper Cake" reminds people that sweets are as scary as war.

1. How much do you know about the author's ideas?

_____Points (1–100 Points).

2. Does this work fit the "black" irony?

Weak □1   □2   □3   □4   □5 Strong

3. How "humorous" is this work?

Weak □1   □2   □3   □4   □5 Strong

4. Does this work conform to the creative concept of "black humor"

Weak □1   □2   □3   □4   □5 Strong

5. Do you think others can understand the author's creative concept?

_____Points (1 – 100 Points).

In this study in which a mode of network questionnaire was adopted, a total of 142 questionnaires were collected including 122 valid questionnaires. There are 34 males and 88 females; the age group contains 5 people under 20 years old, 41 people between 21–40 years old, 69 people between 41–60 years old, and 7 people over 61 years old. The academic qualifications involve 51 persons from research institutions, 58 university graduates, and 13 others. In terms of the background of speciality there are 21 people in art related fields, 32 people in design field, and 69 people in other fields.

4   Results and Discussions

4.1   Overall Evaluation of Black Humorous Works

Table 3 is the average and standard deviation of the overall evaluation on the works by all the participants. For example, can you know the author's creative idea (Q1)? If the average score of work 1 is 69.84 points, and the standard deviation is 18.00 points, it is included in parentheses below. For a second example, the second question (Q2) is this work in line with the "black" taunt? The average and standard deviation of its 5-point score are 3.31 (0.91) each. In light of this, Question 5 (Q5): Do you think other people can understand the author's creative ideas? The average and standard deviation of their objective evaluation are 65.27 (17.11) respectively. The reliability coefficient is 0.927, more than 0.9, which indicates that the reliability level of relevant data is high. The CITC values corresponding to the analysis items of such CITC values are all higher than 0.1, indicating that there is a good correlation between the analysis items and the reliability level is good. In summary, the reliability coefficient of the research data is higher than 0.9, indicating that the high reliability of the data can be used for further analysis.

The differences between male and female participants are as follows: Question 3 in Work 2: To what extent is this work in line with "humor"? At a significant level ($t = 3.02$, $P < 0.01$), it was shown that the average value of female participants (4.07) is significantly higher than that of male participants (3.47). Similarly, Question 4 in Work 2: Is this work in line with the creative idea of "black humor"? At a significant level ($t = 2.52$, $P < 0.05$), the average value of female participants (4.10) was significantly higher than that of male participants (3.67). In addition, Question 4 in Work 4: Does this work conform to the creative idea of "black humor"? At a significant level ($t = 2.63$, $P < 0.05$), it was shown that the average value of female participants (3.34) was significantly higher than that of male participants (2.93). Besides, there is no significant difference in the other works and questions for different participants. As far as age is concerned, there is no significant difference, indicating that in this case study, participants' perceptions of black ridicule and humor were not restricted by age.

Table 3. The average and standard deviation of the overall evaluation on the work by all the participants

Question	P1	P2	P 3	P4	P5	P6	P7	P8	P9
Q1	69.84	78.59	75.65	66.86	71.98	69.38	77.80	72.96	74.15
	(18.00)	(13.65)	(14.57)	(18.06)	(19.55)	(19.54)	(17.52)	(18.49)	(19.43)
Q2	3.31	4.06	3.80	3.35	3.63	3.46	3.95	3.57	3.77
	(0.91)	(0.78)	(0.91)	(0.84)	(0.97)	(1.03)	(1.04)	(0.84)	(1.00)
Q3	3.41	3.89	3.63	3.16	3.59	3.40	3.73	3.39	3.57
	(0.83)	(0.90)	(0.90)	(0.89)	(1.00)	(1.03)	(1.07)	(0.82)	(1.01)
Q4	3.35	3.97	3.70	3.22	3.54	3.39	3.87	3.51	3.69
	(0.86)	(0.80)	(0.87)	(0.80)	(0.99)	(0.98)	(1.03)	(0.86)	(0.99)
Q5	65.27	74.64	71.95	64.75	69.70	66.61	74.32	70.78	72.10
	(17.11)	(14.75)	(16.01)	(16.85)	(18.43)	(20.12)	(18.38)	(17.77)	(18.90)

As far as the participants' academic qualifications are concerned, the data shows that there are significant differences in varying questions on works 1, 2, 7 and 9. For example, Question 1 in Work 2: How well does the work fit the "taunt"? At a significant level ($F = 3.78$, $P < 0.05$), the average value of participants with a background of research institution (3.60) is significantly higher than that of participants with other backgrounds (3.10). Question 1 in Work 2: How much can you know about the author's creative ideas? At a significant level ($F = 5.11$, $P < 0.01$), the average value of the participants with a background of research institution (83.52) is significantly higher than that of other academic participants (74.80). Question 3 in Work 7: How well does this work meet the "humor"? At a significant level ($F = 5.06$, $P < 0.01$), the average value of the participants with a background of research institution (4.05) is significantly higher than that of other academic participants (2.88). Similarly, Question 4 in Work 7: Does this work meet the creative idea of "black humor"? At a significant level

($F = 3.34$, $P < 0.05$), the average value of the participants with a background of research institution (4.10) is significant Higher than that of other academic participants (3.13). For another example, Question 2 in Work 9: How well does this work meet the "taunt"? At a significant level ($F = 3.34$, $P < 0.05$), the average value of participants with a background of research institution (4.10) showed a significantly higher value than that of other academic participants (3.50). In addition, there is no significant difference in the other works and questions for participants with different academic qualifications.

In the work of the questionnaires "Double-collapsed Soldier's Cream", the "taunt" and "humor" questionnaires were both scored high, but the scores on the participants were relatively low. This part means that it is impossible for the participants to judge it as a favorite work that can be deeply explored in the future due to other reasons such as modeling or moral pluralism of the work. However, part of Double-collapsed Soldier's Cream works modeled is obviously different from the molding techniques of other works, and a reversely collapsed state is presented with the works formed by the author's use of extrusion tool, and whether the use of its techniques will cause the viewers' visual impact in the future shall also be paid attention to by the author!

As far as the participants' speciality background is concerned, the data shows that there are significant differences in varying questions in works 1, 4, 7 and 9. For example, Question 1 in Work 1: How much can you understand the author's creative ideas? At a significant level ($F = 4.20$, $P < 0.01$), the average score of other specialities is significantly lower than that of art-related specialities. Question 5 in Work 1: Do you think other people can understand the author's creative ideas? At a significant level ($F = 3.57$, $P < 0.01$), the average score of other specialities is significantly lower than that of art-related specialities. For another example, Question 2 in Work 4: How well does this work meet the "taunt"? At a significant level ($F = 3.06$, $P < 0.05$), the design-related average score is significantly lower than the art-related ones. Question 1 in Work 7: How much can you understand the author's creative ideas? At a significant level ($F = 4.24$, $P < 0.01$), the average score of other specialities is significantly lower than that of design-related specialities. Question 2 in Work 9: How well does this work meet the "taunt"? At a significant level ($F = 5.23$, $P < 0.01$), the average score of other specialities is significantly lower than that of art-related specialities. In addition, there is no significant difference between the remaining works and the questions for participants from specialities. The above data shows that in this case study, the art speciality's perception and cognition of black humor is significantly better than that of design-related and other specialities, and that of the design-related specialities is superior to other specialities.

4.2   Discussion

Regarding the Participants' Response to: Which one of these works do you think is the most "taunting" creative? The result is that Work 7 "Escaper Cake" has the highest number of recognitions 32 people (27.1%), followed by Work 2 "Double Collapsed Soldier's Cream" with 25 people (21.2%), Work 9 "Cake for Soldier Writing Love Letter" with 20 people, Work 3 "Soldiers' Ice Cream" with 19 people (16.1%) and Work 5 "Attacking Soldier's Cream" with 15 people (12.7%), as shown in Fig. 4.

Through paired t test, Works 7 and 2 show no significant difference. At the same time, it shows that in the paired t test, Work 2 is significantly better than Work 9 (t = 3.17, p < .01), Work 3 (t = 3.31, p < .01) and Work 5 (t = 4.65, p < .01). Similarly, Work 7 is significantly better than Work 5 in the paired t test (t = 3.09, p < .01); but there is no significant difference in Works 9, 3 and 5. The above data shows that the ideas of black "taunt" in the nine works can be clearly distinguished in this case study relying on the participant choice of individual evaluation or overall evaluation.

Ask the Participants on: Which one of these works do you think is the most "humorous" creative? The result is the work—(7) The highest number of people who should get the deserter cake is 32 (27.1%), followed by Work 1 (2) Double-collapsed Soldier's Cream (5), Attacking Soldier's Cream (6) and Inverted Soldier's Cream with 16 people (13.3), as shown in Fig. 5. Similarly, through the paired t test, Works 7 and 2 show no significant difference; at the same time, Work 2 is significantly better than Work 5 (t = 4.65, p < .01) and Work 6 (t = 6.10, p < .001) in the paired t test. In addition, Work 7 is significantly better than Work 5 (t = 5.82, p < .01) and Work 6 (t = 5.43, p < .001) in the paired t test; there is no significant difference between Works 5 and 6. In Works 2, 5 and 6, the participants presented significant differences in the individual evaluations, but the differences could not be distinguished in the choice of the overall evaluation, indicating that the participants could not completely distinguish the creativity of nine works with "Humor". The reason why the participants could not clearly distinguish or evaluate the "humorous" ideas in the nine works is worth further exploration.

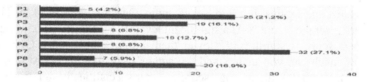

Fig. 4. The most ridiculous works of the participants

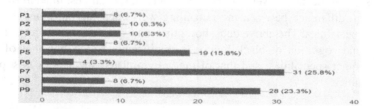

Fig. 5. The most humorous works of the participants

Ask the participants on: Which work do you like the most? The result is that Work 1 (7) Escaper Cake receive the highest recognitions 31 people (25.8%), followed by Work 1 (9) Cake for Soldier Writing Love Letter with 28 people (23.3%) and (5) Attacking Soldier's Cream with 19 people (15.8%), as shown in Fig. 6. Similarly, through the paired t test, there is no significant difference in Works 7 and 9; at the same time, it shows that Work 7 is significantly better than Work 5 in the paired t test (t = 3.09, p < .01). In addition, Work 9 has no significant difference from Work 5 in the paired t test. In addition, there are no significant differences between the nine participants and the five questions among all the participants. From the data in Table 3, it can be shown that Work 2 is the highest evaluated among all five questions, but when the participants evaluate separately, why was Work 7 chosen "Escaper Cake" as the favorite work, it may be "Escape" relative to "Cherry", showing the opposite nature of black taunt and humor, and achieving the true meaning of "black humor", but its real reason is intriguing and worthy of further exploration.

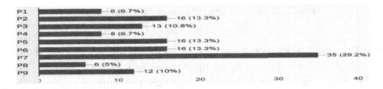

Fig. 6. The most favorites works of the participants

5 Conclusions and Suggestions

Artistic aesthetics highlights personal taste and style, and the form of life aesthetics is displayed everywhere in the food, clothing, living, and entertainment of life. With no need for esoteric philosophical theories, aesthetics naturally appear in life as long as we feel at any time with heart. Black humor is a way for artists to express artistic emotions, and it is also a theory of artistic creation. When people face life difficulties and live a very boring life, how should they face the meaning of life?

Therefore, this article aims to explore how artists express their lyrical emotions through the concept of "black humor" through the art works of artists. Hope that these art works will bring people the joy of finding happiness in suffering, so that they will live through the difficulties of life. At the same time, by learning about how people appreciate and interpret the black humor works of artists, and what kind of life experience these art works can bring to people, the possibility of applying "black humor" to artistic creation is further explored, so as to provide artists with black humorous creations for reference.

The relevant study results of this case study can be summarized as follows:

1. For male and female participants, except for works two for question three, works two and four for question four, the average of female participants is significantly higher than the average of male participants. In addition, there is no significant difference between the other works and the question for different participants.

2. There is no significant difference in terms of age, indicating that in this case study, the participants' perceptions of black taunt and humor are not restricted by age, and they can experience black humor regardless of age.

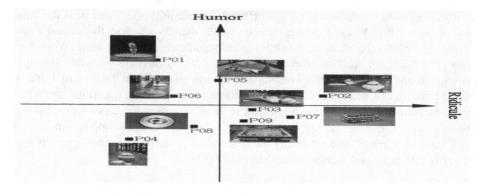

Fig. 7. Cognitive space diagram of black humor.

3. As far as the participants' academic qualifications are concerned, the data show that Works 1, 2, 7, and 9 have significant differences in varying questions. The average value of participants with a background of research institution is significantly higher than that of participants with other academic qualifications. In addition, there is no significant difference between the other works and the questions in the participants with different academic qualifications.

4. As far as the speciality background of participants is concerned, the data shows that in this case study, the art department's perception and cognition of "black humor" is significantly better than that of design-related and other specialities and that of the design-related speciality is superior to that of other specialities, and the reason is worthy of further discussion.

5. Regarding the participants on: Which one of these works do you think is the most "taunting" creative? The data shows that in this case study, the black "taunt" creativity of nine works can be clearly distinguished by virtue of the participant choice of individual evaluation or overall evaluation.

Depending on the study results above, a complete outline of the study case can be understood from the cognitive space diagram of black humor in Fig. 7, that is, the horizontal axis is counted as the "black taunt" dimension, and the vertical axis is regarded as the "humor display" dimension; the preliminary results of this case study can be understood by comparing the works in Table 1 with the data in Table 3. In short, black humor, as a creative idea of artists can be accepted by the public through its creation, and it is undoubtedly an inspiration and is also an affirmation for artists. It can provide artists with future creation through the "black humor" concept for reference. In future research, how "black taunt" and "humorous display" complement each other should be more rigorously explored to show the meaning of black humor through "black" taunt and "humor".

1. This study attempts to use a kind of questionnaire to analyze the perspective of the audience and to observe the distance between the author's ideas and the audience's viewpoints. Looking forward to the preliminary black humor evaluation criteria

produced by this research, to which artists will refer in the future for this research when creating their works, so that created works are closer to people's mind and can help artists more accurately convey their viewpoints when creating conceptual works.

Acknowledgements. The authors would like to thank Professor Rungtai Lin for offering the research framework and valuable suggestions. The authors also wish to thank those who contributed to the research.

References

1. Grace (2012). https://www.zhihu.com/question/20604360/answer/15613512
2. Hsu, C.-Y. (2007). https://www.peopo.org/news/5527
3. Hsu, C.Y. (2008). http://artres.moc.gov.tw/portal_f1_page.php?button_num=f1&cnt_id=107
4. Lin, C.L., Chen, J.L., Chen, S.J., Lin, R.: The cognition of turning poetry into painting. J. US-China Educ. Rev. B **5**(8), 471–487 (2015)
5. Lin, R.: Transforming Taiwan aboriginal cultural features into modern product design: a case study of a cross-cultural product design model. Int. J. Des. **1**(2), 45–53 (2007)
6. Lin, R., Qian, F., Wu, J., Fang, W.-T., Jin, Y.: A pilot study of communication matrix for evaluating artworks. In: Rau, P.-L.P. (ed.) CCD 2017. LNCS, vol. 10281, pp. 356–368. Springer, Cham (2017). https://doi.org/10.1007/978-3-319-57931-3_29
7. Norman, D.A.: Emotional design – Why We Love or Hate Everyday Things. Basic Books, New York (2005)
8. Norman, D.A.: The Design of Everyday Things: Revised and Expanded Edition. Basic books, New York (2013)
9. Pratt, A.R.: Black Humor: Critical Essays. Garland Publishing, New York (1993)
10. Lin, R., Lee, H.-M.: Poetic – The Experience of Poetic Drawing. NTUA, New Taipei City (2015)
11. Schulz, M.F.: Black Humor Fiction of the Sixties: A Pluralistic Definition of Man and his World. Ohio University Press, Ohio (1973)
12. Xuexue (2013). http://www.xuexuecolors.com/coloritem.php?xue=5&id=606
13. Zhihu (2015). https://www.zhihu.com/question/20604360/answer/16424435

Concerning the Perspective of Sound Insulation on Approaches of Interior Design

Wei Lin[1(✉)], Hsuan Lin[2], Zih Yu Huang[1], and Yun Hsuan Lee[1]

[1] School of Architecture, Feng Chia University, Taichung, Taiwan
wlin@fcu.edu.tw, ziyu125673@gmail.com,
a0985233250@gmail.com
[2] Department of Product Design, Tainan University of Technology,
Tainan, Taiwan
te0038@mail.tut.edu.tw

Abstract. In the study of interior design, experience in space perception and related senses is very important. In addition to the visual aesthetic performance, the sound effects of musical instruments, voices, and relative sounds are as important as visual perception. In the process of sound insulation of interior element, the physical performance of sound is presented. The design approaches for the characteristics of space shape, room volume, material, and detailed decoration are based on the above-mentioned design concerns to predict the room sound performance requirements. Effects of sound insulation measurement is mainly based on impulse response, which represents the physical reaction between a certain point in space and the sound source. In the performance design process, different acoustic model evaluation techniques can be used to obtain the impulse response as the basis for sound field performance evaluation. This study explains the correspondence between interior design and sound insulation performance for topics such as sound transmission loss theory, computer simulation, and on-site measurement techniques.

Keywords: Interior design · Sound insulation · Computer simulation · On-site measurements

1 Introduction

The speed of sound waves varies depending on the medium. The speed of sound in an atmosphere of 20 °C is about 343 m/s, and the transmission speed of sound through solids is much faster than air. When sound waves are transmitted from one interface to another, they are reflected on the boundary between the two interfaces. There are similarities between sound waves and light waves. When sound waves are incident obliquely when they contact the interface of an object, the incident angle will be equal to the reflection angle. When the reflection surface is flat and the scale is larger, it is like a mirror reflection effect, specular reflections will occur [1]. If the reflecting surface has a concave-convex texture or decoration, and the wavelength of a certain frequency band is equivalent, the intensity of the reflected sound will be reduced, and the reflected energy will be scattered at various angles, which is called diffuse or diffuse reflections [2, 3].

© Springer Nature Switzerland AG 2020
P.-L. P. Rau (Ed.): HCII 2020, LNCS 12193, pp. 516–525, 2020.
https://doi.org/10.1007/978-3-030-49913-6_42

In addition to the natural physical characteristics of the sounds mentioned above, the use of Sound reinforcement can compensate for the limitations of natural conditions, especially in large hall spaces. Through the use of acoustic equipment, it can provide sufficient volume, adjust the characteristics of the sound and the balance of the vocal part during the performance, and can record or reproduce. For general performance venues, for all audience seats, the volume of the sound reinforcement system must provide more than 85 dB, and the volume of rock performance venues must reach as high as 110 dB. In addition to providing sufficient volume, the sound clarity of the system may also be discussed, the range of output frequency meets the requirements of a high standard. The equipment system consists of sound receiving equipment, reproduction and recording equipment, processing and control equipment, etc., from traditional analog signals to digital signals, the integration of signal workstation systems has become the trend of sound field evaluation and application implement. In terms of the acoustic characteristics of interior space, the radiation of sound in the indoor space will cause a series of reflections. After a distance from the sound source, the sound volume will be mainly controlled by the reflected sound. Apart from the outside distance, the sound volume will not decrease significantly. The scale of the space is also related to the characteristics of the sound distribution. The smaller the interior space and the higher the surface reflection intensity, the greater the volume of sound. An impulse response is an acoustic effect recorded at a certain measurement point (Receiver) in a room, corresponding to one or more sound source points (Source) with a sound producer. An impulse response is a communication tool for acoustic consultants and architects. It can be used to understand the detailed relationship between subsequent reflections (such as early reflections) and direct sounds. It also includes late energy, such as reverberation energy. This response records the arrival time and sound energy of direct sound and various subsequent reflections [4]. In the past fifty years, in the physical study of natural sound in halls, acousticians have successively proposed many acoustic measures (Acoustical measures) to represent several important subjective acoustic elements. Most of these indicators are evaluated by listening to music. The main physical quantities include Reverberation Time (RT), when the sound stops, due to the existence of reflection, the sound does not disappear immediately but gradually decays. This process is called reverberation, and the corresponding physical index is called reverberation time (RT). The phenomenon generally refers to the time duration after attenuation of 60 decibels (dB). In general interior, the reverberation or clarity can be considered as two sides of the condition, that is, when the reverberation is increased, the clarity is decreased. Therefore, considering the two factors of space and time, the performance space required for a specific performance object has a certain scale and material characteristics. Generally, the small space requires high definition, and the reverberation time is short. The planning of the reverberation time (RT) value is recommended to be about (0.6–1 s) according to the space size. Acoustical indices, such as RT30, C80, D50, Ts and EDT, are derived from the impulse response which is based on the International Standard ISO 3382 (Bradley 2004) [5]. Through the distribution of sound absorption and diffusion materials in the indoor space, the initial reflected energy is effectively radiated to the seat. The ideal indoor space is a moderate size of 16.5–49.5 square meters. If the space is less than 13 square meters, there may not be enough space for sound reflection, and the sound easily floods the overall environment, covering too much area, affecting the clarity of the sound. The larger the space volume or the higher the reflection intensity of the surface material, the longer the reverberation time. The size and shape of an interior environment will have a great impact on the sound equipment of the device. The shape and size of the space will affect the path of sound propagation in the space, thus causing a difference in a person's viewing experience. The interior space is between two planes. As a result, sound waves are constantly reflected to form standing waves. Therefore, in spatial planning, eliminate the concentrated sound wave path and let the energy of the sound be evenly distributed in the space. In the interior where the spatial unit is located, it is best to stay away from the environment that may cause noise, such as the side of the road or the adjacent space that generates noise. If it can be an independent enclosed space, it will be more effective in blocking environmental noise and improve the space. Sound quality, play the effectiveness of film and television listening equipment.

2 Visualization of Sound Distribution

In addition to the design of the building space, the sound energy distribution has an impact on the sound filed. In order to further confirm the morphology of indoor sound field performance planning goals and the independence and correlation of acoustic parameters, the computer simulation evaluation technology includes several item-oriented discussions, including sound energy of diffused field to estimate the sound insulation performance of indoor structures evaluation, and finally, after the completion of the verification measurement, an objective test is performed to record the physical performance of real-time condition and explore the corresponding relationship with the objective physical measurement of the room. In this phased study, computer simulation is used to predict and evaluate the sound field model and the sound insulation performance of indoor structures. In the 1960s, Shroeder [6] introduced the basic principles of computer simulation to indoor acoustics. Krotstad [7] first published a paper on computer simulation of indoor sound fields. With the continuous advancement of software and hardware technology, the computer simulation software for hall sound quality has matured and is widely used in hall research on sound quality design and evaluation of sound field characteristics. The computer simulation of the indoor sound field simulates the propagation law of sound waves in the room by establishing a mathematical model of the actual hall according to the geometric acoustic method. The acoustic simulation software uses the Lamber scattering algorithm, and the calculation results are closer to the measured values. Due to the establishment and modification of the digital model and the establishment of the material database, the data environment of these parameters can be used to view the sound quality environment with high accuracy. The relative software was be presented, it can reduce the time needed for the creation of noise contour maps considerably. The development of a fit for purpose software for mapping contours based on measurements. Scanned maps and CAD drawings can be used as backgrounds for future evaluation. The actual measurement is used to draw the sound energy distribution map, and the NoiseAtWork software is used to analyze and draw the distribution curve. The results can be used to establish the optimization plan for the overall distribution of the sound field. Individual environmental factors can be used to verify and hypothesize to construct The model, through the implementation of measurement correspondence, further draws sound pressure level images and verifies sound field models, predicts future scenes and benchmarks for subjective evaluation, and then takes measures. Using the computer simulation of the sound field environment results, the calculation method to perform grid calculations, draw the sound energy distribution curve diagram, which has an intuitive trend and visual representation, and can evaluate the sound field in which it is located under different conditions surroundings. The simulation results provide a lot of information, including the location and strength of sound energy. In some cases, this method has the function of trend prediction, especially under stable sound sources, such as fixed noise sources (fixed mechanical sound), and multiple sound source are conducted for the measurements (See in Fig. 1.).

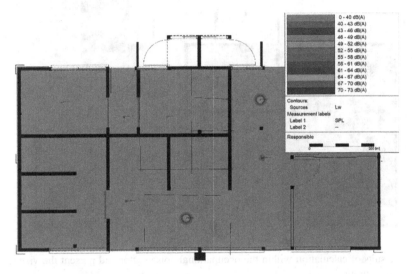

Fig. 1. Multiple standing sound source are conducted for the simulation and calculation with on-site sound energy distribution

The mapping contours presentation is based on measurement results with the equivalent average volume *LAeq* (dB) as the evaluation index and the A-weighted noise intermittently exposed in a certain period of time in the selected position in the sound field are averaged by the energy. The parameter index formula is shown in Eq. 1.

$$LAeq = 10 \log \frac{1}{T} \int_{t}^{t+T} \left(\frac{Pt}{P0}\right)^2 dt \tag{1}$$

LAeq: A-weighted average energy level dB (A) in period time;
T: measurement time in seconds;
Pt: measure sound pressure in Pa;
P0:   reference sound pressure, based on 20 μPa

For different sound sources, measures to reduce sound energy can also be plotted and sorted according to the size of the sound energy results. NoiseAtWork software is used to simulate and draw the sound energy distribution curve to establish the overall distribution of the sound field and the overall distribution profile. Individual environmental factors can be used to verify and hypothesize to build a model. Through the implementation of measurement correspondence, the sound pressure level image and Validate the sound field model, predict future scenarios and explore the impact of sound source energy, and then take corresponding measures. Results can be discussed and evaluated simultaneously (See in Fig. 2).

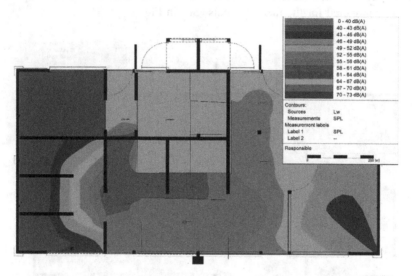

Fig. 2. Results of calculation within the occupational noise sector and present the visualization of mapping contour.

3   Calculation of Sound Insulation for Building Element

Sound insulation performance of building structures through construction system require regulations to reduce noise interference between different units. There are many reasons for the indoor noise environment of the building, including the airborne noise of neighbors and outdoors. Noise is transmitted into the room through building doors and windows, walls and floors, and the vibration of equipment inside the building and the indoor activities of residents constitute in noise environment, which has become one of the causes that bother and affect their quality of life. There are existing regulations on sound insulation and the goal is to strengthen the building's sound insulation structure to reduce noise interference between residential occupants and improve the quality of the home audio environment. Air sound insulation design and floor impact sound insulation design have their application scope. Domestic residential common 150 mm thick RC wall surface cement mortar painted individual household walls, the site sound insulation level can reach more than 50 dB, with good sound insulation performance is equivalent to the requirements of foreign sound insulation benchmarks. The analysis results have the same trend, with high correlation, which shows that the results of the individual household wall test in this study are really valid. In addition, RC bare floor slabs commonly used in domestic housing, and effective countermeasures against impact sounds, have become a source of distressing noise for collective residential residents. As long as the mass per unit area (m) and the Modulus of Elasticity (E) of the panel are known, the sound transmission through a single-layer plate can be approximated to a good accuracy. At low and mid frequency bands, the acoustic transmission loss (TL) is calculated according to the mass law [8, 9]. The prediction formula is shown in Eq. 2.

$$TL = 20 \log(mf) - 48 \text{ dB} \qquad (2)$$

At high frequencies, the coincidence effect weakens the acoustic transmission, and the transmission loss is given by Eq. 3

$$TL = 20 \log(mf) + 10 \log(f/fc) - 44 \text{ dB} \qquad (3)$$

Another simulation of program that can estimate the sound insulation ability of partition walls, floors, ceilings and windows. It can make a more accurate estimation of the sound transmission loss of 1/3 octave and the weighted sound insulation (STC or Rw) which can be used for noise evaluation. It takes account of finite size effects which are very important when predicting small samples such as windows and also for normal elements at low frequencies. The low-frequency sound transmission effect of very important small-sized building structures is considered in the calculation of sound insulation, and it is applied to the estimation of small-sized building structures such as windows and ordinary building structures. As with other estimation tools, simulation is not a substitute for actual measurement. However, according to the comparison with the test data derived from the database, for most building structures and elements, the difference can be within 3 decibels. The materials databases can be filtered to include or exclude materials from most of the countries and it is adapted to most regions in the world. The databases are updated regularly and feedback from users is always welcome to extend and improve the material selections. For the example of calculation for the prediction transmission loss of double panel systems may refer to in 4 different frequency regions. At low frequencies the transmission loss is determined primarily by the mass law. The mass-air-mass resonance frequency of the partition (fo) determined by the mass of the panels and the air gap, the TL increases at 18 dB/octave as the two sides become decoupled. The other region the cavity width becomes comparable to a wavelength at frequency fL the cavity modes couple the panels together and the TL increases at 12 dB/octave. The last concerns is focused on the solid connections act as sound bridges between the two panels and the TL is limited to a constant amount above the mass law, and increases at only 6 dB/octave [10]. The results of double layer of lightly structure for sound insulation calculation as shown in Table 1.

Table 1. The results of insulation calculation for double layer of lightly structure

		Material Description and illustration
50	13.9	
63	13.9	
80	13.7	
100	9.7	
125	13.9	
160	19.7	
200	25.1	120 mm
250	29.7	
315	33.6	
400	36.9	
500	39.9	
630	42.7	
800	44.8	
1000	46.8	
1250	48.6	
1600	50.1	
2000	51.1	
2500	51.3	
3150	48.8	Wall: + 1 x 10 mm Plasterboard + Timber stud (100 mm x40 mm) +
4000	41.5	75 mm Fibre glass (10kg/m3) + 1 x 10 mm Plasterboard
5000	45.7	
Rw		38
C		-4
Ctr		-11

4 On-Site Measurement

Taking into account the current indoor environment and sound field environment quality, conduct a current environmental assessment. The measurement results will provide a basis for the design decision of the construction team. Based on the data measured and analyzed at the site, a preliminary improvement proposal and performance proposal are proposed. With reference to the ISO140-3 the difference of SPL field measurement method, the spatial sound pressure level difference is calculated by Eq. 4. In addition, the correction formula of the opening area is included in Eq. 5.

$$TL = L_1 - L_2 \qquad (4)$$

$$R'w = TL + 10\log S/A \qquad (5)$$

TL: Sound transmission Loss (dB).
$L1$:   Averaged SPL at source room (dB).

L2:   Averaged SPL at receive room (dB).
S: Area of test species (m^2).
A: Absorption coefficient at receive room (dB)

The acoustic parameters in the physical quantities of the indoor sound field are mainly described in terms of Reverberation Time (RT). After the sound energy stops, due to the presence of reflections, the sound does not disappear immediately, but gradually decays. This process is called reverberation, and the corresponding physical index is called reverberation time (RT) as previous mentioned. Evaluation of sound insulation performance of building elements (such as walls, doors or windows) are based on ISO140-3 and ISO717-1 measurement methods to regulate and evaluate performance. Insulation performance standards for most typical building component sound need to be between Rw 45–50 dB, and more than 50 dB is a high-performance sound insulation construction. Rw is a parameter value measured under careful settings and conditions in the laboratory. Under field conditions, it is represented by R'w. For example, the sound transmission problems such as the socket that the opening of the partition wall intersects with the slot, and other lateral sound transmission channels. The noise generated by structural vibration through the structure of the wall must be solved and concerned. According to the ISO standard, the sound insulation performance of the building in the indoor space is evaluated (the openings are all closed). The test frequency band range is 1/1 times the octave 100 Hz to 3150 Hz. In addition to the indoor sound insulation performance test, the volume of the corridor affects the adjacent indoor space. Finally, after clarifying the sound insulation performance, the indoor and speech intelligibility will be significantly improved. The detailed description of the on-site measurements and the corresponding evaluated spaces are described in Table 2. The field measurement results for test specie are listed in Table 3 and 4 according to the performance of the ISO717-1 specification.

Table 2. The detailed description of the on-site measurements and the corresponding evaluated spaces are listed

Measurement parameter	Evaluated room	Detailing description
R'w (dB)	Partition of rooms Windows Doors Building elements	Sound insulation performance test in accordance with ISO 140-3 and ISO 717-1
RT (s)	Receiving room	Room acoustics measurements in accordance with ISO 3382

Table 3. Acoustical parameters with on-site measurement at receiving room are listed

Parameter	Frequency					
	125 Hz	250 Hz	500 Hz	1000 Hz	2000 Hz	4000 Hz
T30(s)	0.62	0.39	0.39	0.45	0.53	0.66
	0.39	0.39	0.45	0.53	0.66	0.39
	0.39	0.36	0.42	0.57	0.61	0.39
	0.41	0.36	0.43	0.57	0.63	0.41
STI	Speech intelligibility reach to STI = 0.65 (Good)					

Table 4. The field measurement results of specification.are listed according to the sound insulation performance of the ISO717-1

Freq.	TL
100	61.6
125	59.1
160	59.2
200	55.3
250	46.4
315	46.7
400	42.2
500	42.7
630	42.2
800	44.0
1000	43.6
1250	43.4
1600	40.7
2000	35.7
2500	35.5
3150	33.0
R`w	40

5 Discussion

In interior design research, the perception of space and related senses is very important. In addition to visual aesthetic performance, the sound effects of musical instruments, sounds and relative sounds are just as important as visual perception. During the acoustic design of the room, the physical properties of the sound insulation were proposed. The design method for the characteristics of space shape, room volume, materials and detailed decoration is to predict the sound performance requirements above design concerns. The measurement of sound insulation is mainly based on the impulse response, which represents the physical reaction between a point in space and the sound source. In the performance design process, different evaluation of sound insulation techniques can be used to obtain the impulse response as the basis for sound field evaluation. This research explains the correspondence between interior design and sound insulation performance for topics such as sound transmission loss theory, computer simulation, and on-site measurement techniques. Some preliminary results are abstracted as followed:

(1) Individual environmental factor can be used to verify and hypothesize to build a model by the simulation and easy to demonstrate the calculation of results with mapping contour for further prediction.
(2) Sound insulation performance of building structures through construction system require regulations by the software to reduce noise interference before the approaches of detailing design.
(3) The on-site measurement verification can be obtained through the analysis of the instrument and digital workstation. After analysis by the digital signal worksta-tion, each parameter must be entered into the simulation software for data analysis and systematically organized.

Acknowledgements. The authors wish to thank Huang Kung Huang, Natural Acoustic Co. for the helps of software assistance, Professor Wei-Hwa Chiang, Dep. of Architecture, National Taiwan University of Science and Technology, and Hwa Hsia University of Technology the kindly assistances during the evaluation phase.

References

1. Barron, Michael: Auditorium Acoustics and Architectural Design. E&FN Spon, London (1993)
2. Beranek, L.L.: Concert Halls and Opera Houses: How They Sound. Springer, New York (1996)
3. Beranek, L.L.: Concert Halls and Opera Houses: Music, Acoustics, and Architecture, 2nd edn. Springer, New York (2004). https://doi.org/10.1007/978-0-387-21636-2
4. Long, Marshall: Archtectural Acoustics. Elservier Academic Press, London (2006)
5. Bradley, J.S.: Using ISO3382 measures to evaluate acoustical conditions in concert halls (2004)
6. Schroeder, M.R.: New method for measuring reverberation time. J. Acoust. Soc. Am. **37**, 409 (1965)
7. Krokstad, A., Strøm, S., Sørsdal, S.: Calculating the acoustical room response by the use of a ray tracing technique. J. Sound Vib. **8**, 118–125 (1968)
8. Sharp, B.H.: Prediction Methods for the Sound Transmission of Building Elements, Noise Control Engineering, vol. 11 (1978)
9. Cremer, L., Heckel, M., Ungar, E.E.: Structure-Borne Sound. Springer, Heidelberg (1988). https://doi.org/10.1007/978-3-662-10121-6
10. INSUL. http://www.insul.co.nz/tech-info. Accessed 1 Feb 2020

Visual Data Storytelling: A Case Study of Turning Big Data into Chinese Painting

Yanru Lyu[1(✉)], Tuck Fai Cheng[1,2], and Rungtai Lin[1]

[1] Graduate School of Creative Industry Design,
National Taiwan University of Arts, New Taipei City 22058, Taiwan
lyuyanru@gmail.com, rtlin@mail.ntua.edu.tw
[2] Graduate School of Applied Cosmetology, HungKuang University,
Taichung City 43302, Taiwan
Kenneth1831@hk.edu.tw

Abstract. Visual data storytelling is a relatively new terminology that has emerged over the last decade. The use of information technology in data visualizing is becoming more common and accessible to users. The artist apply a variety of multimedia, symbols and metaphors to independently create a visual form that expresses data and communicates with real life. The visual data are the media that provide powerful and essential means of communication. If "visual data storytelling" is viewed as a process of communication, it follows naturally that how the artist's performances are conceived, developed, delivered and received, and how the audience is attracted, accurately understanding the data and affected by the data visualization are worth exploring. Therefore, this study is intended to propose a framework focusing on how the conception of the artist affects the creation process and how the creation process is understood by the audience. The artist's creation activities were analyzed through the framework of four steps using a case study of turning "big data" into "Chinese painting." The results showed that the approach could be applied to understanding data visualization and provides artists with an idea of how to concentrate their efforts at the creation stage, the easier to communicate with their audience. In addition, the research framework seems to provide a better way to explore the understanding of how data transforms into art forms, which is clearly worthy of further study.

Keywords: Big data · Data visualization · Storytelling · DIKW model

1 Introduction

In this data-driven era, there are a variety of purposes for data acquisition and application. The information made up of data can not only help people make more intelligent decisions, but also examine their view of the world from a more objective perspective [1]. Transforming data into a form that relies on the human visual system to perceive the embedded information, the resulting visual effect is as simple as discovering the underlying laws in movies [2]. On the one hand, through the research of visualization in computer science, data and facts can be presented rationally and objectively, thus making the data readable. On the other hand, there are parallel

© Springer Nature Switzerland AG 2020
P.-L. P. Rau (Ed.): HCII 2020, LNCS 12193, pp. 526–535, 2020.
https://doi.org/10.1007/978-3-030-49913-6_43

discourses regarding the artistic visualization aesthetics, which mainly focus on the exploration of human emotions and the transmission of inner views, but unfortunately rarely involves [1, 3–5]. As Norman [6, 7] argues in a successful design, visualization has evolved into as a functional art, which not only focuses on usability goals, but also needs to provide memorable, interesting, enjoyable, and engaging experiences. Therefore, more attention needs to be paid to artistic visualization in order to tell the audience something except what it is behind data.

Artistic visualization, as a type of visualization centered on emotional experience, refers to the artist's use of beauty in data by artist to arouse the perception of the audience. Different from the visualization just for usability goal, the goal of artistic visualization is usually to communicate a concern, rather than presenting data. The data is used as material and transformed into a form of beauty that makes relevant patterns visible to demonstrate the authenticity of the concerns [3, 4]. The information anxiety mentioned by Wurman is caused by the gap between what we understand and what we think we should understand [8], which can be bridged by the communication between the outer world and the audience in a meaning way [3]. Consequently, how to communicate is the research focus of artistic visualization.

As one of the most effective means of communication, stories have long served as a medium for conveying information, cultural values, and experiences. In this increasingly computerized world, with the development of technology and culture, there more complex narrative ways for the transmission of information [2, 8]. Visualization is not only about the exploration and analysis of data, but also about eliciting profound emotional and/or intellectual responses [1, 9]. There are countless real-life stories behind the data, which are displayed in ways that depend on what the audience wants to see or hope the audience to see. Therefore, visual data storytelling absorbs the ideas from both the artist/designer and the audience [1, 10].

If "visual data storytelling" is viewed as a process of communication, the following questions are worth exploring. How are the artist's performances conceived, developed, delivered and received? How are the audiences attracted, accurately understood the data, and affected by the visualization? Therefore, this study proposes a framework to explore how the conception of the artist affect the creation process and how the creation process is understood by the audience.

2   Theoretical Background

2.1   DIKW Model

The data-information-knowledge-wisdom (hereinafter referred to as DIKW) model is a common method to explain the human understanding in the perceptual and cognitive space [11]. Nathan Shedroff [8] gives an overview of understanding, that is, a continuum from data to wisdom. Ackoff, R. L. [12] defines data as symbols that has no value until they are processed into a useable form in a given context. Information consists of processed data with more usefulness that can provide answers to "who", "what", "where" and "when" questions. Knowledge is the application of data and information to provide answers to "how" questions. Understanding is the appreciation of "why". Wisdom is the evaluation of understanding. The first four categories are related to the past, while the fifth category deals with the future. Zeleny [13] describes the components of the DIKW model for different purposes, including know-nothing (data), know-what (information), know-how (knowledge), know-why (wisdom), and know-for-sure (enlightenment) beyond wisdom. By integrating several models known as DIKW Hierarchies, Cairo [3] represents the gap that Wurman, R. S [8] describes between the data and the knowledge, and explains the process from reality to the human brain. The unstructured information from outer world can be encoded as data, which is shaped by the communicator. When the audience has a deep understanding of the acquired knowledge, relevant patterns can produce knowledge and even reach the realm of knowledge. Based on the previous studies combined with the DIKW model, the cognitive process from data to wisdom is shown in Fig. 1.

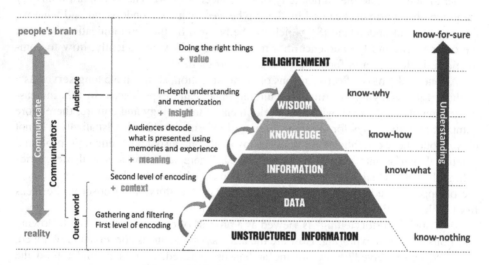

Fig. 1. Congnition from data to wisdom

2.2   Framework of Communication Research

Since the audience cannot gain personal insights directly from abstract data, the communication involving the artist as the communicator encoding and audience decoding is an important part of the discussion. There are six constitutive factors in Jakobson's [14] communication model, which are addresser, addressee, context, message, code, and contact. This model is used to analyze an act of communication in visualization. The artist (addresser) sends a message to the audience (addressee) through his/her visualization work. To be operative, the work (message) requires a story (context) and is mastered by the audience (addressee). The meaning of work must be based on his/her message and on the shared meaning system (code) that makes up the work. Finally, physical channels and psychological connections are established between the artist and the audience (contact), enabling both of them to enter and maintain communication. Of these six factors, each factor determines the corresponding different functions, respectively emotive, conative, referential, poetic, phatic, and metalingual, which will be described in detail below. The emotive function focuses on the attitude or emotion of the artist. The conative function is a kind of orientation toward the audience. In the referential function, the work is related to the real data. The poetic function is the aesthetic expression of data art. For code and contact, the metalingual function is to confirm the code system, and the phatic function is the medium for communication.

Lin et al. [15–18] put forward a framework for communication research that contains three levels of problem, namely technical, semantic, and effectiveness. Firstly, the technical level requires the audience to receive information through his/her senses, that is, how accurately the artist can convey the information through his/her visualization work. Second, the semantic level requires the audience to be able to understand the meaning of the message without misinterpreting, misunderstanding, or even not understanding at all, namely the degree of accuracy with which the audience understands the original meaning of the message. Third, the level of effectiveness involves the audience taking corrective action in accordance with its original meaning, that is, how effectively affect conducts in the way expected. Based on the previous studies [14–20], a research framework combining communication theory with communication and DIKW models is proposed to explore the issue of turning data into story (see Fig. 2).

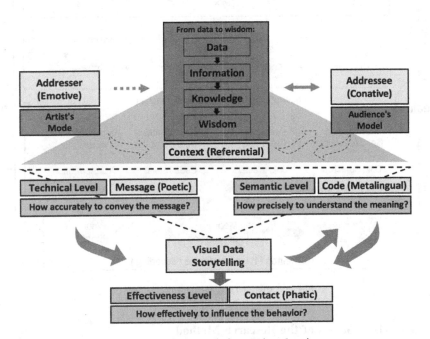

Fig. 2. Research framework for turning data into story

Visualization involves complex issues as interdisciplinary processes. On the basis of the above discussion, the framework in this study can be used for a continuous search for a deeper understanding of the process of visual data storytelling.

3   Methodology

3.1   Visual Data Storytelling Model

According to the studies of Lin [15] and the previous research framework (see Fig. 1), the visual data storytelling model includes three main stages, which are data processing, coding model and visualization works. The model focuses on how to extract the semantic features from data and then then transform these features into art forms, which can be divided into three stages: analyzation, translation and implementation, as shown in the upper part of Fig. 3.

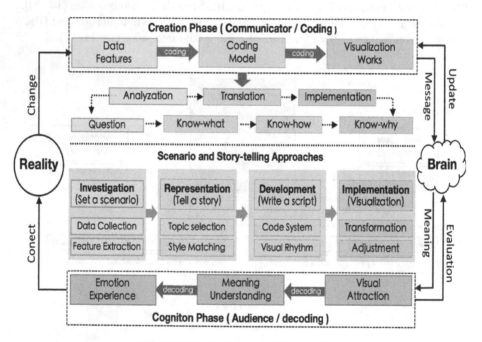

Fig. 3. Visual Data storytelling model

3.2   The Three Stages of the Research Method

As shown in Fig. 3, there are three stages of the visual data storytelling model, including the analyzation stage, translation stage and implementation stage. A further description is given below.

Analyzation Stage: This stage looks for hidden problems in the data. By observation and measurement, data are recorded. The data features are identified during processing, including the outer level of visual form, the mid level of meaning, and the inner level of emotion. Through this process, artists can use the methods and tools of big data analysis to obtain contextual information from useful data.

Translation Stage: The purpose of translation is to explain "what is the problem" and "how to cause the problem". The information from the data is translated into knowledge by associating it with the memory and experience of the audience. At this stage, the artist can relate this knowledge to the problems in modern society, and create an interaction between the reality and the audience's brain.

Implementation Stage: From this stage to the completion from data to wisdom. The implementation stage involves the expression of knowledge related to the data features, the artist's understanding of the meaning of information, his/her aesthetic sensibility, and his/her flexibility to adapt to various media. In this process, the artist's in-depth understanding of knowledge can add value to wisdom. This knowledge is combined with the artist's sense of visual communication to employ these three levels of data features in visualization.

3.3   The Four Steps of Visual Data Storytelling Process

Based on the creation model and the previous studies [10, 15, 21], the big data into story is used in scenario and story-telling approaches is used in scenario and story-telling approaches. In the practical visualization process, four steps are used to transfer data into story, namely, investigation (setting a scenario), representation (telling a story), development (writing a script), and implementation (visualization), as shown in the middle part of Fig. 3. The four steps of this process are further described as follows:

Investigation/Setting a Scenario: Data recorded by observation and measurement is the core of any visualization, which can be found in a lot of places, including experts in the related fields, a variety of online applications, or collections by people [1]. It should be explored after formatting and then used to identify data characteristics, the source of the problem, with a critical eye that includes technical, semantic and effectiveness levels. Through this process, the artist can obtain contextual information from the data.

Representation/Tell a Story: Through the structure of the story, this step aims to inform the audience what the question is about the data. Therefore, based on the previous scenario, the topic can be selected and narrowed down. In order to establish a connection between the story topic and the audience, an externally recognizable style should be used on the topic to make it easier for the audience to understand.

Development/Write a Script: As a step in developing concepts and prototypes, this step focuses on code system, which explores the transformation mechanism from data to visual form. During this step, the scenario and story may require modification to highlight the important point. In addition, this step provides a way to illustrate the story logic with visual rhythm.

Implementation/Visualization: The goal of this final step is to evoke an emotional response of the audience from data to wisdom through a comprehensive visual experience. Therefore, all data features should be listed in a matrix table to help artist examine the transformation effect. Moreover, the artist needs to evaluate the recognition of visualization from three levels, and then update the work based on the result of this evaluation.

Finally, it is necessary to always consider the audience and purpose of the visualization works. In traditional data visualization studies, there have been assessments of usability goals, such as effectiveness and efficiency. Alternatively, There are few approaches to experience goals in the visualization literature [22]. As shown in the lower part of Fig. 3, the process of audience cognition includes three phases of visual attraction, meaning understanding and emotion experience, which are not only the reference for the creation process, but also the three levels matrix of evaluation.

4   Case Study: Turning Big Data into Chinese Painting

Based on the previous discussion, the framework of visual data storytelling is applied to a case study that transforms big data into art forms and tell a story. The work includes more than 100,000 ecological data from 34 cities, including the capital cities of mainland China and Hong Kong, Macao and Taipei, between 2013 and 2019. Based on the features extracted from the data, the coding system on the artistic style of Chinese landscape painting is constructed, with the purpose of making use of the visually attractive style of landscape painting to make the audience pay attention to and reflect on natural ecological issues. In a practical process, four steps are used to transfer ecological data to Chinese paintings (see Fig. 4).

First of all, environmental issues have been the subject of extensive discussion for a long time, and we try to identify some specific problems. Based on the four steps of the visual data storytelling process, the scenario is set through the analysis for the four sets of ecological data, air quality, water quality, temperature and green coverage ratio. By using web crawlers to collect aerial data and manually collect other data from government reports, the statistical analysis method is used to explore the relationship between data, time and cities. The results of the analysis help to find interesting questions. For example, there are significant differences in the air quality index (AQI) among the cities in the south and north, while the cities in the same river basin have similar data trends. According to this data feature, in-depth exploration can be focused on the group of basin-based cities.

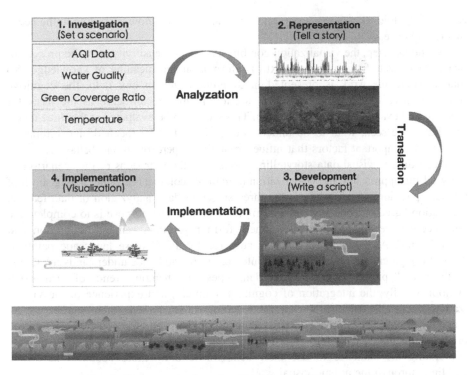

Fig. 4. The process of turning big data into Chinese painting

The four steps and the visualization creation process are described as follows.

Second, in the representation step of telling a story, the topic should be selected according to the data characteristics and what want the audience to know. In this case, although the data set shows that those northern cities are in a harsh environment, there has been a trend of improvement in the recent two years. Therefore, by choosing a theme full of positive hope, this visualization is expected to have an impact on the audience behavior in the future. In order to match the scenario and topic of looking forward to the environment with beautiful mountains and rivers, Chinese landscape painting is used as the main reference style.

The third step is to develop the story by writing a script. In order to communicate effectively, it is necessary to use universal encoding to transform abstract information into concrete perception, so that the audience can easily decode with their memories and experience. For instance, the perception of mountains is usually that the higher the altitude, the greener the color, and the better the air. Consequently, the higher the AQI value, the worse the air quality, which is encoded as a lower altitude and the yellowish color location, and vice versa. Similarly, following encoding rules, other data can be converted into shapes and colors. On the other hand, just like a movie story, visual rhythm can also highlight points and tell vivid stories. In order to make storytelling both poetic and pictorial, the screen slowly scrolls from left to right with background music before triggering the interaction. More label information is displayed rhythmically with interactive events that accompany mouse hover or click. In addition, the story will be told what they want to know or want them to know according to the needs of the audience.

As the last step, the visualization combines aesthetic sensitivity with the process of dealing with data feature, the context of information and meaning of knowledge. No matter where the work is presented in different media in any field, the cognitive processes involved in the visual data storytelling model can serve as the basis for creation and evaluation for visualization. This work can be evaluated at the three levels of what to be seen, what to be understood, and what to be touched, and ultimately identify the important factors that influence audience perception and behavior.

According to visual data storytelling model and the four steps of the scenario and story-telling approaches, the visualization of natural ecological data into a long scroll of Chinese painting is realized from the three stages of data analyzation of data feature, translation based on code system, and implementation. The purpose is to complete the audience's three cognitive levels, namely form perception, semantic cognition and inner feeling. At first, the audience is attracted by the Chinese landscape painting. Then, through careful observation and interaction, the audience understands the theme of the overall picture, as well as the data types and changing trends of each visual symbol. Finally, the integration of cognition, memory, and experience of the visualization touches the audience's response to ecological phenomena, thereby affecting the behavior in natural ecology. The artist's creation process and the audience's cognition process constitute a complete process from "big data" to "Chinese painting", thereby stimulating the audience to use their behavior to draw more beautiful landscape paintings through the artistic visual works.

5   Conclusions and Suggestion

This study proposes a framework of visual data storytelling based on the DIKW model and communication theory, focusing on how the artist affects the creation process from data to visualization, and how the artwork is understood by audience from meaning to insight. Through a case study of transforming "big data" into "Chinese painting", the artist's creation process is analyzed from the four steps of the scenario and story-telling approaches. The results indicate that the approach could be applied to understand data visualization and provide artists with an idea of how to transform the data into art forms and how to tell stories during the creation stage, making it easier for them to communicate with the audience.

The research framework seems to offer a better way to explore the understanding of how "big data" can be transformed into art forms, which clearly deserves further study. Furthermore, detailed creation processes need to be developed in the future to provide artists with specified storytelling procedures for visualization. In addition, it suggests that the audience's cognitive experience be taken into account in the assessment, which is identified as three levels, namely technical, semantic and effectiveness levels.

Acknowledgments. The authors would like to express their sincere thanks to Professor Lin for his guidance in the research. In addition, special thanks to Long et al. for participating in the creation process of the study case in this paper.

References

1. Nathan, Y.: Visualize This: The FlowingData Guide to Design, Visualization, and Statistics. Wiley, Indianapolis (2011)
2. Gershon, N., Page, W.: What storytelling can do for information visualization. Commun. ACM **44**(8), 31–37 (2001)
3. Cairo, A.: The functional Art: An Introduction to Information Graphics and Visualization. New Riders Press, Berkeley (2012)
4. Kosara, R.: Visualization criticism-the missing link between information visualization and art. In: 11th International Conference Information Visualization, pp. 631–636. IEEE, Zurich (2007)
5. Judelman, G.: Aesthetics and inspiration for visualization design: bridging the gap between art and science. In: Paper presented at the proceedings. eighth international conference on information visualisation (2004)
6. Norman, D.A.: Emotional Design: Why We Love (or Hate) Everyday Things. Basic Books, New York (2004)
7. Norman, D.A.: The Design of Everyday Things: Revised and, Expanded edn. Basic Books, New York (2013)
8. Wurman, R.S.: Information Anxiety 2. Que, Indianapolis (2000)
9. Kosara, R., Mackinlay, J.: Storytelling: the next step for visualization. Computer **46**(5), 44–50 (2013)
10. Edward, S., Heer, J.: Narrative visualization: telling stories with data. IEEE Trans. Visual Comput. Graphics **16**(6), 1139–1148 (2010)
11. Chen, M., et al.: Data, information, and knowledge in visualization. IEEE Comput. Graphics Appl. **29**(1), 12–19 (2008)
12. Ackoff, R.L.: From data to wisdom. J. Appl. Syst. Anal. **16**(1), 3–9 (1989)
13. Zeleny, M.: Human systems management: Integrating knowledge, management and systems. World Scientific (2005)
14. Jakobson, R.: Language in Literature. The Belknap Press of Harvard University Press, Cambridge (1987)
15. Lin, R.: Transforming Taiwan aboriginal cultural features into modern product design: a case study of a cross-cultural product design model. Int. J. Des. **1**(2), 45–53 (2007)
16. Lin, R., Lin, P.-H., Shiao, W.-S., Lin, S.-H.: Cultural aspect of interaction design beyond human-computer interaction. In: Aykin, N. (ed.) IDGD 2009. LNCS, vol. 5623, pp. 49–58. Springer, Heidelberg (2009). https://doi.org/10.1007/978-3-642-02767-3_6
17. Lin, C.-L., Chen, J.-L., Chen, S.-J., Lin, R.: The cognition of turning poetry into painting. J. US-China Educ. Rev. **5**(8), 471–487 (2015)
18. Fiske, J.: Introduction to Communication Studies. Routledge, London (1990)
19. Barthes, R.: Elements of Semiology. Hill & Wang, New York (1968)
20. Silverman, K.: The Subject of Semiotics. Oxford University Press, New York (1983)
21. Gao, Y., Wu, J., Lee, S., Lin, R.: Communication between artist and audience: a case study of creation journey. In: Rau, P.-L.P. (ed.) HCII 2019. LNCS, vol. 11577, pp. 33–44. Springer, Cham (2019). https://doi.org/10.1007/978-3-030-22580-3_3
22. Saket, B., Endert, A., Stasko, J.: Beyond usability and performance: a review of user experience-focused evaluations in visualization. In: Proceedings of the Sixth Workshop on Beyond Time and Errors on Novel Evaluation Methods for Visualization, pp. 133–142 (2016)

Research into Development of Auspicious Cultural and Creative Products About Bird-and-Flower Paintings as Decorations for Spring Festival in Guangzhou

Li Ou-Yang[1](✉) and Jie Ling[2,3](✉)

[1] The Guangzhou Academy of Fine Arts, Guangzhou,
People's Republic of China
oylee@163.com
[2] Zhongkai University of Agriculture and Engineering, Guangzhou,
People's Republic of China
47219382@qq.com
[3] Studying School for Doctor's Degree, Shinawatra University,
Bangkok, Thailand

Abstract. The Spring Festival is a traditional festival in China, but there are distinctive regional festival customs across different places. This research intends to focus on auspicious and symbolic decorations for Spring Festival in Guangzhou and adopt bird-and-flower paintings as a means of decorating products, and aims to develop an array of cultural and creative products with regional characteristics based on contemporary daily needs of people through different craftsmanships, colors, expressions and artistic conceptions. This research hopes to stimulate and promote creative life and cultural memory in the new era, advance and enrich the Spring Festival culture in Guangzhou from varied dimensions, enhance people's recognition of traditional festivals, and effectively fuel the economic development of cultural industry based on marrying traditional bird-and-flower paintings in Lingnan with handicraft and by integrating the techniques of graphic and product design.

Keywords: Auspicious cultural · Creative products · Bird-and-flower paintings · Spring festival in guangzhou

1 Presentation of "Flowers" in Traditional Customs of Spring Festival in Guangzhou

Guangzhou is also known as the City of Flowers, since its people are fond of flowers and regard them as part of their lives. In particular, large numbers of flowers and special purchases for the Spring Festival will be put on sale in the market three days before ringing out the Old Year and ringing in the New Year. Aside from purchasing Spring Festival flowers for celebrations in the market, people also deem "Flower Fairs" as an important folk custom, because as a significant medium for prayers in New Year, "flowers" are indispensable items for the New Year.

P.-L. P. Rau (Ed.): HCII 2020, LNCS 12193, pp. 536–547, 2020.
https://doi.org/10.1007/978-3-030-49913-6_44

1.1   Spring Festival "Flower Fair" in Guangzhou

Guangzhou's folk customs are derived from the traditional folk customs of the central plains of China (Xiao 2006). For example, traditional festivals in Canton, such as the Spring Festival, Lantern Festival, Tomb-sweeping Day, Dragon Boat's Festival, Mid-autumn Festival, Double Ninth Festival and Winter Solstice Festival, bear resemblance to the folk customs in the central plains of China. However, the Cantonese folk customs boast their own unique features, especially the life customs of "taking flowers as clothes" and "eating flowers and using fruits as clothes". Flowers and fruits play an essential role in the Cantonese folk customs such as customs in different festivals including flower fair of winter jasmine in the Spring Festival, flower fair in Fangcun District on Human Day, and wearing poet's jasmine to worship Seven Sisters on the Chinese Valentine's Day, and like folk celebrations relating to gods including Shengcai Fair (praying for children and fortune) in the first lunar month, Polo Birth Temple Fair in the second lunar month, and Kamfa Goddess Festival in the fourth lunar month.

Flower fairs have long been held in Guangzhou due to many local flower growers, but it was not until the 1920s that they developed into a proper festival. In 1927, business was dull in Guangzhou, especially flower market. In 1929, "the thriving shops also found it difficult to make a profit, and most industrial and commercial operators lost money". After the founding of the People's Republic of China, Lunar New Year flower fairs gradually picked up, and were familiar to tourists at home and abroad as a distinctive celebration. In 1953, "Lunar New Year flower fairs witnessed an unprecedented gloom. On the nights of the Chinese New Year's Eve and one day before, there were many tourists but few local visitors on the flower fairs in Jianglan Road and Shibafu Road in Xiguan (Liwan District), South Hanmin Road (Yuexue District), and the street in front of Haizhuang Temple (Haizhu District)". After 1956, there were more than 200 flower stands in Jiaoyu Road, specifically, 562, 684, 1,449 and 1,284 in 1961, 1962, 1963 and 1964, respectively. In 1987, the Lunar New Year flower fairs were visited by 3 million people within a short span of three days. In 1966, a three-storey torch was erected in the Lunar New Year flower fair in Xihu Road (Yuexue District), whose foundation comprised over 600 pots of kumquats and calamondins, and more than 1,400 pots of dahlias, pansies, red sages and chrysanthemums. The Lunar New Year flower fairs were since then filled with a sense of celebrations. In 1990, the Lunar New Year flower fairs were opened, with more than 2,300 stands in seven districts, where fish and handicrafts were also available in addition to the traditional Spring Festival flowers.

1.2   Auspicious Connotations of Spring Festival Flowers in Guangzhou

The Spring Festival flowers carry varied meanings of wishes. The meanings of these flowers are connected to traditional Chinese culture, and have become a kind of holiday symbol. Besides, their symbolic meanings are largely associated with the pronunciation of their Chinese names, or their physical characteristics symbolize a certain excellent quality in people. The meanings of symbols commonly used in the Spring Festival are luck, prosperity, longevity, fortune and happiness, such as peony for fortune, reishi mushroom for longevity, lucky bamboo for prosperity, peach blossom for luck and citron for reunion.

The connotation of kumquat in Guangzhou is good luck and great fortune. In the Spring Festival, kumquat is particularly favored by merchants, and they will buy kumquat trees and place them in their commercial premises and homes to express their wishes. During the Spring Festival in Guangzhou, peach blossom carries the connotations of "realizing ambition" and "being lucky in love"; butterfly orchid conveys the meaning of "stroke of luck", and different colors have different connotations (Fig. 1).

Fig. 1. Peach Blossom Spring Festival Guangzhou Huishijia Restaurant. (2020). Source: author's own photograph

1.3   Artistic Expressions of Spring Festival Flowers in Guangzhou

"Suichao" is the first day of the first lunar month, and also called "New Year's Day", "Spring Festival", "Sanchao (first day of the year)", etc. "Suichao tu" (New Year's Painting) is a work to usher in the New Year, praying for good luck, avoiding conflicts and having plenty to eat and wear. Artists of bird-and-flower paintings express their wishes for the New Year by painting "Suichao tu". The motifs of "Suichao tu" fall into three categories including warding off evil spirits, describing customs, and praying with flowers and fruits, with the last category directly relating to flowers.

This kind of paintings often conveys good connotations with homophony of the Chinese names of plants. These paintings also reflect changes in people's life. The collections of "Suichao Tu" by Zhao Chang in the Song Dynasty are the early paintings with a motif of flowers, where he drew peony, narcissus, camellia, peach blossom, bamboo leaves, lakes and stones with exact delineation as well as enriched and bright colours. Dong Xiang in the Song Dynasty painted three containers in his work "Suichao Tu", where varied plants were arranged including cypress tree leaves, plum, camellia, persimmon, reishi mushroom, houseleek and lily. This work was largely drawn in strong lines. Wu Changshuo and Ren Bonian in the Qing Dynasty and Qi Baishi in modern times also drew "Suichao tu" based on their different feelings. Ju Lian also produced many works of this type, such as the "Painting of Elegant Offering for New Year" (size: 28.4 × 30.8 cm) in 1887, where he painted peony, narcissus, chrysanthemum, grapes, peach, papaya, persimmon, etc. In his other work "Suicao Tu" (size: 75 × 26.5 cm) in 1894, he drew peach blossom, peony, narcissus, bergamot, persimmon, grapes, melon, peach, pumpkin, etc. Besides, in the "Painting of

Elegant Offering for New Year" (size: 85 × 35.5 cm) in 1897, he again painted peach blossoms, peony, chrysanthemums, narcissus, citrus, grapes, peach, bergamot, persimmon, reishi mushroom, citron, etc.

2 Insights into Cultural and Creative Products About Bird-and-Flower Paintings

There are two types of techniques for bird-and-flower paintings, namely, fine brushwork and freehand brushwork. Painting the same flower using these two techniques will produce different effects. To be specific, the shapes in freehand brushwork are more relatively impressionistic, where the color or shape is largely similar to, rather than exactly the same as, the natural objects. By contrast, fine brushwork paintings require more precise shapes. For instance, the above two paintings of peach blossoms for good luck were the works of the same painter, but they differ in shape and expression (Figs. 2 and 3).

Fig. 2. Freehand brushwork: Peach Blossom by Zhou. Y. (2007). Source: Zhou (2011).

Fig. 3. Fine brushwork: Peach Blossom by Zhou. Y. (1998). Source: Zhou (1999).

To transform a painting into a product, the primary method now is to transfer part or all of the painting to the surface of the product, and the design of creative products has been completed. However, this is nowhere near the creative design of bird-and-flower paintings. This method can display the whole piece of bird-and-flower painting, but it cannot present the characteristics of such painting. The design of creative products entails considering and integrating the technical and cultural characteristics of products and bird-and-flower paintings, so that the characteristics of such products and paintings can be matched and blended. This paper attempts to probe into how to make innovations from a border-less perspective, and will approach from the following three angles, i.e. association of shape, re-interpretation of meanings and craftsmanship expression.

2.1 Association of Shape – Designing Product Appearance from the Perspective of Shape

The graphic shapes are easily recognized by people, so the content of the bird-and-flower paintings is easily accessible to them. However, those who are strange to the cultural meanings of these paints may just find them very nice without knowing their meanings. The particular meanings of a product are not straightforwardly emphasized in its appearance, but the shape of bird-and-flower paintings will be expressed with the help of products or auxiliary products. In this way, people can first see this shape, and then understand and interpret a product based on their own cultural background.

Appearance of Products. Despite differences in the presentation methods of painting techniques, drawings on paper are two-dimensional works while creative products have both two-dimensional and three-dimensional structures. If a two-dimensional work is converted into a three-dimensional structure one, different methods are required. The design will focus on the external shape of a product, meaning that shapes of elements are adopted to create the appearance of a product. For example, if the object to be designed is peach blossom, then the shape of the product can be directly modeled on that of the peach blossom. This shape is divided into the shape of a product's main part and packaging (Figs. 4 and 5).

Fig. 4. Qing Emperor Qianlong's Enamel Flower Double Boxes for Life Expectation. Source: website of Guangdong Museum, http://www.gdmuseum.com/gdmuseum/_300746/_300758/zx59/431241/index.html

Fig. 5. Qing Emperor Qianlong's Enamel Flower Double Boxes for Life Expectation Guangdong Museum. Source: website of Guangdong Museum, http://www.gdmuseum.com/gdmuseum/_300746/_300758/zx59/431241/index.html

When the shape of the main part draws on that of elements in bird-and-flower paintings, it can be an overall or partial shape. The overall shape means that three-dimensional construction of product is directly modeled on the three-dimensional shape of bird-and-flower paintings; partial modeling means that the design only uses elements in the bird-and-flower paintings as decorations or certain functions in the design. Additionally, shapes of the carriers of bird-and-flower paintings can be a reference too. The traditional carriers of these paintings include hand fans and hanging scrolls. Special shapes have particular meanings in Chinese culture. For instance, gift boxes in such shapes as hexagon, octagon and regular polygon can be traced back to a long time ago, representing endlessness or blessings of luck, prosperity and longevity. Round shape symbolizes reunion, while square shape signifies round sky above square Earth.

Addition or reduction can be employed in reference for packaging of products. Addition means that an external shape or the shape of elements in bird-and-flower paintings can be drawn on and added to the basic shape. On the contrary, reduction means that the packaging of a product can be hollowed out in the shape of elements in bird-and-flower paintings.

Decoration of Products. The two-dimensional language graphics in products with a certain shape plays a paramount role in the design of cultural and creative products. The language of flowers and birds in a work substantially enriches the graphics language, and further, imbues the graphics with the spirit of the times. The traditional language of bird-and-flower paintings is matched with corresponding graphic forms according to the characteristics of products for the Spring Festival as well as their overall shape (Fig. 6).

Fig. 6. Venchi's New Year gift box. Hong Kong (2020). Source: http://tsimshatsui.k11.com/Venchi/post/239894.aspx

Decorative Graphics. The Spring Festival flowers are embedded into the surface of a product as decorative graphics. For example, flowers and branches are rotated around the center as a pivot on the New Year gift box of Venchi, and decorate the surface of the entire round box.

Simplified Graphics. The shape of the Spring Festival flowers is simplified as vector graphics or stylistic graphics for repeated decorations. Such graphics can be used in combination or separately.

Painting Graphics. Painting graphics are based on traditional artistic expressions and learn from the graphics in such artistic forms as bird-and-flower paintings in fine brushwork or in freehand brushwork among traditional Chinese paintings, watercolor bird-and-flower paintings, or pencil drawings.

2.2 Re-Interpretation of Meanings – Designing Product Shape from Extensional Meanings of Bird-and-Flower Paintings

There are two possibilities for the expressions of bird-and-flower paintings in product design. First, the existing products need the symbolic meanings of bird-and-flower paintings to add cultural meanings to them; second, brand-new products are designed based on the extensional meanings of bird-and-flower paintings. The meanings of bird-and-flower paintings are sophisticated and cannot be deciphered at the first glance, so re-interpretation is required. The Bauhaus design style is a preferable re-interpretation medium. After comprehending the Chinese culture, designers can summarize it into a variety of symbols through the Western design thinking, and then enable people in different countries to understand the meanings of these symbols once they see the symbols. Or corresponding symbols of bird-and-flower paintings will show up once people from different countries can enter their own languages, so meanings can be re-interpreted.

When used as symbols, the elements in bird-and-flower paintings can only convey some meanings like technique, color and composition. Therefore, such elements should be connected with the above meanings, and the meanings to be expressed designed. Corresponding elements are selected for design. Although the original paintings are not directly or entirely presented in the product design, the hidden inner connections can also be identified in the product.

Characteristics of Line Drawing. Bird-and-flower paintings in fine brushwork contain a line called modified contour line, which is like a tight and strong iron wire. Some line is called earthworm line, which is outlined in a rounded and segmented fashion and resembles a twisted earthworm. Some line is named nail head with mouse tail, whose first stroke is like a nail and whose last stroke is like a thin mouse tail. The above characteristic symbols can be converted into the ways of font design and the characteristics of lines of shapes.

Characteristics of Color. The heavy-coloring technique in bird-and-flower paintings can exhibit brilliant and magnificent colors, so as to arouse a feeling of sublimity and admiration. By contrast, the techniques of bird-and-flower paintings in freehand brushwork can reveal manifold degrees of black under different penetrations of ink and xuan paper, allowing people to envision an illusory and misty forest. The bird-and-flower paintings of different schools will have varying viewpoints of colors, and the feelings generated by the colors are diverse. Hence, selecting the bird-and-flower paintings and products which express the same characteristics, and designing products with a focus on the symbolic characteristics of colors can bring more diversified imaginations of artistic conceptions to the products.

Characteristics of Composition. Composition refers to the relationship of objects and their position in a picture, and the composition of bird-and-flower paintings is based on a complete system of theories. Designers can design simplified symbols using the theories about the composition of bird-and-flower paintings, and reconstruct the symbols to produce new patterns. Moreover, it can design products from the internal thinking mode to more proactively integrate Chinese and Western cultures.

2.3   Craftsmanship Expression – Considering Material and Structure of Products from Local Craftsmanship

The craftsmanships at which different times and regions are adept have their own characteristics. Traditional bird-and-flower paintings are outlined by professional painters, and then produced by different artisans. For example, cloisonné enamelling during the Ming and Qing Dynasties refer to a technique of enamelling an object whereby flat copper wires are bent into the required shapes onto the cloisons into which enamel paste is applied before the object is fired and polished. Lacquering is a traditional and distinctive Chinese craft, and is a decorative method which is mainly applied to wooden ware. It is divided into three categories, including Maki-e, mother-of-pearl inlay and carved lacquer, of which the first one emphasizes painting while the latter two are mainly ornamental. Famille rose is a process of painting directly on the clay body and then molding by firing. The painting styles are diversified by learning from the techniques of traditional Chinese paintings or decorative patterns. Besides, a single color or a range of colors can be used as appropriate.

Modern design and expressions generally involve printing process, say, UV, gilding, bulging, die cutting, coating, varnishing, bronze printing, spot-color printing, gold and silver powder coating, electrostatic flocking, indentation, etc.

Using traditional or modern techniques alone to express bird-and-flower paintings pose certain limitations in product innovation. If designers only use traditional craftsmanship for expression, perhaps the craftsmanship has been lost, or the long-term costs of craftsmanship do not fit the positioning of a product. In case of using modern process only, there are no barriers to such process, easily giving rise to similarities and to difficulties in gaining competitive edges. Circumstances vary in different places, so do their specialities and craftsmanship characteristics. Therefore, while considering how to slash the production cost of a product, designers should maximize the advantages of local craftsmanship. From the angle of craftsmanship, designers need to merge the characteristics of traditional and modern craftsmanship, and re-define the priorities in designing modern products in connection with bird-and-flower paintings. Meanwhile, they should create new ways of product mix, which is also a desired perspective.

3 Development of Creative Products Based on Bird-and-Flower Paintings as Auspicious Symbols

It is the most important design and development task to develop creative products that can add to the festive atmosphere of the New Year. Auspicious symbols and bird-and-flower paintings are special regional traditions. From the international perspective of the global village, it is a trend to design with symbols easy to understand by people all over the world and with regional characteristics. Therefore, the design technique of Bauhaus coupled with the way of thinking for flower-and-bird paintings can render barrier-free communication.

To this end, we can create a product development model. First, we investigate the market demand and learn special regional crafts to determine which type of products can meet the local demand. Then, we analyze the collected data to help designers identify the type of symbols, themes, and targets. We integrate the idea of creative products based on bird-and-flower paintings with the techniques of flower-and-bird paintings, graphic design, and product design to formulate product development strategies. After releasing products to the market, we collect feedback for iterative development (Table 1).

Table 1. Creative product development model

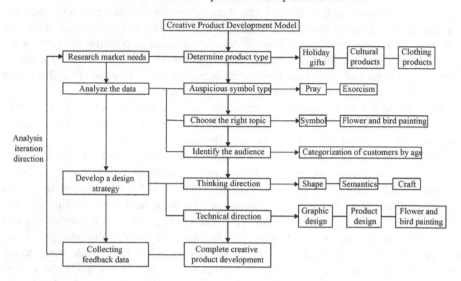

Take the three types of cultural and creative products, namely, Spring Festival gifts, cultural products, and apparel, for example. We analyze how to add auspicious symbols of Guangzhou to the development of creative products based on flower-and-bird paintings and a model.

3.1 Spring Festival Gifts

Product Development Based on Traditional Bird-and-Flower Paintings. Fan products: Round silk fans are a representative gift among men of letters in Suzhou. It is suitable to send them to literati and women. Porcelains with the traditional pattern of bird-and-flower or integrating the processes of Guangdong decorated ware reflect the characteristics of Guangzhou and are gifts or products of choice. Such porcelains have a high cost and are made manually. Hence, such porcelains can be considered for the development of products with a high-end demand or a high development budget.

Development of Gifts Decorated with Bird-and-Flower Paintings. Hexagonal, octagonal, and round gift boxes can be decorated with the pattern of flowers and birds. The grade of gift boxes can be determined by material and process. Moreover, gift boxes can be wrapped with embroidery fabrics to raise their grade. Lacquer boxes are popular and precious gift boxes. The surface is decorated with lacquer paintings of flowers and birds or mother-of-pearl buttons.

Development of Gifts in Flower Shapes. Gift boxes in an unconventional shape can be raised to a higher level through the concept of connotation. A gift box in the shape of a peach blossom will stimulate consumers to think about the connotation of a peach blossom. A peach blossom implies good luck in adventures with men or women in China.

Red Envelopes are Must-have Products for the Chinese New Year. People in Guangzhou give more red envelopes than those in other areas in China during the Spring Festival. As long as you are not married, you can accept a red envelope. Therefore, red envelopes are within the scope of product development. Patterns of bird-and-flower, buzzwords, and special printing skills give collection significance to red envelopes. Each red envelope embodies the Spring Festival culture of Guangzhou (Fig. 7).

Fig. 7. K11 New Year Li-Shi. Hong Kong (2020). Source: https://www.facebook.com/k11ArtMall/posts/10162851990580274

3.2 Apparel

Bird-and-flower painting is a traditional form of art. When added to apparel, including brooches, scarves, and hairpins, flower-and-bird paintings create a unique aesthetic feeling. Generally, more flower-and-bird paintings are applied to women's apparel. However, we can also ponder about how to integrate such paintings into men's apparel. For instance, we can adopt different design contents and forms.

Women's apparel can be given to friends and relatives as gifts. It is relatively easy to apply bird-and-flower paintings to scarves or kerchiefs. Due to the different shapes of scarves, a variety of patterns of flowers and birds can be selected. A bird-and-flower painting can be used in whole or in part. Furthermore, the pop style can be blended with patterns of flowers and birds to produce a special visual effect. Shanghai Tang has added patterns of flowers and birds to its new season of silk scarves.

Bird-and-flower paintings can also be coupled with brooches. The contour of peach blossoms and twigs can be three-dimensional. Petals can be embroidered. The overall effect will be dignified and graceful. Such a brooch is perfect to rest at the clothes or scarf of a woman. The flower series of brooches designed and produced by the Guangzhou studio reflect the local festival feature.

The space of creation for men's apparel can be bigger. Men's kerchiefs, collar buckles, ties, and bow ties are all included. The style and color of design are better to be more low-key and restrained. Embroidery can also be applied to ties, resulting in a different visual effect (Fig. 8).

Fig. 8. Peach Blossom Brooch Guangzhou Youxiu Beauty Studio. Source: author's own photograph

3.3 Cultural Products

Cultural products are a direction of creative product development. The strategy is to present cultural products in a package. A single cultural product can be fragmentary and small. A package of cultural products can share the same design keynote and result in a better effect. You can buy a package for yourself or others. They can also be used as business gifts. Packages can vary in form and content. A stationery package can include pencils, pens, notebooks, and tapes. They can be decorated with Cantonese-style patterns of flowers and birds or abstract patterns of bird-and-flower to raise the aesthetic taste of consumers. Ordinary stationeries will look artistic. Folk customs and regional information are integrated into daily life.

A calendar package can include a calendar, red envelopes, notebooks, and couplets. The element of New Year flowers of Guangzhou can be added to the package. Processes and paper can be designed in an innovative manner. Patterns, processes, and materials can be designed and combined.

Patterns of flowers and birds are applied to furnishing articles, besides brooches, to indicate an auspicious meaning. Such furnishing articles are popular among consumers. During the Spring Festival, people in Guangzhou like to buy flower bonsai in the flower market to decorate their homes. However, such bonsai tend to wither in about one month. In contrast, furnishing articles with patterns of bird-and-flower are not restricted by seasons and can be placed at home all year round.

4 Conclusion

Traditional culture is the most valuable regional resource as well as the most fundamental element of cultural identity. The Spring Festival is not only an important festival in China, but also is celebrated across the cultural circles of overseas Chinese. Thanks to the vast territory and time-honored history of China, festival cultures in different regions have formed their distinctive expressions over the course of historical development. Therefore, the research, development, and promotion of cultural and creative products concerning festivals need to respect local traditional customs, lifestyles and popular cultures. Development strategies for such products should be customized by means of sufficient research and data analysis. Besides, the cultural exchanges between countries should be taken into account, so development of such products should use an internationally common product language. Only in this way can cultural and creative products be incorporated with cultural characteristics of traditional festivals, to serve the purpose of enhancing people's recognition of such festivals, creating cultural life and cultural memory for the new era, and effectively propelling the economic development of cultural industry.

Acknowledgment. Projects: Cultural Comparison of Traditional Festival Products between Guangdong and Hong Kong and Innovation and Development of Cultural and Creative Products (2017WTSCX065).

We thank Guangdong Provincial Department for funding this study.

References

Xiao, F.: Spring festivals and seasonal rites of passage. J. Beijing Normal Univ. (Soc. Sci.) **06**, 50–58 (2006)

Zhou, Y.: Zhou Yansheng Fan Painting Art. Lingnan Fine Arts Press, Guangzhou (1999)

Zhou. Y.: Zhou Yansheng's Collection of Fine Brushwork and Freehand Brushwork. Great Wall Art Press, GuangZhou (2011)

Application of Auspicious Cultural in Metalworking Jewelry Design

Minghong Shi[1,3(✉)], Chi Zhang[2(✉)], Yiwen Ting[3(✉)],
and Po-Hsien Lin[3(✉)]

[1] Shenzhen Technology University,
Shenzhen, Guangdong, People's Republic of China
jun101786@126.com
[2] Beijing Institute of Fashion Technology, Beijing, People's Republic of China
chizhang.c@foxmail.com
[3] Graduate School of Creative Industry Design,
National Taiwan University of Arts, New Taipei City, Taiwan
adingl113@gmail.com, t0131@mail.ntua.edu.tw

Abstract. This paper aims to explore how metal craft creators practices craft to create metalwork jewelry implanted through cultural connotation to finally achieve the communication between the creator and the viewer or wearer, based on the author's personal experience in metalworking creation and by using the research method of constructing three stages of design process. In the example listed, the auspicious culture, as one part of Chinese profound culture, is transformed into the visual form of metalwork jewelry via the artistic language of metalwork creation, facilitating viewers to interpret the concept of the creator through creation, so as to maximize the reading validity of the viewers. Research results show that this research method can be applied in metalworking creation, and effectively help viewers to fully understand the connotation of works. This research provides an advanced way to explore the understanding of how connotation can be transformed into physical form, which is obviously worth studying. This research is divided into three stages. In the first stage, through literature review, by practicing communication cognitive theory and the method to extract situational stories, an evaluation criteria is established. In the second stage, a research framework is constructed to carry out the physical transformation of metalworking art language, and to explore the feasibility of research methods. By taking questionnaire analysis, feasibility of the evaluation method used in metalworking creation is examined and evaluated to check the effectiveness of this research method. In the third stage, relative suggestions are proposed for the reference of further researches.

Keywords: Auspicious culture · Metalwork jewelry · Communication · Cognition

1 Introduction

Artistic creation has been assumed, Art creators arouse the emotions of the audience by art creation, and they make efforts to materialize some specific feelings. However, creators also find it difficult to clarify what exactly this feeling is [2]. For example, a

© Springer Nature Switzerland AG 2020
P.-L. P. Rau (Ed.): HCII 2020, LNCS 12193, pp. 548–558, 2020.
https://doi.org/10.1007/978-3-030-49913-6_45

creator tries to express his feelings from the material beauty he or she feels or the inspiration got from the contemplation of natural things, which, from the perspective of communication theory, can be interpreted as the process of encoding by the artist. Bell claims that the characteristics of works of art lie in the need to arouse people's aesthetic feelings ultimately. And artists feel that their works of art must be appropriate. No matter what aspect a work of art looks like, as long as it expresses the artist's feelings for reality or can arouse others' aesthetic feelings, then this work of art can be regarded as appropriate. As for how to identify an artist's work as appropriate, author thinks that two aspects are needed. One is expression or called encoding and the other is arousing or called decoding. A successful work of art also requires the artist to effectively transmit ideological content of the work to the audience. The process of the audience reading of the artist's work is called decoding.

The author wishes to build a proper mode to express and narrate metalworking creation from the perspective of personal professional field, and then discuss the communication mode and cognitive mode of metalworking creation taking communication cognitive theory. As there are few researches on creation theorization in the field of metalwork jewelry, the author starts researching from a set of metalwork jewelry works ever created to explain the design process from the image level, semantic level and result level. It encodes the content through three levels of communication, and then sends out messages to expect viewers to decode with highest efficiency. Through research and verification, this paper also explores the feasibility of this method, and then builds a metalworking creation model, aiming to provide reference for metalworking creators.

2 Literature Review

Artistic creation has been assumed, discussed and studied by scholars for a long time. As a form of communication, there is an unusual network in it. However, researches conducted on artistic creation weren't launched from perspective of communication until just recently. Communications, an important exposition in 20th century, is a research field introduced in recent 60 years. With the introduction of mass media technology and its explosive increase, the nature and the methods of communication have undergone major changes, and communications itself also accordingly changed at the same pace. The contemporary significance of communications is reflected in many personal communication theories and models that have developed since 1949, when the field emerged. The widespread application of its theories in various fields of culture also shows its contemporary importance [10].

Craig, R. T. believed that communication theories can be practically applied in many aspects of culture, which by the large demonstrated art could change with the development of communication [3]. Goldman, A. pointed that art evaluation requires communication between artists and audiences. Art should not only participate in social context but also be sublimated to interactive experience between artists and audiences [6]. As a powerful means and media of communication, art is also regarded as a process of social interaction. It's a process of how artists' works are conceived, developed, transmitted and accepted, and also a process of how audiences are attracted and accurately understand them. In addition, researches conducted on how audiences are influenced by works are also needed [8]. Mass communication theory provides a metaphysical theoretical basis for encoding and decoding connections among artists, works and audiences, which are three elements of art. Durham, G. and professor Kellner, D. expounded three phenomenons that occurs in the general process of encoding and decoding. The phenomena include correct understanding, controversial understanding and the one that are contrary to the original meaning [4]. Communication relationship includes two actors (the sender and the receiver) as well as the message transmitted and received. The sender translates nonmaterial message into physical medium or carrier to the receiver. Then the receiver translates the medium into the message that sender wants to convey [9]. Based on the theory above, professor Lin, R. constructed a theoretical framework for intercommunication between viewers and artists during creation process in his research on how to transform poetry into paintings, and also a corresponding research framework for art recognition and evaluation [7].

In contemporary art, jewelry is defined as the carrier of time and culture, which has potential capacity to communicate or convey information. We can foresee a whole picture from a small starting point and jewelry serving as a clue through which we can capture the characteristics of an era [1]. Some communication theories can be used in explaining the main communication relations in the process of expounding art forms. Based on three levels of "creative connotation" of art works, which include technical level of shape perception, semantic level of cognition significance and result level of inner feeling, it encodes the "message" of metalworking jewelry and then verify the effectiveness of the research by evaluating the message received by receiver [5].

3   Methodology

3.1   Construction of Three Steps in Design Process

The research adopts communication and cognition theories. And based on theories, this paper constructs a three-steps method in metalworking jewelry design process that have auspicious meanings from technical level of appearance perception, semantic level of significance cognition and result level of inner feeling. And based on those three levels, this paper aims to realize encode mode as shown in Fig. 1.

On the first technical level of shape perception, designers firstly conceive and design auspicious image and then put forward eight auspicious words and expressions according to the design requirement after recognizing the requiring images and contents. At last they select some classic and auspicious elements corresponding to auspicious words and expressions. On the second semantic level of cognition significance, the author combine auspicious indication with Chinese aesthetic, and put forward a three "based on" target, vividly showing appearance based on original topic, clearly

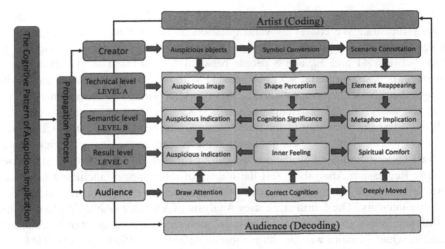

Fig. 1. The cognitive pattern of auspicious implication (compiled by the research)

expressing auspicious meaning based on its original image, truly performing anthro-
pomorphic sense based on the auspicious meaning recognized in common sense.
Namely, in accordance with auspicious indication, the work need to meet the targets
above. The vivid image should give full play to morphological characteristics of the
auspicious elements, so that the audience can clearly understand the image indication
of the work in viewing. And then through the interpretation of the image, the audience
can associate it with auspicious meaning behind metaphor implication. At last, with the
better understanding of the auspicious meaning, the aesthetic spirits of eastern nations
are conveyed. After three "based on" above are met, it constructs a scenario based on
the descriptive content of auspicious words and expressions to design an ideal auspicious pattern. On the third result level of inner feeling, traditional techniques and skills
are applied to create special texture that meet contemporary aesthetic standard, so that
the shape of the work reflects its symbolic meaning. And then through element reap-
pearing, auspicious meaning is conveyed. Final goal is audiences are deeply moved and
comprehend the auspicious metaphor implication and designers' ideas and purpose in
feeling stratification.

3.2 Questionnaire Analysis

After reviewing literature, this research verifies the feasibility of methodology by
attributes assessment and online questionnaire. Questionnaire set questions from
technical level (whether the workmanship is exquisite), semantic level (whether the
work is ingenious) and result level (audiences' feelings about the work), and also set
questions like preference level and creativity intensity of each work. Question 9 is a
single choice to match different works with auspicious words and expressions. Question 10–11 are set as single choice to choose your favorite work and the most auspicious work form eight works.

A total of 51 subjects are divided into four age groups, most of whom are related to the art profession. We collect 51 valid questionnaires, 24 from males and 27 from females. There are 21 people between 19 and 30, 8 people between 31 and 40, 14 people between 41 and 50, and 8 people between 51 and 60. The overall attributes assessment is based on Likert's 5-point scale (1 with the lowest agreement and 5 with the highest agreement) for questionnaire survey. After sorted, the questionnaires collected are analyzed and tested by software SPSS. The first stage takes reliability analysis to test the reliability of the questionnaire. The second stage uses Chi-square test to test whether sex or age can influence subjects' preference degree of eight works and their understandings of auspicious meaning behind the work. The third stage uses Multiple Regression Analysis to test the impact of three factors, including technical, semantic and result factors, on subjects' preference degree of eight works and works' creativity intensity. The fourth stage uses Analysis of Variance (ANOVA) to examine the differences in four age groups in subjects' preference degree and works' creativity intensity. (Questionnaire website: https://forms.gle/JriJWmrbP7M9ngLA8) (Table 1).

Table 1. Questionnaire

Title	Description	1	2	3	4	5
Technical level	Is the workmanship of this work consummate					
Semantic level	Does the work convey auspicious meaning in a clever way					
Result level	How is your auspicious feeling on this work					
Preference	How much do you like this work					
Creative intensity	How is the creative strength of this work?					
Please choose the word you think correspond to each of these eight works						
Which of these eight works do you like best						
Which of these eight works do you think can best reflect the auspicious meaning						

4   Research Results and Discussion

The reliability analysis of the questionnaire aims to discuss the internal consistency of the various dimension of the scale, and the reduction of the Cronbach's alpha from each dimension after deleting one single question, as a reference standard for selecting the question and assessing reliability of the scale. According to questionnaire analysis, Cronbach's alpha is .823. Total relevant situation of the correction of each dimension in single choice ranges from .572 to .783. The situation after deleting alpha coefficient ranges from .744 to .824, which demonstrate the internal consistency between questions is high. Thus the questionnaire has credibility. This research scale table has also been reviewed and revised by experts and scholars proving this questionnaire validity and authority.

4.1 Analysis of Preference Degree of the Works and Understandings of Auspicious Meaning Behind the Works Among Different Genders and Ages

According to the analysis, subjects of different sexes, or from different age groups presents no significant differences in preference degree of the work and understandings of auspicious meaning behind the work. In terms of preference degree of different genders, males choosing products E and H both account for 14.3%, which is highest in male group. Females choosing product H account for 26.5% and who choose product A account for 10.2%. It can be seen from this the product H is the most preferred among men and women, and genders or ages have no impact on their preference degree. A good product is suitable for all ages. In terms of understandings of auspicious behind the works, the percentages of men and women who choose product A are highest, with men accounting for 16% and women account for 14%, namely a total percentage of 30%. It can be seen from this the product A is the product that all people, whether men or women, believe conveying auspicious meaning (Tables 2 and 3).

Table 2. Preference degree of the works among different age groups or genders

Rank	1	2	3	4	5	6	7	8
No.	H	E	D	A	G	F	B	C
Product								
Percentage of Total	26.5	20.4	14.3	12.2	10.2	8.2	6.1	2.0

Table 3. Creativity intensity order judged by different age groups or genders

Rank	1	2	3	4	5	6	7	8
No.	A	E	H	B	D	G	F	C
Product								
Percentage of Total	30.0	20.0	16.0	12.0	12.0	6.0	4.0	0

4.2   Analysis of Preference Degree of the Works from Technical, Semantic and Result Levels

According to test above, product A is the favorite work. Correlation coefficient of product A is analyzed and there is a significant difference. As shown in Table 4 below, the three predictor variables are correlated to product A. The three predictor variables and their correlation coefficients are .209, .439 and .202 respectively. Based on Multiple Regression Analysis in the table below, the correlation coefficient R of overall predictor variable and dependent variable is .685. The explained variation of three predictor variables for product A is 47%, and F value equals 13.869, which reaches a significant level of .000. And among them, the most significant predictor variable is semantic level a2 with β value equaling to .389, which reaches a significant level of .018. The result indicates that three levels are significantly correlated to preference degree of product A. And the preference degree of product A can be jointly explained and predicted from three levels. The most significant level is semantic level.

Table 4. Multiple regression analysis of preference degree from technical, semantic and result levels

Model		B	Std. error	Beta	t	Sig.
Preference to work	Technical level a1	.209	.136	.187	1.533	.132
	Semantic level a2	.439	.178	.389	2.461	.018**
	Result level a3	.202	.122	.239	1.656	.104
	Constant	.148				

R = .685 Rsq = .470 F = .13.869 Sig = .000
*p < .05 **p < .01 ***p < .001

4.3   Analysis of Creativity Intensity of the Works from Technical, Semantic and Result Levels

According to the test above, product H has the highest creativity intensity. The correlation coefficient of product H is analyzed and there is a significant difference. As shown in Table 5 below, the three predictor variables are correlated to product H. The three predictor variables and their correlation coefficients are .330, .349 and .341. The correlation coefficient R of overall predictor variable and dependent variable is .813. The explained variation of three predictor variables for product H is 66.1%, and the F value equals 30.546, which reaches a significant level of .000. And among them, the most significant predictor variable is technical level h1. And β value of technical level equals .280, which reaches a significant level of .022, β value of semantic level h2 equals .314, which reaches a significant level of .034, the β value of result level h3 equals .319, which reaches a significant level of .021. The result indicates that three levels are significantly correlated to people's understandings of creativity intensity. And to a considerable extent, creativity intensity of product H can be jointly explained and predicted form three levels, in order of result level h3, technical level h1 and semantic level h2.

Table 5. Multiple regression analysis of creativity intensity of product H from technical, semantic and result levels

Model	Constant	B	Std. error	Beta	t	Sig.
Preference to work	Technical level h1	.330	.140	.280	2.361	.022*
	Semantic level h2	.349	.160	.314	2.181	.034*
	Result level h3	.341	.143	.319	2.395	.021*
	Constant	−.202				

R = .813 Rsq = .661 F = 30.546 Sig = .000
*p < .05 **p < .01 ***p < .001

4.4 Analysis of Preference Degree of the Works and Creativity Intensity Among Different Age Groups

As shown in Table 6 and according to the ANOVA of different age groups and preference degree of works, there are significant differences among product E, F and G. After test of significance, the F values respectively equal 3.664, 2.836 and 3.405, all of which are below the significant level of .05. According to the result of Scheffe analyzing, people between 51 to 60 prefer works most, while people between 41 to 50 prefer works least. There is no significant difference in ANOVA of different age groups and preference degree, so people's understandings of creativity intensity of eight products designed in the research are almost same for all age. All the average creativity intensity reach more than 3 points except product C whose average creativity intensity is 2.98. The information above demonstrate subjects agree to the creativity intensity of the eight works in the research.

Table 6. ANOVA of different age groups and preference degree of works

Model		SS	DF	MS	F	Sig.	Group(age)	M	SD	Scheffe
e	Between groups	11.546	3	3.849	3.644	.019**	1.19–30(n = 21)	3.33	.966	4 > 1> 2 > 3
	Within groups	49.631	47	1.056			2.31–40 (n = 8)	3.13	.991	
	Total	61.176	50				3.41–50(n = 14)	2.64	1.216	
							4.51–60 n = 8)	4.13	.835	
							Total	3.24	1.106	
f	Between groups	8.968	3	2.989	2.836	.048**	1.19–30(n = 21)	3.48	1.078	4 > 1> 2 > 3
	Within groups	49.542	47	1.054			2.31–40(n = 8)	3.38	.916	
	Total	58.510	50				3.41–50(n = 14)	2.93	1.141	
							4.51–60(n = 8)	4.25	.707	
							Total	3.43	1.082	
g	Between groups	6.203	3	2.068	3.405	.025**	1.19–30(n = 21)	3.67	.658	4 > 2> 1 > 3
	Within groups	28.542	47	.607			2.31–40(n = 8)	3.38	.916	
	Total	34.745	50				3.41–50(n = 14)	3.00	.877	
							4.5–60(n = 8)	4.00	.756	
							Total	3.49	.834	

556   M. Shi et al.

4.5 Analysis of Matching Degree Between the Works and Auspicious Words and Expressions

According to the Confusion Matrix in Table 7, it can be seen that the result of the ninth question about matching degree between eight works and auspicious word and expressions is: 4 works are correctly matched with according words and expressions. Namely, half of them are highly recognized. Product G is correctly matched most so it's easiest to recognize, followed by product H, A and C. Product D and B are correctly matched least so its scenario is the least consistent with auspicious words and expressions. And the others' matching degree can be inferred from the data corresponding to each row and column. The correct matches of product C and the wrong matches of product F, are 17 and 18 respectively, most people mistaking product F for C.

Table 7. Analysis of matches between eight works and auspicious words and expressions

Title	As Longevity As Crane	Crane of Thousands Years' Life	Birthday Wishes from Dual Bats	As Noble As Red-crowned Crane	Crane and Pine with Infinite Youth	Thousands Years old Flat Peach	Enjoy Longevity	Crane with Auspicious Clouds
Item Number	A	B	C	D	E	F	G	H
As Longevity As Crane and Pine	19	12	1	5	11	0	0	1
Crane of Thousands Years' Life	9	5	2	19	6	0	2	6
Birthday Wishes from Dual Bats	4	2	17	4	0	18	3	1
As Noble As Red-crowned Crane	7	10	7	5	5	3	9	0
Crane and Pine with Infinite Youth	4	9	1	16	8	2	0	8
Thousands Years old Flat Peach	4	3	14	2	6	10	7	1
Enjoy Longevity	4	1	5	2	3	3	22	7
Crane with Auspicious Clouds	5	6	4	2	1	8	2	21

5 Summary

1. Among all the subjects, people between 51 to 60 preferred products designed in the research most, and people between 41 to 50 preferred least. There is no difference in preference degree of works and understanding of auspicious meaning behind works among subjects from different age groups. It is obvious that metalworking jewelry with auspicious culture studied in the research can be accepted by all ages, most of whom also highly understand the auspicious meaning behind the works.
2. Different genders and ages neither influence audiences' preference degree nor influence their views on auspicious meaning behind the works. Males and females both preferred product H most. And they all believe the product A has the most auspicious meaning.
3. Technical, semantic and result levels are related to people's preference degree and creativity intensity of products A and H.
4. Semantic level affects the degree of preference of works in the most remarkable way.
5. These three levels are significantly related to the cognition of creativity intensity of product H. Relevance of creativity intensity in product H is in the order of result level h3, technical level h1 and semantic level h2.
6. The product G performs best in matching works with auspicious words and expressions due to its homophonic feature. From the level of shape perception, the image of "cat" and "butterfly" in the works are clear enough for viewers to easily associate them with the title of the work "enjoy longevity". Product F is mistaken for product C because they both have the image of "peach". But in product C, the image of "peach" is bigger than that of "bat". And compared with product F, the image of "peach" is more realistic and vivid. Reasons above may lead to visual confusion. The questionnaire results show that, when matching auspicious words and expressions with the works, we should lay more emphasis on the shape level of the work to make the image of work more prominent and directly perceived when creating.

6 Conclusion and Suggestions

Metalworking jewelry with auspicious meaning need to carry elements that the public prefers, so that the audience can feel the auspicious atmosphere and vibe by watching or wearing jewelry. And such jewelry works also need to resonate with the audiences' hearts and construct the association of scenario. On how to more effectively convey auspicious meaning, the research put forward a three-steps method from technical, semantic and result levels with three "based on", which also combine with oriental aesthetics. And this paper takes scientific assessment and verification to prove the methodology is effective.

According to questionnaire result, the subjects' understandings of the auspicious meaning behind the works are almost consistent. The jewelry with auspicious meaning is more popular and accepted by senior people. They need to understand information in a more direct way compared with young people. It is needed to strengthen the work on technical level to more accurately express the auspicious meaning. Jewelry works should be designed in a more concrete and direct way, so that audience can clearly understand the design ideas that the designers want to express when appreciating the work. Designer should also pay more attention to factors on technical, semantic and result level. In this way, design works will be more creative while deepening the factors on semantic level. Namely, the content of the work ought to be more easily associated with scenario that convey auspicious meanings as much as possible, so that auspicious jewelry can become more popular. Therefore, by constructing a cognitive pattern of auspicious implication from three levels mentioned, jewelry with auspicious meaning can become greatly popular and be well recognized. The research can serve as a reference for metalworking creators and jewelry designers.

References

1. Fei, T.: Jewelry: a carrier of spirit. Art research (2008)
2. Bell, C.T.: Art, pp. 2–15. Createspace Independent Publication, Scotts Valley (2014)
3. Craig, R.T.: Communication theory as a field. Commun. Theory 9(2), 119–161 (1999)
4. Durham, M.G.: Media and Cultural Studies. Wiley-Blackwell, New York (2012)
5. Fiske, J., Jenkins, H.: Introduction to Communication Studies. Routledge, New York (2011)
6. Goldman, A.T.: The Blackwell Guide to Aesthetics, pp. 93–108. Wiley-Blackwell, Malden (2008)
7. Gao, Y., Wu, J., Lee, S., Lin, R.: Communication between artist and audience: a case study of creation journey. In: Rau, P.-L.P. (ed.) HCII 2019. LNCS, vol. 11577, pp. 33–44. Springer, Cham (2019). https://doi.org/10.1007/978-3-030-22580-3_3
8. Lin, R., Qian, F., Wu, J., Fang, W.-T., Jin, Y.: A pilot study of communication matrix for evaluating artworks. In: Rau, P.-L.P. (ed.) CCD 2017. LNCS, vol. 10281, pp. 356–368. Springer, Cham (2017). https://doi.org/10.1007/978-3-319-57931-3_29
9. Maquet, J.: The Aesthetic Experience: An Anthropologist Looks at the Visual Arts, pp. 151–158. Yale University Press, New Haven and London (1986)
10. Wheaton, E.: The artist and the audience: an interdisciplinary study of composer-audience relationships in musical. Communication (2004). https://doi.org/10.22215/etd/2014-10328

The Pilot Study of the Theater of the Bauhaus

Yiwen Ting[1]([⊠]), Minghong Shi[2], Po-Hsien Lin[1], and Rungtai Lin[1]

[1] Graduate School of Creative Industry Design,
National Taiwan University of Arts, New Taipei City, Taiwan
adingl113@gmail.com, rtlin@mail.ntua.edu.tw,
t0131@ntua.edu.tw
[2] Shenzhen Technology University, Shenzhen, Guangdong,
People's Republic of China
jun101786@126.com

Abstract. After the establishment of Bauhaus School, in order to enable students to study across fields, the principal Walter Gropius hopes that the artist Oskar Schlemmer will be responsible for the drama course. From 1923 to 1929, Schlemmer led the Bauhaus theater course, creating the golden age of the Theater of the Bauhaus and becoming synonymous with the Theater of the Bauhaus. The simplest statement he puts forward is that "the human body is a mobile building." «Triadic Ballet» tried to create with the students in a workshop led by Schlemmer in 1912. In 1923, at the Weimar National Theatre, which took ten years of experimentation, Schlemmer developed the potential of exploring theaters in a metaphorical way of dance and machine. This stylized theater dance became an important text for understanding modern art revolution and Bauhaus's stage thoughts. Bauhausdances.org suggested: "Schlemmer influenced the performance theory of Moss Cunningham, John Cage, and Ivan Nicholas." Compared with the research on Bauhaus, such as architecture and product design, the Theater of the Bauhaus is less discussion. However, the forward-looking experiments of the Theater of the Bauhaus «Triadic Ballet have profoundly influenced the integration and development of modern cross-disciplinary performing arts. This study attempts to analyze the Theater of the Bauhaus «Triadic Ballet» proposing the aesthetic view of human body in space, From the perspective of art history, this paper analyzes the contemporary significance of this work in the development of modernist art.

Keywords: The Theater of the Bauhaus · Triadic Ballet

1 Introduction

After the establishment of the Bauhaus, Director Walter Gropius asked painter Oskar Schlemmer to teach drama courses and foster students' interdisciplinary knowledge. Therefore, from 1923 to 1929 when Schlemmer led theater courses in the Bauhaus, the golden age of Bauhaus theater was created. The simplest statement Schlemmer proposed was that "the human body is a moving building," which corresponds to the design concept of the Bauhaus. However, compared with research on the architecture and product design of the Bauhaus, research on Bauhaus theater is relatively scant.

© Springer Nature Switzerland AG 2020
P.-L. P. Rau (Ed.): HCII 2020, LNCS 12193, pp. 559–572, 2020.
https://doi.org/10.1007/978-3-030-49913-6_46

Prospective experiments of the Triadic Ballet of Bauhaus theater have profoundly affected the integration and development of modern interdisciplinary performing arts.

The Triadic Ballet was performed in the Deutsche National theater and Staatskapelle Weimar in 1923. In a decade-long experiment of the ballet, Schlemmer used the metaphorical approach of dance and machines to explore the potential of theater. The current study conducted a qualitative analysis on the Triadic Ballet of in Bauhaus theater and proposed an aesthetic perspective of the human body in a pure space. According to the analytical results, we arranged actual clips of performances of the Triadic Ballet and analyzed the historic importance of this work in the context of modernism in art from the perspective of art history. Our research objectives were as follows: (1) To review the development of Western modern dance, including the concept of the Bauhaus. (2) To investigate and analyze the application of concepts of the Bauhaus in the Triadic Ballet. (3) To apply creative ideas from the Triadic Ballet to practices of artworks.

2   Literature Review

2.1   The Triadic Ballet of the Theater of the Bauhaus

The experimental theater of the Bauhaus has influenced modern dance and theater [30]. Bauhaus theater courses were opened during the early years of the Bauhaus's establishment in the 1920s and an exclusive theater was built when the school moved to Dessau in 1926. During this period, the courses were led by the painter Oscar Schlemmer (1888–1943) with the aim of enabling students to understand the relationship between the human body and space through theater courses. Furthermore, the course objective was to cultivate students' creative thinking through creative displays of performing arts. The Bauhaus Dances Organization in the United States suggested that, "Oskar Schlemmer's theater concepts have influenced the performance theory of modern and postmodern dancers such as Merce Cunningham, Alwin Nikolais, and Robert Wilson" [3].

Research on the Bauhaus has mainly focused on design and architecture, and research on the theater of the Bauhaus is relatively scant. In 1925, a book titled *Die Bühne im Bauhaus* was published in the Bauhaus book series, and was translated into English and published as *The Theater of the Bauhaus* in 1961. The English version included an introduction to Walter Gropius and four essays, namely *Humans and Artistic Shapes* and *Theater* by Schlemmer; *Theatre, Circus, Variety* by Laszlo Moholy Nagy; and *U-Shape Theater* by Farkas Molnár. The shock caused by *The Theater of the Bauhaus* was because of its deconstruction of the traditional concept of theater from two aspects, namely theater space and the human body in space. The concept of theater is related to the building of the theater itself; specifically, it involves the great potential of the building to actualize performances. The concept of the human body in space involves the perfection of performance art, which is particularly true for the four laws of the human body in space proposed by Schlemmer. Under the four laws, the traditional narrative form of dance is abandoned, and dance art creation no longer exists to serve characters but returns to the creation of art itself. Additionally, Schlemmer demonstrated the purity and abstractness of art in modernism through bold experiments.

In the posthumously published book *The Letters and Diaries of Oscar Schlemmer*, Schlemmer wrote that, "Human organism, stands in the cubic and abstract space of the stage; humans and space each have different laws, who will become dominant? In one situation, abstract space changes itself to face and adapt to differences of natural people. In another situation, natural people reshape their image to adapt to abstract space." Furthermore, he asserted that, "Those who are involved in these laws are 'individuals as dancers' who follow the laws of the body and also the laws of space. Whether in an abstract movement, a symbolic dance show, or an empty stage…these dancers are all a medium for transitioning to the great world of theater" [29].

The Triadic Ballet started to be appreciated by dancers in workshops as early as 1912. Part of the ballet's content was published in 1915, it premiered in Stuttgart in 1922, and it was performed in the Deutsche National theater and Staatskapelle Weimar in 1923. For a decade-long experiment of this ballet, Schlemmer used the metaphorical approach of dance and machines to explore the potential of theaters. This ballet, which is least similar to traditional ballet, has become a crucial text for understanding the changes in modern art and the stage ideas of the Bauhaus [30]. Three different methods exist for translating the Triadic Ballet and they were all developed based on three acts and three dancers. German dance critic explained that the word "Triadic" in "The Triadic Ballet" originated from a Greek word that implied three acts and three dancers. The performance of the ballet consisted of three styles, namely solo dance, duo dance, and trio dance. A total of 12 dance poses including circles, triangles, and squares and 18 sets of costumes were also divided into three series [13]. The whole show consisted of three series in yellow, rose, and black and was performed by two male dancers and one female dancer. The dancers changed into 18 sets of costumes and performed 12 sessions of dances, as indicated in the manuscript of the Triadic Ballet by Oskar Schlemmer in Fig. 1.

Fig. 1. Manuscript of the Triadic Ballet by Oskar Schlemmer [28]

2.2   The Development of Modern Dance in the West

After the French King Louis XVI laid the foundation for ballet, the development of dance in the West can be separated into four main periods, namely ballet, modern dance, postmodern dance, and contemporary dance. Modernism rose from the end of the 19th century to the beginning of the 20th century. Arts in modernism are modern departures from Western cultural and artistic traditions centered on rationality [27]. Modern dance was born in that era because of people's opposition to traditional classical ballet. The appearance of the theater of Bauhaus also affected the stage form and experimental spirit of postmodern dance.

The Bauhaus Dances Organization in the United States directly suggested that, "Oskar Schlemmer has influenced the performance theory of modern dancers such as Merce Cunningham, Alwin Nikolais, and Robert Wilson" [3]. The United States is the birthplace of modern dance and a development center of postmodern dance. German modern dance influenced the performance style in modern theaters during the development of Western modern dance. In this study, we sought to answer the question of how the theater of the Bauhaus affected the performance styles of postmodern dance and even contemporary dance. Therefore, the background and importance of the theater of the Bauhaus in modern dance development are examined in this section through organizing the development of modern dance in the United States and Germany.

Overview of the Development of Modern Dance in the United States. The free dance of Loie Fuller (1862–1928) and Isadora Duncan (1877–1927) represents the first generation of pioneers in the development of modern dance in the United States. These two dancers broke from the more than 400-year-old tradition of ballet dancing and overcame the shackles of dance clothes and shoes. Duncan, the mother of modern dance, was inspired by Greek statues and achieved the natural beauty of harmony between man and nature in her works. The first generation of dance pioneers admired nature and freewheeling dance, which influenced the second generation of modern dancers, such as Martha Graham (1894–1991), Doris Humphrey (1895–1958), José Limón (1908–1972), and Merce Cunningham (1919–2009).

In the mid-term development of these dancers in modern dance, they sought the special vocabulary of dance styles and developed their personal dance training systems; for example, the "contraction and release" of Graham and "fall and recover" of Humphrey. Cunningham was inspired by The Chinese I Ching in 1951 and created chance operations. From the 1990s, the Life Forms choreographic software tool was adopted, hailing a new era of computer choreography [24, 26].

After the 1960s, a new generation of dancers suggested that modern dance had evolved to be more distant from the audience compared with ballet and had become an obscure art form only for academics [2]. These dancers optimized an opportunity to publish their dance work when they once gathered at Judson Memorial Church in 1934; specifically, dancers led by Yvonne Rainer announced a postmodern dance manifesto and broke from traditional rules of modern dance; following this, post-modern dances incorporating various styles appeared. For example, Steven Paxton (1939 to present) created contact improvisation, and numerous dance works of Deborah Hay (1941 to present) have been performed outdoors or in public, which are works that have emphasized interpersonal communication. Numerous dancers at this time boldly and creatively performed highly experimental postmodern dances [24–27].

Overview of the Development of Modern Dance in Germany. The father of German modern dance, Rodolf von Laban (1879–1958), opened a dance school in Munich in 1910 and established a dance company in 1912. Laban studied architecture and painting in his early life, which formed the foundation for his research on dance involving the human body in space. In *The World of Dancers* (1920), Laban stated that, "My goal is not to establish guidelines and dogma, but to awaken people's keen insight into dance." The crucial cornerstone of Laban's dance thought was developed from three elements, namely the dance, music, and language of the perfect art of Bacchus emphasized by Nietzsche. Laban established theories for dance itself and continually adopted Nietzsche's spirit of Bacchus as his core principle when exploring the inherent nature of dance moves [35]. Mary Wegman (1886–1973), Laban's most famous student, was the person who truly transformed Laban's dance thoughts into stage practices.

Similar to other modernist artists, the rational principles that people once advocated could be perceived in the dance ideas of Wegman. As revealed by Nietzsche, the distorted and free nature of humans can only be restored by returning to the original impulse of Bacchus. In 1930, Wegman's student Hanya Holm founded a branch of the Wegman School of Dance in New York City. The school brought numerous German expressionist dance performance styles to the United States, and one of its most famous students, Evan Nicholas, became a notable figure in postmodern dance [27].

In 1932, "The Green Table," the classic work of Kurt Jooss (1901–1979), won a gold medal at the First International Choreography Competition in Paris, and became the most internationally influential large-scale choreodrama in the history of German modern dance [24]. Jooss founded the Folkwang Dance School, one of the most famous students of which was the pioneer of dance theater Pina Bausch (1940–2009). Bausch entered Folkwang Dance School in 1955 and received a scholarship to attend the dance division of the Juilliard School in New York in 1960; her teachers included the American second-generation dancers Paul Taylor (1930–2018) and José Arcadio Limón (1908–1972). Bausch returned to Germany to join the Folkwang Ballett Essen in 1962, took over as the art director in 1972, and renamed the dance company Tanztheater Wuppertal Pina Bausch. Bausch's most famous saying was that, "I am not concerned with how people move, but why they move." Her strong dance style cultivated a Tanztheater with complete drama structure, highly integrated means, strong senses of tragedy, and indestructible drama power" [25].

According to the aforementioned development of modern dance in the United States and Germany, we organized the development of Western modern dance, as shown in Fig. 2. The Bauhaus extended the artistic design concepts of shape, space, and color to dance experiments of humans and space, opening up a new experimental field for dance theaters.

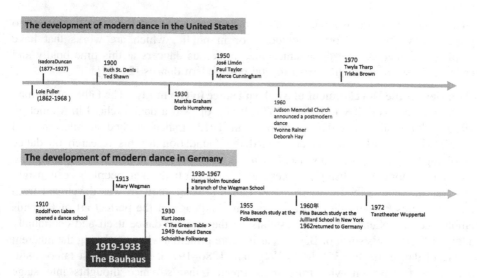

Fig. 2. Development of American and German Modern Dance (organized by this study)

3   Research Design and Method

This qualitative case study analyzed Schlemmer's Triadic Ballet through a literature review and data collation. Figure 3 presents our research process, each stage of which is described in the following paragraphs:

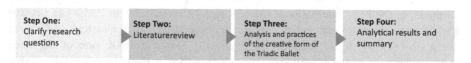

Fig. 3. Research process (organized by this study)

Step One: Clarify Research Questions. This was a preliminary study of the Triadic Ballet of the Bauhaus. To clarify and list the research questions of this study, we organized the theater concepts of the Bauhaus and Schlemmer as well as the influence these concepts had on the style of next-generation performance arts. Subsequently, we determined our research purposes by reviewing relevant literature.

Step Two: Literature Review. Our literature review was divided into two major sections. The first section was on literature related to the theater of the Bauhaus and Schlemmer's Triadic Ballet. Specifically, we depicted the analytical structure of the Triadic Ballet, and practiced the reprinted version of some clips of the Triadic Ballet.

In the second section of the literature review, we organized a linear chart of American and German modern dance from the development history of Western modern dance. The aim was to elucidate the importance of the theater of the Bauhaus in the development of modern dance.

Step Three: Analysis and Practices of the Creative Form of the Triadic Ballet. We analyzed the Triadic Ballet and constructed a creative model for it through the literature review. The model included three major triads, namely space, shape, and color. Additionally, each triad was divided into three triadic elements to explore and analyze the characteristics and creative form of the Triadic Ballet.

We drew the structure of the Triadic Ballet's creations to understand the ballet's creative form. However, because of limitations in time, human power, and resources, we were only able to reprint the first part of the second act. We also made video records of our practices of reprinting artworks to serve as a reference for future research.

Step Four: Analytical Results and Summary. Through the literature review, analysis of the Triadic Ballet's form, and practices of artworks, we sought to understand the background and form of the Triadic Ballet of Schlemmer. Additionally, we drew relevant conclusions to serve as a preliminary study of the form and expression of performance arts and the theater of the Bauhaus.

4 Analysis of the Triadic Ballet of the Theater of the Bauhaus

4.1 Analysis of the Creation of the Triadic Ballet

The Triadic Ballet of Schlemmer was developed based on the theme of "triad" and all forms of art revolve around the three concepts of "triad" throughout the work. This study explained the work by dividing it into core concepts and expression forms, which are described in the following subsections.

Core Concepts: The core concepts of the Triadic Ballet are the triad of space, shape, and color; furthermore, these three core concepts are inseparable from various designs, including costume, move, route, and stage design. In the triad, "space" includes height, depth, and breadth; "shape" includes circles, triangles, and squares; and "color" includes red, yellow, and blue. Therefore, the entire form of the Triadic Ballet is formed around the core concepts of three large triads and three small triads, and we present these concepts and triads in Fig. 4.

Coding of Art Forms: We categorized the expression form of the Triadic Ballet into forms of artistic expression, namely costume design, move design, route design, and stage design, which are described as follows (Fig. 5):

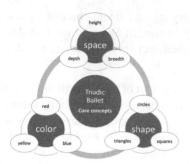
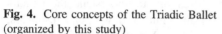
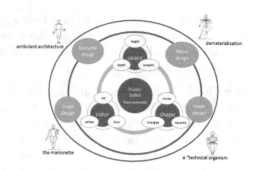

Fig. 4. Core concepts of the Triadic Ballet (organized by this study)

Fig. 5. Analysis of the Triadic Ballet (organized by this study)

Costume Design: A total of 18 sets of costumes were designed according to the core concepts of three large and three small triads. The concept of costume design was created based on the four laws of change in the human body proposed by Schlemmer. These laws show that the human body has four forms, namely ambulant architecture, marionettes, metaphysical organisms, and technical organisms.

Move Design: The dance moves were designed according to the limitations of dance costumes and Schlemmer's four laws of the human body in space. Specifically, circles, triangles, and squares of moves are drawn in space based on the operation of human limbs. This broke from the traditional thinking regarding ballet moves, and the design of moves can be seen to be mostly mechanicalized and coded. The dancers wore masks or had their faces painted white to disguise their human appearance or expressions during the performance; this also achieved the form of a decentralized and technical organism, presenting the human body as an artistic medium on stage. That is, the human body represents the expression forms of ambulant architecture and marionettes.

Route Design: Throughout the work, the dancers' moves in the stage space revolve around and are generated by the concepts of circles, triangles, and squares. Dots, lines, and areas are integrated and operated within a dancer's moves and form a three-dimensional operation mode. For example, the black dancer in the third act can be seen to form her own rotation; furthermore, the revolution of the dancing route, the vertical circle of the dancer herself, the flat circle of the stage floor track, and the vertical space of the stage space all present a circular trajectory of the entire stage in three dimensions (Fig. 6).

Stage Design: In 12 different plays in three acts, each act has a special stage color and background. This creates a different atmosphere, shows different high- and low-level spatial changes, and displays geometric shapes such as circles, triangles, and squares. For example, in "rose" of act two, stars and circles made with lines appear and they complement the dancers' moves and movement tracks, thereby presenting a visual experience of geometric shapes (Fig. 7).

Fig. 6. The "Black Dancer" in the third act [33]

Fig. 7. "Rose" stage of act two [33] (Color figure online)

Art Coding Analysis of the Triadic Ballet: Schlemmer created the Triadic Ballet according to the core concepts of large and small triads and was able to present complete costume, action, route, and stage designs. The core concept is that of forming a complete stage expression through various art forms. Through our literature review and image database analysis, we analyzed the content shown in Fig. 8. Specifically, the Triadic Ballet is separated into three acts. The first act is yellow, which is further divided into parts, and has a more humorous atmosphere; furthermore, moves in the act are presented in a more humorous and brisk fashion. The second act is rose, which has three parts and a grand, serious atmosphere; moreover, the design of moves is relatively grand, and they are presented in groups. The third act is black, which has four parts and a mysterious atmosphere. The move design of the act attempts to present fantasy dance moves through slow rotations and walking. The three acts comprise a total of 12 parts and feature three dancers (two women and one man). They present 18 sets of costumes in turn and perform three dance styles, namely solo, duo, and trio dance.

Core concepts			Art coding					
Color	Space	Shape	Act	Atmo-sphere	Move	Dancer	Form	Costumes
Red	Height	Circles	Yellow	Humorous	Brisk fashion	Female dancer	Single dance	
Yellow	Depth	Triangles	Rose	Serious	Grand	Female dancer	duet dance	18 sets of costumes
Blue	Breadth	Squares	Black	Mysterious	Fantasy	Male dancer	Trio dance	

Fig. 8. Art Coding of the Triadic Ballet (organized by this study) (Color figure online)

Our art coding analysis of the Triadic Ballet revealed that triads were used for stacking from core concepts to art coding when Schlemmer was creating his artistic works. This enabled Schlemmer to present a complete artistic stage performance, even though the entire work only lasts 30 min and its structure is highly conscientious and careful. As shown in Fig. 9, we organized creation models of the Triadic Ballet based on the aforementioned core concepts, art coding, and art forms.

Core concepts			Art coding						Art form	Performance
Color	Space	Shape	Act	Atmo-sphere	Move	Dancer	Form	Costumes	Costume design	
Red	Height	Circles	Yellow	Humorous	Brisk fashion	Female dancer	Single dance		Move design	
Yellow	Depth	Triangles	Rose	Serious	Grand	Female dancer	duet dance	18 sets of costumes	Route design	
Blue	Breadth	Squares	Black	Mysterious	Fantasy	Male dancer	Trio dance		Stage design	

Fig. 9. Creative form of the Triadic Ballet

4.2 Verification Analysis and Practice of the Creation of the Triadic Ballet

We analyzed the creation model of the Triadic Ballet before actually arranging artworks for verification. However, because of limited resources and time, we only selected a part of play from act two (rose) to verify our research outcomes. Additionally, we applied four types of coding to our reproduction:

Costume Reproduction: The manuscripts of Schlemmer were used as prototypes for costume production. Polyurethane and thick paper were used to make a large round skirt and cut the skirt pleats, and the shell shape of the upper body was also hand-carved before being colored for the following reasons: (1) the costume material could not be traced; (2) to ensure the movability of dancers when wearing the costume; and (3) to ensure a complete presentation of the vertical circle of the large round skirt. To conform to Schlemmer's marionettes law, we selected an image of the reprinted version from 1970. Additionally, following the concept of modern clothing's modeling aesthetics, the upper limbs were changed to close-fitting white tights, and the dancer was painted completely in white from the face to neck; the aim was to disintegrate the shape of the human body and fully disguise the emotions of the human face (Fig. 10).

Fig. 10. Process of costume reproduction

Movement Application: We used Schlemmer's manuscripts, letters, and notes and a 1970 reperformance of the Triadic Ballet by the German choreographer Margarete Hastings as our references. Additionally, this study examined Schlemmer's four laws of change in the human body in space, which emphasized two concepts, namely organisms and decentralization. Because of these concepts, we emphasized the cross movement of hands on the chest to represent a figure of eight symbol ("∞") and changed the hand movements of the original fifth position in ballet to connect the two hands together to present a circular symbol. Moreover, when dancers were moving (Burre'), the circle movement of the wrist was exaggerated to show the circular trajectory of the hand movement. Dancers performed with an expressionless white face for the whole parts of the act in addition to coded and mechanicalized moves. This was done to present the grand and serious atmosphere of dance moves set by Schlemmer; specifically, it presented the marionettes, a law of human body functions with respect to space (Fig. 11).

Moves of the "∞" symbol   Change of hand position in   Circular moves of the wrist
                             the fifth position

Fig. 11. Application of moves during the performance

Scenery Reproduction: To show the ratio of the dancer's large round skirt to the large circle, we made a large circle with a diameter of 210 cm. The circle was based on the dancer's height of 165 cm plus the height of a releve' to visually present the spatial ratio of the circle. Subsequently, we recorded the work in a virtual studio and completed the second act against a rose background through dynamic post-production (Fig. 12).

Fig. 12. Creation of stage props and blackground

Route Track: Based on the move designs, the spatial presentation of a large vertical circle, the breadth, depth, and height of space, and the triangle, circle, and square shapes emphasized by Schlemmer, we designed the trajectory of the dancer's movements. Subsequently, we presented the trajectory of the moving space of points, lines, and surfaces, which is shown in Fig. 13.

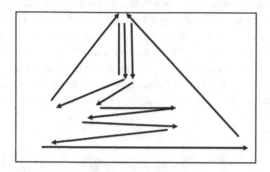

Fig. 13. Route track

5 Conclusion and Recommendations

In this preliminary study on the Triadic Ballet of Schlemmer, we collected data from videos and organized the influence of the Triadic Ballet on the development of modern dance in the West. Furthermore, we analyzed the creative form of the Triadic Ballet through Schlemmer's concepts, and actually arranged and recreated solo dance parts from the second act (rose) to verify its creation model.

(https://www.youtube.com/watch?v=wLCYwKxvSCk&feature=youtu.be)

Our main conclusions are as follows:

1. The creative form of the Triadic Ballet comprises three parts, namely core concepts, art coding, and form coding. These core concepts consist of three large triads and three small triads. The whole work is a highly conscientious and careful form of modernist creation with characteristics including verification and science, purity and abstractness, and rationality and logic.
2. In the development of Western dance history, the Triadic Ballet did not form a dance or move style itself. Nevertheless, Schlemmer extended the artistic concepts of shape, space, and color to the design of the human body and theater space, creating a new experimental field for dance.
3. Schlemmer's four laws of the human body in space initiated a dialogue between dance and technology as well as that between dance and machinery in the form of modern dance theaters. When machinery was involved in a performance, artists integrated all art forms into the theater and new technology created new space for the theater. The medium that the human body plays in the theater has become a crucial topic in today's stage creations.

4. This creation model can be used as a reprint of the whole act of the Triadic Ballet, as well as for understanding the audience's view of the ballet through public performances and quantitative research through questionnaires.

References

1. Baumgarten, A.G.: Aesthetics. Culture and Art Publishing House, Beijing (1987). Translated by Wang Xuxiao
2. Banes, S.: Writing Dancing in the Age of Postmodernism. University Press of New England, Hanover (1994)
3. Bauhaus dance. http://bauhausdances.org/,2019/1125
4. Chen, S., Yen, H., Lee, S., Lin, C.: Applying design thinking in curating model-a case study of the exhibition of turning poetry into painting. J. Des. **21**(4), 1–24 (2016)
5. Fang, W., Gao, Y., Zeng, Z., Lin, B.: A study on audience perception of aesthetic experience in dance performance. J. Des. **23**(3), 23–46 (2018)
6. Lin, B., Xu, M.: A basic study on triadic ballet. J. Inner Mongolia Arts Univ. (1), 117–120 (2016)
7. Goldman, A.: Evaluating art. In: Kivy, P. (ed.) The Blackwell Guide to Aesthetic, pp. 93–108. Blackwell Pub., Malden (2004)
8. Hall, S.: Encoding/decoding. In: Hall, S., et al. (eds.) Culture, Media, Language, pp. 117–127. Hutchinson, London (1980)
9. Jakobson, R.: Language in Literature. Harvard University Press, Cambridge (1987)
10. Jianping, O.: History of World Art Dance Volume. Oriental, Beijing (2003)
11. Martin, J.: Introduction to the Dance. Culture and Art Publishing House, Beijing (1994). Translated by Ou Jianping
12. Kant, M.: Oscar Schlemmer's Triadic Ballet (Paris, 1932) and dance discourse in Germany. Three letters with annotation and a commentary. Dance Res. **33**(1), 16–30 (2015)
13. Landgraf on dance. https://www.ilonalandgraf.com/2014/06/patience-pays/,2019/12/01
14. Langer, S.K.: Problems of Art. Scribner, New York (1957)
15. Langer, S.K.: Feeling and Form. Scribner, New York (1953)
16. Lin, R.: Designing "emotion" into modern products. In: International Symposium for Emotion and Sensibility, KAIST, Korea 27–29 June 2008, p. 11 (2008)
17. Lin, R., Cheng, R., Sun, M.-X.: Digital archive database for cultural product design. In: Aykin, N. (ed.) UI-HCII 2007. LNCS, vol. 4559, pp. 154–163. Springer, Heidelberg (2007). https://doi.org/10.1007/978-3-540-73287-7_20. ISBN 978-3-540-73286-0
18. Lin, R., Qian, F., Wu, J., Fang, W.-T., Jin, Y.: A pilot study of communication matrix for evaluating artworks. In: Rau, P.-L.P. (ed.) CCD 2017. LNCS, vol. 10281, pp. 356–368. Springer, Cham (2017). https://doi.org/10.1007/978-3-319-57931-3_29
19. Lin, R.: Service innovation design for cultural and creative industries – a case study of the Cultural and Creative Industry Park at NTUA. In: International Service Innovation Design Conference, Dongseo University, Korea, 20–22 October 2008, pp. 14–25. (Keynote Speech)
20. Chun, L.: Humanity Dance and Mechanical Principles-From Tridic Ballet (2018). https://kknews.cc/zhtw/culture/pgkz88j.html. Accessed 10 Dec 2019
21. Lu, C., Lin, R.: The influence of bauhaus style on Taiwan design education. Art Apprec. **6**(3), 28–43 (2010)
22. Lu, Y.: Dance Aesthetics. Central University for Nationalities, Beijing (2011)
23. Gang, L.: Reading for Cultural Studies. China Social Science Press, Beijing (2000)

24. Ou, J.: Appreciation of Foreign Dance History and Works. Higher Education, Beijing (2008)
25. Jianping, O.: Dance Appreciation. Jiangsu Education, Nanjing (2009)
26. Liu, Q.: Anthology of Liu Qingyi's Anthology 1-Body Language Study of Modern Dance. Shanghai Music, Shanghai (2013)
27. Liu, Q.: Outline of History of Modern Western Dance. Shanghai Music, Shanghai (2014)
28. Schlemmer, O.: Man and art figure. In: Gropius, W., Wensinger, Ar.S. (eds.) The Theater of the Bauhaus. Wesleyan University Press, Middletown (1961)
29. Schlemmer, O.: The letters and dDiaries of Oskar Schlemmer. Northwestern University Press, Evanston (1990)
30. Smock, W.: The Bauhaus Ideal Then And Now: An Illustrated Guide to Modernist Design. Academy Chicago Publishers, Chicago (2004)
31. Sun, Y., Lin, S., Sun, M.: The evaluation of the classic design in contemporary perspective: reflection on bauhaus hundred years of prosperity. J. Des. 24(3), 49–72 (2019)
32. The influence of Bauhaus style on Taiwan design education. In: Proceedings of the 2009 Process Design Symposium: 90 Years of Bauhaus Review and Prospect, pp. 30–41. Department of Craft Design, National Taiwan University of Arts (2009)
33. Triadic Ballet. https://www.youtube.com/watch?v=rlIiT80dqHE. Accessed 25 Nov 2019
34. Zeimbekis, J.: Why digital pictures are not notational representations. J. Aesthetics Art Criticism 73(4), 449–453 (2015)
35. Zhang, Y.: Western Dance Art from the Perspective of Cultural History Guangxi Normal University Press (2016)
36. Zhu, L.: The language of dance. In: Anthology of Modern Western Art Aesthetics Dance Aesthetics Vol. Original by Mary Wigman. Chunfeng Literature and Art Publishing House, Liaoning Education Press Shenyang (1990)

Study on Restoration-Oriented Digital Visualization for Architectural Trim-Work of Guanlan Hall in Yuanming Yuan

Huan Wang[1], Jue Zhong[2], Wen Li[3], and Cameron Clarke[4(✉)]

[1] Capital Normal University, Beijing 100048, China
whuan@cnu.edu.cn
[2] China Committee of Education Technology (CAET), Beijing 100084, China
juezhong1127@tsinghua.edu.cn
[3] Maryland Institute College of Art, Baltimore 21217, USA
42715024@qq.com
[4] Royal Danish Academy of Fine Arts, Copenhagen,
1435 Copenhagen, Denmark
cameronclarke89@gmail.com

Abstract. Today computing techniques and sophisticated digital tools are changing architectural heritage, conservation and restoration. In this paper, we study the historical architecture of the Yuanming Yuan imperial Garden of Qing Dynasty through an interpretation of historical documents, the communicative value of symbols and construction and develop into photographs and 3D models to express its intangible formal value. Based on the interpretation of the drawings of YangshiFang in the Imperial Household Department (Neiwu Fu), with their account of the complex constructional elements and layout, this paper rebuilds Guanlan Hall in Wanchun Garden at the southern Yuanming Yuan with digital modeling and a VR Exhibition System. The digital modeling recreation of Guanlan Hall creates an immersive communication tool. It gives an experience of the interior trim-work & tectonics of construction, an understanding of the patterns of architectural interior space. We investigate the importance of cultural transmission, which underlines the role of drawing as methodological structure and the role of Handicraft regulation as an instructional experience of research and cultural promotion. By providing a streamlined digital deconstruction process with animation and VR, the 3D model develops a detailed understanding of the Qing Dynasty style architectural trim-work structures and construction processes, contributing to research on the interior design of the Yuanming Yuan and the cultural dissemination of Chinese ancient architecture.

Keywords: Digital modeling · Chinese architectural trim-work · Interior design · Visualization · Virtual reality

1 Background

The massive Chinese royal gardens, Yuanming Yuan (Gardens of Perfect Brightness,"圆明园", or called "The Old Summer Palace") was founded in the 46th year of Kangxi Dynasty (1707) and has undergone a process of continual renovation for more

© Springer Nature Switzerland AG 2020
P.-L. P. Rau (Ed.): HCII 2020, LNCS 12193, pp. 573–594, 2020.
https://doi.org/10.1007/978-3-030-49913-6_47

than 150 years. The Yuanming Yuan covers an area of 3.5 km², with a construction area of 200,000 m², and more than 150 attractions. During its most prosperous period, Yuanming Yuan was a highly functional and delicate imperial space for meetings of the ministers, welcoming of ambassadors, and addressing government affairs (Fig. 1).

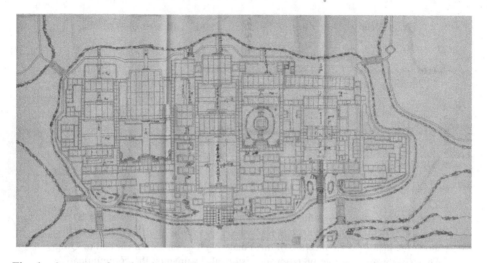

Fig. 1. A masterplan drawing of Jiuzhou Qingyan (the scene of peaceful and continents, "九州清晏") in Yuanming Yuan

From the idea to the realization, the contemporary development of digital modeling in architecture leads to a coordinate rewriting for the multidimensional involvement between model and visualization, especially in the timber structure field of traditional Chinese interiors. First, 3D modeling records building information component types, crafts, prompting a transformation from text and graphics to a digital resource library. Second, expressing by modeling the limitation of process traditional technology for restoration could be neglected and the restoration comparison of multiple periods can be realized in the same model. Besides, digital modeling provides possibilities for visualization of architectural heritage to be utilized in the interpreting and translating of traditional culture. Presently, the technology has achieved display presentations such as 3D animation video, VR visualization, and projection visualization, which makes the interior space more realistic. Here, it also supports research and analysis of building data based on 3D models.

UNESCO puts forward strict requirements for the restoration of the architectural heritage, which brings challenging for the indoor reconstructive restoration of the Yuanming Yuan destroyed buildings since it announced that:

"5. Any proposed intervention should for preference:
a) follow traditional means;
b) be reversible, if technically possible; or

c) at least not prejudice or impede future preservation work whenever this may become necessary; and
d) not hinder the possibility of later access to evidence incorporated in the structure."
(Refers: Principles For the Preservation of Historic Timber Structures, 1999.)

On the one hand, the difficulty of accurately interpret the original construction data was the result of a historical lack of physical and photographic information. The only paintings and archives that clearly marked the period are qualitative descriptions, and it is difficult to determine the original shape and structure at the year of the initial construction. On the other hand, traditional Chinese timber-fame architecture is a combination craft of wood, cave, and painting. Structured components also have decorative patterns and specific materials that run through backward even partly missing with the development of contemporary construction technology. Therefore, the actual reconstruction of a traditional wooden structure form will meet a departure from the original state of "Restoring the Old as the Old".

In this regard, it is necessary to bring vitality and vigor to the static works of buildings in a bid to meet the development through time. If the restoration research can be launched with a 3D model that supports multiple visual expression with visualization technology, it will afford a full realization and restoration research for the heritage conservation and cultural transmission. The study of cultural heritage with digital models is conducive to a liberating design approach and allows for the discovery of cultural characteristics from a contemporary construction perspective. An important role of modeling with this technique is that it supports research for cultural dissemination of the architectural heritage, which arouses an expectation on this kind of destructed and precious heritage restoration in China.

This paper is focusing on an architectural drawings and regulatory compositional approach to support the restoration-oriented modeling, leading to digital visualization of architectural interior space.

2   Introduction to the Construction and Documents of Chinese Traditional Wooden Trim-Work

Chinese architectural documents have more than 4,000 years of history. The first palace site was found in Erlitou during the Xia Dynasty (B.C.2070–B.C.1600), and was of a scale of 10,000 m^2. According to the Han-Dynasty portrait stone and funerary objects, three major wood-structure systems in ancient China, which are column- and-girder style, column and tie style, and multi-beam and flat roof style, had all developed (Fu 2015), particularly those structural components including tou-kung (Dougong, "斗栱"), pillar, and rafter were presumable and administrative. The wooden structure provides the main bearing system that comprehensive created of multiple materials and processes such as tiles, stone, earth, paint, oil, etc. The specific materials and processes are charged by specific craftsmen. The craftsmen-ship promoted through the next decades until the Qing Dynasty, which was the last imperial government, the traditional construction process was sustained by "professional craftsman system ("五行八作")".

Chinese architecture has a prototype that structured into three parts: platform, column or wall, tou-kung, and roof. The platform works as a foundation that is a soil and stone structure to lift the building high; the column and beam joint a timber frame system constructed of wood, and the wall is responsible for enclosing interior functional space. Formal buildings have tou-kung to elevate the roof. Under the eaves, a masonry wall with doors and windows surrounds and separates the inside and outside spaces. Inside the wall is a rich diversity type of wooden decoration, which has the essential effect on dividing the room, guiding the stream of people moving, and embellishing the space that people actually use.

Under the roof, where the main functional and aesthetic space is located, there are interior trim-work and exterior trim-work to divide the room and decorate the surface. Both the interior and exterior trim-work have the shape that transforms from window and door approximately. The exterior trim-work involves Geshan (槅扇), Kanchuang (槛窗), and Zhizhaichuang (支摘窗), while the interior trim-work includes more types of Geshan (槅扇), Bishachu (碧纱橱), Luodizhao (落地罩), Feizhao (飞罩), and etc. Simultaneously compared with other handicrafts, indoor construction requires not only skillful wooden construction techniques and decorative arts, but also integrates the support of much other handicrafts, such as sculptures craft, oil painting craft, gold craft, silver craft, etc. The study of wood decoration is the key to clarify the design approach of interior spaces in the late Qing Dynasty. Unfortunately, the trim-work of the most architectures in Yuanming yuan were destroyed by war and it was restored with great difficulty (Figs. 2 and 3).

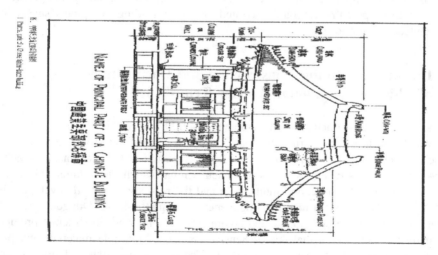

Fig. 2. Principle parts of a Chinese timber-frame building (By Liang Sicheng, 1901–1972)

Fig. 3. A Bishachu of Jianfu Palace in Forbidden (Palace Museum Ancient Architecture Department Architecture and decoration of the Forbidden City 2007.)

3 Approach to the Restoration and Construction for the Trim-Work of Yuanming Yuan

Restoration of Chinese buildings relies heavily on historical construction documents.

Drawings, which work as the professional communicating materials between various departments and the emperor in the project, formatting parallel projection and perspective drawing methods in combination with text annotations to qualitatively record the construction information of the layout, section, and details of the building. For the Yuanming Yuan project, it is identified that the drawings have the fundamental reference for restoration with advantages of professional and intuitiveness for a comprehensive use to infer accurate construction information by comparing and referencing multiple drawings. Similar to the drawing, there is one another historical archive named architecture module ("烫样", Tangyang), which is a structural material in the form of a model, but the Yuanming Yuan's rarely remains.

Books of Handicraft regulations and precedents are standards and references for construction and manufacturing in the traditional period, which retains two authority documents in China's construction history. Beginning in the Tang and Song dynasties, China's cities were highly prosperous therefore construction and handicraft were highly developed. The Ministry for Construction and Handicraft was responsible for managing the city's Civil Engineering projects and compiled the book "Yingzao Fashi"(Treatise on Architectural Methods or State Building Standards, "营造法式") under the supervision of Li Jie, who was the directorate of Buildings and Construction. Until the Qing Dynasty, when was the last highly period of prosperity, the imperial official edited the "Gongcheng Zuofa Zeli" (Technical instructions for the building crafts, "工程做法则例") based on the "Yingzao Fashi" and Edited by Yunli (允禮, 1967–1738). According to the regulated process in the book, the technology, materials, aesthetics, and other factors, the specifications that including styles, sizes, materials, and expenditures, which were regarded as the critical aspects for the construction projects. Apart from the two books, there were Zelis special for specific handicrafts and constructions in Qing Dynasty, such as Neiyan Zuofa (Regulation for Interior Trim-work, "内檐做法") and Yuanming Yuan Neigong Zeli (Regulation and Standards for Yuanming Yuan, "圆明园内工则例"). These books were all revised to Jiangzuo Zeli (Handicrafts Regulation and Precedents Standards, "匠作则例") since they worked to guide the building and palace construction process. Traditional construction established a professional structure system by Handicrafts Regulation and precedents documents for construction management and serves as a professional foundation for contemporary restoration research (Figs. 4 and 5).

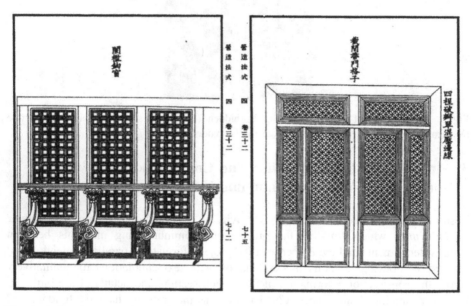

Fig. 4. A drawing page of architectural trim-work in Yingzao Fashi (Yingzao Fashi, 1145, vol 32)

續修四庫全書 史部 政書類

各項裝修做法開後
一計開
凡簷裏安裝槅扇法以飛簷椽頭下皮與槅扇掛
空檻上皮相齊下安槅扇下檻掛空檻分位上
安橫披并替椿分位如無飛簷椽以簷椽頭下
皮與槅扇掛空檻上皮相齊或高壹丈即係安
裝槅扇并上下檻分位簷枋下皮至掛空檻上
皮高叄尺即係安裝橫披并替椿分位掛空檻
又名中檻又名上檻替椿又名上檻
工程做法 卷四十一 十二
凡金裏安裝槅扇法以廊內之穿插枋下皮與槅
扇掛空檻下皮相齊下安槅扇并下檻分位上
安橫披并掛空檻替椿分位
凡次稍間安裝檻窗上替椿橫披掛空檻俱與明
間相齊上抹頭與槅扇上抹頭齊下抹頭與槅
扇羣板上抹頭齊其餘尺寸係風檻榻板檻墻
分位
下檻以面闊定長如面闊壹丈即長壹丈內除

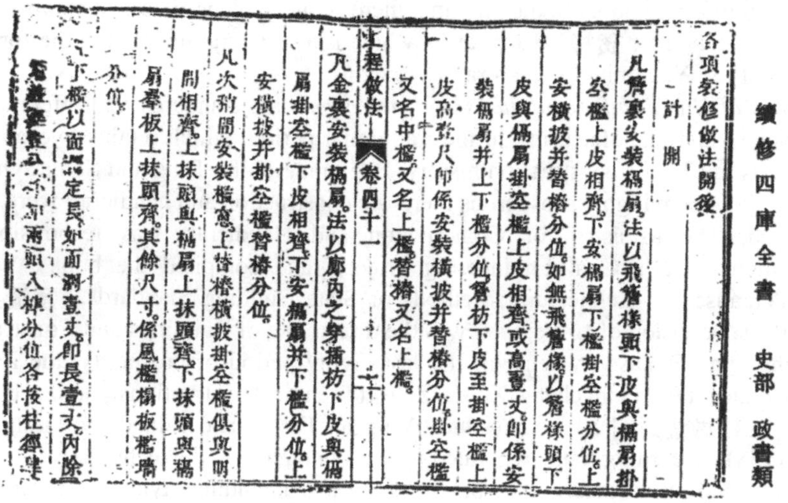

Fig. 5. A page of architectural trim-work in Gongcheng Zuofa Zeli (Gongcheng Zuofa Zeli, 1734, vol 41)

Based on the above, the approach of this paper is to interpret the qualitative trim-work layout from drawings, calculate the missing decorative pattern and component size through the Handicraft Regulations and Precedents of the Qing Dynasty. Followed by a trim-work database of components converting, which for a virtual reconstruction on the Sketchup platform. After being converted into a digital model, 1) the general shape can be transformed into intuitive and intelligible method for understanding, such as images, videos, etc. with the connection of other software platforms. 2) Craftsmanship and techniques, which are invisible behind the shape, can be expressed apparently by means of assignment and translation. 3) Realize a communication between ancient and modern design, explore a process that using projection to base regeneration for primordial space (Fig. 6).

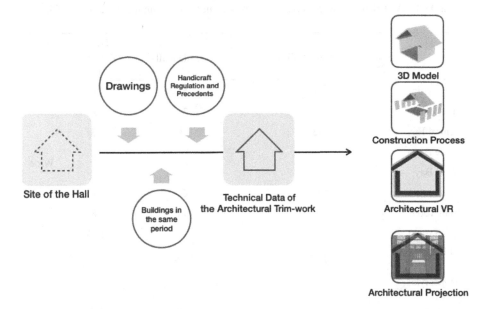

Fig. 6. The approach of Yuanming Yuan Trim-work Restoration by 3D modeling and Digital Visualization for this paper. (By Huan Wang)

4   Case Description

4.1   Overview

The most distinctive features of the Yuanming yuan are the buildings with various architectures, named Hall (formal and main buildings, "厅堂"). The Guanlan Hall located in the "Jiexiu Shanfang" (Cottage with a View of Pretty Mountain, "接秀山房") scenic area is the place where the emperor from Jiaqing to Xianfeng lived. The Guanlan Hall was first built in Jiaqing in the 22nd year (1817). In the "Yang Ji Zhai Conglu" (Yangjizhai Series, "养吉斋丛录"), see the record of the interior eaves decoration of the "Jiexiu Mountain House" undertaken by the Lianghuai Salt Government. And other renovations. In the twenty-four years of Jiaqing (1819), it was converted into a three-house (Juan, "卷") and five-room hall, Guanlan Hall, with gorgeous decoration and rich space. Since then, it has become an important part of the Fuhai Coastal Tour for living and it is also the most magnificent building that set a prototype for Shende Hall (The Hall for the Cultivation of Virtue, "慎德堂") in the Daoguang period. Guanlan Tang is a representative of the garden architecture and interior design in the Qing Dynasty. Similar to the it in the garden, the Shende tang and Tiandi Yijiachuan Dian (the Tiandi family in Qichun Garden, "天地一家春殿"), which have the similar shape and structure in Yuanming yuan (Table 1), preserves few decoration construction documents and hardly been seen in today's Qing Palace (Fig. 7).

Table 1. A survey of three-house and five-room hall in Yuanming Yuan (Unit: Chi)

	Guanlan Hall	Shende Hall	Tiandi Yijiachun Hall	Description
Bay wide	5	5	5	
Bay deep	3	3	3	
Central Bay	13	13	13	
Side Bay	12	12	12	Wide
End Bay	12	12	12	
Porch room	6	6	6	
Main room	23.6	23.6	28	
Porch room	-	-	26.5	Deep
Floor to ceiling	15.7	15.8	15.4	
Hypostyle Column (diameter)	1.3	1.3	1.4	
Peripteral Column (diameter)	13.5	13.6	13	
Scenic area	Cottage with a View of Pretty Mountain (Jiexiu Shanfang"接秀山房")	Peace for all China(Jiuzhou Qingyan "九州清晏"	Garden of gorgeous(Qichuan Yuan"绮春园")	
Period	Jiaqing Emperor	Daoguang Emperor	Tongzhi Emperor	

(1 chi = 1/3 m)

Note. The indoor space between every two roof trusses is called room ("间")

Fig. 7. A photo of Guanlan Hall in Yuanming Yuan (By Huan Wang)

4.2 Construction Materials

Archives. Guanlan Hall's written archives confirm that it was one of the Yuanming yuan's construction projects from September 23rd of Jiaqing emperor's period to the 24th year of Guangxu in Guangxu emperor's period and played as a starting spot for garden touring from the 22nd to 24th years of Guangxu emperor's period. Relevant text files also exist in the Shende Hall drawing file.

Drawings. Nine constructive drawings of Guanlan Hall are survived accordingly leading to a complementarity supports for comprehensive construction information. The drawings involve diverse types with general plan, site plan, trim-work plan, and partial components size drawing, which mention the scale and craft of the building, trim-work, and the surroundings. Among them, Fig. 031-0005 and Fig. 042-0011 are the most detailed, including important information such as the location, type, and size of the trim-work craft. The research sorts out the construction information of Guanlan Hall's drawings shown in the following table (Table 2, Figs. 8 and 9):

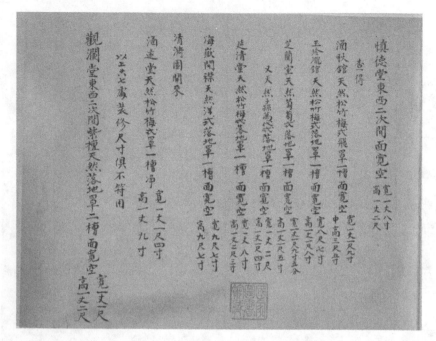

Fig. 8. Written archives of Guanlan Hall. (No. 008-0042-02 of Yangshi Lei's Drawings and Archives of the Summer Palace in the National Library)

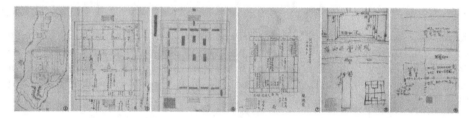

Fig. 9. The construction drawings of Guanlan Hall from the Office of Architectural Designs in this paper. (Yangshifang, lit. "office for architectural of Imperial Household Department (Neiwu Fu))

Table 2. The construction drawings of Guanlan Hall from Yangshi Lei

Number	图名	Name	Size	Date	Description
① 031-0003	观澜堂地盘样	Guanlan Hall Floor Plan	69.0cmX 39.0cm	uni-dentified	Plan: Building, Interior and Surrounds Size: Bay wide, Bay deep, Hypostyle Pillar, Peripteral Pillar, Ku-Ching ("Mirror Base")
② 031-0006-01	观澜堂地盘准底	Guanlan Hall accurate Floor Plan	38.4cmX 79.5cm	uni-dentified	Plan: Building and Surrounds Size: Bay wide, Bay deep
③ 031-0004	观澜堂准样	Guanlan Hall accurate Plan	33.2cmX 28.2cm	uni-dentified	Plan: Building and Interior Size: Bay wide, Bay deep and Components Trim-work: Types and location of Partial Components
④ 031-0005	观澜堂 地盘准底	Guanlan Hall accurate Floor Plan	35.4cmX 26.5cm	uni-dentified	Plan:Building and Interior Trim-work: Types, location, Sizes, and Patterns of Partial Components
⑤ 042-0011	观澜堂地盘装修尺寸准样	Guanlan Hall accurate Trim-work Floor Plan	46.7cmX 29.4cm	August 5th. year of Xianfeng Emperor's period (1855)	Plan:Building and Interior Size: Bay wide, Bay deep Trim-work: Types, location, and Sizes of Partial Components
⑥ 345-0801	观澜堂面宽进深尺寸地盘画样	Guanlan Hall Size floor Plan of Bay Wide and Deep	39.0cmX 41.0cm	uni-dentified	Plan:Building and Interior Size: Bay wide, Bay deep, and Interior Height Trim-work: Types and Sizes of partial Exterior Trim-work components

⑦	005-0009-01	观澜堂平样糙底	Guanlan hall sketch floor plan	13.0cmX 11.0cm	uni-dentified	Plan:Building and Interior Size: Bay wide, Bay deep, and Interior Height Trim-work: Types of Exterior Trim-work
⑧	005-0043	观澜堂西山楼（檐）装修糙底	Guanlan hall sketch floor plan of Western glade Room	21.0cmX 14.0cm	uni-dentified	Size: Wall
⑨	031-0006-02	观澜堂平样糙底	Guanlan hall sketch floor plan	17.5cmX 26.0cm	uni-dentified	Plan: Sectional Building Trim-work: Types and Sizes of Partial Components

Handicraft Regulations and Precedents. Guanlan Hall's Handicraft Regulations and Precedents come from the remaining construction files of the Ministry of Industry (Gong Bu), Imperial Household Department (Neiwu Fu), the Yuanming Yuan Works Agency (Yuanming Yuan Gongchengchu) and other organizations. There are two chapters specifically for exterior trim-work craft, which named Gexiang Zhuangxiu Zuofa (Architectural Trim-work Regulation and precedents, "各项装修做法") from Gongcheng Zuofa Zeli and Neiwu Zhuangxiu Zuofa Xice (A detailed Architectural Trim-work Regulation and precedents of Neiwu Fu, "内务装修做法细册"), and two specifically for interior trim-work craft with a detailed size accounting regulation for every type, which named Neiyan Zhuangxiu(Interior architectural trim-work, "内檐装修") and Neiyang Zhuangxiu Zuofa (Interior architectural trim-work regulation and precedents, "内檐装修做法"). Fortunately, mostly remained Zeli is collections for Yuanming Yuan Work, which kept volumes from eight to thirty separately in Yuanming yuan Zeli. From Guanlan Hall's drawings, only the type and location of the exterior trim-work can be described, while the components' information is not confirmed accurately. The Trim-work Handicraft Regulations and Precedents of both exterior and interior establish a standard for measurement and a reference for the pattern while sizing definition method follows the traditional Chinese architecture modular system, that is, the component size and details of timber-frame are determined by the width and depth measurement of the building.

5   Digital-Modeling Visualization Experiments

Firstly, this paper conducts the construction data from the historical documents to construction dimensions. By comprehensively interpreting the construction information in the drawings and archives of Guanlan Hall, this paper concludes the architectural trim-work from general layout, components to the details. The drawings provide the layout and type of the trim-work, the specific dimensions of important components partly, and the pattern of decoration surface. The handicraft regulation and precedents determine specific dimensional data, materials, and styles of each component that are missing in drawings. The technical data is sorted out as shown in the following Tables 3 and 4, (Fig. 10):

Table 3   Exterior architectural trim-work of Guanlan Hall

Trim-work	Components	Section Size	
		Height (Width)	Thickness
Geshan	Bottom threshold	0.78*②	0.39*
	Middle threshold	0.65*	0.39*
	Top threshold	0.65*	0.39*
	Frame	0.65*	0.39*
	Stile and rail	0.3*	0.42*
Kanzhuang	Frame	0.65*	0.39*
	Stile and rail	0.3*	0.42*
Glasschuang	Stile and rail	0.16	0.2*
	Side wall	1.2	2
	Glass panel	6.65	4.02
	Frame	1.2	2

Table 4   Interior architectural trim-work of Guanlan Hall

Trim-Work	Location		Components	Length	Section Size	
	Width direction	Depth direction			Height (width)	Thickness
Langanzhao		O	Partition	22.3		
			Top threshold		0.45*	0.27
			Top and middle threshold		0.45	0.27
			Middle threshold		0.3	0.27
			Frame		0.42	0.27
			General frame		0.6	0.27
			Panel		3.1	2.85
			Middle open	12.17		

(*continued*)

Table 4 (*continued*)

Trim-Work	Location		Components	Length	Section Size	
	Width direction	Depth direction			Height (width)	Thickness
Langanzhao	O		Partition	10.7		
			Frame		0.35	0.27
			General frame		0.45	0.27
			Panel	4.04	2.84	
			Middle open	3.17		
Kanchuang		O	Partition	10.5		
			Lower wall	10.5	3.45	
			Leaf	6.1	1.6	
			Rail		0.16*	0.18*
Kanchuang	O		Partition	11.7		
			Lower wall	11.7	3.45	
			Leaf	6.1	1.6	
			Rail		0.18*	0.18*
Bishachu	O		Partition	10.7	12.7	
			Leaf			
			Rail		0.18*	0.18*
Tianranzhao	O		Partition	11.7		
			Frame	11.7	0.18*	
			Caven bracing	11.34	4.88–2.44*③	0.12*
Tianranzhao	O		Partition	10.7		
			Frame	11.7	0.18*	
			Caven bracing	11.34	4.88–2.44*	0.12*
Luodizhao		O	Partition	10.5		
			Leaf	6.1	1.6	
			Rail		0.18*	0.18*

Note

① According to Handicraft Regulations and Precedents, the calculation base for the exterior trim-work components' dimensions is the building's bay width, depth and column diameter. This table doesn't include the building dimensions.

② The components' dimension in this table are based on the interpretation of Drawings. Those data marked with "*" is determined through the calculation by the Handicraft Regulation and Precedents accordingly.

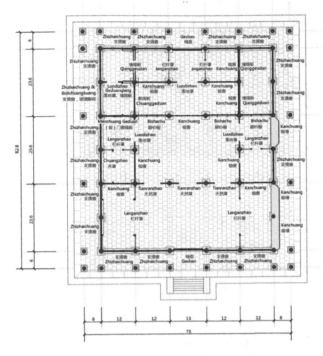

Fig. 10. The architectural trim-work plan of Guanlan Hall from historical document to construction dimension. (By Huan Wang)

In regard to the compiled architectural trim-work data, four digital visualization experiments were attempted, which aimed to explore the digital visualization approach created by Chinese tradition from shallow to deep and from single to multiple.

5.1 Experiment 1 3D Model

3D modeling is not anything new to architecture, however, it is still not universal for interior space visualization in Yuanming Yuan halls as the result of the complicated construction process of traditional Chinese buildings. The first experiment in this study was to generate a digital model by the Sketchup software platform with materials, colors, and patterns according to the intuitionistic presentation on Qing Dynasty. The 3D modeling delivers a component map library as supplementary material for reading drawings when understanding architectural trim-work of traditional style.

This followed by assigning the corresponding decorative pattern to the model and rendering graphics and animation from a people wandering perspective. Graphics are comprehensible to spatial experience effects intuitively, while animation can provide immersive effects in a way of shuttle and walking experience. For the dynamic space design of traditional Chinese space construction, it can effectively break the cognitive barriers from a cross-era perspective (Figs. 11, 12, 13 and 14).

Fig. 11. The prime 3D modeling graphics of Guanlan Hall restoration (By Huan Wang)

Fig. 12. The prime 3D modeling graphics of Guanlan Hall restoration (By Huan Wang)

Fig. 13. The prime 3D modeling graphics of Guanlan Hall restoration (By Huan Wang)

Fig. 14. The prime 3D modeling graphics of Guanlan Hall restoration (By Huan Wang)

5.2 Experiment 2 Construction Processing Motion Graphic

The 3D model-based next extended experiment is to use digital models on expressing the construction process to illustrate the construction logic of traditional Chinese construction visually. Traditional Chinese architecture has a stricter installation logic on the interior structure, as well as the Yuanming Yuan building restoration, come from little more than the Qing Dynasty drawings and documents materials. This is hardly shown in the general 3D renderings, which creates a barrier to cultural communication.

The components were individually disassembled into independent monomers and placed in corresponding positions, and the corresponding relations were connected with the guidelines and additional explanations were provided. Experiment 2, on the one hand, produced production and installation streamline from drawings, Handicraft and regulation precedents, and then components assembly with both graphics and videos. From a cross-cultural perspective, it enables a positive improvement effect from the representation of moving the constructive factors to spatial performance (Fig. 15).

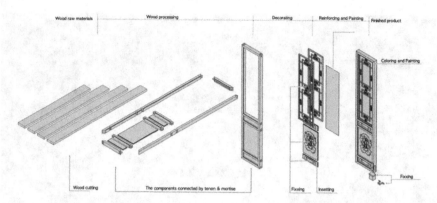

Fig. 15. 3D modeling processing of component construction. (By Huan Wang)

5.3   Experiment 3 VR Panorama

The above two experiments are as regard a visual experience of "standing outside the space". Additional way of communication between the viewer and the traditional period of construction is VR presentation, which is currently used commonly in the industry and information technology. Experiment 3 is to recreate the reality scene of experience. VR technology can compose the feeling of engaging the viewer into the specific space, that is, "stand inside the space", which expands the possibility of restoration research. A rendering plug-in of Sketchup works to connect the selected location immersive graphics accordingly from the VR maps exported for walking experience in the Guanlan Hall.

VR, that is called virtual reality. VR technology projects the images that is virtually shaped in a form of sphere onto the surface from the central point of view to achieve an immersive effect of the viewers when watching from a viewer perspective. The rendering plug-in that captures sketches can transform pictures of selected position for a picture converting that can be recognized by virtual reality headsets or multi-projected environments form an immersive walking experience.

The output visualized image is presented with a mobile phone and Google Cardboard VR. VR motion video were also tried in the study by setting the parameters of light and route in multiple specific scenes in advance. Mobile phones and Google Cardboard VR facilities an improvised but intangible medium to engage the dynamic and situated sensation (Fig. 16).

Fig. 16. 3D model VR panorama modeling graphics of Guanlan Hall (By Huan Wang)

5.4   Experiment 4 Heritage Projection Plan

Aa a ruined site in the Yuanming Yuan, Guanlan Hall is keeping nothing except a stage built in stone and brick. What remains of the building's platform is difficult to trace back to its original appearance. In fact, it is difficult for any other real scene that uses the media to completely shape the subject and its environment, giving people the feeling of being in real space—because those unreal spaces is missing the most extraordinary characteristic of Chinese garden is the flowing-relationship between the interior and exterior of the surroundings. If a rebuilt space with life-size image could be presented in front of the audience, where the site is located and restore the place and scene in a real way in a way, it will bring an experience between viewers and sites to bridge a historical dialogue.

Firstly, before the architectural projection, the illusion of light can be projected according to the reconstructed architectural model the physical scene shaping since it is only finding a ruined site. The basic theory is that when the laser projector projects a virtual ancient building image from four directions of the building, it recreate an artificial scenario for ancient surroundings. In practice, the method of projector mapping (Madmapper or Resolume Arena) technology on heritage architecture has been launched out in the Forbidden City recreation project in China. It has outstandingly advantages on that the projected graphics, patterns, animations or videos can be projected on the traditional Chinese architectural structure without damage. The insufficient aspect is that it is difficult to show the internal structure and space of the building.

Secondly, another method is to build a holographic foil above the ruin site, which is for 3d model's display the on the original site by holographic projection. Holographic projection shows a spacious surround by reshaping the human-scale spatial projection and the real-world projection material diversity. This sort of architectural project can be attempted both inside and outside, which is more flexible than laser architectural projection.

Either way, it can be intuitively displayed to the viewer, realize the feeling of being close to the actual situation, and achieve the purpose of visualizing the significance of spreading culture. But at the same time, both methods are not only expensive and difficult to implement. They are currently at the level of theoretical discussion (Fig. 17).

Fig. 17. Expected effect of projection techniques processing (By Huan Wang)

6   Achievement

In China, urban parks, green spaces or other public green spaces are enthusiastic to design outdoor spaces into the style of the Qing Dynasty form, which sometimes is regarded as a cultural symbol. This may come from the transmission of traditional cultural heritage from visual aesthetics genes and last in the next 50 years continuously. In the actual construction of these design projects, they are often actually operated by craftsmen while the designers cannot present professional drawings of traditional style. Craftsman and designers do not have full communication at the beginning of the project usually therefore it is unavoidable to cause a lot of questions in the traditional-style projects. This research supports traditional construction methods and presents them intuitively. It is a reference for designers, and it is also hoped that by applying this design thinking to traditional construction we can inspire more innovative designs.

3D models can support a renewal of the space shaping analysis of the architecture and garden. From a cultural heritage perspective, the development of critical skills for understanding and communication of architectural characteristics of the Qing Dynasty.

This experience highlights conceptual and procedural statements: Designing Digital Visualization from sketches to textured rendering. Perception and VR (Virtual Reality) engages the user within the environment by generating realistic images, sounds and other sensations that replicate a real environment or create an imaginary setting. By providing a streamlining and deconstruction process, the model develops a comprehensive understanding of Qing Dynasty style architectural structures and construction processes, which contributes to research on the Chinese interior design of Yuanming Yuan.

Acknowledgements. The authors are grateful for the social science financial support provided by "Beijing Municipal Education Commission" (Grant No. SM202010028013).

References

By, R.J.: Smith, The Qing Dynasty and Traditional Chinese Culture. Rowman & Littlefield, Lanhan (2015)

Fu, X.: Architecture technology. In: Lu, Y. (ed.) A History of Chinese Science and Technology, pp. 1–194. Springer, Heidelberg (2015). https://doi.org/10.1007/978-3-662-44163-3_1

Liu, C.: Shen Xiu Si Yong. Tsinghua University Press, Beijing (2004)

Zou, H.: A Jesuit Garden in Beijing and Early Modern Chinese Culture. Purdue University Press, West Lafayette (2011)

Guo, Q.H.: Chinese Architecture and Planning: Ideas, Methods, Techniques. Axel Menges, Stuttgart (2005)

Fu, H., et al.: Chinese Architecture. Yale University Press, New Haven (2002)

Liang, S.: Qing structural regulations. Society for research in Chinese architecture (1934)

Liang, S.: Footnote on Yingzao Fashi. China Architecture & Building Press, Beijing (1981)

Wang, S.: The Collection of Artisan Regulations of Interior Decoration in the Qing Dynasty. China Bookstore Press, Beijing (2008)

Zuofa, G.: (Technical instructions for the building crafts, "工程做法"). In: Yunli 允 禮 et al., vol. 339–340 (1741). Reprint Gugong zhenben congkan: Qingdai zeli. Hainan Chubanshe, Haikou (2000)

Neiyan, Z.: (Interior architectural trim-work, "内檐裝修"). In: Wang, S., et al. The Collection of Artisan Regulations of Interior Decoration in the Qing Dynasty, vol. 6. China Bookstore Press, Beijing (2000)

Neiwu, Z., Zuofa, X.: (A detailed architectural trim-work regulation and precedents of Neiwu Fu, "内务裝修做法细册"). In: Wang, S., et al. The Collection of Artisan Regulations of Interior Decoration in the Qing Dynasty, vol. 4. China Bookstore Press, Beijing (2000)

Zuofa, N.Z.: (Interior architectural trim-work regulation and precedents, "内檐裝修做法"). Collected by Capital Library of China No. 15571

Neiting Yuanming yuan neigong zhuzuo xianxing zeli 内庭圓明園内工諸作現行則例 (Current regulations and precedents on interior handicrafts in the Inner Courts of the Garden of Perfect Brilliance). In: Wang, S., et al. The Collection of Artisan Regulations of Interior Decoration in the Qing Dynasty, vol. 1. China Bookstore Press, Beijing (2000)

Palace Museum Ancient Architecture Department (ed.). Architecture and Decoration of the Forbidden City. Forbidden City Publishing House, Beijing (2007)

National Library. Yangshi Lei's drawings and archives of the summer palace in the national library. National Library Press, Beijing

Historical Archives of the Qing Dynasty. The Summer Palace. Shanghai Ancient Books Press, Beijing (1991)

Wu, X.Y., He, Y., Liu, Y., Song, G.X.: Study of the garden art of Yuanming Yuan Jiuzhou scenic area under the digital vision. Chin. Landsc. Archit. **30**(12) (2014)

He, Y., Yin, L.N.: Translating: bringing lost heritage into our time_a closer look at the case of Yuanming Yuan imperial garden. China Cultural Heritage, April 2014

Jiang, S.Y.: Collection of Palace Zelis of Qing Dynasty. National Library Document Reproduction Center, Beijing (2011)

How to Inherit and Innovate Patterns on the Silk Road in Modern Design

Chuan Wang[✉]

School of Design and Arts, Zhuhai College of Beijing Institute of Technology,
6 Jinfeng Road, Xiangzhou District, Zhuhai 519085, Guangdong, China
21441233@qq.com

Abstract. Goal of Research: To discuss how to inherit and innovate graphs of ancient Silk Road in modern design.

Means of Research: Based on Silk Road's history, this article analyzes Silk Road graphs' values of culture and aesthetics, taking example of three classic patterns of "grape", "honeysuckle" and "treasure flower", and shows their application in modern design, taking example of "caisson ceiling" design and "scroll" pattern.

Result of Research: The usage of Silk Road graphs in modern design has three limits, limit of design, limit of usage and limit of market.

Conclusion: Ways to improve inheritance and innovation of Silk Road graphs in modern design can be teaching Silk Road culture and history in colleges and universities, using new media and putting culture of those graphs into design, binding graphs, culture and products together.

Keywords: Silk Road · Graphs · Modern design · Innovation · Inheritance

1 Introduction

Throughout the world, designers often blend their native traditional culture characters into modern design by usage of classic graphs to highlight their nations' unique classic aesthetics, and thus to promote their traditional culture. As a nation of a long history of more than five thousand years, China teems with ancient constructions and artifacts showing ancient Chinese people's wisdom and beauty, their classic graphs a great fortune of China and the whole world. Graphic patterns from the ancient Silk Road are emblems of those ancient civilizations along the Road, and are important cultural heritage for Chinese people and all the people in the world. It has great cultural value in reviving those old graphs, blending them into modern design through inheritance and innovation. Ways of this inheritance and innovation have recently become a hot spot of research work of relative specialists and scholars.

© Springer Nature Switzerland AG 2020
P.-L. P. Rau (Ed.): HCII 2020, LNCS 12193, pp. 595–605, 2020.
https://doi.org/10.1007/978-3-030-49913-6_48

2   Concept and Background of Silk Road

"Silk Road" became open by the diplomatic work of ZhangQian through Hexi Corridor after ancient Chinese West Han Dynasty's Han Wudi defeated north-east Asia Huns. Silk Road started from West Han's capital city Chang'an, now Xi'an, went through China's north-west territory of Gansu and Xinjiang, and further through Middle Asia and West Asia to Europe. Silk Road connected ancient European and Asian nations, and still acts as a major bridge of trade and communication between China and the countries along the road. Silk Road goes through vast area, passing lots of relics such as Jiayu Pass and Mogao Caves in China and the Buddhas of Bamyan and Loulan outside of China. Those relics and ancient artifacts show characteristics of the cultures along Silk Road and their communication and integration.

3   Cultural and Aesthetic Value of Graphs Along Silk Road

Along Silk Road there were various graphic patterns. Taking advantage of Silk Road's open and growing, ancient cultures, including Ancient Greek Culture, Persian Culture, Indian Culture and more, influenced each other and cultivated beautiful graphic patterns rich in cultural value, continuously innovated by their people based on their original local culture. Graphic patterns of plants are especially well-used and well-known. Below is analysis of cultural and aesthetic values of a few common graphic patterns.

3.1   "Grape" Pattern

"Grape" pattern is one of the most used and seen patterns on Chinese silk textiles, but its origin was from ancient Egypt and Middle East. Grapes were plentiful in ancient Egypt and Middle East, being part of those area's main food source. Lots of ancient Greek ceramics were painted with "grape" pattern. Grape was later carried into China. Because of its dense vines and leaves, grape was deemed as a symbol of multiplication and its graphics was vastly used on silk fabrics. Figure 1 shows a hand draw copy of graphic patterns of some figure's cloths from a China Dunhuang Mogao Cave's fresco. In this picture, the intertwining grape vines and clustering grapes, rich with classic beauty of Chinese tradition, shows ancient Chinese people's good wish for lots of children and ever-lasting lineage.

Fig. 1. [Picture 1] a hand draw copy of graphic patterns of some figure's cloths from a Mogao Cave's fresco, in the age of Early Tang Dynasty

3.2 "Honeysuckle" Pattern

"Honeysuckle" is also a common graphic pattern on Silk Road. Honeysuckle is a common Chinese herb medicine, functioning as alleviator of inflammation and intoxication. Its graphic pattern is a simple yet cunning wavy arrangement of vines and leaves, originated in ancient Greece and influenced by east Rome Culture and Indian culture. Since its entrance into China, "Honeysuckle" pattern was plentifully used on silk cloths, as can be seen on figures on Dunhuang frescos. This pattern was symmetrized and balanced in Tang Dynasty and became a common silk pattern at that time. Figure 2 shows an upper garment of a handmaid on a silk painting excavated in Tulufan, Xinjiang. The silk upper garment is decorated with blue-yellow "Honeysuckle" pattern, showing a wish for health and stability through luxurious beauty.

Fig. 2. [Picture 2] upper garment of a handmaid on a silk painting (Color figure online)

3.3 "Treasure Flower" Pattern

"Treasure flower" is often seen on China's Tulufan Cave's frescos and Mogao Cave's caisson ceilings. This pattern is a compositive pattern, usually of plant pattern elements of both Chinese origin and foreign origin. It is a pattern frequently used on silk textiles since Tang Dynasty, a symbol of the deep merge of oriental culture and occidental culture. "Treasure flower" was prevalent in the age of High Tang Dynasty, with plenty of silk fabrics of this pattern excavated from ancient tombs at lots of places in Xinjiang. Figure 3 shows a silk Pipa bag. On this bag is a typical "treasure flower" pattern, mixing lotus, pomegranate flower and peony, showing not only High Tang Dynasty's aesthetic habit of rich colors, but also its ethos of inclusiveness.

Fig. 3. [Picture 3] a silk Pipa bag of Tang Dynasty.

4 Application of Silk Road Graphic Patterns in Modern Design, Taking Example of a Dunhuang Pattern

4.1 Usage of Dunhuang Caisson Patterns in Modern Design

Caisson ceilings usually are placed on top of rooms or halls like umbrellas, and often are decorated with paintings or relieve. Caisson patterns are typical patterns of Dunhuang and are widely used. There are more than four hundred caisson ceilings in Dunhuang, and most of them are gracefully painted. Placed at tops of caves, caissons are not vulnerable to elements such as sand storm or vandalism, and so were deemed by ancient Chinese people as being capable of subduing fire demon and protecting constructions. The most typical application of Dunhuang caisson patterns in modern design is the Great Hall of the People in China. To stand for the greatness of Chinese people, the Great Hall of the People uses lots of Dunhuang caisson patterns to make grandeur of Chinese style. The central hall on the third floor of the Great Hall of the People is called "the Golden Hall" (see in Fig. 4). The golden hall is mainly golden. Its ceiling, supported by stone pillars, is decorated with Dunhuang style caissons from which golden chandeliers are hung. The caissons give the space layers and depth of traditional Chinese grace.

Fig. 4. [Picture 4] the Great Hall of the People

4.2 Application of Dunhuang Scroll Patterns in Modern Design

Dunhuang Scroll patterns are also one of the most seen traditional Chinese graphic patterns on Silk Road. Duhuang Scroll patterns are mostly composed of honeysuckle, lotus, orchid and peony, arranged in elaborate "S" shaped wavy curves, and thus are named "Scroll" for the curly shapes of the plants. Scroll actually evolved from an older Chinese graphic pattern, honeysuckle, after being integrated with lots of foreign patterns. It is in Tang Dynasty that Scroll came into being as a unique graphic pattern of China, standing for good fortune and goodness. In modern design, Scroll is often seen in planar design, such as poster, wrapping and book cover, being popular in the domain of visual design for its free curvy shaping. Figure 5 shows the cover of Toshiharu Itō's "Copies of Tang Scroll – a biography of decorative graphic patterns". The designer of the book cover is the renowned Japanese designer, Matuda Yuhimasa. The book covers are blue, red and brown, overlaid with golden scroll pattern, harmoniously colorful, noble and yet vivid with a sense of free expression given by the sprawling curves, showing a perfect mix of historical heritage and modern design.

Fig. 5. [Picture 5] book cover of "Copies of Tang Scroll – a biography of decorative graphic patterns". (Color figure online)

4.3   Application of Dunhuang Fresco Graphs in Modern Design

In recent years, countries, especially China, pay more and more attention to Silk Road, and artists and artisans working for enterprises and governments start to put Silk Road graphs into modern design, giving them new usages. At the end of 2018, Tencent and Dunhuang Research Institute put Dunhuang Scarf online on the anniversary of their agreement of "Dunhuang Digital Devoters" plan. Users of Dunhuang Scarf can use wechat to explore the public account, Tencent Cultural Innovation, to find graphs unique to Dunhuang frescos, such as "three rabbits sharing ears" of the No. 407 cave of Mogao, Dunhuang and "hundreds of birds circling Phoenix" of the No. 71 cave of Mogao, to have them printed on customized silk scarves. Customers can choose the graphs and edit them. This program not only interests customers, but also greatly improves innovation of using traditional graphs in modern design. Take example of "digital silk deer" being sold by the team of Tencent Cultural Innovation. This scarf combines the fresco "Life Story of the Deer King" of the No. 257 cave of Dunhuang Mogao, North Wei period and the green landscape on the up-right corner of the fresco "Story of Uṣṇīṣa vijaya dhāraṇī sutra" of the No. 217 cave, High Tang period. This scarf printed its main graphs of nine-colored deer on the background of green landscape, giving itself a unique style of classic fresco, and endowing itself with the Buddhism idea of mercy and intrepidity of the original fresco, making the overtone gentle and kind. Take another example of a Chinese New Year red envelop, a Dunhuang cultural innovation product being sold on Taobao.com (see in Fig. 6 and 7). Red envelops are used by Chinese people for wrapping gift money on traditional holidays or ceremonies. This red envelop printed the graphic pattern, fortunate clouds from the No. 331 cave of Mogao, Early Tang period, together with Chinese glyphs "good fortune", giving itself a graceful tune of traditional Chinese aesthetics. The fortunate clouds and "good fortune" glyphs work harmoniously together to bring a rich sense of wealthiness, showing a great wish for peace, fortune and happiness.

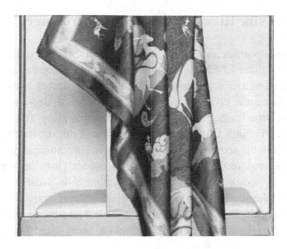

Fig. 6. [Picture 6] "Digital silk deer" (Color figure online)

Fig. 7. [Picture 7] a Dunhuang cultural innovation product, Chinese New Year red envelop (Color figure online)

These cases show Silk Road graphs' Chinese style charm through inheritance and innovation in modern design. There is huge room in applying in modern design those graphs of folktales full of ancient Chinese people's wisdom and merit, and plentiful of material to be utilized in the development of cultural innovation economy. However, market of those graphs is not yet developed, due to most people's lack of understanding of Silk Road's culture and various graphs. Those graphs' inheritance and innovation are hindered by shortage of both customers and esteemed brands.

5 Problems in Silk Roads Graphs' Modern Usage

As one of the most important trade paths, since its open, Silk Road has vastly circulated both economy and culture of China and the west nations along the road. Graphs along the road, on fabrics and artifacts, are delicate with extraordinary historical and cultural value, reflecting Eurasion civilizations' growing path and deposit. In recent years, China has actively broadcasted culture of Silk Road, blending graphic patterns better into modern design. Though Chinese governmental and non-governmental Institutions and departments have vigorously tried to active inter-communication about Silk Road culture both inside and out of China with various activities, except professionals, Chinese and foreign people are still unfamiliar about Silk Road graphs. This shows some problems in inheritance and innovation of Silk Road graphs in modern design, and these problems limits Silk Road culture's influence and hampers its graphs' spread and growth. These problems are summarized into aspects listed below.

5.1 Limits of Silk Road Graphs' Elements

Silk Road graphs are plentiful and various, but those graphs were mostly from the design of ancient artifacts and fabrics, and the biggest challenge of utilizing those graphs in modern design is to harmoniously blend them into modern design without losing their original cultural and aesthetic value. Nowadays the most seen usage of those graphs in modern design is direct copying, like copying the most popular Chinese Dunhuang graphs, caissons, canopies, scrolls, etc., into fabrics, souvenirs, culture innovation products and more. Those copying lacks necessary innovation, and the most important reason behind is that those graphs, though regionally characteristic, are mostly mythic creatures, animals and plants, far away from modern culture and everyday life, and so are limited from being blended into modern design. To meet modern society's growing need for classic Chinese arts, those graphs need proper innovation to meet the high standard of modern design, creating a new aesthetics trend meeting modern design's need for practicality and preserving the original graphs' rich nationality.

5.2 Limits of Media

Silk Road graphs were painted on and engraved in ancient constructions and fabricated in silk works. Now those graphs are mostly used on silk cloths, major constructions and souvenirs, lacking utility though looking good. Take the example of their application in modern cloths. Those graphs are mostly used on apparels of fashion show, but scarcely on casual dressings. The ultimate reason of this limit of media is that Silk Road graphs are still on their way of deeper integration with modern culture to become a fashion. To have a wider media of application, those graphs can be considered to be utilized in stationery, household, electronics and more modern products.

5.3   Limit of Market

Most Chinese people and foreign people now know little of Silk Road graphs. Only Dunhuang graphs are better known in China. This limits the market of Silk Road graphs in modern design, and limited market leads to limited inheritance and innovation in market-directed economy. There are two reasons for the limit of Silk Road graphs' market. The first reason is, except professionals, inside and out of China, common people and even post-secondary students have not deeply learnt Silk Road graphs. Relative education is only for some fields in art. This directly limits the number of potential customers. The second reason is, Silk Road graphs are mostly used on major constructions, souvenirs and fashion show apparels that are at a far distance from common people's everyday lives. So customers usually prefer more practical products than modern products designed with Silk Road graphs, and thus their market becomes more limited. Limit of market obviously has hampered Silk Road graphs' inheritance and innovation in modern design. However, this market can be expanded, as can be seen in the case of Forbidden City cultural innovation products, pursued and admired by vast customers including even young customers. To expand the market, designers need to pay close attention to modern people's aesthetic preference and find the right spots to insert and infuse Silk Road graphs into modern design.

6   Silk Road Graphs' Inheritance and Innovation in Modern Design

Nowadays all countries emphasize their culture's inheritance and growth, to build cultural institution and business more adherent to their nationalities. Silk Road graphs, which are an aggregation of Chinese traditional visual arts, deserve our attention. Its inheritance and innovation in modern design is important to promotion of Chinese traditional culture and communication of all the cultures around the world. To better utilizing Silk Road graphs in modern design, designers have to establish a new mode of Silk Road graphs' inheritance and innovation, adapting themselves to this new epoch, following this new epoch's progress in every aspect of society and breaking out-of-date routines to widen their thoughts. Below are suggestions for better inheriting and innovating Silk Road graphs in modern design, according to the problems mentioned.

6.1   Teaching Silk Road' Culture and History in Post-secondary Schools

For better inheritance and innovation, more people have to know Silk Road and deeply research Silk Road graphs. Attention should be paid in these two aspects. Firstly, lessons of Silk Road graphs should cover more students. They should be taught not only in fields of ceramics, sculpture, painting and other traditional arts majors, but also in more fields such as advertisement design, construction, environmental engineering, fashion design and industrial design, to let more student have a chance to know Silk Road graphs, and thus to promote Silk Road graphs' application in more fields through more students' inspired interest of the graphs. Secondly, students' creativities should be valued. Those creativities will bring new inspiration into Silk Road graphs' application in modern design and new concept of inheritance, that can greatly help Silk Road graphs' inheritance and innovation.

6.2   Developing New Media

Now Silk Road graphs are mainly used on a small number of types of cloths such as silk and souvenirs sold at places along Silk Road. Their aesthetics value is under-exploited. Putting different graphs to different media according to the graphs' individual cultural connotation and thus raising the media's aesthetics value is a good way to inherit and develop the graphs. Take the example of one important Silk Road graph, "Date Palm". Greco-Bactria is an important area in the middle of Silk Road. In Greco-Bactria, many artifacts and relieves have the graph of "Date Palm". "Date Palm" graph is a whole date palm hanging dates or surrounded by intertwining plants. Dates are an important agricultural product of Mesopotamia and East Mediterranean area, and date palms were worshiped as holy trees by ancient Greek and Anatolian people. "Date Palm" graph became prevalent in Western Regions after Hellenistic period. Date Palm graphs were also often used on silk cloths in ancient China. Date Palm graph is bilaterally symmetric, nobly graceful and very decorative. Now in China this graph is only slightly used on silk fabrics. With its style and meaning, Date Palm graph can be considered in modern home decoration, since classics style have gradually become one of nowadays people's major choices. It can be used on doors, windows, curtains and drapes, bringing homes some tune of classics and culture while hinting prosperous lives. In general, when considering new media for Silk Road graphs' inheritance and innovation, we should put enough thought into compatibility of graphs' historical background and choice of media, to genuinely uplift the media's aesthetics value and utility.

6.3   Getting Hold of the Joint Point of Silk Road Graphs and Silk Road Culture's Derivative Products to Use Graphs' Individual Culture as Modern Design's Material

Silk Road graphs are full of ancient people's wisdom along the way. Each group of graphs reflects a region's long history's deposit of culture, customs and life style, vivid with regionality. Nowadays all countries in the world pay heavy attention to preservation of highly regional traditional culture. So we should use Silk Road graphs' culture as modern design's material, forging traditional culture into modern design's ingredients. For Silk Road graphs' inheritance and innovation, we can learn from Forbidden City cultural innovation products that are popular in recent years. "Forbidden City Cultural Innovation" group put Forbidden City's graphs into design of notebooks, pens and pencils, bookmarks, mugs, etc. Those products' Forbidden City's classic style beauty is looked forward to and sought after by lots of young people. Those products not only are usable, but also let customers see and feel everyday living of Ming Dynasty and Qing Dynasty that has long past in history. In Silk Road graphs' inheritance and innovation, graphs, such as China's famous Dunhuang graph patterns, can be used as regional cultural code on various types of modern products, not only stationery, but also home supplies for customers fond of traditional touches in their homes. They can also be used in design of jewelry, bracelet, rings, earrings and more. They can even be transformed into modern and cute emoji, aired on internet. All of these can promote traditional aesthetics in modern design and inspire people to look for Silk Road culture behind the graphs.

6.4 Emphasizing Integration of Traditional and Modern Elements in Design

Modern design is to meet the need of modern economy and social activity. Traditional graphs' Inheritance and innovation in modern design should not be simple printing them on all modern products or randomly mixing and laying them together. New sights and ideas should be put into those traditional graphs, and joint points of traditional graphs and modern design should be found to integrate and sublimate them together, interpreting the graphs' inner traditional culture in a modern way. And modern design of traditional graphs should be commercialize to let it infiltrate into modern life.

7 Summary

Silk Road graphs have high cultural and aesthetic value. As society keeps developing and progressing, people more and more want regionalities and nationalities around the world infused into modern design. So, Silk Road graphs' inheritance and innovation in modern design become especially important. In the process of inheritance and innovation, its popularity should be highly emphasized: how to utilize the graphs in modern design, to let users feel traditional cultural aesthetics while enjoying products' full functionality, and let it become one important way to guide people's learning and inheriting Silk Road culture. In general, in Silk Road graphs' inheritance and innovation in modern design, graphs' cultural meaning should be deeply understood, so that traditionality can be cunningly combined with modernity to show traditional graphs on modern media in a creative way, and finally Silk Road culture can be shown on the world's stage with a brand new stance.

References

1. Jianzheng, C.: Silk road in the view of the grand history of han and tang dynasty. Wenbo **3**, 3–7 (2010)
2. Jixiang, P.: Introduction of Art. Peking University Press, Beijing (2006)
3. Li, Q.: Maritime Silk Road, vol. 5-I, p. 96. Huangshan Publishing House, Hefei (2016)
4. Xiao, Y.: A Silk Road Journey. Northwest University Press, Xi'an (2015)
5. Jie, Y.: Design and promotion of dynamic CI in digital media. Packag. Eng. **37**(10), 13–16 (2016)
6. Xu, L., Wei, S.: Research of mortise-tenon connection's application on new materials. Furniture **5**, 6–10 (2016)

Author Index

Printed in the United States
By Bookmasters